WORLD HISTORY

Preparing for the Advanced Placement® Examination

Ryan

Chiaramonte

402-404 outline

Reviewers

Phil Cox
AP® World History Exam Reader
Broad Run High School
Ashburn, Virginia

David L. Drzonek
AP® World History Teacher
Carl Sandburg High School
Orland Park, Illinois

Ronald P. Eydenberg
College Board® Academic Advisory Council, Past Member
Revere Public Schools
Revere, Massachusetts

Charles Hart
AP® World History Exam Table Leader
Westmont High School
Westmont, Illinois

David Brian Lasher
AP® World History Exam Reader
Northwest Pennsylvania Collegiate Academy
Erie, Pennsylvania

John Maunu
AP® World History Exam Table Leader
Cranbrook/Kingswood High School
West Bloomfield, Michigan

Thomas J. Sakole
AP® World History Exam Sample Selector and Table Leader
Broad Run High School
Ashburn, Virginia

WORLD HISTORY

Preparing for the Advanced Placement® Examination

AMSCO SCHOOL PUBLICATIONS, INC.,

a division of Perfection Learning®

World History: Preparing for the Advanced Placement® Examination
is one of a series of AP® social studies texts first launched with
United States History: Preparing for the Advanced Placement® Examination.

© 2015 Perfection Learning®

www.perfectionlearning.com

2 3 4 5 6 7 8 9 10 EBM 20 19 18 17 16 15

When ordering this book, please specify:

Softcover: ISBN 978-1-62974-845-0 or **1487801**
eBook: ISBN 978-1-62974-944-0 or **14878D**

Printed in the United States of America

Contents

Preface   xi

Introduction: Preparing for the Advanced Placement®
Examination in World History   xii

PERIOD 1: Technological and Environmental Transformations, to c. 600 B.C.E.   1

Chapter 1: From Hunter-Foragers to Settled Societies
Early Humans • Neolithic Revolution • Civilization   2

  Historical Perspectives: Was Farming a Mistake?   11

  Think As a Historian: Historical Argumentation   16

  Write As a Historian: Identify the Thinking Skill   16

Chapter 2: The First Civilizations
Mesopotamia • Egypt • Indus Valley • China   17

  Historical Perspectives: Why Do Civilizations Rise and Fall?   40

  Think As a Historian: Use of Relevant Historical Evidence   45

  Write As a Historian: Understand the Topic   45

Period 1: Review   46

  Thematic Review   46

  Turning Point: Why 600 B.C.E.?   46

  DBQ: Egyptian and Chinese Religions   47

PERIOD 2: Organization and Reorganization of Human Societies, c. 600 B.C.E. to c. 600 C.E. 50

Chapter 3: Classical Civilizations in Greece and Persia
Crete • City-States • Culture • Persia • Alexander the Great   52

  Historical Perspectives: Was Alexander Great?   65

  Think As a Historian: Recognize Periodization   71

  Write As a Historian: Use Chronological Order   71

Chapter 4: The Roman World
   Monarchy • Republic • Empire • Fall   72

 Historical Perspectives: Why Did Rome Collapse?   85

 Think As a Historian: Use Topic-by-Topic Comparison   91

 Write As a Historian: Recognize Appropriate Comparisons   91

Chapter 5: Classical Civilizations in India and China
   Mauryan • Gupta • New Religions • Han   92

 Historical Perspectives: Why Did So Many Belief Systems
             Develop in One Period?   106

 Think As a Historian: Recognize Contextualization   111

 Write As a Historian: Introducing the Topic   111

Chapter 6: Early American Civilizations
   Moche • Mesoamerica • Maya   112

 Historical Perspectives: Were the Mayans Violent?   118

 Think As a Historian: Recognize Historical Interpretations   123

 Write As a Historian: Review the Main Points   123

Period 2: Review   124

 Thematic Review   124

 Turning Point: Why c. 600 C.E.?   124

 DBQ: The Impact of Han China   125

PERIOD 3: Regional and Transregional Interactions, c. 600 C.E. to c. 1450   129

Chapter 7: Byzantine Empire and Kievan Rus
   Byzantine Empire • Kievan Rus   131

 Historical Perspectives: Was Justinian Noble or Ruthless?   140

 Think As a Historian: Synthesis of Information   145

 Write As a Historian: Write an Effective Thesis   145

Chapter 8: Islamic World Through 1450
   Muhammad • Umyyads • Abbasids • Ottomans   146

 Historical Perspectives: What is Islam's Legacy in Spain?   155

 Think As a Historian: Practice Historical Argumentation   160

 Write As a Historian: Use Topic Sentences   160

Chapter 9: Expansion of African Trade
   Bantu Speakers • Trade • Mali • Zimbabwe   161

 Historical Perspectives: Does Africa Have History?   173

 Think As a Historian: Practice Using Historical Evidence   179

 Write As a Historian: Support a Topic Sentence   179

Chapter 10: East Asia in the Post-Classical Period
Sui • Tang • Song • Japan • Korea • Vietnam   180

Historical Perspectives: Who Invented Gunpowder and Guns?   195

Think As a Historian: Practice Historical Causation   201

Write As a Historian: Creating Smooth Transitions   201

Chapter 11: South Asia and Southeast Asia, 600–1450 C.E.
Chola • Islam • Southeast Asia • Angkor   202

Historical Perspectives: Did Islam Alter Indian Culture?   212

Think As a Historian: Practice Using Historical Perspective   218

Write As a Historian: Consider Patterns of Continuity and Change   218

Chapter 12: Western Europe after Rome, 400–1450 C.E
Charlemagne • Feudalism • Crusades • Renaissance   219

Historical Perspectives: Were the Dark Ages Dark?   234

Think As a Historian: Practice Periodization   240

Write As a Historian: Consider the Time   240

Chapter 13: The Mongols and Transregional Empires
Genghis Khan • Batu • Hulegu   241

Historical Perspectives: How Brutal Was Genghis Khan?   249

Think As a Historian: Practice the Skill of Comparison   254

Write As a Historian: Consider the Culture   255

Chapter 14: The Americas on the Eve of Globalization
Mississippians • Toltecs • Aztecs • Inca   256

Historical Perspectives: How Populous Was America in 1491?   265

Think As a Historian: Practice Contextualization   271

Write As a Historian: Anticipate Opposing Arguments   271

Period 3: Review   272

Thematic Review   272

Turning Point: Why 1450?   272

DBQ: Achievements of Sub-Saharan Africa   273

PERIOD 4: Global Interactions, c. 1450–c. 1750 C.E.   276

Chapter 15: Western Europe Expands Its Influence
Reformation • Nation-States • Enlightenment   278

Historical Perspectives: How Did Women Fare in Early Modern Europe?   294

Think As a Historian: Practice Interpretation   300

Write As a Historian: Provide Examples   301

Chapter 16: The Americas in the Early Colonial Period
        Colombian Exchange • European Colonization   302

  Historical Perspectives: How Harsh Were the Spanish?   312

  Think As a Historian: Practice Synthesis   319

  Write As a Historian: Support Generalizations   319

Chapter 17: Africa in the Early Colonial Period
        Songhay • European Contacts • Slave Trade   320

  Historical Perspectives: What Was the Slave Trade's Impact?   328

  Think As a Historian: Recognize Correlation   334

  Write As a Historian: Apply the Skill of Historical Argumentation   334

Chapter 18: Russia Unifies and Expands
        Ivan III • Ivan IV • Peter • Catherine   335

  Historical Perspectives: How Revolutionary Were Peter I's Reforms?   345

  Think As a Historian: Apply the Use of Historical Evidence   352

  Write As a Historian: Explain Causation   352

Chapter 19: Islamic Gunpowder Empires
        Ottomans • Safavids • Mughals   353

  Historical Perspectives: Why Did the Islamic Gunpowder
        Empires Decline?   364

  Think As a Historian: Use Causation   371

  Write As a Historian: Use Generalizations   371

Chapter 20: East Asian Stability Meets Foreign Traders
        Ming • Qing • Japan • Korea   372

  Historical Perspectives: Why Did China Explore and Stop?   380

  Think As a Historian: Recognize Patterns Over Time   386

  Write As a Historian: Use Quotations   386

Period 4: Review   387

  Thematic Review   387

  Turning Point: Why 1750?   387

  DBQ: Peter the Great   388

PERIOD 5: Industrialization and Global Integration, c. 1750 to c. 1900   392

Chapter 21: The Enlightenment, Nationalism, and Revolutions
        France • The Americas • Romanticism • Unification   394

  Historical Perspectives: Was the Enlightenment Positive?   413

  Think As a Historian: Apply Using Periodization   419

  Write As a Historian: Address Contradictory Information   420

Chapter 22: Industrial Revolution, 1750–1900
               Causes • Effects • Responses   421

   Historical Perspectives: What Defines Industrial Society?   433

   Think As a Historian: Apply the Use of Comparison   440

   Write As a Historian: Summarize Information   441

Chapter 23: Turkey, China, Japan, and the West
               Ottomans • Ching Dynasty • Meiji Restoration   442

   Historical Perspectives: How Strong Were the Ottomans?   458

   Think As a Historian: Apply Contextualization   464

   Write As a Historian: Write a Strong First Sentence   464

Chapter 24: Global Links and Imperialism, 1750–1900
               Labor • Africa • Asia • Latin America • Australia   465

   Historical Perspectives: What Was Imperialism's Impact?   477

   Think As a Historian: Apply Interpretation   483

   Write As a Historian: Review the Main Points   483

Period 5: Review   484

   Thematic Review   484

   Turning Point: Why 1900?   484

   DBQ: Women in Japan   485

PERIOD 6: Accelerating Global Change and Realignments, c. 1900 to Present   490

Chapter 25: The World War I Era, 1900–1919
               Causes • Russian Revolution • Combat • Results   492

   Historical Perspectives: Was the Paris Peace Conference a Success? 503

   Think As a Historian: Apply Synthesis   509

   Write As a Historian: Write a Strong Last Sentence   510

Chapter 26: The Interwar Years, 1919–1939
               Internationalism • Depression • Radical Right • Nationalism 511

   Historical Perspectives: What Caused Totalitarianism?   526

   Think As a Historian: Use Argumentation in a Paragraph   532

   Write As a Historian: Use Verb Tenses Carefully   533

Chapter 27: World War II
               Pacific Theater • European Theater • Results   534

   Historical Perspectives: Why Did the Allies Win?   544

   Think As a Historian: Use Causation in a Paragraph   550

   Write As a Historian: Choose Precise Words   550

Chapter 28: The Cold War Era
United Nations • Containment • Berlin • China • Korea   551

  Historical Perspectives: Was the United Nations Effective?   565

  Think As a Historian: Use Comparison in a Paragraph   571

  Write As a Historian: Use Active Voice   572

Chapter 29: Decolonization
Algeria • India • Israel • Africa • Latin America   573

  Historical Perspectives: Why Do Some Countries Develop?   591

  Think As a Historian: Continuity or Change   597

  Write As a Historian: Grouping Information   597

Chapter 30: Post-Cold War World, 1990–Present
Globalization • Environment • Genocide   598

  Historical Perspectives: What Happens Tomorrow?   615

  Think As a Historian: Use Synthesis in a Paragraph   621

  Write As a Historian: Use Commas Correctly   622

Period 6: Review   623

  Thematic Review   623

  Turning Point: Is Today a Turning Point?   623

  DBQ: World War I   624

AP® World History Practice Exam   629

Index   654

Preface

This first edition of *World History: Preparing for the Advanced Placement®
Examination* provides a concise narrative, skills instruction and practice,
multiple-choice questions, essay questions, document-based questions, and
in-text activities designed to help student get ready to take the College Board's
World History AP® Examination. It can be used in several ways:

- a core textbook for a course
- a supplement to a college-level textbook
- a review book in the final weeks before the exam

For teachers, an answer key is available from the publisher.

As of its publication, *World History: Preparing for the Advanced Placement®
Examination* was up to date with all standards and guidelines published by the
College Board. For the latest information on AP® World History courses and
the exam, check the world history section of apcentral.collegeboard.com and
advancesinap.collegeboard.org.

INTRODUCTION

Preparing for the Advanced Placement® Examination in World History

Student enrollment in AP® World History courses has grown over the years. Here are the reasons most often cited for enrolling in the course:

- Evidence that the student has the ability to succeed as an undergraduate
- Increased eligibility for scholarships
- Opportunity to save on college expenses by earning college credit
- Opportunity to test out of introductory college courses
- Evidence that AP® students have better college graduation rates
- Enrichment of the AP® students' high school experience

The placement and credits offered will vary from college to college. The College Board's Web site provides a comprehensive list of colleges and universities that accept AP® examinations and the credits they award for passing scores.

Most students who take AP® courses report that they are more challenging than regular courses; they also report that AP® courses are also more interesting and gratifying. The rewards of taking on the challenges of an AP® program go beyond the scores and placement. They include the development of lifelong reading, thinking, and writing skills as well as an increased enjoyment of history.

This introduction will provide you with background information that will help you understand the structure of the AP® World History exam.

Overview of the AP® World History Exam

This textbook was created to prepare you for the current AP® World History exam. The exam emphasizes the thinking skills used by historians, with a strong focus on themes and related concepts to help deepen your understanding of World History. The three-hour-and-five-minute exam will also include readings, images, and other data sources.

The AP® World History exam will include the components shown in the the table on the next page.

Type of Question	Number of Items	Number of Minutes	Percentage of Score
Multiple-Choice	**70**	**55**	**50%**
Free-Response	**3**	**130**	**50%**
• Document-Based Question	1	50*	
• Continuity and Change-Over-Time Essay	1	40	
• Comparative Essay	1	40	

* includes a 10-minute reading period

Each of these exam components will be explained in this Introduction, along with a guide to sequential skill development to help prepare for the exam.

AP® examinations, including the World History exam, score student performance on a five-point scale:

- *5:* Extremely well qualified
- *4:* Well qualified
- *3:* Qualified
- *2:* Possibly qualified
- *1:* No recommendation

An AP® score of 3 or higher is usually considered evidence of mastery of course content similar to that demonstrated in a college-level introductory course in the same subject area. However, the requirements of introductory courses may vary from college to college. Many schools require a 4 or a 5.

The AP® exams are built differently than basic classroom exams. First of all, the AP® exams are deliberately constructed to provide a wider distribution of scores and higher reliability, increasing the likelihood that test-takers repeating the same exam will receive the same scores. AP® exams, while more difficult than most testing in high school, are also scored differently. The cutoff for a "qualified," or level 3, score may range between 50–60 percent of the possible points. Only a small percentage of students will gain more than 80 percent of the possible points. If you have difficulty with a third or more of the questions on the practice AP® exams, you should not be discouraged. The exam is challenging, but like any challenge, if broken down into manageable steps it can be mastered.

How This Book Can Help

The goal of this textbook is to provide you with the essential content and instructional materials needed to develop the knowledge and the historical thinking and writing skills needed for success on the AP® World History exam. You can find these in the following parts of the book:

- **Introduction.** This section introduces the four thinking skills, five themes, and six periods of the history program. A step-by-step skill development guide is provided for answering 1) the Multiple-Choice questions; 2) the Continuity and Change-Over-Time question and the Comparative Essay questions; 3) the Document-Based Essay question.

- **Concise History.** The 30 chapters of essential historical content and accessible explanation of events are the heart of the book. Each of the six periods is introduced with summaries and key AP® concepts.

- **Maps and Graphics.** Maps, charts, graphs, cartoons, photographs, and other visual materials are also integrated into the text to help you practice analytical skills.

- **Historical Perspectives.** Each chapter includes a section that introduces significant historical issues and conflicting interpretations.

- **Key Terms by Themes.** In each chapter, a list of key terms organized by theme is included to aid in a review of the chapter.

- **Multiple-Choice Questions.** Each chapter contains 10 multiple-choice questions to assess your historical knowledge and skills using a variety of sources.

- **Document-Based Questions.** Each chapter will conclude with one DBQ for practice.

- **Continuity and Change-Over-Time Essay Questions and Comparative Essay Questions.** Each chapter contains a Continuity and Change-over-Time Essay question and a Comparative Essay question. Each also has two additional questions for extra practice.

- **Practice Examination.** Following the final chapter, a complete practice examination is provided.

- **Index.** The index is included to help locate key terms for review.

A separate **Answer Key** is available for teachers and other authorized users of the book, and can be accessed through the publisher's web site.

The Study of AP® World History

Historians attempt to give meaning to the past by collecting historical evidence and then explaining how this information is connected. They interpret and organize a wide variety of evidence from primary sources and secondary texts in order to understand the past. What the readers of AP® World History exams hope to find in a student's work is evidence of his or her ability to think like a historian: to analyze and use evidence and to deal with probing questions about past events. Often there is not one "answer" for such questions, no more than one can find all the answers in any one historical source. AP® teachers and readers are looking for the student's ability to think about history and to support ideas with evidence.

AP® candidates should appreciate how participants in history as well as historians differ among themselves in their interpretations of critical questions in world history. Each chapter of this book thus includes a **Historical Perspectives** feature to introduce some of the issues raised and debated by historians over time. The AP® history exam does not require an advanced knowledge of historiography—the study of ways different historians have used to construct their accounts of the past, or, as some say, "the history of history." Nevertheless, prior knowledge of the richness of historical thought can add depth to your analysis of historical questions.

Students planning to take the AP® World History exam also need to become familiar with and then practice the development of: 1) historical thinking skills, 2) thematic analysis, and 3) the concepts and understandings of the six periods that provide the organization of the content. These three components of the course are explained below for orientation and future reference.

Don't become overwhelmed with this introduction or try to comprehend all the finer points of taking the AP® exam in the first few days or weeks of studying. Mastery of these skills and understandings takes time and is an ongoing part of the study of AP® history. This introduction will become more helpful as a reference after you have studied some historical content and have begun to tackle actual assignments.

Historical Thinking Skills

Advanced Placement® history courses encourage students to become "apprentice historians." A primary means to attain that goal is to begin thinking like a historian. The College Board, which creates the AP® exams, has identified four essential historical thinking skills for AP® World History. Every question on the World History exam will require you to apply one or more of these historical thinking skills. (Essays and document-based questions most often involve more than one skill.) Many of these skills, or "habits of the mind," will already be familiar to you, and will only take some practice to think about them more explicitly. Also, the review questions at the end of each chapter and period require the application of one or more of the four historical thinking skills.

The following paragraphs explain these four AP® historical thinking skills and their corresponding components and provide examples of how you can apply the skills.

Skill 1: Crafting Historical Arguments from Historical Evidence This skill has two components: historical argumentation and the use of relevant historical evidence.

Historical Argumentation Argumentation involves the ability to analyze a question and to address that question through the construction of a plausible and persuasive argument. Historical argumentation requires a focused and analytic thesis supported by relevant historical evidence. The skill also involves the ability to evaluate the arguments and supporting evidence used by others.

Consider the following prompt from a document-based question:

> Using the following documents, analyze similarities and differences in social structure in Europe and Japan when each had feudalism. Identify an additional type of document and explain how it would help your analysis of the social structure of these societies.

This task demands a clear and comprehensive thesis that supports the position with persuasive and relevant evidence. Later in this introduction, writing such an essay will be explained and broken down into manageable steps.

Appropriate Use of Relevant Historical Evidence Use of evidence involves the ability to evaluate evidence obtained from diverse sources, including written primary and secondary sources, art and illustrations, artifacts, maps, and statistical data. You will need to be able to analyze evidence in terms of content, author, purpose, format, audience, and historical context. This use-of-evidence skill also involves the ability to assess the perspective of the author of a historical source, make inferences, draw conclusions, and recognize any limitations or errors in the source. Assessing an author's perspective, or point of view (POV), is one of the things required for a Document-Based Question.

For example, a diary entry of an eighteenth-century cottage industry worker in Britain who was put out of work as a result of technological advances might be one-sided and negative about new technology. That source, however, could provide insights into the social divisions and thinking of the times; and it may be relevant on other issues, such as the conditions of those working for wages as well as early critiques of a capitalist, market-driven economy.

Skill 2: Chronological Reasoning This skill has three components: Historical Causation, patterns of Continuity and Change-Over-Time, and Periodization.

Historical Causation. Recognizing causation involves the ability to identify, analyze, and evaluate the relationships among many historical events and developments as both causes and effects. Historians often try to distinguish between immediate, or proximate, and long-term causes and effects. In addition, some events and developments may have some *correlation* without proof of a direct causal relationship, while others may be only *coincidental*, or without a relationship at all.

The period of the Industrial Revolution is a rich resource for the study of causation. One could argue that the enclosure movement and the resulting migration of workers to industrial cities were *proximate* causes for the Industrial Revolution, but that the growth of population from the agricultural revolution, the development of new technology, and the emergence of capitalism and the market economy were its *long-term causes*. Historians might debate whether new inventions such as the spinning jenny and the water frame were *primary* or *secondary* causes of the breakdown of cottage industries and the rise of huge urban factories. Some might also argue that the bleak nature of industrial labor caused the popularity of entertainment such as soccer and baseball, while others might argue that those sports were only *coincidental* developments. Understanding the multiple causes and effects of historical events involves analyzing and making judgments about their relative significance. Demonstrating this skill is a key component in the essays for the free response section.

Patterns of Continuity and Change-Over-Time Thinking about continuity and change over time involves the ability to recognize, analyze, and evaluate the dynamics of history over periods of time of varying lengths, often investigating important patterns that emerge. The study of themes in history (explained later in this introduction) is often the tool of choice to understand continuity and change over time.

Britain's industrialization shows *continuities and changes over time* in class structure. Britain began the period as a highly stratified society with the monarch at the top; powerful nobles next on the social pyramid; a small middle class of bankers, merchants, and lawyers next; and small landowners and craftspeople at the bottom. Through the upheavals of industrialization, stratification remained a *continuity*, but *change* did occur, as new groups and classes arose. At the bottom now were factory workers and coalminers—the *working class*. Industrialization also expanded a new *middle class* of managers, office workers, small business owners, and professionals. Toward the top of the hierarchy (but still below the monarchy) were wealthy industrialists, who eclipsed the landed aristocracy in power.

Periodization Periodization involves the ability to analyze and organize history into blocks of time, or periods. Periods in history are often identified as starting and ending with significant turning points, such as the beginning or conclusion of a war. While historians recognize that periodization is a useful tool in the organization of history, the choice of specific dates depends on what a historian considers most significant, such as a particular political, economic, social, or cultural theme. Historical thinking involves not only being aware how a historian's point of view will shape choices about periodization, but also how periodization can, for example, change a historical narrative from a political perspective to an economic or foreign affairs perspective.

For example, readers will note developments explained in the context of one period that did not occur in that period. Such overlap demonstrates how different purposes or themes affect periodization and how events and developments do not always fit into defined periods. Period 5 (1750-1900) focuses on industrialization and globalization, yet Chapter 24 of that period (The Industrial Revolution) refers to developments of the early 1700s, such as the agricultural revolution and the impact that competitive Indian cotton had on Britain's cottage industries. Although these developments occurred during Period 4 (Global Interactions), they were important precursors to the Industrial Revolution, since they created conditions—population growth and economic competition—that helped bring about the Industrial Revolution.

Skill 3: Comparison and Contextualization Historical thinking involves the ability to compare and contrast historical developments as well as the ability to contextualize the developments, or connect them to particular circumstances. Both the skills involve the ability to step back and, from different perspectives, discover commonalities and differences that help broaden one's historical understanding.

Comparison Comparison involves the ability to describe, compare, contrast, and evaluate two or more historical events or developments in the same or different eras or periods. It also involves the ability to identify, compare, contrast, and evaluate a given historical event or development from multiple perspectives.

Again using the period of the Industrial Revolution, twentieth-century historians have compared and contrasted the struggle to improve conditions in the early factories and mines to the growth and change in the labor union movement of the twentieth century.

Contextualization This skill involves the ability to see how a specific event or development fits into the context of larger and broader historical developments often on the national or global level.

For example, historians can better understand the movements to improve social and economic conditions for working class families during Britain's Industrial Revolution in the context of the Enlightenment ideas and the spirit of revolution that were so widespread across Europe at that time. Contextualization is a necessary skill for the Change-Over-Time Essay, and demonstrating it will maximize your score.

Skill 4: Historical Interpretation and Synthesis Historical interpretation involves the ability to describe, analyze, evaluate, and construct diverse interpretations of the past and to determine the context and points of view of primary and secondary sources. This thinking skill also involves understanding how particular circumstances and contexts shape historians' interpretations of past events. It challenges historians and students alike to avoid interpreting the past in terms of the present and to understand the tentative nature of many existing judgments about the past.

In a 2008 interview, British historian David Cannadine explained how historians' changing interpretations can impact the understanding of a period, such as the Industrial Revolutions and the periods leading up to it.

> In the 1960s and 1970s everybody was interested in causes, and in explanation and in change . . . . and there's a whole set of books that have titles like *The Making of the English Working Class, The Origins of Modern English Society, The Origins of American Politics*, and *The Crisis of the Aristocracy.* Everybody was concerned with change, with the explanation, with causes, with crisis . . . .
>
> Whereas I think over the last 20 years or so that's all been put on one side, and what people are now interested in is meaning and understanding, and trying to get a sense that earlier worlds are different,

and we just need to understand how they operated. The difficulty with the change view was that everything was always perpetually in motion, and that clearly wasn't true. The problem with the meaning and understanding view is it's not clear how we get from there to here, because according to that nothing ever seems to change.

Historians, as we can see, often "rewrite" or revise interpretations of history as a result of changes in society, personal perspectives, the discovery of new sources and information, and, above all, the asking of new questions. Questioning is a primary tool that historians use to "peel back the onion skin" in order to discover new interpretations of the evidence. As is often repeated, "The quality of one's history is determined by the quality of one's questions."

Synthesis. Historical synthesis involves applying all of the other historical thinking skills as well as drawing from and fusing knowledge and methods from diverse sources and disciplines in order to build a new and persuasive understanding of the past. Synthesis thus involves the combining of diverse and contradictory evidence to create a many-sided and broad interpretation of the past.

William McNeill ended his landmark book *The Rise of the West* with a conclusion in which he attempted to synthesize lessons learned from an exhaustive study of human history. The following lines capture a small part of his historical synthesis.

> The two-edged nature of power is nothing new in human affairs. All important new inventions have both freed men from former weakness and deficiency and enslaved them to a new regimen. The hardy hunter surely despised the first farmers, bowed down by the heavy labor of the fields; and through long subsequent centuries barbarian freemen regularly scorned the servile habits of their civilized contemporaries. Yet these repugnances never for long arrested the spread of agriculture or civilization. Civilized history, likewise, as this book has tried to show, may be understood as a series of breakthroughs toward the realization of greater and greater power . . . .

Of course, the expectations for an AP® World History student in a 40-minute essay or a 50-minute DBQ are more modest, but they do include developing a clear thesis that deals with all parts of the question and taking into account conflicting evidence and diverse interpretations.

Course Themes

Each AP® World History exam question is also related to one or more of five course themes. These five themes will help you think about the main ideas that are central to the study of world history. The themes include the study of interactions with the natural environment, the development and interaction of cultures, the building and expansion of states as well as the resulting conflict, the dynamics of economic systems, and the development and change of social structures and gender roles.

Each theme includes a list of related key topics, to make the themes more concrete and to facilitate cross-period investigations and to help identify trends and processes that have developed over centuries in different parts of the world.

Each chapter in this book includes a review list of important names, places, events, and concepts used in that chapter, "Key Terms Organized by Theme." To help you recognize thematic connections in the chapter, the entries in the list are grouped under subheads for each them. These subheads are listed below in parentheses after the full name of the theme.

Theme 1: Interaction Between Humans and the Environment (Environment)

Sub-Themes:

- Demography (the study of human populations) and disease
- Migration
- Patterns of settlement
- Technology

This theme focuses on the interplay between the natural environment and human society. Since prehistoric times, humans have interacted with the environment in numerous ways—as hunters, fishers, farmers, pastoralists; these interactions have led to patterns of migration and settlement based on factors such as climate and available flora and fauna. Interaction with the environment intensified with population growth and migration. Cities grew, trade networks flourished, and diseases devastated regions. With the Industrial Revolution, environmental exploitation increased exponentially to the present day, as population growth and sophisticated new technologies have increased our mastery over the environment.

Theme 2: Development and Interaction of Cultures (Culture)

Sub-Themes:

- Religions
- Belief systems, philosophies, and ideologies
- Science and technology
- The arts and architecture

This theme explores world cultures, including ideas, beliefs, ideologies, and knowledge—those within societies and those shared between societies. Students should be able to explain ways in which religions, philosophies, and technical and artistic accomplishments demonstrate how groups in a society see themselves and others, and how they respond to challenges. Students should understand that when societies interact and share cultures, people produce new ideas and behaviors, and this can affect developments in other themes. For example, a student might be asked how various religions shape gender roles, or how various philosophies influence government structures or economic systems. By comparing different cultures, students learn unique aspects of each culture as well as cultural trends across societies.

Theme 3: State-Building, Expansion, and Conflict (State-Building)

Sub-Themes:

- Political structures and forms of governance
- Empires, nations, and nationalism
- Revolts and revolutions
- Regional, transregional, and global structures and organizations

This theme explores how societies have built and maintained hierarchical systems of rule as well as the conflicts generated by these processes. Students are encouraged to compare political structures (such as kingdoms, empires, and nation-states) across time and place, as well as interactions among such structures. Continuity and change are reflected through focus on stability and conflict (internal and external). Students should examine and compare various forms of state development and expansion, cultural and ideological foundations, and social structures in differing contexts. This theme also explores different types of states, such as autocracies and constitutional democracies. Finally, students should be able to explain interstate relations, such as warfare and diplomacy, as well as the importance of international organizations. Nationalism, revolutions, and global structures and organizations are particularly relevant to Period 5 (c. 1750 to c. 1900) and Period 6 (c. 1900 to Present).

Theme 4: Creation, Expansion, and Interaction of Economic Systems (Economics)

Sub-Themes:

- Agricultural and pastoral production
- Trade and commerce
- Labor systems
- Industrialization
- Capitalism and socialism

This theme explores systems that societies have developed to exploit their environments to produce, distribute, and consume goods and services across time and place, including major transitions in economic activity, such as the beginnings of agriculture, the growth of industrial production, the development of new labor systems, and the ideologies, values, and institutions (such as capitalism and socialism) that sustained these systems. Students should pay close attention to patterns of trade and commerce between societies, particularly to the relationship between regional and global trade networks and their effects on economies, cultural and technological diffusion, migration, state formation, social classes, and interaction with the environment. Industrialization, capitalism, and socialism are particularly relevant to Period 5 (c. 1750 to c. 1900) and Period 6 (c. 1900 to Present).

Theme 5: Development and Transformation of Social Structures (Social Structures)

Sub-Themes:

- Gender roles and relations
- Family and kinship
- Racial and ethnic constructions
- Social and economic classes

This theme explores relations among human beings, including ways that societies group their members and reinforce these groupings with norms that govern interactions. Social stratification comprises distinctions based on family and kinship systems as well as hierarchies of gender, race, ethnicity, wealth, and class. Students should be able to analyze social categories, roles, and practices—how and why they were created, maintained, and transformed. Students should be able to analyze how transformations of social structures were related to other historical shifts, including those in political economy, cultural expression, and human ecology.

Historical Periods

AP® World History is also based on a framework of six chronological periods. These periods are listed and briefly explained below with the correlated chapters from this book. According to the College Board, questions on the exam will be divided chronologically as shown below.

Period	Percentage of Questions
1: Technological and Environmental Transformations, to c. 600 B.C.E.	5%
2: Organization and Reorganization of Human Societies, c. 600 B.C.E. to c. 600 C.E.	15%
3: Regional and Transregional Interactions, c. 600 C.E. to c. 1450	20%
4: Global Interactions, c. 1450 to c. 1750	20%
5: Industrialization and Global Integration, c. 1750 to c. 1900	20%
6: Accelerating Global Change and Realignments, c. 1900 to Present	20%

Period 1: Technological and Environmental Transformations, to c. 600 B.C.E. (Chapters 1–2) The period from the migrations of Paleolithic hunting-foraging bands to the formation of the earliest civilizations deals with the "peopling" of the earth, the rise of Neolithic agricultural groups, and the development and interactions of early agricultural, pastoral, and urban societies.

Period 2: Organization and Reorganization of Human Societies, c. 600 B.C.E. to 600 C.E. (Chapters 3–6) These chapters follow the development of dynasties, states, and empires in Persia, Greece, Rome, China, South Asia, and the Americas. The chapters trace the development of religious and cultural traditions as well as the emergence of transregional trade and communication networks.

Period 3: Regional and Transregional Interactions, c. 600 C.E. to c. 1450 (Chapters 7–14) During this period, transregional networks expanded. As empires collapsed and were reconstituted, new state forms emerged; interregional contacts encouraged technological and cultural exchanges. Innovations stimulated agricultural and industrial production, with consequences such as the revival of cities, which had declined as a result of factors such as invasion and disease.

Period 4: Global Interactions, c. 1450 to c. 1750 (Chapters 15–20) With the globalizing of networks of communication and trade as well as new developments in navigation, Western Europe expanded its worldwide influence as far as East Asia; colonies arose in the Americas and Africa; the silver, spice, and sugar trades created the first truly global exchange of goods and people; Russia attempted modern reforms amid autocratic rule; and Turkic Empires rose and declined in Asia and the Middle East.

Period 5: Industrialization and Global Integration, c. 1750 to c. 1900 (Chapters 21–24) During this period, industrialization brought great changes to the way goods were produced and consumed, but also to the global economy, social relations, and culture. Industrialized nations expanded their empires in search of raw materials and markets, leading, in response, to the formation of states, such as Meiji Japan, as well as to anti-imperialist resistance, nationalism, revolution, and reform, all supported by the rise of Enlightenment thinking. For different reasons, the new global economy brought significant increases to global migration, resulting in many consequences and reactions.

Period 6: Accelerating Global Change and Realignments, c. 1900 to the Present (Chapters 25–30) During this period, technological advances have altered how humans understand the natural world, as new technologies enabled great population growth while threatening ecological balances. The period has been one of unprecedented global conflict, in a struggle between overthrowing and maintaining existing political orders as well as between conflicting ideologies. As a result of the challenges of war and economic collapse, states have developed new forms of control, such as state-run economies. In addition, new international organizations of political and economic governance have arisen.

Each period will be introduced with an overview of the key concepts of the period from the College Board's curriculum. The College Board provides a detailed factual content outline for the course, with a list of key concepts and sub-concepts, accessible in the AP® World History Curriculum Framework on the College Board Web site (apcentral.collegeboard.com; enter Course Home Pages). The key concepts and sub-concepts are flexible enough to allow the use of a variety of relevant historical evidence to support them. The authors of this textbook have reviewed all of the concepts in the College Board's curriculum framework and have written the historical content of this text to ensure that it definitively illustrates and supports these concepts. The goal of the historical content in this text is not to cover every historical fact, but to deal with the essential evidence and understandings needed to address the challenges of the AP® World History exam.

Preparing for the AP® Exam Questions

History, like any field of study, is a combination of subject matter and methodology. The historical skills and themes are methods or tools to explore the subject matter of history. One cannot practice these skills without knowledge of the historical content and understanding of specific historical evidence. The following section provides suggestions for development of another set of skills useful for answering the questions on the AP® exam. Again, the "mastery" of these skills, particularly writing answers to AP® questions, takes practice.

In this section, the two parts of the AP® exam in World History will be explained with suggestion on how to develop the skills related to each different kind of questions in the exam: 1) Multiple-Choice Questions and 2) Free-Response Questions.

1. Answering the Multiple-Choice Questions

The College Board asks 70 multiple-choice questions (MCQs) on the AP® World History exam, and students will have 55 minutes to complete this section. The value of MCQs will be 50 percent of the student's score; and each MCQ will assess one or more historical thinking skill and will also require historical knowledge from the content of AP® World History. Some questions will be related to the analysis of a "stimulus," such as a primary or secondary source; images, such as artwork, cartoons, and photos; or data, including graphs, charts, and maps. Each question will have one BEST answer and three distracters. The questions will place less emphasis on simple recall and more emphasis on the use of evidence and the other historical thinking skills.

This textbook provides preparation for the multiple-choice question section of the exam through the 1) Key Terms by Theme and 2) Multiple-Choice Questions at the end of each chapter. In addition, the practice AP® exam at the end of the book includes 70 multiple-choice questions. The MCQs in this book are similar in form and purpose to those appearing on the AP® exam but are also designed to review the content and understanding of the chapter.

Analyzing the Stimulus. In the AP® exam, some multiple-choice questions will be introduced with a stimulus, such as a map, graph, table, picture, or excerpt from a source. When analyzing a stimulus, the familiar questions of "Who? What? When? Where? and Why?" can help spark your thinking. Beyond these questions, one of the most important question to ask is, "What is the point of view of the author, artist, or speaker?" Consider the following excerpt by Simon Bolivar, leader in the fight for independence by Spanish colonies in South America during the nineteenth century.

> Do not adopt the best system of government, but the one which is most likely to succeed. . . . for it must be admitted that there is nothing more difficult in the political world than the maintenance of a limited monarchy. Moreover it must also be agreed that only a people as patriotic as the English are capable of controlling the authority of a king and of sustaining the spirit of liberty under the rule of scepter and crown.

The multiple-choice questions about this excerpt will test your understanding of it. (This will be easier after you have studied Bolivar and the colonial revolutions in Latin America.) In addition, the questions will focus on one or more historical thinking skills. Below are topics of multiple-choice questions that could be asked about this excerpt.

- Comparison: What comparison is Bolivar suggesting between the English and the colonists he is leading?

- Contextualization: Which of the following best describes how Bolivar's statement fits into the context of its historical period?

- Historical Argumentation: Which of the following best summarizes the argument presented by Bolivar?

Making a Choice. You need to read the stem (the question or statement before the choices of possible answers) of any MCQ and all four choices carefully before you choose your answer. More than one choice may appear to be correct at first, but you must select the BEST answer. If you are not immediately confident which answer is best, start by eliminating answers you recognize as incorrect. Choices that include words that reflect absolute positions, such as "always," "never," or "exclusively," are seldom correct, since historical evidence can rarely offer such absolute certainty. Also keep in mind the need to make judgments about the significance of a variety of causes and effects.

Should you guess on the AP® exam? Yes: The exam format does not penalize for guessing, since points are not deducted for incorrect answers. So, you should answer every question. Obviously, though, the process of first eliminating a wrong answer or two before guessing increases your chances of choosing the correct answer.

Budgeting Your Time. The AP® History exam allows 55 minutes to answer the 70 questions. Fifty-five minutes does not allow enough time to spend two or three minutes on difficult questions. For questions involving a passage, chart, or picture, read the question first. If you find a question is hard, make a guess and then come back to it later if you have time.

Recommended Activities. Practicing sample multiple-choice questions is important before the exam, if for no reason other than to reduce the number of surprises over the format of the questions. However, for many students, the review of content through multiple-choice questions is not the most productive way to prepare for the exam. The purpose of the chapter content in this text is to provide a useful and meaningful review of the essential concepts and evidence needed for the exam. By reviewing the essential facts in the historical content, you will better recall and understand connections between events, which is extremely important for applying the historical thinking skills.

2. Answering the Free-Response Essay Questions (Document-Based Question, Continuity and Change-Over-Time Essay Question, Comparative Essay Question)

On the AP® World History exam, test takers will answer three essay questions. While a Document-Based Question is the first of the three, it will be presented last in this introduction because once you have developed your essay writing skills, you will be better prepared to write a competent answer to the Document-Based Question.

The other two essay questions will be a Continuity and Change-Over-Time Essay and a Comparative Essay. Test takers will have 40 minutes to answer each of these two questions. Before you begin to write, take 5 to 10 minutes on each question to identify key points and plan the structure of your essay.

Your essay responses will be evaluated on the following criteria:

A. Argumentation: Develops a thesis or relevant argument that addresses all parts of the question, including the historical thinking skill or skills addressed.

B. Use of Evidence: Supports the thesis using specific evidence clearly linked to the thesis.

C. Targeted Historical Thinking Skill: Effectively uses an additional and relevant thinking skill, such as causation, periodization, or interpretation.

D. Synthesis: Synthesizes the argument, evidence, and context in a coherent and persuasive essay.

Development of Essay Writing Skills. AP® candidates will most benefit from starting the practice of writing AP® history essays as early as possible. Instead of writing and rewriting complete essays until all elements are mastered, it is helpful first to break down the skills needed to write an effective AP® history essay into sequential steps. The following steps have proved useful in developing the skills needed to answer the essay questions:

1. Analyze the question.
2. Organize the evidence.
3. Develop a thesis.
4. Write an introductory paragraph.
5. Write the supporting paragraphs and conclusion.
6. Evaluate the essay.

1. Analyze the question. Taking the time to consider what the question *really* asks is often overlooked in the rush to start writing. Stop and ask yourself, *What exactly is the question asking? What are the targeted historical thinking skills? Causation? Comparison, Continuity and Change-Over-Time? Periodization?* Read over the question or prompt two or more times. What are the key words or phrases in the question? Underline them. They could be verbs such as "analyze," "explain" "support," or "refute." All questions have one thing in common: They demand the use of historical thinking skills and analysis of the evidence. An essay answer will not receive full credit by simply reporting information. Therefore, the student should be on guard for questions that start out with the verbs "identify" or "describe." Such a question is usually followed by "analyze" or some other more complex thinking skill. Consider, for example, this AP® essay question:

Describe the forms of government developed by TWO of the following monarchies and analyze similarities and differences between the two governments.

- Abbasids
- Tang
- Mayans

For this essay, it is not enough simply to describe the two forms of government you choose; you must also *analyze the similarities and differences* between the two forms of government.

Consider this important advice for any AP® essay question: *If you think that you can write an essay without making some judgment that results in a thesis statement, you have not understood the question.*

After the judgments needed to complete the essay are clear, all the parts of the question need to be identified. The AP® History exam has made some questions easier to understand by clearly structuring the question's parts, as in the above question on the forms of government of three monarchies. More often, however, the two, three, or more aspects of the question are embedded in one sentence, as in this example:

> Analyze continuities and change in China's political and economic policies from 1900 to the present.

This question asks the student to analyze *continuities* and *change* in China's policies in both *politics* and *economics* since 1900. If a student fails to deal with all parts of the question, the essay would receive a lower score. It may take only a few seconds to identify key historical thinking skills as well as the essential components of the essay question. If you take the trouble to do so, you will understand the question better and avoid the mistake of writing a perfectly good essay that receives little or no credit because it answered a question that was not asked.

Recommended Activity. As an initial skill-building activity, analyze the essay questions at the end of Period 1. *Underline* the key words that indicate what the writer should do and circle the words that indicate the specific parts or aspects of the content that need to be addressed.

2. Organize the Evidence. Many students start writing their answers to an essay question without first thinking through what they know, and they often write themselves into a corner. Directions for the AP® History exam advise students to spend some time planning before starting to write the essay question. This advice emphasizes how critical it is first to identify what you know about the question and then organize your information. A recommended practice is to make a brief outline or table summarizing what you know about the question, which should take about five minutes. A sample outline is provided on the next page. It shows the topics that could be treated in answering the essay question concerning China's politics and economics since 1900. The table has places to list both continuities and changes for both politics and economics. The entries are short themes, with specific examples noted in parentheses.

Question: Analyze continuities and change in China's political and economic policies from 1900 to the present.		
	Continuity	**Change**
Politics	• Authoritarian government (last emperors, warlords, Mao) • Limits on individual freedom (Cultural Revolution in 1966, Tiananmen Square in 1989) • Rivalry with Japan (legacy of 1895, Twenty-One Demands in 1915, World War II from 1931 to 1945) • Strong nationalist feeling (identity as powerful country)	• Type of government (by emperors before 1912, briefly a republic after 1912, Communists after 1949) • Relationship with the United States (ally in World War II, rivals in Korea and the Cold War, détente beginning in 1972 led to more trade) • Degree of centralization (warlords in 1920s, the more centralized under Communists after 1949)
Economics	• Most populous country in the world • Rural areas poorer than urban areas • Merchants and traders important (Chinese merchants common outside of China)	• Relationship with foreigners (anti-imperialist in the Boxer Rebellion in 1900, extensive trade recently) • Role of rural farmers (peasants at first, organized into communes after 1958, private ownership began returning in 1981) • Prosperity (poor for most of the period, famines killed 20 million after the Great Leap Forward, greater prosperity in recent decades)

Recommended Activity. Practice identifying the type of evidence you will need to answer questions by setting up an outline, table, Venn diagram, or other graphic organizer for each of the Continuity and Change-Over-Time Essay questions and each of the Comparative Essay questions in Chapter 1. You do not have to fill in the details.

3. Develop a thesis. After you see the evidence that you know, you can write a thesis statement that you can support. A strong thesis, or argument, is an essential part of every AP® History essay answer, and it should be restated in the conclusion as exam readers look at the first and last paragraphs when scoring this point. Surprisingly, many students seem to have difficulty taking a position necessary to build a strong argument. Some are afraid of making a mistake. But think about the nature of history. History does not offer the certitude of mathematics or the physical sciences. Disagreement over the interpretation of the historical evidence develops because of the limitations of the evidence available and the differing perspectives of both participants and historians. AP® readers are looking not for the "right answer" but for a writer's ability to interpret the evidence and use historical support for that interpretation.

A thesis must be more than a restatement of the question. A thesis requires taking a position on the question. Below is one possible thesis statement that uses the information shown in the previous table.

> Whereas political independence and economic development were common themes in China from 1900 to the present, the political system changed from an imperial-Confucian based dynasty to a nationalist government to a communist one-party state, and the economy became an industrial and export-driven economy by century's end.

This statement is straightforward and it takes a position on the issues raised by the question. This interpretation will provide the organizing argument that guides the development of the essay.

Recommended Activity. Work with a partner or in groups of three. Each of you should write a prompt that might appear on a test based on a current event in the news. Exchange prompts. Then write a thesis statement in response to your partner's prompt. Compare and discuss your thesis statements using these guide questions.

- Does the thesis take a position?
- Does the thesis offer an interpretation of the question?
- Does the thesis help organize ideas for an essay?

4. Write the introductory paragraph. The main point of the first paragraph is to state a thesis clearly that addresses the question. A clear thesis is not only what the readers of the essay will look for, but it sets the organization for the rest of the essay. An effective introductory paragraph may also provide the context of the question and a preview of the main arguments that will be developed in the subsequent paragraphs. However, this additional information should not distract from the thesis statement.

The model for an expository, five-paragraph essay illustrates how a well-organized essay relates back to an effective introductory paragraph. This model also emphasizes the importance of restating the thesis as the supporting paragraphs are developed. However, do not conclude from this model that an essay should consist of five paragraphs. The total number of paragraphs and sentences is for the writer to determine. What the model does suggest is that the introductory paragraph is crucial because it should shape the full essay, including the arguments to be developed. If the introductory paragraph is properly written, the rest of the paper will be less challenging to write, since you have already organized your information.

Recommended Activity. Practice writing introductory paragraphs for the essay questions at the end of each period. Next, follow up the introductory paragraph with an outline of the supporting paragraphs. For each paragraph, list historical evidence that you will link to the thesis. The exercise of writing an introductory paragraph and an outline of your supporting paragraphs helps in two ways. First, it reinforces the connection of the main points in the introduction to the supporting paragraphs. Second, it requires you to think in terms of historical evidence before you start writing a complete essay.

5. Write the supporting paragraphs and conclusion. The number and length of the paragraphs forming the body of the essay will vary depending on the thesis, the main points of your argument, and the amount of historical evidence you present. To receive the highest score, the AP® candidate also must explain how specific historical evidence is linked to the thesis. Each essay will also have an additional targeted historical thinking skill. The chart below shows the main focus of an essay based on key words in the prompt.

Key Words in the Question	What an Essay Should Do
Analyze, analysis	Examine the parts of a topic by identifying and commenting on the nature and relationship of these parts in order to explain why things happen
Cause, causation	Describe and analyze causes and/or effects of a historical development, illustrated with specific examples
Compare, comparison	Describe and analyze reasons for similarities and/or differences in historical developments with specific examples
Continuity and Change-Over-Time	Describe and analyze similarities and differences across time with specific examples
Periodization	Analyze the way historical events are grouped together because they share certain traits or are divided by turning points

Besides your ability to address the targeted thinking skill, your essay will be evaluated on how well you synthesize relevant historical evidence and present the context of the question. For example, in the sample question above, the context of the Cold War and the rise of Communism is essential to understanding the political and economic policies of China during that time.

Your goal is not to fill up a specific number of pages but to write an insightful, persuasive, and well-supported paper. Many students fail to achieve the full potential of their essay because they simply list a few generalities or a "laundry lists" of facts, and they do not answer the full question. Keep in mind that the readers of your essay are not looking for a retelling of history, or "stories." They will be grading you on your ability to craft an analytical essay that supports an argument with specific evidence. A short yet concise essay in which every word has a purpose is better than an essay bloated with fillers, flowery language, and interesting stories.

Your conclusion should restate the thesis. In addition, it should answer the larger question of "So what?" That is, the conclusion should provide the context and explain why the question is relevant in a broader understanding of history.

Here are some tips to keep in mind as you start practicing the writing of history essays for the AP® exam.

Write essays in the third person and in past tense. Write your essay in the third person, avoiding use of the first person ("I," "we"). Also, write in the past tense, except when referring to documents or sources that currently exist (e.g., "the document implies"). Readers also prefer the active voice over the passive voice, because it is more effective in explaining cause and effect (e.g., "Wealthy investors built factories in Britain." is in the active voice; "Factories were built in Britain." is in the passive voice).

Use precise words. Use words that clearly identify persons, factors, and judgments. Avoid vague verbs such as "felt." Use stronger verbs instead such as "insisted," "demanded," or "supported." Also, avoid vague references, such as "they" and "others." Use instead specifics, such as "China's Communist leaders." Avoid absolutes, such as "all" and "none." Rarely in history is the evidence so absolutely conclusive that you can prove that there were no exceptions. Use verbs that communicate judgment and analysis, such as "reveal," "exemplify," "demonstrate," "imply," and "symbolize."

Define or explain key terms. The majority of questions will deal with specific terms (such as "hunter-foragers" "agricultural revolution," "society," or "civilization"), and an essential part of your analysis should be an explanation of these terms.

Anticipate counterarguments. Consider arguments against your thesis to show that you are aware of opposing views. The strongest essays confront conflicting evidence. This is often called a concession or conciliatory paragraph, and is best used directly following your thesis.

Remain objective. Avoid rhetoric, especially on social issues. The AP® test is not the place to argue that one group were racists, or that one group were the "good guys" while another were the "bad guys." And do not use slang terms like "bad guys!"

Communicate the organization and development of your argument. Each paragraph in your essay should develop a main point that is clearly stated in the topic sentence. It is also good practice to provide a few words or a phrase of transition to connect one paragraph to another.

The conclusion should focus on the thesis. Restate the thesis in a fresh and interesting manner or explain its significance. The conclusion should not try to summarize all the data or introduce new evidence. If you are running out of time but have written a well-organized essay with a clear thesis that is supported with evidence, your conclusion can be very short. As noted earlier, stating your thesis in the conclusion is important because the readers look for the thesis point in the first and last paragraph.

Recommended Activity. Your first effort to write an AP® History essay will be a more positive experience for all involved if it is an untimed assignment. After gaining confidence in writing the essay, you should try your hand at a timed test similar to that of the AP® exam (40 minutes for the essay). The purpose of such practice is to become familiar with the time constraints of the exam and to learn ways of (1) improving the clarity as well as the efficiency your writing, and (2) gaining insight into the type of information needed. The feedback from these practice tests—whether from teachers, peers, or self-evaluation—is essential for making progress.

6. Evaluate your AP® essay. More essay writing does not necessarily produce better essays. Breaking down the process into manageable steps is one key for improvement. Peer evaluation as well as self-evaluation can also help you internalize the elements of an effective essay and learn ways to improve. The activity below provides a set of questions about how effectively an essay achieves the elements that the AP® readers look for in their grading. The use of the essay-evaluation techniques can help AP® candidates better understand the characteristics of an excellent essay.

Activity: Evaluation of the Essay

1. Introductory Paragraph Underline the thesis and circle the structural elements identified in the introduction. How effectively does the introductory paragraph prepare the reader for the rest of the essay? How might you improve the introductory paragraph?

2. Thesis Is the thesis clear? Does it deal with all parts of the question?

3. Analysis Does the body of the essay provide analysis of the question? Does the body reflect the argument and controlling ideas stated in the introductory paragraph? Does the body acknowledge opposing points of view? How could the analysis be improved?

4. Evidence Is the thesis supported clearly with substantial, relevant information? What significant additional information or evidence could have been used for support?

5. Errors What minor or major errors in fact or analysis does the essay display?

6. Presentation How well organized and persuasive is the essay? Does paragraph composition, sentence structure, word choice, or spelling add to or detract from the essay? Identify areas that need improvement.

Recommended Activity. Teacher evaluation and self-evaluation of essay work is initially less threatening than peer evaluation, but once a level of confidence is established, peer-evaluation can help you become a better writer and is often the most useful form of feedback. Below is a generic scoring guide for the essay based on the College Board's rubrics for the essay. Use the guide to evaluate your work and internalize the characteristics of a strong essay.

Scoring Guide: Continuity and Change-Over-Time Essay

Below is the scoring guide for the Continuity and Change-Over-Time Essay. The first table is for the "Basic Core: Competence" level.

Attribute	What Readers Look For	Historical Thinking Skill Applied	Maximum Possible Points
Thesis	An acceptable thesis answers all parts of the question and addresses the global issues and the time period or periods specified.	• Argumentation • Patterns of Continuity and Change-Over-Time	1
Response	The essay addresses all parts of the question. The parts do not have to be addressed evenly.	• Argumentation	2
Support	The essay supports the thesis with appropriate historical evidence.	• Argumentation	2
Context	The essay uses relevant world historical context to explain continuity and Change-Over-Time.	• Contextualization	1
Analysis	The essay analyzes the process of continuity and Change-Over-Time.	• Patterns of Continuity and Change-Over-Time • Causation	1
Subtotal	The essay as a whole combines information effectively.	• Synthesis	7

Essays awarded a seven on the "Competence" measures are considered for two possible additional points on the "Expanded Core: Excellence" level.

Attribute	What Readers Look For	Historical Thinking Skill Applied	Maximum Possible Points
Varied	• The thesis is clear, analytical, and comprehensive. • The essay analyzes all relevant issues of the question. • The essay provides ample historical evidence to support the thesis. • The essay links with relevant ideas, events, and trends in an innovative way.	Varied	2
		Total possible points	9

Scoring Guide: Comparison Essay

Below is the scoring guide for the Comparison Essay. The first table is for the "Basic Core: Competence Level."

Attribute	What Readers Look For	Historical Thinking Skill Applied	Maximum Possible Points
Thesis	An acceptable thesis compares and contrasts the issues or themes specified and answers all parts of the question.	• Argumentation • Comparison	1
Response	The essay addresses all parts of the question. The parts do not have to be addressed evenly.	• Argumentation	2
Support	The essay supports the thesis with appropriate historical evidence.	• Argumentation	2
Comparison	The essay makes at least one relevant, direct comparison.	• Comparison	1
Analysis	The essay analyzes at least one reason for a similarity or difference identified in a direct comparison	• Comparison • Causation	1
Subtotal	The essay as a whole combines information effectively.	• Synthesis	7

Essays awarded a seven on the "Competence" measures are considered for two possible additional points on the "Expanded Core: Excellence" level.

Attribute	What Readers Look For	Historical Thinking Skill Applied	Maximum Possible Points
Varied	• The thesis is clear, analytical, and comprehensive. • The essay analyzes parts of the question thoroughly. • The essay provides ample historical evidence to support the thesis. • The essay relates comparisons to larger global context.	Varied	2
		Total possible points	9

3. Answering the Document-Based Question (DBQ)

The AP® World History exam includes one Document-Based Question (DBQ). You will be given 50 minutes to answer, including 10 minutes for reading the documents. To receive a top score, you will need to refer to all of the documents in your analysis. The grading of DBQs will also place more emphasis on understanding the background of the documents. You are expected to include at least one or more of the following in your analysis of each document.

- The purpose of the document and the key words that explain how the document relates to the question
- The intended audience of the document
- Details that demonstrate the author's point of view
- The historical context
- How the documents may be grouped with other documents
- How an additional source could amplify missing information or bias

The initial difficulty of answering a DBQ largely disappears if you remember that it builds on the skills for writing responses to the essay questions. The same skills apply here.

- Write a thesis statement that addresses all parts of the question
- Build argumentation supported by relevant specific evidence
- Use targeted historical thinking skills, and
- Synthesize

The only difference is that you must analyze and refer to up to 10 primary and secondary sources in your supporting arguments. The focus in answering the DBQ, just as in the essay, is to develop a strong thesis that deals with all parts of the question. This sample DBQ illustrates how important it is to identify and address all parts of the prompt.

Analyze major changes and continuities in the social, economic, and political conditions of women during the eighteenth and nineteenth centuries in France and Great Britain.

An effective answer will have to address the targeted thinking skill: continuity and change. It will also have to show the social, economic, *and* political conditions, in *both* France *and* Great Britain for the period.

The greatest mistake a writer can make in answering a DBQ is to write little more than a descriptive list of the documents. The arrangement of the documents in the DBQ should not control the organization of the essay. Rather, the documents should be grouped or categorized based upon the themes in the question. Analyze the documents in terms of evidence to be linked to the thesis, and integrate them into a well-organized and persuasive essay.

As you use this textbook, you will deal with numerous documents or "stimuli" before practicing the first DBQ. There is one DBQ in the review section at the end of each of the six periods, and another one in the Practice Exam at the end of the book. Use these practice DBQs to develop your historical thinking skills as well as the writing skills needed for answering the DBQ on the exam.

Here are some tips for writing an effective DBQ.

1. Use the first 10 minutes to read and make marginal notes on the documents. As in the Essays, take time to formulate a thesis that will address all parts of the question before you start writing. The key historical thinking skills to be developed for the successful writing of a DBQ are use of evidence, argumentation, and synthesis, but each DBQ will also have a targeted thinking skill.

2. Brief references to the documents are enough. Because the readers already know the content of the documents, there is no need to quote them at length. A reference to the document's author or title is enough. Many writers simply site the document number in parentheses, such as (Doc. 1), because it is quicker. Readers like this system as well, because it is simple and clear.

3. Use all of the documents. They are all important. However, recognize that each one represents a point of view and some might contain information that is not accurate.

Some documents may seem to be irrelevant to your thesis and its defense but may be used to show your understanding of the other side of the question and the context in which the document was created. Part of the challenge of the DBQ is to demonstrate your judgment about the sources based on your knowledge of historical period.

Recommended Activities As a prewriting activity for the DBQs, work with a small group of classmates to read a document and discuss the author's point of view, purpose, historical context, and intended audience.

A practice scoring guide for DBQs based the College Board's grading rubrics is provided on the next page. (Check apcentral.collegeboard.com for updates.) Use this guide to evaluate your work and to internalize the criteria for writing a strong DBQ essay.

Scoring Guide: Document-Based Question

Below is the scoring guide for the Document-Based Question. The first table is for the "Basic Core: Competence" level.

Attribute	What Readers Look For	Historical Thinking Skill Applied	Maximum Possible Points
Thesis	An acceptable thesis addresses all parts of the question and states a position that can be supported.	• Argumentation • Other skills depend on the topic of the question	1
Use of Documents	The essay addresses all of the documents and demonstrates that the writer understands them.	• Argumentation • Other skills depend on the topic of the question	1
Support	The essay supports the thesis with appropriate historical evidence or key words or phrases from each of the documents.	• Argumentation • Other skills depend on the topic of the question	2
Point of View	The essay analyzes the point of view in at least two documents.	• Use of Historical Evidence	1
Analysis	The essay analyzes the documents by grouping them in two or three ways.	• Argumentation • Use of Historical Evidence • Other skills depend on the topic of the question	1
Additional Sources	The essay identifies and explains the need for one type of appropriate additional document or source.	• Argumentation • Use of Historical Evidence	1
Subtotal	The essay as a whole combines information effectively.	• Synthesis	7

Essays awarded a seven on the "Competence" measures are considered for two possible additional points on the "Expanded Core: Excellence" level.

Attribute	What Readers Look For	Historical Thinking Skill Applied	Maximum Possible Points
Varied	• The thesis is clear, analytical, and comprehensive. • The essay shows insightful analysis of the documents. • The essay uses documents persuasively as evidence to support the thesis. • The essay analyzes the documents in multiple ways, such as grouping them or synthesizing information. • The essay includes relevant "outside" historical content that is not specifically mentioned in the documents. • The essay explains why additional types of document(s) or sources would be useful.	Varied	2
		Total possible points	9

Review Schedule

Plan how you will prepare to take the AP® World History exam. Set a schedule for your review of each period of history. You might spread your review over a long or a short amount of time. Many AP® candidates find that study groups are helpful. The following is a sample of a review schedule using this text. It assumes the review will take place over eight weeks:

Week 1: Review writing skills and content to c. 600 C.E. (Chapters 1–2)

Week 2: c. 600 B.C.E. to c. 600 C.E. (Chapters 3–6)

Week 3: c. 600 C.E. to c.1450 (Chapters 7–10)

Week 4: c. 600 C.E. to c.1450 (Chapters 11–14)

Week 5: c.1450 to c.1750 (Chapters 15–20)

Week 6: c.1750 to c.1900 (Chapters 21–24)

Week 7: c.1900 to the present (Chapters 25–30)

Week 8: Complete and review practice test

Staying with a schedule requires discipline. This discipline is greatly strengthened if a study group chooses a specific time and place to meet and sets specific objectives for each meeting. Some individuals may find it more productive to create a review schedule for themselves. If this review text has been used in conjunction with a history course, your familiarity with the essential content and skills developed in this book should make it an even more convenient and efficient review tool.

Regions

Exam questions often ask about specific regions of the world. These regions are shown on the following maps:

WORLD REGIONS — A BIG PICTURE VIEW

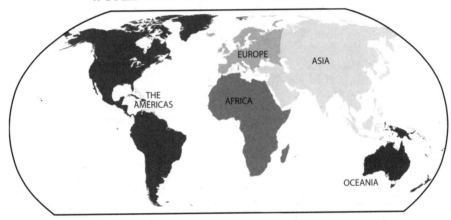

WORLD REGIONS — A CLOSER LOOK

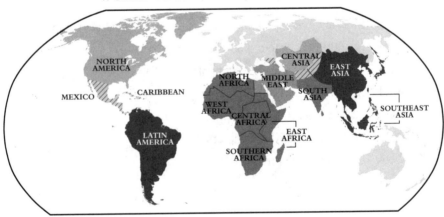

Source: *AP® World History Course and Exam Description.*

PERIOD I: Technological and Environmental Transformations, to c. 600 B.C.E.

Chapter 1 *From Hunter-Foragers to Settled Societies*

Chapter 2 *The First Civilizations*

Period Overview

From their origins in East Africa, nomadic humans slowly migrated across the earth, hunting and foraging for food. The development of farming and herding around 8000 B.C.E. (10,000 years ago) was revolutionary. With a more dependable food supply, villages grew into cities, people specialized in jobs, powerful states emerged, and people developed the first writing systems. Trade expanded, spreading new goods and ideas more rapidly than before. By 600 B.C.E., Mesopotamia, India, Egypt, China, Mesoamerica, and the Andes had impressive civilizations that would provide the core of later civilizations in their regions.

Key Concepts

1.1 Big Geography and the Peopling of the Earth

  I. Archeological evidence indicates that during the Paleolithic era, hunting-foraging bands of humans gradually migrated from their origin in East Africa to Eurasia, Australia, and the Americas, adapting their technology and cultures to new climate regions.

1.2 The Neolithic Revolution and Early Agricultural Societies

  I. Beginning about 10,000 years ago, the Neolithic Revolution led to the development of new and more complex economic and social systems.

  II. Agriculture and pastoralism began to transform human societies.

1.3 The Development and Interactions of Early Agricultural, Pastoral, and Urban Societies

  I. Core and foundational civilizations developed in a variety of geographical and environmental settings where agriculture flourished.

  II. The first states emerged within core civilizations.

  III. Culture played a significant role in unifying states through laws, language, literature, religion, myths, and monumental art.

Source: *AP® World History Course and Exam Description.*

From Hunter-Foragers to Settled Societies

"Civilizations take ages to be born, to settle, and to grow."
—Fernand Braudel, *A History of Civilizations*

Achieving an understanding of early human history is difficult. But even though prehistoric peoples did not have a written language, they left evidence of how they lived in their bones and in their *artifacts,* objects made by people in the past. For example, the size and composition of skeletons can suggest how well nourished people were. Chipped stones indicate they made tools with sharp edges. The remains of burnt logs show they used fire. And since prehistoric people often buried their dead with jewelry and religious tokens, they left clues about what they considered valuable. By studying these physical remains, people today can trace the movements of the earliest humans across the globe, understand how they traded with each other, and learn about the new technologies they developed.

Migrating Across the Globe

Modern humans, the group *Homo sapiens sapiens,* first appeared in East Africa between 200,000 and 100,000 years ago. They survived by hunting animals and foraging for seeds, nuts, fruits, and edible roots, so they are labeled as *hunter-foragers* or hunter-gatherers. Always on the search for food, they migrated from place to place, gradually expanding the region of human settlement. If the population became too dense in one area or if the climate shifted, they might be pushed to move. Other times, they might be pulled to a new region by new sources of food or fresh water. As people encountered new climates and environments, they developed new cultural patterns and new forms of technology.

One force pushing migration was climate change. As the climate warmed and cooled, animal and plant habitats shifted. People adjusted by following the animals and plants. Each time the climate cooled—a dip in the average daily temperature of several degrees—habitats would shift toward the equator and glaciers would grow, covering up land. As the climate warmed, habitats would shift away from the equator and more land would open up for occupation. As the animals and plants moved, so did people.

During one cooler period, so much water froze into ice that the ocean levels fell as much as 400 feet below today's level. The level was low enough that land connected northeastern Asia and what is now Alaska. This land, now submerged under the Bering Strait, provided a bridge between Asia and the Americas. Nomadic hunters followed herds of animals that wandered across this land. When temperatures increased and ocean levels rose, these people, the first Americans, were cut off from their Asian ancestors. Over time, they slowly moved farther south along the coast.

By 10,000 B.C.E., possibly far earlier, humans lived on every continent except Antarctica. In each region, people developed distinctive cultures.

The Paleolithic Period

The early years of human history are part of the *Paleolithic Period,* which began 2.5 million years ago and ended about 10,000 years ago (8000 B.C.E.). Because humans used stone tools and weapons in this period, it is often called the Stone Age. In addition to stone, people made tools from wood, animal bones, and antlers. Many of their tools included a sharp point or blade. For example, they had digging sticks for uncovering roots they could eat, and they had spears, harpoons, and arrows for killing animals.

Adapting to the Environment As people migrated in search of animals and edible plants, they found certain tools to be particularly useful in the new environment they encountered. For example, as they moved into cooler climates as far north as the tundra, they needed scrapers for cleaning the flesh off of animals' skins they wore for warmth. In the warmer regions such as the tropics, nets for catching fish were particularly valuable. As they reached the coasts of the Mediterranean Sea and the Pacific Ocean, they built strong rafts to venture out onto the water. In forested areas, they used axes to cut down trees to make shelters. People adapted technology to new conditions.

MIGRATION OUT OF AFRICA

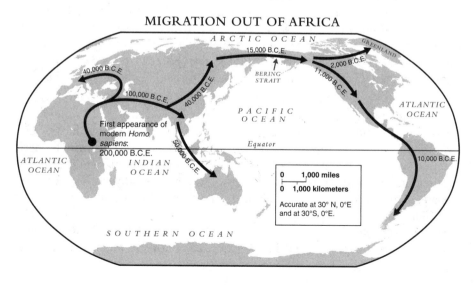

Control of Fire One of the greatest accomplishments of people in the Paleolithic Period was to learn to control fire. It changed their lives by providing

- light to allow them to see better after the sun went down
- heat so they could live in colder climates than before
- protection against wild animals
- smoke to pacify bees, which made obtaining honey easier
- help in hunting by scaring animals to race to their death over a cliff

Possibly the most influential use of fire was to prepare food. Cooking made protein-rich and starchy foods (both hunted and foraged) easier to digest and, hence, more nutritious.

Hunter-Forager Society As early humans developed new technology, they also established more complex social structures. At the center of society was the nuclear family, which then expanded outward to include ties between related families. Several related families that moved together in search of food were called a *kinship group.* A typical group might include 20 to 40 people. Smaller groups might have difficulty finding enough food. Larger groups would use up the food supply of an area more quickly, which would require more frequent moving. Kinship groups were often nearly self-sufficient. They could make most or all of what they needed to survive.

Though kinship groups traveled on their own and were close to self-sufficient, they were not isolated. They were often part of a larger group of relatives called a *clan.* And sometimes multiple clans combined into still larger units called a *tribe.* An individual did not have to be related to other members to be considered part of a tribe. The tribes were formed for purposes of group hunting or mutual defense from enemies and were usually led by chiefs and priests.

Between groups at each level of organization—kinship group, clan, and tribe—people were also tied together by trade. Besides trading goods such as tools and clothing, they also traded people. A person from one group might join another group to help balance out the size of each group. Through these trades in goods and people, ideas spread. People learned new methods for making tools, new thoughts about religion, and new information about the world.

Roles in Society Since early people did not leave written records, most modern knowledge of them comes from the study of artifacts. However, in modern times, anthropologists have also studied hunter-forager groups whose way of life probably resembles that of earlier nomads. From these modern studies, scholars have inferred that Paleolithic groups probably were relatively egalitarian. They did not have many layers of leaders, and only small differences separated the poorest and the wealthiest individuals in a kinship group.

Functions in hunter-forager societies were often divided by gender. These societies were *patriarchal,* ones dominated by men. Paleolithic males took charge of hunts, warfare, and heavy labor. Paleolithic women gathered and

Source: iStockphoto

The oldest known paintings were created about 40,000 years ago..

prepared food and looked after the children. Anthropologists believe that the women breast-fed their children for as long as five years, a practice that provided high nutrition for the children as well as a very rudimentary form of family planning. (Test Prep: Write a paragraph connecting early hunter-forager groups with such groups in Russia. Read about the Slavic peoples on page 137)

Religion and Art Paleolithic people developed a system of religious beliefs centered around the worship of gods they associated with the forces of nature. The belief that animals, rivers, and other elements of nature embody spirits is called *animism*. The first religious leaders were probably *shamans*, people believed to have special abilities to cure the sick and influence the future. Ritual sacrifices to these gods and evidence of burial practices suggest a belief in the afterlife that dates back 100,000 years. Evidence of artistic expression has been found in the form of cave paintings, which date back to 32,000 years ago, and musical instruments, such as flutes, dating to 30,000 years ago. Paleolithic art may have been connected to religious ceremonies.

Neolithic Revolution

Around 10,000 years ago (8000 B.C.E.), as the climate was warming up from an Ice Age, a collection of social and political developments coalesced into what is called the *Neolithic Revolution*, a set of dramatic changes in how people lived based on the development of agriculture. These changes are sometimes called the Agricultural Revolution. This "revolution" did not happen instantaneously, nor did it occur everywhere at the same time, nor did it affect everyone directly. For example, the Neolithic Revolution in China dates to 5000 B.C.E., whereas in the Middle East, it can be dated to around 8000 B.C.E. It can be characterized by several major developments:

1. agriculture
2. pastoralism
3. specialization of labor
4. towns and cities
5. governments
6. religions
7. technological innovations

Agriculture Taking advantage of a warmer global climate following the end of the last Ice Age, some hunter-forager cultures learned to grow crops by putting seeds of wild plants into the ground. They gave up their nomadic way of life to stay in one place and take up *agriculture,* the practice of raising crops or livestock on a continual and controlled basis. As they learned to plant, tend, and harvest crops, people found they often had a *surplus,* or more than they needed for themselves. The development of agriculture occurred first in lands just east of the Mediterranean Sea. It also occurred independently at several other places and from these places spread throughout the world.

These early farmers domesticated the crops that were already growing wild in their region: wheat and barley in Southwest Asia, millet in Northern China, rice in Southeast Asia, and maize (corn) in Mesoamerica. As cultivation of these crops spread, the natural diversity of plants in a region decreased. With that change came reductions in the diversity of insects and animals that depended on the other crops.

The availability of these farmed crops also made the diets of people less diversified. Usually people in an area would grow just one or two crops, and they would eat foods prepared with those crops at every meal. People continued to hunt animals and to gather wild fruits and nuts when seasonably available, but overall the farmers' diets lacked the variety of full-time hunter-foragers. By cultivating just one or two plants, they eliminated other plants that had been part of people's diets.

Pastoralism Even before people settled down as farmers, people in Africa, Europe, and Asia had begun to tame wild animals so they could be brought up to live with humans, a process called *domestication*. The first animal that people domesticated was the dog. Initially, humans employed dogs to assist with hunting and to provide warnings about the approach of dangerous animals. Goats were domesticated next. They provided both meat and milk. Other animals were domesticated soon after—cattle, horses, sheep, pigs, and chickens—that provided labor or food. As people began to keep larger herds of animals, they began to lead them from one grazing land to another. Their way of life is called *nomadic pastoralism,* or simply pastoralism, because it was based on people moving herds of animals from pasture to pasture. Like hunters and foragers, pastoralists were mobile. Like farmers, pastoralists controlled their food supply. Pastoralism first emerged in grassland regions of Africa and Eurasia.

Domestication of Plants and Animals						
Area	18,000 to 15,000 B.C.E.	15,000 to 12,000 B.C.E.	12,000 to 9,000 B.C.E.	9,000 to 6,000 B.C.E.	6,000 to 3,000 B.C.E.	3,000 to 1 B.C.E.
Europe	• Dogs			• Sheep • Pigs • Goats • Cattle	• Wheat	
Middle East			• Cattle • Barley • Wheat	• Goats • Sheep		
Africa				• Cattle	• Sorghum	• Rice
Asia			• Rice • Pigs	• Millet • Cattle		
Americas				• Maize • Squash	• Beans	

Like farmers, pastoralists made the shift away from hunting-foraging hoping to create a more dependable food supply for themselves. And like farmers, pastoralists affected the environment dramatically. At times, pastoralists would allow their animals to graze an area so heavily that the animals would destroy the grass. When rains came, without grass to hold the soil in place, the soil would wash away and the land became infertile.

However, pastoralists were unlike farmers in one important way: While farmers settled in one place, pastoralists moved regularly. Hence, while farmers accumulated belongings, pastoralists usually owned very little. And while farmers had only a little contact with people in other communities, pastoralists were in contact with new items and new ideas. Over the past

10,000 years, pastoralists have played an important role in spreading ideas and trading goods among people. (Test Prep: Create a chart comparing Paleolithic pastoralists with later pastoralists such as the Mongols. See page 241.)

Specialization of Labor The growth of agriculture and pastoralism reduced plant and animal diversity, but the surpluses of food they produced led to dramatic changes. For the first time in history, some workers were free to focus on tasks other than producing food. Some people became *artisans,* people who made objects people needed, such as woven clothe or pottery. Others became *merchants,* people who buy and sell goods for a living. Still others became soldiers, religious leaders, or politicians. This process of allowing people to focus on limited tasks is called the *specialization of labor.*

The impact of specialization of labor was far-reaching. Freed from work on the farms, artisans made weapons, tools, and jewelry. A merchant class, engaged with trading these objects, emerged. The surplus of food and goods, combined with the needs of religious ceremonies and a rudimentary system of taxation, led to the invention of writing, which was first used to keep records about trades and tax payments. People later began to use writing to communicate with one another, to record descriptions of events, and to write down religious stories. The development of writing marked the transition from prehistory to history.

Growth of Villages, Towns, and Cities The food surplus encouraged both a growth in population and an opportunity to do work not related to producing food. Permanent dwellings and villages and towns multiplied as tribes abandoned their nomadic lifestyles and, eventually, some cities emerged. With the change in food production came *social stratification.* This means that some people accumulated wealth in the form of jewelry and other coveted items and by building larger and better decorated houses. The idea of private property became increasingly important. People with more wealth or more power to control the surplus formed an elite. In general, the elites were men.

One of humankind's first cities was *Jericho,* which was built on the west bank of the Jordan River. The oldest evidence of human settlement there dates from about 9000 B.C.E. Another ancient city, *Catal Huyuk,* in present-day Turkey, was founded in 7500 B.C.E. along a river that has since dried up. The city existed for about 2,000 years, but its well-preserved remains have helped modern people understand life long ago. Although both cities were significant population centers, and while Jericho has tremendous significance in the Judeo-Christian tradition, neither city became a major site of an emerging civilization.

Governments The surplus of food also led to the creation of governmental institutions. People had to work together to clear land and, in many places, provide irrigation to water the crops. To coordinate these efforts required a government. And if the community produced a surplus, powerful leaders were required to supervise how it was used, and soldiers were needed to protect it from other groups. Priests were needed, not only to supervise religious ceremonies, but also to explain how the behavior and rulings of leaders were based on religious doctrine.

The leaders of farming communities and towns developed the earliest forms of government. Those who owned the most land or livestock became the wealthiest and thus the most powerful. They became the leaders of local governments.

Religions Given the unpredictable nature of weather and longer-term climate changes, Neolithic farmers experienced temporary interruptions and problems, just as farmers do today. Moreover, agricultural land could lose its fertility through *overfarming* unless it was left fallow or it was fertilized, usually by the spreading of animal manure. Pastures could erode due to *overgrazing,* or the continual eating of grasses or their roots, without allowing them to regrow. As people tried to persuade the spirits of nature to help with their crops and herds, religious ceremonies became more elaborate. These ceremonies became so important and elaborate, a special class of *priests* and *priestesses* developed to conduct them.

In some regions, new religious beliefs became highly organized before 600 B.C.E. For example, along the eastern coast of the Mediterranean Sea, the Hebrews emerged under the leadership of Abraham. They were among the first religious groups to worship only one deity, a practice called *monotheism*. In South Asia, the Vedic religion included a variety of deities and a heavy emphasis on rituals. In what is now Iran, a teacher named Zoroaster inspired the religion of Zoroastrianism, which focused on the eternal battle between two forces, one good and one evil.

Technological Innovations Societies advanced as people adopted new tools and skills. In some cases, these advances were probably made in one place. In other cases, they were made in several places independently. Either way, most people learned about new technology through trade, war, or other forms of contact with other societies:

- To store food and carry water, they invented waterproof clay pots. People shaped pots out of wet clay and then hardened them in fire. Sometimes people decorated the pots before firing by etching designs on them. Since these pots are one of the artifacts that has lasted thousands of years, they provide insight into how people lived and what they thought was important.

- People improved on the drilling stick, creating a plow. The plow could be pulled by oxen or other animals, which made cultivating crops much easier. In addition, turning over the soil disrupted the growth of weeds, which enabled crops to grow better and increased their yield.

- The development of the wheel with an axle revolutionized transportation and trade. A wheeled cart could transport a load with about 3 percent of the effort needed to drag it. People could transport everything more easily, from grain for overseas trade to stones for building monumental architecture. Adding wheels to a plow made planting crops easier.

- The production of *textiles,* items made of cloth, included several steps. Weavers, who were usually women, learned to spin hair from animals or fibers from plants into threads and then weave the threads into cloth. Workers would often decorate the textiles by dying the threads and making patterns. All of this work was usually done in the home.

- People gradually learned *metallurgy,* the science of the study of metals. They replaced their stone tools and weapons with ones made from metal, a process made easier as they learned to heat metals with fire. They first used *copper,* which they found in a pure state in the ground. Through experimentation, they learned that melting tin and copper together made a stronger metal, *bronze.* This metal marked such an advance that it gave the period a new name: the *Bronze Age,* which began at different locations at different times but generally between 3300 and 2300 B.C.E.

The First Civilizations

The seven developments of the Neolithic Revolution that began around 8000 B.C.E. created the foundation for a new form of human society to emerge over several thousand years. This new form is *civilization,* a large society with cities and powerful states. In early civilizations, many people continued to hunt and forage, often mixing those activities with farming or herding.

Trends that began to emerge in the Neolithic Revolution became even stronger in the early civilizations. For example, society became more stratified into clearly different socio-economic classes, human impact on the environment became more intense, government and religious and military institutions became larger and more complex, and trade increased. Elites grew more powerful as they became increasingly wealthy. The gap between the rich and the poor grew wider, and the relative power of men and women in society diverged more noticeably. Most societies became *patriarchies,* ones ruled by men. (Test Prep: Write a paragraph comparing the Neolithic Revolution with the Industrial Revolution. See pages 421–433.)

The first four civilizations that grew out of the Neolithic Revolution developed independently in river valleys scattered around the earth. The first one was in Southwest Asia, in the valleys of the Tigris and the Euphrates, a region called Mesopotamia. The next three were in the Nile River valley in Egypt, the Huang He (Yellow) River valley in China, and the Indus River valley in India. Two other early civilizations, in Mesoamerica and the Andes Mountains, were not tied closely to a major river valley.

All six of these civilizations developed ways of life, such as language, religious beliefs, and economic practices, that would heavily influence successor civilizations in their regions. Because of their influence, they are examples of *core and foundational* civilizations.

HISTORICAL PERSPECTIVES: WAS FARMING A MISTAKE?

Scholars of prehistoric life disagree about the benefits and costs of the development of agriculture and pastoralism. Biologist and geographer Jared Diamond called the development of agriculture the "worst mistake in the history of the human race." He argued that reducing the variety of food in people's diets increased malnourishment. Relying on fewer food sources made people more susceptible to famine. Living in concentrated settlements increased everyone's risk for disease. Together, Diamond concluded, these changes reduced the average life span.

In contrast, evolutionary psychologist Steven Pinker argued that agriculture and pastoralism reduced violence. He cited studies that suggest that hunter-forager societies had high murder rates and frequent warfare. These societies were dangerous because they lacked governments strong enough to maintain peace.

Evolutionary anthropologist Jay Stock saw both negatives and positives in the Neolithic Revolution. From a study of 9,000 skeletons from ancient Egypt, he found that hunter-foragers who lived before the agricultural revolution averaged 5 feet, 8 inches tall. However, those who lived in the first several thousand years after the development of farming averaged 4 inches shorter. Still, he noted the long-term benefits of agriculture: "Without the surplus of food you get through farming, we couldn't have the runaway technological innovation we see today."

KEY TERMS BY THEME

ENVIRONMENT	STATE-BUILDING	SOCIAL STRUCTURE
overfarming	Jericho	kinship group
overgrazing	Catal Huyuk	clan
		tribe
CULTURE	**ECONOMICS**	patriarchal
artifacts	textiles	artisans
Homo sapiens sapiens	specialization of labor	merchants
Paleolithic Period	copper	social stratification
Neolithic Revolution	bronze	priests
monotheism	hunter-forager	priestesses
Bronze Age	agriculture	
civilization	surplus	
core and foundational	domestication	
	nomadic pastoralism	

1. Which statement best summarizes the variety of changes that resulted from people learning to use fire?

    (A) Fire improved the diet of early humans.

    (B) Fire made domestication of animals easier.

    (C) Fire allowed people to use metals for the first time.

    (D) Fire altered the relationship between men and women.

2. The key development that allowed people to begin settling into permanent communities was

    (A) the use of stone tools

    (B) the advent of the pastoral lifestyle

    (C) the development of agriculture

    (D) the invention of writing

3. Why might historians use 8000 B.C.E. to mark the beginning of a period in human history?

    (A) People began to practice agriculture for the first time.

    (B) People moved out of Africa for the first time.

    (C) People domesticated animals for the first time.

    (D) People developed writing for the first time.

4. Which best describes the relationship between Paleolithic kinship groups?

    (A) Because kinship groups were self-sufficient, they had almost no contact with other groups.

    (B) While kinship groups traveled separately, they traded goods, members, and ideas.

    (C) Since life was so difficult, kinship groups depended heavily on each other for survival.

    (D) Anthropologists have not yet found physical remains of Paleolithic cultures.

5. Which generalization best describes where the first four civilizations developed?

    (A) They all emerged on separate continents.

    (B) They all grew up along seacoasts.

    (C) They all developed in the same climate zone.

    (D) They all formed in river valleys.

6. The development of classes of people specializing in particular types of labor, such as artisans, priests, scribes, and merchants, in early civilizations was most likely made possible by
   (A) the invention of writing
   (B) surplus food
   (C) patriarchal relationships
   (D) trade between groups

Question 7 refers to the excerpt below.

Wheels are the archetype of a primitive, caveman-level technology. But in fact, they're so ingenious that it took until 3500 B.C. for someone to invent them. . . .

   The tricky thing about the wheel is not conceiving of a cylinder rolling on its edge. It's figuring out how to connect a stable, stationary platform to that cylinder.

   The stroke of brilliance was the wheel-and-axle concept," said David Anthony, a professor of anthropology at Hartwick College and author of *The Horse, the Wheel, and Language* (Princeton, 2007). "But then making it was also difficult.

—Natalie Wolchover, "Why It Took So Long to Invent the Wheel,"
Scientific American. March 6, 2012.

7. Using the excerpt and information in the text, which statement best describes the advances in technology made by Paleolithic people?
   (A) Technological advances showed their creativity.
   (B) They invented new forms of technology systematically.
   (C) The wheel was developed in different regions at the same time.
   (D) They viewed advances in technology as a sign of luck.

8. Early cities such as Catal Huyuk and Jericho are important to historians and other scholars because they
   (A) include several famous cave paintings
   (B) demonstrate how urbanization changed culture
   (C) were the sites of the first domesticated animals
   (D) provide the first evidence of trade among people

Question 9 refers to the table below.

World Population to 5,000 B.C.E.	
Year	Population (in millions)
1 million B.C.E.	0.1
300000 B.C.E.	1.0
25000 B.C.E.	3.3
10000 B.C.E.	4.0
5000 B.C.E.	5.0

Source: Michael Kremer, "Population Growth and Technological Change: One Million B.C. to 1990," *The Quarterly Journal of Economics,* Vol. 108, No. 3 (Aug. 1993), 681–716.

9. Which statement is best supported by the evidence in the table?
   (A) The population of hunter-foragers varied greatly.
   (B) Human population grew more rapidly after the Neolithic Revolution.
   (C) A decline in population caused people to adopt nomadic pastoralism.
   (D) Warfare prevented the population from increasing.

10. Which of the following illustrates a major change in how human societies were organized as the Neolithic Age progressed?
   (A) Humans stopped gathering food and began to hunt and fish.
   (B) Allegiance to divinely approved hereditary leaders replaced tribal societies.
   (C) Settled societies with specialized skills emerged in a growing number of places.
   (D) Nomadic pastoralism replaced agriculture in a growing number of societies.

CONTINUITY AND CHANGE-OVER-TIME ESSAY QUESTIONS

Directions: You are to answer the following question. You should spend 5 minutes organizing or outlining your essay. Write an essay that:

- Has a relevant thesis and supports that thesis with appropriate historical evidence.
- Addresses all parts of the question.
- Uses world historical context to show continuities and changes over time.
- Analyzes the process of continuity and change over time.

1. Analyze continuities and change in the diet of people before and after the development of agriculture beginning around 8000 B.C.E.

Questions for Additional Practice

2. Analyze continuities and change in religion before and after the Neolithic Revolution.

3. Analyze continuities and change in culture between period before the Neolithic Revolution and the modern period.

COMPARATIVE ESSAY QUESTIONS

Directions: You are to answer the following question. You should spend 5 minutes organizing or outlining your essay. Write an essay that:

- Has a relevant thesis and supports that thesis with appropriate historical evidence.
- Addresses all parts of the question.
- Makes direct, relevant comparisons.
- Analyzes relevant reasons for similarities and differences.

1. Compare and contrast how people in nomadic societies and people in the first settled societies interacted with the environment.

Questions for Additional Practice

2. Compare and contrast the effects of technological innovations on the development of early agricultural and pastoral societies during the Neolithic Revolution.

3. Compare and contrast social stratification in hunter-forager societies and in the first settled societies.

In a historical argument, a historian provides evidence to support an answer to a question about the past. Evidence is specific information that is based on facts or reasons, not unsupported opinions. *For each of the following questions, which statement below it would be most useful in an argument answering it?*

1. What caused early agricultural and pastoral societies to become more stratified?

    A. The development of wheeled vehicles contributed to a growing division between most people and a few wealthy elites.

    B. The development of wheels was very important in human history.

2. Why does the amount of sculpture, painting, and other forms of art increase as a society moves from hunting and gathering to agriculture?

    A. Agricultural societies can produce enough surplus food that people can devote more time to creating art.

    B. People created art long before they developed agriculture, and they continued to do so after they settled into permanent communities.

When answering an essay question, note the type of thinking that the question is asking you to demonstrate. For example, *analyze* and *evaluate* are different thinking skills. *Analyze* means to examine the parts of something; you often analyze information when you want to explain why something happened. In contrast, *evaluate* means to identify the positive and negative aspects of something or to determine its significance. *In each of the following questions, which word states the type of thinking the answer should express?*

1. Compare the role of women in hunter-forager and agricultural societies between 10,000 B.C.E. and 600 B.C.E.

2. In a paragraph, describe life in a hunter-forager society.

3. The Neolithic Revolution made government more important. Explain why this change happened.

4. Plows, axles, textiles, and iron were technological innovations in early societies. Select one of these and assess its significance.

5. Contrast religion before and after the Neolithic Revolution.

2

The First Civilizations

Create Babylon, whose construction you requested! Let its mud bricks be molded, and build high the shrine!

—The Epic of Creation, 1st Millennium B.C.E., a Sumerian version of how the world began.

Four of the first civilizations emerged in river valleys. In one or more of these, as well as in other early civilizations, people developed large urban areas, extensive trade, formal legal codes, sophisticated writing systems, and other critical developments that have become standard features of civilizations ever since.

The Sumerians

In Southwest Asia, the *Tigris* and *Euphrates* rivers flow south from modern-day Turkey through what is now Iraq to empty into the Persian Gulf. The area between these two rivers was once known as *Mesopotamia*, which comes from a Greek word meaning "between rivers." Because so many ancient civilizations arose there, the region is now called "the cradle of civilization." A larger area, the *Fertile Crescent*, overlaps with Mesopotamia but also includes an area to the west, along the Mediterranean coast.

The geography of Mesopotamia presented numerous agricultural benefits. Frequent flooding from the Tigris and Euphrates would leave deposits of silt, which made the soil very fertile. The water and fertile soil of Mesopotamia, combined with a warm climate, provided the resources the Neolithic people who lived in the region needed to begin farming.

Sometime before 5000 B.C.E., a group of nomadic pastoralists called *Sumerians* migrated into Mesopotamia, settling alongside people already living there. Over time, these new migrants created the civilization of *Sumer*. They built cities, canals to carry river water to fields, and dams to control the rivers' unpredictable flooding. The first complex governments arose to coordinate these tasks. While Sumer is not a separate country today, the civilization it created provided the core and the foundation of several other civilizations in the Middle East, and its influence is evident throughout the world today.

Sumerian Government By 3000 B.C.E., some cities in Sumer were home to between 2,000 and 10,000 people. By 2700 B.C.E., the largest city, *Uruk*, had a population of 50,000. Most city dwellers were farmers, who made daily trips to the countryside to work in the fields.

SUMERIA AND OTHER CITY-STATES AND EMPIRES

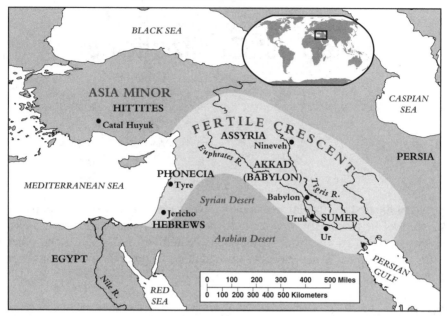

Each Sumerian city and the land it controlled formed a *city-state*, which typically covered several hundred square miles. The city-states were independent, each with its own government. Since the Sumerians believed that land belonged to the gods, the first rulers were the city-states' priests. They assigned fields to the farmers, distributed the harvested crops at the city's temple, and managed all trade.

As the Sumerian city-states grew in size and number, they began to compete with each other for land and water. Wars resulted. To defend themselves, urban governments built massive stone walls around their cities. They also organized armies. Over time, Sumerian military leaders became more important than priests. These military rulers, called *kings,* ruled over a territory known as a *kingdom*. Religion and politics were blended in Sumerian civilization in the sense that kings were also high priests. This practice helped increase social stability, since the king was perceived as being a direct link between the people and the gods.

Sumerian Religion The people of Sumer were *polytheistic,* worshiping many gods. They believed that the gods controlled the natural forces around them. The priests explained the gods' will to the people and directed worship at the temple. To win the gods' favor, Sumerians made offerings and prayed that the gods would cause the rivers to flood at the right times for growing crops.

Because the floods were so important—and so uncertain—in Mesopotamia, satisfying the gods was very important to Sumerians. This may explain why they devoted so much effort and wealth to constructing monumental architecture that was religious. They placed temples and altars in large stepped pyramids, called *ziggurats*. They believed that the gods punished humans in this life for bad behavior, but they did not believe in reward or punishment after death. Instead, they believed that the dead simply turned to dust.

Sumerian Economy and Trade Sumerians learned to farm the land intensely. As a result, they were able to produce an agricultural surplus, which had all of the effects described in Chapter 1, particularly a *division of labor*. Many Sumerians engaged in work other than producing food. They made pottery, wove cloth, cast utensils in bronze, and engaged in other crafts.

The agricultural surplus also allowed Sumerians to trade extensively, not only throughout the region of Mesopotamia but transregionally with other civilizations. While some of the trade was over land, they also sailed seven-person canoes into the Mediterranean Sea and through the Persian Gulf and into the Arabian Sea. Major trade goods included gold from Egypt and tin from Persia. Through their trading networks, the Sumerians obtained goods from even farther away. They traded for beads, wood, resin, lapis lazuli, and obsidian that originated in Southeastern Africa, from the region that is the present-day country of Mozambique. From India, they obtained pearls, copper, and ivory. Many of these trade items were used by artists to create impressive and ornate sculptures and jewelry, much of which had religious significance.

Sumerian Social Structure As Sumerians became more specialized in their work, distinctions between classes became sharper. And as the society grew wealthier, the gap between the poor and the rich increased. One sign of the increase in social stratification was that a new class of nobles and wealthy landowners joined priests and kings at the top of society. The middle classes comprised merchants, farmers, and professionals such as architects. Hired workers made up the lower class. At the very bottom of society were slaves— foreign prisoners of war or Sumerian families who could not pay their debts. About 40 percent of the people living in Sumerian cities may have been slaves. Many people were needed to build the massive stone structures in cities and to create and maintain the vast irrigation systems in the countryside that formed the basis of Sumer's wealth.

Women in Sumer Upper-class Sumerian women enjoyed some freedom. They could own property and have incomes separate from those of their husbands. However, only their boys attended school; their girls were educated at home. Also, all marriages were arranged by men.

Cultural and Scientific Contributions To manage their surplus crops, manufacturing, and trade, the Sumerians needed to keep records. To accomplish this, they created the world's first writing system, called *cuneiform*, which consisted of marks carved onto wet clay tablets. (This early writing gives us the modern expression of "set in stone" because once the tablets had been hardened in ovens, the markings were unchangeable.) The development of a complex writing system required the emergence of a separate class of people who were skilled at cuneiform. Called *scribes*, these individuals were charged first with record-keeping and later with the writing of history and myths.

Cuneiform wedges (left) were the first writing system. Phoenician letters (above) became the basis for the modern alphabet used by writers of English and many other languages.

Sumerians made several advances in thought and technology. They pioneered many important inventions related to farming, including carts and metal plows, as well as sundials and a 12-month calendar with which the Sumerians attempted to predict the flooding of the Tigris and Euphrates rivers. A final noteworthy invention was the Sumerian number system, which was based on 60. They used 60 because it could be divided into whole segments by 2, 3, 4, and 5. Today, people still divide an hour into 60 minutes, a minute into 60 seconds, and a circle into 360 degrees.

It was during the time of Sumer's power that *The Epic of Gilgamesh*, perhaps the oldest written story on the earth, was produced. It was originally composed on 12 clay tablets in cuneiform script. The epic concerns the adventures of a real Sumerian king named Gilgamesh who ruled the city-state of Uruk somewhere between 2750 and 2500 B.C.E. From *The Epic of Gilgamesh*, historians know something about the people who lived in the land between the Tigris and Euphrates rivers in the 2nd and 3rd millenniums B.C.E and what they valued in a leader. (Test Prep: Write a paragraph comparing Gilgamesh with the Greek heros in Homer. See page 56.)

Sumerian Decline Mesopotamia had supplies of water and fertile land, so it attracted other groups who wanted to control the region. And because there were few natural barriers to prevent invasions, and because of the independent nature of the city-states, the Sumerian city-states fell to invaders around 2300 B.C.E. However, the culture they developed became the core and foundation of later empires in the region.

The Babylonian Empire

Sometime during the several centuries following the decline of Sumer, a new weapon appeared in Mesopotamia: the compound or composite, bow. This bow combined wood with animal bone or horn to make a stronger, and hence more deadly, bow. It was either developed in Mesopotamia or by nomadic pastoralists in central Asia. The bow gave its first users an advantage over rivals.

Around 1900 B.C.E., a Persian people from what is now Iran invaded and took control of Mesopotamia. The invaders built a new capital city called Babylon, so they became known as the *Babylonians*. They would eventually control a large territory that included diverse cultural groups, called an *empire*.

King Hammurabi The Babylonians' most powerful king was *Hammurabi*. He conquered all of Mesopotamia and ruled for more than 40 years, until about 1750 B.C.E. Hammurabi abolished local governments and appointed officials who were responsible only to him. Later, he reorganized the tax structure. These changes made it easier for his representatives to collect the tax and also increased the amounts collected. The taxes were used primarily to maintain irrigation canals to improve agricultural productivity.

Hammurabi is famous for creating a set of laws: the *Code of Hammurabi*. He had the 282 laws carved into stone monuments, one of the first instances of laws being put into writing for everyone to see. Hammurabi's laws dealt with topics such as property rights, wages, contracts, marriage, and various crimes.

The Code's main purpose was to protect people's rights. It was built on the idea of "an eye for an eye." That is, the punishment should fit the crime, often very precisely. For example: "If a builder builds a house for someone, and does not construct it properly, and the house that he built falls in and kills its owner, then that builder shall be put to death. If it kills the son of the owner, then the son of that builder shall be put to death."

Hammurabi's system of justice, though harsh, was not as violent or unpredictable as the retribution people often carried out when they felt injured. By replacing individual vengeance with a well-publicized system administered by government, Hammurabi brought greater stability and justice to society.

Babylonian Society and Culture Babylonian culture resembled that of Sumer in several ways. For example, Babylonians adopted many of the Sumerians' religious beliefs and was a *patriarchal* society, one dominated by men. However, under Babylonian rule, women enjoyed more rights than the women in Sumer had. Babylonian women could be merchants, traders, and even scribes. Marriages were arranged by parents. A Babylonian woman could leave her husband if he was cruel, although she could not divorce him. However, if she did leave him, she could take her property with her.

Some Babylonians were skilled astronomers. They could accurately predict the movement of planets and eclipses of the moon. From this knowledge, they devised a lunar calendar. In Babylonia, *astronomy*, the study of objects outside Earth's atmosphere, was linked to the Babylonians' religious practices of fortune-telling and *astrology*, predicting the future by studying movements of stars and planets.

The Phoenicians

The *Phoenicians* occupied parts of present-day Lebanon, Israel, and Jordan around 3000 B.C.E. With strong sailing ships, the Phoenicians developed a wide trade network across the Mediterranean Sea, even venturing into the eastern Atlantic Ocean. The Phoenicians exported cedar logs, colorful textiles, glass, and pottery, among other items. The Phoenicians were at their peak from 1200 to 1100 B.C.E., during which time they expanded their empire around the Mediterranean. *Carthage,* a Phoenician colony on the coast of North Africa, became a significant outpost in the region.

The Phoenicians are remembered for developing an *alphabetic script,* a system of symbols (letters) that represent the sounds of speech, as an alternative to cuneiform around 1000 B.C.E. The Phoenician 22-letter alphabet was a great help to increased trade, and it was later modified by the Greeks and Romans, who spread the alphabet across their empires. It is now used by much of the Western world. The Arabic and Hebrew alphabets also evolved from the basic system pioneered by the Phoenicians. (Test Prep: Create a chart comparing the Phoenician alphabet with the Chinese writing system. See page 35.)

The Hebrews

The *Hebrews*, whose descendants became known as *Israelites* and later as *Jews,* lived in the region of Canaan—present-day Israel, Palestine, and Lebanon. What historians know of Hebrew civilization comes partly from their sacred writings, the Hebrew scriptures, which Christians have traditionally referred to as the Old Testament. In addition, archeologists have unearthed a great deal of information about the Hebrews. According to Hebrew scriptures, Canaan was founded by *Abraham* who left Mesopotamia to settle there in approximately 2000 B.C.E. Today, Jews, Christians, and Muslims all trace their religious heritage to him.

A severe drought in Canaan forced some Hebrews to migrate to Egypt where they were later enslaved for several centuries. According to Hebrew scriptures, about 1300 B.C.E., the Hebrews were led out of Egypt by *Moses* and eventually returned to Canaan. Moses also introduced the *Ten Commandments,* a code of conduct that became very influential in areas dominated by Christianity.

Monotheism Like most other groups, the early Hebrews were polytheistic. However, they were one of the first groups to adopt *monotheism,* a belief in only one deity.

Division and Diaspora Over the following centuries, the Hebrews divided into two separate kingdoms, which weakened their power. The two kingdoms were conquered by the Assyrians and the Babylonians, and the descendants of Abraham were enslaved for the second time in their history. Now known as Israelites, many fled or were driven out of their homes. This movement was the beginning of the *Jewish Diaspora,* the spreading of Jews throughout the Mediterranean world and the Middle East. Jews were able to return to Jerusalem only after the Persians, who were more tolerant of religious diversity, conquered the region in 539 B.C.E.

However, Persian rule did not last. As less tolerant rulers controlled the region, Jews again suffered discrimination. Many migrated to North Africa, southern Europe, and elsewhere, continuing the Jewish Diaspora. Because of this movement of people, Jewish ideas and culture spread and would eventually spread throughout the world. While the Jews did not have their own country, they did maintain a strong sense of identity.

The Geography of Africa

Geographers have divided Africa into four major climate zones:

1. A Mediterranean climate zone, with its mild seasons and temperate weather, consists of a strip of land along the northern edge of Africa— the southern coast of the Mediterranean Sea.

2. A desert zone consists of the continent's two deserts—the *Sahara* in northern Africa and the *Kalahari* in southern Africa.

3. The rain forest zone stretches east to west and lies on both sides of the equator. Though many people think of rain forest as typical of Africa, this zone makes up only about 10 percent of the continent.

4. The final climate zone is the savanna, made up of broad grasslands with small trees and shrubs. Two major bands of savanna are located just north and south of the tropical rain forest zone. Ten thousand years ago, the northern savanna band was much larger, covering much of the area that is now the Sahara.

Ancient Egypt

The *Nile River* begins in the interior of Africa and flows north to empty into the Mediterranean Sea. In ancient times, rich black soil covered the banks and delta of the river, making the length of the Nile ideal for agriculture, especially wheat, barley, and the papyrus plant, which was used for writing material and also for making baskets, sandals, and other items. Annual floods would deposit silt, replenishing the soil. (Since the building of the Aswan Dam in 1968, the Nile River no longer experiences annual flooding.)

Introduction of Agriculture and Pastoralism In the Nile River Valley, people began to practice agriculture and pastoralism around 6000 B.C.E. or 5000 B.C.E. From people in Mesopotamia, Egyptians learned to grow wheat and barley. From people living in the grassy savanna land to the south, Egyptians learned to grow gourds, watermelons, and sorghum and to raise donkeys and cattle. Over the span of two thousand years, Egyptians domesticated animals, began mining copper to make jewelry and tools, and had enough agricultural surplus for towns to emerge. Just as the Sumerian civilization influenced later

AFRICA CLIMATE ZONES

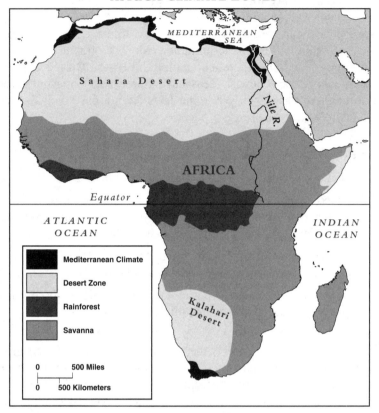

people in Mesopotamia, so the earliest Egyptian civilization became the core and foundation of later ways of life in the Mediterranean world.

However, Egypt was making these advances as the climate was changing. Beginning around 5000 B.C.E., declining rainfall across North Africa was causing *desertification,* the creation of desert-like conditions. The Sahara was growing larger and dryer, and the savanna region was growing smaller.

Like the Sumerians, the Egyptians dug irrigation canals to spread the floodwaters and increase the amount of land they could farm. Indeed, some scholars think that the Egyptians may have learned this technology from trading with the Sumerians. The Egyptians may also have learned from the Sumerians about the wheel, the plow, bronze-making, and writing.

Transportation and Trade The wind blows south through the Nile Valley from the Mediterranean Sea. This geographic feature allowed early Egyptians to use the Nile River for transportation and trade. They could move south against the Nile's current by putting sails on their boats. To travel north, all they had to do was let the current carry them. As a result, Egyptians not only traded locally, but traded through the region of northeast Africa. From the mouth of the Nile, traders engaged in transregional trade with Mesopotamia.

Another feature of the Nile that promoted Egypt's prosperity was that it flowed through a vast desert. The dry lands to the west and east provided natural barriers against attacks. While invaders attacked Mesopotamia many times, Egypt developed for more than 1,300 years before its first major invasion.

Early Governments Desertification brought more people to settle near the Nile River. The need to work together to feed this larger population caused local chiefs to emerge. Strong leaders gradually united the towns into two kingdoms. One was Lower Egypt, in the north, where the Nile flows into the Mediterranean. The other, Upper Egypt, was farther south and more upstream. Around 3100 B.C.E., *King Menes* united the two kingdoms, a turning point in Egyptian history. Menes also established his capital at the city of Memphis, located at the southern end of the Nile Delta.

Historians have divided much of subsequent ancient Egyptian history into three long periods of stability: the *Old Kingdom, Middle Kingdom*, and *New Kingdom*. Separating this periods were shorter ones of turmoil.

The Old Kingdom (2660–2160 B.C.E.) Unlike Mesopotamia, which remained divided into city-states during the third century B.C.E., Egypt began developing a strong central government. The king or queen leading this government is now known as a *pharaoh,* although the term did not come into use until the New Kingdom. From Memphis, the kings and queens ruled as *theocrats*, rulers holding both religious and political power. Egypt's kings wielded their considerable authority to undertake extensive building projects, including the famous pyramids.

Since Egyptians believed that the pharaohs were descended from the gods and were immortal, they supported great efforts to preserve and honor their bodies after death. Most of Egypt's large pyramids were built during the Old Kingdom as tombs for rulers. Each pharaoh's body was preserved as a mummy and placed in a pyramid with jewelry and other items for use in the afterlife.

At first, all land belonged to the pharaoh, who appointed the governors and other government officials in each of the kingdom's provinces. Some pharaohs rewarded their officials with land as payment for their services. Over time, these lands and positions began to be passed from father to son. A class of nobles eventually developed as a result.

As the noble class grew stronger, some of them began to challenge the authority of the pharaohs. The pharaohs' power was further weakened by a period of drought, which resulted in famine and starvation. This all led to civil unrest, rivalries among the provinces, and the collapse of the Old Kingdom. The kingdom again split into Upper Egypt and Lower Egypt. For more than 100 years, civil wars swept Egypt as nobles competed for power and the throne.

The Middle Kingdom (2040–1786 B.C.E.) In 2040 B.C.E., Mentuhotep II took power. He moved the capital to Thebes, farther south on the Nile, and reunited Egypt under a central government, reducing the power of the provincial governors and eventually gaining control over all of Egypt. (Test Prep: Write a paragraph comparing Mentuhotep II's takeover of Egypt to similar takeovers in history. See chart on page 73.)

The pharaohs of the Middle Kingdom had a different approach to governing than had their predecessors. To encourage loyalty, they had statues and other art created that pictured them as wise and caring protectors of the people. These images, along with writings that gave the same message, were part of a great renewal in art, religion, and literature. Many temples to the gods were built during this period.

Pharaohs used their power to construct huge irrigation projects that increased the size of Egypt's farmland. In addition, they expanded their country's borders. Their armies pushed east to control the Sinai Peninsula and south into Nubia, which was rich in gold and other resources.

The Middle Kingdom ended after an invasion by a pastoral nomadic people called the *Hyksos* from modern Syria. The Hyksos used their superior technology—horse-drawn chariots and greatly improved bows and arrows—to defeat the Egyptians.

The New Kingdom (1570–1070 B.C.E.) The Hyksos occupied Egypt for a short period of time. As Egyptians learned to use the same battle technology, they were able to defeat the Hyksos, beginning the era known as the New Kingdom. Using the newly powerful army, pharaohs expanded southward into Nubia and north into Mesopotamia. Through negotiation and conquest, Egypt gained access to highly prized resources such as bronze and wood.

Around 1350 B.C.E., the pharaoh *Akhenaton* tried to change Egypt's religion. He called for the worship of one god, a sun god called *Aten*. Such a change would have dramatically changed the role of priests in Egyptian society. Many priests opposed worshiping just one god, and Akhenaton's struggle with them disrupted Egypt and weakened his power. After his death, Egypt's old religion was restored. Moreover, the priests became more powerful than ever.

A powerful pharaoh, *Ramses the Great*, took the throne around 1290 B.C.E. He remained in power for a remarkably long time—nearly 67 years—during which he successfully expanded the empire into Southwest Asia. Ramses built more temples and erected more statues than any other pharaoh. However, Egypt's empire had become a tempting target for invaders. One of these were the *Hittites*, who had a military advantage over the Egyptians because they were beginning to use iron tools and weapons. Although Ramses made peace with the attacking Hittites, his successors lacked his power and skills.

After Ramses' death, Egypt began a long period of decline. Besides carrying out expensive but failed wars against neighbors, Egypt suffered from repeated invasions from Libyans, Kushites, Assyrians, the Persians, the Macedonians, and the Romans, among others. Combined with internal revolts, these dismantled the once-mighty Egyptian Empire. Egypt did not regain its independence until modern times.

Egyptian Society The social hierarchy in Egypt was complex, with royal families, nobles, and priests at the top. Artisans worked in shops attached to temples and were paid by the government. Below this class was a large lower class, predominantly of farmers. Farmers' crops belonged to the owner of the land—the government, a temple, or a noble family. In addition to doing their own farming, farmers were required to work on irrigation and other government construction projects. Below the farmers—at the lowest level—were the slaves, who usually hailed from lands conquered by Egypt. Except for slaves, all classes of people were equal under the law, but Egypt's class system was very rigid. It was difficult to advance from one class to a higher one. (Test Prep: Create a chart comparing Egyptian society with Indus Valley society. See page 30.)

Egyptian women had more rights and freedoms than most ancient women. They could own property, make contracts, divorce, and pursue legal disputes in court. Two women, Hatshepsut and Cleopatra, even became pharaohs. A few women held posts at temples. However, most women were not educated. They usually did not take part in government and had little political power.

Religion Like the Mesopotamians, the ancient Egyptians were polytheistic, worshiping many gods. Among these were Ra, the sun god; Osiris, the god of life and death; and Isis, wife of Osiris, who was the goddess of nature. The gods were represented by statues and small idols. People believed that the god was present in these objects. They prayed and made offerings to the god to win the god's favor and protection.

The Egyptians believed in life after death. At first, this belief applied only to pharaohs. Later, it was extended to all people and even animals. But the Egyptians believed the body must be preserved for the dead to have an afterlife. Some people were mummified and buried in tombs. *Mummification* involved removing the body's internal organs, drying the body with salts, and packing its insides and wrapping it with chemically treated cloth. The body was then put in a sealed coffin. Only the rich could afford mummification. Poor people were buried in the desert, where the dry environment preserved their bodies.

Continuous Egyptian Culture The long periods of unity under the Old, Middle, and New Kingdoms allowed a stable Egyptian culture to develop. This culture remained largely intact, even when Egypt was ruled by outsiders. In fact, invaders often adopted aspects of Egyptian culture.

Egyptian Writing By about 3000 B.C.E., people in the Nile Valley were using a form of picture-writing known as *hieroglyphics*. This writing system was much like the Sumerians' cuneiform, with the addition of symbols that represented ideas and sounds. Instead of writing on clay tablets, however, the Egyptians found a better material. They mashed *papyrus*, a type of plant that grew along the Nile River, using its fibers to create a type of paper; indeed, the English word "paper" comes from this plant's name. The *Book of the Dead* was a paper book that Egyptians put in the coffins of dead pharaohs and some nobles; each version of the book was different since it told the story of the dead person. The Egyptians also wrote hieroglyphs on the inside walls of tombs of the mummified dead to tell stories of the dead.

Scientific Contributions Ancient Egypt's pyramids and temples were engineering marvels, built with great accuracy using simple tools and surveying instruments. Egyptians cut the massive stone blocks used in their construction in distant quarries in the desert and transported them to a construction site. They then moved these heavy blocks up ramps to their place on the pyramid. Egyptians developed math and engineering skills to build the various pyramids.

Monumental architecture such as pyramids in Egypt (upper) and ziggurats in Mesopotamia (lower) reflected the power of early governments to organize workers to build large structures.

The ancient Egyptians developed a number system based on 10 that was very much like the system we use today. They had knowledge of the concept of fractions as well as whole numbers. Their knowledge of geometry helped them to build the pyramids and to restore the boundaries of fields after a flooding of the Nile. They also developed a calendar based on a year that contained 365 days. The calendar was created to track the stars for religious purposes and to monitor the flooding of the Nile.

The practice of mummification gave the ancient Egyptians much knowledge about the human body—knowledge that many future civilizations would draw upon and benefit from. Egyptian physicians were able to set broken bones, amputate limbs, and stitch up wounds. They soaked cloth bandages in honey to prevent infection. They used plants and herbs to relieve pain and to treat conditions like asthma. Nevertheless, adult life expectancy was only about 35 years, and about one-third of ancient Egyptians died in infancy.

Nubia, Kush, and Axum

Just south of Egypt, three other ancient kingdoms developed. Though none were as wealthy as Egypt was at its peak, each prospered through regional trade along the Nile River, and carried on transregional trade across the Red Sea.

Nubia Nubia emerged in the Upper Nile Valley around 3500 B.C.E. Egyptian traders went to Nubia in search of gold, ivory, incense, cattle, animal skins, and slaves. Nubians were recruited to serve as mercenaries in Egyptian forces. Nubia was basically an agricultural country, growing most of the same crops and raising the same domesticated animals as Egypt. Unlike Egypt, though, the flood plain was not as wide. Therefore, Nubian farmers had to make more use of irrigation networks to water their fields.

The Nubians were heavily influenced by Egyptian culture, in part because of their close proximity to the land of the pharaohs. For example, the Nubians built Egyptian-type pyramids and palaces. They also worshiped some of the Egyptian gods and adopted Egyptian burial practices. However, the Nubians retained some of their gods as well. Likewise, the Nubians used Egyptian hieroglyphics in writing, but they also developed their own script, which was alphabetic.

Nubia lasted for nearly a thousand years before falling into decline, only to reemerge as the kingdom of *Kush,* around 2500 B.C.E.

Kush Kush remained dependent on Egypt, only establishing some political and cultural independence by about 1000 B.C.E. Kush even conquered Egypt briefly before they themselves were overthrown by the Assyrians in 663 B.C.E. Even without control of Egypt, however, Kush became an important kingdom economically, trading with the Roman Empire, India, and Arabia. Kushites exported slaves as well as ivory, gold, and cattle. The Kushites mined iron ore from which they made tools and weapons in furnaces fueled by timber. The city of Meröe was a particularly important trade center.

Kush enjoyed its greatest power from about 300 B.C.E. to 100 C.E. Afterward, their power and influence declined, partly because of *deforestation*. Kushites cut down trees in order to make the charcoal used in smelting iron. In the 340s C.E., Kush was conquered by the civilization of *Axum*.

Axum The civilization of Axum was founded on the plateau of present-day Ethiopia in the first century C.E. Its capital city was also called Axum. The state had an agricultural economy, with farmers using plows to cultivate wheat, barley, and millet. Axumites also established a successful trading colony on the Red Sea called Adulis, where traders sold products from the African interior (such as hides, ivory, and slaves) in exchange for money or products from India, Arabia, and the Roman Empire. Adulis and Axum as a whole grew rich by taxing foreign trade and by requiring conquered lands to pay tribute.

Because of their trading connections with the Roman Empire, some Axum people converted to Christianity. The religion's popularity continued to increase, helping to create a more cohesive society. In 330 C.E., Christianity was decreed the official religion of Axum by then-king King Ezana.

The Axumites defeated the Kushites in Meröe in the 340s C.E. In the 500s, Axum expanded its territories to include modern Yemen, on the Arabian Peninsula. From Arabia, Axum borrowed a script for its written language.

Axum began to decline around 600 C.E. However, Axum remained strong enough to counter efforts by Muslims to convert Axumites to Islam in the seventh and eighth centuries. Christianity continues to be the dominant religion in the area (Ethiopia)—about two-thirds of Ethiopians are Christians today.

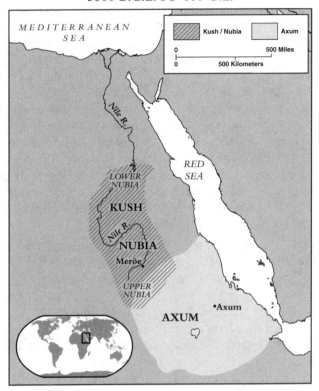

NUBIA, KUSH, AND AXUM,
3500 B.C.E. TO 600 C.E.

Indus Valley Civilizations

Like civilizations in Mesopotamia and Egypt, the *Indus River Valley* civilizations developed near water and became the core and foundation of later civilizations in the region. Between 2500 and 2000 B.C.E., indigenous peoples of the Indian subcontinent, known as *Dravidians*, established two sophisticated urban centers in the Indus River Valley: *Harappa* and *Mohenjo-Daro*. Their written language, mainly in the form of pictographs, has not yet been deciphered, but it seems to be loosely connected to the Dravidian languages still existing in contemporary southern and central India. Archaeologists came to know about Harappan society's existence only in the 1920s.

Much of the archaeological evidence from Harappa and Mohenjo-Daro sites comes from a collection of artifacts as well as the remains of city walls and numerous buildings. Archaeological remains reveal evidence of an advanced civilization with division of labor. Jewelers, potters, architects, and artists all resided within these cities. Archeologists can infer that a social hierarchy existed in the Indus Valley because the foundations of homes in the Harappa's center were found to be of varying sizes. And since most residents, rich and poor, had private toilets that drained into a municipal sewage system, the cities must have had sophisticated technology and urban planning.

Agriculture and the Environment Because so few residents of Mohenjo-Daro and Harappa were farmers, archeologists conclude that rural areas were providing ample amounts of food to these urban areas. Evidence also shows that Harappans traded by sea and land with Sumer and Egypt and by land with the societies in eastern India. If civilization can be defined by the existence of an agricultural surplus and a resulting division of labor among a society's residents, then the Indus Valley societies should be considered civilized.

Environmental degradation probably caused the gradual decline and eventual disappearance of the Harappan and Mohenjo-Daro civilizations. Their people removed so many trees from their lands that this deforestation caused the soil to erode. Another possible reason for the disappearance of the Harappan and Mohenjo-Daro societies is the ferocious and temperamental Indus River, which often flooded. Floods could have destroyed their cities as well as the cities' remains. Earthquakes are considered to be another possibility.

Aryan Migrations and Interactions Very few, if any, features of Harappan society are found today in South Asia. The group that arrived 500 years after its decline left a more lasting mark on South Asian culture. *Aryans*, Indo-European-speaking peoples originally from Central Asia, traveled from Persia through the Hindu Kush Mountains over a period of several centuries, beginning in 1500 B.C.E. The nomadic, pastoral Aryans brought the first horses into India. Native Indian peoples were no match for Aryan warriors on horseback and in horse-drawn chariots. Over time, Aryan settlements and culture spread east along the Ganges River and its surrounding plains.

Importance of Clans Each Aryan tribe was divided into *clans*, each with its own territory and each headed by a male chief who ruled with advice from a committee of clan members. Unlike Egypt, the people had no central government, and at times, the clans fought each other. The first Aryans continued their herding lifestyle, raising horses, cattle, goats, and sheep. Eventually, though, most of them settled in villages and began to farm, intermingling with the native peoples. Wheat and barley were their main crops, but they also grew sugar cane, gourds, peas, beans, and other vegetables.

Although poor transportation made trade difficult, other types of goods gradually appeared in their villages. Early trade was by *barter*—a system by which one thing is exchanged for another. By 500 B.C.E., though, their use of silver and copper coins led to an increase in trade and in the number of craftspeople and merchants.

Aryan Language Aryans brought their sacred language, *Sanskrit*, with them to South Asia. At first, stories were passed orally from generation to generation, but sometime between 1200 and 1000 B.C.E., the Aryans developed a writing system. While most literary and religious works were recorded in this language, they also had a commonly used tongue which would eventually evolve into *Hindi*. Due to the Aryans' Indo-European origins, Sanskrit shares similarities to Latin, another *Indo-European language*. For example, the word for *king* in Latin is *rex*, and the word for *king* in Sanskrit is *raja*. Sanskrit continues to be studied by religious scholars, while Hindi is still spoken widely among many northern Indian societies.

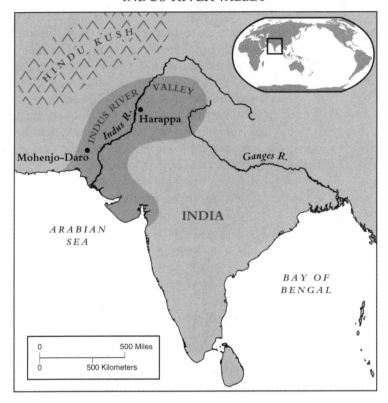

Aryan Religious Traditions The *Vedas*, Sanskrit for "knowledge," are a collection of Aryan religious hymns, poems, and songs. The *Rig-Veda* is the most famous; it sheds light on ancient Indian society, particularly the conflicts that occurred between the Dravidian and the Aryan peoples. The *Rig-Veda* outlined proper priestly (*brahmin*) behavior, which included performing several daily rituals honoring the gods. These responsibilities placed brahmins in a position of authority in Indian society. The importance of the Vedas in Indian spiritual life had waned a bit by 500 B.C.E. as Vedic knowledge began to meld with the spiritual contributions made by Dravidians.

Aryan and Dravidian Beliefs Many aspects of the Aryans' language, religious traditions, and social organization continue today in South Asia. Their interactions with indigenous peoples of India, particularly the Dravidians, also had a lasting impact on Indian society.

The late *Vedic Age* (800–400 B.C.E.) was marked by the Aryans' growing awareness of Dravidian beliefs. The interaction of both traditions came to fruition in the *Upanishads*, a collection of religious thought that illuminated several new religious concepts: *brahma, dharma, karma,* and *moksha.*

Brahma is an overarching, universal soul that connects all creatures on Earth. Each individual human being is not a separate entity; his or her individual soul is not the essence of truth or reality. An individual soul is not terribly important; one must try to escape a cycle of life and death and join the universal soul, brahma. In order to escape the seemingly endless cycle of birth and rebirth, one must perform righteous duties and deeds, known as one's dharma. This dharma then determines one's karma, or fate, in the next life. If someone's soul carries a heavy karmic burden, then one could perhaps be reborn as a lower-class person or even in a lower life form.

Conversely, a person who performs good deeds throughout life is believed to have good karma, which in turn may help his or her soul in a future life. A soul's ultimate goal should be to attain *moksha,* or eternal peace and unity with brahma. Believers can attain moksha through intense meditation and the casting off of worldly pleasures.

The *Upanishads* is a foundational text for the set of religious beliefs that later became known as Hinduism. It is historically significant because it reflects the blending of Aryan and Dravidian religious values, and also because it reflects the social structures of Ancient India.

China's First Civilization

The fourth core and foundational river civilization developed in eastern China. China includes two major rivers, the *Huang He* (Yellow) and the *Chiang Jiang* (Yangtze). The Chiang Jiang stretches almost 4,000 miles across central China. The Huang He, while shorter at 2,400 miles, connects China's northern interior to the Yellow Sea. The river takes its name from the deposits of *loess*, a type of fertile soil that is yellow in color. For thousands of years, the flooding of the Huang He has deposited this silt across a wide area.

In addition to the advantage of the two rivers, much of eastern China experiences a reliable, moderate climate. Meanwhile, two geographical features protected China from invasion: the Gobi Desert in the west and the world's tallest mountain range, the Himalayas, in the southwest.

As early as 6500 B.C.E., Neolithic people of the Yangtze Valley were growing rice. Then around 5800 B.C.E., people began farming near the Huang He. Their main crops were soybeans and a grain called millet. By 3000 B.C.E., groups along the Huang He had taken up rice farming, too. Meanwhile, both groups had begun domesticating chickens and pigs.

According to Chinese tradition, the first silk production also began around 3000 B.C.E. People wove fine silk cloth from the threads of silkworms, which fed on the leaves of the region's mulberry trees. They also made items from copper and carvings from a precious stone called jade.

China's First Rulers Although ancient Chinese civilization faced no outside threats, villages along the Huang He were sometimes attacked by nomadic peoples who lived in the nearby hills. According to Chinese legend, a man named Yu brought order to the region around 2100 B.C.E. He organized projects to build roads to encourage trade, create ditches to control flooding, and drain swamps to create farmland. He also organized the region's villages into zones for defense and placed each zone under a local leader who reported to him.

Yu passed his power to his son Qi, and with his rule what is known as the *Xia Dynasty* began. (A *dynasty* is a series of rulers who all belong to the same family.) The Xia Dynasty lasted for about 400 years. Little is known about the

Xia Dynasty, since the early Chinese had no writing system. The only written information about the Xia kings was recorded more than a thousand years later. In recent times, though, archeologists have unearthed evidence that a Xia kingdom did indeed exist.

The Shang Dynasty Around 1750 B.C.E., a local leader named Tang overthrew the Xia king and took power. This event marked the beginning of the *Shang Dynasty*, which ruled for the next 600 years. During this time, Shang rulers conquered neighboring peoples, establishing an empire. From a succession of capital cities, the Shang kings wielded tremendous economic and religious power. (Test Prep: Create a chart comparing the Shang with other empires of its time, such as the New Kingdom in Egypt (page 26), Mohenjo-Daro in India (page 30), and the Sumerians in Mesopotamia (page 17).)

Economy, Technology, and Trade The Shang economy was primarily based on agriculture. Most people were peasants, but others worked at skilled crafts, making pottery, carving jewelry from ivory and jade, and crafting weapons, tools, wheels, and other items from bronze. Artisans and merchants lived in the capital and in towns across the empire. The bronze technology came from Southwest Asia via migrating Indo-European peoples who settled in what is now western China. Traders also brought tin from Southeast Asia and jade from Central Asia.

The Shang rulers controlled the copper and tin mines in China, and they kept a monopoly over the production of bronze in the country. Their bronze weapons and armor and their horse-drawn chariots made them stronger than anyone who dared to oppose them. The Shang kings and their nobles waged frequent wars on enemies inside and outside the empire, capturing prisoners who were then enslaved or slaughtered as sacrifices to the gods.

EARLY DYNASTIES IN CHINA, TO C. 400 B.C.E.

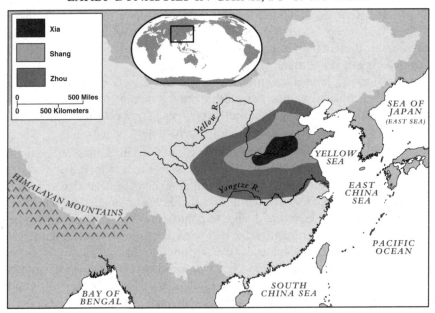

Religion Like other early river civilizations, the Shang were polytheistic. They believed that several different gods controlled the forces of nature. The gods worshiped during the Shang Dynasty included gods of the sun, moon, clouds, and wind. Efforts to communicate with the gods produced the earliest known examples of writing from the Shang period. People would inscribe questions for the gods on oracle bones, which were turtle shells, oxen bones, or the bones of other animals. Then they would insert heated pins into the oracle bones. The heat would cause cracks to form, and the cracks could be interpreted to gain an answer to the question. Shang kings relied on the bones to tell them such things as whether to attack an enemy and if the crops would be successful.

China's long tradition of *ancestor veneration* also began during the Shang Dynasty. The ancient Chinese believed that the spirits of their ancestors could speak to the gods for them. They made offerings to their ancestors, hoping to win their favor. The Shang kings made almost daily sacrifices to the ancestors, seeking the gods' help in making their rule a success. There was no organized priesthood in ancient China.

Historians know that ancient Chinese believed in life after death because objects were buried with the dead for their use in the afterlife. When a king or noble died, some of his servants and pets were killed so that they could travel with him to the next world.

Cultural and Scientific Contributions The Shang developed a written script of *pictographs*, or graphic symbols, each of which represented an idea, concept, or object, rather than representing a single sound, as letter systems do. Like other early writing systems, the Chinese one was very complicated, and as in Mesopotamia and Egypt, usually only scribes could read and write. The written script invented during the Shang Dynasty is the forerunner of the script used by Chinese today.

Standard systems of measurement helped the Shang rule the empire. Their calendar had 12 alternating months of 29 and 30 days. Royal astronomers added extra days as needed to get to a 365-day year.

The Shang made contributions in the arts as well. Shang artisans created bronze castings, ivory carvings, silk garments, and white clay pottery. The first Chinese musical instruments also appeared during the Shang Dynasty. Drums, bells, stone chimes, and a simple wind instrument called an ocarina played melodies that have long been lost to time.

The End of the Shang Dynasty Like all civilizations, the Shang Dynasty experienced a rise and fall. Over time, the Shang kings had become weaker, and in 1045 B.C.E., a military man named Wu raised his own army and challenged Shang rule. The king was killed, the Shang Dynasty ended, and Wu established the *Zhou Dynasty* in its place.

The Zhou Dynasty Zhou kings ruled for about 900 years, making their dynasty the longest in Chinese history. The first 200 years of Zhou rule has become known as China's first *Golden Age*, a period in a society of relative peace, prosperity, and innovation.

The success of the Zhou Dynasty resulted from the kings' abilities to centralize and hold power, bringing stability to the region. They also expanded the territory under their control, making the reach of the Zhou Dynasty much larger than what the Shang's had been. Another key element in the Zhou leaders' success was the introduction of a concept called the *Mandate of Heaven*, which was the idea that a just ruler's power was bestowed by the gods. Zhou kings were thus referred to as "sons of heaven." However, invasions or natural events such as a severe earthquake were often taken as signs that a ruler no longer had the Mandate of Heaven. The Zhou had used the concept to justify overthrowing the Shang. This became a precedent. Throughout China's history, the overthrow of rulers has been justified by the charge that a particular ruler had lost the Mandate of Heaven. (Test Prep: Write a paragraph comparing the Mandate from Heaven with the "divine right of kings." See page 284.)

Source: Shutterstock

During the Shang Dynasty, people wrote on tortoise shells.

Government The Zhou kings expanded their territory to such an extent that eventually they could not control it directly. Instead, the kingdom divided into many regions, each under the control of relatives or loyal friends who owed allegiance to the king. These regions functioned much like city-states. The local rulers governed as they wished, paying taxes to the king and providing soldiers for his army. From time to time, the regional leaders had to visit the king's court to proclaim their loyalty. The Zhou kings also made alliances with kings who ruled territory along their borders. These alliances protected the Zhou kingdom by helping to shield it from invasion by nomadic peoples from the north and west. The network of regional rulers, with relationships based on mutual defense agreements, created the basics of *feudalism,* which would reappear in many cultures later in history.

The Zhou governmental system broke down over time as regional authorities began to assert themselves. Some stopped sending the collected taxes to the king, keeping the money for their own use. Some stopped sending soldiers to serve under the king and instead formed their own armies.

Developments in metals also affected the central-regional power balance. Bronze weapons continued to be important, but the Chinese began using iron weapons during the Zhou Dynasty. Regional rulers grabbed centers that produced iron and bronze weapons, which were sometimes then used against the Zhou rulers and each other.

Trade and Agriculture China experienced great changes during the long Zhou rule. Internal trade expanded and there was some foreign trade. The first Chinese money came into use in the form of copper coins, with different ones minted in different regions.

The development of iron technology around the sixth century B.C.E. (the Iron Age) changed Chinese agriculture. Using iron tools, Chinese peasants built dikes, reservoirs, and irrigation canals to better control their water supply. Iron plows drawn by oxen allowed more land to be farmed and more food produced than ever before. This resulted in a steady population growth.

Most Chinese were peasant farmers who did not own the land they lived on. They lived in small villages and farmed the village fields together. They also had to devote a number of days of labor each year to work on roads, canals, and other local projects. (Test Prep: Create a chart comparing China's work requirement with the Incan mit'a system in the fifteenth century C.E., see page 261; and the French corvée system in the nineteenth century C.E., see page 417.)

Urbanization The trade among the regions led to the growth of towns and some cities. These urban areas needed artisans and metal production workers, although this class of people remained small. Merchants set up shops in towns and cities, selling goods from around China. Those cities that were seats of national or regional power attracted administrators, soldiers, scribes, and others.

Zhou Achievements Another reason why the Zhou Dynasty is considered a "golden age" is the large number of technological achievements attributed to it. The Zhou military benefited from the invention of the crossbow and the iron sword, and armies also began using mounted cavalry in this period. Meanwhile, Zhou farmers developed plows and improved irrigation systems in order to better exploit the waters of the Huang He and Yangtze rivers. Last but not least, roads were improved, which bolstered trade and brought increased contact with outsiders.

The Decline of the Zhou Dynasty By the 800s B.C.E., the Zhou kings had begun to lose control. Uprisings by local leaders combined with invasions from the west combined to weaken the central government. By the 400s B.C.E., the Zhou kings had little power outside their own city-state. The other states of the Zhou kingdom fought among themselves for control.

The First American Civilizations

In response to the varied climates and geographic regions in the Americas, people evolved into distinctive cultures as they moved from place to place. By 3000 B.C.E., some of the indigenous peoples, possibly first in Mexico, discovered that food could be grown and harvested, not simply gathered from wild plants. One of the first important plants to be grown by the indigenous Americans was *maize* (corn). This plant, native to the Western Hemisphere, was domesticated from wild types into several different varieties. Other important native crops were beans, potatoes, peppers, pumpkins, cotton, and tobacco.

The Chavin About the same time human settlements developed in *Mesoamerica* (Central America and what is now Mexico), settlements began near the Andes Mountains. For example, along the coast of what is now Peru, the *Chavin civilization* existed from around 1000 to 200 B.C.E. The center of the Chavin civilization was Chavín de Huántar, a ceremonial center north of Peru's current capital of Lima. Chavín de Huántar was home to an elaborate temple made of white granite and black limestone. Since these materials are not native to the region, they had to be obtained by trade. Drainage ditches were built under the temple to prevent flooding during rainy seasons. Shamans interpreted the temple's many sculptures and carvings.

Most of the Chavin people lived in the valleys, growing cotton, maize, potatoes, and quinoa, a grain used for food. In addition to growing crops, the Chavin relied heavily on llamas. These animals provided meat, often eaten in a dried form known as jerky; wool, woven into clothes; and transport, for carrying goods. Like earlier river valley civilizations in Afro-Eurasia, they developed irrigation systems. Because of their agricultural surpluses, the Chavin population increased, and the Chavin developed three urban centers, each with more than 10,000 people.

The Chavin developed impressive techniques in gold, silver, and copper metallurgy. They learned how to solder pieces together by melting metal. The Chavin are also remembered for the artistry of their pottery and cotton textiles, including making fishnets out of cotton thread.

Although the Chavin people were closely tied to each other by religion, their political structure was weak. Once the religious authority went into decline, there was little to hold the Chavin together, and their civilization dissolved into various regional groups.

The Olmec Mesoamerica would become home to several advanced civilizations. The foundation, or core, of all of these was the *Olmec*. Their language, beliefs, art, and athletics influenced the later civilizations such as the Maya and the Aztec. The Olmec flourished in east and central Mexico from around 1200 to 400 B.C.E. The climate was warm and humid, so crops grew well. Like other early civilizations, the Olmec were primarily agricultural, growing corn, beans, squash, and avocados.

And like many early civilizations, the Olmec developed near water. Several small rivers crossed their land, so fresh water was plentiful and transportation was easy. They carried on a flourishing trade with regions as far as 250 miles away, obtaining jade and obsidian, out of which they made jewelry, sculptures, and religious symbols. The Olmec produced small carvings of jaguars, snakes, feathered serpents, and figures that were half human and half animal. But the Olmec are most famous for carving enormous basalt monuments of human heads. About 17 of these have been found, with the largest about 10 feet tall and weighing many thousands of pounds. Thousands of slaves were used to drag and float the heavy basalt blocks from sites 50 miles away.

The Olmec also built large structures. They created large earthen pyramids, under which they buried jewelry, sculptures, mirrors, and mosaics. They built arenas for playing a kind of ball game that may have had religious significance—and may have been deadly for the losers.

The Olmec developed a calendar, a numbering system that included a zero (rare among early number systems), and the first writing system in the Americas. The system used *glyphs,* pictures and symbols of real objects. While many traits of Olmec culture, including their language, their use of feathered serpents, and their ritual ball game, provide the core and foundation of later cultures in Mesoamerica, later writing systems in Mesoamerica do not seem to be based on the one of the Olmec.

The Pacific Peoples

The first people arrived in *Oceania,* the vast region in the Pacific Ocean that includes New Guinea, Australia, and more than a thousand other islands, about 60,000 years ago. They were hunter-foragers. Because of an Ice Age, sea levels were lower and distances between islands were less. Thus, these migrants would have needed little more than a raft to go from island to island.

The Austronesian Speakers The *Austronesian-speaking people* probably originated in southern China and later moved to Taiwan and the Philippines. Around 5000 to 2500 B.C.E., they began to migrate to New Guinea also. They already were farmers and herders and introduced agriculture to the people of New Guinea. The Austronesians assimilated with the existing population. Agriculture, however, did not spread to Australia's *aboriginals*, who remained hunter-foragers.

During the next 1,000 years, the Austronesian people migrated by boat across a distance of over 10,000 miles. To the east, they went from one Pacific Island after another. By then, they had developed double-hull canoes that could go vast distances, reaching the islands of *Polynesia,* including Samoa, Hawaii, Easter Island, and New Zealand. Another group of Austronesians migrated west all the way to the African island of Madagascar. Wherever they went, they took along pigs, chickens, yams, and taro so they could maintain their agricultural way of life. They supplemented this food by hunting and fishing.

Easter Island The people who settled on *Easter Island* divided into clans, with a chief for each clan. One chief ruled over all of the clans. They constructed large stone statues that represented ancestor-gods. For a long time, the Easter Islanders carried on trade with other islands, even though distances to these islands were vast. They cultivated sweet potatoes, which they probably first obtained from the coast of South America. From Easter Island, the growing of sweet potatoes spread to other Pacific islands, including New Zealand.

Gradually, the population of Easter Island grew until the island became overpopulated, lacking enough resources to support the people. Easter Island suffered deforestation. This environmental crisis, coupled with civil unrest and wars between island factions, caused the population size to plummet sometime before Europeans first visited the island in 1722 C.E.

One of the ongoing questions that historians ask is why certain cultures at certain times become innovative and prosperous and then seem to lose their ability to develop new ideas, to improve the lives of their citizens, and to influence other countries. For example, why did the Sumerians develop the first writing system? Today, why has China, in less than a century, risen from crushing poverty to become a world power?

Among the first and most influential Europeans to write about why civilizations develop was a German, Oswald Spengler (1880–1936). In his *Decline of the West* (1917), Spengler viewed civilizations as the expression of an idea, often seen most clearly in its art or architecture. He theorized that civilizations go through a cycle akin to the four seasons: during the "spring" of a civilization, it develops agriculturally; during the "summer," towns and cities emerge; in the "autumn," the civilization develops large cities and centralized governments; finally, in the "winter," the civilization declines as it becomes involved in materialism, imperialism, and its resulting cynicism or *nihilism,* the rejection of moral or ethical principles. Since the process is cyclical, cultures go through it repeatedly.

French historian Fernand Braudel (1902–1985) saw the development of civilization as the building of a web of relationships between people through trade and communication. His perspective heavily influenced later approaches to world history. In contrast to Braudel's emphasis on physical objects, British historian Christopher Dawson (1889–1970) argued that religion is the bond that builds these relationships and civilization. According to Dawson, "religion is key to history." Both of these world historians rejected the cyclical view of history suggested by Spengler and others. Recent world historians have emphasized the role of geography and environment. For example, British historian Felipe Fernández-Armesto, in *Civilizations* (2000), viewed the development of civilization as a response to its immediate environment.

KEY TERMS BY THEME

ENVIRONMENT
Tigris and Euphrates
Mesopotamia
Fertile Crescent
Carthage
Sahara
Kalahari
Nile River
desertification
Indus River Valley
environmental
  degradation
deforestation
Huang He
Chiang Jiang
loess
Mesoamerica
maize
Oceania
Polynesia

ECONOMICS
division of labor
barter

CULTURE: RELIGION
polytheistic
ziggurats
astronomy
astrology
Hebrews
Israelites
Jews
Abraham
Moses
Ten Commandments
monotheism

Jewish Diaspora
Aten
mummification
Aryans
Hindi
Vedas
brahmin
Vedic Age
brahma
dharma
karma
moksha
ancestor veneration
Golden Age

CULTURE: LITERATURE
scribes
The Epic of Gilgamesh
cuneiform
alphabetic script
hieroglyphics
papyrus
Book of the Dead
Indo-European
  language
Sanskrit
Rig-Veda
Upanishads
pictographs
glyphs
Austronesian-speaking
  people

SOCIAL STRUCTURE
patriarchal
clans
feudalism

STATE-BUILDING:
  KINGDOMS
Sumerians
Sumer
Uruk
city-states
king
kingdoms
Babylonians
empire
Phoenicians
Old Kingdom
Middle Kingdom
New Kingdom
Hyksos
Hittites
Kush
Axum
Dravidians
Harappa
Mohenjo-Daro
Chavin civilization
Olmec
Easter Island
aboriginals

STATE-BUILDING:
  LEADERS
Hammurabi
Code of Hammurabi
King Menes
pharaoh
theocrats
Akhenaton
Ramses the Great
Xia dynasty
dynasty
Shang Dynasty
Mandate of Heaven
Zhou Dynasty

1. How did the Phoenicians first use the alphabet they created?
   (A) To correctly perform complex religious rites
   (B) To rule their many subjects
   (C) To facilitate their wide-ranging, trade-based empire
   (D) To record and promote their democratic legal code

2. Which of the following is the best example of the type of question the Chinese would use oracle bones to help them answer?
   (A) Why does the moon change its appearance?
   (B) Why does rain become snow?
   (C) How long is a trip from one city to another?
   (D) Which day is best for the army to attack an enemy?

3. The Hittites successfully conquered their neighbors because they
   (A) invented the bow and arrow
   (B) used iron weapons extensively
   (C) were experts in guerilla warfare
   (D) had more soldiers than other groups

4. How are the religions of Judaism, Christianity, and Islam similar?
   (A) They all trace their history to Abraham.
   (B) They all were founded in Egypt.
   (C) They all began as monotheistic.
   (D) They all controlled a country throughout history.

5. How did geography affect cultural interaction in the early history of Southwest Asia?
   (A) Daunting mountains protected the people from invasion.
   (B) Rich deposits of marble provided areas with goods to trade.
   (C) Isolation from other civilizations made trade difficult.
   (D) Lack of natural barriers led to repeated conquests.

6. Materials used to build Chavín de Huántar are evidence that the Chavin
   (A) traded with people outside of their region
   (B) developed a strong central government to rule the civilization
   (C) understood sophisticated principles of construction
   (D) had similar ideas about beauty as the Olmec

Question 7 is based on the following excerpt.

If a man knocks the teeth out of another man, his own teeth will be knocked out.

7. The above excerpt from the Code of Hammurabi is based on the idea of
    (A) one's punishment depends on one's status
    (B) a person should not put another person to death
    (C) one will go to heaven or hell depending on how one behaves in life
    (D) the punishment should fit the crime

8. Elements of Sumerian and Babylonian culture such as irrigation projects, calendars, astrology, and the worship of nature deities demonstrate
    (A) the influence of the Hebrews
    (B) the importance of the cycles of nature in their lives
    (C) that superstition stunted the development of practical skills
    (D) the inability of those two peoples to collaborate effectively

9. The Royal Road of the Persians exemplifies
    (A) remarkable advances in technology
    (B) the empire's devotion to their king
    (C) skill at managing a large, diverse empire
    (D) cultural borrowing from the Sumerians

10. Egypt's periods of stability and prosperity generally happened when Egypt
    (A) was reducing trade with other empires
    (B) was practicing monotheism
    (C) was ruled by a strong central government
    (D) was facing a threat of invasion

CONTINUITY AND CHANGE-OVER-TIME ESSAY QUESTIONS

Directions: You are to answer the following question. You should spend 5 minutes organizing or outlining your essay. Write an essay that:

-   Has a relevant thesis and supports that thesis with appropriate historical evidence.
-   Addresses all parts of the question.
-   Uses world historical context to show continuities and changes over time.
-   Analyzes the process of continuity and change over time.

1. Analyze continuities and change between 3000 B.C.E. and 1000 B.C.E. in the economy or the political system of Mesopotamia.

Questions for Additional Practice

2. Analyze continuities and change in ONE of the following aspects of culture in the Fertile Crescent from 3500 B.C.E. to 500 B.C.E.:
    *   systems of writing
    *   religion
    *   arts and architecture

3. Analyze continuities and change in technology in between 5000 and 600 B.C.E. in ONE of these regions:
    *   Egypt
    *   India
    *   China

COMPARATIVE ESSAY QUESTIONS

Directions: You are to answer the following question. You should spend 5 minutes organizing or outlining your essay. Write an essay that:
*   Has a relevant thesis and supports that thesis with appropriate historical evidence.
*   Addresses all parts of the question.
*   Makes direct, relevant comparisons.
*   Analyzes relevant reasons for similarities and differences.

1. Analyze similarities and differences in culture between Mesopotamia and Egypt.

Questions for Additional Practice

2. Analyze similarities and differences between the religious developments of the Hebrews and the Aryans.

3. Analyze similarities and differences in political systems in TWO of the following regions before 600 B.C.E.:
    *   Mesopotamia
    *   Egypt
    *   China

THINK AS A HISTORIAN: USE OF RELEVANT HISTORICAL EVIDENCE

Use relevant evidence. Evidence is irrelevant if it uses the wrong culture, wrong time period, wrong topic. For example, if the question asks about the first civilizations in Mesopotamia, facts about Sumer are more relevant than facts about Egypt. *For each claim below, evaluate the relevance of the statements below it:*

1. The Assyrians were successful at warfare.

   a. Assyrians learned from Central Asian pastoralists to use chariots.

   b. The Assyrians adopted much of the culture of the Sumerians.

2. Abraham was an influential religious leader.

   a. Canaan includes sites holy to Jews, Christians, and Muslims.

   b. Abraham was originally called Abram.

3. The year 539 B.C.E. was a key date in Middle Eastern history.

   a. Jews rebuilt the temple in Jerusalem.

   b. The Persians were a pastoral tribe that settled in what is now Iran.

WRITE AS A HISTORIAN: UNDERSTAND THE TOPIC

In writing an essay, be clear about the topic. Students sometimes do not read an essay question closely and so they write about examples from the wrong region, wrong time period, or wrong theme. *For each essay question below, explain whether the examples are relevant to the topic:*

1. Did the first civilizations of the Middle East built impressive cities?

   a. The roads and sewer systems of early India were remarkable.

   b. Some cities in Mesopotamia had populations of 30,000.

2. How did warfare shape the first civilizations in the Middle East?

   a. The conquest of the Middle East by the Roman Empire shaped the religious and political development of the region.

   b. The Hittites' use of iron made them successful at war.

3. Compare and contrast the impact of the Sumerians and the Jews on later cultures.

   a. Sumerians used 60 as the basis for the number system.

   b. Jews had two major rebellions against Roman rule.

PERIOD 1: Review

Thematic Review

Directions: Briefly answer each question in paragraph form.

1. **Interaction Between Humans and the Environment** How did the agricultural revolution in Southwest Asia change the relationship between people and the environment?

2. **Development and Interaction of Cultures** Analyze how the relationship between the cultures of Sumer and Babylonia. How was this similar to the relationship between the Olmec and the Maya?

3. **State-Building, Expansion, and Conflict** How did the agricultural revolution lead to the development of kings and to greater warfare?

4. **State-Building, Expansion, and Conflict** How do the achievements in architecture in Mohenjo-Daro and in ancient Egypt both reflect the process of state-building?

5. **Creation, Expansion, and Interaction of Economic Systems** Analyze how forms of transportation and types of trade goods affected the trade between Mesopotamia and the Indus Valley.

6. **Development and Transformation of Social Structures** Analyze the similarities and differences of the systems of record-keeping that emerged in the Mediterranean and the Shang Dynasty.

TURNING POINT: WHY 600 B.C.E.?

Historians today often use 600 B.C.E. to mark the end of the early period in human history because it reflects a global perspective on the past, not a focus on one particular region. By that date, core and foundational civilizations had developed in several parts of the world and they had established regional and transregional trade routes. Soon after 600 B.C.E., revolutionary developments in religion and thought would occur in China, India, and Greece.

However, historians in the past usually focused more on their own cultures than on the entire world. As a reflection of this focus, they often selected other dates as turning points based on which events were most important in that culture's history. For example, European historians often used 753 B.C.E. as a turning point in history because it marked the founding of the Roman Kingdom. Chinese historians traditionally organized histories around dynasties of emperors, so 600 B.C.E. was not as significant as 1046 B.C.E., the founding of the Zhou Dynasty, or 256 B.C.E., the end of that dynasty.

DOCUMENT-BASED QUESTION

Direction: The following question is based on the accompanying Documents 1–7. (The documents have been edited for the purpose of this exercise. Documents in later DBQs will be longer.)

This question is designed to test your ability to work with and understand historical documents. Write an essay that:

- Has a relevant thesis and supports that thesis with evidence from the document.
- Uses all of the documents.
- Analyzes the documents by grouping them in as many appropriate ways as possible; does not simply summarize the documents individually.
- Takes into account the sources of the documents and analyzes the author's point of view.
- Identifies and explains the need for at least one additional type of document.

You may refer to relevant historical information not mentioned in the documents.

1. Using the following documents, analyze similarities and differences in religious beliefs and practices in Egypt and China in the period before 600 B.C.E. What additional types of documents would be most helpful in furthering your analysis?

Document 1

Source: *Pyramid Texts* (c. 2425–2300 B.C.E.) describing a dead Egyptian pharaoh's passage to the afterlife.

The king ascends to the sky among the gods dwelling in the sky. He stands on the great [dais], he hears (in judicial session) the (legal) affairs of men. Re finds thee upon the shores of the sky in this lake that is in Nut (the Sky-goddess). 'The arriver comes!' say the gods. He (Re) gives thee his arm on the stairway to the sky. 'He who knows his place comes,' say the gods. O Pure One, assume thy throne in the barque of Re and sail thou the sky.

Document 2

Source: *Book of the Dead,* a guide for use in the Egyptian afterlife, 1567–1085 B.C.E.

Hail great god, lord of the place of the Two Goddesses of What is Right.
I have come before you so that you may bring me to see your perfection. . . .
I have not impoverished the divine herd (people);
I have committed no crime in place of What is Right;
I have not known (explored) nothingness;
I have not done any evil; . . .
I have not slighted a servant to his master;
I have not caused affliction;
I have not caused hunger;
I have not caused grief;
I have not killed;
I have not harmed the offering-cattle

Document 3

Source: Interpretations of cracked bones in the Shang Dynasty of China (c. 1554–1040 B.C.E.).

"If the king joins with Zhi [Guo] (an important Shang general) to attack the Shaofang, he will receive [assistance]."
"Lady Hao's (a consort of Wu Ding) childbearing will be good."

Document 4

Source: *The Book of Rites,* compiled in China during the Zhou Dynasty.

"Of all things by which men live, li [rituals, ceremonies, and customs] is the greatest. . . . [The sacrifices, music, and prayers] aim to bring down the Lord on High, as well as ancestral deities from above. The relation between the ruler and ministers is then rectified; generous feeling between father and son is maintained; elder and younger brothers are harmonized: the high and low find their own positions; and the proper relationship between husband and wife is established. This is what is called "securing the blessings of Heaven.""

Document 5

Source: An Egyptian carving showing the Pharaoh Seti (ruled c. 1294–1279 B.C.E.) making an offering to Osiris, the god of death, afterlife, and resurrection.

Source: Shutterstock

Document 6

Source: Chariots in a Chinese grave, Shang Dynasty (c. 1554–1040 B.C.E.).

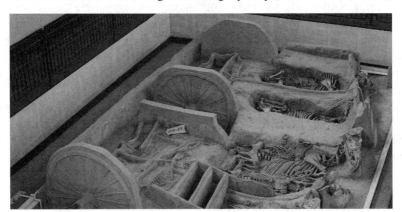

Source: Wikimedia Commons / Danielinblue

Document 7

Source: Herodotus (c. 484–425 B.C.E.) writing about Egyptian religion.

Such Egyptians as possess a temple of the Theban Jove, or live in the Thebaic canton, offer no sheep in sacrifice, but only goats; for the Egyptians do not all worship the same gods, excepting Isis and Osiris, the latter of whom they say is the Grecian Bacchus.

PERIOD 2: Organization and Reorganization of Human Societies, c. 600 B.C.E. to c. 600 C.E.

Chapter 3 *Classical Civilizations in Greece and Persia*

Chapter 4 *The Roman World*

Chapter 5 *Classical Civilizations in India and China*

Chapter 6 *Early American Civilizations*

Period Overview

The 1,200 years between 600 B.C.E. and 600 C.E. saw the rise of great empires that became the core foundations of later civilizations in much of the world. The Roman and Byzantine and Persian in western Eurasia, the Maurya and Gupta in South Asia, the Qin and Han in East Asia, the Maya in Mesoamerica, and the Moche in the Andes provided security for merchants and several built roads so trade flourished, linking people across regions. Goods and ideas flowed along land routes, such as the Silk Roads crossing Eurasia and the Trans-Saharan routes in Africa, and across sea routes in the Mediterranean and the Indian Ocean. Trade fostered the growth of great cities, such as Rome and Alexandria on the Mediterranean, Chang'an in China, and Teotihuacan in Mesoamerica.

However, the strength of these empires brought challenges. Empires grew so large that governing distant lands became difficult and defending long borders became expensive. Trade provided pathways for devastating diseases to move from one region to another. Population growth increased demand for food, and the resulting expansion of agricultural land caused soil erosion and deforestation. Prosperity produced intense concentrations of wealth. Each great empire eventually declined, suffering from decentralization of political power, reductions in trade, and lower urban populations.

No other period in history had such influential developments in belief systems. Judaism and Christianity spread throughout the Roman Empire. In India, the evolution of the Vedic beliefs that would eventually form Hinduism also included the development of a caste system. In China, three systems of thought became widespread and continue to this day: Buddhism, with its emphasis on understanding human suffering; Confucianism, with its emphasis on social harmony and rituals; and Daoism, with its emphasis on the interplay between humans and nature. In Greece, philosophers emphasized logic and observation rather than faith as ways to understand the world.

Key Concepts

2.1   The Development and Codification of Religious and Cultural Traditions

    I. Codifications and further developments of existing religious traditions provided a bond among the people and an ethical code to live by.

    II. New belief systems and cultural traditions emerged and spread, often asserting universal truths.

    III. Belief systems affected gender roles. Buddhism and Christianity encouraged monastic life and Confucianism emphasized filial piety.

    IV. Other religious and cultural traditions continued parallel to the codified, written belief systems in core civilizations.

    V. Artistic expressions, including literature and drama, architecture, and sculpture, show distinctive cultural developments.

2.2.   The Development of States and Empires

    I. The number and size of key states and empires grew dramatically by imposing political unity on areas where previously there had been competing states.

    II. Empires and states developed new techniques of imperial administration based, in part, on the success of earlier political forms.

    III. Unique social and economic dimensions developed in imperial societies in Afro-Eurasia and the Americas.

    IV. The Roman, Han, Persian, Mauryan, and Gupta empires created political, cultural, and administrative difficulties that they could not manage, which eventually led to their decline, collapse, and transformation into successor empires or states.

2.3.   Emergence of Transregional Networks of Communication and Exchange

    I. Land and water routes became the basis for transregional trade, communication, and exchange networks in the Eastern Hemisphere.

    II. New technologies facilitated long-distance communication and exchange.

    III. Alongside the trade in goods, the exchange of people, technology, religious and cultural beliefs, food crops, domesticated animals, and disease pathogens developed across far-flung networks of communication and exchange.

Source: *AP® World History Course and Exam Description.*

3

Classical Civilizations in Greece and Persia

The purpose of [my research] is to prevent the traces of human events
from being erased by time, and to preserve the fame of the important and
remarkable achievements produced by both Greeks and non-Greeks. . . .

—Herodotus, *The Histories*. Trans. Aubrey de Sélincourt (New York: Penguin Group, 1972).

While Egypt was in its Middle Kingdom, Babylon was rising in Southwest Asia; the Harappans were giving way to the Aryans in India, and the Shang dynasty was on the horizon in China. At the same time a distinctive Greek culture was developing at the eastern end of the Mediterranean. The origins of this culture were in the Minoan and Mycenaean kingdoms. Many centuries later, as the Greek historian Herodotus wrote in his *Histories*, Greek culture would flourish in several city-states, giving rise to a Golden Age of innovative ideas in philosophy, literature, and art. After the Golden Age ended, two powerful military leaders emerged: Philip II and then Alexander the Great. Each spread Greek culture as they conquered lands in and around the Mediterranean and Southwest Asia. These areas, influenced by classical Greek culture, became known as the Hellenistic kingdoms.

Early Mediterranean Civilizations

Two cultures that emerged on the islands and along the northern coast of the eastern Mediterranean Sea had long-term impact. They provided a foundation for later developments in Greece.

Crete The Minoans lived on an island in the Aegean Sea called *Crete*. Because they had many harbors but little fertile soil, they relied on trade, and grew rich through trade with Greece, Phoenicia, Egypt, and Asia Minor. They decorated their homes with paintings and other decorations. The Minoans built a beautiful city on Crete called *Knossos*—for a while, the wealthiest city on the Aegean. No writing from the *Minoan civilization* in Crete has been deciphered, but the existence of artifacts all around the Mediterranean testifies to Cretan influence in the period around 2000 B.C.E. The wealth of the Minoans, their skill as builders, and their experience as seafarers gave rise to stories of a legendary King Minos in Knossos and of Daedalus and the maze.

Mycenae The city of *Mycenae*, on the mainland of Greece, was probably never conquered by the Minoans, yet it contained artifacts revealing a number of Minoan cultural influences. In addition, the presence of amber from the north and ivory from Syria are testimony to Mycenae's widespread trade in the area. Both the Minoan and the Mycenaean civilizations declined in what is sometimes called a "dark age" starting around 1100 B.C.E. and lasting until about 750 B.C.E. However, their arts and culture, as exemplified in frescoes, statuettes, jewelry, and even the presence of indoor plumbing at the *Knossos Palace* complex, continued to spread to the Greek mainland, Southwest Asia, and North Africa. This spread of culture would become an ongoing example of continuity, not only in the Mediterranean area and Southwest Asia, but also throughout emerging Europe.

CRETE, MYCENAE, AND GREEK CITY-STATES

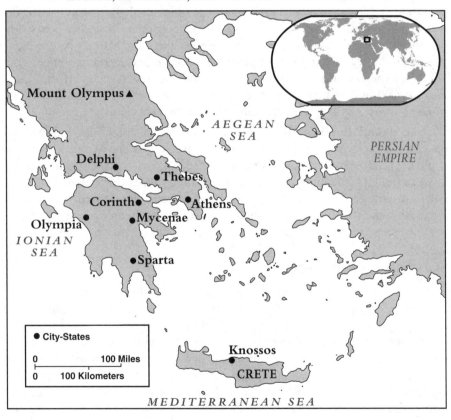

Rise of the Greek City-States

Geography's influence on Greece is easy to see. The Greek mainland is a giant peninsula that juts into the Mediterranean, and the surrounding waters include many small islands. These islands and the mainland's long, irregular coastline made seafaring and trade important. Traveling on Mediterranean sea lanes, Greeks transported grain, timber, gold, and other metals from one point to another, growing prosperous and connecting cultures as they did. Like sea-faring cultures throughout history, the Greeks became open to new ideas and technology from their trading partners. For example, when Phoenicians developed an alphabet that made writing and reading easier, the Greeks quickly adopted it with all the benefits of more efficient communication.

Geography also shaped Greek politics. Numerous islands, mountainous terrain, and lack of rivers separated one Greek tribe from another. The disconnected terrain long prevented the Greek people from uniting under one government. Instead, they usually had independent local governments. Greece was separated into *poleis* (city-states; singular—*polis*). Over the course of Greece's history, these poleis would at times be allies and at times be enemies. Access to the sea also helps to explain how Greece developed in competition with an expanded Persian empire, a competition that resulted in the great *Persian Wars* of the fifth and fourth centuries B.C.E. These wars were described in *The Histories* by the first great Greek historian, *Herodotus*.

Social and Political Systems Citizenship of a polis was confined to males—Greece was a patriarchy—and only free ones. Slaves and foreigners could not be citizens. A polis could call upon its citizens to defend their lands as *hoplites* (infantry members), sometimes fighting against other poleis. Different poleis in Greece had different types of government. In a *monarchy,* a king ruled the state. In an *aristocracy,* nobles ruled. In an *oligarchy,* a few wealthy landowners and *merchants* ruled. In a *democracy,* all citizens participated.

Sparta's Military Society

Two of the most powerful poleis were *Sparta* and *Athens*. While both were city-states, they differed greatly from each other. Sparta remains famous for developing a society organized around producing a powerful military.

Sparta's focus on developing soldiers began with child-rearing. Boys were taken away from their mothers beginning at age seven and raised with extensive training and endurance lessons to make them solid soldiers. To prepare them for the harsh life of a soldier, boys suffered physical abuse, went without food, and were ridiculed for showing any sign of weakness. When grown, men served in the active military or in the reserve until age 60.

With Spartan men serving in the military, *Spartan women* ran their households with greater freedom than did other Greek women. Free Spartan women received an education, could own property, and were not secluded in their homes. They won praise for staying fit and participating in athletics so they would bear healthy sons to increase the size of the army. A significant responsibility for women was the inculcation of Spartan values in their children.

For example, children learned the values of the state religion, which developed around the kings, who also served as the supreme priests.

To enable men to serve in the military and women to focus on bearing children and raising them to be soldiers, Spartan society relied on *helots*, or slaves, to do agricultural labor needed to feed everyone. Helots were generally captives resulting from Spartan raids on their neighboring inland.

Keeping helots under control and supporting the military were key functions of the Spartan government. The government was run by an oligarchy that shared power between two kings. Ideas originating from outside the polis were discouraged as destabilizing, and social life was tightly controlled. Spartans believed that top-down government power was necessary for a stable and prosperous society.

Athenian Democracy

Today, Sparta is remembered for creating a military society and *Athens* for its political and intellectual achievements. Early governments of Athens were *monarchies*, followed by a period of aristocracy. *Solon*, a reform-minded aristocrat who lived in the sixth century B.C.E., became known as a wise ruler who improved life in Athens. He is credited with setting free many Athenians enslaved for debt and limiting the amount of land any one man could own.

Politics As Athens and other Greek city-states increased their trade with one another, they developed prosperous merchant classes. However, the merchants resented those who held a monopoly on political power. As men of wealth and property, merchants thought that they should have more of a voice in government. When the *aristocrats* refused these demands, the merchants joined small farmers to support *tyrants*—leaders who seized power with the people's support. By 650 B.C.E., tyrants had overthrown the aristocrats in most city-states.

At first, the tyrants were popular. They lowered taxes and ended the practice of enslaving people who could not pay their debts. They also gave citizens a greater voice in matters that affected their lives. Over time, though, some tyrants alienated their supporters by abusing their power.

Democracy During the 500s B.C.E., most Greek city-states overthrew their tyrants. Some poleis returned to governments ruled by aristocrats or kings, but Athens and others turned to democracy. For a while, Athens was a *direct democracy*, a government in which all citizens could vote directly on laws and other issues in a large assembly. By contrast, in a *representative democracy*, citizens elect leaders to represent them and give those leaders powers to make laws and govern. The democratic Athenian government was comprised of nine top officials called *archons*, a council of nobles, and a citizen assembly.

Pericles Perhaps the most famous name of all in the Greek government was that of *Pericles*, whose period of rule in Athens is sometimes called the Golden Age (461–429 B.C.E.) During his reign, the *Parthenon*, a great temple in Athens that had been destroyed in war with Persia, was rebuilt. Pericles is credited with reforms to government such as transfer of power to an assembly.

He created the Council of 500, which served as an ongoing government of Athens, and he developed the People's Courts, which ruled on charges of legal violations.

Women For women and slaves in Athens, life was hard. They were excluded from government service and from voting. Women could not own any property beyond personal items. They did not receive an education. If women had matters to settle in court, they had to employ a male guardian. Upper-class women always had to be accompanied by a man when they left home. Early marriages and exclusion from most of public life kept women isolated. Women were believed to be intellectually inferior to men and thus incapable of being satisfying relationship partners. (Test Prep: Create a chart comparing the treatment of women in Greece with their treatment in Egypt and China. For Egypt see page 27; for China see page 101.)

Athenian Philosophy

Perhaps as a result of having seaports and welcoming trade connections with the outside world, new ideas flourished in Athens. The arts, mathematics, and literature created by Athenians formed the basis of academic disciplines still studied in schools worldwide. Two epic poems, the *Iliad* and the *Odyssey,* have been recited, read, and studied every since they were presumabley composed by a Greek poet named Homer around the ninth century B.C.E. .

Socrates One influential Greek thinker was *Socrates*. His emphasis on continually asking questions to systematically clarify another person's ideas and to identify the core of them became known as the *Socratic Method*. Socrates was eventually put to death by the Athenian government for questioning the state religion.

Plato A student of Socrates, *Plato*, kept his teacher's ideas alive. Plato opened a school called the *Academy*, where he taught students to question the nature of ideas such as good, evil, justice, and beauty. Departing from the oral tradition of philosophy, Plato wrote *dialogues*, teachings presented as discussions between Socrates and his pupils. In the dialogue known as *The Republic*, Plato described an ideal society ruled by a government that rested upon a concept of justice and ethical values. While many Athenians advocated democracy, Plato did not. Instead, in *The Republic,* Plato envisioned a society composed of workers, warriors, and "philosopher kings." This last group would be intelligent and rational enough to make decisions for the good of the whole state.

Aristotle One of Plato's students, *Aristotle*, also became a famous Athenian philosopher. Aristotle wrote on a range of topics, from how to organize government to the qualities of good literature. He might be best known for his ideas about ethics. Aristotle believed in avoiding extremes in behavior. For example, moderate courage was a virtue. Too little courage made one a coward; too much made one fool-hardy. Aristotle called this emphasis on moderation the *Golden Mean.*

Aristotle emphasized gaining knowledge through *empiricism,* trusting what one learned from observation and evidence of the senses, rather than emphasizing intuition or religious beliefs. Aristotle also focused on *logic,* the science of the formal principles of reasoning. However, unlike modern scientists, Aristotle and other Greeks did not emphasize experiments. An additional contribution by Aristotle was his work *Poetics*, which for the first time set down definitions of tragedy and comedy in the theater, as well as definitions of epic and lyric poetry. Such systematic writings about philosophy, literature, and the arts constituted a new development in the Mediterranean world. The ideas of Socrates, Plato, Aristotle, and other Greek thinkers provided the foundation for European thought for centuries. (Test Prep: Write a paragrapho comparing Greek philosophers with influential thinkers in other cultures. See page 100 for Confucius and page 9 for Zoroaster.)

Athenian Religion and Culture

Greek religion was based on an influential set of myths. Through these stories, rather than through specific teachings about ethics, most Greeks expressed their ideas about right and wrong behavior and the role of gods in their lives. Books and movies about Zeus, Hercules, Odysseus, and other Greek mythological figures remain popular today. Over time, as contact increased between Greeks and other groups, such as Persians and Egyptians, Greek religion became more *syncretic,* combining ideas from different sources. For example, the deity Serapis combined elements of the Greek Zeus, the Egyptian Osiris, and other deities into one.

Greek religion and literature were closely connected. Attendance at religious functions, of which theater was often a part, was considered a civic duty. Some Greek playwrights, including *Euripides* and *Sophocles*, used the myths of the gods as convenient literary devices for their plays. Although the term "satire" comes from a later Roman form of drama, there were certainly satirical sections in the Greek *comedies*, plays in which a character triumphs over hardship. The most prolific author of comedies was *Aristophanes*, who wrote 40 plays, including *Lysistrata* and *The Birds.*

Aeschylus and Euripides wrote *tragedies*, dramas that deal with death, war, justice, and the relationships between gods and ordinary people. For example, *Prometheus Bound* by Aeschylus tells the tale of how Prometheus steals fire from Zeus, gives it to humans, and then suffers eternal punishment. *The Trojan Women* by Euripides describes how Athenians slaughtered people they captured in the Trojan War. Greek tragedies and comedies influenced William Shakespeare of the sixteenth century and continue to influence modern playwrights today.

Architecture and Art Religion was also connected to the distinctive Greek architectural style, a style exemplified by the *Parthenon* in Athens. This massive stone building, rectangular but elegant, featured rows of tall columns on all sides and was topped by a slanted roof. In a panel sitting along the top of the columns, artists carved friezes illustrating Greek myths.

The Olympic Games Religion also provided the context for athletic competitions. Unlike modern sports, which emphasize keeping records of who ran the fastest and who jumped the farthest, Greek sports emphasized rituals. For example, before competing, athletes would provide offerings to show their respect for the gods. Beginning around 776 B.C.E., the Greeks held Olympic games every four years. Athletes from all the city-states gathered in one spot, Olympia, to compete in various sports. Wars among the city-states commonly would be suspended for the duration of the games so that athletes and spectators could assemble. Thus, even though there was not a centralized state of Greece, the Olympic Games helped create a common feeling of "Greekness." The games continued for over one thousand years, ending around 400 C.E. The games were restarted in 1896.

Greek Colonies

Starting around the eighth century B.C.E., the Greek city-states began establishing colonies around the Mediterranean, partly because the Greeks' population growth was outstripping the food supply. Some Greeks moved willingly to the colonies, others less willingly. The reluctant ones drew lots to see who would emigrate.

In a typically Greek spirit of independence, the colonies were allowed a large measure of autonomy, but each maintained a shared culture with its home city-state. Some of the largest of these colonies were located on the island of Sicily at *Syracuse* and *Agrigentum*, on the Italian Peninsula at Naples, on the coast of France at Marseilles, and on the western coast of Asia Minor.

Geography had a decided impact on the Greek city-states, as it has on every state. French historian Fernand Braudel wrote that "the poor, precarious soils along the Mediterranean, combined with an uncertain, drought-afflicted climate, spurred ancient Greek and Roman conquest." Additionally, the arid and temperate climate of Greece allowed for outdoor teaching in the schools of philosophy such as Plato's Academy. Further, the climate provided an ideal setting for outdoor theater competitions where highly developed literary genres such as tragedy and comedy appeared. Access to the sea encouraged colonization and trade, interactions that exposed the Greeks to new ideas that brought change while maintaining elements of Pan-Hellenic continuity.

Persian Empire

Beginning in 559 B.C.E., under the leadership of *Cyrus the Great* (ruled 559–529 B.C.E.) the *Persians* conquered most of the lands from the Aegean Sea (west of Turkey) to the borders of India. After 30 years of rule, Cyrus was succeeded by his son *Cambyses*, who conquered Egypt and parts of Southeast Europe. Their empire became known as the *Achaemenid Empire,* sometimes called the First Persian Empire. It united three of the earliest centers of civilization—Mesopotamia, Egypt, and India—into one powerful empire, covering a territory almost the size of the United States. It was the largest, most diverse empire the world had yet seen, including more than 70 distinct ethnic groups

THE PERSIAN EMPIRE UNDER THE ACHAEMENIDS

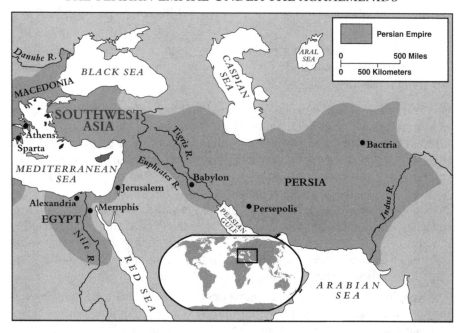

The Reign of Darius Like rulers in Egypt and China and other places, Persian rulers supported their legitimacy with claims that they ruled by divine right. However, their power rested upon their own abilities to build and hold an empire. Ruling such a large empire in an era when transportation and communication were so slow required new ways of thinking about power. Under *Darius I* (ruled 522–486 B.C.E.), Persia divided lands it conquered into provinces so that the king's policies announced in the capital of Persepolis could be administered throughout the empire. Then, rather than simply demand the loyalty of rulers who were selected locally, Darius created a new position— *satrap,* a ruler of a province who was responsible to the emperor, not to local leaders. Finally, inspectors, called "The Eyes and Ears of the King," traveled to each province and reported to the king on the behavior of the satraps. The provincial structure, with satraps and inspectors, created an efficient administrative bureaucracy.

To pay for this bureaucracy, Darius instituted regular tax payments. The flow of tax dollars into the government enabled the Persians to fund several magnificent projects under Darius.

- The capital city, *Persepolis,* which was located in what is now Iran, became a celebrated city, featuring an impressive royal palace and celebrating the artistic traditions of several groups in the empire.

- The *Royal Road,* which spanned some 1,500 miles across the empire, was the most famous of the network of roads built to encourage trade. Darius added an efficient courier service with postal stations along this road.

- Darius also instituted the construction of *caravanserai,* which were combination inns and markets for people traveling the Royal Road by camel caravan.

- The empire instituted a *common currency* that was accepted across the empire. This made trade simpler thereby uniting the empire and promoting prosperity.

Toleration While Persians centralized political power, they did not try to enforce religious and cultural uniformity in their empire. Darius I, in particular, allowed ethnic groups to retain their cultural identity and tolerated religious diversity as long as people paid their taxes and contributed soldiers to the military force to maintain the empire. His successor, *Xerxes* (519–465 B.C.E.) built a Gate of All Nations (also called Gateway of Xerxes) at an entrance to Persepolis to show that he was honoring all his subjects. Persian toleration of diversity was an unusual policy, one that made the Persian Empire unlike other empires of its time. (Test prep: Write a paragraph comparing and contrasting religious toleration under the Persians with later examples of the policy. See page 152 for Isamic rule in Spain.)

Religious Beliefs One of the most important legacies of the Persians was the spread of *monotheism,* the belief in only one god. Although monotheism also appeared in other cultures, most people in Southwest Asia were polytheistic before the Persian prophet *Zarathustra* (c. 660 B.C.E–583 B.C.E.) began teaching a new faith, *Zoroastrianism.* This faith was based on belief in only one god, Ahura Mazda, or the "wise lord." The religion also believed in a god of darkness and other lesser gods, none of which were to be worshipped. Zoroastrianism also taught the concepts of *heaven and hell.* After death, good people would be rewarded in heaven, while the evil ones would be punished in hell. Originally, priests called *magi* had passed Zarathustra's teachings orally from generation to generation. Then later, a collection of written texts based on Zarathustra's beliefs, the *Avestas,* was produced, which helped spread the religion. Zoroastrianism's monotheistic principle and other teachings may have shaped the development of Judaism and Christianity.

Society Persian society had much the same social stratification as earlier empires of the region. However, because of its size, it had a larger class of educated, well-paid government workers. This bureaucracy included accountants, administrators, tax collectors, and translators.

Similarly, the number of slaves in Persia was much greater than in other empires. Farmers owned slaves, using them as agricultural laborers, and their numbers increased as agricultural production increased. Other slaves were servants to city-dwellers, and still others were owned by the government and used to build roads, large buildings, and irrigation systems throughout Persia.

Even though Persian society was patriarchal, women were allowed to own and manage property, and if they worked in a shop, they were allowed to keep their wages. Common Persian women engaged in economic activities, including weaving textiles and trading them for food for their families. Divorce was possible. Some aristocratic Persian women wore veils, mainly to advertise their social status.

Environment and Technology The Persians irrigated their fields, as did other civilizations in Southwest Asia. The Persian method, however, was innovative: underground canals, called qanat, were used to reduce the evaporation of the water as it traveled to the fields. Qanat were especially common in the arid Iranian Plateau of central Persia.

Trade The Persians conducted much trade along the Persian Road and other land routes. They also conducted trade by sea. For example, ivory and gold came from Turkey; cedar and woolen fabrics from Phoenicia; wine and oil from Greece; and grain, textiles, and papyrus from Egypt.

Persia vs. Greece

As the Greek city-states expanded east and the vast Persian empire expanded west, the two clashed over territory. The conflict began in Asia Minor. In Asia Minor, Persians occupied several Greek colonies. Around 499 B.C.E., some of these conquered Greek areas rebelled in campaigns knows as the *Persian Wars*. Athens and Sparta formed an alliance to help the rebel colonies. In 490 B.C.E., at the city of *Marathon* in mainland Greece, an outnumbered Athenian army defeated the Persian forces of Darius, who then withdrew from Greece.

Xerxes again tried to push westward. He organized a force of thousands and attacked Greece, defeating a few hundred Spartans and their allies at the *Battle of Thermopylae*. After their victory, the Persians captured and burned Athens. In reaction, the Athenians and their allies formed the *Delian League*. When the Persians later met the Athenians at sea, the Athenians won the naval *Battle of Salamis*. Soon, the Greeks won other sea and land battles, forcing the Persians to retreat to their homeland.

Decline of Persia The cost of the battles with the Greeks severely damaged the Persian Empire. Further, Xerxes began to take a less tolerant attitude toward non-Persians in the empire. Together, these forces began to undermine the strength of the Persian Empire.

Athens-Sparta Rivalry The alliance among Greek city-states did not last. Athens expected other city-states to pay taxes to it, which the latter resented. Chief among these was Sparta, which revolted against Athens, beginning the *Peloponnesian War* (431–404 B.C.E.). With the help of its Greek allies in the *Peloponnesian League,* Sparta defeated Athens and became the dominant power in Greece.

The Rise of Macedonia

As Persia weakened and the Greeks divided, a new power arose in Macedonia, a region on the northern edge of the Greek world. *Philip II* resolved to conquer and unite the Greek city-states and then conquer Asia Minor. He quickly conquered all of the Greek city-states except Sparta. However, Philip II's further plans were cut short when he was assassinated in 336 B.C.E. He was succeeded by his son Alexander, who immediately began the conquests that would earn him the name *Alexander the Great* and extend Greek influence all the way to India.

Alexander and the Hellenistic World During Alexander's 13-year campaign, he governed his far-flung conquests by picking native residents to help him rule. For example, in present-day Iran he allowed local Persian administrators to run that part of the empire. Alexander cemented his relations with leaders in the area by marrying several Persian women and urging his leading generals to do the same. In Egypt, he founded the great city of *Alexandria*, which would become a center of Hellenistic culture and a major seaport. (The historical *Hellenistic Period* takes its name from the Greek word *Hellenes*, meaning "Greeks.") The *Ptolemy dynasty* eventually built a library at Alexandria, the largest library of the ancient world, as well as the Alexandrian Museum, a place where scholars did research.

As a result of Alexander's conquests, Greek language, architecture, mythology, and philosophy became widespread. Small colonies of Greeks were established all over the Hellenistic world, even as far as Bactria, a region in what is now Afghanistan. The continuity of Greek culture held strong even as Greek governmental unity declined. An example of such continuity can be seen in the Greco-Buddhist art from the areas in South Asia, another region visited by Alexander's forces. Temples show influences in Greek columns and some statues show the Buddha in Greek clothing.

Formation and Fall of the Kingdoms Alexander's death in 323 B.C.E. at the age of 32 ushered in a time of chaos. The central administration of the empire collapsed. Alexander had failed to designate an heir, so his generals battled with one another to establish their own kingdoms. Instead of one powerful empire, the Greek-influenced lands became divided into several. Chief among the generals/rulers were the *Seleucids* in Asia and the *Ptolemies* in Egypt. Smaller monarchies controlled Pergamum in Asia Minor, the area around Sparta, and the area around Athens. These regions would eventually fall to the Roman Empire. For example, Athens and other city-states fell to the Romans in the first century B.C.E. The break-up of the Greek empire did not mean the end of Greek culture. Much of it was adopted by the Romans. Greek teachers and doctors were highly prized as slaves in Rome because they transmitted a culture admired by the Roman upper classes. (Test Prep: Write a paragraph comparing and contrasting Alexander Darius. See page 59.)

Other Empires in Persia

Though the great Achaemenid empire of Cyrus, Darius, and Xerxes ended, their ideas lived on. The later rulers of Persian lands kept many of their innovations in administration.

Greece, along with India, developed some of the first forms of drama. Greek plays (upper) were often simple productions that taught that people had to suffer to learn. In contrast, Indian drama (lower) often used dance and frequently had happy endings.

Seleucids The *Seleucids* who ruled Persia from 305 to 83 B.C.E. encouraged Greeks and Macedonians to settle there as colonists. They kept Achaemenid's bureaucratic system, but the satraps often revolted against their Macedonian rulers. The Seleucids lost control of their eastern lands to the Parthians and were finally replaced by the Romans.

Parthians Originally nomadic peoples from Central Asia, the *Parthians* ruled over what is now Iraq, Iran, and much of the land bordering western India, beginning in 247 B.C.E. Their capital city was Ctesiphon. They kept the Achaemenid's satrap system of governing. In the first century C.E., they prevented the Roman Empire's army from marching east beyond Syria. Neither side could conquer the other. Border towns and surrounding areas would change hands as victories were won by one side or the other. In 224 C.E., the Parthians were defeated by the *Sassanids*.

Sassanids During the Sassanid dynasty (224–651 C.E.), the government promoted Zoroastrianism and persecuted Christians, whom it suspected as being sympathetic toward the Christian Roman Empire. The Sassanid Empire was large but not as large as the Parthian Empire had been. For example, it did not control Armenia (to the north) nor Bactria (to the east).

Comparing the Greek and Persian Empires

Persia and Greece established the two great empires of the eastern Mediterranean area. They shared many similarities. Both empires covered large territories. They had wide cultural influence. They allowed most women few rights, although some women did become influential in Achaemenid court.

The two empires had very different religious traditions. Darius of Persia had the following inscription carved in three languages on a monument: "I am Darius, the great king . . . from antiquity . . . by the grace of Ahuramazda." Note that he attributed his reign to Ahuramazda, the one deity of the Zoroastrians. In contrast to the Persians' monotheism, the Greeks had a pantheon of gods. They had gods and goddesses for each aspect of life.

Greeks and Persians also viewed unity within their empires differently. The Persians showed high tolerance for diverse customs and traditions throughout their empire. They had one emperor in control, though they allowed for local autonomy. In contrast, the Greeks were more united culturally through language, religion, and traditions such as the Olympic games. However, the Greeks were less united politically. The city-states fought one another and joined together only when threatened with invasion.

The two empires demonstrate the power of syncretism. They became more alike during the Hellenistic period. For example, when Alexander the Great conquered territories from the Persians, he adopted their system of local administration. In addition, the excellent postal system of the Persians, combined with the use of coins that developed around the Mediterranean, facilitated trade that made the entire region more prosperous. Trade helped form a cultural synthesis of Persian astronomy and Zoroastrianism with Greek language, literature, gods, mystery cults, and various styles of government. The blending of these elements shaped the context for the next great empire of the Mediterranean world: the Roman Empire.

Whether historians consider Alexander great or not depends on which aspects of his life strike them as most important. Victor David Hanson, reviewing several recent books on Alexander, described the range of views from "drunken . . . psychopath" to "the Aristotelian who tamed Asia . . . with gentle firmness and romantic elán." One of the first historians to write about Alexander was the Roman historian Arrian Flavius Arrianus, who was impressed by the Macedonian's conquests. Arrian lived about four centuries after Alexander in an empire that inherited much of its culture from the Greeks. To Arrian, Alexander was a great leader who united people under his rule, created a large area where trade could flourish, and brought peace between long-time rivals Greece and Persia. Like many Romans, Arrian seemed little bothered by the costs of creating a large empire.

But these costs did bother English historian George Grote. Writing in the late 1800s, Grote was appalled by the bloodshed that resulted from Alexander's drive to win personal glory. Alexander executed thousands of conquered soldiers or villagers at a time. Maybe hundreds of thousands of people died in the wars Alexander carried out. To Grote, Alexander and his father, Phillip, were simply "brutalized adventurers."

More recently, Paul Cartledge combined aspects of both Grote and Cartledge in his evaluation of Alexander. Alexander was certainly brutal, but his brutality was common for his times. And his conquests, once completed, offered the possibility, according to Cartledge, of a "peaceful, multi-ethnic coexistence."

Two other British historians were less forgiving than Cartledge. Peter Green pointed out that many of the benefits brought by Alexander vanished upon his death. "The empire he built collapsed the moment he was gone; he came as a conqueror and the work he wrought was destruction." Alexander brought peace and unity, but only briefly. After his death, his generals fought one another and broke up his empire. Whatever the benefits that Alexander brought, they did not survive long enough to be worth the costs. And John Keegan, the preeminent military historian of the past century, concluded that Alexander's "dreadful legacy was to ennoble savagery—to which all who opposed his will were subject—in the name of glory."

KEY TERMS BY THEME

CULTURE: WRITERS & LITERATURE
Herodotus
The Histories
Homer
Iliad
Odyssey
Plato
The Republic
Aristotle
Poetics
Avestas
Aristophanes
Aeschylus
The Trojan Women
Euripides
Sophocles

CULTURE: ARCHITECTURE
Parthenon
Persepolis
Knossos Palace

CULTURE: PHILOSOPHY & RELIGION
Socrates
Socratic Method
Academy
Golden Mean
logic
empiricism
syncretic
Zoroastrianism
Zarathustra

ENVIRONMENT
qanat

STATE-BUILDING: LEADERS
Cyrus the Great
Delian League
Cambyses
Darius I
Xerxes
Peloponnesian League
Philip II
Alexander the Great
Solon
Pericles
Ptolemies

STATE-BUILDING: GOVERNMENTS
Poleis (polis)
monarchies
aristocracy
oligarchy
tyrants
democracy
direct democracy
representative
   democracy

STATE-BUILDING: KINGDOMS AND WARS
Crete
Knossos
Minoan civilization
Mycenae
Syracuse
Agrigentum
Persian Wars
Marathon
Battle of Thermopylae
Battle of Salamis
Persians
Achaemenid empire
Seleucids
Parthians
Sassanids
Athens
Sparta
Alexandria
Hellenistic Period

SOCIAL STRUCTURE
hoplites
archons
helots
satraps
aristocrats
merchants
Spartan women

ECONOMICS
caravanserai
common currency
Royal Road

1. One of the main reasons for the prosperity of Minoan civilization was that it
   (A) adopted the alphabet of the Mycenaeans
   (B) developed a strong trade network
   (C) was heavily influenced by Greek culture
   (D) defeated the Spartans in the Peloponnesian War

2. Geography most affected the development of the *poleis,* or Greek city-states, in which of the following ways?
   (A) The geography provided an urban center for a region surrounding it.
   (B) The mountains separated the regions so that they did not unite under one government.
   (C) The unnavigable seas made development difficult due to the lack of agriculture and trade.
   (D) The geography assured that there was no contact with other Mediterranean cultures.

Question 3 refers to the excerpt below.

Comfort, therefore, not condolence, is what I have to offer to the parents of the dead who may be here. Numberless are the chances to which, as they know, the life of man is subject; but fortunate indeed are they who draw for their lot a death so glorious as that which has caused your mourning, and to whom life has been so exactly measured as to terminate in the happiness in which it has been passed.

–Pericles, *The Funeral Oration,* 431 B.C.E.

3. The quote above is intended to convince parents of those who died in the Peloponnesian War that
   (A) their children died for the worthy cause of defending Athens
   (B) they should protest the war to save the lives of young Athenian men
   (C) there is no glory in death, even in war
   (D) the Peloponnesian League is winning the war

4. Which statement best describes the status of women in the Greek city-states?

   (A) They were coveted by men as intellectual companions.

   (B) They were allowed to own property and to reclaim their dowries when widowed.

   (C) They were allowed more independence in Sparta than in Athens.

   (D) They walked freely on the streets of Athens without male companions.

5. Athens differed from the city-states of ancient Mesopotamia because it

   (A) was a democracy at times

   (B) carried on trade with Egypt

   (C) included a large slave population

   (D) had a religion with many deities

6. Why were satraps used in the Persian Empire but not in Greece?

   (A) Persia was a land empire while Greece was a sea-based culture.

   (B) Persia was very large while Greek city-states were small.

   (C) Trade was more important in Persia than in Greece.

   (D) Persia included people of many religious faiths while Greeks all shared the same religion.

7. Which of these served the same role in the Persian Empire as the sea did for Greece?

   (A) the Royal Road

   (B) the common currency

   (C) qanat

   (D) Persepolis

8. One way people benefited from the conquests of Alexander the Great was that

   (A) the Greek Olympics became more closely tied to the practice of traditional Greek religion

   (B) the Greek language developed an alphabet that made writing more efficient

   (C) he dramatically increased cultural and economic connections between South Asia and the Mediterranean world

   (D) he introduced the idea of Greek concept of religious toleration to the Persians, who had not practiced it before

9. Comparing the Greece of the sixth to fourth centuries B.C.E. and the Hellenistic period following the death of Alexander the Great most clearly illustrates which of the following conclusions?

(A) Use of the Greek language for literature and business declined.

(B) Greek art and architecture became less admired and imitated.

(C) There was uniformity of religion throughout the Mediterranean as a result of Greece's victories over of the Persians in each period.

(D) Greek governmental unity and alliances declined so that conquest of the Eastern Mediterranean was easier for the rising Roman Empire.

Question 10 refers to the table below.

	Greek City-State A	Greek City-State B
Total Population	140,000	108,000
Citizens As Percentage of Total Population	25% to 30%	5% to 10%
Form of Government	Democratic	Oligarchic
Military	Strong navy	Strong army

Source: Information adapted from "Two Faces of Greece." pbs.org.

10. The table above describes Athens and Sparta. Which statement below best uses evidence from the table to indicate which is Athens?

(A) A is probably Athens because it was a very small city-state.

(B) A is probably Athens because it had a high percentage of citizens.

(C) B is probably Athens because it was oligarchic.

(D) B is probably Athens because it built its society around its army.

CONTINUITY AND CHANGE-OVER-TIME ESSAY QUESTIONS

Directions: You are to answer the following question. You should spend 5 minutes organizing or outlining your essay. Write an essay that:

- Has a relevant thesis and supports that thesis with appropriate historical evidence.
- Addresses all parts of the question.
- Uses world historical context to show continuities and changes over time.
- Analyzes the process of continuity and change over time.

1. Analyze continuities and change in the policies on religion and trade of Darius and Xerxes.

Questions for Additional Practice

2. Analyze continuities and changes between Greek city-states in the period before Alexander the Great and the communities of the Hellenistic Period following the Alexander's death in 323 B.C.E.

3. Analyze continuities and change in Greece between 800 B.C.E. and 300 B.C.E in ONE of the following aspects of life:
   • state-building, expansion, and conflict
   • culture

COMPARATIVE ESSAY QUESTIONS

Directions: You are to answer the following question. You should spend 5 minutes organizing or outlining your essay. Write an essay that:
   • Has a relevant thesis and supports that thesis with appropriate historical evidence.
   • Addresses all parts of the question.
   • Makes direct, relevant comparisons.
   • Analyzes relevant reasons for similarities and differences.

1. Analyze similarities and differences in the fall of TWO of the following kingdoms or empires:
   • the empire of Alexander the Great
   • the Achaemenid Empire
   • the Minoan kingdom

Questions for Additional Practice

2. Compare the role of women in Greek city-states around the time of Pericles and in Ancient Egypt under the pharaohs.

3. Compare the political structures of the Persian Empire with that of ONE of the following:
   • Sumeria in Ancient Mesopotamia
   • Egypt under the Pharaohs
   • China under the Shang and Zhou Dynasties

THINK AS A HISTORIAN: RECOGNIZE PERIODIZATION

Periodization helps tame the grand sweep of history into manageable time spans. Historic periods can be marked in many ways, including wars, changes in climate, or technological innovations. *Which TWO statements below best illustrate periodization?*

1. Sparta is remembered for creating a military society in which boys underwent rigorous training as soldiers.

2. Women, slaves, and foreigners could not be citizens in the poleis of early Greece.

3. The years from Socrates to Aristotle marked the start of a new way of thinking about ideas.

4. Greece's many small islands and long, irregular coastline made seafaring and trade important in ancient Greece.

5. During the Persian Wars, Greek city-states rebelled against Persian rule and eventually forced the Persians to retreat, ushering in an era of fortune.

WRITE AS A HISTORIAN: USE CHRONOLOGICAL ORDER

Chronos was the Greek word for time that is measured by sundial or clock—that is, orderly and predictable. From that comes the word *chronological*. A chronological approach examines events in the order in which they occur. *Which THREE of the sentences below cue you that the writer's approach is chronological?*

1. A distinctive Greek culture developed in the early Mediterranean civilizations; centuries later in the Golden Age, Greek culture would flourish again.

2. Infighting among city-states in Greece ended a period of fortune, partly caused by Athens' demand that the other city-states pay it taxes.

3. During his 13-year campaign, Alexandra's conquests included Egypt, which eventually became a center of Hellenistic culture.

4. Greece was so influential in the Hellenistic world that its influences showed in South Asia's art, architecture, and clothing.

5. Early governments of Athens were monarchies, followed by a time in which aristocrats ruled.

4

The Roman World

tu regere imperio populos, Romane, memento
(hae erunt artes), pacique imponere morem,
parcere subiectis et debellare superbos. . . .

'   *You, Roman, remember to rule the peoples with power*
(these will be your arts), to graft custom onto peace, to spare the conquered,
and to subdue the proud. . . .

—Anchises to Aeneas, Virgil's *The Aeneid*, 6.851–3, Translated by Sue Gilmore

Although the quotation above appears in Latin and English, its source, *The Aeneid*, combines a Greek story from Homer with settings in Southwest Asia, North Africa, Sicily, and, finally, the Italian Peninsula. This epic by the Roman poet Virgil thus brings together in one work many of the cultural combinations presented in the previous chapter. Additionally, the epic accurately forecasts the cultural, political, and military legacies of the Roman Empire, continuities still apparent in much of the world. *The Aeneid* displays for the reader Virgil's ideal of leadership, an ideal he was anxious to pass on to his patron, Augustus Caesar. Virgil's lessons might have helped the Roman Empire survive had it been followed by *all* the Roman emperors.

Rome as a Monarchy (c. 753–509 B.C.E.)

Like the earlier Greek civilization, Roman civilization developed on a giant peninsula. But while geography hindered Greek unity, it did not prevent Italian unity. For example, the *Apennine Mountains*, which run the length of that peninsula, are less rugged than the mountains of Greece. The Apennines did not prevent trade or travel in ancient times.

Etruscans and Latins The city of Rome owes much of its early history to the combining of three groups, often warring but sometimes collaborating: *Etruscans*, *Latins*, and Greeks. The Etruscans were settled in the northern Italian Peninsula when Rome was yet a village on seven hills. They later mingled with the less advanced Latins of central Italy. They gained an alphabet from the Greek colonists of southern Italy, with whom they traded.

As shown by the remarkable tombs still existing in Italy, Etruscan skills included building with stone. The Etruscans mined iron, copper, and tin and made metal weapons and tools. Similarly, Etruscans were probably responsible for the roads and temples of this early Roman period, as well as for military tactics displayed in battles.

Political Traditions According to tradition or myth, the village on seven hills that would become *Rome* was always welcoming to outcasts and outsiders, and it grew accordingly. Tradition also suggests that local tribes agreed to have a rotating kingship, which began with Romulus (the supposed son of the war god Mars). According to legend, Romulus killed his twin brother Remus after an argument about where to locate the new city, and gave his name to the city in 753 B.C.E.

More certain than these stories are the accomplishments of the early Romans. They drained swamps, which gave them a large amount of fertile land, significantly more than the Greek city-states had. They found nearby sources of drinking water and metal ores. The site that became Rome, 15 miles up the *Tiber River* from the *Tyrrhenian Sea*, was good for trade and yet far enough from the ocean to be easily defended against sea-borne attackers. It would soon become the central point for interaction with other settlements in Italy.

Comparing Early Forms of Government				
Civilization	Form of Government	Leading Individual or Body	Characteristics	Relationship Between Government and Religion
Egypt: Middle Kingdom	Dynasty, highly centralized	Pharaoh	Hierarchy of appointed officials under the pharaoh	Pharaoh was seen as both a ruler and a god
Greece: Athens City-State	Direct democracy, highly decentralized	• The Assembly (all citizens) • Council of 500 (chosen by lottery) • Courts (magistrates chosen by lottery)	Males over 18 were considered citizens, and they could participate in government	Religion was separate from government but influential
China: Han Dynasty	Dynasty, centralized	Emperor with advice from officials	Officials chosen by Emperor based on skill and knowledge following Confucian ideas	Religion was mostly separate from functions of government
Rome: Republic	Republic, centralized	Emperor and Senate	Citizens elect senators	Religion was separate from government but influential

From Monarchy to Republic

Government in Rome evolved as a practical response to both improvements and domestic pressure for protection. By the early 500s, when Tarquinius Superbus (Tarquin the Proud), ruled the city, he was a tyrant. He was also the final monarch of early Rome. Opposition to his rule arose among the *patricians*, or wealthy landowners. In 509 B.C.E., they overthrew him. But instead of creating another monarchy, they established a government of elected officials—a *republic*. It was a representative government, not a direct democracy like Athens had for a while. At first, only the wealthiest and the most prestigious Roman citizens were represented in the *Senate*. Holding tenure for life, senators increased in number to about 300 during the fourth century B.C.E.

Plebeians and Magistrates Most Romans were *plebeians*—small farmers, tradespeople, craftsworkers, and common soldiers. Gradually, they began to call for political reforms so they could have a say in government. In 287 B.C.E., they won the right to be full citizens. They got their own assemblies—the Assembly of Tribes and the Assembly of Centuries—where plebeians could pass laws and select *magistrates,* officials who carried out the day-to-day operations of government. The Senate and the assemblies also acted as courts, deciding disputes between people and trying accused lawbreakers.

Tribunes Additionally, new officials called *tribunes* were elected to represent the plebeians. They could exercise veto power in the Senate, although the ever-practical senatorial politicians often included these representatives of the "plebs" in their leadership circles in order to keep favor. These patron-client relationships became an important part of political as well as social life. A senator used his lower-class clients to bolster his prestige, to serve as "extras" who would cheer him through the streets or mourn at family funerals and greet arriving banquet guests. In return for these duties, the clients were granted a measure of protection and, sometimes, rations of bread and wine.

Consuls The most important magistrates were two *consuls.* They were elected by Roman citizens to preside over the government and to serve as commanders of armies in military campaigns. One consul could block the acts of the other by saying *"veto,"* which is Latin for "I forbid it." This is one of the earliest examples of *checks and balances*—a way of dividing power to keep any part of government from becoming excessively powerful. (To read about how checks and balances are used in the government of the United States, see a government textbook.)

Rule of Law Inequities in the unwritten system of laws brought about unrest and strikes from the plebeians and their leadership. One government response was to display the *Laws of the Twelve Tables* publicly (c. 450 B.C.E.). Putting written laws in the full view of the public provided a check on the injustices of the judiciary system, an important concept built into numerous later constitutions. The Laws of the Twelve Tables dealt with almost every aspect of life—including business transactions, property boundaries and penalties for crimes. More laws and political institutions evolved as the need for them arose. (Test Prep: Create a table comparing the Laws of the Twelve Tables with the Code of Hammurabi. See page 21.)

Rule of law created a career path for lawyers. Rich and powerful senators and merchants brought legal cases, often against corrupt officials. One of the greatest members of the legal profession was *Cicero*, trained in writing and oratory by Greek teachers as well as Roman ones. His elegant writing is still studied today for its clarity, preciseness, and persuasiveness. The existence of courts, references to legal terms, and entire orations given in the course of lawsuits testify to the significance of the rule of law in the Republic.

Roman Expansion

After overthrowing its own king, Rome encouraged central Italy's other city-states to revolt against the Etruscans. After the city-states were free of Etruscan rule, the Romans conquered them. By 275 B.C.E., Rome controlled the entire Italian Peninsula.

Adept leaders and smoothly organized armies became the Roman trademark. Equally helpful in running the large area they had conquered was the extension of privileges to the conquered peoples. Citizenship was often the reward for supplying troops and tribute to Rome. Later, small Italian cities demanded the privilege of providing soldiers and money so their residents could become Roman citizens.

Greece and Gaul As Rome extended its power into southern Italy, it developed conflicts with Greeks over control of Greek colonies. In 275 B.C.E., the Romans defeated a Greek army that had invaded Italy to protect the Greek colonies there. Then, in a series of four wars between 215 and 148 B.C.E., Rome defeated Macedonia, in northern Greece. The Romans went on to take control of what remained of the empire created by Alexander the Great. In addition, the Romans moved north and west to conquer parts of Gaul, a territory that is part of what is now France.

Carthage and Beyond One of Rome's largest conflicts was with *Carthage*, a city-state across the Mediterranean on the north coast of Africa. Carthage had once belonged to the Phoenician Empire but had since created its own empire by conquering parts of Spain. Rome and Carthage both wanted to control the Mediterranean trade. They fought a series of three wars between 264 and 146 B.C.E., the *Punic Wars*. When the Romans finally captured Carthage in 146 B.C.E., they destroyed the city, enslaved its population, and, according to legend, salted the land to make it infertile, thereby condemning Carthage to poverty for years to come. Today, ending a war with the complete destruction of an enemy is known as a *Carthaginian peace*.

The victory over Carthage gave Rome control of a large empire, including North Africa, Spain, and Sicily. The Romans later rebuilt Carthage and maintained a colony there. It became the empire's fourth-largest city. Roman armies also conquered swaths of modern Syria, Egypt, Britain, and Germany by the middle of the first century C.E.

However, conquest was not permanent. For example, centuries later, in 439 C.E., the nomadic *Vandals*—who had invaded North Africa from Spain—took Carthage, and in 455 they conquered Rome itself.

Soldiers All citizens between ages 17 and 46 who owned land were required to serve in the Roman *legions*. These large armies were needed to fight wars and to guard the expanding empire. Most soldiers were poor farmers. When they entered the army, many sold their small farms to wealthy patricians. The patricians combined their purchases to create huge estates, known as *latifundia*. While some soldiers settled elsewhere in the empire once their services were complete, many others came to Rome. Around the time of Julius Caesar, Rome's population was probably more than one million people and growing.

Roman Society

Patricians and plebeians were influential in Roman society. Less powerful were two other groups: slaves and women.

Slaves Most slaves were foreigners captured during Rome's wars. They were brought to Italy to work in homes and on the large farms of wealthy Romans. The latifundia of the patricians required an ever-increasing number of slaves. Except in poor families, raising and educating Roman children was carried out by slaves, often Greek ones. Among wealthy Romans, some slaves even ran the households.

With conquests increasing, the number of captives available for slavery grew. Conditions of slavery became harsher, especially after the *Spartacus Rebellion* in 73 B.C.E. when a slave named Spartacus led one of the largest slave revolts in history. Roman soldiers killed thousands of rebels before the revolt was crushed, and another 6,000 slaves were captured and executed by crucifixion.

The existence of so many slaves slowed down growth and innovation in the Roman economy. Slave labor was so cheap that landowners had little incentive to develop new technology.

Decline of Small Landholders The low cost of slave labor was one of two factors that caused a decline in the number of small landowners. Independent farmers and tenants could not compete successfully against production by slaves. In addition, the years many small farmers spent in the military cost many of them their land. As time passed, large estates absorbed more and more of the holdings that had previously been farmed by the small landowners.

Women In early Roman society, women faced many forms of discrimination. Only men could be citizens. Women could not vote. In married couples, men owned all the family property and headed the households. However, young women of high social position usually received some level of education. Further, women could inherit property and other forms of wealth from their fathers, which gave them influence with their husbands. (Test Prep: Write a paragraph comparing the role of women in Roman society with the role of women in classical India. See page 95.)

Civil Wars

Strong Roman military leaders completed numerous conquests in the last two centuries B.C.E. Each leader raised armies through promises of land; these promises lead to the existence of personal armies more loyal to individual leaders than to Rome. For example, *Gaius Marius, Lucius Pompey Magnus*, and *Julius Caesar* were all popular and successful generals whose troops were devoted to them. In the following generation, the same would be true for *Marc Antony* and *Octavian* (later known as *Augustus*). Clashes between vying groups of Romans thus became civil wars in which generals opposed one another for leadership of the state.

The conflict between generals for power in Rome reached a decisive point in the first century B.C.E. One general, Marius, was a "new man" not born to the senatorial class. He was elected six times to the consulship. The other consul, Sulla, came from a more patrician family. Sulla was successful over Marius during their lifetime. However, Marius' nephew Julius Caesar would prevail and drive Sulla from the city. Caesar was a *popularis*, an aristocrat whose strength was based on his support from the common people of Rome, such as the plebeians, rather than just other elites. His armies had finally become too powerful for the representative government of the Republic to prevail.

End of the Republic Julius Caesar, after vanquishing his major foe, Pompey, and becoming sole consul, became dictator for life in 46 B.C.E. He accomplished major reforms such as revising the calendar, increasing the size of the Senate, extending citizenship, and granting land to some poor veterans. Caesar also added conquests for Rome as far away as the German forests and Egypt. However, frightened by his power and influence, a group of conspirators attacked and killed him on the famous "Ides of March" (March 15, 44 B.C.E.). Competition between the two remaining generals—Octavian and Marc Antony—led to the downfall of the Republic and the establishment of the Roman Empire.

Having defeated conspirators at Philippi (in Macedonia), Antony and Octavian turned on each other, first temporarily dividing the Roman lands between them, east and west. However, at the *Battle of Actium* on the Ionian Sea in 31 B.C.E., Octavian defeated Antony and proclaimed himself sole ruler of Rome.

The Roman Empire (27 B.C.E.–476 C.E.)

With the help of a Senate grateful for an end to the civil war, Octavian began to mold Rome into the image he wanted. His goals were to strengthen family values, keep the peace, and promote prosperity. The result was a hugely successful, well-governed empire that extended throughout the Mediterranean. One Roman historian quoted Octavian as saying, "I found Rome a city of bricks and left it a city of marble." Octavian was proclaimed "Augustus Caesar," and the next 200 years became known as *Pax Romana,* or Roman peacetime. (Test Prep: List the similarities and differences between the Pax Romana with the Pax Mongolica (Mongolian peace). See page 243.)

Roads and Defenses Rome built a network of roads that made movement of trade goods, written orders, and soldiers and their provisions easier. In addition, Rome built fortresses and walls to protect strategic cities and transportation points.

Social Classes The social and political hierarchy established in the days of the Republic continued into the Empire Period. Some upward mobility was possible: a new *equestrian class* was available to male Roman citizens whose property was valued at 400,000 sesterces (at a time when Roman legionaries were making about 900 sesterces per year). Equestrians could hold positions of authority in government but not ones as influential as those occupied by senators and their families.

The senatorial class became the instrument of Augustus and later rulers by which they directed the affairs of the empire. However, Augustus and his successors made clear that their will was absolute. Augustus offered a tax bonus to members of this class who had more than two children because he wished to see the numbers of the aristocracy increase.

THE ROMAN EMPIRE

Lower classes, no longer as ably represented in their popular assemblies, were nevertheless pacified by free games and grain and the possibility, however unlikely, of advancing in the social order. Slavery continued to increase as both businesses and large estates increased. Greek slaves were in high demand as physicians and teachers, maintaining the continuity of Greek culture. Slaves could sometimes buy their freedom, becoming newly rich "freedmen," but slaves who ran away and were caught received the brand "F" for *fugitivus* on their foreheads.

Women During the Empire Period, the rights of women expanded over what existed in early centuries. For example, women could divorce—many upper class women did so in the tumultuous times preceding the takeover by Augustus. They also began to exercise more property rights as new inheritance laws allowed them to gain and keep control of property. Typical of their increasing influence was their presence as near-equals in social events, something made clear by the art and literature of the period. Even without political rights, the economic worth of women who ran businesses gave them some political influence.

Roman histories and literature abound with frequent references to strong, educated women. This shows that Roman women had more influence than their counterparts to the east in the Hellenistic world, in India, or in China. One avenue to independence opened for widows whose husbands and fathers had both died, leaving the women to start handling their own affairs.

Law Not least of the accomplishments of the Augustan era were those in law. Although Cicero had been killed in the purges undertaken by Antony, Roman law continued to spread to all parts of the empire. For example, it was Roman law that allowed the Christian apostle Paul to insist on being taken to Rome for trial as a citizen—a journey that would aid in the establishment of the early Christian Church in Rome.

Literature and Philosophy As well as operating under the rule of law, Augustus saw himself also as a patron of literature. Famous writers such as *Virgil* and Horace were recipients of his generosity, as was *Ovid* until Augustus banished him to the far edge of the Black Sea (perhaps because Ovid wrote love poetry). Historians such as Livy and Tacitus carried on the tradition of Roman literature in the first century C.E. Philosophers such as Seneca did as well. Seneca would become the tutor of the infamous Nero, an emperor symbolic of decadent rulers during the long and gradual decline of the Roman Empire.

Roman writers were heavily influenced by Greek traditions. For example, writers of the early Empire continued to use Greek forms for poetry. Further, Greek ideas lay behind such Roman philosophies as *Epicureanism,* which promoted living simply, enjoying the pleasures of life, and not focusing on appealing to the gods. Another Roman philosophy based on Greek ideas was *Stoicism,* which emphasized that people should learn to accept the will of the gods and remained detached from pleasure and pain. Romans attempted to find the answers to questions about all aspects of life—from the existence of gods to the meaning of life to how to live ethically.

Roman Religion

Syncretism played a key part in many aspects of Roman culture, including religion. For example, they frequently fused local Latin deities with the Greek pantheon of gods. Roman homes had an altar for the local divinities, but the family also went to temples and state celebrations carried out under the auspices of the chief priest, or *pontifex maximus*. Romans required everyone to practice the state religion. However, like the Persians, they tolerated the practice of additional religions as well. Unlike the Persians, many of whom were monotheistic Zoroastrians, the Romans were polytheistic.

State Religion Polytheistic and tolerant, Roman leaders praised their state gods such as Jupiter and Minerva for showing favor as they built their empire. The temple to Vesta, for example, had a group of priestesses who guarded the sacred flame of Rome. Such priestesses grew wealthy and influential in the city. An additional aspect of state religion that would grow more apparent after the death of Augustus was worship of the emperor.

Personal Religion Lares and Penates, old gods believed to protect the household, were still worshipped in the years of the Roman Empire. These gods were the objects of various household rituals. But Romans who yearned for more spiritual beliefs also joined *mystery cults*, religious groups whose followers were promised an afterlife if they underwent secret rituals and purification rites. Some Romans joined in the rites called Eleusinian mysteries (originating in Greece) and the cult of Isis (from Egypt).

Jews Under Roman Rule The Jewish religion consolidated in Jerusalem in what is known as the Second Temple period (530 B.C.E. to 79 C.E.). Jewish scholars codified the Hebrew scriptures, which included Mesopotamian cultural and legal influences brought back to Jerusalem from the Babylonian exile.

The Romans captured Jerusalem in 37 B.C.E. Cicero and other Roman writers of the late Republic and early empire were interested in the religion of the Jews. While Romans might have added the Jewish deity to their pantheon, they were not willing to give any deity exclusive worship. Conflicts between Jews and Romans resulted in three Jewish rebellions in the first two centuries C.E. Roman victories, and resulting persecution of the Jews, caused many Jews to flee their homes in the region around Jerusalem, continuing the diaspora begun in earlier centuries.

The situation of Jewish citizens was complicated by the Roman tendency to treat educated Jews with more deference than other "barbarian" groups in the empire. These circumstances positioned Jews to become scapegoats and objects of prejudice, a situation that would be repeated centuries later in history.

Christianity

Into this Jewish community emerged the figure of *Jesus*, who challenged traditional religious leaders and was regarded as a troublemaker by Roman officials. Followers of Jesus spread his teachings throughout the Roman world. By the end of the first century C.E., *Christianity* was emerging as a distinct form of Judaism and was on its way to becoming a separate religion altogether. Christianity was most popular among the urban poor, slaves, and women throughout the empire. Like the mystery cults and the philosophies of Epicureanism and Stoicism, Christianity appealed to people hungry for answers about the harshness of life and hopeful of an afterlife. The intellectual, political, and religious ferment of the first century C.E. was fertile ground for Christian teachings.

Source: Thinkstock

Source: Thinkstock

While Christianity emphasized worship of God and Buddhism focused more inwardly, people in both traditions constructed large, solid-looking buildings that reflected the strength of their members' commitment to their beliefs.

Peter and Paul One of the people particularly important in spreading the ideas of Jesus and shaping Christianity was *Peter* (died in 64 C.E.) He knew Jesus and was one of his first followers. Peter eventually came to Rome and is today regarded by the Roman Catholic Church as the first pope.

According to the Bible, *Paul* was a Jew who had a sudden, dramatic conversion to Christianity while traveling on a road leading into Damascus.

Though born during the lifetime of Jesus, Paul probably never met him. Paul spread the gospel according to Jesus around the Mediterranean by preaching at many of the great Hellenistic cities such as Ephesus and Corinth. Educated in the Hellenistic tradition of argument and teaching, Paul inspired other preachers as well before he died around 65 C.E.

Features of Emergent Christianity One trait of early Christianity was a focus on living simple lives isolated from society. This allowed members to concentrate on worship and reflection. Over time, some of these people joined together to form *monasteries*, buildings or collections of buildings where people devote their lives to the practice of a religion.

A second trait was *martyrdom*, a willingness to die rather than give up one's beliefs. Romans allowed people to worship their own gods, but they required people to respect the deities of the official state religion. Christians refused to do this, and thousands were imprisoned, tortured, and killed. Despite persecution, Christianity grew stronger. In 313 C.E., the Roman Emperor *Constantine* declared the religion to be legal in the *Edict of Milan*. Constantine became the first Christian emperor. In 330 C.E., he moved the seat of government to Constantinople. Under subsequent Roman emperors, the Christian religion became the official religion of the empire. (Test Prep: Outline the developments of Christianity up to the Byzantine Empire. See pages 131–134.)

A third trait of early Christianity was the appearance of written accounts about the development of the religion. These included four documents describing the life of Jesus, now known as the Gospels according to Matthew, Mark, Luke, and John. They also included several letters written mostly by Paul to early fellowships, advising the members and commenting on the teachings of Jesus. Together, the Gospels and the letters form the core of what is now called the New Testament, a significant part of the Christian Bible.

St. Augustine As Rome entered its darker days, corruption, poor leadership, and encroaching barbarian hordes were common themes. In the fifth century C.E., a monk in Roman North Africa who would come to be known as *St. Augustine of Hippo* (354–430 C.E.) began to write the book *City of God*. Although many written works of St. Augustine survive, this one is particularly important because it points out the existence of a duality: even though the city of God on earth (Rome) might fall to "the barbarians," the city of God in heaven would remain. Tensions that would later culminate in the *separation of church and state* are also present in this work.

Transregional Trade Networks

St. Augustine's work in Roman North Africa illustrates the spread of Christianity to all parts of the Roman Empire and beyond. Christians also brought their religion to Mesopotamia, Persia, and India and even into Central Asia by way of the trade route connecting communities in Europe and Asia called the *Silk Roads*. The overland roads were *transregional* in that they connected regions of various civilizations over long distances. They took several different routes, depending upon the climate, the friendliness of the territories being crossed, and the number of bandit attacks in a given period. Most of the traders took routes through Central Asian cities such as Samarkand and Tashkent. Some went through Indian cities such as Pataliputra and into the city of Kathmandu in Nepal. Traders often paid a portion of the goods as tribute to local lords to allow safe passage through their territories. Overland routes from China separated at the desert town of Dunhuang, one going north, one straight west, and one to the south. The routes overland generally converged at Constantinople, and from there goods went to Rome either overland or by sea. (Test Prep: Create a chart comparing the spread of Christianity with the spread of Zoroastrianism and the spread of Buddhism. See pages 60 and 99.)

Sea Routes Rome also conducted extensive trade to the east across water. Maritime commerce continued across the Indian Ocean as monsoons permitted. Up the Red Sea, after touching at Africa, goods at last reached the port of Rome at Ostia.

Although pirates were a constant problem, the waters of the Mediterranean were more easily navigated than those of an ocean because of smaller distances and numerous island stopping places. The Romans lacked sophisticated navigational equipment, but they still made truly amazing trips as far north as the Scylly Islands (the British islands most southerly from the coast of Wales), from which Roman ships brought back tin.

New Technology and New Goods A major advancement that made its way westward from Central Asia was the *stirrup* for mounted warriors. Stirrups provided greater stability for riders, which made horses easier to ride and control and, hence, more useful. Other goods—silks and spices and especially gold—were much prized by the upper classes of the Roman Empire. Not only did China grow wealthy from trade with Rome, but other cities along the Silk Roads (and increasingly on the trans-Saharan routes across northern Africa) also benefited from that trade. The markets of Samarkand, for example, introduced new fruits and vegetables, as well as rice and citrus products from Southwest Asia, to Europe. In East Africa, a large variety of imports and exports overlapped, suggesting a healthy trading economy. (Test Prep: Write a paragraph comparing the effects on trade of the stirrup and the camel saddle. See pages 165–166.)

Decline of the Empire

From its peak in size and strength, Rome began a slow, uneven decline that began after the third century C.E. For example, the population of Rome declined from over one million to under 100,000.

Population Decline One cause of the waning population was directly related to the empire's expansion. The Silk Road brought trade and wealth, but it also introduced devastating epidemics. In the second century C.E., Rome experienced a marked decline in population caused by plagues of smallpox, and measles. Epidemics killed as many as one-quarter of the population in some cities. Diseases spread again in the third and fourth centuries, and yet again in the sixth century. With the decline in population came a decline in trade, which led to slower economic activity and fewer taxes for the Roman state. As tax revenues dipped, Roman roads and aqueducts were not repaired as often and armies were not paid as regularly. Armies mutinied and trading became less safe, which continued the downward spiral of the empire's wealth and power.

Environmental Problems The success of Roman culture led to population growth around the Mediterranean region. Increasing demand for lumber, for buildings, and for fuel led to deforestation. Increasing demand for food led to overgrazing and farming marginal lands, resulting in soil erosion.

Challenges from Non-Romans The growth of the empire resulted in a larger area to defend. The empire had traditionally been able to absorb non-Romans, such as the Germanic Visigoths who settled in the empire and adopted an agricultural lifestyle in the second century. However, in the fifth century, the Huns led by Attila moved into Gaul from farther east. Their westward progression forced other peoples—the Visigoths, Ostrogoths, Vandals, and Franks—ahead of them into the empire. These additional groups settled around Western Europe and North Africa.

The turmoil from so much movement proved too widespread for Roman soldiers to handle. The Visigoths even sacked Rome in 410 C.E. The last Roman emperor was replaced by a Germanic ruler—Odovacer— in 476. From that period on, the remains of the empire were governed from Constantinople. (Test Prep: Write a paragraph comparing the breakup of the Roman Empire with the breakup of the Han Empire. See page 105.)

Legacies of the Romans

The decline of the Roman Empire did not mean the end of their influence. The empire divided into two parts under *Diocletian* (ruled 284–305), with Rome remaining the capital of the western portion and Byzantium remaining the capital of the east. The eastern portion flourished for many more centuries. Only the western portion continued to decline. However, Roman influence can be seen throughout the world today but most strongly in Europe, Southwest Asia, and the United States.

Law and Government One clear inheritance from the Romans in the United States is the system of representative government with a Senate and House of Representatives as provided for by the U.S. Constitution. The writers of that document, such as James Madison, were students of Roman history, and they consciously adopted Rome as a model. Other institutions, such as checks on the legislators provided by the judiciary and independent courts abiding by the rule of law, can also be traced to the Romans.

Architecture The architectural feature known as the dome and paved roads are contributions of the Romans. Roman columns, temples, and amphitheaters can still be seen today throughout the world. Magnificent examples of aqueducts are scattered throughout Southern Europe and the Mediterranean area. Other practical innovations include large urban sewers as well as under-floor heating in urban homes. Excavations at two Roman cities, Pompeii and Herculaneum, attest to Roman building skills. The Romans put their considerable expertise in engineering to work in both public and private buildings. What remains of Roman structures reflects a solid style obviously built for permanence.

Military When Caesar declared to the Roman Senate in his report on the success of war in Asia Minor, "*Veni, vidi, vici*" ("I came, I saw, I conquered"), it was both a statement of fact and an apt description of his military tactics. Roman armies were efficient and organized, and they have served as models for militaries all the way to modern times. Legionnaires were disciplined to fight in small, flexible units as well as large troops of armored infantry. Army engineers developed extensive *catapults,* devices used to hurl stones a great distance, and *siege devices* such as battering rams, along with bridges and military camps that were laid out efficiently and established with great speed.

Literature Poets, playwrights, historians, and philosophers from classical Rome are still read today. The epic of Virgil, the comedies of Plautus (such as *Miles Gloriosus*, on which the modern comedy *A Funny Thing Happened on the Way to the Forum* is based), and the historical works of Seneca are but a few examples. Roman mythology can be seen in literature, movies, and advertising.

Language Last, and maybe most importantly, the Latin language provided the basis for the family of the European languages called the Romance languages, which include Italian, Romanian, Spanish, Portuguese, and French. English, though not a Romance language, traces over half of its words to Latin or one of the Romance languages.

Rome's influence remains strongly evident today. Similarly, the legacies of two other classical empires in Asia have left powerful legacies: Han China and the Gupta Empire.

HISTORICAL PERSPECTIVES: WHY DID ROME COLLAPSE?

Historians have come up with many explanations for Rome's decline. Why did a region of prosperity and innovation become one in which people had less wealth and less ability to overcome new problems? One Internet site listed 210 reasons. Some historians argue that the empire grew too large to be governed with the technology of the time. Others argue that the empire's wealth was wasted by too many wars of conquest. Or that too many leaders became too corrupt. Or that too many common citizens became too lazy.

One of the most provocative theories comes from the eighteenth-century English historian Edward Gibbon. He partially blames Christianity, with its emphasis on peace, forgiveness, and devotion to God, for undermining the Roman values that built the empire: military conquest, ruthless destruction of opponents, and intense loyalty to the Roman leaders.

Canadian historian Arthur Boak, in his 1921 book *A History of Rome to 565 A.D.,* saw a wide-ranging "transformation in society." "Private industry languished, commerce declined, the fields lay untilled; a general feeling of hopelessness paralyzed all initiative." To Boak, the main culprit in the decline of Rome was the "change from a regime which encouraged individual initiative to a regime of status." In other words, people became less honored for what they actually did, such as running a farm or a business successfully, and more impressed by the wealth or titles their ancestors had accumulated.

One of the more innovative theories in recent years is that Rome collapsed because of health problems caused by the heavy use of lead in aqueducts and dishes. This is an example of historical interpretation that has been made possible by new techniques for gathering information from artifacts.

KEY TERMS BY THEME

STATE-BUILDING		SOCIAL STRUCTURE
republic	Octavian	patricians
Senate	Battle of Actium	plebeians
magistrates	*Pax Romana*	equestrian class
tribunes	Constantine	
consuls	*Edict of Milan*	**CULTURE**
checks and balances	St. Augustine	Virgil
Laws of the Twelve	separation of church	*The Aeneid*
Tables	and state	Ovid
Cicero		Epicureanism
Carthage	**ENVIRONMENT**	Stoicism
Punic Wars	Apennine Mountains	Syncretism
Vandals	Etruscans	*pontifex maximus*
legions	Latins	mystery cults
latifundia	Rome	Jesus
Spartacus Rebellion	Tiber River	Peter
Marius	Tyrrhenian Sea	Paul
Sulla	catapults	Christianity
Pompey Magnus	siege devices	martyrdom
Julius Caesar	stirrup	
Marc Antony		

1. In what way were the Minoan and Etruscan civilizations most similar?
    (A) Neither left many written sources so historians have been forced to rely heavily upon archaeology to study the civilizations.
    (B) Both depended upon large navies to transport goods to Greek colonists located around the Mediterranean.
    (C) Both joined with nearby tribes to establish monarchies which persisted into modern times.
    (D) Both shared a similar religion, as shown in their art and literature.

2. The Roman Republic featured which of the following?
    (A) Senate, representative government, rule of law
    (B) Mandate of Heaven and civil service exams
    (C) Rule by two tyrants and an oligarchy
    (D) Separation of religious functions from those of the state

3. Which statement best summarizes how Romans viewed Greece?
    (A) Romans rejected Greek religion.
    (B) Romans considered Greeks fit only for slavery.
    (C) Romans saw themselves as part of Greek culture.
    (D) Romans prized Greek art and hired Greek tutors.

4. Which most influenced trade in Afro-Eurasia during the first several centuries C.E.?
    (A) The existence of large, stable empires
    (B) The appearance of sophisticated navigational equipment
    (C) The introduction of the stirrup for mounted warriors
    (D) The establishment of the papacy in Rome

5. Which statement probably provides the strongest evidence of the increasing influence of women in the public sphere of imperial Rome?
    (A) Women could not vote nor hold office although they ran households.
    (B) Women could inherit property from their fathers, giving them economic influence and some ability to influence politics.
    (C) Roman literature has references to strong, educated women while Roman art shows them participating in social occasions.
    (D) Women were allowed to divorce by the reign of Augustus.

6. The two documents *Edict of Milan* and the *City of God* are significant because they provide the foundations for
   - (A) epicureanism and Judaism becoming increasingly accepted philosophies
   - (B) the success of empire as a form of government as the Senate increased its power
   - (C) the desirability of making all males citizens of the empire when they fought in the Roman army
   - (D) the legal foundations for Christianity and the dual existence of church and state in Rome

7. Which factor best explains why estates belonging to Roman patricians became very large?
   - (A) Veterans preferred living in cities to living in rural areas.
   - (B) Small landowners sold their lands to patricians when they entered the army.
   - (C) Imports began to exceed exports, particularly of grain.
   - (D) Peacetime allowed for lower taxes so patricians could afford more land.

8. Which statement about the decline of Rome is most plausible?
   - (A) Like Egypt, economic differences among social classes became so small that people lost incentive to work hard.
   - (B) Like Persia, the empire became so large that protecting trade routes became difficult and expensive.
   - (C) Like Greece, Rome began to weaken when new religious beliefs began to challenge traditional ones.
   - (D) Like Sumeria, the Romans failed to develop solid institutions and innovations that would be stable and lasting.

9. Which of the following statements about slaves in the Roman Empire is most accurate?
   - (A) Most slaves came from northern and central Africa and were racially homogeneous.
   - (B) Many slaves rejected Christianity because it emphasized humility.
   - (C) Conditions for slaves improved after a large rebellion led by Spartacus.
   - (D) Slaves carried out the raising and educating of children in wealthy families.

Question 10 refers to the following map.

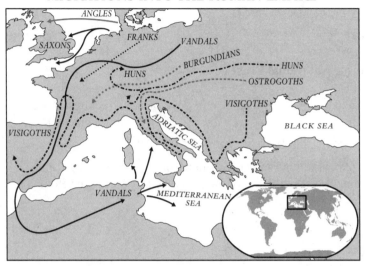

MIGRATIONS INTO THE ROMAN EMPIRE

10. What conclusion can be made about the decline of the Roman Empire based on the map above?

   (A) Rome's ability to resist invaders was reduced by the nonviolent messages of Christianity.

   (B) Invaders into the Roman Empire came primarily from north and west Africa.

   (C) A unified force of "barbarians" attacked Rome from the north.

   (D) Attacks from multiple directions overwhelmed Roman soldiers.

CONTINUITY AND CHANGE-OVER-TIME ESSAY QUESTIONS

Directions: You are to answer the following question. You should spend 5 minutes organizing or outlining your essay. Write an essay that:

- Has a relevant thesis and supports that thesis with appropriate historical evidence.

- Addresses all parts of the question.

- Uses world historical context to show continuities and changes over time.

- Analyzes the process of continuity and change over time.

1. Analyze continuities and change between Greece and Rome between 500 B.C.E. and 500 C.E. in TWO of the following areas:
   - religion
   - gender roles
   - military conquest

Questions for Additional Practice

2. Analyze continuities and change in government structures in the Mediterranean world between the rise of city-states in ancient Mesopotamia and in the later city-states of Greece.

3. Analyze continuities and change in problems faced by the Roman government before the fall of the Republic and during the Roman Empire.

COMPARATIVE ESSAY QUESTIONS

Directions: You are to answer the following question. You should spend 5 minutes organizing or outlining your essay. Write an essay that:
   - Has a relevant thesis and supports that thesis with appropriate historical evidence.
   - Addresses all parts of the question.
   - Makes direct, relevant comparisons.
   - Analyzes relevant reasons for similarities and differences.

1. Analyze similarities and differences in the role of women in the Roman Republic and in ONE of the following civilizations:
   - Han China
   - Mauryan and Gupta India

Questions for Additional Practice

2. Analyze similarities and differences between slavery in Rome (both the Roman Republic and the Roman Empire) and slavery in ONE of the following cultures:
   - Egypt under the pharaohs
   - Greece in the age of Pericles

3. Analyze similarities and differences in the importance of transregional trade in the Roman Republic and in the Persian Empire under Darius.

THINK AS A HISTORIAN: USE TOPIC-BY-TOPIC COMPARISON

Topic-by-topic comparison shows the differences and/or similarities between two topics, whether you are comparing Christopher Columbus to contemporary explorers with their sights set on Mars or Alexander the Great to Napoleon Bonaparte. *Which TWO of the thesis statements below exemplify topic-by-topic comparison?*

1. Social class was paramount in the Roman Empire. The lower class had meagre opportunity to advance; the equestrian class held some positions of authority; the senatorial class wielded the most power.

2. Two "isms" focused on contrasting visions of life. Epicurianism promoted enjoying earthly pleasures. In contrast, stoicism emphasized that people should submit to the will of the gods.

3. Cultism was common in the Roman Empire with members of some cults promised an afterlife if they underwent secret rituals and purifications.

WRITE AS A HISTORIAN: RECOGNIZE APPROPRIATE COMPARISONS

Historians often compare events or individuals in order to highlight trends or distinctive traits. Comparisons work best when the two developments are in the same category—two empires that declined—rather than two completely dissimilar topics—Julius Caesar and Egyptian pyramids. *Which THREE of the questions or statements below are most appropriately answered by a comparison essay?*

1. Why did both the early Roman and Greek civilizations develop on peninsulas?

2. What do the stone tombs built by Etruscan masons indicate about their society?

3. Describe the similarities between a monarchy and a republic.

4. Identify three ways that discrimination in Rome against slaves and against women differed.

5. Why do historians consider paved roads a great achievement by the Romans?

5

Classical Civilizations in India and China

Your business is with action alone, not by any means with the fruit of the action. . . . Having recourse to devotion, perform actions, casting off all attachment, and being equable in success or ill success.

—*The Bhagavad Gita*, c. 400 C.E

The *Bhagavad Gita* is part of one of the most important writings in the Hindu tradition, *The Mahabharata*. It emphasizes carrying out one's duty as determined by one's birth and on separating oneself from any "attachment" to the effects of one's actions or any other worldly concerns. These emphases became vital themes not only in Hinduism but also in Buddhism, one of several new religions to emerge in India and China between 600 B.C.E. and 600 C.E. In addition to these new religions, new social and governmental structures, such as India's caste system and China's civil service system, emerged that still influence life in those countries today.

Social Organization: The Caste System

The Aryan people who began to settle throughout the Indian subcontinent around 1500 B.C.E. developed a very well-defined social hierarchy that is now known as the *caste system*. Westerners typically use the word "caste" to describe India's social order because the Portuguese used the word *casta* (class) when they first noticed a distinct social hierarchy during their sixteenth-century travels to India. Aryans originally used the word *varna*, meaning "color," to distinguish between themselves (who had "wheat-colored complexions") and the darker-skinned Dravidians. Intermarriage between the two groups occurred often enough that now most physical distinctions are undetectable.

The Caste System in India		
Caste Name	**Function**	**Occupations**
Brahmins	The priestly and learned class	Spiritual leaders, teachers
Kshatriyas	The warrior and ruling class	Rulers, military elite, nobility, property owners
Vaishyas	The merchant and artisan class	Traders, agriculturalists, money-lenders, smiths
Shudras	The peasant and serf class	Unskilled servants for upper three classes, serfs

The Four Castes Caste identities formed around the kinds of occupations and social roles people held in ancient India. A distinct social hierarchy developed, leading to four basic castes: *brahmins*, or people of the priestly class; *kshatriyas*, or the warrior class; *vaishyas*, or merchants and artisans; and *shudras*, or peasants and serfs.

Dalits The lowest rung in the hierarchy consisted of people outside of all the varnas. People once called *untouchables*, now known as *dalits*, performed the most unpleasant work in society, such as disposing of dead bodies and cleaning sewer systems. Their work was so dirty that touching them would supposedly pollute members of the castes.

Evolution of the Caste System Over hundreds of years, the caste system expanded to include the groups that formed around new occupations and groups of people that migrated into the subcontinent. Hundreds of *jatis*, or subcasts, developed within each original caste to accommodate a more complex society.

India long ago outlawed discrimination against dalits, or any caste. However, signs of the caste system are still present. For instance, a last name can reveal a person's social position or his or her family's ancestral occupation. In rural areas, dalits still carry out the least hygienic work. Among the educated urban elite, some people consider caste when considering marriage choices.

New Religions Emerge in India

Individual reflection and meditation became the focal points of two new religions, *Jainism* and *Buddhism*, which emerged in northern India during the late sixth century and the fifth century B.C.E.

Jainism Founded by *Mahavir Jain*, who was born in the 500s B.C.E., Jainism drew on ideas first expressed in the traditional Hindu texts known as the *Upanishads*. The *Upanishads* stated that all creatures on Earth were part of a larger soul, or *Brahma*. Mahavir Jain reasoned that because each living creature was part of Brahma and thus possessed a godly soul, individuals should show mercy to all animals. Thus, Jainism's followers took steps to do no harm. They adhered to strict vegetarian diets; they wore masks over their mouths to avoid swallowing insects; and only a few engaged in farming because it involved killing pests.

As a result of its demanding lifestyle, Jainism gained few followers. However, Jainism's ethical standards, including its doctrine of *ahimsa,* or nonviolence, influenced later generations. For example, Mahatma Gandhi's steadfast commitment to nonviolence stemmed from his belief in ahimsa. Today, followers of Jainism make up a small percentage of India's religious population, but many Hindus identify Jainist ethics within their own beliefs.

Buddhism During Jain's lifetime, a young member of the warrior class, a kshatriya, sought a different path toward salvation. *Siddhartha Gautama* was unfulfilled with the life he led among the pampered young elite. In about 530 B.C.E., he became aware that suffering plagued the human race, and he set out on a quest to discover why. Gautama left his family and became an *ascetic,* someone who rejects worldly pleasures and lives a life of self-denial. According to legend, as he meditated for days underneath a bodhi tree, he came to several realizations that he called *enlightenment.* Afterwards, Gautama called himself Buddha, or "the enlightened one," and his disciples came to be known as Buddhists.

Buddhist doctrines are summarized in the *Four Noble Truths*: (1) all life involves great suffering; (2) all suffering stems from desires for worldly pleasures and material things; (3) suffering can end when one eliminates all of one's earthly desires; and (4) desire can be eliminated by following Buddhism's eight-fold path. This path requires an individual to meditate, reflect, and refrain from the pursuit of earthly pleasures. The goal is, over time, to detach oneself from worldly affairs. Detachment leads to enlightenment, which leads to a peaceful state in the afterlife known as *nirvana.* Reaching nirvana would mean ending the cycle of birth and rebirth, and the pain that goes with it.

Comparing Indian Spiritual Traditions While Buddhism, Jainism, and Hinduism all were built on a belief in inward reflection and a hope to end the cycle of *reincarnation*, only Hindus believed that one's caste has anything to do with one's *karma.* Buddhists and Jains rejected the rigid social hierarchy of the caste system. They believed that it was inconsistent with the ideals of showing mercy to all people and detaching oneself from worldly matters.

Buddhism spread quickly throughout India. It was more accessible to most people than either Hinduism or Jainism. Buddhism became quite popular with members of lower castes because of its rejection of the caste system. Buddhist teachings were not in Sanskrit, the ancient language of educated elites, but in local dialects that stemmed either from Hindi or Dravidian languages. By the fifth century B.C.E., as would Christians 500 years later, Buddhists established *monasteries.*

Duty in Hinduism In the same era that Jainism and Buddhism developed, the late sixth century and the fifth century B.C.E., Hinduism was also spreading. Epic poems such as the *Mahabharata* (an excerpt of which opens the chapter) and the *Ramayana* were transmitted orally, which made them widely accessible in an era when few people could read. These poems communicated Vedic lessons through epic tales of heroism, romance, and adventure.

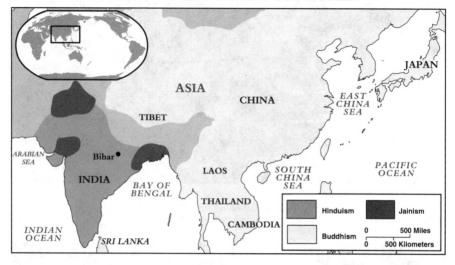

For example, the quotation from the *Mahabharata* that opens this chapter instructs Arjuna to fulfill his caste duties without worrying about the fruits of his actions on Earth. The message sent to listeners was simple: Do not worry about meditating or practicing asceticism in a quest for eternal peace. Performing one's *dharma* should be the goal if one wants to end the birth/rebirth cycle.

Gender Roles The epic poems also taught lessons about gender roles. In the *Ramayana,* the female protagonist, Sita, follows her husband, Ram, dutifully as he is unfairly exiled to the forest for 14 years. Even during a long separation from her husband, Sita is an obedient and faithful wife. Sita's unselfishness and devotion provided a model for how wives should subordinate themselves to their husbands. Inequality in gender relations, while common in religions throughout the Classical period, remained a prominent feature of India's social history even in the Modern Era. For example, only men could become monks; women typically did not get educated.

The *Ramayana* and the *Mahabharata* remain widely read among Hindus today. They are still part of India's cultural fabric.

Mauryan Empire

Of all the continuities in Indian history, spirituality and social organization stand out the most. Strong political centralization does not. Rarely has the entire region of South Asia been unified under one government.

For example, Persian armies invaded the Indus Valley from the west and made it part of their empire about 520 B.C.E. Almost 200 years later, the Greek ruler Alexander the Great defeated the Persians and took over their empire. In 327 B.C.E., he led his army into the Indus Valley and added it to his conquests. Alexander left India two years later, after his troops mutinied.

Source: Thinkstock

Hinduism includes many religious rituals performed by priests leading a community of people (above). In contrast, Buddhism focuses more on individual reflection (below).

Source: Thinkstock

However, two dynasties did manage to wield centralized authority over most of the subcontinent at times: the Mauryans and the Guptas.

The *Mauryan Dynasty* emerged in the fourth century B.C.E. The kingdom of Magadha had grown in prominence, for there were no other comparable competitors in Northern India. Then, under a conqueror named *Chandragupta Maurya,* the kingdom began consolidating and seizing control of additional territory. At its height, during the third century B.C.E., the Mauryan Empire established a centralized government throughout most of the subcontinent. With the exception of the land south of the *Deccan Plateau* (in central India), all of India and modern-day Pakistan was under Mauryan control.

Mauryan Government The Mauryan Empire was divided into segments called *provinces*. Each province had a capital city and was ruled by a prince who governed as representative of the emperor. Each prince was assisted by a *council of ministers*, while another council advised the emperor.

The provinces were divided into *districts* governed by a minister. Each minister was in charge of the district's bureaucrats, whose jobs ranged from maintaining public health to regulating trade. These local officials were usually hired from among the people of each district.

The army kept peace in the empire, and a large spy system kept the government informed of any unrest that was brewing. The high costs of Mauryan government were paid for by heavy taxes on landowners and the value of the crops that farmers raised.

Ashoka Maurya Chandragupta's grandson is undoubtedly the most celebrated of all Mauryan rulers. In the beginning of his career, *Ashoka Maurya*, who ruled 268–232 B.C.E. and is often called *Ashoka the Great,* was a ferocious warrior. He brought large regions of east-central India under Mauryan control. His attack on the eastern Indian kingdom of *Kalinga* was especially brutal, with as many as 100,000 people killed on each side.

As Ashoka gained dominion over this and other lands, the military experiences he had affected him spiritually. The destructive battles against Kalinga prompted him to reconsider his responsibility for causing so many deaths. After that campaign, he converted to Buddhism and ended his violent ways. Ashoka became a strong advocate for Buddhism, building monasteries and sending missionaries to far-flung regions of the empire, even to neighboring kingdoms such as *Ceylon* (modern-day Sri Lanka) and *Bactria* (a kingdom west of the Indus River established by Alexander the Great's Greek descendants). Ashoka's support of Buddhism encouraged his subjects to convert, another factor for Buddhism's surge in popularity.

Ashoka's Achievements Ashoka became well known after this point as an effective governor, instead of as a conqueror. He established an efficient tax-collecting system, which provided a steady revenue stream for the government based in the capital city *Pataliputra* (today known as Patna), near the *Ganges River*. The tax revenue allowed the government to build roads that connected commercial centers, which encouraged trade and travel within the vast empire. One long road connected cities in the northeast with cities in the northwest. Ashoka also ended slavery and required that servants be treated fairly.

One of Ashoka's most famous actions was to inscribe his administration's policies and philosophies on rocks and pillars throughout the kingdom. Like Hammurabi's Code, the *Rock and Pillar Edicts* kept the public informed of the law. This united the empire under a central power.

Instead of making war on neighboring regions, Ashoka promoted peace through diplomacy by sending out ambassadors and Buddhist missionaries. Some of his ambassadors travelled as far as Greece and Egypt. One result of Ashoka's foreign policy was an increase in foreign trade. Taxes on trade within the empire provided additional income for the government.

Decline of the Mauryan Dynasty Despite Ashoka's accomplishments, the Mauryan Dynasty fell apart about 50 years after his death in 232 B.C.E. No Mauryan leader that followed showed the same talent for governance nor the ability to control an expanding government. Over time, the army became ineffective and government officials became idle. In this power vacuum, two invading empires from the northwest briefly attempted to rule the subcontinent: first Bactria and then the *Kushan Empire* ruled from around 180 B.C.E. to 180 C.E. Both the Bactrian and the Kushan empires stretched from Central Asia into northern India.

Trade in Goods and Ideas Despite the invasions and foreign control, India became an important trading crossroads during this period. Silk and other goods from China passed overland through northern India to the Mediterranean Sea. Indian merchants obtained spices and gemstones from kingdoms in Southeast Asia. They traded these items, plus Indian textiles and other merchandise, with the Romans and other peoples along the Mediterranean Sea.

In addition to overland routes, goods were carried in ships from ports along India's west coast to ports on the Red Sea and along the Persian Gulf. From there, traders went overland to Egypt or to the Mediterranean Sea. These *Indian Ocean sea lanes* also connected Indian ports with East Africa and Indonesia. Mauryans even had regular trading relations with the Romans.

Conquest and trade brought new cultures and ideas into India. For example, Indian art styles were influenced by Greek and Roman art. The statues called *Gandhara Buddhas* uniquely combined Greek and Roman artistic traditions with native Indian art.

Gupta Dynasty

The second (and last) major Indian dynasty of the Classical Era was the *Gupta Dynasty*. Though the size of the empire was smaller than the Mauryans' had been, the Gupta Era, which began in the late third century C.E. and ended in 550 C.E., was a Golden Age for India. During the peak of the dynasty's power, trade increased with foreign merchants. Perhaps because their predecessors—the Kushans—had come from foreign lands to the west, the Gupta Dynasty had extensive contact with European merchants as far west as Rome. India thus became an important destination on the *Silk Roads*. (See the map on page 135.)

Governing the Empire Like the Mauryan rulers, the Guptas divided their empire into provinces. In some cases, they kept former kings as provincial rulers. Other provinces were ruled by Gupta princes. All of these officials were responsible to the emperor in the Gupta capital city, Pataliputra. The city became the intellectual and cultural center of the empire.

Scientific and Mathematics Achievements Like the Mauryan ruler Ashoka, the Guptas helped improve health care in their empire. They built free hospitals and encouraged advances in medicine. Indian physicians pioneered surgical procedures to set broken bones and transplant skin grafts. They performed the first *inoculations*—infecting a person with a mild form of a disease so that immunity would develop. Doctors in Southwest Asia and Europe eventually adopted these and other Indian medical practices.

Other Indian advances shaped the modern world. For example, Indian mathematicians developed the numerical symbols 0 through 9 that we use today. They are called *Arabic numerals* rather than Indian because they were introduced into Europe by Arab peoples, who had learned about them through trade with India.

Gupta Religion As in other Classical cultures, religion was a dominant force. In India, it was particularly noticeable in education, art, and literature. Hindu children from upper castes studied the *Vedas* and other great works of literature in school. Entire universities were devoted to the study of specific subjects, including government, astronomy, math, art, painting, and architecture. One of the most ancient universities in the world was in *Nalanda,* located

Source: Paul Trafford / Wikimedia Commons

Statues of Buddha are common, although Buddhists do not worship him as Christians worship Jesus.

in northeastern India. In *Sarnath*, in north central India, Buddhist scholars established a university devoted entirely to the study of Buddhist teachings. With strong support from the Gupta government, painting, sculpture, and literature flourished.

While religion was important, unified practice of it was not. Both the Mauryan Empire and the Gupta Empire allowed religious freedom. With the Guptas' support, Hinduism spread to become India's major religion, which it remains today.

Spread of Buddhism Contacts increased with China, not only because of the Silk Roads trade, but but also because many Chinese were curious to learn about Buddhism. Monasticism had spread throughout South Asia, encouraging the intense study of the religion. Buddhist shrines became popular pilgrimage locations for the religion's followers. Chinese missionaries visited Buddhist sites as early as the fifth century C.E., thus paving the way for Buddhism to spread in China. Buddhism ended up gaining many more followers in East Asia and Southeast Asia than in South Asia.

Decline of the Gupta Dynasty Regionalism forms one of South Asia's historical continuities. As a result of the subcontinent's ethnic diversity and vast number of languages, any administrative power had to make deliberate efforts to unify the country. Though the Guptas presided over an economically vibrant dynasty, they were unable to organize a highly centralized bureaucracy. Unlike Ashoka Maurya, who traveled constantly within the empire to keep close watch over its affairs, the Gupta emperors took a hands-off approach to governing. This led to growing disunity among the far-flung regions of the empire.

Invasions by nomads from the northwest, the *White Huns*, brought the final downfall of the Gupta Dynasty. The Gupta Dynasty had begun to shrink by the end of the fifth century, when the White Huns conquered Northern India. By 500, these Huns had taken over western India, which destroyed the Gupta Empire's trade with Rome. Around 550 C.E., the Gupta Dynasty became the last of the great Eurasian empires of the first century C.E. to collapse. (Test Prep: Create a chart comparing the impact of the nomadic invasions of India with similar invasions of Rome and China. See page 84 for Rome and pages 242–245 for the Mongolian invasion of China.)

Three Great Philosophical Traditions

While India was only rarely united by a centralized government, China often was. However, during the declining centuries of the Zhou, China suffered a period of instability. During this period, most Chinese followed a simple animistic belief in natural objects and forces and veneration of the souls of the dead. This animism was coupled with shamanism, in which a shaman, or spirit guide, mediated the connection between the everyday world and the spirit world. Over time, however, three significant new schools of thought evolved: Confucianism, Daoism, and Legalism.

Confucius The philosopher K'ung Fu-tzu, known today as *Confucius,* was born around 551 B.C.E., while the Zhou dynasty was in decline. Historians have sorted through the many stories about his early life and have reached the following conclusions. Confucius was probably born into poverty. He might have had a number of different jobs as part of the Chinese bureaucracy, all the while developing his own thoughts about the individual's relationship to the state. A falling-out with local powers in his home state led Confucius to travel across China, speaking to people and gaining disciples as he went.

The ideas of Confucius became the foundation of the belief system of *Confucianism.* After Confucius died, his disciples compiled his teachings, and probably added some of their own thoughts, in a complex work called the *Analects* (*Selected Sayings*). (Test Prep: Write a paragraph comparing the *Analects* with the Christian Bible. See page 82.)

The Teachings of Confucius During this very turbulent time in China's history, the ideas of Confucius appealed to many people because he argued for respecting social hierarchies and traditions. "Good government consists in the ruler being a ruler, the minister being a minister, the father being a father, and the son being a son." (*Lunyu* 12.11) He focused on behavior in everyday life, not on beliefs about any deity. For example, he taught the importance of family, respect for one's elders, and reverence for one's ancestors. He believed that conducting the proper rituals would lead to social harmony.

Confucius also believed in what is called the Golden Rule—"do unto others as you would have them do unto you"—a tenet important in many other moral and philosophical traditions, including Christianity and Judaism. Confucius preached humility and the importance of virtue, which he defined as treating others properly. He even applied this principle to China's government and kings. The teachings of Confucius affected Chinese beliefs and values more than any other philosophy and continue to be important in twenty-first century China.

Confucianism and the Family Largely because of Confucianism, the family became the most important unit in Chinese society. The status of a man's family, not his wealth or accomplishments, determined his place in society. A family typically included the mother and father, their sons and sons' wives, and any unmarried daughters. All family members lived in the same house and shared household duties.

The father was the head of the household. The older he was, the more respect and authority he had. Fathers arranged the marriages of their children and grandchildren. Upper-class fathers also decided on their sons' education and careers. This all fell under the concept of *filial piety,* which can be defined as the duty of family members to subordinate their needs and desires to those of the male head of the family, or its ruler.

Women had few rights and were not usually educated. They were expected to remain subservient to men and boys, regardless of age. Although mothers and mothers-in-law were greatly respected, married daughters tended to be treated like servants in the husband's households.

Daoism *Daoism* (also spelled Taoism) dates back to the late 500s B.C.E., at the time of the Zhou Dynasty. The origins of Daoism are shrouded in mystery, but its founder is usually said to be *Laozi,* also called the Old Master. As happened with Confucius, Laozi had many disciples who collected his teachings. The followers gathered the Old Master's ideas together in the *Dao De Jing (The Classic Way and the Virtue).*

In Daoism, followers seek happiness and wisdom by way of the path, or *dao.* To follow the dao is to renounce worldly ambitions and society and instead to seek harmony with nature. A key symbol of Daoist philosophy is the Yin and Yang, in which two sides come together in harmony: the Yin, or humanity's submissive and "feminine" side, and the Yang, or humanity's aggressive and "masculine" side. The goal, as understood in Daoism, is to keep the two sides in balance. Daoism appealed to China's peasants because of their connection to natural forces and the land. These ideas had wide influence in China. Medical doctors focused on restoring the natural balance among the forces in a person's body. Poets wrote about nature and human involvement with it. Scholars tried to understand the natural properties of metals and how one might be transformed into another. Architects attempted to create structures that integrated well with their natural surroundings.

Comparing Daoism and Greek Mythology			
Topic	Taoism Only	Both Taoism and Greek Mythology	Greek Mythology Only
Nature of Deities	• Represent abstract ideas • Are benevolent • Are detached from human affairs	• Pantheon of separate deities that oversee every aspect of society	• Have human characteristics • Can be be petty, jealous, and vengeful • Can intervene in human affairs
Hierarchy among Deities	• The Great High God has abstract deities above him	• One head deity who rules over other gods	• The head deity, Zeus, has no deities above him
Relationship Between People and Deities	• People can become deities		• Deities can procreate with humans, producing demigods
Common Themes	• Inner peace • Balance between opposites (yin/yang)		• War and love • Heroic action
Afterlife	• A state of non-being		• A tangible place, Hades

Legalism Creating a sharp contrast to Confucianism and Daoism was the third philosophical tradition of China's Classical period, Legalism. As the name suggests, the philosophy of Legalism was less concerned with questions of the meaning of life, and more with how people behaved. Since human nature was understood to be essentially bad, Legalists believed that society needed a system of strict laws and punishments to control people. Because most citizens, according to Legalism, should live their lives as either farmers or soldiers, education was not considered to be especially necessary. Legalists argued that society should discourage people from becoming teachers, merchants, poets, or artists. Another tenet of legalism was collective responsibility of a family or community for every member. One should observe one's relatives and neighbors and turn them into authorities if they break the law.

Legalism was led by two philosophers, *Han Fei Zu* and *Li Si*. Their ideas struck a chord with many people during the often-violent Qin Dynasty (see below). However, after that dynasty ended and the following dynasty brought greater stability, Legalism faded. It failed to have the long-term impact of either Confucianism or Daoism.

The Qin Dynasty in China

The instability of the Zhou ended when, in 221 B.C.E., an ambitious leader named Qin Shihuangdi raised his own army and defeated what remained of the Zhou leaders. One by one, he also conquered the nearby regional authorities, taking control of all of China and establishing his own dynasty. The Qin (or Ch'in) dynasty was brief, lasting only until 207 B.C.E., but memorable—in part due to the cruelty of its leader.

Not content to just be king, the title claimed by Qin, *Shihuangdi,* means "first emperor." He created a very centralized state with all of the government under his personal control. In particular, he abolished local laws and appointed magistrates to replace local leaders. Books that were not in keeping with Qin's own beliefs were burned, and hundreds of scholars were buried alive. Anyone who resisted his authority could be executed or sent into exile. Many dissenters were sent north, to work on building a network of walls to keep out invaders—workers who died while building these walls were buried within the walls themselves. Hundreds of thousands of people were conscripted to construct the northern walls and to toil on other infrastructure projects. (Test Prep: Write a paragraph connecting the Qin walls with the Great Wall of China. See pages 181 and 373.)

Achievements of Qin Dynasty Despite his despotism, Qin did much to change China in ways that won him praise.

- He expanded the size of the Chinese empire, mostly to the south and the west.

- He gave peasants the right to own land.

- He standardized the Chinese script, which had developed many local variations during the Shang dynasty, thereby making communication and trade easier.

- He standardized coinage as well as weights and measures. These steps greatly aided commerce.

- He ordered the building of canals and roads, which improved trade.

Qin's most remarkable legacy was not discovered until 1974 when his tomb was unearthed. Inside Qin's tomb, which had gone untouched for 2000 years, were more than 7,000 life-sized soldiers made out of terra-cotta—an army for the afterlife. Each soldier was unique, demonstrating a level of realism that had not been seen in Chinese art to this point. (Test Prep: List the differences and similarities between Qin's royal burial with the burial of the pharaohs of Egypt. See page 27.)

In 210 B.C.E., Qin died, and his son took the throne. However, four years later, in 206 B.C.E., a Qin general led a revolt. The rebels killed the emperor and the entire royal family, and the rebel general seized power. He and his family began the *Han Dynasty,* which lasted for more than 400 years.

The Han Dynasty

Han Wudi (who ruled 141–87 B.C.E.) was the Han Dynasty's most significant emperor. He oversaw a vast expansion of the empire, as China invaded and took over Korea and northern Vietnam. Wudi also sent Chinese forces into Central Asia, almost all the way west to Bactria, to defeat the nomadic *Xiongnu*

Source: Shutterstock

Source: LACMA

While Confucians honor early generations by keeping ancestor tablets in their homes (left), Daoists honor nature through painting (right).

peoples, who had been raiding Chinese villages for years. To maintain control of the new western lands, Wudi relocated landless Chinese farmers into Central Asia to establish agricultural colonies.

Central Government Meanwhile, at home, Wudi expanded the efficient, centralized government started by the Qin. One of his most important accomplishments was the introduction of a *civil service examination*. Under this system, people were hired based on their test-taking abilities instead of their personal or family connections. Because at first not many young men were qualified for government positions, Wudi created a national university to prepare them for employment. The combination of the exams and the university began China's tradition of having a well-trained and highly respected bureaucracy to administer government policies. As a result, China prospered for many years.

Wudi's rule—and the period immediately following—is sometimes referred to as the *Pax Sinica*, Chinese Peace. During this period, the country enjoyed peace, the economy grew, and the population increased. As the common people prospered, so did the rich, who created a thriving market for luxury goods.

Silk Roads Trade Traders moved Chinese products west along a series of routes that became known as the *Silk Roads*. This trade brought China into contact with the Roman Empire. The Silk Roads would also eventually bring Buddhism into China from Central Asia.

Silk production increased greatly during Emperor Wudi's rule. Because Chinese silk was of such high quality, silk and silk garments could be sold as far away as the Roman Empire, Mesopotamia, Persia, and India.

Paper, Calendar, and Farming Chinese science and technology prospered under Han rule. The Chinese invented paper around 100 C.E. and calculated the current calendar year of 365.25 days. Improvements to the iron plow and developing a yoke that did not put presure on an animal's windpipe made farming more productive.

Capital Cities The city of *Chang'an* was the capital of the Han Empire as well as its cultural center. Surrounded by a wall, the city had parks, many homes, and some palaces. Chang'an served as the eastern end of the Silk Roads. Many of its residents were bureaucrats and people who served bureaucrats. Later in the Han dynasty, because of civil unrest in Chang'an, the capital city was moved to Luoyang in eastern China.

Disease, Inequality, and Unrest The Pax Sinica did not last. One problem for the late Han dynasty was the spread of diseases, which came to China along the Silk Roads with the movement of traders and other migrants. Smallpox, measles, and bubonic plague were the most destructive of these epidemic diseases, which reduced the population of China by as much as one-fourth. (Test Prep: Create a Venn Diagram based on the impact of epidemic diseases in the Han and Roman Empires. See pages 83–84.)

Another problem was economic. Many small farmers had to give up their lands to large landowners to satisfy their debts. Inequality increased as a small number of landholders came to own more and more of the land. One non-Han emperor, Wang Mang (who ruled 9–23 C.E.), attempted to redistribute land from large landowners to landless peasants. However, this land reform was not well received, creating more unrest and leading to his replacement by a member of the Han family. In 126 C.E., peasants began what became a series of revolts, which further weakened Han rule.

Subsequent Han emperors also failed to address the land distribution problem and the associated famines. This inspired more peasant uprisings, most notably the *Yellow Turban Rebellion*—so named because of the scarves worn by the peasants involved. The death toll probably reached several million, making it one of the bloodiest conflicts in the world before the 1900s. The dynasty came to an end when the emperor was overthrown in 220 C.E. and China was divided into three kingdoms.

India and China Trade

While the Himalayas separated the centers of civilization in South and East Asia, the eastern Indian Ocean and the South China Sea connected them. These routes were part of a vast trading network linking most of Afro-Eurasia. Sailors in Indian Ocean made several technological advances that facilitated trade. The astrolabe and improvements to the compass allowed sailors to navigate more precisely. The sternpost rudder enabled them to control the direction of a ship more accurately. Determining monsoon patterns helped them to plan their trips more safely and use winds more effectively. This network would make possible the spread of religion, technology, and goods to shape the next period in human history.

HISTORICAL PERSPECTIVES: WHY DID SO MANY BELIEF SYSTEMS DEVELOP IN ONE PERIOD?

The years from 800 B.C.E. to 200 B.C.E. were a fertile time for new religions and ways of thought. Confucianism, Buddhism, Taoism, Jainism, Greek philosophy, and Jewish monotheism all emerge from this period. Historians have debated how to explain the rise of so many systems of belief and thought in a 600-year period. In a 1949 book, German philosopher Karl Jaspers called these years the "axial age" because they formed the foundation for later thought in several major civilizations. Jaspers noted most of these systems developed on their own—they were not all offshoots of one development in one place. They all emerged in small states, often in the period when one great empire was declining and a new elite was arising. In 2006, Karen Armstrong, a British author who has written several widely read books on religion, published *The Great Transformation*. She expanded on the idea of an axial age, arguing that the violence and suffering of the times spurred people to be more reflective, which led to new systems of thinking.

Another British scholar, Diarmaid McCulloch, called the idea of an axial age "an optical illusion." He suggested that people became no more reflective at a certain time in history, but that humans' ability to write had developed to the point that they could write down their thoughts.

Others have suggested that any clustering of new belief systems in this period is insignificant. Several of the world's most influential religions developed outside of this period. Two major traditions, Hinduism and Judaism, came earlier. Three others, Sikhism and the two largest faiths in the world, Christianity and Islam, came later. In addition, several new faiths have arisen in the last two centuries, including Baha'ism in the Middle East and Falon Gong in China.

KEY TERMS BY THEME

STATE-BUILDING
provinces
council of ministers
districts
Ashoka Maurya
Kalinga
Ceylon
Bactria
Pataliputra
Ganges River
Rock and Pillar Edicts
Kushan Empire
Gupta Dynasty
Mauryan Dynasty
Chandragupta Maurya
White Huns
Han Dynasty
Pax Sinica
Shihuangdi
Xiongnu
civil service
   examination
Yellow Turban
   Rebellion

CULTURE
Vedas *Upanishads*
Brahma
dharma
karma
Mahavir Jain
Jainism
Buddhism
ahimsa
Siddhartha Gautama
ascetic
enlightenment
Four Noble Truths
Bhagavad Gita
Mahabharata
nirvana
reincarnation
monasteries
Ramayana
Gandhara Buddhas
inoculations
Arabic numerals
Nalanda
Sarnath

Confucius
Confucianism
Daoism
Dao De Jing
dao

SOCIAL STRUCTURE
caste system
varna
brahmins
kshatriyas
vaishyas
shudras
untouchables
dalits
jatis

GEOGRAPHY
Deccan Plateau

ECONOMICS
Indian Ocean sea lanes
Silk Roads

MULTIPLE-CHOICE QUESTIONS

1. Emperor Ashoka's sending of ambassadors and Buddhist missionaries to other countries reflected his
   - (A) steadfast opposition to Alexander the Great
   - (B) determination to rule nonviolently through dharma
   - (C) strong support for Hindu traditions
   - (D) lack of tolerance for religious diversity

2. The Pax Sinica and Pax Romana were similar in that both
   - (A) ended suddenly when pastoral nomads began attacking communities
   - (B) were periods of peace when trade prospered
   - (C) reflected the influence of a religion that emphasized peace
   - (D) lasted only the lifetime of a single ruler

Questions 3–4 refers to the excerpt below.

> To know the masculine and be true to the feminine
>   is to be the waterway of the world.
> To be the waterway of the world is to flow with the Great Integrity,
>   always swirling back to the innocence of childhood.
> To know yang and to be true to yin is
>   to echo the universe.
> To echo the universe is to merge with the Great Integrity,
>   ever returning to the infinite.

> —Verse 28, *Dao De Jing*, trans. Ralph Alan Dale

3. The excerpt above expresses Daoism's vision of

    (A) a better world by dominating and using nature

    (B) peace through education in natural science

    (C) harmony as people let the natural world guide their actions

    (D) how feminine values should overrule masculine violence

4. Followers of which system of thought would most object to the above statement?

    (A) Legalism

    (B) Hinduism

    (C) Confucianism

    (D) Jainism

5. Which of these rulers followed policies toward religious unity in his empire similar to those practiced by Ashoka?

    (A) Darius

    (B) Qin Shihuangdi

    (C) Akhenaton and other Egyptian pharaohs

    (D) Roman empires before Constantine

6. One important contribution of classical India to other societies is

    (A) the belief in reincarnation

    (B) the effective, unified governance

    (C) the war chariot

    (D) an easy-to-use number system

7. With which statements would Confucius agree with most strongly?

    (A) People should be free to find and pursue their true calling in life.

    (B) Men and women should share power equally.

    (C) Treating others properly is the key to a good society.

    (D) Scholars are less valuable to society than are merchants.

Question 8 refers to the following Venn diagram.

Hinduism
- Important writings: Rig-Veda and Mahabharata
- Several deities that are expressions of a single God

Buddhism
- Two main traditions, Theravada/Hinayana and Mahayana
- Doctrines include the Four Noble Truths

8. Which statement would fit in the section where the two circles overlap in the above Venn diagram?

   (A) Widely followed in Indian today

   (B) Teach that individuals go through repeated cycles of birth and death

   (C) Focus on obedience to a single deity

   (D) Were founded upon the teachings of one individual

9. Which statement best summarizes the relationship of Jainism to Hinduism and Buddhism?

   (A) Jainism is a variation of Hinduism.

   (B) Jainism shares all of the traits that Hinduism and Buddhism share.

   (C) Jainism shares aspects of Hinduism and Buddhism, but is separate from them.

   (D) Jainism is unlike Hinduism and Buddhism in all of its basic beliefs and pratices.

10. Which of the following is most accurate about the spread of Buddhism?

    (A) It grew after it began to emphasize the worship of local dieties.

    (B) It remained closely linked to Hinduism.

    (C) It became more popular outside the country of its origin than inside.

    (D) It did not change as it spread from one culture to another.

CONTINUITY AND CHANGE-OVER-TIME ESSAY QUESTIONS

Directions: You are to answer the following question. You should spend 5 minutes organizing or outlining your essay. Write an essay that:

- Has a relevant thesis and supports that thesis with appropriate historical evidence.

- Addresses all parts of the question.

- Uses world historical context to show continuities and changes over time.
- Analyzes the process of continuity and change over time.

1. Analyze continuities and change in religion in India between the Vedic age and the age of the Mauryans and Guptas.

Questions for Additional Practice

2. Analyze the changes and continuities that occurred in political structures in India during the Classical Era.

3. Analyze the continuities and change of the Chinese interaction with other cultures beginning with the Zhou era and ending with the Han era.

COMPARATIVE ESSAY QUESTIONS

Directions: You are to answer the following question. You should spend 5 minutes organizing or outlining your essay. Write an essay that:
- Has a relevant thesis and supports that thesis with appropriate historical evidence.
- Addresses all parts of the question.
- Makes direct, relevant comparisons.
- Analyzes relevant reasons for similarities and differences.

1. Analyze similarities and differences in the economic systems of the Gupta and Mauryan Empires.

Questions for Additional Practice

2. Analyze similarities and differences in the decline of TWO of the following empires:
- Roman
- Han
- Mauryan and Gupta

3. Analyze similarities and differences in Confucianism and TWO of the following religions or systems of thought:
- Greek philosophy from Socrates to Aristotle
- Greek and Roman religion prior to Christianity
- Christianity

THINK AS A HISTORIAN: RECOGNIZE CONTEXTUALIZATION

To contextualize is to look at an idea, event, person, or situation together with everything that relates to it. After you place events in context, you begin to see themes and patterns emerge in history and ultimately you understand how laws, institutions, customs, and other factors give rise to a particular period in time. *Which THREE of the following statements or questions explore context?*

1. In the Bhagavad Gita, the warrior Aryuna hesitates to go into battle, in part because he does not want to fight against members of his own family on the opposing side.

2. The caste system in India began around 1500 B.C.E. and consisted of four castes: brahmins, kshatriyas, vaishyas, and shudras.

3. In the fourth century B.C.E., the Mauryan Dynasty grew to prominence because it had no other comparable competitors in Northern India.

4. By 180 B.C.E., India was controlled by foreigners. Nonetheless, the region became an important trading crossroads between China and the Mediterranean.

WRITE AS A HISTORIAN: INTRODUCING THE TOPIC

Starting an essay with a sentence or two of general or background information on the topic establishes the context for the rest of what you write. For example, to answer a question about the significance of the office of satrap, you could start by noting that as empires grew larger, they needed new methods of controlling local regions. *For each question below, select the sentence that best provides context for the topic.*

1. Discuss the weaknesses of the Greek government that led to its decline.

   a. Greece's fragmented landscape made uniting under a single government difficult.

   b. Alexander the Great spread Greek culture far beyond the traditional borders of Greece.

2. Describe the significance of theater in Greek culture.

   a. Greek plays heavily influenced William Shakespeare.

   b. Many of the leisure activities stemmed from facets of the Greek religion and were used to mimic or please the gods.

6

Early American Civilizations

It was from within the places called Paxil and Cayala that the yellow ears of ripe maize and the white ears of ripe maize come from. . . . Thus was found the food that would become the flesh of the newly framed and shaped people.

Popol Vuh, "The Discovery of Maize"

The early centers of civilization in the Americas, in the Andes Mountains and in *Mesoamerica*, produced several great civilizations. Two of the most significant ones in the Andes were the *Chavin* and later the *Moche*. In Mesoamerica, the *Olmecs* were a foundational civilization that heavily influenced two later groups, the *Mayan* and Aztec civilizations.

The Moche

After the Chavin, described in Chapter 2 the next major civilization to develop in the Andes was the Moche, which arose around 200 B.C.E. and lasted until 700 C.E. Developing in the Moche and Chicham river valleys in what is today northern Peru, the Moche expanded outward into the valleys through both population increase and conquest.

Architecture Moche rulers supervised the building of a number of monumental structures centered around two temples. One was the *Huaca del Sol* (Temple of the Sun), a stepped pyramid. The other was the *Huaca de la Luna* (Temple of the Moon), a terraced platform. Both were made out of unfired adobe bricks. The Moche built a fortified city around these two temples. To assist in agriculture, the Moche built extensive irrigation networks, bringing water from rivers to fields via ditches. This was necessary since the civilization experienced fluctuations in rainfall from year to year. (Test Prep: Create a table that compares Moche architecture and agriculture with developments in Egypt. See page 23.)

Economy and Trade The Moche grew a variety of crops, including corn and beans, often in irrigated fields. Among the animals they kept were llamas. Llamas provided transport up and down the steep mountains, fibers to produce textiles, and dung to fertilize crops.

As in Mesopotamia and other places where agriculture developed, an agricultural surplus in most years allowed the culture to develop an artisan class. Artifacts created by the Moche included ceramic water jars, which

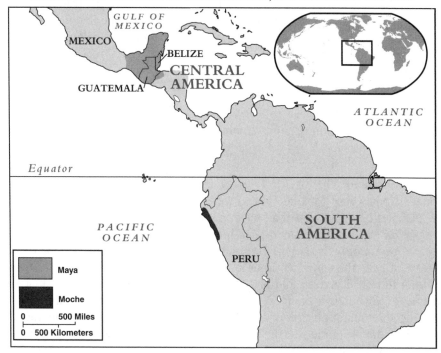

were painted with images of rulers, slaves, warriors, priests, healers, gods, plants, and animals. Moche artisans also made beautiful jewelry and other objects from gold, silver, and copper. Their textiles were made from the wool of the alpaca and vicuña and from cotton.

Trade was mostly local, between Moche communities. Without large boats or wheeled vehicles, long-distance trade would have been difficult.

Society and Religion The complex Moche social structure was organized around *ayllus*, which were small communities based on the idea of communal work. Members of an ayllu believed they all shared the same mythical ancestor. This meant that even people who were biologically unrelated could still be considered part of the extended family of the ayllu through this shared ancestor. When a woman married, she would join her husband's ayllu, while still maintaining membership in her own. Like many people in cultures around the world in this era, the Moche venerated their ancestors.

Like the Maya in Mesoamerica (see following pages) and other early cultures, the Moche had important ceremonial centers where they conducted religious rituals. Some of the Moche rituals included human sacrifice at times. And like other early cultures, religion and government were closely linked. Like the Greeks, they believed in many gods, gods who often acted with the same emotions and passions as humans, but at time with greater powers.

Disappearance of the Moche Strong social cohesion kept the Moche civilization vibrant for nine centuries. However, it eventually vanished as a distinctive culture, perhaps because of climate changes—the region experienced

30 years of unusually heavy rains followed by 30 years of drought. These weather events might have seriously weakened the Moche civilization because Moche leaders gained some of their authority by claiming to be able to predict the weather. Whatever the cause, scholars believe that Moche civilization probably ended in violence and civil war.

Mesoamerica

The Olmec civilization declined in power, but it left a strong legacy on later cultures in the region. They adopted aspects of the Olmec language, religion, and economy.

Teotihuacan The city of *Teotihuacan* was founded around 150 B.C.E. not far from where Mexico City is today. Its name comes from a word in the Nahuatl language that may have meant "birthplace of the gods." With a population eventually numbering in the hundreds of thousands, Teotihuacan grew to be not only the largest city in the Western Hemisphere, but one of the largest cities in the entire world of its time. The city's orderly growth—it was laid out in a grid pattern and had multistory apartment buildings—suggests that the expansion was planned and regulated by a strong government.

The ceremonial portion of the city featured many important monuments, including the Pyramid of the Sun, the Pyramid of the Moon, and the Temple of Quetzalcoatl, named for a prominent god who was portrayed as a feathered serpent. A long road called the Avenue of the Dead connected these monuments. Priests and nobles, who were at the top of the social hierarchy, lived in extravagant homes. Peasants and artisans, who occupied the lower rungs of the social structure, dwelt in apartments within multiunit dwellings. (Test Prep: Write a paragraph comparing Teotihuacan with another city with orderly growth, read about Mohenjo-Daro on page 30.)

The city itself was surrounded by fields, which supported intensive agriculture; many of Teotihuacan's people were farmers and peasants, although there was also considerable regional trade. One of the city's main exports was *obsidian* (hard glass rock) deposits that were found in the area. Teotihuacan also thrived because of its many artisan workshops. Artisans tanned animal hides into leather and made pottery, obsidian tools, and weapons.

Decline Teotihuacan reached its peak around 500 C.E. and then began to decline, for reasons historians have not agreed upon. Sometime between 600 and 650 C.E., a large fire burned much of the city. Some of Teotihuacan's people settled in the Mayan lowlands and may have been incorporated into the Mayan civilization.

The Mayans

Around 1500 B.C., the Mayan people began to establish small settlements. Over time, the villages grew as the Mayans developed an advanced civilization. Mayan civilization reached its height between 250 and 900 C.E. That is sometimes called its *Classic Period*. At its peak, as many as 2 million Mayans populated the region. They stretched over the southern part of Mexico in much of what is now Belize, Honduras, and Guatemala. Most lived in or near one of the approximately 40 cities that ranged in size from 5,000 to 50,000 people.

Agriculture To provide for the large population of city dwellers, the Mayans practiced what is called *slash-and-burn agriculture*. They created fields by cutting down trees and plants in a patch of forest and then burning them. The resulting ashes fertilized the soil. The *Maya* also terraced fields to limit erosion of the land that they had cleared on hillsides. They drained swamps and built irrigation systems to water their crops. For meat, the Mayans hunted deer. Eventually, the Mayans would learn to raise deer.

The Mayans' chief crops were corn, beans, and squash, referred to as the Three Sisters. Since the Mayans lacked draft animals, they seeded and harvested by hand. It was men's work to seed and harvest, while women prepared food and, if needed, raised deer.

Source: Thinkstock

Mayan pyramids, with steps going up the side, were similar to Mesopotamian ziggurats. Similarly shaped architecture can be found from Spain and Algeria to China and Indonesia.

Cities The Mayans, using only stone tools, cut and shaped limestone blocks to build religious centers. By 200 C.E., these centers grew into cities with temples, palaces, and plazas for public gatherings. The most important temples were located on top of pyramids, to be closer to the heavens. The pyramids were up to 200 feet high—as tall as a 20-story building. They also served as observatories for Mayan astronomers.

Mayan Government The main form of Mayan government was the *city-state,* each one ruled by a king and consisting of a city and its surrounding territory. Most rulers were men. However, when no male heir was available or old enough to govern, Mayan women ruled. Wars between city-states were common, and sometimes the winner absorbed the loser. However, people rarely fought to control territory. More often they fought to gain *tribute*—payments from the conquered to the conqueror—and captives to be used as human sacrifices during religious ceremonies.

Each Mayan king claimed to be descended from a god. The Mayans believed that when the king died, he would become one with his ancestor-god. The king directed the activities of the elite scribes and priests who administered the affairs of the state. Royal rule usually passed from father to son, but kings who lost the support of the people were sometimes overthrown. The common people were required to pay taxes, usually in the form of crops, and to provide labor to the government. City-states had no standing armies, so when war erupted, governments required citizens to provide military service. No central government ruled all Mayan lands, although often one city-state was the strongest in a region and would dominate its neighbors.

Mayan Religion The Mayans worshiped many deities. Among the most important were those of the sun, rain, and corn. Priests held great power in Mayan society, a sign that religion had a major role in Mayan life. Women could be priests, and at least one god (the goddess of the Moon) was female. Priests led religious ceremonies and festivals at regular times based on the Mayan calendar. They made offerings to the deities so that prayers might be answered. As mentioned above, these offerings sometimes involved human sacrifice. War captives were killed in temple ceremonies as offerings to the gods.

The Mayans participated in a ball game—with features similar to today's basketball and soccer—as part of the religious ritual. Players used their feet, hips, and legs, but not their hands, to move a ball through a hoop. Losers may have been sacrificed to the gods. (Test Prep: Write a paragraph tracing connections between the Olmec and Mayan religions and sports. See pages 38–39.)

Science and Culture The Mayan people have sometimes been called the "Greeks of the New World" because of their cultural achievements. Mayan science and religion were closely linked. Priests studied the heavens and calendars to predict the future and to decide if a time was right for war.

Although they had no telescopes, the Mayans were among the best astronomers of early times. An observatory, the *Caracol*, located in the city of *Chichén Itzá*, was built around 1000 C.E. Priests predicted eclipses of the sun and calculated the phases of the moon accurately. Indeed, their understanding of mathematics and astronomy, especially their observations of Venus from the Caracol, enabled Mayan priests to design a calendar more accurate than one used in Europe at the time. The Mayans' advanced study of mathematics included the concept of zero and calculations that totaled in the hundreds of millions.

The Mayans also had the most advanced writing system of all the early American civilizations. Their writing used pictures and symbols akin to the *hieroglyphics* of the Egyptians, but with more than 850 different characters. The symbols were carved into a type of paper made from tree bark, which was sometimes bound together into books.

They decorated buildings, clay pots, and monuments with their history and other messages. Public buildings often had carved stone reliefs. The Mayans carved wood, although little of it has survived, and jade, when they could get it. Since the Mayans lacked metal tools, they carved using flint. In addition to carvings, the Mayans created vivid paintings on walls, as well as on pottery used as grave offerings.

Early Writing Systems				
Culture	Time Developed	What Symbols Represent	Approximate Number of Symbols	Direction of Reading Symbols
Sumeria (cuneiform)	c. 3500 B.C.E.	Pictures	1,500	Originally top to bottom, but changed to left to right
Egypt (hieroglyphics)	c. 3400 B.C.E.	Pictures and sounds	700	Varied from text to text
China	c. 1500 B.C.E.	Pictures and words	varied	Right to left and top to bottom
Phoenecia (alphabet)	c. 1500 B.C.E.	Sounds	22	Right to left
Maya	c. 250 B.C.E.	Pictures and words	850	Left to right in 2-symbol columns

Decline of Mayan Cities Around 900 C.E., a variety of related changes came together to cause rapid changes in Mayan culture. Population growth had made cities crowded. The destruction of forests caused environmental damage. Stresses between cities led to increasing wars. The climate shifted, which resulted in many years of drought. The combination of these changes made living in cities difficult, and the urban population began to decline rapidly. Mayans began to abandon their cities and resume a rural life. The descendants of this culture still live in the region today, and more than 7 million people speak a variety of Mayan languages. Their religion combines two traditions: Mayan beliefs and Roman Catholicism. (Test Prop: Write an outline comparing the early Mayans with their descendants. See page 262.)

Environmental Problems Facing the Mayans and Romans		
Issue	Mayans	Romans
Wetlands	Desertification reduced wetland areas	Wetlands spread
Forests	Biodiversity of forests reduced	Overuse of trees for manufacturing
Soil	Silt clogged rivers	Soil became poor from excessive farming
Weather	Prolonged droughts	
Crop Production	Crop output decreased	Crop failures
Grazing	Did not graze animals significantly	Overgrazing of domesticated animals

HISTORICAL PERSPECTIVES: WERE THE MAYANS VIOLENT?

After the Mayans began moving out of cities around 900 C.E., the surrounding jungle quickly reclaimed the area. So when Spaniards began exploring southern Mexico and central America in the 1500s and 1600s, the great buildings and pyramids had been swallowed up by plants. The Spaniards heard stories about great ruins in the jungles, but not until the 1800s did scholars begin to uncover and study them. For example, the greatest known Mayan site, at Tikal, was unknown to people from outside the region until 1848.

As scholars began to uncover Mayan sites, they struggled to decipher the Mayan writing system. The first breaks came as they understood numbers and references to stars and planets. Hence, the first interpretations of Mayan culture focused on their great achievements in math, astronomy, and art. In addition, as more and more buildings and carvings were uncovered, people focused on the Mayans' achievements in art. The publication of *A Study of Mayan Art* by Herbert Spinden in 1913 brought wider public attention to all that the Mayan had accomplished.

During the mid-1900s, archeologists began to fill in their interpretation of what they saw. The great interpreter of Mayan culture during this period was a British archeologist, Eric Thompson. His 1954 book, *Rise and Fall of Maya Civilization,* portrayed a fairly peaceful and successful culture.

However, as linguists slowly made headway into deciphering more and more Mayan writing, the interpretation of Mayan culture changed. Instead of reading about only astronomical observations, scholars began to read about wars between cities, deadly struggles for political power, and sacrifices for religious purposes. In 1986, Linda Schele and Mary Miller organized an art exhibit, "The Blood of Kings: A New Interpretation of Maya Art." The Mayan, once viewed as so peaceful, were now understood to have a strain of violence in their culture as well.

Then, in 2006, the release of a Hollywood movie, *Apocalypto,* carried this understanding to a wildly inaccurate extreme. The Mayan were portrayed as bloodthirsty, evil savages enthralled with torture and mass executions. This unhistorical depiction led scholars of the Mayan to speak out in an effort to correct the public perception. If the Mayan were not as peaceful as scholars once thought they were, they were not as brutal as the people portrayed in the movie.

KEY TERMS BY THEME

STATE-BUILDING	ayllus	Caracol
city-state	Mesoamerica	Chichén Itzá
tribute	Olmec	
	Teotihuacan	**ENVIRONMENT**
CULTURE	Maya	obsidian
Moche	Mayan	slash-and-burn
Huaca del Sol	mother civilization	agriculture
Huaca de la Luna	hieroglyphics	
	Classic Period	

MULTIPLE-CHOICE QUESTIONS

1. Which is a sign that Teotihuacan had a strong government?
   - (A) Streets were built on a grid pattern.
   - (B) Priests had larger homes than did peasants.
   - (C) Most people were involved in agriculture.
   - (D) A large fire burned much of the city.

2. Unlike the Mayan, the people of Teotihuacan lived
   - (A) in one large city instead of many small cities
   - (B) mostly in lowlands that were often swampy
   - (C) much closer to the equator, so it was warmer
   - (D) primarily on small farms along rivers and streams

3. In which way were the Moche and the Mayan similar?
   - (A) Both developed a system of writing.
   - (B) Both featured an Avenue of the Dead.
   - (C) Both emphasized the idea of communal work.
   - (D) Both saw their power decline when the climate changed.

4. Which of the following describes civilizations in South America but not in Mesoamerica?
   - (A) People developed a writing system.
   - (B) People viewed the jaguar as a deity.
   - (C) People used llamas extensively for producing wool and transporting goods.
   - (D) People held ritual ball games that sometimes involved human sacrifice.

5. One similarity between the Chavin and the Moche is that both
   (A) carried on extensive trade by sea with the Maya
   (B) lived primarily in the higher elevations of the Andes
   (C) made jewelry and ritual items out of jade
   (D) constructed irrigation ditches to aid farming

Question 6 refers to the image below.

Source: Thinkstock

6. The Mayan pyramid shown above is similar to the Egyptian pyramids because both demonstrated
   (A) the ability of the society to organize a large labor force
   (B) the need to build structures for defense against invaders
   (C) the syncretism between an older and a newer culture
   (D) the value people placed on creating tombs for its leaders

7. Which statement uses the term *ayllu* accurately?
   (A) An *ayllu* was a large community led by one ruler.
   (B) All members of an *ayllu* were related biologically.
   (C) Women could belong to more than one *ayllu*.
   (D) The purpose of an *ayllu* was to share work.

Questions 8–10 refer to the following table.

Sulfur Level in Yucatán Peninsula Soil	
Year	Percentage of Sulfur in Sediment
500	6%
600	5%
700	7%
800	15%
900	15%
1000	4%
1100	3%
1200	3%

Source: "Drought and the Ancient Maya Civilization." ncdc.noaa.gov.
Higher sulfur content in sediment indicates drier conditions.

8. Which of these statements about the 800s and 900s does the data support?

(A) Mayan cities probably suffered from drought.

(B) Mayan cities probably increased food exports.

(C) Moche cities probably raised fewer alpaca.

(D) Moche cities probably experienced increased flooding.

9. Which conclusion does the table best support?

(A) Immigration to the region increased during the ninth century

(B) Population decline began around the year 1000.

(C) Population of the region began to increase after the year 1000.

(D) Interregional trade peaked in the ninth and tenth centuries.

10. By the tenth century, what demographic phenomena was happening in the Yucatan peninsula?

(A) People were immigrating to South America.

(B) Citizens were abandoning the cities for the countryside.

(C) Mayan cities were growing in size.

(D) Diseases were spreading rapidly in the region.

CONTINUITY AND CHANGE-OVER-TIME ESSAY QUESTIONS

Directions: You are to answer the following question. You should spend 5 minutes organizing or outlining your essay. Write an essay that:

- Has a relevant thesis and supports that thesis with appropriate historical evidence.
- Addresses all parts of the question.
- Uses world historical context to show continuities and changes over time.
- Analyzes the process of continuity and change over time.

1. Analyze continuity and change in the size of Mayan cities between 1500 B.C.E. and 1000 C.E. and why this is significant.

Questions for Additional Practice

2. Analyze the continuities and changes in the societies and cultures of Mesoamerica from the Olmec through the Mayans.

3. Analyze the continuities and changes in the influence of geography on the Chavin and the Moche in the centuries prior to 700 C.E. .

COMPARATIVE ESSAY QUESTIONS

Directions: You are to answer the following question. You should spend 5 minutes organizing or outlining your essay. Write an essay that:

- Has a relevant thesis and supports that thesis with appropriate historical evidence.
- Addresses all parts of the question.
- Makes direct, relevant comparisons.
- Analyzes relevant reasons for similarities and differences.

1. Compare how the governments in the Andes and in Mesoamerica between 600 C.E. and 1200 C.E. controlled their citizens using ONE of the following:
   - trade
   - religion

Questions for Additional Practice

2. Compare how people interacted with the environment in the early civilizations of the Americas and among the Austronesian peoples of the Pacific Islands.

3. Compare the Mayan civilization with Han China in TWO of the following areas:
   - government
   - religion and art
   - culture

THINK AS A HISTORIAN: RECOGNIZE HISTORICAL INTERPRETATIONS

To interpret is not only to state facts, but also to explain the meaning and impact of those facts. Historians interpret facts by putting them into context and connecting them with other information, not just letting them stand isolated on their own. Often, interpretation is rooted in a comparison. To say a city was small, or a battle was influential, or an individual was powerful suggests a comparison with other cities, battles, or individuals. *Which TWO of the following are the best examples of interpreting facts?*

1. Around 1500 B.C., the Mayans began to establish settlements.

2. Pyramids were up to 200 feet high—as tall as a 20-story building.

3. Unlike Egyptian women, Mayan women could be priests.

4. Today, more than seven million people speak Mayan languages.

WRITE AS A HISTORIAN: REVIEW THE MAIN POINTS

Use words such as *significant* and *paramount* to cue readers that you are making an important point. *Which word in each statement suggests that the statement is making a main point?*

1. The most prominent early centers of civilization in the Americas were the Chavin and the Moche in the Andes, and the Olmecs, Mayan, and Aztecs in Mesoamerica.

2. Historians today believe the Moche civilization vanished primarily because of climate change—30 years of rain followed by 30 years of drought.

3. Teotihuacan thrived for several key reasons: a strong government, a large population, orderly growth, and superb natural resources.

4. Mayan farming was successful due to these crucial techniques: slash-and-burn agriculture, the terracing of fields to limit erosion, swamp draining, and the building of irrigation systems.

PERIOD 2: Review

Thematic Review

Directions: Briefly answer each question in paragraph form.

1. **Interaction Between Humans and the Environment** Compare how geographic factors affected unification in Greece and in Rome.

2. **Development and Interaction of Cultures** How did religion influence other aspects of culture in Greece, the Gupta Empire in India, and the Mayan civilization?

3. **State-Building, Expansion, and Conflict** Compare the ways two of these leaders administered their empires: Alexander the Great, Augustus Caesar, and Ashoka Maurya.

4. **State-Building, Expansion, and Conflict** Analyze the similarities and differences between Mayan city-states and those in Greece.

5. **Creation, Expansion, and Interaction of Economic Systems** Explain how the Silk Roads were connected to sea-based trade routes in the Indian Ocean and Mediterranean Sea.

6. **Development and Transformation of Social Structures** How did the Indian caste system compare with the social hierarchy in Rome?

TURNING POINT: WHY C. 600 C.E.?

Historians today often use 600 C.E. to mark the end of what some call the Classical Era in world history. By that date, the last of the several great empires of Eurasia had collapsed and been transformed. This date was also just before the rise of Islam and the expanded cultural interactions that occurred as a result of Islamic conquests and trade. The period after 600 was also marked by renewed importance of the Middle East.

However, many earlier European historians who focused on the importance of the Roman Empire chose the fall of the Western Empire in 476 C.E. as the key turning point. Historians of the Americas would likely choose a later date between 700 and 900 C.E. when the Moche and Mayan civilizations declined.

DOCUMENT-BASED QUESTION

Direction: The following question is based on the accompanying Documents 1–10. (The documents have been edited for the purpose of this exercise.)

This question is designed to test your ability to work with and understand historical documents. Write an essay that:

- Has a relevant thesis and supports that thesis with evidence from the document.
- Uses all of the documents.
- Analyzes the documents by grouping them in as many appropriate ways as possible. Does not simply summarize the documents individually.
- Takes into account the sources of the documents and analyzes the author's point of view.
- Identifies and explains the need for at least one additional type of document.

You may refer to relevant historical information not mentioned in the documents.

1. Using the following documents, compare and contrast the factors that made Cyrus the Great and King Ashoka successful rulers. Explain how another type of document could help you analyze the reasons behind these two rulers' success.

Document 1

> **Source:** The Cyrus Cylinder, written in Babylonian script, describing Cyrus's conquest of Babylon in 539 B.C.
>
> My vast troops marched peaceably in Babylon, and the whole of [Sumer] and Akkad had nothing to fear. I sought the welfare of the city of Babylon and all its sanctuaries. As for the population of Babylon . . . I soothed their weariness, I freed them from their bonds. . . .
>
> All kings who sit on thrones, from every quarter, from the Upper Sea to the Lower Sea, those who inhabit remote districts and the kings of the land of Amurru who live in tents, all of them, brought their weighty tribute into Shuanna, and kissed my feet. From Shuanna I sent back to their places to the city of Ashur and Susa, Akkad, the land of Eshnunna, the city of Zamban, the city of Meturnu, Der, as far as the border of the land of Qutu—the sanctuaries across the river Tigris—whose shrines had earlier become dilapidated, the gods who lived therein, and made permanent sanctuaries for them . . . .

Document 2

Source: A Jewish historian, Josephus, writing in the first century C.E., describing the departure of the Jews from Babylon.

"KING CYRUS TO SISINNES AND SATHRABUZANES SENDETH GREETING.

I have given leave to as many of the Jews that dwell in my country as please to return to their own country, and to rebuild their city, and to build the temple of God at Jerusalem on the same place where it was before. I have also sent my treasurer Mithridates, and Zorobabel, the governor of the Jews, that they may lay the foundations of the temple, and may build it sixty cubits high, and of the same latitude, making three edifices of polished stones, and one of the wood of the country, and the same order extends to the altar whereon they offer sacrifices to God. I require also that the expenses for these things may be given out of my revenues.

Document 3

Source: a Greek historian, Xenophon, writing in the fourth century B.C.E. about Cyrus the Great.

[Cyrus speaking to his father Cambyses] As for enforcing obedience, I hope I have had some training in that already; you began my education yourself when I was a child by teaching me to obey you, and then you handed me over to masters who did as you had done, and afterwards, when we were lads, my fellows and myself, there was nothing on which the governors laid more stress. Our laws themselves, I think, enforce this double lesson:—'Rule thou and be thou ruled.' And when I come to study the secret of it all, I seem to see that the real incentive to obedience lies in the praise and honor that it wins against the discredit and the chastisement which fall on the disobedient.

Document 4

Source: a Greek historian, Xenophon, writing in the 4th century B.C.E. about Cyrus the Great.

And he would bring more modesty, he hoped, into the hearts of all men if it were plain that he himself reverenced all the world and would never say a shameful word to any man or woman or do a shameful deed. . . . And his people, he thought, would learn to obey if it were plain that he honored frank and prompt obedience even above virtues that made a grander show and were harder to attain. Such was his belief, and his practice went with it to the end.

Document 5

Source: a Greek historian, Xenophon, writing in the fourth century B.C.E. about Cyrus the Great.

So it was that Cyrus called a council and spoke as follows: "Gentlemen and friends of mine, you are aware that we have garrisons and commandants in the cities we conquered, stationed there at the time. I left them with orders simply to guard the fortifications and not meddle with anything else. Now I do not wish to remove them from their commands, for they have done their duty nobly, but I propose to send others, satraps, who will govern the inhabitants, receive the tribute, give the garrisons their pay, and discharge all necessary dues." . . .

With these words he assigned houses and districts to many of his friends among the lands he had subdued: and to this day their descendants possess the estates, although they reside at court themselves. "Now," he added, "we must choose for the satraps who are to go abroad persons who will not forget to send us anything of value in their districts, so that we who are at home may share in all the wealth of the world. For if any danger comes, it is we who must ward it off."

Document 6

Source: Edict 3 of King Ashoka, 257 B.C.E.

Twelve years after my coronation this has been ordered—Everywhere in my domain the Yuktas, the Rajjukas and the Pradesikas shall go on inspection tours every five years for the purpose of Dhamma instruction and also to conduct other business. Respect for mother and father is good, generosity to friends, acquaintances, relatives, Brahmans and ascetics is good, not killing living beings is good, moderation in spending and moderation in saving is good.

Document 7

Source: Edict 5 of King Ashoka, 257 B.C.E.

In the past there were no Dhamma Mahamatras but such officers were appointed by me thirteen years after my coronation. Now they work among all religions for the establishment of Dhamma, for the promotion of Dhamma, and for the welfare and happiness of all who are devoted to Dhamma. . . . They (Dhamma Mahamatras) work for the proper treatment of prisoners, towards their unfettering, and if the Mahamatras think, "This one has a family to support," "That one has been bewitched," "This one is old," then they work for the release of such prisoners.

Document 8

Source: Edict 6 of King Ashoka, 257 B.C.E.

In the past, state business was not transacted nor were reports delivered to the king at all hours. But now I have given this order, that at any time, whether I am eating, in the women's quarters, the bed chamber, the chariot, the palanquin, in the park or wherever, reporters are to be posted with instructions to report to me the affairs of the people so that I might attend to these affairs wherever I am.

Document 9

Source: Edict 12 of King Ashoka, 257 B.C.E.

Beloved-of-the-Gods, King Piyadasi, honors both ascetics and the householders of all religions, and he honors them with gifts and honors of various kinds. But Beloved-of-the-Gods, King Piyadasi, does not value gifts and honors as much as he values this—that there should be growth in the essentials of all religions. Growth in essentials can be done in different ways, but all of them have as their root restraint in speech, that is, not praising one's own religion, or condemning the religion of others without good cause. And if there is cause for criticism, it should be done in a mild way.

Document 10

Source: Edict 13 of King Ashoka, 257 B.C.E.

Beloved-of-the-Gods, King Piyadasi, conquered the Kalingas eight years after his coronation.[25] One hundred and fifty thousand were deported, one hundred thousand were killed and many more died (from other causes). After the Kalingas had been conquered, Beloved-of-the-Gods came to feel a strong inclination towards the Dhamma, a love for the Dhamma and for instruction in Dhamma. Now Beloved-of-the-Gods feels deep remorse for having conquered the Kalingas. Indeed, Beloved-of-the-Gods is deeply pained by the killing, dying and deportation that take place when an unconquered country is conquered.

PERIOD 3: Regional and Transregional Interactions, c. 600 C.E. to c. 1450

Chapter 7 Byzantine Empire and Kievan Rus

Chapter 8 Islamic World Through 1450

Chapter 9 Expansion of African Trade

Chapter 10 East Asia in the Post-Classical Period

Chapter 11 South Asia and Southeast Asia, 600-1450 C.E.

Chapter 12 Western Europe after Rome, 400-1450 C.E.

Chapter 13 The Mongols and Transregional Empires

Chapter 14 The Americas on the Eve of Globalization

Period Overview

Large empires, often rooted in revivals of core and foundational cultures that had developed in earlier history, emerged after 600 C.E. Though Rome had fallen under the power of non-Romans, most of the empire once ruled from there continued, with a new name, the Byzantine Empire. The capital moved to the city of Constantinople. In eastern Europe, the city of Kiev became the capital of an empire blending Slavic and Scandinavian influences and based on the prosperous trade between the Baltic Sea in the north and the Black Sea in the south. Following the teachings of Muhammad, followers of Islam carried their faith quickly throughout southern Asia and parts of Africa and Europe. They created centers of great intellectual achievement in Baghdad and Spain. In Africa, increased trade across the Sahara and along the east coast pulled Africa more deeply into global trade than ever before.

The revival of a united China resulted in great prosperity and innovation under the Tang and Song dynasties. While India was often divided, it had periods of unity and prosperity, and new trade-based empires emerged in Southeast Asia. In the 1200s, the Mongols, a group of Central Asia nomads, emerged and conquered lands from central Europe to the Pacific Ocean, creating the largest land empire in human history. While the conquest came with great devastation, the unity of so much territory under the rule of one group allowed trade to flourish once again across Eurasia, with new ideas and technology spreading easily.

In the Americas, the two regions that had produced large regional empires in early periods did so again. The Aztecs in Mesoamerica created a loose federation of cultural groups under their control, while the Incas in the Andes created a more united empire, one linked by extensive trade.

Key Concepts

3.1 Expansion and Intensification of Communication and Exchange Networks

    I. Improved transportation technologies and commercial practices led to an increased volume of trade, and expanded the geographical range of existing and newly active trade networks.

    II. The movement of peoples caused environmental and linguistic effects.

    III. Cross-cultural exchanges were fostered by the intensification of existing, or the creation of new, networks of trade and communication.

    IV. There was continued diffusion of crops and pathogens throughout the Eastern Hemisphere along the trade routes.

3.2 Continuity and Innovation of State Forms and Their Interactions

    I. Empires collapsed and were reconstituted; in some regions, new state forms emerged.

    II. Interregional contacts and conflicts between states and empires encouraged significant technological and cultural transfers.

3.3 Increased Economic Productive Capacity and Its Consequences

    I. Innovations stimulated agricultural and industrial production in many regions.

    II. The fate of cities varied greatly, with periods of significant decline, and with periods of increased urbanization buoyed by rising productivity and expanding trade networks.

    III. Despite significant continuities in social structures and in methods of production, there were also some important changes in labor management and in the effect of religious conversion on gender relations and family life.

Source: *AP® World History Course and Exam Description.*

7

Byzantine Empire and Kievan Rus

"Justice is the constant and perpetual wish to render every one his due. The maxims of law are these: to live honestly, to hurt no one, and to give every man his due."

—*Corpus Iuris Civilis*

By 330 C.E., the eastern half of the Roman Empire had become wealthier and more important than the western half. Thus, Emperor Constantine made the city of *Byzantium* the capital of the empire and renamed it *Constantinople* in his own honor. Today, this city is known as Istanbul. Later, in 395, the Roman Empire was divided administratively into completely separate empires, a western one ruled from Rome and an eastern one ruled from Constantinople. As explained in Chapter 4, the western empire declined until it was taken over by German invaders in 476. However, the eastern half, the *Byzantine Empire* grew and prospered.

The capital and cultural center of the Byzantine Empire, Constantinople was located on the European side of the *Bosporus Strait*. That narrow body of water connects the Black Sea and the Sea of Marmara, which in turn connects to the Mediterranean. The city's location made a center of trade connecting Europe and Asia. This brought the city great wealth, and made it a blending of strong European and Asian influences.

The Byzantine Empire

As the map shows, by 527 C.E., the Byzantine Empire stretched over large swaths of the lands bordering the Mediterranean, including North Africa, Spain, Italy, Greece and the rest of the Balkans, and Southwest Asia. In addition to the capital of Constantinople and its surroundings, the empire also controlled the city of Rome.

As the wealthy capital of an expanding empire, Constantinople faced attacks from Germanic invaders. That is why strong, wide stone walls were built around Constantinople. Similar defenses were strengthened in other Byzantine cities. The Byzantines fought repeated battles on their eastern border with the powerful Sassanid Empire based in Persia. The two empires fought for control of land in Asia Minor and Syria.

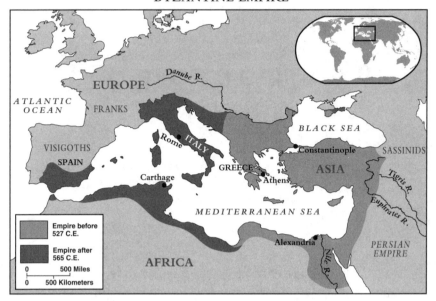

BYZANTINE EMPIRE

- Empire before 527 C.E.
- Empire after 565 C.E.

0   500 Miles
0   500 Kilometers

Byzantine Government The Byzantine government was highly centralized. A vast imperial bureaucracy brought continuity to the empire even during periods of unrest and war. Although the empire enjoyed comparatively long periods of peace, it did experience instability, mostly caused by power struggles over succession to the throne.

Justinian the Great Along with his wife Empress Theodora, Emperor *Justinian I* (ruled 527–565) oversaw a revitalization of Constantinople. Most notably, a Christian church called *Hagia Sophia* was expanded, and its large dome became a focal point of the city's architecture. According to legend, when a Russian visitor in the tenth century saw the spectacular church, he commented, "There God dwells among men."

Another of Justinian's significant contributions was the revival of the legal traditions of Rome. Justinian's collection of laws was called the *Corpus Iuris Civilis* (*Body of Civil Law*), although it is often referred to simply as the Justinian code. The code remained a foundation of legal knowledge in Europe until the nineteenth century. (Test Prep: Write a paragraph comparing Justinian with another leader who codified the law, Hammurabi. See page 21.)

Under Justinian, the Byzantine Empire expanded its territory. In the east, Byzantine forces under General Belisarius defeated the Sassanids. This established the eastern border of the empire. In the west, the Byzantines conquered parts of North Africa, southern Spain, Sicily, and Italy. The expansion, however, was expensive. The Byzantine Empire was nearly bankrupt by the time Justinian died in 565.

Byzantium after Justinian After Justinian's reign, the borders of the Byzantine Empire contracted. *Bulgars* (Turkic people originally from Central

Asia) took over much of the Balkans. Germanic tribes reoccupied much of Italy. Arab peoples took over Syria, Egypt, and the rest of North Africa, spreading the Islamic faith. The Islamic forces put Constantinople under siege twice, but the Byzantines were able to hold them off. In the 800s and later, the Byzantine Empire was able to expand again. (Test Prep: Write a paragraph connecting the Byzantine Empire with later events in the Balkans, see page 355.)

Heraclius Unlike previous Byzantine emperors, *Heraclius* (ruled 610 to 641) spoke Greek rather than Latin. During his reign, the attention of the empire was largely focused toward the east and resisting numerous invasions from Islamic forces in the Near East and Sassanid forces in Asia Minor. Although Heraclius never attained complete victory over the invaders, he did manage to greatly reduce the power and influence of the Sassanids in Southwest Asia.

Leo III Conflicts between the Byzantine Empire and Islamic forces continued into the next dynasty, known as the Syrian, which took power in 717. The first Syrian ruler, Leo III (ruled 717 to 740), defeated and reclaimed much of the Near Eastern territory lost by his predecessor, and gained additional lands in Asia Minor.

Source: Thinkstock

Source: The Walters Art Museum

Three neighboring faiths developed various traditions about the portrayal of people in art. Fearful that people would worship art as a false idol, many Islamic artists portrayed no people at all (above, left). In contrast, Roman Catholic artists often portrayed Jesus (above, right). Orthodox artists showed the influence of both traditions, while some focused on non-religious figures, such as Queen Theodora (below).

Source: Dreamstime

Leo III's greatest impact was on religion. He instituted a controversial policy of *iconoclasm*, the practice of opposing the veneration of religious images and icons. In this policy, he may have been influenced by Islam, which had a strong tradition against realistic renderings of religious figures such as Jesus and the prophet Muhammad. Leo III ordered all images and paintings in churches be either covered or destroyed. Opposition to his policy was strongest among monks in the Byzantine Empire, and it was not accepted by the popes.

Basil II Ruling from 976 to 1025, Basil II resumed the successful expansion of the Byzantine Empire started by Justinian four centuries earlier. In the Balkans, Byzantine forces defeated the Bulgars at the *Battle of Kleidion* in 1014. He also conquered some territory in eastern Asia Minor.

Religion The Byzantine Empire was a *theocracy*, meaning that there was no separation between the state and the church. The religious leaders were essentially a department of the government. The emperor appointed the head of the church (the *patriarch*) and sometimes even dictated what sermons should be delivered to local congregations. (Test Prep: Write a paragraph comparing the role of religion in Byzantium and in China. See page 182.)

Many *monasteries* and other religious communities were founded throughout the Byzantine Empire during the 300s and 400s. Monks and nuns lived in these centers of prayer and work. They provided aid to the people in times of natural disasters. The monasteries did not become centers of scholarship and education, however, as those in Western Europe did. As mentioned earlier, most monks and nuns opposed iconoclasm; they wanted to keep the icons in churches and monasteries.

The Byzantine Empire believed strongly in proselytizing, spreading their faith to others. They sent Christian missionaries abroad in hopes of converting nonbelievers such as the Bulgars and Moravians in Central Europe.

The Missionary Cyril The most famous and successful missionary was named Cyril. In about 863, Cyril created his own alphabet, which was loosely based on Greek, to help him spread not only the word of God but also literacy in general. This Cyrillic alphabet was adopted by Russians and people who spoke many of the Slavic languages—the family of languages used in Eastern Europe. The tradition of Christianity practiced in the Byzantine Empire, which later became known as the Eastern Orthodox tradition, continues to be practiced in much of Eastern Europe today, even though the empire dissolved centuries ago.

Conflict with Rome Over time, tensions increased between the Eastern wing of the church in the Byzantine Empire and the Western wing, centered in Rome. The controversy over Leo III's iconoclastic policy was just one point of contention between the two branches. There was also disagreement over the authority of the Pope, and over whether Rome was the central city of Christendom. Tensions came to a head in 1054, when a *schism,* or separation, split the Roman Catholic Church in Western Europe and the *Eastern Orthodox Church* in Southeastern Europe and Russia. (Test Prep: Write an outline comparing the schism of 1054 with the Reformation. See page 278.)

AFRO-EURASIAN TRADE NETWORKS

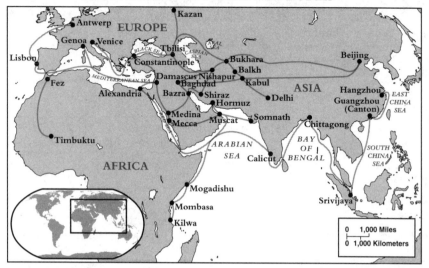

Trade and Prosperity A major reason the Byzantine Empire endured for almost a thousand years was its strong economy. Due to the location of Constantinople, trade flourished with lands bordering the Mediterranean, with Northern Europe, and with China and India via the Silk Roads. There was so much Byzantine trade that people around the Mediterranean used a Byzantine gold coin as a common currency.

In addition, silk weaving developed as an important industry in the empire as early as 550, again adding fuel to Byzantium's economy. The government regulated this industry in order to prevent the formation of business monopolies.

The Byzantine economy also had a strong agricultural component. The labor was provided by peasants, most of whom were not free. They could not leave the land of their landowner because of either laws that prohibited it or debts that they could not pay to their landlord. From time to time, the Byzantine government tried to break this bond. The government's *theme system* offered peasants their freedom if they agreed to join the imperial military service. Also, the emperors mandated limits as to how much land any one landlord could own.

Concentration of Wealth Imperial efforts to create an agricultural economy with many small landowners were not successful. Land became concentrated in the hands of fewer and fewer people, which led to increasing peasant revolts. In addition, as landowners became more powerful, they were able to resist tax collections more easily than could small landowners. As a result, tax income declined, weakening the Byzantine government.

Free Peasant Revolts Free peasants were one step above peasants in the economic hierarchy. They were "free" in that they contracted with landowners and paid rent for the land they worked. They were one of the main sources of taxes and recruits for the government. Periodically, the nobility tried to force free peasants into peasant status to increase their income or land holdings. Predictably, such tactics sparked revolts, including one led by Basil the Copper Hand (928–932) and one led by Ivaylo (1277–1280).

Afro-Eurasian Trade Goods		
Trade Center	**Imports**	**Exports**
Novgorod (Russia)	Spices, silk, steel, horses, jewels	Furs, honey, wax, wool, linens, slaves
Timbuktu (Africa)	Textiles, horses	Salt, gold, slaves
Swahili city-states (Africa)	Porcelain, jewelry, glass, textiles	Ivory, exotic animals, gold, slaves, cotton, glass beads
Hangzhou (China)	Cotton, wool, ivory, gold, silver	Silk, rice, spices, porcelain, tea, paper
Calicut (India)	Horses, glassware, porcelain, satin	Spices, jewels, gold, cotton, silk
Baghdad (Arabia)	Textiles, slaves, porcelain	Textiles, leather, paper, books
Melaka (Indonesia)	Porcelain, paper, textiles, sugar, salt	Rice, pepper, spices, tin, aromatic woods
Venice (Italy)	Spices, silk, jewels	Metals, salt, wheat, wines, oils

The Arts Arts, literature, and education flourished during the Byzantine Empire. They were nearly all religious in nature. Literature of the period focused on the importance of seeking salvation by obeying God's will. Books and songs were written detailing the lives of Jesus and Mary, as well as a large number of Christian saints. Fine artists were likewise focused on devotional work, such as icons and mosaics depicting Christian themes and *illuminated manuscripts* of the Bible, which were elaborately decorated with colored illustrations and flecked with silver and gold. Byzantine art proved highly influential on later generations, both in Europe and in Islamic cultures.

Education Education during the Byzantine Empire was likewise dominated by religion. Schools run by the Eastern Orthodox Church taught a wide variety of subjects, including philosophy, math, medicine, and law—all with a religious point of view. The *University of Constantinople* was founded in 850; many of its students were trained for service in the vast Byzantine bureaucracy, while others focused on copying the classical writings from Ancient Greece and Rome.

Life in the City The city of Constantinople, wealthy from its position as a trade center, became known for the lavish homes of its aristocrats, its beautiful churches, and the impressive imperial palace. Like Rome, even the common people went to public baths. Other gathering spots were restaurants, taverns, and the *Hippodrome,* a large stadium like the Coliseum in the Rome. The other large cities of the Byzantine Empire, such as Antioch, Thessalonica, and Trebizond, had similar attractions, but none had an imperial palace and none rivaled Constantinople in grandeur.

Decline and Fall The expenses of constant conflict on both its eastern and western borders, combined with the reluctance of the wealthy to pay taxes and the unrest among the common people, slowly undermined the strength of the Byzantine Empire. The declining strength can be seen in a series of military defeats spread out over four centuries. In 1071, a group that originated in the steppes of central Asia known as the Seljuk Turks defeated Byzantine forces in the *Battle of Manzikert*. After this defeat, the Turks gradually took more and more territory in Asia Minor.

Around that same time, Byzantine forces clashed with a new power in the Mediterranean—the *Normans* from northern France. The Normans took control of Sicily and southern Italy from the Byzantines in 1071. (For more about the Normans and their invasion of England in 1066, see Chapter 12.)

Another major setback for the Byzantines came in the early 1200s. As you will read later, in 1095, the Byzantine Emperor Alexius I asked the pope to call upon Roman Catholics in Western Europe to help fight against the Turks in the region of the Middle East called the Levant, an area many Christians called the "Holy Land." The result was a series of military expeditions, called the *Crusades,* in which knights and commoners from Western Europe traveled to the Levant with hopes of seizing control for Christianity. During the Fourth Crusade (1202–1204), soldiers from Western Europe gathered in the Italian city of Venice to prepare to sail to the Levant. However, the Venetians persuaded, or possibly coerced, crusading European knights to sack their trading rivals in Constantinople first.

The Byzantine Empire continued to shrink. By the fifteenth century, the remnant of the empire was concentrated solely in Europe. In 1453, the Ottoman Turks, who had replaced the Seljuk Turks in western Asia Minor, conquered Constantinople, marking the end of the Byzantine Empire.

Slavic Peoples and the Origins of Russia

Historians know little about the earliest history of the Slavs. They originally populated the steppes to the northeast of the Black Sea. By about 500 B.C.E., three identifiable Slavic-language groups began to emerge:

- East Slavic, which evolved into Ukrainian and Russian

- West Slavic, which evolved into Polish, Slovak, and Czech

- South Slavic, which evolved into Serbian, Croatian, and Slovenian

At first, the Slavs lived a hunter-forager lifestyle, which was dictated by their environment. In the forested north, the soil in the area was fertile, but the growing season was short. By contrast, the steppes to the south enjoyed a longer growing season but the land was too tough to plow with existing technology.

The Rise of Kievan Rus The East Slavs made contact with people of Northern Europe known as *Vikings* around 800. As you will read in Chapter 12, the Vikings expanded from their homeland in Scandinavia west into England, south into Western Europe, and east into Slavic territory. They moved south and east along river routes, including Europe's fourth longest river, the extensive

Dnieper River, flowing from Russia, Belarus, and the Ukraine to the Black Sea. By the end of the ninth century, the Vikings had taken control of the area and ruled over the Eastern Slavs. Viking rulers were called *Rus*, a word that later became the source of the name *Russia*. In the early 900s, under the Viking ruler *Oleg*, a settlement on the Dnieper River became the Principality of Kiev (see the map), also called *Kievan Rus.*

Kievan Rus was essentially a collection of city-states, which were allowed to govern themselves as long as they paid tribute to the main ruler, the Grand Prince of Kiev. Ruling Kievan Rus was a council of *boyars,* or nobles. The boyars elected the prince of Kievan Rus when a vacancy occurred and served as a war council during times of conflict. Since the boyars represented the people they governed, the system is sometimes considered an early form of democracy. However, membership in this council was limited to Viking military leaders.

KIEVAN RUS, 750 TO 1130

Kiev Converts to Christianity As discussed above, the Byzantine Empire sent missionaries to convert the people of Kievan Rus to Orthodox Christianity. These conversion attempts were motivated not only by the basic desire to spread the religion, but also by worries that an organized, pagan Kievan Rus would present a potential political threat to the empire.

Conversion formally succeeded in 989, when Prince Vladimir I ("the Great," ruled 980–1015) of Kievan Rus married the sister of the Byzantine emperor. As part of the agreement, Vladimir had to convert to Orthodox Christianity, as did all of his subjects. With Eastern Orthodox Christianity thus established as its official religion, Kievan Rus became increasingly linked to the empire, both culturally and politically. Byzantine advisers, priests, and teachers were sent to Kiev. Hundreds of wooden onion-dome churches were built, in imitation of the style of Byzantine churches, and the monastic tradition came to Kievan Rus. In terms of politics, the imperial control of the church became widely accepted in Russia. Despite the conversion of the ruling elite in Kievan Rus, pagan traditions survived among the peasants for centuries.

The Golden Age of Kievan Rus The "golden age" of Kievan Rus took place during the tenth and eleventh centuries, when the civilization enjoyed both a strong government and a cohesive society. The first great leader of the Golden Age was Vladimir I, the ruler who oversaw the conversion of Kievan Rus to Christianity. He also expanded the western border of his kingdom. The second great leader was Vladimir's son, Yaroslav I (ruled 1019–1054). He is known as Yaroslav the Wise because he promoted education, and he codified the legal system, *Russkaya Pravda* ("Russian Justice").

The Slave Trade The rulers of Kievan Rus engaged in some trade with Baghdad to the southeast and Baltic ports to the northwest. The major trading partner, however, was the Byzantine Empire. The Kievan princes organized annual expeditions to Constantinople to sell honey, hides, furs, and timber, but mostly to sell slaves. Kievan Rus had no agricultural surplus; indeed, they had more people than they could support. So each fall, the princes would demand tribute from various Kievan towns and agricultural areas, calling for a certain number of peasants from each community to be sent to Kiev as slaves. The slaves were then transported to Constantinople by boats on the annual trade expedition. (Test Prep: Write a paragraph comparing slavery in Kievan Rus to slavery in Africa. See page 171.)

In return for slaves, the Kievan princes received gold coins and other riches of the Byzantine Empire. When the princes were not satisfied with these exchanges (as in 860, 907, and 1043), they sent naval expeditions to raid Constantinople.

The Decline of Kiev The increasing dependence of Kievan Rus on the Byzantine Empire proved to be its undoing. Kievan trade delegations found it hard to reach Constantinople due to the invasion of nomadic groups from central Asia, such as the Pechenegs of the steppe south of Kiev. As Byzantium's economic fortunes declined, so too did Kiev's. In 1169, northern Russian princes took advantage of Kiev's weakness by sacking the city. They did so again in 1204.

Less than forty years later, in 1240, Kiev was invaded by the largest and most powerful group from Central Asia, the Mongols, who took over and stayed for almost 250 years. During this period, the so-called Khanate of the Golden Horde occupied the steppe and exacted tribute from those Russian princes living in the forests to the north. The Mongols were not interested in occupying the forests, preferring the grassy steppe for their grazing herds of horses. By the time the Mongols were finally defeated by Russian forces, the Byzantine Empire had fallen. (The Mongols are discussed in more detail on page 241.)

Novgorod One of the largest city-states in northern Kievan Rus was Novgorod. According to legend, Novgorod was founded by a Scandinavian, Rurik, in the tenth century. An influx of German merchants, Finns, Swedes, and Slavs over four centuries created a multicultural city with a population of around 400,000. Novgorod prospered through trade, connecting the Baltic Sea and Black Sea regions along the Volga and Dneiper river routes. Products traded included furs, honey, and tar produced in the north; cloth and metals from farther west in Europe; and grains from farther east in Russia. Novgorod's growth was representative of the growth of many cities between 800 and 1300. During this period, a warming climate caused agricultural productivity to increase, which resulted in greater surplus goods for trade. Novgorod became independent from Kievan Rus in the twelfth century. However, like many cities in this era, it was eventually absorbed by a growing empire. In the fifteenth century, a newly organized Russian empire would seize control of Novgorod.

HISTORICAL PERSPECTIVES: WAS JUSTINIAN NOBLE OR RUTHLESS?

One of the first writers to evaluate Justinian was Procopius, who was a top advisor to Justinian's top military leader, Belisarius. In his extensive public writings, Procopius praised Justinian as a capable and honorable leader. However, he also wrote *Secret History,* a scathing account of Justinian and his rule. This account remained hidden until long after the death of Procopius. It was finally published in 1623. The disparity between the public and private writings of Procopius leaves many questions. Was the *Secret History* the truth that Procopius was unwilling to publish because he knew it would destroy his career? Was it a work of jealousy that should not be taken seriously? Was it simply an example of how leaders appears flawed to those who know them best?

For the next several hundred years, European historians generally praised Justinian. Like him, they were living in a world in which leaders were praised for expanding their borders, especially to spread Christianity. Otto of Freising, a twelfth-century German bishop writing during the Crusades called Justinian a "most zealous and Christian monarch" who "triumphed gloriously."

As historians focused more on non-religious forces in history, they praised him less for expanding Christian territory and more for his reforms, such as his law code that standardized legal practice in the empire. Some historians have become more critical. For example, Peter Heather, in *The Restoration of Rome: Barbarian Popes and Imperial Pretenders,* attacks Justinian's style of rule as "authoritarianly chaotic," and his actions as brutal. "By Roman or indeed any standards, Justinian was an autocratic [ruler] of the worst kind. It worried him not a jot to slaughter his own citizens in huge numbers to keep himself in power, not to launch speculative attacks on neighboring states with much the same end in mind, no matter what the collateral damage."

KEY TERMS BY THEME

STATE-BUILDING
Byzantium
Corpus Juris Civilis
Heraclius
Basil II
Battle of Kleidion
Byzantine Empire
Justinian I, "the Great"
Battle of Manzikert
Crusades
Fourth Crusade
Normans
Slavs
Vikings
Rus

CULTURE
Leo III iconoclastic
    policy
iconoclast
Hagia Sophia
theocracy
patriarch
monasteries
Cyril
schism
Eastern Orthodox
    Church
theme system
Cyrillic alphabet
illuminated
    manuscripts
Bulgars

University of
    Constantinople

SOCIAL STRUCTURE
Hippodrome
Oleg
Dnieper River
Kievan Rus
boyars
Prince Vladimir I, "the
    Great"
Yaroslav I, "the Wise"
Russkaya Pravda

ENVIRONMENT
Constantinople
Bosporus Strait

MULTIPLE-CHOICE QUESTIONS

1. One difference between the government in Constantinople and the government of Rome was that only the Byzantine Empire

    (A) was ruled by a theocracy

    (C) had a unified body of laws

    (C) traded with more regions in Asia and Eastern Europe

    (D) gave basic rights to women

Question 2 refers to the following excerpt.

Oh, justice! The deed of the supreme high priest! Nay, of one who claimed to be the leader of the whole world as indeed the Latins assert and believe, but this, too, is a bit of their boasting. For when the imperial seat was transferred from Rome hither to our native Queen of Cities, and the senate and the whole administration, there was also transferred the arch-hieratical primacy.

—From "The Alexiad," written by Anna Comnena
in the twelfth century.

2. The transfer described in the passage probably refers to

    (A) a transfer in cultural leadership from Rome to the Normans

    (B) an increase in trade between Rome and Kievan Rus

    (C) a decrease in Rome's prosperity during the Crusades

    (D) a shift of power from Rome to Constantinople

Questions 3 and 4 refer to the following table.

Byzantine Empire Budget		
Year	Budget for Soldiers' Pay (in millions of Byzantine gold coins)	Total Budget (in millions of Byzantine gold coins)
300	5.0	9.4
450	2.2	7.8
518	3.7	8.5
540	5.1	11.3
565	5.0	8.5
641	1.5	3.7
668	0.7	2.0
775	0.6	1.9
842	1.3	3.1
959	1.9	3.9
1025	3.0	5.9

Source: Adapted from Warren Treadgold, *A History of the Byzantine State and Society.* Stanford: Stanford University Press, 1997. Pages 145, 277, 412, 576.

3. Which statement is best supported by the information in the table above?
   (A) Pay to soldiers usually accounted for more than half of the empire's budget.
   (B) The wealth of the empire reached its peak under Justinian.
   (C) The cost of governing the empire grew steadily between 300 and 1025.
   (D) The salary paid to individual soldiers was higher in 300 than in 450.

4. Which statement is consistent with the evidence in the table?
   (A) The Byzantine government spent heavily on military actions.
   (B) Ivaylo led a revolt by free peassants.
   (C) A schism split the Roman Catholic and Eastern Orthodox Church.
   (D) Leo III led a campaign against icons.

5. The success of both the Byzantine Empire and Kievan Rus shows
   (A) the value of extensive trade along water routes
   (B) the benefits of a powerful military for seizing new territory
   (C) the impact of Viking culture in this era
   (D) the drawbacks of selling people into slavery

6. The Seljuk Turks, the Pechenegs, and the Mongols all
   (A) originated as identifiable groups in the steppes of Central Asia
   (B) adopted Orthodox Christianity through contact with the Byzantine Empire
   (C) fought either for or against the Byzantines at the Battle of Manzikert
   (D) emerged as military powers for the first time in the 900s

7. What do iconoclasm, Heraclius's choice of language, and ideas about theocracy have in common?
   (A) All reflect differences between Rome and Constantinople.
   (B) All were fundamentally political rather than religious issues.
   (C) All were responses to invasions by outsiders.
   (D) All showed the influence of Greek culture.

8. Which statement best explains why Constantinople became so wealthy?
   (A) Constantinople formed an alliance with the wealthier empire of Kievan Rus.
   (B) It carried out successful military conquest against the Sassanids.
   (C) The use of the Justinian Code protected the rich against peasant revolts.
   (D) The city's location on key water routes made it a center of trade.

9. Which event created a long-lasting connection between the Slavic principality of Kievan Rus and the Byzantine Empire?
   (A) The building of a canal connecting the Danube and the Dnieper rivers
   (B) The Russian acceptance of the Eastern Orthodox faith
   (C) Invasions from the west forcing Kiev to ally with Constantinople to the south
   (D) The Byzantine Empire's defeat of Kiev at the Battle of Manzikert

10. Justinian and Yaroslav the Wise are both famous for
   (A) creating a law code that was used in their empires
   (B) expanding their empires through conquest
   (C) being the first people in their lands to convert to Christianity
   (D) uniting separate territories into one empire

CONTINUITY AND CHANGE-OVER-TIME ESSAY QUESTIONS

Directions: You are to answer the following question. You should spend 5 minutes organizing or outlining your essay. Write an essay that:

- Has a relevant thesis and supports that thesis with appropriate historical evidence.
- Addresses all parts of the question.
- Uses world historical context to show continuities and changes over time.
- Analyzes the process of continuity and change over time.

1. Analyze how political transformations in the eastern Mediterranean contributed to continuities and changes in the economy and cultures of the Byzantine Empire during the period c. 500 C.E. to 1450 C.E.

Questions for Additional Practice

2. Analyze continuities and changes in Christianity in Byzantium and Constantinople between c. 200 and 1450.

3. Describe continuities and changes in the relationship between the Byzantine Empire and Kievan Rus from 1000 to 1453.

COMPARATIVE ESSAY QUESTIONS

Directions: You are to answer the following question. You should spend 5 minutes organizing or outlining your essay. Write an essay that:

- Has a relevant thesis and supports that thesis with appropriate historical evidence.
- Addresses all parts of the question.
- Makes direct, relevant comparisons.
- Analyzes relevant reasons for similarities and differences.

1. Compare how the Byzantine Empire perserved Roman ideas with how Rome perserved Classical Greek ideas.

Questions for Additional Practice

2. Compare the power of the Byzantine Empire with ONE of the following:
   - Imperial Rome
   - Han China

3. Compare the development of Constantinople with Novgorod or Athens.

THINK AS A HISTORIAN: SYNTHESIS OF INFORMATION

When synthesizing, you draw together traits to create a whole. When you listen to songs by the same singer, for example, you may hear a common mood or theme that defines his or her distinctive sound. *Which ONE of the following statements is the best example of synthesis?*

1. The strength of the Byzantine Empire was based on its vigorous economy, centralized government, and strong defensive walls.

2. Agricultural labor in the Byzantine Empire was provided by peasants.

3. During the Crusades, knights and commoners from Western Europe traveled to the Levant in hopes of seizing control of the land for Christianity.

4. The Golden Age of Kievan Rus, a collection of city-states, took place during the tenth and eleventh centuries.

WRITE AS A HISTORIAN: WRITE AN EFFECTIVE THESIS

In answering an essay question, include a thesis statement in the introduction that clearly states your argument. The thesis should be stated using specific language and include only information directly relevant to the question. *In the each exercise, choose the more effective thesis statement.*

1. What made the Byzantine Empire so strong?

   a. The Byzantine Empire, based in its capital of Constantinople, thrived because of a combination of political and economic features.

   b. The Byzantine Empire's strong centralized government and diverse economy helped it flourish.

2. What cultures influenced Kievan Rus society?

   a. The Byzantine Empire's religious influence on the Kievan Rus society resulted in a heavy Christian presence in the city-states.

   b. Outside influences can be seen in the religion of Kievan Rus.

3. Compare and contrast the governmental systems of the Byzantine Empire and Kievan Rus culture.

   a. While the Byzantine Empire was led by strong leaders who had consolidated power, Kievan Rus had a Grand Prince who, because of the boyars who ruled in the city-states, was less powerful.

   b. The Byzantine Empire and Kievan Rus differed in their government much the same way that Sparta and Athens differed, with one focused more on its military and one more on cultural achievements.

8

Islamic World Through 1450

Allah will admit those who embrace the true faith and do good works to gardens watered by running streams.

—*The Quran,* Chapter 47

The fastest growing major religion in the world today, Islam, is rooted in faith in one God, Allah, as taught by several prophets. The last of these prophets was *Muhammad* (570–632 C.E.), who lived in the desert lands of the Arabian Peninsula.

In the course of the first century after Muhammad's life, Islam expanded rapidly, reaching from Persia to Spain. Today, Islam remains the predominant religion in the Arab countries of the Middle East and North Africa, as well as in non-Arab countries such as Iran, Pakistan, Indonesia, and Niger.

Pre-Islamic Bedouin Culture

In the sixth century, the *Bedouins* were well established in the Arabian Peninsula. Their culture was mostly nomadic, tribal, and polytheistic. In each clan or tribe, a sheikh ruled with consent of a tribal council. Shaping a sheikh's decisions was a feeling of allegiance to other clans or tribes in the region. *Polygyny,* in which a man has more than one wife at a time, was allowed, partly as a way to care for widows whose husbands had died in raids or warfare.

Although polytheistic, the religion of the Bedouins included worship of a supreme deity: *Allah.* Each tribe had a sacred stone, but the most revered of all was a large black stone at the city of *Mecca.* The entire tribe was a part of the religion, and there was no separate class of priests. Tribal values emphasized honesty and generosity. All of these features—except polytheism—would provide some continuity when incorporated into Islam.

Land trade routes via camels formed the basis of the Arabian economy. When fighting calmed between two nearby empires, the Byzantine to the north and the Sassanid to the north and east, water travel by the Red Sea and Arabian Sea became more popular than overland routes and the Bedouin trade caravans suffered. The Bedouins had to compete with the coastal merchants and traders, whose wealth was growing.

Muhammad and Islam

Muhammad was born into the Bedouin world in 570. He became a caravan manager. In the course of his work, Muhammad regularly came into contact with Christians, Jews, and Zoroastrians. Muhammad married a rich widow in Mecca and settled there. Over the course of many years, he experienced revelations that he attributed to an angel of the deity he referred to as Allah. These revelations were later collected by those who had heard his message in the *Quran* (also spelled *Koran*, meaning "recitation"). Muhammad criticized polytheism, tribal loyalties, and commercial practices in his society. He called for social justice, including alms for the poor.

The Spread of Islam Slowly at first, Muhammad's ideas spread through his preaching. According to tradition, it took Muhammad three years to gather 30 people to follow Allah. Muslims, those who accepted Muhammad's teachings, viewed him as a great prophet, the final one in a line that included Abraham, Moses, and Jesus. But Muslims did not, and do not today, worship Muhammad as divine. This contrasts with the position of Jesus in Christianity, who is considered divine by almost all Christians.

Muhammad's teaching led to conflict with Mecca's existing leaders. They rejected the idea that Muhammad was the agent of the one true deity and began to persecute his kin and those who worshipped Allah. Due to the persecution, Muhammad and his followers fled the city in 622 and escaped to *Medina* (the flight is called the *Hegira*). There he formed the first Muslim community. Muhammad returned ten years later to conquer Mecca and declare the building housed the sacred black stone there—the *Ka'aba*—a shrine of Islam.

During Muhammad's lifetime, most of the Arabian Peninsula was united under Islam. Conditions in Arabia contributed to the rapid spread of Islam. A drought, combined with the desire of the rulers of Islam to extend their trade routes, encouraged the new converts to move out of the Arabian Peninsula. As they moved, they carried their faith with them and introduced it to others. Islam was also expanded through military conquest. But after an area was conquered, Islamic rule was relatively tolerant: No one was forced to convert to the faith. If conquered peoples paid a tax, they could become exempt from military service. The strong allegiance among Arabs to Islam and the egalitarian nature of the religion attracted many new converts.

Core Theological Principles of Muhammad Islam emerged as the third great world religion to come from Southwest Asia. Like the other two, Judaism and Christianity, Islam was a monotheistic faith that honored Abraham and other prophets. Because of these similarities, followers of Islam showed great respect toward these other *People of the Book*. Core theological principles of Islam include: the ideas of salvation and hope of an afterlife; the importance of submission to the will of Allah (the one true God); and a belief in the Quran as the sacred book providing guidance and laws for the followers.

Islam in Practice To put these principles into practice, Muslims have a core set of obligations that have become known as the *Five Pillars*:

1. Believing in only one God—Allah
2. Praying five times daily
3. Giving alms to the poor
4. Fasting during the month of *Ramadan*
5. Making a pilgrimage to Mecca once in a lifetime

Another principle of Islam, and the most controversial one today, is the concept of *jihad,* or struggle to strive in the way of Allah and to improve both oneself and society. While many Muslims view jihad as an inner struggle, some have interpreted it as a requirement to go to war to preserve and extend Islam.

Shariah Developed by Muslim scholars after the death of Muhammad, the Islamic code of law called *shariah* outlines behavioral requirements for daily life. For example, it requires morality and honesty, and bans gambling, eating pork, and drinking alcohol. Polygymy is permitted in some circumstances, but Muhammad attempted to limit the practice to four wives. Also, Muslims were cautioned not to enslave Muslims, Christians, or Jews. Countries that in recent years have based their laws on shariah include Iran, parts of Nigeria, Afghanistan, Libya, Oman, Saudi Arabia, Sudan, and Yemen.

The First Four Caliphs and Umayyads

At Muhammad's death in 632, his followers split over who should become the leader of the Islamic community. Some supported his father-in-law, *Abu Bakr*. Others advocated for Muhammad's cousin and son-in-law, *Ali*. Abu Bakr won the dispute and took over as *caliph,* or head of state. He was responsible for guiding the Islamic world in accordance with the dictates of the Quran. Ali, who lost the dispute, eventually become the fourth caliph.

This succession dispute divided Islam into factions that still exist today. The supporters of Abu Bakr became the Sunni group, or *Sunnis*. They consider the first four successors the "Rightly Guided Caliphs." Supporters of Ali became the *Shia* group, also known as *Shiites*. They consider Ali the first true caliph. Today, about 85 to 90 percent of Muslims are Sunni. Shia are strongest in Iran and Iraq. The term *Dar al-Islam* has come to refer to all of Islamic culture, including Shia and Sunni. (Test Prep: Make an outline comparing the division in Islam with the schism in Christianity. See page 134.)

As caliphs conquered lands beyond the Arabian Peninsula, they spread Islam, the Arabic language, and the cultivation of cotton, sugar, and citrus crops. Abu Bakr led raids into and seized land from the Byzantine Empire based in Constantinople and the Persian Sassanid Empire. Political conquest often led to religious conversion, but not always. Muhammad had taught that people should not be forced to become Muslims. Further, the conquering forces had a financial reason not to require religious conversion. Because Muslims were exempt from certain taxes, conversions reduced on tax collections.

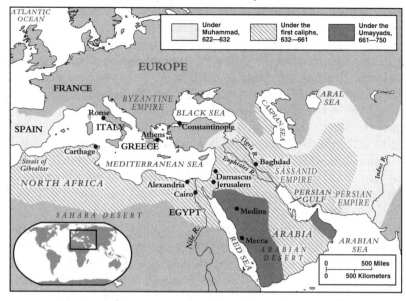

Ali, the fourth caliph, ruled from 656 until he was assassinated in 661. At that time, a network of merchants from Mecca, aided by capable generals and strong armies, assumed power. They founded the *Umayyad Dynasty*. This Sunni dynasty moved its capital to *Damascus*, from where it governed its huge empire for approximately 90 years. Ultimately, the Umayyads' control reached as far west as Gibraltar, in the Iberian peninsula, and as far east as India. They controlled the largest territory of anyone since the Roman Empire.

Followers of Ali, however, resisted the Umayyad leaders, causing Shia beliefs to develop political as well as religious components. Their community leader became known as *imam* rather than caliph.

Umayyads and Abbasids

By the end of 90 years, the Umayyad rulers had grown weak and corrupt. In 750, their capital, Damascus, fell to a group known as the *Abbasids*. The new rulers founded a new city for their capital, *Baghdad*. Situated in an ideal spot for trans-Eurasian trade, Baghdad soon rivaled Constantinople in both wealth and population, and the Abbasid Caliphate became one of the most powerful and innovative empires of its time.

Baghdad's Influence In addition to serving as a capital city, Baghdad became a center of learning. Although the paper-making process originated in China, the invention of techniques to make thicker, more useful paper was an achievement of Baghdad. A cataloguer of books in the tenth century listed thousands of existing titles and authors, many from lands far from the caliph's court. The expansion of the intellectual world of Baghdad represented a "golden age" of learning.

The Influence of Persia When Islam was brought to Persia in 651, Arabic was the official language, and non-Arab believers such as Persians were treated as second-class citizens. In the ninth century, Persian Muslims began a movement against the privileged status of Arabs, arguing that the practice went against the Islamic principles of brotherhood and equality. Through such efforts, Persians were able to convert to Islam while maintaining their distinctive Persian culture and language. During the Islamic Golden Age that followed, Persia contributed remarkable scholars, scientists, and poets. The polymath known to the West as Avicenna (980–1037) advanced the science of medicine and wrote on numerous topics, including astronomy, geography, and logic. Rumi (1207–1273) was a Persian poet, theologian, and jurist. His poetry, mostly written in Persian, has been influential not only in Persia, but around the world. Rumi's teachings became the basis of the Sufi movement within Islam, which is described on page 155.

Problems for the Abbasids Even as Baghdad flourished in intellectual areas, the rulers confronted difficulties with tax collection and control of far-flung provinces. Grain and produce reached the city as partial payment for taxes from provincial governors, so the central administration tried to standardize tax collection to be in cash only. Administrators hoped that this reform would better support the government and minimize corruption by provincial officials.

Over time, the political empire became increasingly hierarchical with an ever-growing bureaucracy. *Viziers* (prime ministers) would communicate the will of the ruler to the people—the ruler himself was often seated behind a screen. Being a ruler was a dangerous occupation and leaders faced frequent assassination attempts. Some were successful.

Comparing Islamic Empires		
Abbasid Empire	**Both**	**Umayyad Empire**
Location: Southwest Asia and North Africa *Capital:* Baghdad	*Branch of Islam:* Sunni *Ethnicity of Leaders:* Arab *Foreign Policy:* spread influence of Islam	*Location:* Southwest Asia, North Africa, and Southwest Europe *Capital:* Damascus and then Córdoba

Invasions and Trade Shifts

In the 1100s and 1200s, the Abbasid Empire suffered from a problem that plagued many prosperous empires in history: attacks from outside groups. Four different groups successfully assaulted parts of the Abbasid Empire. All came from the west or north.

Mamluks Originating from Egypt, the *Mamluks* were a Turkic group that had formerly been military slaves. They took control of Egypt and established an empire across North Africa.

Source: LACMA

Gold coins minted under the Abbasids were widely used in the Mediterranean region.

Seljuk Turks Like the Abbasids, the Seljuk Turks were Muslims. They originated from Central Asia. They seized parts of the Middle East, including Baghdad itself. Their leader took the title *sultan*, reducing the Abbasid caliph to the role of chief Sunni religious authority. The Turks almost immediately began threatening the neighboring Byzantine Empire.

Crusaders The conquest by the Seljuk Turks brought a third invader to the region: Crusaders from Europe. Under the Abbasids, Christians could travel easily to and from their holy sites in and around Jerusalem. When the Seljuk Turks limited this access, Christians in Europe organized Crusades to reopen access. The Crusades will be described in more detail in Chapter 12.

Mongols The fourth group to attack the Abbasid Empire were among the most famous conquerors in history: the Mongols. Like the Seljuk Turks, they hailed from Central Asia. The Mongols conquered what was left of the Abbasid Empire in 1258, and pushed Seljuk Turks out of Baghdad. They continued to push westward, but were stopped in Egypt by the Mamluks. The Mongols will be described in more detail in Chapter 13.

Economic Challenges The Abbasids faced economic as well as military challenges. In particular, trade patterns were shifting. Baghdad lost its traditional place on the southern Silk Roads route when goods began to move more frequently along northern routes. Over time, Baghdad lost population and its canals fell into disrepair and the countryside could not sustain the agricultural needs of the urban population. Slowly, the infrastructure that had made Baghdad a great city fell into decay.

Islamic Rule in Spain

While the Umayyads ruled only briefly in the Middle East, they had more success farther west. In 711, after Muslim forces had defeated Byzantine armies across North Africa, they successfully invaded Spain from the south. They designated *Córdoba* as their capital for Spain. They rapidly expanded northward, sending forces into France.

Battle of Tours The Islamic military was turned back in 732 when it lost the *Battle of Tours* against Frankish forces. This defeat, rare for Islamic armies during the 700s, marked the limit of rapid Islamic expansion into Western Europe. Most of the continent remained Christians, but Muslims ruled Spain for the next seven centuries. (Test Prep: Write a paragraph tracing the Islamic influences on Spanish culture. See also pages 227–229.)

Prosperity Under Islam Like the Abbasids in Baghdad, the Umayyad rulers in Córdoba created a climate of toleration with Muslims and Christians coexisting easily. They also promoted trade, with Chinese and Southeast Asian products entering Spain, and through it the rest of Europe. Many of the goods in this trade traveled aboard ships called *dhows*. These ships, first developed in India or China, had long, thin hulls that made them excellent for carrying goods, though less useful for conducting warfare. The influence of Islamic architecture can still be seen in Spain today. Impressive buildings were constructed during this period, such as the palaces and fortresses of the *Alhambra* (thirteenth century), built outside present-day Grenada.

Scholars in Spain The Islamic state in Spain known as al-Andalus, became a center of learning. Córdoba had the largest library in the world at the time. Among the famous scholars from Spain was *Ibn Rushd,* known in Europe as *Averroes* (twelfth century). He wrote influential works on law, secular philosophy, and the natural sciences. Another great scholar of ethics during this period was Maimonides, who was Jewish.

Social and Cultural Life

Over time, the Islamic world fragmented politically but advanced culturally. Trade brought in new goods and fresh ideas. In addition to the cities of Baghdad and Córdoba, Cairo in Egypt and Bukhara in central Asia developed great universities.

Islamic centers of learning were not limited to the study of religious teachings. Indeed, in the sayings of the prophet Muhammad is the injunction to "Go in quest of knowledge even unto China." Islamic scholars translated Greek literary classics into Arabic, saving the works of Aristotle and other Greek thinkers from oblivion. Scholars also brought back mathematics texts from India and techniques for paper-making from China. Medical advances in hospital care improved in cities such as Cairo, while doctors and pharmacists studied for examinations for licenses that would allow them to practice. Writers such as the Persian *Omar Khayyám,* author of *The Rubaiyat,* created works that remain well known throughout the world today.

Centers of Learning in the Islamic World		
Name	Location (Date Founded)	Specialty
House of Wisdom	Baghdad (c. 762)	Mathematician Al-Khwarizmi established basis of algebra
University of Al Karaouine	Fez, Morocco (859)	First university in the world to offer degrees
Library of al-Hakam II	Cordoba, Spain, (c. 961)	Library contained several hundred thousand volumes
Al-Azhar University	Cairo, Egypt (972)	University offered undergraduate and postgraduate degrees
Al-Nizamiyya University	Baghdad (1065)	University offered free education

Social Classes in the Islamic World Before the era of Muhammad, farmers and sailors were more common in the Arabian Peninsula than pastoral nomads. However, it was the nomads who led the camel caravans that built trade relationships between coastal and interior dwellers. As always, with trade in goods came the spread of ideas. Trade between the Byzantine and Islamic empires led to contact of people in the Arabian peninsula with Christianity and Judaism. Even as society changed, kinship remained the most important aspect of social relations in the early Islamic world. Clan members felt strong loyalty to one another, just as they had in the Bedouin world.

However, the increase of trade along the Red Sea caused the growth of a powerful merchant elite in many cities. Both Mecca and Medina in Muhammad's day were stops on the long-distance camel routes. In these cities, mosques and shariah came to provide a common base for social and cultural life.

In the non-Arab areas of Islamic expansion, control by Islamic caliphs led to some discrimination toward non-Arab converts, though usually not open persecution. This discrimination gradually faded in the ninth century. The caliph's soldiers, who were forbidden to own territory they had conquered, sometimes chose to remain in the armies of the caliphates because they received regular salaries. The presence of a permanent military force that kept order but did not own property allowed life for most of the inhabitants of the countryside to remain virtually unchanged. However, people paid tribute to Islamic caliphs rather than to Byzantine rulers.

Commerce and Class The role of merchants in Islamic society was more prestigious than in other societies in Europe and Asia at the time. Muhammad himself had been a merchant, as had his first wife. Merchants could grow rich from their dealings with far-flung trade routes across the Indian Ocean and Central Asia. They were esteemed as long as they maintained fair dealings and gave to charity in accord with the pillars of the Islamic faith.

Slavery Although Islam allowed slavery, Muslims could not enslave other Muslims. Also exempt were Jews, Christians, and Zoroastrians. Slaves were often imported from Africa, Kievan Rus, and Central Asia, but the institution of hereditary slavery did not develop. Many slaves converted to Islam, after which their owners freed them. Once liberated, their children were considered freeborn.

Slave women might find themselves serving as concubines to Islamic men who already had wed their allotment of four wives. Slave women were allowed more independence—for example, to go to markets and to run errands—than the legal wives. Only slave women were permitted to dance or perform musically before unrelated men. This opportunity sometimes enabled female slaves to accumulate enough money to buy their freedom.

Free Women in Islam

Some of the practices now associated with Islam were common cultural customs in Central Asia and the Byzantine Empire before the time of Muhammad. For example, women often covered their heads and faces. This practice solidified under Islam, with most women observing *hijab*, a term that can refer either to the practice of modest dress in a general sense or to a specific type of covering. (Men there also often wore head coverings of various sorts, from turbans to skull caps.) While women could study and read, they were not supposed to do so in the company of men not related to them.

Muhammad's Treatment of Women Muhammad raised the status of women in several ways. He treated his wives with love and devotion. He insisted that dowries, the price a prospective husband paid to secure a bride, be paid to the future wife rather than to her father. He forbade *female infanticide,* the killing of newborn girls. Maybe most important, Muhammad's first wife was an educated woman with her own business, which set a pattern for recognition of women's abilities.

The Status of Women Overall, Islamic women enjoyed a higher status than Christian or Jewish women. Islamic women were allowed to inherit property and retain ownership after marriage. They could remarry if widowed, and they could receive a cash settlement if divorced. Under some conditions, a wife could initiate divorce. Moreover, women could practice birth control. Islamic women who testified in a court under shariah were to be protected from retaliation, but their testimony was worth only half that of a man. One gap in the historical record is written evidence of how women viewed their position in society. Most of the records created before 1450 were written by men.

As elsewhere, the rise of towns and cities resulted in new limitations on women's rights. Their new status might best be symbolized by the veil and the harem. *Harems,* dwelling areas set aside for women and eunuchs, were made up of wives, concubines, and the children of these women.

Sufism

As Islam spread, it became more varied. In some areas, particularly in India and Persia, Islamic groups called *Sufis* began to appear. Notable for their shaved heads, Sufis followed rituals and ecstatic chants in attempts to unite with God. Sufi groups abstained from earthly pleasures and some used whirling dancing to express religious ecstasy. Unlike Muslims who focused on intellectual pursuits such as the study of the Quran, Sufis emphasized introspection to grasp truths that they believed could not be understood through learning. The rise of Sufism may have begun as a mystical response to the perceived love of luxury of the early Umayyad caliphate.

HISTORICAL PERSPECTIVES: WHAT IS ISLAM'S LEGACY IN SPAIN?

An old saying is that the Muslims needed seven years to conquer Spain and the Christians needed seven centuries to reconquer it. Historians have viewed those seven centuries of Islamic rule in Spain in many ways. In the early 1800s, people in the United States knew little about Islam. So, when writer Washington Irving put together a collection of tales and observations about the Muslim era in Spain, under the title *Tales of the Alhambra* in 1832, he focused on how exotic and romantic the era was. The book was very popular when it was published, and is still widely available today.

In the first half of the twentieth century, as Spanish nationalism grew stronger, historians looked for the roots of what made Spain distinctive from other countries in Europe. A Spanish historian who spent most of his life in Argentina, Claudio Sánchez-Albornoz, found these roots in pre-Islamic era. He argued that the essential character of Spanish culture was established before Muslims arrived, persisted during their rule, and reemerged when they were forced out. In other words, Albornoz viewed the impact of the Muslims on modern Spain as relatively minor. In contrast, Américo Castro, a Spanish historian who taught for many years in the United States, argued that the impact of Islam was immense. Castro concluded that the fusion of Islamic culture with older Spanish traditions was what made Spain "Spanish."

In recent years, clashes between Christians and Muslims have prompted historians to focus less on Spanish national identity and more on how Islamic rulers of Spain created a culture of tolerance. For example, Yale professor Maria Rosa Menocal, in *Ornament of the World: How Muslims, Jews and Christians Created a Culture of Tolerance in Medieval Spain,* published in 2002, praised Spain as a place where scholars "saw no contradiction in pursuing the truth, whether philosophical or scientific, or religious, across confessional [religious] lines."

KEY TERMS BY THEME

STATE-BUILDING
Abbasid
Baghdad
viziers
Seljuk Turks
sultan
Mamluks
Córdoba
Battle of Tours

SOCIAL STRUCTURE
Muhammad

CULTURE
Bedouins

polygyny
Allah
Mecca
Quran (Koran)
Medina
Hegira
Ka'aba
People of the Book
Five Pillars
jihad
Ramadan
shariah
Abu Bakr
caliph

Ali
Sunnis
Shias
Dar al-Islam
Umayyad Dynasty
Damascus
imam
dhows
Averroes
Alhambra
Omar Khayyám
The Rubaiyat
female infanticide
dowries
hijab
Sufis

MULTIPLE-CHOICE QUESTIONS

1. Which of the following is the best example of how Islam, during and after the time of Muhammad, adopted aspects of the traditional religion of Bedouin culture?

    (A) The respect for the ideas expressed in the Koran

    (B) The importance of the black stone known as the Ka'aba

    (C) The requirement to follow the principles of shariah

    (D) The ban on enslaving Jews, Christians, and Zoroastrians

2. The division of Islam between Sunnis and Shias was similar to other conflicts in history that began as

    (A) a dispute between upper and lower classes

    (B) a rivalry over who should succeed an important leader

    (C) a battle for control of a natural resource

    (D) a debate over how to interpret a law

3. Between the eighth century and the eleventh century, Baghdad became

    (A) an important city in the Byzantine Empire

    (B) an important center of learning and distribution point for books

    (C) the most important city in the Umayyad empire

    (D) the most important city on the northern Silk Roads

4. The attack by the Seljuk against the Abbasids in 1055 is an example of,
   (A) nomads attacking a settled society
   (B) Persians attacking Arabs
   (C) ocean-going invaders attacking a land-based empire
   (D) invaders being pushed to move from outside pressures

5. Which of the following statements best describes the Islamic rule of Spain between the eighth and fifteenth centuries?
   (A) Spain slowly became part of the Abbasid Empire.
   (B) Spain had to fight off attacks by the Seljuks and Mamluks.
   (C) Muslims built a culture of religious toleration.
   (D) The Battle of Tours marked the beginning of Islamic influence in Spain.

6. Free women in the Islamic world enjoyed which of the following rights?
   (A) They could speak publicly in marketplaces.
   (B) They could participate in dance performances in mixed groups.
   (C) They could serve as imams or priests in local mosques.
   (D) They could divorce and own property in certain circumstances.

7. What impact did urbanization have on the status of women in the Arabian Peninsula?
   (A) Their status remained relatively the same because it reflected religious values.
   (B) Their status rose because they had more employment opportunities.
   (C) Their status declined since they performed fewer tasks raising food.
   (D) Their status rose because some joined the upper class or royalty.

8. From the time of Muhammad to 1450, which of the following best describes the movement of the knowledge of technological advances?
   (A) They often began in the Islamic world and moved to Europe.
   (B) They often began in Europe and moved to the Arabian Peninsula.
   (C) They often began on the edges of the Islamic world and moved to the Arabian Peninsula.
   (D) They often began and remained in the Arabian Peninsula.

9. Which factor was most responsible for the decay of Baghdad in the thirteenth century?

(A) Islam had lost its popularity in the area.

(B) The city had become overpopulated.

(C) Huge amounts of wealth were invested in city infrastructure.

(D) The conquering Turks fought each other more than they maintained the city.

Question 10 refers to the following excerpt.

> I saw my Lord with the eye of my heart.
> He said, "Who are you?" I said, "I am You."
> You are He Who fills all place.
> But place does not know where You are.
> In my subsistence is my annihilation;
> In my annihilation, I remain You.

—Mansur al-Hallaj (c. 858–922), Persia

10. Which phrase most accurately explains something about al-Hallaj's views about religion or politics?

(A) "I am You" suggests he is a Sufi.

(B) "You are He who fills all places" suggests he is an Umayyad.

(C) "With the eye of my heart" suggests he is a Sunni.

(D) "In my subsistence is my annihilation" suggests he is Mamluk.

CONTINUITY AND CHANGE-OVER-TIME ESSAY QUESTIONS

Directions: You are to answer the following question. You should spend 5 minutes organizing or outlining your essay. Write an essay that:

- Has a relevant thesis and supports that thesis with appropriate historical evidence.
- Addresses all parts of the question.
- Uses world historical context to show continuities and changes over time.
- Analyzes the process of continuity and change over time.

1. Analyze the continuities and changes in the role of women in the Middle East between c. 500 and c. 1450.

Questions for Additional Practice

2. Analyze continities and changes in the spread of Islam from 622 to 1450.

3. Analyze the continuity and change in the economy and society in the Abbasid Dynasty from 750 to 1258.

COMPARATIVE ESSAY QUESTIONS

Directions: You are to answer the following question. You should spend 5 minutes organizing or outlining your essay. Write an essay that:

- Has a relevant thesis and supports that thesis with appropriate historical evidence.
- Addresses all parts of the question.
- Makes direct, relevant comparisons.
- Analyzes relevant reasons for similarities and differences.

1. Compare the city of Cordoba under Islamic rule with ONE of the following cities:
   - Chang'an in Han China
   - Athens in Classical Greece
   - Persepolis in the Achaemenid Dynasty

Questions for Additional Practice

2. Compare the spread of Islam with the spread of Christianity. How were the two processes similar and different?

3. Analyze the similarities and differences in culture between the Umayyad and Abbasid dynasties.

THINK AS A HISTORIAN: PRACTICE HISTORICAL ARGUMENTATION

A historical argument includes an analysis that is carefully written and supported by facts and evidence. It is not simply a statement of fact, such as "Baghdad was the largest city in the Abbasid Empire." Nor is it a personal preference or unsupported opinion such as "I like the Abbasids more than the Umayyads." *Which TWO of the following statements are the best examples of a historical argument?*

1. Islamic rule was relatively tolerant because it did not punish people who did not convert to Islam.

2. The core principles of Islam, Christianity, and Judaism are more similar than different. All consider Abraham an important figure.

3. In the century following Muhammad's death, Islam spread through the Middle East, North Africa, and South Asia.

4. Of all of the invaders who attacked Baghdad, the Mongols were the most interesting.

WRITE AS A HISTORIAN: USE TOPIC SENTENCES

Add clarity to an essay by starting each body paragraph with a clear and concise topic sentence that introduces the main point of the paragraph. *For each item, select the best topic sentence for an essay about Islam.*

1. First body paragraph

   a. Islamic nations differed from other religious states since they had different beliefs regarding social structure.

   b. Compared to women of Judaism and Christianity, Islamic women enjoyed more privileges such as inheriting land and the right to independent thinking.

2. Second body paragraph

   a. A class of merchants arose in some Islamic states due to the growth of trade.

   b. The economy grew in the Muslim world through many different factors.

3. Third body paragraph

   a. Shariah law governed over the people of Islam, and served as the basis for moral code in Muslim states.

   b. Islam directly affected the legal system of the state.

9

Expansion of African Trade

After that the chief of the poets mounts the steps of the pempi [a raised platform on which the ruler sits] and lays his head on the sultan's lap, then climbs to the top of the pempi and lays his head first on the sultan's right shoulder and then on his left, speaking all the while in their tongue, and finally he comes down again. I was told that this practice is a very old custom amongst them, prior to the introduction of Islam, and that they have kept it up.

—Ibn Battuta, c. 1352

Ibn Battuta's commentary on Mali society sheds light on the cultural forces at work in Sub-Saharan Africa during the fourteenth century. A scholar from Morocco on the northwest coast of Africa, he was well versed in Islamic law, also known as shariah. Islamic governments in Mogadishu and Delhi sought his advice and welcomed him to their lands. Ibn Battuta's travelogue has made him a legend among historians, who point to his life as an example of how Islam's phenomenal growth increased connections among cultures of Asia, Africa, and southern Europe. Islam's arrival in Africa did not produce massive conversions among Africans. Nevertheless, the Islamic Empire's presence in Africa profoundly affected politics, economics, and culture within many African societies. As Ibn Battuta's account makes clear, in those African societies that had adopted Islam, many of their long-standing traditions remained. Sub-Saharan Africa's history between the spread of Islam and the period of European colonization is one of both cultural continuity and tremendous change.

The Migrations of Bantu-Speakers

Historians and linguists have long studied the spread of people of the Bantu language group from its beginning in modern-day Nigeria and Cameroon to the east and south, eventually covering about one-third of the continent of Africa. They propose that the spread of this language group was the result of the migration of the Bantu-speaking peoples and their interactions with local groups along the way. Most historians believe that rather than arriving en masse like a conquering horde, the migrations involved small groups of people who spoke Bantu moving from one point to another.

When the Bantu-speakers started to migrate from West Africa around 3000 B.C.E., they brought an agricultural economy with them. They cultivated yams and oil palms, skills that they may have picked up from peoples living along the Nile. Because of the success with these crops as well as with two grains, millet and sorghum, they produced a surplus of food. This enabled the population of the Bantu-speaking peoples to increase, prompting part of the population to move to new areas. Perhaps the fertility of the land decreased from overuse, providing another incentive to move on. The Bantu-speakers spread their knowledge of agriculture to the forest peoples they encountered, who were hunter-foragers.

One of the most important crops for the Bantu-speakers came long after the migration had begun. Between 300 and 500 B.C.E., Indonesian seafarers, traveling across the Indian Ocean, introduced bananas to Sub-Saharan Africa. The nutrition-rich food led to a spike in population. Many Indonesians settled on the island of Madagascar, whose spoken language even today is part of the Austronesian family of languages. Bananas allowed the Bantu-speaking peoples to migrate to places where yams did not easily grow. To grow bananas, farmers increased land for cultivation, which enriched diets and inspired more population growth.

The Bantu-speakers' migration was possible because of their technology skills. They built canoes and traveled up and down West Africa's and Central Africa's rivers. In addition, by 500 B.C.E., they had iron-making technology, which enabled them to make more efficient tools for clearing land and weapons for warfare. This technology gave them an edge over other peoples they encountered, including the Batwa of the Congo Basin, people formerly known as pygmies. The Bantu-speaking peoples defeated many tribes in battle, absorbing many of the defeated into their own population. Thus, there was considerable assimilation and displacement of other African peoples.

The Bantu-speaking peoples brought their infectious and parasitic diseases with them as they moved. For example, malaria was common in West Africa, where the Bantu-speakers had some immunity to it from long exposure. The people they met in the forests, however, had no such immunity. (Test Prep: Write a paragraph comparing the spread of disease by the Bantu-speaking peoples to the spread of disease by Europeans in the Americas. See page 303.)

By 2000 B.C.E., the Bantu-speakers had reached Lake Victoria and the other Great Lakes of East Africa. There they met nomadic pastoral peoples and adopted the practice of raising sheep and cattle. From the Great Lakes, they began moving south. By 400 C.E., people who spoke Bantu had reached South Africa, where the migration ended.

Societies Because the migration of people who spoke Bantu covered such vast distances and took place over such a long period of time, there came to be much variety among various Bantu-speaking groups. Generally, they formed close-knit communities that settled in small villages. Their societies were matrilineal, which means that villagers would trace their ancestry through their mothers, not their fathers. Some Bantu-speakers dropped the agricultural economy because the geography of some places better supported nomadic pastoralism or hunting-foraging.

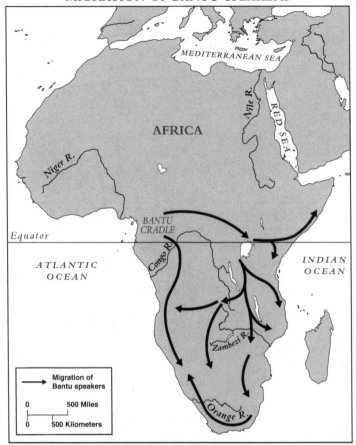

Religion Bantu-speakers generally believed that a single god had created the world, and that many spirits inhabited it. People did not worship the god directly but sent messages to him through spirits. Many Bantu-speaking peoples practiced a type of ancestor veneration, in that they believed that after death, spirits remained on Earth to guide the living. (Test Prep: Write a paragraph comparing the ancestor veneration of the Bantu-speakers and the Chinese. See page 35.)

Arts Belief in the spirit world inspired the Bantu-speaking peoples to create masks and sculpted figures to represent dead ancestors. Music was also an important part of worship and ceremony. Bantu-speakers used instruments such as drums, flutes, and horns to create not only religious music but also secular music to accompany work. The Bantu-speakers also had an impressive tradition of story-telling—a spoken literature that was passed down the generations.

Political Structures in Inland Africa

By 1000 C.E. agriculture had emerged through most of Sub-Saharan Africa. Because of the sedentary nature of agriculture, communities had to form increasingly complex political relationships in order to govern themselves.

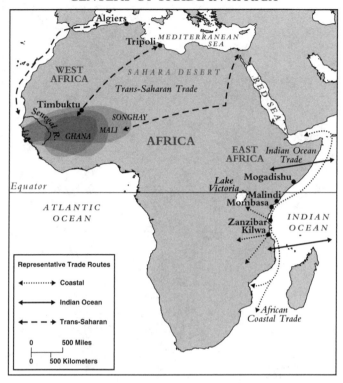

CENTERS OF TRADE IN AFRICA

In contrast to most Asian or European societies, states in Sub-Saharan Africa did not centralize power under one dominant figure or a strong central government. Instead, communities formed kin-based networks, where families governed themselves. A male head of the network, a chief, mediated conflicts and dealt with neighboring groups. Groups of villages became districts, and a group of chiefs decided among themselves how to solve the district's problems.

As populations grew, kin-based networks became more difficult to govern. Competition among neighbors increased, which in turn increased fighting among villages and districts. Survival for small kin-based communities became more challenging. Though many such communities continued to exist in Sub-Saharan Africa until the nineteenth century, larger kingdoms grew in prominence, particularly after 1000 C.E. For example, hierarchical political structures emerged in the Congo River basin. (Test Prep: Write a paragraph contrasting the decentralized political systems of the Bantu-speaking peoples with more centralized systems. See page 320.)

Islam's Impact on Trade

Because of their small scale, the traditional kin-based societies of Sub-Saharan Africa did not trade on a global level. As in South Asia, Sub-Saharan Africa increasingly traded with other parts of the world and learned of Islam at the same time. Merchants and Islam arrived via two routes: across the Sahara and over the Indian Ocean.

Trans-Saharan Trade While the East African Coast had been fairly well populated for many centuries before the arrival of Islam, few societies had inhabited the Sahara Desert because its arid climate made it nearly impossible to farm. Though nomadic communities did conduct some trade across the Sahara, the volume of trade increased exponentially with the arrival of Islamic merchants in the seventh and eighth centuries.

Camels and Trade Merchants from Southwest Asia traveled across the Sahara on camels. Native to the Islamic heartland (Arabia), camels began to appear in North Africa in the third century B.C.E. Camels, accustomed to the harsh, dry climate of the Arabian Desert, adapted well to living in the Sahara. Compared to horses, camels can consume a large quantity of water at one time (over 50 gallons in three minutes) and not need additional water for a long stretch of time. They began to replace horses and donkeys after 300 C.E.

As use of the camel spread, people developed as many as 15 types of camel saddles for different purposes.

- South Arabians developed a saddle in which the rider sits in back of the hump, which makes riding easier because the rider can hold onto the hair of the hump.

- Northern Arabians developed a saddle for sitting on top of the hump, putting them high in the air, which gave them greater visibility in battles.

- Northern Africans developed a saddle that allowed them to sit in front of the hump. Being near the head gave the rider the best possible control over the camel.

- Somalis in Eastern Africa, who were semi-nomadic and needed to carry their possessions with them, designed a saddle for carrying loads.

By the end of the eighth century C.E., the trans-Sahara trade had become famous throughout Europe and Asia. Gold was the most precious commodity traded. West African merchants acquired the metal from the waters of the Senegal River, near modern-day Senegal and Mauritania. Foreign traders came to West Africa seeking not only gold, but also ivory and slaves. In exchange, they brought salt, textiles, and horses. For more than 700 years, trans-Saharan trade brought considerable wealth to the societies of West Africa, particularly the kingdoms of Ghana and Mali.

Indian Ocean Trade Trade has a long history on the East Coast of Africa. Coastal cities such as Kilwa (in modern Tanzania), Malindi (in modern Kenya), and Mogadishu (in modern Somalia) traded among themselves from the time the Bantu-speaking peoples brought agriculture to the region about 2000 B.C.E. International trade also had existed there for centuries, before the founding of Islam: merchants from India, Southeast Asia, and Persia all made contact with coastal cities of Africa via the Indian Ocean. Greek and Roman mariners as well had traveled down the Red Sea to trade with the region.

By the eighth century C.E., Islamic merchants had rejuvenated maritime trade, which had declined in the centuries after the fall of the Han, Gupta, and Roman civilizations. The Indian Ocean trade created thriving city-states, sometimes known as the Swahili city-states. "Swahili," which literally means "coasters," referred to the inhabitants of bustling commercial centers, such as Kilwa, Mombasa (in modern Kenya), and Zanzibar (in modern Tanzania). The traders of the Zanj Coast, as it was known in Arabic, sold ivory, gold, and slaves to their Arab trading partners, as well as more exotic goods such as tortoise shells, peacock feathers, and rhinoceros horns. In exchange, the "Zanj" cities acquired Chinese porcelain, Indian cotton, and manufactured ironwork. Trade was so vigorous with East Asia that Chinese porcelain remains a common find among the ruins of Swahili cities.

Trade brought considerable wealth to the cities on the East African coast. Architectural ruins in Kilwa suggest the wealth and grandeur that once existed there. For example, most buildings had traditionally been constructed of mud and clay. However, at the Indian Ocean trade's height, many mosques and wealthy merchants' homes were made of stone or coral.

Comparing Pack Animals			
Animal	Location	Benefits	Drawbacks
Camel	Northern Africa and Sub-Saharan West Africa	• Able to travel long distances • Can eat thorny plants and drink salty water found in deserts • Has long eyelashes that protect against desert winds • Only animal that can cross deserts • Does not spook easily	• Requires high level of salt to stay healthy • Can be very aggressive and even vengeful • Cannot be controlled with a bit • Cannot be boarded in a stall
Ox	Eurasia and the Americas	• Has high level of stamina • Can pull heaviest loads • Unlikely to stray or be stolen • Can survive on local grazing • Tolerates various climates and diets	• Moves slowly compared to other pack animals • Requires more water and food than other pack animals
Horse	Worldwide	• Can run at high speeds • Can be controlled with a bit • Can be used in battle • Can adapt to most climates and terrains	• Requires grain to keep fit • Spooks easily • Can be stolen easily • Strays easily • Less sure-footed than other pack animals • Cannot tolerate high heat
Llama	Americas	• Maintains traction in mountains • Has calm disposition • Requires little water • Adapts well to cold and mountainous climates	• Cannot pull heavy loads • Can carry less than other pack animals • Cannot tolerate high heat

Political Structures of West and East Africa

Several kingdoms benefited from the increased wealth that the trans-Saharan and Indian Ocean trades brought to Africa. In West Africa, the kingdoms of *Ghana* and *Mali* emerged. In East Africa, the Swahili Coast's prosperity produced the powerful kingdom of Zimbabwe.

Ghana Nestled between the Sahara and the tropical rain forests of the West African coast, the kingdom of Ghana was not in the same location as the modern nation of Ghana. Historians believe that the kingdom had been founded during the fifth century, at least two centuries before the time of Muhammad, but Ghana reached its peak of influence from the eighth to the eleventh centuries. Ghana's rulers sold gold and ivory to Muslim traders in exchange for salt, copper, cloth, and tools. From Ghana's capital city, *Kumbai Saleh,* the king ruled a centralized government aided by nobles and an army equipped with iron weapons.

Source: Daderot / Wikimedia Commons

Source: Thinkstock

The gold artifacts (upper) were part of the valuable trans-Saharan trade in West Africa. The modern photo of foods and spices (lower) shows the types of goods that have been popular in the Indian Ocean trade in East Africa since the eighth century C.E.

Mali By the twelfth century, wars with neighboring societies had permanently weakened the Ghanaian state. In its place arose several new trading societies, the most powerful of which was Mali. The government of Mali profited from the gold trade, but it also taxed nearly all other trade entering West Africa; and, therefore, became even more prosperous than Ghana had been. Most of Mali's residents were farmers, who cultivated sorghum and rice. However, the great cities of *Timbuktu* and *Gao* accumulated the most wealth and developed into centers of Islamic life in the region. Timbuktu in particular became a world-renowned center of Islamic learning. By the 1500s, books created and sold in Timbuktu brought prices higher than most other goods.

Mali's founding ruler, Sundiata, became the subject of legend. His father had ruled over a small society in West Africa in what today is Guinea. When his father died, rival groups invaded, killing most of the royal family and capturing the throne. They did not bother to kill Sundiata because the young prince was crippled and was not considered a threat. In spite of his injury, he learned to fight and became so feared as a warrior that his enemies forced him into exile. His time in exile only strengthened him and his allies. In 1235, Sundiata, "the Lion Prince," returned to the kingdom of his birth, defeated his enemies, and reclaimed the throne for himself.

WEST AFRICAN KINGDOMS

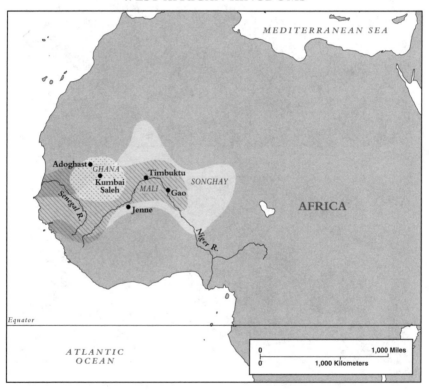

Sundiata's story made him beloved within his kingdom, but he was also an astute and capable ruler. Most scholars believe he was a Muslim and used his connections with others of his faith to establish trade relationships with North African and Arab merchants. Sundiata cultivated a thriving gold trade in Mali. Under his steady leadership, Mali's wealth grew tremendously.

Mansa Musa In the fourteenth century, Sundiata's grand-nephew, *Mansa Musa,* brought more fame to the region. However, Mansa Musa was better known for his religious leadership than for his political or economic acumen. A devout Muslim, Mansa Musa began a pilgrimage in 1324 to Mecca, Islam's holiest city. His journey, however, was unlike that of any ordinary pilgrim. Mali's prosperity allowed him to take an extraordinarily extravagant caravan to Arabia, consisting of 100 camels, thousands of slaves and soldiers, and gold to distribute to all of the people who hosted him along his journey. His pilgrimage displayed Mali's wealth to the outside world.

Mansa Musa's visit to Mecca deepened his devotion to Islam. Upon his return, he established religious schools in Timbuktu, built mosques in Muslim trading cities, and sponsored those who wanted to continue their religious studies elsewhere. Though most West Africans continued to hold onto their traditional beliefs, Mansa Musa's reign deepened the support for Islam in Mali. However, in less than 100 years after Mansa Musa's death, the Mali kingdom was declining. By the late 1400s, the Songhay Kingdom had taken its place as the powerhouse in West Africa. In spite of Mali's fall, Mansa Musa's efforts to strengthen Islam in West Africa succeeded: the religion has a prominent place in the region today.

Zimbabwe Zimbabwe was the most powerful of all the East African kingdoms between the twelfth and fifteenth centuries. It was situated between the Zambezi and Limpopo rivers in modern-day Zimbabwe and Mozambique. Zimbabwe built its prosperity on a mixture of agriculture, grazing, trade, and, above all, gold. Zimbabwe had rich gold fields, and it traded with the Swahili city-states as well as with Persia, India, and China. Just as in Ghana, the kings taxed any gold that traveled through the land.

As in the Swahili cities, a testament to the kingdom's wealth can be seen through its architecture. Though most houses in the region had traditionally been constructed from wood, by the ninth century chiefs had began to construct their "zimbabwes", the Bantu word for "dwellings", with stone.

By the end of the thirteenth century, a massive wall of stone, 30 feet tall by 15 feet thick, surrounded the capital city, which became known as the *Great Zimbabwe.* The stone wall was the first large one on the continent to be built without mortar. Inside the wall, most of the royal city's buildings were made of stone. In the late fifteenth century, nearly 20,000 people resided within the Great Zimbabwe. However, overgrazing so damaged the surrounding environment that residents of the bustling capital city abandoned it by the end of the 1400s. The wall still stands in the modern country of Zimbabwe.

Social Structures of Sub-Saharan Africa

Sub-Saharan Africa's small communities, instead of having strong central governments ruling over large territories, were organized around several structures: kinship, age, and gender. As described earlier in this chapter, kinship connections allowed people to identify first as members of a clan or family. Age was another significant social marker. An 18-year-old could do more hard labor than a 60-year-old, but younger people often relied on the advice of their elders. Thus, communities divided work according to age, creating age grades or age sets. Finally, gender had an influential role in social organization. Men dominated most activities that required a specialized skill; for example, leather tanners and blacksmiths were typically men. Women generally engaged in agriculture or gathering food. They also took the primary responsibilities for carrying out domestic chores and raising their family's children.

Women's Roles in Sub-Saharan Africa As mentioned before, some societies were matrilineal, in which kinship passed from the mother to her children. This did not necessarily mean that these societies were matriarchal, with women holding power over men. Indeed, most Sub-Saharan communities were patriarchal. Even so, some examples of female empowerment did exist. For example, Ibn Battuta observed that in West Africa, a man did not pass on his inheritance to his sons. Instead, he willed it to his sister to pass onto her sons.

Though many Africans had converted to Islam, they did not adopt all of its norms concerning gender. Women and men who were not married mixed freely and openly, and women often did not veil themselves. Several reasons could account for the different customs between Africa and Southwest Asia. Wearing the hijab (a veil that covered the head and chest) was a practice in Southwest Asia before the time of Muhammad, so it may have been considered a cultural tradition, not a religious requirement. Sub-Saharan societies had their own gender norms that predated the new ones that arrived with Islam, and such traditions did not change quickly.

Slavery in Sub-Saharan Africa and Southwest Asia Slavery had been a long-standing tradition in Africa before Europeans arrived. Prisoners of war, debtors, and criminals all became slaves. Private property did not exist in many kin-based societies, so some people instead accumulated slaves in order to increase their wealth and social status.

The arrival of Islam and global trade increased the volume of slaves in Africa. Slaves were precious commodities along the trans-Saharan and the Indian Ocean trading routes. Arab and Southwest-Asian merchants imported millions of Africans from the Swahili trading cities. These slaves were uprooted from their lives and brought to entirely different lands with unfamiliar languages and traditions. Arab traders preferred women over men and put them to work as servants, as opposed to agricultural workers. Female slaves often became concubines. Male slaves were used in the military or, sometimes, became high-ranking eunuchs (castrated men) in royal courts.

Comparing Three Types of Slavery			
	Chattel	**Domestic**	**Debt Bondage**
Description	Slaves were the legal property of the owner.	Slaves served as cooks, cleaners, or other household workers.	People became slaves, sometimes through mutual agreement, to repay a debt.
Examples	Common in the Americas, sixteenth century to nineteenth century	Common in Classical Greece and Rome; the Middle East	East Africa before the fifteenth century; European colonies in the Americas
Was enslavement permanent?	Yes	Often	Not in theory, although many slaves never regained freedom
Were the children of slaves automatically slaves?	Yes	Often	Children often inherited the debts of their parents
Did slaves have any rights?	No	Some: laws or customs might prevent a master from selling a slave	Some: laws or customs might limit how severely a master could punish a slave

Slaves and others from the East Coast of Africa were known in Arabic as Zanj. Between 869 C.E. and 883 C.E., slaves working on sugar plantations in Mesopotamia mounted a series of revolts. One of these, led by Ali bin Muhammad, became known as the Zanj Rebellion. Ali bin Muhammad, along with the 15,000 slaves he organized, captured the city of Basra, in modern Iraq, and established a splinter government. Ten years after the original revolt, Mesopotamian forces quashed the rebel forces and killed Ali bin Muhammad. The size and length of time before it was defeated make the Zanj Rebellion one of the most successful slave revolts in history.

The Indian Ocean slave trade between Africa and Southwest Asia continued well into the nineteenth century, somewhat longer than the Atlantic Ocean slave trade between Africa and the Americas. You will read more about the Atlantic Ocean trade in Chapter 17.

Cultural Life in Sub-Saharan Africa

Playing music, creating visual arts, and storytelling were important aspects of African cultural life, as they were in many other cultures around the world, because they provided enjoyment and helped marked rituals such as weddings and funerals. In Africa, these activities carried additional significance. Because traditional African religions included ancestor veneration, song lyrics provided a means of communicating with the spirit world. African music usually had a distinctive rhythmic pattern, and vocals were interspersed with percussive elements such as handclaps, bells, pots, or gourds.

Visual arts also commonly served a religious purpose. For example, metalworkers created busts of past rulers so that ruling royalty could look to them for guidance. Artists in Benin, West Africa, were famous for their intricate sculptures in iron and bronze.

The Griot Literature, as it existed in Sub-Saharan Africa, was oral. *Griots,* or storytellers, were the conduits of history for a community. Griots possessed encyclopedic knowledge of family lineages and the lives and deeds of great leaders. The groits were also adept at music, singing their stories and accompanying themselves on instruments such as the kora—a 12-string harp.

The griots were both venerated and feared as they held both the power of language and of story. It was said that a griot could sing your success or sing your downfall. By telling and retelling their stories and histories, the griots preserved a people's history and passed that history on from generation to generation. Kings often sought their counsel regarding political matters. It has been said that when a griot died, it was as though a library had burned.

Until recently, it was thought that the position of griot was held exclusively by men. But in many parts of Africa, women were also trained as griottes. They would sing at ceremonies and special occasions, such as before a wedding. For example, the griotte would counsel the bride to not talk back if her mother-in-law abused her or reassure the bride that if things got too bad, she could always come back home. It is thought that the griotte provided women with a sense of empowerment in a male-dominated society.

Swahili: A Syncretic Language The arrival of Islam brought with it cultural changes. Apart from spreading the new faith, the presence of Islamic merchants on the Indian Ocean coast influenced the developing language of Swahili, a Bantu language melded with Arabic vocabulary. Today, Swahili is spoken by various groups in the African Great Lakes region as well as other parts of Southeast Africa. It is the official language of four countries in central and east Africa: Democratic Republic of the Congo, Kenya, Uganda, and Tanzania. In addition, it is one of the official languages of the African Union.

Religion Christianity had first entered Egypt and Ethiopia during the first century C.E., but the spread of Islam had weakened its influence in the region of Ethiopia known as Axum. In the twelfth century, however, a new ruling kingdom there enthusiastically embraced Christianity and ordered the building of 11 massive churches made entirely of rock.

From the twelfth through the sixteenth centuries, Ethiopia was a virtual island of Christianity on the continent of Africa. Because of its isolation from both the Roman Catholic Church and the Eastern Orthodox Church, Ethiopian Christianity developed independently. People combined their traditional faith traditions, such as ancestor veneration and beliefs in spirits, with Christianity to create a distinct form of faith. This religious syncretism was apparent in the construction in the 11 rock churches noted above, which are still used today. Carved rock structures had been a feature of Ethiopian religious architecture since the second millennium B.C.E.

Attitudes among non-Africans toward African history have gone through a revolution in past century and a half. For most societies during most of African history, people did not keep written records. History was oral: it consisted of the long, detailed accounts of the past as told by griots. As contact with Europe, Southwest Asia, and South Asia increased, writing spread through the continent, and with it the idea that history was a story based on written records. Since Africans did not have written records, they became, in the eyes of Europeans, people without a past. This idea persisted among Europeans well into the 1900s. For example, in 1965, one of England's most prominent historians, Hugh Trevor-Roper, declared that Africa's past was nothing more than "barbarous tribes in picturesque but irrelevant quarters of the globe."

By the time of Trevor-Roper's comment, the dismissive attitudes toward African history had already begun changing. In the late nineteenth century, one pioneer in the effort to validate African history was Edward Wilmot Blyden. He was born to free black parents in the West Indies in 1832. Unable to gain admission to universities in the United States, Blyden migrated to Liberia and became involved in its development. He eventually became a diplomat and Liberia's Secretary of State. Though a Christian all his life, Blyden argued that Islam was an important unifying force among Africans because it was not the religion of colonizers. Blyden became an leading advocate of the Pan-African movement, an effort to build a common African identify among the diverse peoples of the continent.

Another African political leader, Leopold Senghor of Senegal, became the leading advocate for the study of African history and culture in the mid-twentieth century. Senghor, who served as president of Senegal for 21 years, argued that Africans not only had a history, but also a distinctive heritage that they should preserve and take pride in.

More recently, as globalization has made historians more aware of how interconnected people have been throughout history, historians have treated Africa as a full participant in history. Among the leaders in this shift in perspective has been Ross Dunn, a historian in the United States associated with the San Deigo State University. His 1986 book *The Adventures of Ibn Battuta, a Muslim Traveller of the Fourteenth Century* revealed to many scholars the diversity in Africa as well as the links among communities in Africa, Asia, and Europe as early as the 1300s.

KEY TERMS BY THEME

ENVIRONMENT
malaria
bananas
Congo River

CULTURE
Ibn Battuta
camel saddle
hijab
eunuchs
Ali bin Muhammad
Zanj Rebellion
griots
rock churches
San

ECONOMICS
Indian Ocean trade
trans-Saharan trade
Kumbai Saleh
Timbuktu
Gao
Kilwa
Swahili city-states
Mombasa
Zanj Coast

SOCIAL STRUCTURE
matrilineal descent
kin-based networks
age grades (or age sets)

STATE-BUILDING
chief
Kongo Kingdom
Ghana
Mali
Sundiata
Mansa Musa
Mecca
Songhay
Zimbabwe
Great Zimbabwe

1. As Bantu-speakers migrated throughout Sub-Saharan Africa, they spread the use of
    (A) gold and silver
    (B) slash-and-burn agriculture
    (C) a uniform language
    (D) the Islamic faith

2. One parallel between the importation of bananas to Africa and the spread of rice cultivation in East Asia was that both resulted in
    (A) increased trade with other countries
    (B) a higher death rate from the introduction of new diseases
    (C) higher migration from rural areas to cities
    (D) rapid population growth

3. One similarity between the increase of trade across the Sahara and trade along the eastern coast of Africa was that both
    (A) developed new technologies that used iron
    (B) depended primarily on networks among Bantu-speaking peoples
    (C) resulted in the spread of Islam
    (D) led to a rapid increase in a new form of labor, slavery

4. The most important global impact of Islam coming to Sub-Saharan Africa was that
    (A) the region participated more in interregional trade than before.
    (B) the Islamic faith became more militant
    (C) religious wars erupted in the region
    (D) diseases indigenous to the African continent spread throughout Eurasia

5. Trans-Saharan trade shows the importance people in northern Africa placed on
    (A) trading for luxury items for the wealthy
    (B) obtaining iron for making weapons.
    (C) purchasing horses for use by farmers.
    (D) obtaining salt for preserving and flavoring food.

6. Unlike the empires of Ghana, Mali, and Songhay, the empire of Zimbabwe was
   (A) directly involved in the Indian Ocean trade
   (B) linked to the Middle East by trade
   (C) heavily influenced by Islam
   (D) based on trade in gold

7. Which of the following situations would reflect the highest status in a Sub-Saharan culture during the time period 600–1450?
   (A) A young man who owned many cows
   (B) An elderly man who served on a council of elders
   (C) A young woman who became the fourth wife of a tribal chief
   (D) An elderly woman whose son was the best hunter in the village

8. Which best explains why veiling never became universally accepted by Sub-Saharan Africans who converted to Islam?
   (A) Veiling was a custom in Southwest Asia, not a religious requirement.
   (B) Religious customs usually weaken as a faith spreads to new areas.
   (C) Sub-Saharan Africa's climate was too hot for women to wear veils.
   (D) Religion was less significant to Bantu-speakers than to Arabs.

Question 9 refers to the excerpt below.

Gold was at a high price in Egypt until they came in that year. The mithqal did not go below 25 dirhams and was generally above, but from that time its value fell and it cheapened in price and has remained cheap till now. The mithqal does not exceed 22 dirhams or less. This has been the state of affairs for about 12 years until this day by reason of the large amount of gold which they brought into Egypt and spent there . . . .

—Al-Umari, 1324

9. The excerpt describes one of the results of a trip by
   (A) a traveler from Morocco to Southwest Asia
   (B) an explorer from Spain to Mesopotamia
   (C) a king from Mali to Mecca
   (D) a prophet from Mecca to Medina

Question 10 refers to the image below.

Source: Thinkstock

10. The above image shows a Christian church in East Africa carved out of rock. The building demonstrates how people

   (A) adapt new ideas to local conditions

   (B) modify old structures for new uses

   (C) blend new and old religious beliefs

   (D) combine new technology with old traditions

CONTINUITY AND CHANGE-OVER-TIME ESSAY QUESTIONS

Directions: You are to answer the following question. You should spend 5 minutes organizing or outlining your essay. Write an essay that:

   • Has a relevant thesis and supports that thesis with appropriate historical evidence.

   • Addresses all parts of the question.

   • Uses world historical context to show continuities and changes over time.

   • Analyzes the process of continuity and change over time.

1. Analyze the changes and continuities in African culture before and after the arrival of Islam in the seventh and eighth centuries.

Questions for Additional Practice

2. Analyze the changes and continuities in political and cultural life in West Africa from 600 to 1450.

3. Analyze the continuities and changes in trade in East African kingdoms from 600 to 1450.

COMPARATIVE ESSAY QUESTIONS

Directions: You are to answer the following question. You should spend 5 minutes organizing or outlining your essay. Write an essay that:
- Has a relevant thesis and supports that thesis with appropriate historical evidence.
- Addresses all parts of the question.
- Makes direct, relevant comparisons.
- Analyzes relevant reasons for similarities and differences.

1. Discuss the similarities and differences in the interaction between Islam and African religions and between Christianity and African religions from 600 to 1450.

Questions for Additional Practice

2. Compare and contrast women's status in Sub-Saharan Africa with women's status in ONE of the following Post-Classical civilizations from 600 to 1450.
   - Southwest Asia
   - China
   - India

3. Discuss the differences and similarities in economics and politics between the Swahili city-states and the cities of the Mali Kingdom.

Historical evidence comes from many sources, from ruins to eyewitness accounts in diaries and letters. To use historical evidence requires asking questions of the source. For example, Who created this evidence? Why did he or she make it? Whom was it created for? How did people use it at the time? *Describe the kind of evidence that might be used to answer or explain the following questions or statements:*

1. What cultural forces were at work in Sub-Saharan Africa during the 14th century?

2. How important was belief in the spirit world to the Bantu-speaking peoples?

3. Explain how wealth from the Indian Ocean trade was displayed in the Swahili city-states.

4. How and why did griots, or storytellers, become the keepers of history in their communities?

5. In what ways did visual arts serve a religious purpose in the Sub-Saharan world?

WRITE AS A HISTORIAN: SUPPORT A TOPIC SENTENCE

The topic sentence of a body paragraph in an essay should be supported with facts and informed judgments. You can achieve this support through using specific names, dates, and examples that relate to the focus of your topic sentence. *Select the TWO sentences that most clearly support a paragraph that begins with this topic sentence: Foreign influences on religion were strong in the kingdoms of Mali and Zimbabwe.*

1. The strong influence of Islam in East Africa can be seen in the large amount of Arabic in the language of Swahili.

2. Weddings and funerals often included musical rituals that consisted of communicating with the spiritual world.

3. Although most African communities lacked a written language, elders passed on important knowledge through song lyrics.

4. The people of Ethiopia combined Christianity with traditional beliefs in spirits and ancestor veneration.

5. In present-day Africa, Islam dominates many countries as a major religion.

10

East Asia in the Post-Classical Period

All the birds have flown up and gone;
A lonely cloud floats leisurely by.
We never tire of looking at each other –
Only the mountain and I.

—Li Bo, "Alone Looking at the Mountain" (date unknown)

Poet Li Bo (701–762 C.E.) was one of the most accomplished artists of the Tang era in China. Many of his poems, such as the one above, describe someone contemplating nature. Others focus on attending parties and other ways people enjoy life with friends. These themes, both positive and uplifting, seem to reflect the buoyancy of Post-Classical China. During the 600 years of the Tang and Song dynasties, China enjoyed great wealth, political stability, and fine artistic and intellectual achievements. These years were a golden era in Chinese history.

During the Post-Classical period, China dominated East Asia. Its neighbors, including Korea, Japan, and Vietnam, developed vibrant and distinctive cultural traditions, but each also displayed China's influence.

Political Structures in China

After the collapse of the Han Dynasty in the third century C.E., China fell into a state of anarchy for nearly 400 years. People suffered from reduced trade and greater political turmoil until the short-lived *Sui Dynasty* (581–618 C.E.).

Unity under the Sui Dynasty Emperor Sui Yangdi unified China through violence and repression. Successful military expeditions to the south expanded the reach of China's government. He also sent troops into Korea and Central Asia. Sui Yangdi ruled through harsh, dictatorial methods, which made dissent risky.

Grand Canal The greatest accomplishment of the dynasty was the inception of the construction of the *Grand Canal*. This ambitious public works project involved thousands of conscripted peasants working for many years. The idea behind the canal was to provide a means of transporting rice and other crops from the food-rich Yangtze River valley in the south to populous northern China and the center of government of Luoyang. At the southern end of the

Grand Canal was the city of *Hangzhou*, which expanded greatly during the Sui Dynasty because of the increased trade. It was during the Sui Dynasty that the city leaders had a defensive wall built around the city. The Sui used conscripts also to reinforce the "Long Wall" in the north begun by earlier dynasties. (The Long Wall would later become part of the Great Wall of China.)

Downfall of the Sui The rule by the Sui lasted only 40 years. People complained about high taxes needed to pay for the expensive military escapades, the conscription of laborers for the building projects, and the emperor's dictatorial ways. The emperor was assassinated in 618, and the dynasty ended.

Tang Dynasty

The short Sui Dynasty prepared the way for the longer, more influential *Tang Dynasty* (618–907 C.E.). During this period, China enjoyed relative prosperity and stability. Rulers extended the territory of the Chinese Empire. At its height, the Tang Dynasty extended west to Central Asia, north to Manchuria, and south into modern-day Vietnam.

Tributary System The Tang Dynasty dominated its neighbors. The Chinese viewed their country as the *Middle Kingdom*, a society around which the whole world revolved. At the very least, China was the center of a *tributary*

SUI AND TANG EMPIRES

system, an arrangement in which other states had to pay money or provide goods to honor the Chinese emperor. For example, the *Silla Kingdom* in Korea was not part of China, but it had to pay a large tribute to the emperor. The tributary system cemented China's economic and political power over several foreign countries, but it also created stability and stimulated trade for all parties involved.

Tang emperors also expected representatives from tributary states to perform a ritual *kowtow,* a requirement in which anyone greeting the Chinese emperor must bow his or her head until it reached the floor. This act was a way to acknowledge China's superior status.

Tang Accomplishments The Tang Dynasty had some notable achievements. Emperor Tang Taizong (ruled 627–649) further developed modes of transportation that had begun during the Sui Dynasty, such as roads and canals, as well as postal and messenger services. His government successfully reduced the dangers from bandits.

Tang Taizong expanded the empire's bureaucracy, which developed into an important and ongoing feature of Chinese government. Candidates for the bureaucracy had to pass an extremely rigorous civil service examination. The exam system had a tremendous impact on Chinese culture. Since the examination was difficult, education became increasingly important in China, a development that fostered economic growth for many centuries. Further, serving in the bureaucracy was highly regarded. So, just as communities today might take pride in producing an Olympic athlete or a noted actor, communities in China took pride in their natives who won a good position working for the government. Though most bureaucrats earned their positions in government, some were appointed. Aristocratic families had greater access to high-level positions in the bureaucracy than did any other group.

Spread of Buddhism In 629, a Chinese Buddhist monk named *Xuanzang* left China to go on a pilgrimage to India, the birthplace of Buddhism. He traveled west on the Silk Roads to Central Asia, then south and east to India, which he reached in 630. Along the way and in India he met many Buddhist monks and visited Buddhist shrines. In order to gain more insight into Buddhism, he studied for years in Buddhist monasteries and at Nalanda University in Bilar, India—a famous center of Buddhist knowledge. After 17 years away, Xuanzang finally returned to China, where people greeted him as a celebrity. He brought back many Buddhist texts, which he spent the rest of his life translating into Chinese. These writings were highly instrumental in the growth of Buddhist scholarship in China.

An Lushan By the eighth century, the Tang Empire already showed signs of weakness. Emperor *Hsuan Tsung* (ruled 712–756) was not devoted to administering the affairs of government and became distracted by his favorite concubine, Yang Guifei. A military leader named An Lushan orchestrated a rebellion involving about a hundred thousand soldiers, overthrowing Hsuan Tsung in 755. Finally, an army of *Uighurs,* an ethnic group living in Central Asia on land controlled by China, arrived from the west to restore power to the government and defeat the rebels. The rebellion did tremendous damage.

The death toll from the fighting, combined with the starvation and disease associated with the conflict, reached the millions and maybe the tens of millions. It was probably one of the most devastating wars in human history. The Tang survived, but they never fully recovered their power. They had to pay an annual tribute to the Uighurs. The Tang Dynasty finally collapsed in 907.

Song Dynasty

The *Song Dynasty* began in 960 and lasted until 1279. Because nomadic pastoralists from Manchuria invaded its lands, captured the northern part, and set up their own empire (the *Jin*, with a capital in Beijing), the Song came to rule a smaller region than the Tang had. Nevertheless, China under the Song was quite prosperous, and the arts flourished.

Bureaucracy and Meritocracy Under the Song, China's bureaucracy expanded, and the number of bureaucratic positions in government increased. Moreover, Emperor Song Taizu made special efforts to expand the educational opportunities to young men of the lower strata so they could pass the civil service exams. Though the poor were still extremely underrepresented in the

SONG AND JIN EMPIRES

bureaucracy, the Chinese system of meritocracy allowed for more upward mobility than any other hiring system of its time.

However, under the Song Dynasty, the bureaucracy had gotten so large it contributed to the empire's weakness. By creating more positions within the bureaucracy and by paying these officials quite handsomely, Song Taizu increased the costs of government enough that it began drying up China's surplus wealth.

Another problem was that Song Taizu and other emperors asked some bureaucrats to be responsible for military affairs. Government officials, who were together known as the *scholar gentry,* had studied in-depth the teachings of Confucius and the Chinese classics, but they were not experts in military tactics and strategy. Their lack of expertise left Chinese armies more vulnerable to nomadic incursions.

A Shifting Capital Because of threats from nomads, the Song Dynasty moved its capital from *Chang'an* (the modern city of Xian) about 530 miles to the east, to *Kaifeng.* In 1127, under continuous pressure from incursions by nomads, the empire was forced to move its capital again, this time 400 miles further south, to Hangzhou.

The *Southern Song Dynasty* survived until 1279, when the nomadic Mongol Empire vanquished the government and established the *Yuan Dynasty.* In the years leading up to the Mongol conquest of China, the Song Empire had been paying tribute to the Mongol nomads as a way to stave off conquest. However, this tribute was not enough to save China from Mongol domination.

Economic Developments in Post-Classical China

The Tang Dynasty's efforts to promote agricultural development, improve infrastructure, encourage foreign trade, and spread technology led to rapid prosperity and population growth during the Song Dynasty. For the first 150 years under the Song, China may have grown faster than any country ever had.

Land Reform Reforms in agriculture spurred economic growth. As was the case in many societies of the era, a feudal hierarchy prevented most people from owning any land or from owning sufficient land to live on. As discussed earlier, Wang Mang attempted to redistribute land during the Han Dynasty, when social tensions reached their peak. This created widespread unrest and weakened the Han Dynasty permanently.

Six hundred years after Wang Mang's failed reforms, the Tang Empire reintroduced an *equal-field system,* which attempted to ensure that all Chinese families had a parcel of land to cultivate. The empire's intent was not humanitarian; its goal was to wrest power away from the landed aristocracy. This reform proved effective for about 100 years, resulting in an increase in rural wealth. In the eighth century, though, the landed aristocracy used their money and power to bribe government officials to let them keep owning their land. Though the equal-field system reform did not last, rural wealth did grow, and increased prosperity provided some stability for the countryside.

Agricultural Productivity Agriculture prospered also because of new methods of production. The Chinese put manure (both human and animal) on the fields to enrich the soil. They built elaborate irrigation systems using ditches, water wheels, pumps, and terraces to increase productivity. New heavy plows pulled by water buffalo or oxen allowed previously unusable land to be cultivated.

Under the Tang Dynasty (618–907), *fast-ripening rice* (also known as Champa rice) added to Chinese agricultural surpluses. This grain is native to northern Vietnam, which came under the control of China during the Tang Dynasty. Fast-ripening rice allowed peasants in the warmer agricultural region of southern China to grow two crops a year. Thus, both land redistribution and food surpluses were instrumental in spreading China's prosperity.

Because of the Sui Dynasty's construction of the Grand Canal, one of the biggest infrastructure efforts of its time, agricultural products from southern China traveled more easily to the less fertile lands of northern China. The Grand Canal moved the centers of agricultural production of China from the barren north to the fertile south.

In most societies in world history prior to the time of the Song, agricultural goods dominated the economy and trade. Song China produced more nonagricultural goods for commercial use than any earlier civilization. Two of these goods stand out: porcelain and silk. Under the Song, China went through *proto-industrialization,* a phase that precedes and enables full industrialization later, earlier than Western Europe. (Test Prep: Write a paragraph comparing China's proto-industrialization with the cottage industries of Western Europe. See page 287.)

Urbanization Like the Abbasid civilizations, Song China featured growing urban areas. Chinese cities impressed Marco Polo, a visitor from Western Europe's most sophisticated urban area—Venice. Polo wrote extensively about the high levels of urbanization he saw in the thirteenth century.

> They use paper money as currency. The men as well as the women are fair-skinned and handsome. Most of them always dress themselves in silk, as a result of the vast quantities of that material produced in Hangzhou, exclusive of what the merchants import from other provinces.

Hangzhou was large—it was home to about one million people—but other Chinese cities were larger. Chang'an had about two million. However, Hangzhou was the center of culture in southern China, the home of poets such as Lu Yu and Xin Qiji. And, located at the southern end of the Grand Canal, it was a center of trade. Like other important cities of the era, such as Novgorod in Russia, Timbuktu in Africa, and Calicut in India, the city grew and prospered as its merchants imported and exported goods. This trade brought diversity to Hangzhou, including a thriving community of Arabs.

Tax Policy The Song reduced the requirement that people labor for the government. Instead, they paid people to work on public projects. This increased the money in circulation, thereby promoting economic growth.

Metal, Gunpowder, and Guns Iron and steel production increased greatly in China as people developed their skills in smelting, the process of separating a metal from ore. One major advance in metal production was to convert coal into coke, a process that removes many of the impurities found in coal. By using coke, the Chinese could make metal that was stronger and make better plows, weapons, and bridges.

During the ninth century, Chinese researchers, trying to find elements that might lead to longer or even eternal life, discovered that blending certain ingredients created a powder that, when touched with a flame, exploded. This was gunpowder. They soon learned to use gunpowder to produce both entertaining fireworks displays and weapons. The first guns were made in the Song Dynasty. Over centuries, the technology of making gunpowder and guns spread from China to all parts of Eurasia via traders on the Silk Roads and through the movement of nomadic peoples such as the Mongols along the steppe, the long stretch of grasslands from Mongolia to Hungary.

Foreign Trade As discussed in earlier chapters, interregional trade along the Silk Roads created many intercultural connections during the Classical Era. After the collapse of classical civilizations such as the Roman and Han empires, activity on the Silk Roads declined dramatically. However, by the eighth and ninth centuries, Arab merchants from the Abbasid Empire revived the land route of the Silk Roads as well as sea routes in the Indian Ocean. Tang China had much to offer the newly revived global trade network, including the compass, paper, and gunpowder. China exported porcelain, tea, and silk. From other parts of Asia, China imported cotton, precious stones, pomegranates, dates, horses, and grapes. These luxury goods appealed to the upper class of Chinese society, whose members reveled in their country's newfound affluence.

To manage the increasing trade, China developed new financial systems. Because copper coins became too unwieldy to transport for everyday transactions, the government developed a system of credit known as *flying cash*. This allowed a merchant to deposit *paper money* under his name in one location and withdraw the same amount at another location. Merchants and tax collectors used abacuses to calculate their transactions. The system of flying cash became the model for the banks of the modern era. Later, Chinese governments would prohibit private individuals and businesses from making paper money, reserving that right for themselves.

Advances in naval technology allowed China to control trade in the South China Sea. Chinese scientists developed the *magnetic compass* and improved the *rudder*, both of which helped aid navigation and ship control along the seas. The Chinese *junk*, developed in the Han Dynasty, was a boat similar to the Southwest Asian dhow (discussed in Chapter 8), had multiple sails and was as long as 400 feet—at least triple the size of the typical Western European ship of its time. The hull of a junk was divided into compartments. The walls making these divisions strengthened the ship for rough voyages at sea and made sinking less likely.

Innovations in Commerce, 500 B.C.E. to 1603 C.E.			
Financial Instrument	Description	Origin Date	Early Location
Coin	Minted precious metals (silver, bronze, gold) with own inherent value	c. 500 B.C.E.	Lydia, Turkey
Caravanserai	Inns along trade routes where travelers could trade, rest, and replenish	c. 500 B.C.E.	Persian Empire
Paper Money	Currency in paper form	c. 800 C.E.	China
Hanseatic League	First common market and confederation of merchant guilds	1296 C.E.	Germany
Banking House	Precursor to modern bank	c. 200 B.C.E.	China
Bill of Exchange	A written order without interest which binds one party to pay a fixed sum to another party at a predetermined date in the future	c. 700 C.E.	China

Social Structures in China

Through most of Chinese history, the majority of people lived in rural areas. The Tang and Song eras were no exception. However, this was the first time in China's history when urban areas grew in prominence. At the height of the Song Dynasty, China was the most urbanized land in the world, boasting several cities containing more than 100,000 people. The largest cities, Chang'an, Hangzhou, and Guangzhou, were cosmopolitan metropolises— active centers of commerce with many entertainment options to offer. Taverns, restaurants, street vendors, markets, theaters, and specialty shops filled with imported luxuries were all available to residents of these bustling cities, many of which were located on the southeastern coast of China. The size and wealth of these cities amazed foreign visitors and traders, who came from as far away as Italy.

New Social Class Though urbanization represented a significant development in China's economic and social landscape, life in rural areas grew more complex as well. As discussed earlier, the Song Dynasty expanded the bureaucracy immensely, opening up opportunities for well-paying jobs to men of modest backgrounds. This expansion created an entirely new social class, the *scholar gentry*. They soon outnumbered the aristocracy, which was comprised of landowners who inherited their wealth. The scholar gentry were educated in Confucian philosophy, had more money than their ancestors, and, because of their numbers, became the most influential social class in China.

Other Classes Three other classes ranked below the scholar gentry: farmers, artisans and craftsmen, and the merchant class. Merchants were considered by the gentry as the lowest in rank because they didn't produce anything new; they merely profited from the exchange of others' handiwork and labor. Even so, the merchant was often quite wealthy and held considerably more influence in society than their rank would suggest.

Role of Women As in many societies, in China, men ruled and women assumed subordinate roles. China's patriarchal society strengthened during the Song and Tang dynasties. One distinctive constraint on women's activity in China was the practice of *foot binding*, which began during the Song Dynasty. From a very young age, girls from aristocratic families had their feet wrapped so tightly that the bones did not grow naturally. Though the small feet were considered a sign of beauty, foot binding was quite painful and often made it difficult for women to walk. Many women had to use canes to get around, and some had servants carry them to their desired destinations. Because it restricted a woman's movement, foot binding was not prevalent among rural peasants. Thus, a bound foot signified social status, something particularly desired when choosing a suitable mate. Often, such practices have served to restrict women and thus limit their contributions to the public sphere.

CHINESE WOOD-BLOCK PRINTING

Source: Thinkstock

With the development of wood block printing in China, people could make multiple copies of art or written texts without laboriously copying each by hand.

Intellectual and Cultural Developments

Perhaps because of China's increased affluence, better-educated populace, and extensive contact with foreign nations, intellectual pursuits (technology, literature, and visual arts) thrived during the Tang and Song eras.

Paper and Printing The Chinese had invented paper as early as the second century C.E., and they developed a system of printing in the seventh century. They were the first culture to use *wood-block printing*. In that method, an artist carves a block of wood so that the carved parts of the wood will appear as blank spaces on the page. The artist then coats the remaining raised parts of the block with ink, and the mirror image of the block is created when pressed against a page. A Buddhist scripture produced in the seventh century is thought to be the world's first wood-block printed work. (For more on the Gutenberg press, see page 278.)

Reading and Poetry The development of paper and printing expanded the availability of books. Though most peasants were illiterate, China's privileged classes had increased access to literature. Confucian scholars not only consumed literature at a tremendous rate, they also were the major producers of literature throughout the Post-Classical Era. The Tang and Song dynasties' emphasis on schooling created generations of well-rounded scholar-bureaucrats with leisure time on their hands, which they might spend composing romantic verses or dabbling in painting. These members of a privileged class were the world's first "Renaissance men."

The secular backgrounds of many writers were revealed in their poetry. For example, *Li Bo*'s verse of the eighth century was light and airy; his subjects were love, friendship, and the pleasures of wine. (See the example at the beginning of the chapter.) His writing stands in contrast to the more somber poetry of *Du Fu*, in the same century. Du Fu is known as the "poet-historian" of China's Post-Classical Era. As the Tang Dynasty began to crumble, Du Fu's writing dealt with the hardships of daily life. The works of these two prolific writers continue to be read in modern times.

Painting Another art form that flourished during the Post-Classical Era was landscape painting. Landscape in Chinese literally means "mountain-water." Human figures on the canvas are miniscule in comparison to the work's vast empty spaces or mountains. Daoism's emphasis on nature shows itself in these paintings.

Religious Diversity in China

Many Chinese respected the ideals of Daoism and combined Daoist beliefs with Confucianism. The two belief systems existing alongside each other in people's everyday beliefs and practices. For example, the scholar gentry who created meditative landscape paintings were also well-versed in Confucianism. However, Confucians and Buddhists did not coexist comfortably.

Buddhism had come to China from its birthplace in India via the Silk Roads. Its presence is evident during the anarchic period between the later Han and the Sui dynasties. However, its popularity became widespread during the Tang Dynasty. The seventh century Buddhist monk Xuanzang was instrumental in building Buddhism's popularity in China.

Buddhism and Taoism Monks introduced Buddhism to the Chinese by relating its beliefs to Daoist principles. For example, Buddhism's idea of dharma became translated as dao ("the way"). Eventually, Buddhist doctrines combined with elements of Daoist traditions to create the syncretic faith *Chan Buddhism*, also known as *Zen Buddhism*. Similar to Taoism, this new form of Buddhism emphasized direct experience and meditation as opposed to formal learning based on scripture.

Thanks to this religious syncretism, Buddhism's popularity in China grew immensely. Monasteries—homes of monks—appeared in virtually every major city, which became a problem in itself for the Tang bureaucracy. Wealthy converts donated large tracts of land to monasteries, which did not pay taxes, annoying the Confucian bureaucracy.

More broadly, it was difficult for many leaders of the Tang Dynasty, which considered itself the "Middle Kingdom"—the center of world affairs—to accept that a foreign religion would have such prominence in society. Buddhism's popularity, which drew individuals away from China's native religions, made Daoists and Confucians quite jealous. Thus, during the eighth century, Tang officials ordered that Buddhist monasteries be closed and their lands seized. Nevertheless, Chan Buddhism remained popular among ordinary Chinese citizens.

Buddhism and Neo-Confucianism The Song Dynasty was somewhat friendlier towards Buddhism, but it did not go out of its way to promote the religion, preferring to emphasize China's native traditions, such as Confucianism, which itself went through changes. Buddhism's presence had been so strong that many Confucians had begun to adopt its ideals into their daily lives. The development of printing had made Buddhist scriptures widely available to the Confucian scholar gentry. In spite of themselves, the scholars found that they appreciated the thoughtfulness that Buddhism devoted to issues of the soul and the meaning of life. Thus, *Neo-Confucianism*, another syncretic faith, evolved in China between 770 and 840. Neo-Confucianism is a social and ethical philosophy, not a religious belief, that combines rational thought with the metaphysics of Taoism and Buddhism. This new incarnation of Confucianism also became immensely popular in the countries in China's orbit, including Japan, Korea, and Vietnam.

Japan

Though the "Middle Kingdom" was powerful, Japan, Korea, and Vietnam had their own political and cultural traditions. That said, China cast a long shadow over its neighbors. During the Post-Classical Era, these societies were forced to adapt to the rise of China and grapple with the changes that its predominance brought to their lands.

Fear of China During the Post-Classical Era, Japan's isolation was interrupted by China's emergence as a global power. Though China did not invade Japan during this time, it did have a presence in nearby Korea, which troubled the Japanese government. Japanese officials worried that the "Middle Kingdom" would soon be encroaching upon their land.

Under Prince *Shotoku Taishi* (lived 574–622), of the dominant Yamato region, Japan responded by attempting to implement Chinese practices in Japan. For example, the prince wrote a new constitution that consolidated power for all of Japan in one ruler. He argued for a centralized government with a merit-based system of selecting bureaucrats. He hired skilled Chinese laborers to come to Japan to share their knowledge in various crafts and construction. The court also sent Japanese nobility to China to study Chinese culture. They promoted Buddhism and Confucianism as supplements to Japan's traditional Shinto religion, and introduced wood-block printing to Japan (Test Prep: In a paragraph compare Japan's reaction to China with its reaction to Western powers in the 1800s. See page 454.)

Religious Affiliations in Japan Today			
Religion	**First Widely Practiced in Japan**	**Source**	**Perecentage of Japanese***
Shinto	Prehistoric period	Developed in Japan	84
Buddhism	Sixth century C.E.	China	71
Christianity	Sixteenth century C.E.	Portugal	2
Other	Various	Various	8

Source: The World Factbook. cia.gov.

* Many Japanese consider themselves followers of more than one religion.

Taika Reforms After Shotoku's death, his successor enacted other reforms, known as the *Taika Reforms*, in 646. One goal of the reforms was increasing efficiency; the other was to wrest control of society from the landed aristocracy. The new laws put all farmland under government ownership, which meant that all taxes would be paid directly to the central government, rather than the nobility. This was a major blow to the power of the feudal lords and a large step toward creating a powerful centralized government.

In the 710, the *Fujiwara clan* took control of the government and moved the capital city to *Nara*, which was built in the style of China's capital city, Chang'an. Indeed, the Fujiwara Clan continued in the tradition of Shotoku in modeling itself after Tang China in many ways.

Return to Decentralized Government Eventually, however, the power of the aristocracy was too strong, and in 794 the current emperor moved the capital back to *Heian*, where the emperor had more support. Unlike the Chinese emperors, the emperor of Japan was merely a figurehead to whom the Japanese people gave respect. In the Post-Classical Era, power truly rested in the hands of the Fujiwara family.

Leaders of the empire during the Heian Period (794–1185) still tried to emulate Chinese political traditions. They were not successful, though, as Heian Japan slipped back into a pattern of political decentralization. Though the government had instituted an equal-field system similar to China's, it failed because of the nobility's influence. The merit-based bureaucracy actually served to strengthen the nobility because the civil service examination was not open to all social classes.

The Tale of Genji Although leaders of Heian Japan failed to consolidate government power, their cultural achievements are notable. Literature flourished during this period. A woman named *Murasaki Shikibu* wrote *The Tale of Genji*, arguably the world's first novel. It is a classic of world literature about Genji, an imperial prince. *The Tale of Genji* is not only a melancholy story of love and the passing of time, but it is also a window into the life of aristocratic Japan.

Military Rule Political weakness and aristocratic greed caused the downfall of the Heian court. Thereafter, the *Minamoto clan* rose to power. From the end of the twelfth century until the late sixteenth century, power would stay in the hands of the Minamoto family, which installed a *shogun*, or military ruler, to reign supreme. This shogun was separate from the emperor, who had even less power during this period than before. While the Nara and Heian courts tried to emulate China's scholarly and courtly traditions, the Minamoto shogunate emphasized military prowess.

Because power became decentralized under the Minamoto clan, noble families returned to battling over estates. To protect their lands, nobles recruited *samurai*, professional warriors who, in return for their sacrifice, received clothing, shelter, and food from their landlord. In the absence of any army or central political force to stabilize the society, the samurai played a central role in the 400-year period (the Kamakura and Muromachi shogunates) after Heian Japan fell. (Test Prep: Make an outline in which you compare Japanese samurai with knights of medieval Europe. See page 223.)

Feudalism For hundreds of years, Japan had been a feudal society without a centralized government. Landowning aristocrats, the *daimyo*, battled for supreme power over the land, while the majority of people worked as rice farmers.

Japanese feudalism was similar to European feudalism, which is described in Chapter 12. Both featured very little social mobility, and both systems were built upon hereditary hierarchies. In Japan, peasants, known as serfs, were born into lives of economic dependency, while samurai were born into their roles as protectors, and daimyo were born into lives of privilege. In Europe, the three groups were serfs, knights, and nobles.

What distinguishes Japanese feudalism from that of Europe was that the daimyo enjoyed much more power than the nobility in Europe did. The daimyo ruled over vast stretches of land and, in reality, were more powerful than either the emperor or the shogun. By contrast, Europe's hierarchy placed the monarch above the nobility. Though there were periods when authority of the monarch waned and power was distributed among nobility, the main centralized power structure of European feudalism would not change until the Modern Industrial Era.

In Europe, the ideal knight held to the code of chivalry, with duty to countrymen, duty to God, and duty to women, the latter expressed through courtly love and the virtues of gentleness and graciousness. In Japan, the code was known as *bushido*, and stressed frugality, loyalty, the martial arts, and honor unto death.

Korea

Since it shared a land border with China, Korea had a much more direct relationship with China than Japan. The Tang Dynasty demanded that representatives of the Korean Silla Kingdom perform the ritual kowtow when meeting the Chinese emperor and become a tributary state of China. In order to appease the Chinese, the Korean Kingdom agreed. Giving tributes to China had its benefits: Korea began receiving valuable Chinese exports to which it may not have otherwise had access.

Similarity to China Through its tributary relationship, Korea and China were in close contact. Thus, Korea emulated many aspects of China's politics and culture. For example, it modeled its capital city, *Kumsong*, on Chang'an. It centralized its government in the style of the Chinese. Culturally, Koreans adopted both Confucian and Buddhist beliefs. The educated elite studied Confucian classics, while Buddhist doctrine attracted the peasant masses. Koreans adopted Chinese written characters, even though it was difficult because the two languages were not the same.

Korean Bureaucracy The Korean landed aristocracy held such power over Korean society that certain Chinese reforms were never implemented. Though there was a Korean civil service examination, it was not open to peasants. Thus, there was no truly merit-based system for entering the bureaucracy.

Vietnam

Vietnam's adversarial relationship with China stands in stark contrast to Korea's peaceful one. The Vietnamese realized the benefits of new technology and trade, but they did not willingly give up their own identity to China.

Trade The Han Dynasty had expanded south into Vietnam during the Classical Era. It did not significantly alter Vietnam's culture or government, though it did bring trade to this Southeast Asian land. In exchange for Chinese silk, the Vietnamese exported tortoise shells, ivory, peacock feathers, and pearls.

Relationship with China Several aspects of Vietnamese culture differed from Chinese culture, which is why so many resisted Chinese incursion into their lifestyles. For example, women in Vietnamese culture enjoyed greater independence in their married lives than did Chinese women in the Confucian tradition. While the Chinese lived in extended families, the Vietnamese preferred *nuclear families* (just a wife, husband, and their children). Vietnamese villages operated independently of a national government; political centralization was nonexistent.

Sinification, or the assimilation of Chinese traditions and practices, was not welcomed wholeheartedly in Vietnam. Vietnamese schools educated their students in Chinese, which led the Vietnamese to develop their own written language based on Chinese characters. They still retained their spoken language, however, which is not at all related to the Chinese language. (Test Prep: Write a paragraph in which you compare and contrast the way Vietnam dealt with the Chinese language with the way Korea dealt with the Chinese language. See page 193.)

Although Vietnam adopted a merit-based bureaucracy of educated men, the Vietnamese system did not function like the Chinese scholar-bureaucracy. Instead of loyalty to the emperor, scholar-officials in Vietnam owed more allegiance to the village peasants. In fact, Vietnamese scholar-officials often led revolts against the government if they deemed it too oppressive. Vietnamese women resented their inferior status under the Chinese, as well as Confucian practices such as *polygyny* (the practice of having more than one spouse at the same time).

As the Tang Dynasty began to crumble in the eighth century, Vietnamese rebels took the opportunity to drive out China's occupying army. In their battles against the Chinese, they showed a strong capacity for *guerilla warfare*, perhaps due to their deep knowledge of their own land.

In spite of Vietnamese efforts to maintain the purity of their own culture, sinification did occur. For example, the majority of the Vietnamese converted to Buddhism and became serious adherents to the faith. Politically, Viet kingdoms modeled their palaces after those in China, but with less grandeur and opulence. Formal education continued to be conducted in Chinese.

HISTORICAL PERSPECTIVE: WHO INVENTED GUNPOWDER AND GUNS?

The development of gunpowder and its use in guns revolutionized world history. While the Chinese took credit for developing both gunpowder and guns, European historians were skeptical because they doubted the Chinese had the technological ability. For example, Henry Hime, a British military officer, argued in his 1904 book, *Gunpowder and Ammunition: Their Origin and Progress,* that the Chinese "possessed little genius for mechanical or chemical inventions" so they had probably "obtained their first gunpowder and firearms from the West."

Europeans slowly acknowledged Chinese contributions to the technologies that led to the development of guns. They first recognized that the Chinese had invented gunpowder, and that knowledge of the explosive substance had been carried by traders and the Mongols to Europe in the thirteenth century. However, European historians continued to argue that the Chinese had used gunpowder only for fireworks, not for weaponry. Historian Jack Kelly, in a recent book about the history of gunpowder, noted that historians had not moved much beyond Hime's argument in their views of Chinese abilities. "The notion of China's benign relationship with gunpowder sprang in part from Western prejudices about the Chinese character. Some viewed the Chinese as dilettantes who stumbled into the secret of gunpowder but couldn't envision its potential. Others saw them as pacifist sages who wisely turned away from its destructive possibilities."

The next step was for Europeans to acknowledge that the Chinese historians were correct, and that the Chinese had begun using gunpowder to make early forms of guns since the tenth century. British scholar Joseph Needham revolutionized western attitudes toward China with his multi-volume work *Science and Civilization in China.* Begun in 1954, it continued after Needham's death under other scholars and now includes more than 25 volumes. By 1986, Needham called the development of gunpowder "no doubt the greatest of all Chinese military inventions." And he concluded that the Chinese had developed the first gun "before other peoples knew of the invention at all."

KEY TERMS BY THEME

ECONOMICS
equal-field system
fast-ripening rice
proto-industrialization
flying cash
paper money
magnetic compass
rudder
junk
wood-block printing

SOCIAL STRUCTURES
nuclear family
sinification
polygyny
Xuanzang
Hsuan Tsung
An Lushan
scholar gentry
daimyo

STATE-BUILDING
Sui Dynasty
Grand Canal
Hangzhou
Tang Dynasty
Middle Kingdom
Silla Kingdom
tributary system
Song Dynasty
Southern Song
    Dynasty
Tang Taizong
Song Taizu
Chang'an
Kaifeng
Yuan Dynasty
Ming Dynasty
Minamoto clan
shogun
samurai
Kumsong
guerilla warfare

CULTURE
kowtow
Uighurs
foot binding
Li Bo
Du Fu
Chan (Zen)
    Buddhism
Neo-Confucianism
Shotoku Taishi
Taika Reforms
Fujiwara clan
Nara
Heian
Murasaki Shikibu
The Tale of Genji
bushido

MULTIPLE-CHOICE QUESTIONS

1. Why are the Tang and Song dynasties often thought of as China's Golden Age?
   (A) Foreign workers built the Grand Canal and rebuilt the Great Wall.
   (B) It was a period of wealth and stability.
   (C) Women gained more rights.
   (D) Trade brought large quantities of gold into China.

2. One long-term impact of the civil service examination system in China was
   (A) to place a high value on learning
   (B) to reduce corruption in government
   (C) to allow equal opportunities for men and women
   (D) to decentralize the government

3. Why is China during the Song Dynasty (960–1279) often regarded as the most upwardly mobile civilization of the time?

(A) Gender equality became an active goal.

(B) Talented officers were needed to lead the army as they conquered new territories.

(C) Chinese meritocracy rewarded gifted men.

(D) Confucian principles expected the status quo to be constantly tested.

4. Which statement best summarizes the influence of the bureaucracy during the Song Dynasty?

(A) It promoted foreign trade, but it made tax collection difficult.

(B) It made managing the empire more efficient, but it was very expensive.

(C) It ended corruption, but it weakened the scholar gentry class.

(D) It strengthened Buddhism, but it undermined Confucianism.

Question 5 refers to the excerpt below.

When she was young, Lingshou was intelligent and fond of study. Her speech was clear and beautiful; her nature modest and unassuming. Taking no pleasure in worldly affairs, she was at ease in secluded quiet. She delighted in the Buddhist teaching and did not wish for her parents to arrange her betrothal.

—Shi Baochang's "Lives of Nuns" (c. 516)

5. Which phrase of the above quotation would the followers of Confucius find the most praiseworthy?

(A) "intelligent and fond of study"

(B) "at ease in secluded quiet"

(C) "delighted in the Buddhist teaching"

(D) "did not wish for her parents to arrange her betrothal"

6. In which of the following ways did China most influence Japan in the Post-Classical period?

(A) Both countries consistently had powerful central governments.

(B) Both countries had military rulers with more power than the emperor.

(C) China's emperors sent scholars to tutor the Japanese emperor.

(D) Japan sent emissaries to China to learn styles of art and literature.

7. One source of conflict between Chinese Buddhism and Confucianism was that
    (A) Confucianism emphasizes accomplishment in this world, while Buddhism emphasizes what happens after death
    (B) Buddhism is based on gender equality, while Confucianism teaches a hierarchical ordering in relationships
    (C) supporters of Buddhism charged that Confucians encouraged class conflict in society
    (D) supporters of Confucianism charged that Buddhist monks made no visible contributions to Chinese society

8. Which is the best example of one way Neo-Confucianism represented syncretism?
    (A) Neo-Confucians discounted filial piety in favor of an all-pervasive soul.
    (B) People spread Theravada Buddhism throughout Southeast Asia.
    (C) The scholar gentry class began to contemplate the existence of the soul and the meaning of life.
    (D) China allowed more classes of people to take the civil service exam.

9. Though the Koreans had to kowtow to the Chinese, one advantage in the tributary relationship was that
    (A) China subsidized the Korean education system
    (B) Korea and China had a healthy trade relationship
    (C) China protected Korea from Japanese and Mongolian incursion
    (D) the Korean peasantry benefited from a weakened nobility

Question 10 refers to the graph below.

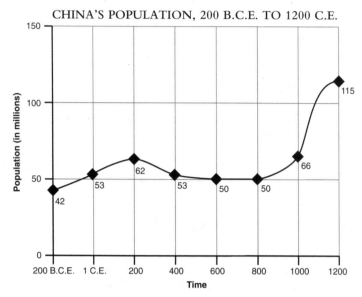

CHINA'S POPULATION, 200 B.C.E. TO 1200 C.E.

Source: Population data adapted from Quamrui Ashraf and Oded Galor, "Cultural Assimilation, Cultural Diffusion and the Origin of the Wealth of Nations." voxeu.org, September 13, 2007.

10. Based on this graph, the two periods when China's population increased the most were also periods when

(A) foreign trade was decreasing rapidly

(B) Buddhism was practiced most widely

(C) the political situation was unstable

(D) the central government was strong

CONTINUITY AND CHANGE-OVER-TIME ESSAY QUESTIONS

Directions: You are to answer the following question. You should spend 5 minutes organizing or outlining your essay. Write an essay that:

- Has a relevant thesis and supports that thesis with appropriate historical evidence.
- Addresses all parts of the question.
- Uses world historical context to show continuities and changes over time.
- Analyzes the process of continuity and change over time.

1. Analyze the continuities and changes in transregional trade between East Asia and ONE of the following regions between 600 and 1450:
   - South Asia
   - Southeast Asia
   - Japan

Questions for Additional Practice

2. Trace the continuities and changes in Japanese political culture from the reign of Prince Taishi until the Minamoto period.

3. Trace continuities and changes in China from the Shang to the Tang dynasties in the relative power of the central and local governments.

COMPARATIVE ESSAY QUESTIONS

Directions: You are to answer the following question. You should spend 5 minutes organizing or outlining your essay. Write an essay that:

- Has a relevant thesis and supports that thesis with appropriate historical evidence.
- Addresses all parts of the question.
- Makes direct, relevant comparisons.
- Analyzes relevant reasons for similarities and differences.

1. Analyze the similarities and differences between the Song and Tang dynasties in ONE of the following areas:
   - centralization of government
   - trade and economic development
   - technological innovation

Questions for Additional Practice

2. Compare and contrast China's relationship with TWO of the following three societies during the Post-Classical period:
   - Korea
   - Japan
   - Vietnam

3. Compare and contrast the Song and Abbasid empires in TWO of the following areas:
   - the role of religion
   - the significance of trade
   - the reasons for decline

THINK AS A HISTORIAN: PRACTICE HISTORICAL CAUSATION

Tests will ask you why an event, trait or trend took place. Statements describing causation often use words and phrases such as *because, consequently, therefore, as a result*, and *which led to*. *In each pair of sentences, select the one that most clearly expresses historical causation.*

1. a. China dominated East Asia during the Sui and Tang periods, even though Korea, Japan and Vietnam also had vibrant cultures.

   b. China's innovations in technology and government brought about its domination of East Asia during the Sui and Tang periods.

2. a. The Sui Dynasty lasted for a comparatively short time by historical standards.

   b. The Sui Dynasty fell soon after its expensive military expeditions.

3. a. Xuanzang contributed to the spread of Buddhism in China.

   b. Buddhism spread throughout East Asia in the seventh century.

WRITE AS A HISTORIAN: CREATING SMOOTH TRANSITIONS

To help readers follow your argument, use transitions to connect sentences. Each sentence should express one main idea, and the transitions should express the relationship between ideas. Using transitions will transform your essay from a listing of facts into an essay that ties thought and ideas together into a whole. *In each exercise, identify a transition word to connect the first and second sentences.*

1. The Sui Dynasty centralized power tightly. _____, the Tang Dynasty flourished as power became less consolidated.

2. Wang Mang made futile attempts to address these problems. _____ the following dynasties did the same.

3. Agricultural reforms resulted in success. _____, China also began industrialization to diversify its economy.

4. Most people in China lived in rural areas. _____ agriculture was the most important part of its economy.

5. China was progressive in economics and government systems. _____, the overbearing patriarchy oppressed women as in most societies during this period.

South Asia and Southeast Asia, 600–1450 C.E.

Where do you search me?
I am with you
Not in pilgrimage, nor in icons . . .
Not in temples, nor in mosques
Neither in Kaba nor in Kailash . . .
Not in yogic exercises . . .
In but a moment of search
Says Kabir, Listen with care
Where your faith is, I am there.

—Guru Kabir (lived 1440–1518)

The devotional poem by *Guru Kabir*, an Indian mystic, illustrates a major cross-cultural interaction: the mosques and Kaba [Ka'aba] of Islam appear side by side in the poem with the temples and the sacred mountain known as *Kailash* of Hinduism. The juxtaposition in the poem mirrors the interaction between the two faiths in history. Although Hindus and Muslims did not always enjoy peaceful relations in South Asia and Southeast Asia, the interactions of cultures and peoples created dynamic changes not only in religious thought, but also in politics, economics, art, and architecture.

Political Structures in South Asia

Political centralization was not common in South Asian history. After the Gupta Dynasty that had dominated South Asia collapsed in 550 C.E., ending the so-called Golden Age or Classical Era of Indian history, disunity returned to most of the region for most of the next 1,000 years. Northern and southern India developed separate political structures, while local rulers in all parts of the subcontinent created strong power bases for themselves. The power of local rulers made it difficult for centralized rule to exist, but easy for wars to occur. Not until the rise of the Mughal Empire later in the sixteenth century would a single empire, and peace, dominate the area (See Chapter 19).

Political Structures in Southern India Southern India was more stable than northern India. Two centralized governments did manage to succeed in overcoming political regionalism and fragmentation for periods after the fall of the Gupta.

The first, the *Chola Kingdom*, reigned over southern India for more than 400 years (850–1267 C.E.). During the eleventh century, the kingdom extended its rule to Ceylon, the large island just south of India that is today known as Sri Lanka. Its geographic location allowed its navy access to the waterways of the Indian Ocean and the Bay of Bengal. At the height of the Indian Ocean trade, the Chola Kingdom's ships were traveling as far east as the South China Sea, a distance of more than 3,000 miles. The kingdom's power began to wane when natives of Ceylon, who were ethnically Sinhalese, drove out the Chola invaders. This dealt a fatal blow to Chola rule, reducing it to a small-scale, regional kingdom.

The second kingdom was in the northern region of southern India, known as *Vijayanagar*, a name that in English means "the victorious city." Vijayanagar had its roots when the Delhi Sultanate based in Delhi (which is discussed below) sent two brothers, Harihara and Bukka, to extend its rule to southern India. These brothers had been born as Hindus and converted to Islam for the sake of upward mobility. When they left the region controlled by the Delhi Sultanate, they took this opportunity to return to the religion of their birth and to establish their own kingdom. Vijayanagar existed from the mid-1300s until the mid-1500s, when a group of Muslim kingdoms overthrew it.

Political Structures in Northern India Northern India experienced a great deal more upheaval than did southern India. While the Himalayas protected India from invasions from the north and east, numerous mountain passes in the northwest allowed four separate invasions by Muslim armies. Each of these attacks created instability and disruption in a region that had been mostly Hindu and Buddhist. Over time, the Islamic presence in the region grew.

One of the first invasions came in the eighth century C.E. Soldiers from Umayyad Empire descended upon *Sind*, a region of northwestern India in present-day Pakistan. However, unlike the Umayyad expansion into northern Africa and Spain, the Umayyad incursion did little to change the everyday lives of the Hindus, Muslims, and Zoroastrians in the region. The Sind's geographic location, on the eastern fringes of the *Dar al-Islam*, kept it isolated from the seat of empire in Damascus. Its regional princes were also adept at wielding their local power when necessary, thus limiting the Muslim conquerors' influence.

A second invasion came three centuries later, and it had greater impact. *Mahmud of Ghazni* conquered the *Punjab* region, controlling much of what is present-day Afghanistan and Pakistan. During the eleventh century, Mahmud's armed forces plundered northern India's Hindu temples and Buddhist shrines for their riches and erected mosques on Hindu and Buddhist holy sites—actions that did little to endear Islam to the Indian people. Mahmud's efforts to convert Indians did not succeed.

Almost 150 years after his death, Ghazni's successors managed to conquer Delhi and much of South Asia north of the Deccan Plateau. Their *Delhi Sultanate* reigned for 300 years, from the thirteenth through the sixteenth centuries. *Delhi*, located in north-central India, was the sultans' seat of power. India's present-day capital city, New Delhi, is located near this older city. However, the sultanate never organized an efficient bureaucracy in the style of the Chinese, which made it difficult for the sultans to impose their policies in a land as vast and diverse as India. The sultans attempted to extend their rule to southern India, but in the late thirteenth century they became more focused on defending themselves from an onslaught by the Mongol army from the northwest. The Mongols had already demolished the Abbasid Empire and its once-magnificent imperial city of Baghdad. Although the Mongols never managed to conquer South Asia, the sultans of Delhi did not maintain control of northern India forever. The Mughal Empire, yet another foreign Islamic empire, rose to power in India during the middle of the sixteenth century. (Test Prep: List the similarities and differences between the Delhi Sultanate and the Mughal Empire. See page 353.)

The presence of Islam in northern India dominated the political history of the era. These "foreign" rulers may have created resentment among native Indians. For example, the Delhi Sultanate imposed a *jizya*, or tax, on all non-Muslim subjects of the empire. For some Indians, the tax was an incentive to convert to Islam. But despite the strong Islamic presence in the region, local kingdoms continued to play a major role in India's decentralized political landscape.

Economic Structures in South Asia

Dar al-Islam might be considered the world's first global empire. Its vast reach connected societies from Northern Africa to Eastern Europe, from Southwest Asia to South Asia. Even before missionaries and imperial armies spread Islam around the world, Islamic merchants traveling to non-Muslim lands in search of trading partners were paving the way. In fact, Arab merchants had been traveling to South Asia for centuries before Islam began expanding. Islamic merchants' connections to the Dar al-Islam combined with developments in sailing technology to transform the Indian Ocean into an economic hot spot during the post-classical era. South Asia, with its location in the center of the Indian Ocean, benefited enormously from the trade in the *Indian Ocean Basin*. (Test Prep: Write a paragraph comparing the Islamic global empire with the later British Empire. See page 465)

Merchants in Diasporic Communities		
Merchant Community	**Region(s)**	**Products**
Muslim	China, Indian Ocean Basin, Europe	Silk, paper, porcelain, spices, gems, woods, gold, salt, amber, furs
Chinese	Southeast Asia, Africa	Cotton, tea, silk, metals, opium, salt
Sogdian	Main caravan merchants along Silk Road, China	Silk, gold, wine, linens
Jewish	China, India, Europe	Glass beads, linens, dyes, spices

Source: Iranica Online. "Sogdian Trade" http://www.iranicaonline.org/articles/sogdian-trade

Trade in the Indian Ocean Basin Although the Indian Ocean trade had existed as early as 200 B.C.E., the expansion of Islam connected more cities than ever before. Trading partners existed in East Africa, East and Southeast Asia, and South Asia. Muslim Persians and Arabs were the dominant seafarers and were instrumental in transporting goods to port cities across the Indian Ocean. Cities on the west coast of India, such as *Calicut,* Quilon, and Cambay, became thriving centers of trade due to interactions with merchants from East Africa and Southwest Asia.

Calicut, especially, became a bustling port city for merchants in search of spices from southern India. Foreign merchants from Arabia and China met in Calicut to exchange goods from the West and the East, respectively. Local rulers welcomed the presence of Muslim and Chinese merchants, as it brought the city wealth and prominence in the Indian Ocean Basin.

Specialized Products As the Indian Ocean trade grew, so did the demand for specialized products. Every region involved in the trade had something special to offer their trading partners.

- India became known for the high quality of its fabrics, particularly cotton. In addition, merchants traveled to India in search of meticulously woven carpets as well as high-carbon steel (used for knives and swords), tanned leather, and artisan-crafted stonework. Merchants also sought pepper from India's southern coastal cities.

- Modern-day Malaysia and Indonesia became known as the *Spice Islands* because of the fragrant nutmeg, cinnamon, cloves, and cardamom they exported.

- Slaves, ivory, and gold came from the Swahili coastal cities of Mombasa, Mogadishu, and Sofala.

- China exported silks, and Chinese porcelain became coveted worldwide, which is why people in the West still refer to their fancier dishes as "fine china."

- From Southwest Asia came horses, figs, and dates.

Monsoon System and Sailing Technology Knowledge of *monsoon winds* was essential for trading in the Indian Ocean. In the winter months, winds originated from the northeast, while in the spring and summer, they blew from the southwest. Thus, merchants had to time their voyages carefully, often remaining in port cities for months at a time, depending on when favorable winds would come their way. As a natural consequence, these merchants interacted with the surrounding cultures and peoples of the region. In fact, many Arab and East African merchants stayed in western Indian port cities permanently because they married the women they met there. Thus, these merchants from the Dar al-Islam were the first to bring Islam to southern Asia, not through missionary work or conquest, but through intermarriage. Their children would generally be brought up as Muslims.

Travelers needed ships capable of navigating the Indian Ocean's winds. Arab sailors used sailing technology to aid their travel. It is debatable whether Arab sailors invented the triangular *lateen sails* that they used, but the sails were popular because sailors found that the triangular shape could easily catch winds coming from many different directions. Chinese sailors during the classical period had invented the *stern rudder,* which gave their ships more stability and made them easier to maneuver. Their small wooden dhows dominated the seas during the post-classical era. Trade facilitated the rapid spread of sailing technology across the many lands bordering the Indian Ocean in this period.

Religion in South Asia

Religion has always held a dominant place in South Asian history, and the post-classical era was no exception. Prior to the arrival of Islam, the majority of South Asians practiced Hinduism, while a smaller number identified themselves as Buddhists. South Asians encountered a starkly different religion when Islam arrived. While Hindus pray to many gods, Islam is strictly monotheistic. Hindu temples and artwork are replete with pictures of deities, while Muslims disapprove of any visual representation of Allah. While Hindus have a hierarchical caste system, Islam calls for the equality of all believers. Hindus interpret their religion loosely, in part because there are several sacred texts. Muslims need only look to the Quran for spiritual guidance.

The Arrival of Islam The relationship between Hindus and Muslims has shaped the history of South Asia since the seventh century, and it continues to shape regional culture and politics today. Islam entered India both forcefully and peacefully. Mahmud of Ghazni destroyed Hindu and Buddhist shrines as he spread Islam. But while Islam was a *proselytizing religion*, meaning that it actively sought converts, Muslim rulers found early in their reign that forcing their Hindu and Buddhist subjects to convert was not successful. Thus, most converts came to Islam voluntarily. As discussed, many Muslim merchants in the Indian Ocean trade moved to Indian port cities and married. Their wives often ended up converting to their husband's religion.

With its emphasis on the equality of all believers, Islam also attracted low-caste Hindus who hoped that conversion would improve their social status. In this sense, Islam in India was like Christianity in the Roman Empire. Each had special appeal to the people who suffered the most under the existing social structure.

The largest numbers of converts, however, were Buddhists. Corruption among the monks and raids on monasteries by early Muslim conquerors left the Buddhist religion disorganized. The spread of Islam helped make Buddhism a minority religion in its place of birth. (Test prep: Make and outline comparing the spread of Islam in South Asia to the spread of Buddhism in China. See page 182.)

Interaction of Islam and Hinduism The most successful messengers of Islam were *Sufis*, who converted large numbers of people to Islam. Sufis were mystics who did not focus on the strict doctrines of the religion, instead emphasizing an individual's personal connection to a higher power. Sufis even allowed converts to continue certain rituals not at all recognized by Islam. Their sincerity and openness to all faiths made Sufi mystics effective missionaries.

Perhaps due to the popularity of Sufism, Hinduism began focusing on personal devotion to God. Devotional groups developed during this period. They focused on a person's spiritual connection or devotion to an individual god, the lord Shiva or Vishnu, for example. The cults became popular also because they preached personal salvation.

In the twelfth century, the *Bhakti Movement* emerged in southern India, emphasizing love and devotion to God. This movement was especially appealing to many believers because it did not discriminate against women or people of low social status. *Mira Bai*, a female poet of the sixteenth century, became one of the most famous figures of the Bhakti Movement. Her songs of devotion to the Hindu lord Krishna are still popular in India.

The only Bhakti poet who became famous than Mira Bai is the one whose words open this chapter. Guru Kabir reminded those who seeking religious truth to look to themselves. He stressed that conventional sources of spirituality, whether Hindu or Muslim, were not the true sources of religion. Instead, he insisted that people focus on their personal faith and develop an emotional connection to God.

Though Kabir was born a Muslim, his beliefs did not fit comfortably within any particular religion. By the end of his life, he was preaching that a single God came in many forms—as Allah, Shiva, or Vishnu. Bhakti devotees failed to meld Hindu and Muslim beliefs, but they, as well as the Sufis, attempted to build bridges between the two religious communities.

Social Structures in South Asia

The arrival of Islam did little to alter the basic structure of society in South Asia. India's caste system is its strongest historical continuity. While obviously inequitable, it lent stability to a politically decentralized land. The caste system was quite flexible and able to accommodate newcomers. Muslim merchants and migrants, even though they were not Hindu, found a place for themselves within the caste hierarchy based on their occupation. These *jatis, or* subcastes, operated like workers' guilds, soon becoming absorbed into the social fabric of Indian society. (Test Prep: Write a paragraph comparing the caste system with its original structure. See page 92.)

At the same time, most of those who tried to escape the grip of the caste system failed. The low-caste Hindus who converted to Islam as a way to improve their social status usually did not achieve that goal. Although they may have found spiritual peace with Islam, low-caste individuals required more education and opportunities for better jobs, not just a new religion, to help them escape their low status in life.

Likewise, Islam did not alter gender relations greatly in South Asia. Women in the Hindu tradition were confined to a separate social sphere, and Islamic women received similar treatment. In Southeast Asia, however, women

Source: Thinkstock

Religious structures in India often demonstrate syncretism in architechture. This one combines towers common in Hindu temples with domes common in Islamic mosques.

enjoyed more independence. In spite of the differing expectations about gender norms, Islam's arrival did little to change the way women were treated.

It should be noted that as Islam spread, the ways in which it was practiced varied, depending on the cultures of the people who converted to the religion. Thus, converts in South and Southeast Asia found ways to accommodate a new faith, but most people did not jettison their time-honored traditions in the process.

Cultural Achievements in South Asia

Indian cultural and intellectual achievements had a profound impact on the Islamic world. Indian scientific learning, particularly in algebra and geometry, was translated into Arabic. Mathematicians from India traveled to Baghdad to instruct the Abbasids on the finer points of Indian intellectual achievements, and Arab astronomers and mathematicians added to the body of knowledge begun by their Indian counterparts. The number system we now use, which is often referred to in the West as "Arabic numerals," in fact originated among Indian mathematicians.

In India itself, sultans erected buildings melding the intricate artistic details of Hindu art with the geometric patterns preferred by Islamic architecture. The city of Delhi is replete with examples of Islamic architecture built during the Delhi Sultanate. One famous example, the *Qutab Minar*, still stands in the southern part of the city. Rulers from the Delhi Sultanate built an elaborate mosque on top of a Hindu temple, and used materials for the mosque from nearby Hindu and Jain shrines. Towering over the mosque is the Qutab Minar itself, a gigantic leaning tower, the tallest structure in India today. Historians debate the reason for its construction; one obvious function is its presence as a symbol of Islamic influence and, at one time, dominance of northern India.

An entirely new language developed among Muslims of South Asia: *Urdu*. It had influences from Sanskrit-based Hindi, as well as from Arabic and Farsi, a Persian language. Urdu takes the grammatical pattern of Hindi, spoken among North Indians, and melds it with much of the vocabulary of Arabic, with some Farsi as well. Spoken today, Urdu is the official language of Pakistan. Its elegant sound works well with spoken literature and poetry, and its creation is a testament to the cultural interactions that took place within South Asia during the Delhi Sultanate.

Southeast Asia

The lands of Southeast Asia—now the modern countries of Indonesia, Malaysia, Cambodia, Thailand, Laos, and, to a lesser extent, Vietnam—were all heavily influenced by South Asia. Indian merchants had contact with these Southeast Asian lands as early as 500 B.C.E. The merchants introduced Indian goods such as gold, silver, metal goods, and textiles to the region and brought back its fine spices.

Through trade, Southeast Asia was also introduced to the Indian religions of Hinduism and Buddhism. The *Ramayana* and *Mahabharata* epics were especially popular among the *Funan* rulers of the first century to sixth century C.E., because the epics served to reinforce ideas of kingship. These rulers— whose kingdom included parts of modern-day Vietnam, Cambodia, and Thailand—conducted royal business in Sanskrit and even adopted the Sanskrit word for king, *raja*, as a way to refer to themselves. Though most of their subjects worshipped local deities or spirits associated with nature, over time Hinduism came to be accepted in the larger culture. Funan rulers profited from the India-China trade by controlling a thin stretch of land on the Malay Peninsula that many merchants used as a shortcut between the two countries. The rulers extracted a fee from all traders who used it. The Funans developed an extensive irrigation system on their lands that helped increase agricultural production. The system was destroyed, however, after peoples from the north— the Chams and *Khmers*—invaded and occupied the Funan kingdom.

During the post-classical period, several kingdoms attempted to control Southeast Asia, including the Srivijaya (670–1025), Singosari (1222–1292), and

TRADING EMPIRES IN SOUTHEAST ASIA

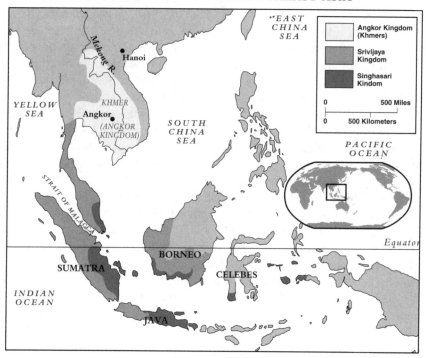

Majapahit (1293–1520). However, the *Angkor Kingdom*, also known as the Khmer, situated near the Mekong River, was the most successful of all. The reasons for Angkor's success have been debated by historians. A leading theory states that the kingdom's sophisticated irrigation and drainage systems led to greater economic prosperity. Irrigation allowed farmers to harvest rice crops several times a year, and drainage systems reduced the impact of the heavy monsoon rains. The Angkor kingdom lasted for more than 500 years (889–1431), controlling land in what is now Cambodia. Its capital was *Angkor Thom*.

The royal monuments at Angkor Thom are evidence of Indian cultural influences on Southeast Asia. Founded by rulers in the eighth century with the help of Indian advisors, the city of Angkor Thom was built to house the king and display the grandeur of his rule. Hindu artwork and sculptures of Hindu gods abounded in the royal city. Building resumed in the twelfth and thirteenth centuries, when Khmer rulers, who had become Buddhist, added Buddhist sculptures and artwork to the complex without destroying any of the Hindu artwork. The entire complex covered about two square miles and was surrounded by a large moat.

During the same period, the ornate and majestic Buddhist temple complex of *Angkor Wat* was constructed, one-half mile from Angkor Thom. In 1451, the Thais invaded the area, forcing the Khmers out. Nevertheless, ruins of the magnificent structures in Angkor Thom and Angkor Wat still stand, testifying not only to the greatness of Southeast Asian culture, but also to the powerful influence of Indian culture on the region.

Source: Thinkstock

The great temple complex at Angkor Wat, in both its architecture and its use, reflects the interaction between Hinduism and Buddhism in Southeast Asia.

Islam A discussion of Southeast Asia would not be complete without a discussion of Islamic influences. Islam's movement into the Indian Ocean region was not very different from its expansion elsewhere. The first Southeast Asian Muslims were local merchants who converted in the 700s, in hopes of having better trading relations with the Islamic traveling merchants who arrived on their shores. Islam was most popular in urban areas at the time. Over the centuries, Islam spread to Sumatra, Java, and the Malay Peninsula.

Sufis did their missionary work in Southeast Asia, as well. Because of Sufis' tolerance for local faith traditions, many people of Indonesia, for example, felt comfortable converting to Islam because they were still allowed to honor local deities.

One Muslim city-state, *Melaka*, also spelled Malacca, became wealthy by building a navy and by imposing fees on ships that passed through the Strait of Melaka, a narrow inlet that many ship captains used to travel between ports in India and ports in China. The Sultan of Melaka became so powerful in the 1400s that he expanded the state into Sumatra and the southern Malay Peninsula. Similar to city-states in East Africa, Italy, and the Americas, Melaka's prosperity was based on the trade rather than agriculture or mining or manufacturing. The sultanate ended when the Portuguese invaded the city in 1511.

HISTORICAL PERSPECTIVE: DID ISLAM ALTER INDIAN CULTURE?

The entrance of Islam into the predominantly Hindu land of India beginning in the seventh century has lead to a debate among historians about how Islam affected traditional Hindu culture. The debate is similar to ones over other cases when a group of migrants or invaders introduce a new culture into an existing one. For example, historians debate how much Bantu-speakers influenced the cultures they encountered as they migrated through Africa, or how much American Indian culture shaped the culture of the Europeans who settled in the Americas after 1492.

Historian Graham Fuller is among those who argued that the impact of Islamic culture on India was large: "An India without its Mughal fusion civilization would have been a culturally far less rich place." This fusion can be seen most clearly in how people express themselves: in the music, art, and architecture of India. Several scholars have noted that the first image that comes to mind for many people when they think of India is the Taj Mahal, which was built by a Muslim.

Other experts downplay the impact of Islam on Indian culture. For example, Brookings Institution scholar Stephen P. Cohen was struck by the contrast between how India reacted to Islam and how other countries reacted. According to Cohen, Islam overwhelmed many of the other cultures in came into contact with as it moved across Northern Africa and through Asia. For example, in parts of the Middle East and Northern Africa, only traces of pre-Islamic culture remain. In constrast, Cohen claims that India kept much of its traditional culture: "Islam did not destroy Indian civilization." India, despite centuries of rule by leaders who practiced Islam, remained a predominantly Hindu land. "The absorptive power of Indian society has always been impressive," Cohen concluded.

Puja Mondal, writing about the impact of Islam on Indian society took a middle position. "Islamic and Hindu traditions have interacted, synthesized, and also remained insulated." The two religions and cultures have existed side by side in India for hundreds of years, each influencing the other in ways large and small, but they have remained separate. The division between the Hindu majority and the Muslim minority continues to be a key issue in Indian politics today.

KEY TERMS BY THEME

GOVERNMENT
Dar al-Islam
Chola Kingdom
Vijayanagar
Sind
Mahmud of Ghazni
Punjab
Delhi Sultanate
Delhi
jizya
Funan
raja
Khmers
Angkor Kingdom
Melaka

ENVIRONMENT
monsoon winds
lateen sails
stern rudder

CULTURE
Kailash
Guru Kabir
proselytizing religion
Sufis
Bhakti Movement
Mira Bai
Qutab Minar
Urdu
Ramayana
Mahabharata
Angkor Thom
Angkor Wat

SOCIAL STRUCTURE
jatis

ECONOMICS
Indian Ocean Basin
Calicut
Spice Islands

1. One major difference between the political structures of South Asia and East Asia in the six centuries following 600 C.E. was that
   (A) South Asia was often fragmented under several governments, while East Asia was often ruled by one centralized government
   (B) South Asian governments attempted to expand their borders, while East Asian governments were content with the size of their territory
   (C) South Asian societies isolated foreigners while East Asian societies promoted interaction with non-Asians
   (D) South Asia was dominated by secular rulers while East Asia was controlled by religious leaders

2. Which was a result of Northern India being invaded more frequently than Southern India after 600 C.E.?
   (A) Northern India developed a centralized government before Southern India did.
   (B) Northern India was more motivated to develop a large standing army.
   (C) Northern India was less politically stable than southern India was.
   (D) Northern India became impoverished from lack of trade.

3. The primary reason merchants were so successful at increasing the size of Dar al-Islam by moving into South Asia and Southeast Asia was that
   (A) invading soldiers helped them force people to convert to Islam
   (B) members of the upper classes were attracted to Islam's emphasis on equality
   (C) intermarriage with local women helped spread the faith
   (D) Muslim traders exported newly converted African slaves into the region

4. How did contact with China assist Muslims in the spread of Islam across South Asia and Southeast Asia?
   (A) Repeated attacks by Chinese military forces in South Asia weakened the empires there.
   (B) Chinese merchants introduced Muslim merchants to the Khyber Pass, the historic invasion route into the subcontinent.
   (C) Many Chinese converted to Islam and became allies with armies from the Middle East.
   (D) The adoption of Chinese sailing technology by Muslim traders allowed them to increase their activity in the Indian Ocean.

5. Buddhism declined in South Asia after
   (A) Islam was introduced from the west
   (B) Hinduism adopted many of its features
   (C) Jainism developed into a separate faith
   (D) Zoroastrianism spread throughout northern India

6. Urdu is similar to Swahili because each one was
   (A) spoken widely in the past, but no longer is
   (B) developed to help people read the Koran
   (C) created by blending Arabic with one or more other languages
   (D) used primarily by poets who were Muslims

7. The surviving buildings in the Angkor Kingdom display a melding of which two religions?
   (A) Buddhism and Islam
   (B) Islam and Hinduism
   (C) Hinduism and Buddhism
   (D) Buddhism and Daoism

Question 8 refers to the excerpt below.

The Hindus believe that there is no country but theirs, no nation like theirs, no kings like theirs, no religion like theirs, no science like theirs. They are haughty, foolishly vain, self-conceited, and stolid. They are by nature niggardly in communicating that which they know, and they take the greatest possible care to withhold it from men of another caste among their own people, still much more, of course, from any foreigner. . . . Their haughtiness is such that, if you tell them of any science or scholar in Khorasan and Persia, they will think you to be both an ignoramus and a liar. If they traveled and mixed with other nations, they would soon change their mind, for their ancestors were not as narrow-minded as the present generation is.

> —from *Alberuni's India* by Al-Beruni, Muslim scholar
> at the court of Mahmud of Ghazni, early eleventh century,
> translated by Edward C. Sachau

8. Based on the excerpt, which statement best reflects Al-Beruni's opinion about Indian society in the eleventh century?
   (A) The Hindu caste system encouraged a free exchange of ideas.
   (B) Hindu scholars had little knowledge outside their own culture.
   (C) Hindu scholars had nothing of value to offer to Muslim scholars.
   (D) Hindus placed little value on learning.

9. The Funan rulers of Southeast Asia appreciated the scriptures of Hinduism, including the *Ramayana* and *Mahabharata*, because they

(A) encouraged ideas of kingship

(B) encouraged trade with other lands

(C) respected local deities

(D) served as a bulwark against the Islamic faith

Question 10 refers to the map below.

WIND PATTERNS

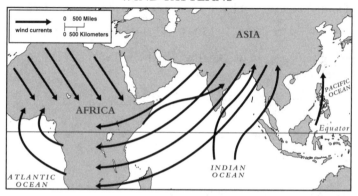

10. Which statement is best supported by the information on the map?

(A) Strong wind patterns prevented desertification in Africa and Asia.

(B) Indian Ocean traders needed knowledge of wind patterns to time their voyages.

(C) Varying wind patterns prevented airborne diseases from spreading in the Indian Ocean Basin.

(D) South Asia was less affected by monsoon winds than Europe was.

CONTINUITY AND CHANGE-OVER-TIME ESSAY QUESTIONS

Directions: You are to answer the following question. You should spend 5 minutes organizing or outlining your essay. Write an essay that:

- Has a relevant thesis and supports that thesis with appropriate historical evidence.

- Addresses all parts of the question.

- Uses world historical context to show continuities and changes over time.

- Analyzes the process of continuity and change over time.

1. Analyze continuities and changes in the practice of religion in ONE of the following regions between 600 and 1450:
   - South Asia
   - Southeast Asia

Questions for Additional Practice

2. Analyze continuities and changes in the social structure of South Asia between 600 and 1450.

3. Analyze continuities and changes in the trade in the Indian Ocean Basin between 600 and 1450. Address both economic and cultural interactions.

COMPARATIVE ESSAY QUESTIONS

Directions: You are to answer the following question. You should spend 5 minutes organizing or outlining your essay. Write an essay that:
- Has a relevant thesis and supports that thesis with appropriate historical evidence.
- Addresses all parts of the question.
- Makes direct, relevant comparisons.
- Analyzes relevant reasons for similarities and differences.

1. Analyze similarities and differences in the governments of TWO of the following states between 600 and 1450:
   - Chola Kingdom
   - Delhi Sultanate
   - Angkor Kingdom

Questions for Additional Practice

2. Analyze similarities and differences in the political structures or the role of religion in TWO of the following cities in the period 600 to 1450 C.E.:
   - Calicut
   - Delhi
   - Angkor Thom

3. Analyze similarities and differences between Sufism and the Bhakti Movement between the arrival of Islam in India in the seventh century and the high point of the Bhakti movement in the twelfth century.

THINK AS A HISTORIAN: PRACTICE USING HISTORICAL PERSPECTIVE

When analyzing a source, identify and then evaluate the perspective of its writer. A writer's age, gender, wealth, and ethnicity are among the many influences that shape his or her view of the world, and each of these helps determine what the writer considers worth recording.

1. Which perspective about religion would a Sufi most likely express?

    a. The obliteration of sacred Hindu sites by Muslims will result in an increase of converts to Islam.

    b. Religion is an intimate and personal bond between an individual and a higher power that does not necessarily subscribe to a doctrine.

    c. Connecting to a specific god in a polytheistic religion can help people reach personal salvation.

2. Which perspective about the social hierarchy would a person of a lower caste in India most likely have?

    a. Converting to Islam might increase the opportunity to receive equal treatment.

    b. Trade is a significant aspect to the lives of people in this caste.

    c. Women who practice Hinduism receive better treatment than Muslim women.

WRITE AS A HISTORIAN: CONSIDER PATTERNS OF CONTINUITY AND CHANGE

A key to understanding the past is recognizing patterns of continuity and change over time. Patterns can encompass anything from the founding of empires to the quest for minority rights. *Which of the following statements would be most useful in an essay that emphasizes continuity over time and which would be best used to emphasize change over time?*

1. The Chola Kingdom and later the Vijayanagar Kingdom—each ruled large portions of Southern India.

2. Starting in the eleventh century, Muslim armies brought new religious beliefs to Northern India.

3. Religion has held a dominant place in South Asian history for more than 3,000 years.

4. One sign of this process was that Funan rulers adopted the Sanskrit word for king, raja, to refer to themselves.

12

Western Europe After Rome, 400–1450 C.E.

I should not wish to be Aristotle if this were to separate me from Christ.

—Peter Abelard, Letter 17 to Heloise (1141)

Following the breakdown of the Roman Empire in 476 C.E., Western Europe entered a period of chaos known as the Middle Ages or the medieval period. Roman rule was replaced by a collection of Germanic tribal kingdoms that fought one another for power and territory. The first 500 years of the medieval period, until 1000 C.E., are often referred to as the Early Middle Ages. Some historians, however, call this period the "Dark Ages," because learning was less widespread than in Roman times and cities were in decline. Moreover, roads were in disrepair and the ancient practice of barter returned to replace the Roman coinage system. Nevertheless, Western Europe remained somewhat connected to the wider world in this period; coastal towns still participated in global trade by way of the Mediterranean Sea.

The years 1000 to 1450 are often called the High Middle Ages. In this later period, European learning and trade began to flourish once again. The French thinker Peter Abelard (1079–1142) quoted above exemplified this rebirth of learning in European society. Although he was the son of a knight, he chose to study philosophy, especially the logic of Aristotle. As a monk and theologian, Abelard used these logical methods to address seeming contradictions in Roman Catholic Church teachings and practices. In spite of his critical writings, Abelard remained faithful to the Church throughout his life.

Political and Social Structures of the Early Middle Ages

In contrast to the large Roman Empire of the past, smaller, less-centralized states developed in the Early Middle Ages. The *Franks*, despite their name, were not French at all but Germanic. They established an early capital in Paris. *King Clovis* (ruled 481–511) became the first monarch to unite all the Frankish tribes and was also the first Roman Catholic ruler of the Franks. However, government under his heirs was unstable. In a recurring historical pattern, succession problems haunted those who tried to establish a centralized monarchy in Western Europe. (Test Prep: Write a paragraph comparing the succession problems in medieval Europe with those that followed the death of Alexander the Great. See page 62.)

Carolingian Dynasty *Charles Martel* was a military leader of the Franks who led Christian forces of northern France, Belgium, and western Germany to defeat the Muslims at the *Battle of Tours* in 732. This victory stopped the expansion of Muslim forces into northern Europe, although most of the Iberian Peninsula, present-day Spain and Portugal, remained under Muslim control. This caliphate came to be known as Al-Andalus and is discussed in more detail in Chapter 8.

Martel founded the *Carolingian Dynasty* of the Frankish kingdom and ruled from 737 to 741. His son Pepin (ruled 752–768) consolidated his power by getting the pope to declare his right to the throne, increasing his legitimacy over rivals.

Pepin's son *Charlemagne* ruled the Frankish kingdom from 768 to 814. In exchange for conquering Lombardy in Italy, Charlemagne was named Emperor of the Romans by the pope in 800. As emperor, he led a force east that defeated the Saxons and converted them to Christianity. With relative peace established, Charlemagne encouraged church-based education and used regional administrators to help govern his empire. Although no lasting centralized government developed, Charlemagne's rule foreshadowed the coming of the *Holy Roman Empire*. The Carolingian Dynasty lasted only through its division among the grandsons of Charlemagne.

Comparing Carolingians and Tang China Numerous political similarities existed between the Carolingians in France and the Tang Dynasty in China (618–907). Both used religion to legitimize their rule, placed a high value on education, and attempted to control the nobles through regional administrators. In addition, both were successful in repelling invaders. For example, Charles Martel in Europe turned back the Muslims at Tours in 732, and Li Yuan, the Duke of Tang, defeated nomadic border peoples and agrarian rebels in 615.

Despite these similarities, the two political systems faced opposite outcomes. The splitting of the Carolingian Kingdoms in 814 led to the intensification of feudalism and local power. In contrast, China entered a period of great prosperity under a strong central government. China's rulers built the Grand Canal to facilitate its rule in two ways: maintaining better contact with southern Chinese regions and providing a better way for those regions to send tribute. The Tang prosperity led to more international contacts through the now-safer Silk Road, with its fortified command posts and garrisons of soldiers. The challenging civil service exams, which required an expanded educational system in China, were unknown in Europe.

While leaders in both Western Europe and China used religion to legitimize rule, ideologies differed as a result of the religious and philosophical trends in each area. The Roman Catholic Church provided the major ideology for Western Europe, and leaders sought legitimacy through their relationships with the papacy. Chinese rulers thought to be legitimate claimed to have the Confucian Mandate of Heaven, but Confucianism and Buddhism vied for influence in China. *Empress Wu* (ruled 665–705) tried to make Buddhism a state religion, but persecution of Buddhists followed her reign, and Confucianism triumphed until the twentieth century.

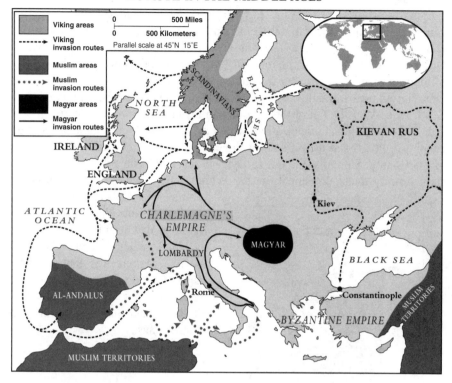

EUROPE IN THE MIDDLE AGES

String of Invasions

As with the decline and fall of the Roman Empire, outside invaders pressured Western European kingdoms and contributed to the decentralization and chaos in the region. As noted earlier, Muslim armies moved up from the south until they were defeated at Tours in 732.

Vikings A second group of invaders Scandinavian *Vikings* (also known as *Norsemen*) came from the north. They traveled in light *longships* that enabled sailors to travel far inland on rivers as well as conduct coastal raids on seas. These longships were frightening vessels, with dragons on the prows and fierce sailors aboard. Carrying as many as fifty men each, longships had banks of oars and a single large sail.

Beginning in the ninth century, these Scandinavians, from present-day Norway, Denmark, and Sweden, landed in England, Ireland, France, Belgium, and harbors up and down the European coastline. From settlements in *Iceland* they reached *Greenland*, and then a coastal area of North America that they named *Vinland*. They also made inroads into neighboring Russia along its rivers. This route was one way that Western Europe kept in touch with Constantinople and, through it, with the rest of the Arab and Islamic world. The Mediterranean trade routes were still in use as well. Byzantine and Islamic coins have been found as far northwest as Poland, perhaps evidence of a far-flung Viking trade with Kievan Rus, as discussed in Chapter 7.

Magyars A third wave of invaders, the *Magyars,* came from the east. Originally from Central Asia, the Magyars encroached on the Byzantine Empire soon after the fall of Rome and went on to settle in present-day Germany, Italy, and France. The Magyars, whose modern descendants live in Hungary, were slowly assimilated into Christianity and came under the control of the monarchs of central Europe after the tenth century.

The political instability of Europe in this period might be compared with South Asia. After the fall of the Carolingian Dynasty in 888 in Western Europe, little effective political organization existed until the creation of the Holy Roman Empire in 962. Even then, much of the empire's power existed at the pleasure of the Church. Similarly, the Gupta Dynasty in South Asia collapsed in the late sixth century under pressure from the White Huns (also known as Hunas) of Central Asia, so there was only loose political organization in India until Mahmud of Ghazni came to power in 998. A major difference between the two regions was that a single major religion unified Europeans, while multiple relgions, especially Hinduism and Sunni Islam, divided South Asians.

Source: Thinkstock

The Viking longship (left) was more sturdily built than the dhow (below), which made it more durable but slower.

Source: Thinkstock

Feudalism: Political and Social Systems

While kings fought, they needed people to protect their lands. Kings paid nobles with land called *fiefs*; the amount of land owned determined a person's wealth. In return, these landowners, called *lords*, promised to fight for the king. The lords were the kings' *vassals*, people who owed service to another person. Lords could have their own vassals if they had enough land to spare. For example, lords could hire *knights* to fight for them by offering them a piece of land. The knights would be the vassals of the lords and owe the lords service. This system of obligations, called *feudalism*, was widespread in Europe from the 800s to the 1200s. (Test Prep: List the similarities and differences between the feudalism in Europe and feudalism in Japan. See page 193.)

Feudalism was a mutually beneficial relationship of free persons. Sanctioned by oaths of loyalty, the system cut down on losses to robbers and bandits, provided equipment for fighters who could hope to become knights, and gave land in return for service of the lord. A king controlled larger areas of land and could give larger fiefdoms to lords loyal to him. Local lords often represented the only law and order in their areas, and their power was absolute.

The feudal system incorporated a *code of chivalry* as a way to resolve disputes and to show etiquette. Since women were to be protected, the code put them on a pedestal while not investing them with any significant additional importance. In practice, women did not have many rights.

Manorial System Large fiefs or estates were also referred to as *manors*. The *manorial system* provided both economic self-sufficiency and defense. Manor grounds were small villages that often included a church, a blacksmith shop, a mill, and presses for making cider, wine, or oil, in addition to the homes of peasants known as *serfs*. Serfs, while not slaves, were tied to the land, and they could not marry or travel without permission from their lords. In exchange for protection provided by the lord of the manor, they paid tribute in the form of crops, labor or, in rare cases, coins. Children born to serfs also became serfs.

Less than ten percent of land was cultivated in the Early Middle Ages and climatic conditions were wet and cold. As both weather and technology improved around the ninth century, the amount of arable or farmable land gradually increased. Agriculture became more efficient toward the end of the Middle Ages due to several developments. The *three-field system,* in which crops were rotated in and out of three fields, came into use.

- One field was planted to wheat or rye, crops that provided food.

- A second field was planted to legume plants such as peas, lentils, or beans. These plants made the soil more fertile by adding nitrogen to it.

- A third field was allowed to remain fallow, or unused, each year.

Technological developments included windmills and several new types of plows. Heavier plows with wheels were developed to deal with the type of soil in areas north of the Alps, while lighter plows were sufficient for the soil in southern Europe. Drawn at first by oxen, the plows became more efficient and swift after the invention of the *horse collar* to yoke teams of horses. Riding horses became easier, too, when the use of *stirrups* spread from Central Asia to Europe about the seventh century. Stirrups distributed the rider's weight more evenly over the horse's back, saving the horse discomfort and back injury while helping the rider to be more secure.

The manor produced everything that people living on it required, limiting the need for trade or contact with outsiders. Many serfs spent their entire life on a single manor, unaware of what was happening in the rest of Europe. A serf might not see more than 100 different people in an entire lifetime.

The languages that almost everyone understood—Latin and German— evolved as areas developed their own *dialects*, or regional ways of speaking. Over time, the Latin dialects developed into new *vernacular languages*, such as French, Italian, and Spanish. Latin remained the formal language used by clergy, scholars, and lawyers, while the vernacular languages were used by common people. Literary works developed in these new languages as well.

Comparing Social Classes in Europe and Asia Social classes were hierarchical in both Western Europe and Asia. While some similarities existed between the feudal system of Western Europe and the caste system of South Asia during the post-classical period, European feudalism allowed for more social mobility. While the practice of serfdom became hereditary in some areas, it was never as restrictive as was the position of untouchables in the Hindu caste system. In addition, knights could receive additional fiefs for services rendered to their lords, and *squires*, who served the knights, could rise to knighthood through deeds of valor. Moreover, the Church offered priests opportunities for upward mobility.

In Tang China (618–907), the emperor ruled a strong central government supported by an efficient bureaucracy. Although there was a class of aristocrats, there were few large estates as land ownership was more widespread than in Europe. Merchants were not as frowned upon as they were in Western Europe, as profit-making was not despised to the extent that it was by the Catholic Church. A scholar-gentry class also developed under the Tangs.

Organized religions in both Western Europe and South Asia provided some opportunities for women through convent life in the Christian areas and Jainist or Buddhist religious communities in South Asia. Women in Tang China were better off now than they were later under the Song Dynasty (960–1279) when foot-binding came into fashion.

Roman Catholic Church during the Middle Ages

In 1054, the Christian Church experienced a division, often called the *Great Schism*, and split into two branches: the Roman Catholic and the Orthodox. The Roman Catholic Church continued to dominate Western Europe until the Reformation in the sixteenth century, while the Orthodox Church was strong farther east, into Russia. (See page 134 for more on the Great Schism.)

The Roman Catholic Church was extremely influential during the Middle Ages. Indeed, it was the only authority that covered much of Europe. Many factors helped the Church keep its influence. First, few people knew how to read or write. Most Church staff, however, were literate. If common people needed something written or read, they asked a Church official to do it. Most manors had a small church and a priest on the grounds.

The Church established the first universities in Europe. Because the Church led in the area of education, most of the great thinkers of the Middle Ages were Church leaders. All artists, even the great ones, worked for the Church. The insides of Church buildings were decorated quite beautifully with paintings, statues, and stained-glass windows. Most artwork focused on religious themes as it was one way to educate the illiterate serf and peasant class.

In addition, the Church held power in the feudal system. If a lord displeased the Church, the Church could discipline or pressure the lord in various ways. For example, it might cancel religious services for his serfs. This distressed the serfs, who would pressure the lord to do what the Church wanted.

Organized similarly to the Roman Empire, the Roman Catholic Church had an extensive hierarchy of regional *bishops*, who owed allegiance to the *pope*, the supreme bishop in Rome. The bishops selected and supervised local *priests*. Missionaries spread Christianity through Europe, providing a common identify even as regional monarchies and vernacular languages developed.

To consolidate power, a Roman document called the *Donation of Constantine* from the eighth century provided the Church with "evidence" that the pope should assume political as well as spiritual authority. The Donation of Constantine was later discovered to be forged. Nevertheless, the influence and power of the papacy increased as exemplified by the pope An example of the papal authority was his ability to inspire members of the aristocracy of Europe to embark on the Crusades, beginning in 1095, discussed later in the chapter.

After the Great Schism in 1054, the authority and influence of the papacy in the West seemed assured. However, that influence waned when French pope Clement V was selected. He refused to relocate to Rome and established instead the papacy in France from 1309 to 1377. This period of nearly 70 years is sometimes referred to as the *Babylonian Captivity*, a reference to the Jewish exile in the sixth century B.C.E. During this period, a second candidate for pope and then a third arose for the head of the Church—all at the same time.

Monasticism Although clergy withdrew to monasteries to meditate and pray, they remained part of the economies of Western Europe. The monasteries had the same economic functions of agriculture and protection as other manors. Although they took vows of poverty and supported charities in their communities, the clergy also wielded considerable political influence, and some monasteries became quite wealthy. Wealth and political power led to corruption. The *Cluniac Reforms*, originating from the monastery at Cluny, France, in the eleventh century, attempted to reform the Church from within. Eventually, corruption, as well as theological disagreements, drove reformers such as John Wycliffe, John Huss, and Martin Luther to part ways with the Catholic Church. (Test Prep: Write a paragraph comparing this period in Church history with the Reformation. See page 278.)

Political Trends in the Later Middle Ages

Stronger monarchies that developed in the later Middle Ages displayed two common characteristics that increased the power of the monarchy at the expense of feudal lords: a growing bureaucracy to carry out the monarch's decisions and an organized army that was controlled by the monarch. In many instances, the desire of people for representation and the desire of monarchs for strong absolutist government conflicted. Sometimes the desire for power also created tension between monarchs and the pope.

Capetian France When the Carolingian Dynasty split into three sections in 987, the western Frankish nobles chose Hugh Capet as their king. The area was called Gaul by the Romans and had been part of Charlemagne's empire; by the time Hugh Capet became king, it was called the "Kingdom of the French." In spite of his title, however, Capet held little real power. It would be left to later kings, such as Philip II (ruled 1180–1223), to develop the first real bureaucracy.

Not until Philip IV (ruled 1285–1314) did the first *Estates-General*—a body to advise the king that included representatives from each of the three legal classes, or *estates,* in France: the clergy, nobility, and commoners— meet. Although the French kings consulted this Estates-General when necessary, they did not exact regular taxes from the upper two estates, the clergy and nobility. Consequently, the Estates-General had little power. The clergy and nobility felt little responsibility to protect a government that they were not financing, a problem that only continued to increase in France up to the eve of the French Revolution of 1789.

Holy Roman Empire The German king *Otto I* was crowned Holy Roman Emperor in 962, hearkening back to Charlemagne's designation as Emperor of the Romans. Otto's successors survived the power struggle with the papacy over the *lay investiture controversy* of the eleventh and twelfth centuries. The dispute was over whether a secular leader, rather than the pope, could invest bishops with the symbols of office. It was finally resolved in the Concordat of Worms of 1122, when the Church achieved autonomy from secular authorities. The Holy Roman Empire remained vibrant until it was virtually destroyed during the Thirty Years' War (1618–1648), from which it never recovered. The Empire came to an end with Napoleon's invasion in 1806.

Norman England The *Normans* were descendents of Vikings who settled in the northwest corner of France, a region know as Normandy. In 1066, a monarch of Normandy known as *William the Conqueror* invaded England and ruled kingdoms on both sides of the English Channel. He presided over a tightly organized feudal system, using royal sheriffs as his administrative officials. William also standardized law codes issued by his royal court.

In time, objections to the power of William and his successor Norman monarchs were responsible for limits on that power in England. First, the *Magna Carta*, signed by King John in 1215 under pressure from leading nobles, required the king to observe certain rights, such as the right to a jury trial before a noble could be sentenced to prison. Also, the nobles won the right to be consulted on the issue of scutage (a form of tax placed on a knight who wanted to "buy out" of military service). Finally, the first *English Parliament* was formed in 1265. These developments increased the rights of the English nobility, but not of the general population.

In the first full parliamentary meeting in 1265, the *House of Lords* represented the nobles and Church hierarchy, while the *House of Commons* was made up of elected representatives of wealthy townspeople. Eventually the power of these two legislative bodies in England became stronger than that of similar bodies on the European continent. The course of English feudalism led to modern democracy for the individual. By contrast, Japanese feudalism developed on a similar course, but it emphasized rights of the group rather than protection of the individual through checks on those in authority.

In the *Hundred Years' War* (1337–1453), the tables were turned between the rival monarchies: this time England invaded France. Although the English retained only the port of Calais in France as a result of the war, a strong sense of unity evolved in both countries during the period. Another result of the war was the spreading use of gunpowder. Invented by the Chinese and brought to the Middle East by Mongols, gunpowder was in use in Europe by the fourteenth century. The Mongols also popularized the use of horses in Europe.

In addition to conquering England, the Normans in the eleventh century also conquered Sicily, taking control of that Mediterranean island from Muslims. In the same century, other Christian forces began taking control of Spain from Muslim rulers. This *reconquista* or reconquest was finally completed in 1492.

High Middle Ages

By the year 1000, the growth of new states and Europeans' increasing interest in foreign goods were leading Western Europe toward a more expansive and progressive period. Both the development of new states and greater trade were brought about in part by the Christian Crusades and the weakening of feudalism at the local and regional levels. These social and political changes would culminate in a new form of monarchy, and a spirit of Renaissance or rebirth, both of which would greatly affect three key areas: commerce, class relations, and gender roles. European lords and knights were ready to stop fighting one another and had retreated from actual battles in favor of more *tournaments*, organized competitions that included *jousts*, combat between knights using blunt weapons, which also became social occasions.

Christian Crusades

Just as Europeans fought to drive Muslims out of Europe, they also sought to reclaim control of the *Holy Land*, the region of Palestine in the Middle East that contains sites of spiritual significance to Jews, Christians, and Muslims. European Christians had enjoyed access to these lands for centuries, even after they came under the control of Muslims. This access was reduced, however, when the Seljuk Turks took control of the region around 1071.

Social and economic trends of the eleventh century added to the pressure among Europeans to invade the Middle East. Rules of *primogeniture*, in which the eldest brother in a family inherited the entire estate, left a generation of younger sons with little access to wealth and land. The landed nobles saw a military campaign as a way to divert the ambitions of these restless nobles as well as unemployed peasants, who often pillaged the lands of neighboring lords. Furthermore, merchants began to desire unfettered access to trade routes through the Middle East. The combination of these religious, social, and economic pressures resulted in a series of European military campaigns between 1095 and the 1200s in the Middle East known as the *Crusades*.

Politics shaped the manner in which the Crusades were conducted. Tensions between popes and kings and between different rulers strengthened the intention of the Church to take control. The Church could also use its spiritual authority to recruit believers. Sinners were promised heaven and, of more immediate concern, relief from their required acts of atonement and penance, if they would join the Crusade. Support also came for the Eastern branch of Christianity as well. Alarmed by news of the persecution and massacre of Christian pilgrims by Seljuk Turks, the Orthodox patriarch at Constantinople appealed to Pope Urban II to help retake the Holy Land from Islamic control.

The First Crusade Of the four major Crusades, only the first was a clear victory for the forces of Christendom. They conquered Jerusalem in July 1099. However, when Muslim forces under Saladin regained control of Jerusalem in 1187. (Test Prep: Create a timeline tracing the spread of Islam up through the Crusades. See pages 147 and 152.)

The Fourth Crusade During the fourth and last major Crusade (1202–1204), *Venice*, a wealthy city-state in northern Italy, had a contract to transport Crusaders to the Middle East, which they referred to as the Levant. However, Venice was not paid all of what was due, so the Venetians persuaded the Crusader debtors first to sack Zara, an Italian city, and then Constantinople, a major trade competitor of Venice. The Fourth Crusade never made it to the Holy Land. Eventually, Islamic forces prevailed in the Levant.

Effects of Crusades Knowledge of the world beyond Western Europe increased as Crusaders encountered both the Byzantine and Islamic cultures. The encounter also increased demand in Europe for newfound wares from the East. In opening up to global trade, however, Western Europeans also opened themselves to disease. The plague, referred to as the *Black Death*, was introduced to Europe by way of trading routes. A major epidemic broke out between 1347 and 1351. Additional outbreaks occurred over the succeeding decades. As many as 25 million people in Europe may have died from the plague. With drastically reduced populations, economic activity declined in Europe. In particular, a shortage of people to work on the land had lasting effects on the feudal system.

The Crusades posed a temporary answer to some of the growing challenges to the Church from reformers and monarchs. The pope's call for military conquests of the Holy Land brought fighting forces of Western Europe together under the Christian banner and stopped squabbling among local rulers. For the longer term, exposure to new ideas from Byzantium and the Muslim world would contribute to the Renaissance and the subsequent rise of secularism.

Economic and Social Change

The Crusades were just part of the changes occurring in Europe. Other forces were also causing an increase in trade and knowledge.

Commerce Local economic self-sufficiency in Europe gradually gave way to an interest in goods from other European areas and from far-flung ports. The Crusades helped pave the way, as lords and their armies of knights brought back fabrics and spices from the East. Despite the inroads on the Byzantine Empire by the Ottoman Turks, the Silk Road trade routes remained in operation, as did sea routes across the Mediterranean Sea and the Indian Ocean. China was still eager for Europe's gold and silver, and Europe was growing more eager than ever for silk, tea, and rhubarb. Global trade increased. Although Europeans had not yet found a route around the Cape of Good Hope at the southern tip of Africa, they had been making overland trips across Europe for many centuries.

In the late thirteenth century *Marco Polo*, an Italian native from Venice, visited the court of Kublai Khan. Polo's captivating descriptions of the customs of the people he met intrigued Europeans. For example, he wrote a history of the Mongols in which he described their practice of multiple marriages and of drinking mare's milk. Curiousity about Asia skyrocketed, stimulating interest in *cartography,* or mapmaking.

Social Change Growth in commerce caused the development of a small *bourgeoisie*, a middle class, also known as *burghers*. The social pyramid of Western Europe thus evolved to have clergy and nobility at the top, large numbers of urban poor and serfs at the bottom, and a growing middle class of shopkeepers, merchants, craftspeople, and small landholders in the middle. The early beginnings of a middle class took shape as Europe joined the Byzantine Empire and Muslim nations in long-distance exchanges of money and goods. Social structures became more fluid, with new emphasis on economics rather than on purely Christian ideals or on military defense and conquest.

Changes in Agriculture Population growth in the Middle Ages after the tenth century resulted from decreases in Viking raids and improvements in agricultural methods for producing food. This agricultural surplus encouraged the growth of towns and of markets that could operate more frequently than just on holidays. The need for more labor on the manors, particularly after the fourteenth-century plagues, gave serfs more bargaining power with lords. Urban growth was hampered after about 1300 by a five-century cooling of the climate known as the *Little Ice Age.* Lower temperatures reduced agricultural productivity, so people had less to trade and cities grew more slowly.

Hanseatic League In the thirteenth century, cities in northern Germany and in Scandinavia formed a commercial alliance called the *Hanseatic League.* Controlling trade in the North Sea and the Baltic Sea, member cities of the league, such as Lubeck, Hamburg, and Riga, were able to drive out pirates and monopolize trade in goods such as timber, grain, leather, and salted fish. League ships would leave the Baltic and North Seas and round the Atlantic Coast of Western Europe, proceeding to the ports of the Mediterranean, where they might pick up valuable goods from Arab caravans. The league lasted until the mid-seventeenth century, when national governments became strong enough to protect their merchants.

Guilds Associations of craftspeople or merchants, *guilds* originated in the towns. Each occupation was separately organized into its own guild. These organizations regulated rules for apprenticeships, helped families of injured or killed workers, and exercised some degree of quality control. Since economic influence was centered in the guilds, they could apply pressure against a local lord or monarch. The centralized states of the High Middle Ages were not yet ready to take on the regulatory and social functions exercised by such groups, so the guilds retained much of their power until early modern times.

Urban Life Dirty and unsanitary, the streets of medieval towns were dangerous for passersby as slop pails were dumped from windows and the resulting raw sewage on the ground spawned rats and fleas. Fire was an ever-present threat since buildings were constructed mostly of wood in the upper stories. Overcrowding was a severe problem because buildings huddled within defensive walls had no room to expand. In most of Western Europe, roughly 5 percent of the population lived in towns, but in the Italian peninsula and the Low Countries in the thirteenth century, the number was around 20 percent.

Towns that could afford it had an outstanding feature—a cathedral in the new Gothic style, which replaced a style common since the mid-eleventh century known as *Romanesque*. Rectangular in shape with stone vaulted ceilings, *Romanesque cathedrals* rested upon massive pillars and walls, and windows were few and narrow. These traits created a dark and forbidding appearance. Beginning in the middle of the twelfth century, the new *Gothic cathedrals* were lighter and airier, featuring architectural details such as arches; spires; stained-glass windows; *gargoyles*, which were exaggerated carvings of humans or animals designed to serve as water spouts; and *flying buttresses*, in which the buttresses, or supports, were extended outward from the wall to a stone foundation, rather than running alongside the wall.

Gender Roles Women found their rights eroding as a wave of patriarchal thinking and writing accompanied the movement from an agricultural society to a more urban one. Men thought that less education was necessary for women, even though women often managed manor accounts. However, Christine de Pisan of Venice strongly challenged the idea that women could not be literate. She herself wrote prose and poetry in praise of women's accomplishments, including *The Book of the City of Ladies*. Women in religious orders had more opportunities to demonstrate their administrative skills than most other women of the time.

Some women were allowed to become guild members and artisans, although not all had property rights. Women in Islamic societies tended to enjoy higher levels of equality, particularly in parts of Africa and Southeast Asia.

Learning Scholarship in the medieval period was almost entirely in the hands of the Church and its clergy. For example, medical advances were almost unknown in Western Europe, since Church authorities believed that sin was the cause of illness. In their minds there was little need to look for other answers.

Nevertheless, had it not been for scribes in the monasteries, few manuscripts would have been saved and much more classical literature would have been lost in the days before the revival of learning in the Renaissance. Aristotle's writings were the foundation for most of the learning of the period, along with Saint Jerome's translation of the Bible into Latin, called the *Vulgate Bible*, created in the late Roman Empire period.

Scholasticism Like Peter Abelard, author of the quotation that opened the chapter, *Thomas Aquinas* in the thirteenth century tried to reconcile Aristotelian knowledge with Christian faith, a system of study called *Scholasticism*. He argued that faith was not endangered by logical thinking. Aquinas's view would open the way for the secularism and Christian humanism of the Renaissance, as well as for the later Enlightenment ideas of progress, reason, and natural law.

Religious Orders Various groups of monks and nuns, usually living in vowed communities, known as *religious orders* of the Catholic Church, advanced Europe's progress, both by keeping learning alive and by promoting practical advice, such as better agricultural methods. Orders such as Benedictines, Franciscans, Dominicans, and Knights Templar followed their own regulations while combining clerical, missionary, and secular duties.

After their founding during the Crusades, the *Knights Templar* combined the functions of knights and monks. They not only fought to reclaim the Holy Land from the Muslims but also cared for the sick and injured. To the north, the *Teutonic Knights* fought pagan Slavs near the Baltic Sea and introduced Christian missions and churches there.

Universities Often sharing books when attending lectures, students at the *University of Paris* in the twelfth century could study liberal arts or theology. In response to disputes between students and townspeople, universities set up *colleges*, boardinghouses for scholars, which were sometimes divided according to students' nationality or discipline. The university granted students licenses to teach after they completed years of study and passed an examination.

Cambridge and *Oxford* universities were founded in England in the twelfth century, preceded in Europe only by a university in Italy at Salerno, the *Salerno Medical School*, founded in the ninth century. Teaching at Salerno was based on knowledge handed down from the time of Hippocrates, Greek physician Galen (129–217 C.E.), who lived in the area that is now Turkey, and on medical information available from ongoing learning in the Arab world. Although Galen was a skilled surgeon for his time and advanced in the study of anatomy, anatomy in that period was almost wholly based on a study of animals rather than humans.

Comparing European and Abbasid Universities Both Western European universities and the cultural centers of the Abbasids with their capital in Baghdad were interested in recording and preserving classical works from Greece and

Rome. In the case of the Abbasid culture, this classical knowledge was combined with new developments coming from India, as well as from other parts of the Islamic world. The Western universities used Latin as the language of pedagogy and focused on liberal arts such as rhetoric, in addition to theological studies. Arabic and Persian were the languages of the Abbasids; their new ideas in math and science used a number system originally from India but later called "Arabic" numbers. Arabic became the language of science for this time period.

As noted above, medical advances were slow to arrive in Western Europe. By contrast, the best hospitals in the world were in the Arabic-speaking world. One reason for the difference may be due to religious sanctions. The Muslims did autopsies and conducted research with human cadavers; in Europe the church prohibited operating on cadavers.

A Persian, *Avicenna* (980–1037), is probably the best-known scholar of the time and is sometimes called "the father of modern medicine." He wrote *Canon of Medicine*, which for 600 years served as a reference book for medical students and doctors. Manuscripts of this work have survived in both Latin and Arabic translations.

The advances of the Southwest and East Asian civilizations were ahead of those in medieval Europe, although Western Europe was quick to catch up after its slower start. Absorbing new goods and ideas would lead Europeans to vast exploration and expansion in the coming centuries, using Asian technology such as paper and agricultural tools. Muslims believed that Europeans were backward and even dirty. Europeans believed Muslims were pagan infidels; some considered them inhuman. As Western Europeans became more open to new ideas and as more unified political units looked toward protection and expansion of their own trade, conflict seemed inevitable.

Renaissance

The expansion of trade, as well as the growth of an agricultural surplus in Western Europe, led to a revival of interest in learning and the arts. In addition, a growing middle class with access to money was able to patronize craftspeople and teachers. The *Renaissance* was characterized by a revival of interest in classical Greek and Roman literature, art, civic virtue, culture. Scholars recovered and studied decaying manuscripts and wrote secular literature. Part of the Reniassance was *humanism,* the focus on individuals rather than God. Humanists focused on education and reform. For example, handbooks of behavior flourished in the fifteenth and sixteenth centuries, as people began to consider not only their place in heaven but also their place in the world. Cultural changes in the Renaissance, such as the increased use of vernacular language, propelled the rise of powerful monarchies, the centralization of governments, and the birth of nationalism. (Test Prep: List some of the elements of classical Greece and Rome revived by the Renaissance. See pages 56 and 79.)

Southern Renaissance In the city-states of Italy and in Spain, the focus of the Renaissance was still clearly under Church domination and patronage. For example, the writer *Dante Alighieri* (1265–1321) used a religious framework for *The Divine Comedy*, which features hell, purgatory, and heaven. Nevertheless, the inquiring spirit of the Renaissance is apparent in Dante's reverence for pagan writers, fearlessness in his criticism of corrupt Church officials, and, most important, his use of the Italian vernacular rather than Latin.

The Renaissance popes were the patrons of famous artists of the Renaissance, and many of the most important sculptures and paintings have religious subjects. As the Renaissance in the south continued until the sixteenth century, a close connection with the Church remained, even as secular thought grew.

Northern Renaissance By 1400, the Renaissance spirit was established in northern Europe as well, where there was great emphasis on piety among *lay people*, those who were not members of the clergy. At the same time, there was an increasing interest in understanding the physical world. *Geoffrey Chaucer*, writing in *The Canterbury Tales* in the late 1300s, portrayed a microcosm of middle-class occupations in England, including several Church positions. His social satire of monks who loved hunting and overly sentimental nuns provided an example of humanism in that Chaucer focused on worldly secular life while still acknowledging the importance of the Church and occupations connected with it. Like Dante a century earlier, Chaucer chose a vernacular, Middle English, for this work, although many of his other writings were in Latin.

LEADING CITIES DURING THE RENAISSANCE IN EUROPE

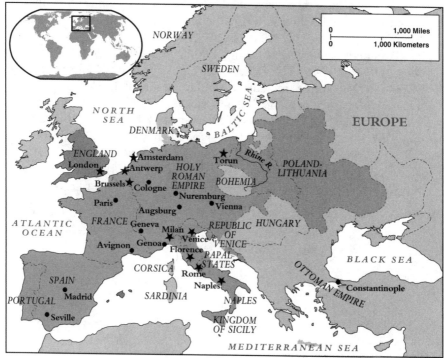

Subsequent events in northern Europe reflect the influence of the Renaissance—for example, on the political front, the development of newly centralized monarchies in England and France. Northern Renaissance art differed from the religious and classical art of Italy, in that it often reflected middle-class occupations and peasant celebrations. A priest from the Netherlands, *Desiderius Erasmus*, author of *In Praise of Folly*, was the most influential northern humanist of the late fifteenth century. Scientists such as *Nicolaus Copernicus* (1473–1553), originally from Poland, showed the increasing interest in understanding the physical world, an interest that would sometimes lead to conflict with the Catholic Church.

HISTORICAL PERSPECTIVES: WERE THE DARK AGES DARK?

The Florentine poet *Petrarch* (1304–1374) is given credit for coining the term "Dark Ages" to describe Europe in the centuries immediately following the fall of the Western Roman Empire. According to nineteenth-century scholars such as Theodor Mommsen, in his essay "Petrarch's Conception of the 'Dark Ages,'" Petrarch was referring to the separation of Europe from its legacy of Greek and Roman classical literature and its failure to produce more such literature. In his book, *The Dark Ages*, the nineteenth-century essayist and historian Samuel Maitland made the argument that scholars should see the "Dark Ages" as dark in two ways: "Do we mean ages which were dark in themselves, and with respect to those who lived in them? Or, do we mean that they are dark to us, and that it is very difficult for us to form a clear idea of them?"

Twentieth-century author William Manchester wrote in *A World Lit Only by Fire* (1992), "The Dark Ages were stark in every dimension." Manchester's examples included the failure of monarchs to keep up the imperial infrastructure of the Romans, the omnipresence of violence and disease, and the bloodthirstiness of tribes such as the Huns. At the same time, the twentieth-century translator of medieval works A.T. Hatto called the Middle Ages "the lively centuries which we call dark." Hatto subscribed to Maitland's second use of the term "dark" to designate the period as simply obscure and not well understood by modern readers.

KEY TERMS BY THEME

STATE-BUILDING: HISTORICAL FIGURES
King Clovis
Charles Martel
Charlemagne
Empress Wu
Otto I
William the Conqueror

STATE-BUILDING: STATES & PEOPLES
Franks
Carolingian Dynasty
Holy Roman Empire
Vikings
Norsemen
Iceland
Greenland
Vinland
Magyars
Normans
Venice

STATE-BUILDING
Battle of Tours
Estates-General
estates
lay investiture controversy
Magna Carta
English Parliament
House of Lords
House of Commons
Hundred Years' War
reconquista
Holy Land
Crusades
Knights Templar
Teutonic Knights

SOCIAL STRUCTURE
lords
vassals
knights
feudalism
serfs
squires
bishops
pope
priests
primogeniture
bourgeoisie
burghers
lay people

CULTURE: LITERATURE & LEARNING
dialects
vernacular languages
University of Paris
colleges
Cambridge
Oxford
Salerno Medical School
Avicenna
Renaissance
humanism
Dante Alighieri
The Divine Comedy
Geoffrey Chaucer
The Canterbury Tales
Desiderius Erasmus
In Praise of Folly
Nicolaus Copernicus
Petrarch
Vulgate Bible
Thomas Aquinas
Scholasticism

CULTURE: ARCHITECTURE
Romanesque cathedrals
Gothic cathedrals
gargoyles
flying buttresses

CULTURE: RELIGION
Great Schism
Donation of Constantine
Babylonian Captivity
Cluniac Reforms
religious orders

CULTURE
code of chivalry
tournaments
jousts
Romanesque

ECONOMICS
manors
manorial system
Hanseatic League
guilds
cartography
Marco Polo

ENVIRONMENT
longships
fiefs
three-field system
horse collar
stirrups
Black Death
cartography
Little Ice Age

1. Which statement best describes how gunpowder technology spread throughout Eurasia?
    (A) The Mongols transferred knowledge of guns from China to Europe.
    (B) European feudal lords developed guns and then use of guns spread eastward.
    (C) Religious influence slowed the adoption of new weapons among Europeans.
    (D) Gunpowder was invented simultaneously in China and Europe.

2. How was the influence of Dante and Chaucer similar?
    (A) Both stimulated renewed interest in classical culture.
    (B) Both reflected the influence of Arab thought in their writings.
    (C) Both encouraged people to write their own poetry.
    (D) Both promoted the spread of vernacular languages.

3. The hierarchical organization of the Roman Catholic Church (pope, bishops, and priests) can be most closely compared to which of the following institutions?
    (A) European manorial system
    (B) International trade organizations
    (C) medieval universities
    (D) Western Roman Empire

4. Which of the following occurred as a result of the Crusades?
    (A) Christians took control of the Holy Land for several centuries.
    (B) European rulers were less likely to fight one another or the pope.
    (C) Many Europeans immigrated permanently to Southwest Asia.
    (D) Exposure to new ideas contributed to the development of the Renaissance.

5. One avenue of advancement for women during the Middle Ages was
    (A) attending universities established just for women
    (B) joining Christian armies of the Crusades
    (C) becoming administrators of Catholic convents
    (D) exercising extensive property rights

6. Which of the following was an effect of the fall of Rome in 476 C.E. in Western Europe in the Early Middle Ages?

(A) Strong nation-states with large standing armies developed.

(B) Cities, transportation, and trade all declined.

(C) Latin quickly disappeared as a spoken language.

(D) The bubonic plague spread rapidly.

Question 7 is based on the following table.

Medieval English Society, c. 1086			
Social class	Approximate population	Percentage of population	Percent of land owned
King, nobles, and top religious leaders	200	Less than 1%	80%
Knights	1,000		
Freemen	340,000	17%	20%
Serfs	1,460,000	73%	Serfs did not own land. They farmed small holdings (15 acres or less) owned by a lord in exchange for rent or service.
Slaves	198,000	10%	Slaves did not own land.

Source: Adapted from J. P. Sommerville, "Medieval English Society," faculty.history.wisc.edu.

7. Which statement about medieval English society is best supported by the information in the table?

(A) Most of the land was controlled by very few people.

(B) Only members of the aristocracy were able to own land.

(C) Most people in England owned at least a small amount of land.

(D) Less than half the population farmed land owned by others.

8. What was the purpose of guilds in the Middle Ages?

(A) to gain more legal rights for members of the nobility

(B) to improve and regulate specific occupations

(C) to invest in long-distance trade and shipping

(D) to organize peasants to agitate for better agricultural practices

Question 9 is based on the following excerpt.

"There are many seeming contradictions and even obscurities in the innumerable writings of the church fathers. Our respect for their authority should not stand in the way of an effort on our part to come at the truth. The obscurity and contradictions in ancient writings may be explained upon many grounds, and may be discussed without impugning the good faith and insight of the fathers. . . .

"All writings belonging to this class are to be read with full freedom to criticize, and with no obligation to accept unquestioningly; otherwise the way would be blocked to all discussion, and posterity be deprived of the excellent intellectual exercise of debating difficult questions of language and presentation. But an explicit exception must be made in the case of the Old and New Testaments. In the Scriptures, when anything strikes us as absurd, we may not say that the writer erred, but that the scribe made a blunder in copying the manuscripts, or that there is an error in interpretation, or that the passage is not understood. . . ."

—from *Sic et Non* (*Yes and No*) by Peter Abelard, 1120

9. Which of these statements is best supported by the information in the excerpt?
    (A) Abelard strongly supported all writings of Church officials past and present.
    (B) Abelard accepted teachings in the Bible but rejected the pope's authority.
    (C) Abelard left the Church because he disagreed with its teachings.
    (D) Abelard believed that questioning some Church writings was beneficial.

10. Which statement best describes the relationship between Europeans and the Islamic world in European Middle Ages?
    (A) The two worlds remained isolated from each other.
    (B) The Islamic world was known primarily for its piracy against European ships.
    (C) Both cultures had negative and false views of one another.
    (D) Europeans encouraged Muslims to attend their universities.

CONTINUITY AND CHANGE-OVER-TIME ESSAY QUESTIONS

Directions: You are to answer the following question. You should spend 5 minutes organizing or outlining your essay. Write an essay that:

- Has a relevant thesis and supports that thesis with appropriate historical evidence.
- Addresses all parts of the question.

- Uses world historical context to show continuities and changes over time.
- Analyzes the process of continuity and change over time.

1. Analyze continuities and changes in trade in ONE of the following movements in Western Europe during the Middle Ages:
   - Crusades
   - Viking migrations

Questions for Additional Practice

2. Analyze continuities and change in the role of the Roman Catholic Church in Europe from 600 to 1450.

3. Analyze continuities and changes in how feudalism and the manorial system effected political structures and economies in medieval Europe.

COMPARATIVE ESSAY QUESTIONS

Directions: You are to answer the following question. You should spend 5 minutes organizing or outlining your essay. Write an essay that:
- Has a relevant thesis and supports that thesis with appropriate historical evidence.
- Addresses all parts of the question.
- Makes direct, relevant comparisons.
- Analyzes relevant reasons for similarities and differences.

1. Analyze similarities and differences in the forms of government developed by the Carolingians and ONE of the following.
   - Tang Dynasty
   - Abbasid Dynasty

Questions for Additional Practice

2. Analyze similarities and differences in European art and cultural life during TWO of the following periods:
   - Early Middle Ages
   - High Middle Ages
   - Renaissance

3. Compare and contrast the social structures of feudalism in Europe and Japan during the period 600 to 1450.

THINK AS A HISTORIAN: PRACTICE PERIODIZATION

The way historians group events into time periods reflects what they consider important. *Which THREE of the following statements best demonstrates an understanding of periodization?*

1. In terms of trade and urbanization, the years from 476 to 1054 shared little in common with the years before or after.

2. Abelard was another great thinker in the philosophical tradition that began with Aristotle in the fourth century B.C.E. and continues with thinkers such as Alasdair MacIntyre, who was born in 1929.

3. Charlemagne's empire existed briefly; it marked a change in how people living in Europe viewed themselves.

4. The Roman Catholic Church had an extensive hierarchy of regional bishops who owed allegiance to the pope.

5. The Fourth Crusade had more in common with the economic motives of the late Middle Ages than with the religiously motivated earlier crusades.

WRITE AS A HISTORIAN: CONSIDER THE TIME

To fully understand a source, think about the context in which it was written. How did the historical circumstances affect the writer's views? Someone writing about astronomy in the 1100s would have different views than someone writing today. *For each sentence, select the statement that provides the most relevant information about the context.*

1. A writer in a German city in 1070 sadly predicts the decline of Christian authority.

   a. The Great Schism in 1054

   b. The Norman Conquest of England in 1066

2. A writer in France in 1250 sees increasing power for feudal lords.

   a. Mongols conquer Russia in 1239

   b. King John signed the Magna Carta in 1215

3. A writer in London in 1350 predicts the world is about to end.

   a. The Black Death killed two to three million Europeans between 1347 and 1351.

   b The English and the French have been at war since 1337.

13

The Mongols and Transregional Empires

Swarming like locusts over the face of the earth, they [the Mongols] have brought terrible devastation to the eastern parts [of Europe], laying it waste with fire and carnage. After having passed through the land of the Saracens [Muslims], they have razed cities, cut down forests, overthrown fortresses, pulled up vines, destroyed gardens, killed townspeople and peasants.

—Matthew Paris, from the *Chronica Majora* (1240)

The *Mongols* of central Asia marched across much of Eurasia throughout the thirteenth century, leaving destruction and chaos in their wake. The reputation of the Mongols for slaughter spread even farther than their actual conquest. Matthew Paris had no firsthand knowledge of the Mongols as he wrote from the safe vantage point of a Benedictine abbey in England. Like Paris, most writers of the time focused on Mongol atrocities. However, in their quest for blood and treasure, the Mongols also sparked a period of interregional connection and exchange at a level that the world had not experienced in a thousand years.

The Mongols and Their Surroundings

In the twelfth century, the Mongols were multiple clans of nomadic pastoralists living north of the *Gobi Desert* in East Asia. Life on the arid Asian steppes was harsh, and it shaped the Mongol culture. Mongols were pastoral nomads who herded goats and sheep and were also hunter-foragers. They expected everyone, male and female, to become skilled horse riders, and they highly valued courage, in hunting and warfare. The Mongols were surrounded by other tribes—the Tatars, the Naimans, the Merkits, and the powerful Jurchen in northern China. The Mongols coveted the relative wealth of tribes and kingdoms that were located closer to the Silk Roads and had easier access to luxury goods such as silk clothing and gold jewelry. These early Mongols dressed plainly in long robes and pants made of pelts and had few possessions other than a *yurt*, a circular, felt-covered tent; horses; and some basic tools used in hunting and herding.

Genghis Khan

The Mongol leader Temujin, born in 1162, spent the early decades of his life creating a series of tribal alliances and defeating neighboring groups one by one. He formed key friendships and married his oldest son to the daughter of a neighboring *khan,* or king. Temujin was intensely focused on building power, This meant that he sometimes appointing talented nonfamily members to positions over family members. And it often meant he would be ruthless. For example, he killed his own stepbrother. He considered personal loyalty the best way to run his growing kingdom. In 1206, Temujin gathered the Mongol chieftains at a meeting called a *kuriltai* where he was elected khan of the Mongolian Kingdom. He took the name *Genghis Khan,* or "ruler of all."

The Beginning of Conquest In 1210, Genghis Khan and his troops headed east and attacked the powerful Jin Empire, which had been established by the *Jurchens* a century earlier and now ruled Manchuria, Inner Mongolia, and northern China. Its capital was the city of Zhongdu, present-day Beijing. Genghis Khan earned his reputation as a terrifying warrior during this campaign; anyone who resisted was brutally killed in retribution. Sometimes the Mongols wiped out the civilian populations of entire towns after defeating their armies. Stories of Khan's brutality spread in advance of his new westward campaigns, inducing some leaders to surrender before an attack. In 1219, Khan conquered both the Central Asian *Kara Khitai Empire* and the Islamic *Khwarazm Empire* farther west. By 1227, Genghis Khan's *khantate,* or kingdom, reached from the North China Sea to eastern Persia. (Test Prep: Write a paragraph comparing Genghis Khan with Alexander the Great. See page 62.)

Genghis Khan at War The skilled and fearsome soldiers under Genghis Khan's command made his empire possible. Mongolian soldiers were strong riders and proficient with the short bow. They were also highly disciplined, and Khan developed an efficient command structure. Groups of 10 warriors operated as a unit with one soldier in command of the rest. These groups of 10 were then similarly organized into larger groups, up to 10 groups of 1,000 warriors each called *tumens*. In addition, the cavalry units were divided into heavy and light cavalry: Heavy cavalry wore more armor and carried more weapons than the light cavalry.

To help with communication between units, a messenger force was created whose members rode for days without stopping, even sleeping on their horses while continuing to ride. With the help of Genghis Khan, the Mongolian armies developed special units that mapped the terrain so that they were prepared against attacks and knew which way to go to attack their enemies. Their military strategies extended to surprise and craft. For instance, Mongol forces frequently deployed a band of warriors smaller than that of their enemy, retreating in feigned defeat; usually, enemy forces pursued the retreating Mongols, who then amassed larger forces to confuse and outflank the enemy.

When coming upon an enemy settlement, Genghis Khan sent a small group ahead to ask for surrender. If the enemy refused, he killed all the aristocrats.

Craftsworkers, miners, and others with skills, such as the ability to read and write, were recruited for the Mongol Empire. Others were used as laborers for tasks such as carrying looted goods back to the Mongol capital or as fodder in the front lines of battles.

Mongols quickly incorporated into their military the weapons and technology of the peoples they conquered. For example, when they conquered parts of China and Persia, they exploited the expertise of captured engineers who knew how to produce improved *siege weapons*, such as portable towers used to attack walled fortifications and catapults that hurled stones or other objects. To keep contact with the far reaches of the empire, Genghis Khan created a type of pony express, except instead of carrying written letters riders carried oral messages.

Genghis Khan at Peace Those who expected Genghis Khan to govern the way he made war were surprised. The period of Eurasian history between the thirteenth and fourteenth centuries is often called the *Pax Mongolica*, or Mongolian peace. Genghis Khan established the capital of his empire at *Karakorum*, near the center of what is now the modern country of Mongolia. In constructing the city and establishing his government, he consulted with scholars and engineers of Chinese and Islamic traditions. Genghis Khan may have been responsible for more new bridges than any other ruler in history. (Test Prep: List the similarities and differences between the Pax Mongolica and the Pax Romana. See page 77.)

The social policies of Genghis Khan were liberal for the day. For example, he instituted a policy of religious tolerance throughout the empire, which was quite unusual in the thirteenth century. Freed from years of warfare, Genghis Khan's soldiers took charge of protecting the Silk Road, making it safe for trade. New trade channels were also established between Asia, the Middle East, Africa, and Europe. Those who survived the conquests by the Mongols and their descendants benefited from the reinvigoration of trade routes that had not been heavily used since the days of the Roman and Han Empires.

Genghis Khan's Successor Genghis Khan died while fighting the *Tangut Empire*, south of the Gobi Desert, in 1227. His chosen successor was his third, and reportedly his favorite, son, *Ogodei* (also spelled Ogedei), who was formally elected emperor by the Mongolian chiefs in 1229.

Ogodei's skills as a military leader could not compare with his legendary father, but under his leadership the Mongol Empire did continue to expand, making inroads into modern-day Georgia, Armenia, and Azerbaijan, as well as capturing land in the Indus Valley and southern China and invading Korea in 1231.

Ogodei also worked to bring a more efficient bureaucracy to the Mongolian Empire, and invested in the greater development of the capital, Karakorum. He wanted to build a permanent city with buildings rather than the traditional Mongol yurts.

Transfer of Knowledge by the Mongols and the Crusaders			
Empire	**Primary Areas Connected**	**Science/Technology Transferred**	**Ideas Transferred**
Mongols	East Asia, Europe, and the Middle East	• Better bridges • Methods of printing • Use of gunpowder • Advances in astronomy	• Increased religious tolerance • Greater respect for artisans and merchants • Islam
Crusaders	Europe and the Middle East	• Advances in chemistry • Algebra • Medicines for reducing pain • Skills at tunneling for military attacks • New siege weapons	• Islam • Christianity • Arabic numerals • Chess • Romantic literature

Mongolian Empire Expands

Three of Genghis Khan's grandsons set up their own khanates, further expanding the empire into Asia and Europe.

Batu and the Golden Horde In 1236, *Batu* led a Mongolian army of 100,000 soldiers into Russia, which at the time was a loose network of city-states and principalities. Batu's army, which came to be known as the *Golden Horde,* marched westward, conquering the small Russian kingdoms and forcing them to pay tributes. In 1240, the capital city of Kiev was destroyed and looted.

The Golden Horde continued pushing westward. An initial period of sympathy for the Mongols, based on religious toleration and promotion of trade, evaporated when Western Europe saw the Golden Horde conquer a Christian region, Russia. In 1241, Batu led the Golden Horde into a successful military encounter with Polish, German, and French knights under the leadership of King Henry of Silesia. Soon afterward, Batu defeated a force of Hungarian knights. He next set his sights on Italy and Austria, but fate intervened. Back in Karakorum, Ogodei Khan died, As a result, Batu called off the attacks, and returned home to attend the funeral and to see to issues of succession. By the time Batu returned to Europe, he had apparently lost interest in conquering Western Europe. Instead he established a new capital on the Volga River, called *Sarai.*

The Mongols ruled northern Russia by working through existing Russian rulers, who sent regular tributes. The Mongols chose this form of indirect rule because they did not want to live in the forests. The rulers of the city-state of *Moscow* began collecting additional tributes, which they set aside to develop an army to resist the Mongols, and began building an anti-Mongol coalition among the Russian city-states. This coalition, under Moscow's leadership, rose up against the Golden Horde and defeated it in 1380 at the *Battle of Kulikovo.* After this battle, Mongol influence began to decline. By the mid-sixteenth century, Russia had defeated all of the descendant khans of the Mongols except the Crimean Tatars, who were not defeated until the late eighteenth century. (Test Prep: Create a timeline tracing the history of Russia under the Mongols up to the emergence of modern Russia. See page 335.)

The Mongols had long-lasting impact on Russia. As elsewhere, Russia suffered widespread devastation and death from the Mongol attacks. But once the destruction by the Golden Horde was over, Russia began to recover. The invasions prompted Russian princes to improve their military organization and to accept the value of more centralized leadership of the region. In addition, three centuries of Mongol rule severed Russia's ties with much of Western Europe. As a result, Russia developed a more distinctly Russian culture than it had before, and resistance to the Mongols created the foundation for the modern Russian state.

Hulegu and the Islamic Heartlands While Batu led the western armies, *Hulegu*, another grandson of Genghis Khan, took charge of the southwest region. In 1258, Hulegu led the Mongols into the Abbasid territories, where they destroyed the city of Baghdad and killed the caliph, along with perhaps 200,000 residents of the city.

MONGOL EMPIRES IN THE THIRTEENTH CENTURY

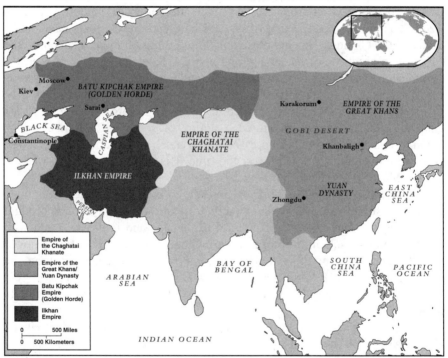

Hulegu's Mongolian armies continued to push west, threatening more of the Middle East. In 1260, however, they were defeated as a result of a temporary alliance between the Muslim Mamluks, under their military leader *Baibars,* and Christian Crusaders in Palestine. Both religious groups viewed the Mongols as serious threat.

At the time of this defeat, Hulegu's kingdom, called the *Il-khanate*, in Central Asia stretched from Byzantium to to the Oxus River, which is now called the Amu Darya. Mongols ruled this kingdom, but Persians served as ministers and provincial and local officials. The Mongols found that this arrangement resulted in maximum tax collection.

Eventually, Hulegu and most of the other Mongols living in the Il-khanate converted to Islam. Before this conversion, the Mongols had tolerated all religions in Persia. After the conversion, however, Mongols supported massacres of Jews and Christians.

Kublai Khan and the Yuan Dynasty Meanwhile, in the eastern part of the Mongolian Empire, a grandson of Genghis Khan, *Kublai Khan*, set his sights on China, which was then ruled by the Song Dynasty. China was a more formidable opponent than those faced by the other khans, and Kublai's armies spent the years from 1235 to 1271 attempting to conquer China. In 1260, Kublai assumed the title of Great Khan, and eleven years later finally defeated the Chinese. Hewing close to Chinese tradition rather than enforcing Mongolian practices of leadership and control, Kublai Khan established the *Yuan Dynasty*. He rebuilt the capital at Zhongdu, which had been destroyed by the Mongols in 1215, calling it *Dadu.*

Kublai Khan proved to be skilled at governing a large, diverse territory. Like his grandfather, he instituted a policy of religious tolerance, which inspired loyalty in formerly oppressed groups such as Buddhists and Daoists, who were out of favor in China at the time. His policies were also tolerant toward Muslims and Christians.

With these and other reforms and the protection of the Mongolian armies, most Chinese initially enjoyed the rule of the Great Khan; he brought prosperity to China because of cultural exchanges and improved trade with other countries, including European ones. Chinese arts and literature enjoyed a golden period during the Yuan Dynasty. For example, Wang Shifu wrote the still-popular play *The Romance of the West Chamber* during this period. It is the story of two young lovers who overcome obstacles until they are finally allowed to marry.

Also during this time, the 17-year-old Venetian *Marco Polo* first visited China. After Polo returned to Italy in 1295, he wrote a book about his trip. However, many Europeans refused to believe his descriptions of China's size, wealth, and wonders. Only when other Europeans followed Polo's route to China did people widely accept that China was prosperous and innovative.

Despite Kublai Khan's adoption of many Chinese customs, Mongolian leaders eventually alienated many Chinese. They hired foreigners for the government rather than native-born Chinese. By promoting Buddhists and Daoists and dismantling the civil service exam system, the Mongols distressed the Chinese scholar-gentry class who were often Confucians. Although the official policy was one of tolerance, the Mongolians tended to remain separate from the Chinese and prohibited non-Mongols from speaking Mongolian.

Just as Batu had reached the limit of Mongol expansion to the west, the Mongolian rulers of China failed to expand beyond China. Starting in 1274, the Yuan Dynasty tried and failed to conquer Japan, Indochina, Burma, and the island of Java. These defeats suggested to the already disenchanted Chinese population that the Mongols were not as fearsome as they once had been. In the 1350s, the secret *White Lotus Society* began quietly organizing to put an end to the Yuan Dynasty. In 1368, *Zhu Yuanzhang*, a Buddhist monk from a poor peasant family, led a revolt that overthrew the Yuan Dynasty and founded the *Ming Dynasty* (1368-1644).

The Mongols' defeat in China paralleled a general decline in their power elsewhere, and the empire began to shrink. The Golden Horde had lost its territory by about 1369, while Central Asian territories were conquered by Tamerlane, also known as Timur the Lame, at around the same time. (Test Prep: Create a map or series of maps showing the different empires and countries that emerged in the same territory after the fall of the Mongol Empire. See pages 353–363.)

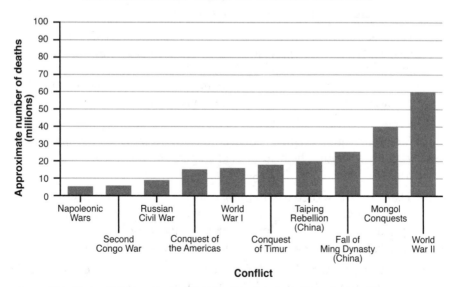

TEN DEADLIEST WARS IN WORLD HISTORY

Source: White, Matthew (2012). Atrocities: The 100 Deadliest Episodes in Human History. New York, NY: W. W. Norton. p. 271, 578. ISBN 9780393345230.

What Was the Long-Term Impact of the Mongolian Invasions?

The Mongolian invasions played a key role in history in many ways, positive and negative.

- Mongols conquered a larger area than the Romans, and their bloody reputation was usually well-earned.

- During the period known as the Pax Mongolica, Mongols revitalized interregional trade between Asia, the Middle East, Africa, and Europe. The Mongols built a system of roads and continued to maintain and guard the trade routes.

- The Mongols ruled successfully due to their understanding of centralized power, a capacity that would transfer in many cases to the occupied civilizations. The Mongols devised and used a single international law for all their conquered territories. Thus, after the Mongols declined in power, the kingdoms and states of Europe, Asia, and Southeast Asia continued or copied the process of centralizing power.

- The Mongol conquests helped to transmit the fleas that carried the bubonic plague, termed the Black Death, from southern China to Central Asia, and from there to Southeast Asia and Europe. It followed familiar paths of trade and military conquest. The Black Death had a huge impact on Europe, killing one-third of the population there in a few years, and had similar effects on other areas, including North Africa, China, and Central Asia. South Asia and Sub-Saharan Africa were spared because there were few trading ports in those regions.

- Mongol women led more independent lives than women in other societies of the time. In their nomadic culture, women tended flocks of sheep and goats in addition to raising children and providing meals for the family. Since they rode horses like Mongol men, the women wore the same kind of leather trousers. Mongol women could remarry after being widowed and could initiate divorces.

- Mongol fighting techniques led to the end of Western Europe's use of knights in armor. The heavily clad knights could not react in time to the Mongols' use of speed and surprise.

- The era of the walled city in Europe also came to an end, as walls proved useless against the Mongols' siege technology. The cannon is considered by some a Mongol invention, cobbled together using Chinese gunpowder, Muslim flamethrowers, and European bell-casting techniques.

- Males in Western Europe replaced their tunics and robes with the Mongol-style pants and jacket combination.

HISTORICAL PERSPECTIVE: HOW BRUTAL WAS GENGHIS KHAN?

Was Genghis Khan a brutal destroyer who murdered millions, or was he a great unifier who promoted prosperity by unifying most of Eurasia?

Many historians emphasize that Khan was a bloodthirsty tyrant. Military historian Steven R. Ward writes that "Overall, the Mongol violence and depredations killed up to three-fourths of the population of the Iranian Plateau." Total deaths attributed to the Mongols during his rule and the rule of his descendants often reach the tens of millions. Stories of his massacres of innocent people and of using unarmed civilians to protect his own soldiers show him to have little regard for human life.

Others historians focus more on Khan's role as a great leader and hero. Mongolian scholars, showing their national pride in their most famous countryman, argue that his reputation for brutality has been exaggerated. As historians from Europe and the United States have focused more on trade and toleration, they have noted the benefits of the Mongols' rule. Genghis Khan forged a united China and established a system of Eurasian trade that renewed the links between China and Europe that had lapsed. Further, the Mongols were open to ideas and tolerant of different religions. Khan believed in a meritocracy, and he established one writing system across his empire. His rule opened the way for new systems of laws, for trade, and for cultural expansion.

One Persian historian takes a position broad enough that everyone can agree with: "Genghis was possessed of great energy, discernment, genius, and understanding, awe-inspiring, a butcher, just, resolute, an over-thrower of enemies, intrepid, sanguinary, and cruel."

KEY TERMS BY THEME

STATE-BUILDING
Mongols
khan
kuriltai
Genghis Khan
Jurchens
khanites
Kara Khitai Empire
Khwarazm Empire
Pax Mongolica
Karakorum
Tangut Empire
Ogodei
Batu

Sarai
Golden Horde
Moscow
Battle of Kulikovo
Hulegu
Baibars
Il-khanate
Kublai Khan
Yuan Dynasty
Dadu
White Lotus Society
Zhu Yuanzhang
Ming Dynasty

ENVIRONMENT
Gobi Desert
yurt

TECHNOLOGY
tumens
siege weapons

CULTURE
The Romance of the West Chamber
Marco Polo

Question 1 is based on the following image.

Source: M. Gauci / Library of Congress

1. The image above shows a European's drawing of Kublai Khan and his advisors being carried into a battle. The image suggests that Europeans
   (A) thought that the Mongols tried to avoid going to battle
   (B) believed that elephants were more effective than horses in battle
   (C) saw the Chinese as very similar to Europeans
   (D) were impressed by Kublai Khan's power

2. How did the Mongols' lifestyle contribute to their military supremacy?
   (A) Their religious practices made them willing to die in battle.
   (B) Their skill on horseback made them expert cavalry fighters.
   (C) Their navigation skills gave them an advantage in naval battles.
   (D) Swift runners provided communication among military units.

3. What military policy practiced by the Mongols might have influenced cities to voluntarily give up without a fight?
   (A) Mongols sent advance emissaries offering payments of gold in exchange for not going to battle.
   (B) Mongols often treated the enemy citizenry better than they were treated by their own leadership.
   (C) The Mongols would wipe out the civilian population of towns resisting their advance as a warning to others.
   (D) The Mongols bought off the surrounding countries and groups, denying the defenders any possible allies.

4. One result of the Pax Mongolica was
   (A) increased transregional trade
   (B) creation of a united Europe
   (C) greater conflict between China and India
   (D) the spread of Christianity in Asia

Question 5 is based on the following excerpt.

By 1257, Hulegu had reached western Persia. From there he sent emissaries to the caliph telling him to raze the walls of Baghdad and fill in the moat and come in person to make obeisance to Hulegu. The caliph replied that with all of Islam ready to defend him, he did not fear. He advised Hulegu to go back where he came from. The Mongol army had recently received reinforcements from other Mongol hordes, and a contingent of Christian cavalry from Georgia.

—From "Invaders: Destroying Baghdad"
by Ian Frazier, *The New Yorker*, April 25, 2005

5. Which is the most likely explanation for the presence of the Christian cavalry from Georgia?
   (A) Christians were trying to prevent Hulegu from attacking them.
   (B) Christians hoped a show of force would prevent a Mongol invasion of Europe.
   (C) Christians and Mongols both wanted the defeat of Muslims.
   (D) Hulegu needed the expertise of Christian cavalry to achieve victory.

6. The long-term impact of Russian resistance to the Golden Horde was
   (A) the complete destruction of many Russian towns and cities
   (B) the conversion of many Russians to Buddhism
   (C) the improvement of Russia's relations with the West
   (D) the primacy of Moscow among Russian city-states

7. Kublai Khan's defeat of the Song Dynasty in China was different from other Mongol conquests because he
   (A) converted to the Buddhist religion of the conquered
   (B) modeled his government on Chinese traditions
   (C) gave most government posts to native-born Chinese
   (D) conquered the land, pillaged its wealth, and then left

8. Which of the following happened as a result of Mongol rule in China?
   (A) Chinese literature and art flourished during the period.
   (B) The civil service examination system became stronger.
   (C) The government supported the work of the Confucian scholars.
   (D) The Chinese emperor of the Song Dynasty remained in power.

9. Which of the following was a positive long-term impact of the Mongol invasions on Europe?
   (A) Economic self-sufficiency of nations
   (B) The strengthening of city fortifications
   (C) The spread of centralized governments
   (D) Improved agricultural techniques

10. The Mongols' nomadic culture differed from more settled western cultures in that Mongols
   (A) developed a caste-like social structure
   (B) had greater equality between the sexes
   (C) placed a greater value on material possessions
   (D) practiced a single, monotheistic religion

CONTINUITY AND CHANGE-OVER-TIME ESSAY QUESTIONS

Directions: You are to answer the following question. You should spend 5 minutes organizing or outlining your essay. Write an essay that:

- Has a relevant thesis and supports that thesis with appropriate historical evidence.
- Addresses all parts of the question.

- Uses world historical context to show continuities and changes over time.
- Analyzes the process of continuity and change over time.

1. Analyze continuities and change in ONE of the following aspects of Mongolian society from the rise of Genghis Khan to the end of the Mongolian empire:
   - Form of government and warfare
   - Trade
   - Cultural practices

Questions for Additional Practice

2. Analyze continuities and change in ONE of these regions that reflect Mongol influences:
   - Eastern Europe and Russia
   - Southwest Asia
   - China

3. Analyze continuities and change in regional trade during the era of the Mongol conquests.

COMPARATIVE ESSAY QUESTIONS

Directions: You are to answer the following question. You should spend 5 minutes organizing or outlining your essay. Write an essay that:
- Has a relevant thesis and supports that thesis with appropriate historical evidence.
- Addresses all parts of the question.
- Makes direct, relevant comparisons.
- Analyzes relevant reasons for similarities and differences.

1. Analyze similarities and differences between Mongol rule in TWO of the following regions:
   - Russia
   - Southwest Asia
   - China

Questions for Additional Practice

2. Compare the impact of the Mongol and Hellenistic Empires.

3. Compare the status of women in Mongolian and Song Chinese societies.

THINK AS A HISTORIAN: PRACTICE THE SKILL OF COMPARISON

In a comparative essay, alternate between the topics you are comparing. That is, compare them detail by detail rather than describing one topic completely and then shifting to the other topic. *Which THREE of the statements below best reflect the skill of comparison?*

1. As a conqueror and warmaker, Genghis Khan was terrifyingly brutal, but his reign afterwards was so tranquil that some call it the "Pax Mongolica."

2. Kublai Khan proved himself skilled at governing a large territory and instituting a policy of religious tolerance.

3. The arrival of the Golden Horde was destructive to Russia, but there were also some benefits, including improved military organization.

4. Starting in 1274, the Yuan Dynasty tried and failed to conquer Japan, Indochina, Burma, and the island of Java.

5. Ogodei, the third and believed to be favorite son of Genghis Khan, became his successor. He was not as skilled a military leader as his father, but under his leadership the Mongol Empire continued to expand.

WRITE AS A HISTORIAN: CONSIDER THE CULTURE

In an essay examining a specific topic, consider the cultural setting of the topic. For example, in evaluating the Mongols' success in warfare, consider the role of horses in their culture. *Choose the background information most relevant to the following sentence.*

1. The period when Ghengis Khan ruled most of Asia is sometimes referred to as the Pax Mongolica.

   a. Religious tolerance became an accepted aspect of life under Ghengis Khan.

   b. Khan ruled harshly and maintained repute as a frightening combatant.

2. Kublai Khan helped China experience economic success during his rule.

   a. The prosperity allowed Chinese literature and arts to flourish.

   b. Kublai Khan enabled cultural exchanges and improved relationships between countries, which facilitated global trade.

3. During the thirteenth century, Russia was forced to create a more centralized political system, specifically regarding their military.

   a. The invasion of the Golden Horde helped Russians realize the flaws of their fragmented government.

   b. While Batu controlled Russia, the representatives from city-states were required to send tributes to the Mongolians.

The Americas on the Eve of Globalization

And when he [the priest] had laid him upon it [the stone table], four men stretched him out, his arms and legs. And already in the hand of the fire priest lay the [knife] . . . and then, when he has split open the breast, he at once seized his heart. And he whose breast he laid open was quite alive.

—Account of Aztec sacrifice from Fray Bernardino de Sahagún, *The Florentine Codex*, 1577

Following the decline of the Olmecs and the Maya in Mesoamerica, new civilizations emerged, such as the Toltecs and the Aztecs. In the Andes, following the Moche came the Inca. The first large-scale civilization in North America was the Mississippian. All of these civilizations developed complex societies that included large urban centers, extensive government bureaucracies, and well-developed religious belief systems. In addition to archaeological evidence, much of what we know about these cultures comes from writings by Europeans who came to the Americas beginning in the late fifteenth century. Fray Bernardino de Sahagún, who is quoted above, was a Spanish Franciscan missionary who arrived in Mexico in 1529. He learned the Aztec language and spent about 30 years observing the Aztecs and asking them about their culture. His work is seen as an early example of anthropological writing that presents a fairly accurate account of Aztec civilization.

The Mississippian Culture

The first large-scale civilization in North America emerged between the 700s and 1500s C.E in what is now the eastern United States. Since it started in the valley of the Mississippi River and spread east, it is known as the *Mississippian* culture. While other cultures built monumental buildings, it built enormous earthen mounds, some of which were as tall as a hundred feet and covered an area the size of 12 football fields. Most were pyramid-shaped or oval-shaped, but some were built in the form of various animals; one large one in Wisconsin was shaped like a man. Some of these mounds have been preserved into the present day, including sites in Illinois and several in Mississippi near Tupelo, Jackson, and Natchez.

Economy and Culture The Mississippian people practiced relatively large-scale agriculture, using the rich soil of the river valley. Corn, beans, squash, and tobacco were among their main crops. Their farming methods and arts suggest some contact with the Maya, but such a link has never been proven.

Like the Maya, Mississippian people lived in large towns that controlled smaller nearby villages. Each town was built around a plaza and had one or more large earthen mounds. Atop some mounds, the Mississippian people built temples made of wood. The largest town was *Cahokia*, in present-day Illinois. Around 1250, the population of Cahokia was about 40,000—a population greater than that of London at the time. Cahokia, like other cities around the world in this era, such as Tenochtitlan, Venice, Timbuktu, and Hangzhou, was a trading city.

Other Mississippian towns were smaller, but all were centers of crafts and commerce. Artwork and manufactures included clay pottery, engraved shells, and various goods made from stone, leather, wood, feathers, and copper. Crafts made of bears' teeth from the Rocky Mountains and turtle shells from the Gulf of Mexico suggest that transregional trade was widespread. Other trade networks reached the Great Lakes and the Atlantic Coast.

Like most other North American Indians, the Mississippian people were practiced animism: They believed that the natural world was filled with spirits. The spirits of animals were considered especially powerful, and hunters carried out ceremonies to honor the spirits of game that they killed. Priests were thought to communicate with the spirits and they served as healers. Although the

THE AMERICAS, 800 TO 1492

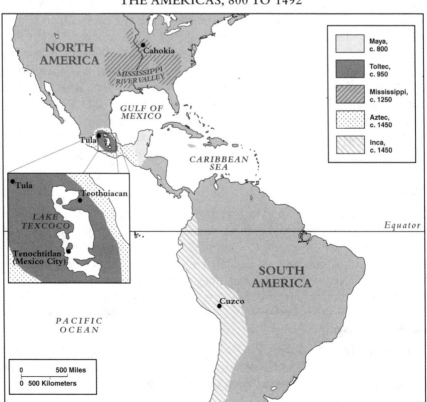

Mississippian people fought with other Indian groups, their religious beliefs prohibited warfare among their own settlements.

Government and Society The Mississippian society had a rigid class structure. A chief called the *Great Sun* ruled each large town; directly beneath the Great Sun was an upper class of priests and nobles. The next level down consisted of the common people: farmers, hunters, merchants, craftspeople, and laborers. At the bottom of society were slaves, who usually were prisoners of war. Women did most of the farming, while hunting was a male responsibility. The Mississippian people had a *matrilineal society*, which means that social standing was determined by the woman's side of the family. For example, when the Great Sun died, the title passed not to his own son, but to a sister's son.

The Decline of Mississippian Civilization Cahokia was abandoned around 1450, and within another 150 years other large Mississippian cities were abandoned. Historians are not sure what caused the decline of the civilization. One theory posits that flooding or other weather extremes caused crop failures and the collapse of agricultural economy needed to sustain the populations of the large cities. Another theory suggests that diseases introduced by the European decimated the population.

The Toltec

The *Toltec* built a capital at *Tula* in northern Mesoamerica by around 950. At its height, Tula had a population of 60,000. The Toltecs were ruled by a warrior aristocracy, wealthy landholders who were also military leaders. Over time, the Toltecs dominated the region by extracting tribute from conquered peoples.

In the tenth century, the Toltec conquered Mayan settlements in southern Mexico and the Yucatán Peninsula. The Toltec religion was a continuation of the cult of *Quetzalcoatl*, borrowed from the Mayans. There may have been other borrowings from the Maya as well. Scholars have noted the architectural similarities between Tula and the Mayan city of *Chichén Itzá*. By 1150, the Toltec had fallen into decline and no longer dominated Mesoamerica. (Test Prep: Create a graphic connecting the Toltec and Mayan civilizations. See page 114.)

The Aztecs

The *Aztecs*, also known as the Mexicas, claimed the legacy of the Toltecs, but in fact the Aztec originated from a different part of Mexico. They were originally hunter-gatherers who migrated to central Mexico from the north in the 1200s C.E. In 1325, they founded their capital *Tenochtitlán* on the site of what is now Mexico City. Over the next 100 years, they conquered the surrounding peoples and created an empire that stretched from the Gulf of Mexico to the Pacific Ocean. (Test Prep: Write a brief outline comparing the conquests of the Aztecs to those of the Mongols. See page 241.)

Capital City The Aztecs used geography for protection and defense by locating Tenochtitlán on an island in the middle of a swampy lake. As the city grew, they scooped up mud from the lake bottom to create more land for buildings and for fields to farm.

Tenochtitlán eventually grew to almost 200,000 people, making it not only the largest city in the Western hemisphere but also one of the largest in the world. At the center of the city, the Aztecs built a pyramid that rose some 150 feet into the air. This *Great Pyramid* and other pyramids, temples, and palaces were made of stone. The Aztecs built their houses mainly of wood, with roofs made from reeds.

Agriculture On *Lake Texcoco*, the Aztecs built floating gardens called *chinampas* to increase the amount of space for food production. The structures were constructed by fencing off a section of the lake bed with woven sticks. Mud and weeds were then added to bring the level of the soil up to the height of the lake. Crops grown in the chinampas supplemented the maize and other staples grown with traditional agricultural practices elsewhere.

The Aztecs dug ditches to use lake water to irrigate their fields and to drain parts of the lake for more land. They used plant and animal wastes as fertilizer and built stone terraces on the sides of the surrounding mountains to prevent erosion. They harvested trees, grown at altitudes too high and cold to farm, in order to provide wood for fires and building materials. To carry out all these tasks, they used only hand tools. Like other early American peoples, the Aztecs did not use wheeled vehicles. And like most groups outside of the Andes, they had no pack animals, either, so they walked between settlements and carried everything themselves. (Test Prep: Create a graphic showing the technology used by the Aztecs and that used in ancient Mesopotamia. See pages 17–12.)

Government, Economy, and Society As the Aztecs conquered much of Mesoamerica, they developed a *tribute system* that insured their dominance in the short-run. Conquered people were forced to pay tribute, surrender lands, and perform military service. Tribute included practical goods such as food, cloth, and firewood, as well as luxury items such as feathers, beads, and jewelry. Most of the luxury goods were distributed to the Aztecs noble class. The Aztecs allowed local rulers to stay in their positions to serve as tribute collectors. This allowed for Aztec political dominance without direct administrative control. In exchange, the conquered people were extended Aztec protection.

To administer the empire, the Aztecs grouped city-states into provinces. They moved warriors and their families to each province's capital to make sure the province remained under Aztec control. In addition, an Aztec official was stationed in each capital to collect tribute from local officials.

Aztec government was a theocracy (rule by religious leaders). At the top was the emperor, known as the *Great Speaker,* who was the political ruler as well as a divine representative of the gods. Next in the social hierarchy were land-owning nobles, who also formed the majority of Aztec military leadership. These nobles owned all Aztec lands, renting some to commoners to farm. The rest was farmed for landowners by slaves. Next in rank were scribes and healers, followed by craftspeople and traders. A special merchant class called *pochteca* traded in luxury goods. Below the traders were the peasants and soldiers.

At the bottom of Aztec society were slaves, many of whom were war captives. Aztec people could be enslaved as well, usually because they did not pay their debts or were being punished for crimes. Besides being used for labor, slaves were also offered up as sacrifices in religious ceremonies.

Religion The intricate and complex religion of the Aztecs was central to their society. They worshipped an ever-evolving pantheon of hundreds of deities, many of whom were considered to have both male and female aspects. Among the most important gods were Huitzilopochtli, a sun god and also a god of war; Tlaloc, a rain god; Quetzalcoatl, a god of wind and of knowledge; and Xipe Totec, a god of agriculture and fertility. Worship among the Aztecs involved a great many rituals and feast days as well as *human sacrifice*. The Aztecs believed that the gods had sacrificed themselves in order to create the world—thus human sacrifice and blood-letting, also called auto-sacrifice, was a sort of repayment and atonement for human sin. Human sacrifice probably had a political component, in the sense that it demonstrated the great might of the Aztec Empire in dramatic fashion. The number of human sacrifices may never be known. Much of the information about Aztec society comes from Spanish invaders, who may have exaggerated the extent of human sacrifice in order to make the Aztecs seem more deserving of conquest.

Culture The Aztecs had a 365-day calendar that they adopted from the Maya. Like the Maya, they used it to mark their religious ceremonies. The Aztecs made beautiful objects out of gold, silver, and precious stones, and also wove fine cloth. They had a system of picture writing that resembles the ideographs of the Maya.

Trade Network Utilizing and extending trade routes established by the Maya and other groups before them, the Aztecs traded as far north as present-day San Luis Obispo and as far south as present-day Costa Rica. They also traded along the Pacific coast as well as the Gulf and Caribbean Sea coasts. They traded goods obtained from tribute, such as cloth, cacao, and rubber balls, for shells, feathers, and precious stones.

Role of Women Women played an important role in the Aztec tribute system since they wove the valuable cloth that local rulers demanded as part of the regular tribute. As the demand for cloth tribute increased, an Aztec husband might obtain more than one wife in order to be able to pay the tribute. While most Aztec women worked in their homes, some became priestesses, midwives, healers, or merchants. A few noble women worked as scribes to female members of royal families. Therefore, at least these few women knew how to read and write.

The Decline of the Aztecs By the late fifteenth century, the Aztec Empire was in decline. The Aztecs' comparatively low level of technology—such as the lack of wheeled vehicles and pack animals—meant that agriculture was arduous and inefficient. Food preparation was similarly difficult; the basic act of grinding maize by hand consumed 30 to 40 hours per week per family. The Aztecs' commitment to military victory and constant need for more human sacrifices induced the leadership to expand the empire beyond what it could reasonably govern. Finally, the extraction from conquered people of more and more tribute, not to mention sacrifice victims, served to inspire more resentment than loyalty. The Aztecs ruled an empire of unwilling subjects who were ready to revolt when given a chance. The arrival of Europeans in the Americas gave them that chance. The combination of European diseases that killed hundreds of thousands of Aztecs, the strength of the invading army of Spaniards led by Hernán Cortés in 1519, and the readiness of conquered people to rebel against Aztec rule brought the empire to a rapid crash.

The Inca

In the early fifteenth century, *Cuzco*, in what is now Peru, was a small center of one of several competing tribes. In about 55 years, through a series of military victories, Cuzco became the capital of the Inca Empire, which extended from present-day Ecuador in the north to Chile in the south.

Origins In 1438, the son of a tribal ruler conquered the Chanca peoples. He assumed control from his father and gave himself the title *Pachacuti* (ruled 1438–1471), which means "transformer" or "shaker" of the earth. Pachacuti's military victories transformed the Incan state into a full-fledged empire. Pachacuti's son *Yupanqui* took control in 1471 and expanded the empire even farther, conquering the state of Chimu in the north. Yupanqui's rule ended in approximately 1493, and his successor *Huayna Capac* focused on consolidating and managing the many lands conquered by his predecessors.

Government, Economy, and Society In order to rule the extensive territory efficiently, the Incan Empire was split into four provinces, each with its own governor and bureaucracy. Conquered leaders who demonstrated loyalty to the empire were rewarded. In contrast to the Aztec methods, conquered people did not have to pay tribute; rather, they were subject to the *mita system*, mandatory public service. Men between the ages of 15 and 50 provided agricultural and other forms of labor, including the construction of roads.

The Inca required that all conquered peoples adapt to their ways. They established schools to teach them *Quechua*, the Inca language, as well as religion and history. Conquered peoples were sometimes moved to new lands far away to weaken their resistance to Inca rule.

As in feudal Europe, the Inca Empire had few market towns and little trade conducted by individuals. However, the government engaged in some long-distance trade. The Inca economy was based on agriculture. The main crops included maize, potatoes, tomatoes, squash, peanuts, coca, and cotton. Most Incan families produced their own food and clothing, but they were required to turn over a portion of their crops to their local ruler. The ruler stored these crops in warehouses that the Inca built across the empire. In times of famine, people were fed from these warehouses. (Test Prep: Write a paragraph comparing the Inca economy with the economy of feudal Europe. See page 223.)

Religion A central part of Incan religion involved *royal ancestor veneration*, a practice sometimes referred to as a *royal ancestor cult*. Dead rulers were mummified and continued to "rule" as they had in life and were thought to retain ownership of their servants, possessions, and property. Thus, Incan rulers could not expect to inherit land or property upon assuming power. This practice was a partial motivator for the constant expansion of the empire.

The name Inca means "people of the sun," and indeed *Inti*, the sun god, was arguably the most important of the Incan gods. Inca rulers were considered to be Inti's representative on the earth. As the center of two critical elements in Incan religion—honoring of the sun and royal ancestor veneration—the Temple of the Sun in Cuzco formed the core of Incan religion.

Each god had his or her own temples and priests. Most temples were small, so priests conducted religious ceremonies outside them. The Inca followed a 30-day calendar, each month featuring its own religious festival.

Priests were consulted before importance actions. To the Inca, the gods controlled all things and priests could determine the gods' will by studying the arrangement of coca leaves in a dish or by watching the movement of a spider. Priests diagnosed illnesses, predicted the outcome of battles, solved crimes, and determined what sacrifices should be made to which god.

Sacrifices were offered on every important occasion. Corn, guinea pigs, and llamas were burned as sacrifices. Serious events such as famines, plagues, and defeat in war called for human sacrifices—although scholars do not believe that human sacrifice was practiced with the same frequency as it probably was with the Aztecs. Many of those sacrificed were provided by conquered peoples.

Comparing Three American Civilizations			
	Maya	**Aztec**	**Inca**
Region	Southern Mexico and Central America	Central Mexico	Andes region of South America
Period	400 B.C.E.–1517 C.E.	1200–1521 C.E.	1200–1572
Crops	Corn, beans, squash	Corn, beans, squash, tomatoes	Corn, cotton, potatoes
Trade	Moderate	Extensive	Limited
Religion	Polytheistic; king sacred; some human sacrifice	Polytheistic; sun god is principle deity; some human sacrifice	Polytheistic; some human sacrifice
Government	Organized city-states each with a king; war for tribute	Powerful king; centralized; war was for captives; tribute	King center of empire; war is for conquest; mita system
Technology and Thought	Math; writing; step pyramids; accurate calendar	Step pyramids; chinampas; acccurate calendar	Terraces; irrigation; waru waru agricultural technique; roads; medicine; masonry
Reasons for Decline	Cities abandoned, possibly a result of drought and deforestation	Conquered subjects rebelled when Spanish under Cortés attacked	Civil war and Spanish forces killed and enslaved populations

Source: DEA / G. DAGLI ORTI / Granger, NYC

Source: Thinkstock

Two ways people expanded the land on which to grow crops were the construction of chinampas in Mesoamerica (upper) and the development of terraces in China (lower). Like the Chinese, the Incas also created terraced fields in the sides of mountains.

Inca religion also had an element of animism, in the sense that Incas believed that elements of the physical world could have supernatural powers. These *huaca*, as they were called, could be large geographical features such as a river or the peak of a mountain, or they could be very small objects such as a stone, a plant, or a built object, such as a bridge.

Achievements In mathematics, the Inca developed the *quipu,* a system of knotted strings used to record numerical information for trade and engineering and for recording messages to be carried throughout the empire. Inca artisans created beautiful everyday ceramic objects as well as tools and weapons from copper and bronze. The Inca were also skilled stone workers. They made remarkable structures using a mortarless technique of precise-fitted stones.

In agriculture, the Inca developed sophisticated terrace systems for the cultivation of crops such as potatoes and maize. The terraces utilized a technique called *waru waru*, raised beds with channels that captured and redirected rain to avoid erosion during floods and that stored water to be used during dry periods.

The Inca were especially good road-builders. Using captive labor, they constructed a massive roadway system called the *Carpa Nan*, with some 25,000 miles of roads used mainly by the government and military. Runners were sent to and from Cuzco and outlying parts of the empire to carry official messages. Like the roads constructed by the Romans, Persians, and Chinese, the Incan roads united a far-flung empire. However, the Carpa Nan would also greatly assist the Spanish when they invaded in the sixteenth century.

Decline Upon the arrival of Spanish conquistador Francisco Pizarro in 1532, the Incan Empire was in the midst of a civil war of succession after the death of emperor Huayna Capac, Some scholars believe that the civil war weakened the Incan army, thus making it easier for Pizarro's forces to prevail. Others believe that other factors such as diseases introduced by the Europeans led to the decline. By 1572, the Spanish had killed or enslaved the native populations, thereby ending the Incan Empire. (Test Prep: Make a timeline tracing the fall of the Aztec and Inca civilizations after initial contact with the Spanish. See pages 302–307.)

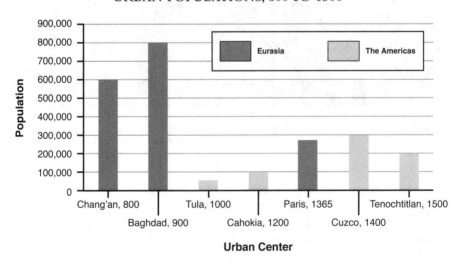

URBAN POPULATIONS, 800 TO 1500

The first Europeans to arrive in the Americas sensed that the land they were settlling on had once been more densely populated. For example, in the 1620s, William Bradford, a leader in the Pilgrim settlement in Massachusetts observed that "The good hand of God favored our beginnings . . . [by] sweeping away multitudes of the natives . . . that he might make room for us." The "sweeping away multitudes" occurred through disease epidemics. While the Pilgrims were the first permanent settlers in Massachusetts, by the time they arrived, European diseases had already killed most of the native inhabitants. Similarly, in most places, European germs reached natives before European people. Hence, population estimates by early Europeans were almost always of a post-disease population that was far smaller than population had been at its peak some years earlier.

Rather than rely on inaccurate estimates, A.L. Kroeber, a pioneer in the field of anthropology, tried a different method. In 1934, he published a population number based on a regional approach. For each region of the continents, he estimated how many people could be supported by the land and resources given the technology of the people living there. He then added up the figures for the total for the Americas. Kroeber estimated that the total population of the Americas before Columbus was about 8.4 million.

Three decades later, another anthropologist, Henry Dobyns, tried to use make use of the early observations by first calculating the "depopulation rate." Based on a few small, but relatively reliable estimates for populations in specific areas, he concluded that the Indian population after being devastated by disease was about 1/20th of what it was at its peak. Applying this to the more reliable estimates of post-contact population, he estimated that the population of the Americas at its peak was between 90 and 112 million people.

The debate over the pe-Columbian population of the Americas continued. Historians called "low counters," such as David Henige at the University of Wisconsin, rejected the high estimates of Dobyns and others. In his 1998 book, *Numbers from Nowhere: The American Indian Population Debate,* Henige argued that the hard demographic data doesn't exist so support these numbers, and that they were based on unrealistic assumptions.

In contrast, "high counters" pushed their estimates far higher than the one by Dobyns. For example, science writer Charles Mann argued that argued that the population of the Americas might have been as high as 200 million before Columbus.

KEY TERMS BY THEME

GOVERNMENT
Mississippian
Great Sun
Toltec
Aztec
tribute system
Great Speaker
Inca
Pachacuti
Yupanqui
Huayna Capac

ENVIRONMENT
Cahokia
Tula
Tenochtitlán
Lake Texcoco
chinampas
Cuzco
Carpa Nan

SOCIAL STRUCTURE
matrilineal society
mita system

CULTURE
Quetzalcoatl
Chichén Itzá
Great Pyramid
human sacrifice
Quechua
royal ancestor
   veneration
royal ancestor cult
Inti
huaca
quipu
waru waru

ECONOMY
pochteca

1. Early American civilizations that believed in animism believed that
   (A) animals should never be sacrificed
   (B) only human beings had souls
   (C) physical objects could have spiritual power
   (D) there were rational explanations for all natural phenomena

2. In which way were the Aztecs similar to the Egyptians?
   (A) They used pack animals to move materials.
   (B) They had wheeled vehicles for transporting goods.
   (C) They developed an alphabet for recording information.
   (D) They used slave labor to build their society.

3. What earlier civilization possessed a religion most similar to that of the Inca?
   (A) The Greeks during the time of Pericles
   (B) The Egyptians under the pharaohs
   (C) Zoroastrians of Southwest Asia
   (D) Buddhists of East Asia

4. Unlike the Mississippian culture or the Incas, the Aztecs successfully constructed
   (A) large earthen mounds
   (B) a city on a lake
   (C) an extensive network of roads
   (D) waru waru to expand their agricultural land

5. The most important reason the Aztec practiced human sacrifice was probably to
   (A) decrease the population
   (B) advance medical knowledge
   (C) pay their debts to their enemies
   (D) appease the gods

6. Which of the following is a common characteristic shared by the Mississippian, Aztec, and Inca cultures?
   (A) Organization of labor for massive building projects
   (B) An egalitarian society
   (C) The deification of Quetzalcoatl
   (D) A great respect for the accomplishments of women

7. Compared to societies in Afro-Eurasia, societies in Mesoamerica
   (A) did not use pack animals
   (B) worshiped sun gods more widely
   (C) placed less value on precious metals and stones
   (D) allowed women to have less power and opportunity

Question 8 is based on the following image.

Source: Cahokia Mounds State Historic Site, painting by William R. Iseminger

8. Which conclusion about life in Cahokia is best supported by the image?
   (A) All common people lived outside the mound complex.
   (B) Few people in Cahokia engaged in agriculture.
   (C) The mound complex was the political and religious center of the society.
   (D) Cahokia declined due to a lack of fresh water.

9. A major difference between the Inca and the Aztecs in their treatment of conquered people is that the Inca
   (A) required labor rather than payment of tribute
   (B) treated conquered people more harshly
   (C) refrained from enslaving their captives
   (D) allowed conquered people to retain their culture

Question 10 is based on the following excerpt.

Floating idly down the tranquil canals of Xochimilco, it's easy to forget you are still within the limits of one of the world's most overcrowded and polluted cities.

White herons soar past lines of trees that waft gently in the breeze. Insects buzz. Flowers bloom. Farmers in flatbed canoes pole silently along the waterways, ferrying flowers and crops their ancestors have cultivated on man-made islands since the Aztec era. . . .

Another project seeks to rebuild chinampas the way the Aztecs did—using reeds and mud from the canal bed to create rich, undulating gardens. Trees known as ahuejotes are planted around the edge of the garden, and their roots eventually lock the site in place.

Aztec farmers slathered the straw beds with rich canal mud, producing as many as five crops a year on the same tiny plot. . . .

> —Gretchen Peters, "Urban Sprawl Begins to Swamp Old Canals."
> *The Christian Science Monitor*, September 19, 2002.
> latinamericanstudies.org

10. Based on the information in the excerpt, what is the main reason the Aztecs used mud in building chinampas?

   (A) To fertilize their crops

   (B) To eradicate disease

   (C) To deepen the canals

   (D) To control pests

CONTINUITY AND CHANGE-OVER-TIME ESSAY QUESTIONS

Directions: You are to answer the following question. You should spend 5 minutes organizing or outlining your essay. Write an essay that:

- Has a relevant thesis and supports that thesis with appropriate historical evidence.
- Addresses all parts of the question.
- Uses world historical context to show continuities and changes over time.
- Analyzes the process of continuity and change over time.

1. Analyze continuities and change in governance in ONE of these regions between 600–1450 C.E.:

   - Mesoamerica
   - Andean region

Questions for Additional Practice

2. Analyze continuities and change in ONE of the following aspects of life
    in Mesoamerica from the Maya up to the Spanish conquest of the Aztecs:
    - politics and government
    - religious practices
    - cultural achievements

3. Analyze continuities and change in the economy of the Andean region of
    South America between 600 and 1450.

COMPARATIVE ESSAY QUESTIONS

Directions: You are to answer the following question. You should spend
5 minutes organizing or outlining your essay. Write an essay that:

- Has a relevant thesis and supports that thesis with appropriate
  historical evidence.
- Addresses all parts of the question.
- Makes direct, relevant comparisons.
- Analyzes relevant reasons for similarities and differences.

1. Analyze similarities and differences in agricultural practices and trade in
    TWO of the following civilizations:
    - Mississippian
    - Aztec
    - Inca

Questions for Additional Practice

2. Analyze similarities and differences between the social structures of
    TWO of the following civilizations:
    - Mississippian
    - Aztec
    - Inca

3. Analyze similarities and differences in location, architecture, and
    population between Tenochtitlán and ONE of the following cities:
    - Baghdad
    - Constantinople

THINK AS A HISTORIAN: PRACTICE CONTEXTUALIZATION

Establishing context is important for historians. Context helps show how an event, a person, a place, or a practice fits into the narrative of history. Provide as much context as you can by answering as many of the five *Ws* as possible: *Who, What, Where, When,* and *Why. Which THREE of the essay titles below provide the MOST context?*

1. Mayan Religious Beliefs During the Classic Era, 250–900 C.E.

2. The Agriculture of the Mississippians

3. Mayan Influences upon Mississippian Farming Methods

4. Mesoamerican Pyramid-Building Techniques

5. Two Agricultural Legacies: Aztec Chinampas and Incan Terraces

6. The Geography of the Aztecs

WRITE AS A HISTORIAN: ANTICIPATE OPPOSING ARGUMENTS

To strengthen arguments in your writing, acknowledge and address opposing arguments. Such acknowledgment will display to the reader that you are open-minded and willing to consider all views. *Identify the words or phrases in each passage that show that differing arguments are acknowledged.*

1. Admittedly, the Spanish invaders may have exaggerated much of their experiences with the Aztec people to portray them as animalistic, but evidence of human sacrifice and territorial wars exists.

2. Many people assume that the Aztecs and Incan civilizations closely resemble each other; however, they share few similarities and separately developed rich cultures.

3. Some fault the Aztecs for not exploiting the wheel. (The Aztecs knew of the technology as evidenced by toys with wheels.) What they fail to consider is the fact that the Aztecs did not have draft animals to pull wheeled vehicles.

4. While there is evidence that the decline of the Mississippian culture was caused by the introduction of diseases by Europeans, there is also evidence that crop failures before Europeans arrived made life in the large cities unsustainable.

PERIOD 3: Review

Thematic Review

Directions: Briefly answer each question in paragraph form.

1. **Interaction Between Humans and the Environment** Compare agricultural practices in at least two of these regions: China under the Tang dynasty, African regions where Bantu-speaking people migrated, Mesoamerica under the Aztec, and the Incan Empire.

2. **Development and Interaction of Cultures** Compare the ways that China and India influenced the cultures of Southeast Asia.

3. **State-Building, Expansion, and Conflict** Analyze similarities and differences in the effects of foreign invasion on the Byzantine Empire, Kievan Rus, and Song Dynasty in China.

4. **Creation, Expansion, and Interaction of Economic Systems** What was the effect of Islam on trade in the Indian Ocean basin?

5. **Development and Transformation of Social Structures** Compare the role of women in at least two of these regions: Africa or Southeast Asia under Islamic influence, Medieval Europe, areas under Mongol rule, Mesoamerica under the Aztec.

TURNING POINT: WHY 1450?

Historians today often use 1450 to mark the beginning of the early modern era in world history. Some key events around that time include the beginning of the Ottoman Empire and the printing of the Gutenberg Bible using movable type, which signaled a revolution in printing and learning. The dominance of the Indian Ocean trade ended about 1450, and the era of European exploration marked a shift to a period of truly global interaction and Western dominance that still continues. Some historians point to 1492, the beginning of the Columbian Exchange, or more broadly to the year 1500 as the turning point. Others cite the rise of Genghis Khan in 1206 as a turning point, considering the lasting effects of Mongol rule across much of Asia.

DOCUMENT-BASED QUESTION

Direction: The following question is based on the accompanying Documents 1–9. (The documents have been edited for the purpose of this exercise.)

This question is designed to test your ability to work with and understand historical documents. Write an essay that:

- Has a relevant thesis and supports that thesis with evidence from the document.
- Uses all of the documents.
- Analyzes the documents by grouping them in as many appropriate ways as possible. Does not simply summarize the documents individually.
- Takes into account the sources of the documents and analyzes the author's point of view.
- Identifies and explains the need for at least one additional type of document.

You may refer to relevant historical information not mentioned in the documents.

1. Using the following documents, analyze the political, economic, and social achievements of the empires of the Sub-Saharan region before their extensive involvement with European trade networks. Identify an additional type of document and explain how it would help your evaluation of these achievements.

Document 1

Source: Egyptian official on Mansa Musa during his royal visit in Cairo during the fourteenth century

This man Mansa Musa, spread upon Cairo the flood of his generosity: there was no person, officer of the court, or holder of any office of the Sultanate who did not receive a sum of gold from him.

Document 2

Source: Description of the city of Timbuktu by Leo Africanus in the early sixteenth century

Here are many doctors, judges, priests, and other learned men that are well maintained at the king's costs. Various manuscripts and written books are brought here . . . and sold for more money than other merchandise.

Document 3

Source: Travels to the Kingdom of Mali, by Ibn Battuta (mid-fourteenth century)

Among their good qualities is the small amount of injustice amongst them, for of all people they are the furthest from it. Their sultan does not forgive anyone in any matter to do with justice. Among these qualities, there is also the prevalence of peace in their country, the traveler is not afraid in it nor is he who lives there in fear of the thief or of the robber by violence.

Document 4

Source: Description of wax process used in making bronze sculpture in Benin by a Hausa artisan, fifteenth century

In the name of Allah the Compassionate, the Merciful. This account will show how the [Benin] figures are made. This work is one to cause wonder. Now this kind of work is done with clay, and wax, and red metal, and solder and lead, and fire. . . . Next it is set aside to cool, then [the outside cover of clay] is broken off. Then you see beautiful figure.

Document 5

Source: Ubaydallah al-Bakri, resident of al-Andalus (Cordobá, Spain), who never travelled to Africa but based these observations on interviews with travelers, 1068

The city of Ghana consists of two towns situated on a plain. One of these towns, which is inhabited by Muslims, is large and possesses twelve mosques. . . . In the environs are wells with sweet water, from which they drink and with which they grow vegetables. The king's town is six miles distant from this one and bears the name of Al-Ghaba. Between these two towns there are continuous habitations. The houses of the inhabitants are of stone and acacia wood.

Document 6

Source: Benin bronze head, sixteenth century

Document 7

Source: Account on East Africa by Duarte Barbosa (c. 1480–1521), an agent of the Portuguese government

And the manner of their traffic was this: they came in small vessels named zambucos from the kingdoms of Kilwa, Mombasa, and Malindi, bringing many cotton cloths, some spotted and others white and blue; also some of silk and many small beads, grey, red, yellow, which things come to the said kingdoms from the great kingdom of Cambray [northwest India] in other great ships. And these wares the said Moors who came from Malindi and Mombasa paid for in gold at such a price that those merchants departed well pleased. . . .

Document 8

Source: Bronze head for a staff in the shape of a coiled snake, from the Igbo-Ukwu people in Nigeria (9th century)

PERIOD 4: Global Interactions, c. 1450–c. 1750 C.E.

Chapter 15 Western Europe Extends Its Influence

Chapter 16 The Americas in the Early Colonial Period

Chapter 17 Africa in the Early Colonial Period

Chapter 18 Russia Unifies and Expands

Chapter 19 Islamic Gunpowder Empires

Chapter 20 East Asian Stability Meets Foreign Traders

Period Overview

The voyage by Christopher Columbus in 1492 that connected the Eastern and Western Hemispheres set off dramatic changes around the world. Europeans and Africans carried to the Americas plants such as sugar and rice as well as horses and other animals that transformed indigenous cultures. Most important, Europeans brought germs of diseases such as smallpox and measles that ravaged the native population. From the Americas, Afro-Eurasia received nutritious new plants such as corn, tomatoes, and potatoes that led to population growth, which in turn led to greater economic growth.

The technological innovations, such as the astrolabe and improved ship designs, that made Columbus's voyage successful also made transoceanic trade between Europe, Africa, and Asia easier. Through these links, Buddhism, Christianity, Islam, and Neoconfucianism spread to new regions, often blending with existing beliefs and traditions. For example, Latin Americans combined indigenous beliefs with Christianity. As belief systems spread, they often changed the relationships between men and women and family structures.

The expansion of global trade reshaped relationships among classes. Coerced and semi-coerced labor, including slavery in the Americas, serfdom in Russia and Japan, and the hacienda system in Latin America, spread. In many urban areas, a growing class of merchants and entrepreneurs emerged. The mixing of ethnic groups resulted in groups such as mestizos, mulattos, and creoles that had not been common in earlier history.

The increase in trade resulted in new states and empires. In West and Central Africa, trade-based states emerged. Along the coasts of Africa and South Asia, Europeans established webs of trading posts that were the beginnings of maritime empires. In the Americas, Europeans settled more widely, seizing more land. In China, South Asia, the Middle East, and Russia, land-based empires expanded.

The expanding connections among cultures and the increase in wealth created changes in the arts. For example, Europe experienced the Renaissance, a rebirth of interest in classical culture that resulted in impressive new styles in painting and sculpture. Miniature paintings became a highly regarded art form in the Middle East and South Asia. New forms of literature produced great writers, such as Shakespeare and Cervantes in Europe, as well as new forms of expression, such as kabuki theater in Japan.

Key Concepts

4.1. Globalizing Networks of Communication and Exchange

I. In the context of the new global circulation of goods, there was an intensification of all existing regional trade networks that brought prosperity and economic disruption to the merchants and governments in the trading regions of the Indian Ocean, Mediterranean, Sahara, and overland Eurasia.

II. European technological developments in cartography and navigation built on previous knowledge developed in the classical, Islamic, and Asian worlds, and included the production of new tools, innovations in ship designs, and an improved understanding of global wind and currents patterns—all of which made transoceanic travel and trade possible.

III. Remarkable new transoceanic maritime reconnaissance occurred in this period.

IV. The new global circulation of goods was facilitated by royal chartered European monopoly companies that took silver from Spanish colonies in the Americas to purchase Asian goods for the Atlantic markets, but regional markets continued to flourish in Afro-Eurasia by using established commercial practices and new transoceanic shipping services developed by European merchants.

V. The new connections between the Eastern and Western Hemispheres resulted in the Columbian Exchange.

VI. The increase in interactions between newly connected hemispheres and intensification of connections within hemispheres expanded the spread and reform of existing religions and created syncretic belief systems and practices.

VII. As merchants' profits increased and governments collected more taxes, funding for the visual and performing arts, even for popular audiences, increased.

4.2. New Forms of Social Organization and Modes of Production

I. Traditional peasant agriculture increased and changed, plantations expanded, and demand for labor increased. These changes both fed and responded to growing global demand for raw materials and finished products.

II. As new social and political elites changed, they also restructured new ethnic, racial, and gender hierarchies.

4.3. State Consolidation and Imperial Expansion

I. Rulers used a variety of methods to legitimize and consolidate their power.

II. Imperial expansion relied on the increased use of gunpowder, cannons, and armed trade to establish large empires in both hemispheres.

III. Competition over trade routes, state rivalries, and local resistance all provided significant challenges to state consolidation and expansion.

Source: *AP® World History Course and Exam Description.*

15

Western Europe
Extends Its Influence

Paris is well worth a Mass.

—Henry of Navarre, King of France (ruled 1589–1610)

The year 1453 is a useful starting date for the early modern period in European history. That year, Constantinople fell to the Turks and the Ottoman Empire became a major power. The mid-1400s saw the end of a wave of plagues, the conclusion of the Hundred Years' War between France and England, and the invention of the Gutenberg printing press followed by an increase in literacy. The Italian Renaissance was well underway by this time. The artist and inventor *Leonardo da Vinci*, painter of the *Last Supper* and *Mona Lisa*, was born in 1452, while fellow artist *Michelangelo*, painter of the ceiling of the Sistine Chapel in Rome and sculptor of the *David*, would be born in 1475. After the long, slow political and economic development of the Middle Ages and recovery from numerous challenges, several countries in Europe of 1453 were becoming hegemonic powers as increasingly wealthy nations launched major explorations and established colonies around the world.

Christianity, a dominant force in Western Europe, would split into many factions in the sixteenth and seventeenth centuries. The quote above was attributed to French king *Henry IV*, often known as *Henry of Navarre*, after he converted to Catholicism for the sake of solidifying his throne. His action demonstrates the willingness of monarchs to think like the *Politiques*, moderates who approached ruling with practicality rather than theology. Henry IV's rule saw increasing emphasis on national sovereignty, which became more and more absolute in France until reaching a high point with Louis XIV (ruled 1643–1715). Henry IV also sanctioned religious toleration of the *Huguenots*, French Calvinists. The forms of government that developed in this period varied from the absolutism of France to parliamentary government in England.

Many important developments of the period 1450–1750 involved European expansion overseas. Two of these will be covered in Chapter 16: new maritime empires in the Americas and the establishment of the Columbian Exchange.

Protestant Reformation

The Roman Catholic Church faced many challenges in the European shift from feudalism to nationalism. International in organization and influence, and boasting a large bureaucracy of its own, the Church was also noted for corruption. Efforts to curb corruption resulted in numerous Church councils and reform movements, such as the *Cluniac Reforms* (950–1130). Efforts at reform, however, were unsuccessful.

Theological disagreements began to surface as well. *John Wycliffe* and the *Lollards* in England in the late fourteenth century argued that priests were unnecessary for salvation. Wycliffe was vilified for translating parts of the Bible into the English vernacular to make it available to the mass of believers, who neither read or understood Latin. The *Hussites*, followers of *Jan Hus* in Bohemia, were declared heretics for beliefs similar to Wycliffe's. Jan Hus himself was burned at the stake. *Huldrych Zwingli* in Geneva campaigned for a religion that would follow the exact teachings of the scriptures. He was opposed, for example, to such ideas as celibacy of the clergy because the rule was imposed long after the scriptures were written.

The power of the Church suffered during the so-called Babylonian Captivity (1309–1378), when the papacy was located in France rather than in Rome. The "Captivity" gave French rulers greater influence over the Church, even the ability to decide who should be pope. Newly centralizing rulers who coveted Church lands and authority began confiscating wealthy Catholic monasteries and sometimes established their own churches. In the eyes of believers, the Church suffered further when it failed to stop the Black Death. (Test Prep: Write a paragraph connecting the Reformation with the problems of the medieval Church. See pages 224–225.)

Lutheranism In 1517, *Martin Luther*, a monk in Wittenberg, Germany, a part of the Holy Roman Empire, presented his *95 Theses* to Church leaders at the university there. Luther objected to the sale of *indulgences*, which granted a person absolution from the punishments for sin. Along with theological interests, the Church had economic and political interests in continuing the sale of indulgences: the Church needed the money generated by the practice. Moreover, the Elector of Brandenburg needed money to maintain his position in the Holy Roman Empire. Luther also hoped to reform other abuses within the Church, such as *simony*, the selling of church offices. Pope Leo X excommunicated Luther in January 1521. Luther and his followers, who were known as Protestants because of their protests against Church practices, soon established a separate church, which became known as the Lutheran Church.

Luther was not a political revolutionary. He did not threaten to replace any government. Nor did he respond to pleas from German peasants to support their rebellions. He was a theological revolutionary. His ideas had social impact on the clergy, as well as on women. Lutheranism taught that women could have direct access to God just as men could and that women had significant roles in the family. However, Protestants generally did not organize convents. As a result, Protestant women did not have the opportunity to become leaders in convents the way Roman Catholic women did.

Calvinism The French theologian *John Calvin* broke with the Church around 1530. In 1536, he authored *The Institutes of Christian Religion* and helped reform the religious community in Geneva, Switzerland. *The elect,* those *predestined* to go to heaven, ran the community, which was based around plain living, simple church buildings, and governance by the elders of the church. Calvin's followers in France were called Huguenots. Other offshoots of Calvinism included the *Reformed Church of Scotland*, led by John Knox, and the *Puritans* in England and later in Boston, who wanted to purify the Church of England of Catholic remnants. Historian and sociologist Max Weber pointed out that an important socio-economic impact of Calvinism is contained in the phrase "Protestant work ethic." Calvinists were encouraged to work hard and reinvest their profits; prosperity ostensibly showed their position among the elect.

Anglicanism The last of the three major figures of the Reformation was the king of England *Henry VIII* (ruled 1509–1547). Henry wanted a male heir to succeed him. So after his wife gave birth to several daughters, Henry asked the pope's permission to annul his first marriage so he could marry another woman, *Anne Boleyn*. But the pope, worried about the reaction of the very powerful emperor of the Holy Roman Empire, *Charles V,* who was the nephew of Henry's wife, refused. Henry, with the approval of the English Parliament, went his own way by setting himself up as head of the new Church of England, or *Anglican Church*, one that would be free of control by the pope in Rome. Two of Henry's daughters, Mary Tudor and Elizabeth I, would later rule.

Counter-Reformation or Catholic Reformation

The Roman Catholic Church, all-powerful in Europe since the fall of Rome, did not sit quietly by and let the Reformation groups take over. Instead, it embarked on a vigorous *Counter-Reformation* to fight against the Protestant attacks. A three-pronged strategy yielded such gains for the Church that it remains the largest Christian denomination in the world:

- The Church increased the use of the *Inquisition*, which had been established in the late twelfth century to root out and punish nonbelievers. The Inquisition sometimes allowed the use of torture to achieve its ends.

- The *Jesuits*, or Society of Jesus, a religious order founded in 1540 by Ignatius of Loyola, undertook missionary activity in Europe and abroad.

- The *Council of Trent* (1545–1563) corrected some of the worst of the Church's abuses and concentrated on reaffirming the rituals such as marriage and other sacraments improving the education of priests, and publishing the *Index of Prohibited Books, writing that the Church considered dangerous to one's faith if read.*

The Counter-Reformation was successful in that Catholicism remained predominant in the areas of Western Europe near the Mediterranean Sea. Moreover, later colonies of the European powers often followed the lead of the home country in religion. Therefore, most of the people in the Spanish, Portuguese, and French colonies became Catholic.

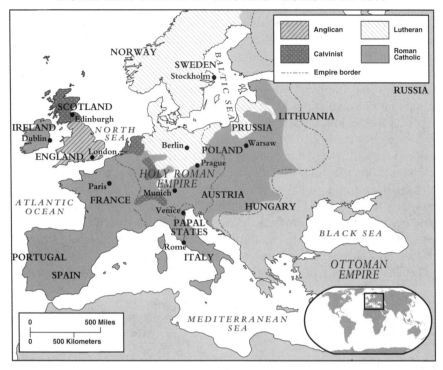

Charles V abdicated as ruler of the Holy Roman Empire in 1555, discouraged by his inability to stop the spread of Lutheranism. He left Spain to his son *Philip II* and the Holy Roman Empire to his brother Ferdinand. Philip II took the Catholic crusade to the Netherlands and ruled its 17 provinces from 1556 to 1581. He later tried to conquer and convert England, but in 1588, English naval power, aided by bad weather, famously defeated his *Spanish Armada*.

Wars of Religion

Europe's growing religious diversity often led to wars. In 1546 and 1547, the forces of Charles V fought the German Lutheran *Schmalkaldic League*. This conflict resulted in the 1555 *Peace of Augsburg*, which allowed each German state to choose whether its ruler, and therefore its inhabitants, would be Catholic or Lutheran. Those subjects who did not wish to accept a ruler's choice of religion could move to another state where their preferred religion was practiced.

In France, meanwhile, the Catholic monarchy warred with the Huguenots for nearly half a century until Henry IV switched from Protestant to Catholic in 1593, evidently believing that "Paris is well worth a Mass." He became the first Bourbon on the French throne and, at least temporarily, granted religious tolerance in the 1598 *Edict of Nantes*.

The final great religious war was the *Thirty Years' War* (1618–1648), which involved most of Europe. The war culminated in the *Peace of Westphalia*, which allowed each area of the Holy Roman Empire to decide on one of three religious options: Lutheranism, Roman Catholicism, or Calvinism. The war led to economic catastrophe. Troops fighting in the war were compensated by being allowed to loot. The war also resulted in diseases and hunger, depopulating Bohemia, the Netherlands, and the Italian and German states. The war's conclusion in 1648 left the religious map of Europe much as it is today, with France, Spain, and Italy still predominantly Catholic; England with a Protestant state church; and the northern areas of Europe becoming either Lutheran or Calvinist. The treaty provision allowing rulers of various areas of the Holy Roman Empire to choose a denomination gave the countries and duchies much more political autonomy than they had had previously. Consequently, the states of Prussia (now part of Germany) and Austria began to assert themselves, although they still formally belonged to the Holy Roman Empire. Prussia began its reliance on a strong military partially in response to the devastation caused by the Thirty Years' War.

Religious Schisms			
Religion and Region	**Schism**	**Leaders**	**Nature of Dispute**
Buddhism in India	Theravada and Mahayana (around 300 B.C.E. to 100 C.E.)	• Four councils held after the Buddha's death	Disagreement between emphasis on personal meditation (Theravada) and public rituals and compassion (Mahayana)
Islam in Middle East	Sunni and Shia (632 C.E.)	• Abu Bakr • Ali	Disagreement over the rightful successor to Muhammad as leader of the Islamic community
Christianity in Europe and Byzantine Empire	Roman Catholics and Orthodox (1054 C.E.)	• Pope Leo IX • Patriarch of Constantinople, Michael Cerularius	Disagreement over the authority of the pope and differences in rituals
Christianity in Europe	Roman Catholics and Protestants (1517 C.E.)	• Martin Luther • John Calvin • King Henry VIII	Disagreements over the role of faith, the role of the clergy and the pope, and how to interpret the Bible

Source: Wikimedia Commons, Summer rest in the shadow of thatched houses, Wu Li / Szilas

Source: Wikimedia Commons / Bentheim Castle, Jacob Isaakszoon van Ruisdael, National Gallery of Ireland

During the religious turmoil in Europe and political turmoil in China in the seventeenth century, artists in both places (China, upper; Europe, lower) commonly portrayed scenes in nature.

Emergence of the Modern Nation State Under New Monarchs

The *new monarchies* of the Renaissance developed in Europe as a result of the desire of certain leaders to centralize power by controlling taxes, the army, and many aspects of religion. The new monarchs included the Tudors in England, the Valois in France, and *Queen Isabella and King Ferdinand* in Spain. In each area, bureaucracies increased and the power of the middle class grew at the expense of lords and the churches. For example, the new monarchies moved to curb the private armies of the nobility.

By the end of the sixteenth century, this centralization coalesced into a system of government that led to absolute sovereignty in England and France. In England, the Stuart king *James I* (ruled 1603–1625) wrote *The True Law of Free Monarchy*, asserting that the monarch was free to make the laws—an assertion with which Parliament did not agree. In France, Henry IV (ruled 1589–1610) listened to his advisor *Jean Bodin*, who advocated the *divine right of the monarchy,* the claim that the right to rule was given to a king by God. These developments foreshadowed the developments of a national monarchy and the modern, centralized nation-state in these areas. Yet by the eighteenth century, Parliament predominated in England, and divine-right monarchy predominated in France until the French Revolution.

English Civil War and Evolution of Constitutionalism

The *English Civil War*, sometimes called the *Puritan Revolution*, broke out in 1642 between supporters of the Stuart monarchy and supporters of Parliament, many of whom were Puritans. The dispute was mainly over what powers Parliament should have in relation to those of the monarch. However, the roots of the conflict can be traced back to the Magna Carta (1215) and the foundation of the English Parliament in 1265. A more recent document, the *Petition of Right* (1628), restated the proposition that the monarch could not levy taxes without Parliament's consent, imprison persons without charge, or quarter soldiers in a private home without permission. Although *Charles I* signed the document, he proceeded to ignore it and did not call a meeting of Parliament for 11 years. By 1642, he was at war with Parliament, a war in which he would lose both his throne and his head.

Although Parliament and its leaders *Oliver Cromwell* and his son Richard Cromwell were in the ascendancy during much of the Civil War, in 1660 a compromise was reached to allow for the return of the monarchy. *Charles II*, who had been in exile in France, became the new Stuart king.

His son, *James II*, succeeded Charles in 1685, resulting in a complete break with Parliament once again. Many in England feared that James II was about to convert to Catholicism and force the country to follow suit. In 1688, a group of lords invited *William and Mary*, the Protestant monarchs of the Netherlands, to become joint rulers of England. As a result of this event, known as the *Glorious Revolution*, James II fled the country. In 1689, William and Mary signed the *English Bill of Rights*, which assured individual civil liberties. For example, legal process was required before someone could be arrested and detained. The Bill of Rights also guaranteed protection against tyranny of the monarchy by requiring the agreement of Parliament on matters of taxation and raising an army. Although the *Toleration Act of 1689* granted freedom of worship to non-Anglicans, the law said that the English monarch had to be Anglican since he or she would be head of the Church of England.

Two philosophers explored the idea of a *social contract,* an agreement under which people gave up some of their rights in exchange for the benefits of living in a community under the protection of a government. In *The Leviathan* (1651) Thomas Hobbes feared weak government. He emphasized the need for a government that was strong enough to protect people from each other. In *Two Treatises of Government* (1690) John Locke feared excessive government. He emphasized the need for a government with enough restraints on it to protect people from tyranny. Locke argued that people had a right and even a duty to rebel against a government that exceeded its legitimate power.

Absolutism Increases in France

In contrast to developments in England, the French government became more absolute in the seventeenth and eighteenth centuries. Building on the ideas advocated by Jean Bodin, advisor to Henry IV, Louis XIII (ruled 1610–1643) and his minister *Cardinal Richelieu* moved to even greater centralization of government and development of the system of *intendants*. These intendants were royal officials sent out to the provinces to execute the orders of the central government. The intendants themselves were sometimes called "tax farmers" because they oversaw the collection of various taxes in support of the royal government. During the reign of the "Sun King," *Louis XIV* (ruled 1643–1715), the intendants helped to implement the financial system put into place by his finance minister Jean-Baptiste Colbert. Among other reforms, Colbert sought to make French manufactured goods more competitive by creating the *Five Great Farms*, an area free from internal taxes.

Louis XIV strongly espoused a theory of divine right and ruled as a virtual dictator. His aims were twofold, just as those of Richelieu had been: he wanted to hold absolute power and expand French borders. Therefore, the spacious and elegant palace at *Versailles* became a political instrument where he entertained the nobles and kept them from conducting business elsewhere, such as fomenting rebellion in their home provinces. Like Peter the Great's city, Saint Petersburg, Louis XIV's grand buildings at Versailles helped to highlight his power. The palace at Versailles, for example, could accommodate hundreds of guests in its apartments and gardens. During the rule of Louis XIV, some ten thousand employees worked in the palace or on the grounds. Louis declared that he was the state: "L'etat, c'est moi." He combined in a very real sense both the lawmaking and the justice system in his own person—he was absolute. In the long run, his and his successors' refusal to share power with the nobility weakened the French government. (Test Prep: Create a table comparing Louis XIV and Peter the Great. See page 338.)

Desiring to expand the borders of France, Louis XIV reorganized his army to carry on a number of wars. For example, he gained the throne of Spain for the Bourbon family, thereby precipitating the *War of the Spanish Succession* (1701–1714). However, the *Peace of Utrecht* (1713) stipulated that the same person could not hold the thrones of France and Spain simultaneously. In paying for his wars, Louis XIV contributed to the economic problems of France—financial woes that contributed to the French Revolution of 1789. (Test Prep: Create a cause/effect chart linking the policies of Louis XIV to the French Revolution. See page 399.)

Scientific Revolution

While the Renaissance was gradually ending in southern Europe around 1600, in the north scientific thinking was on the upsurge. For example, in 1620 English scientist and philosopher Francis Bacon developed an early scientific method called *empiricism*, which insisted upon the collection of data to back up a hypothesis. Science was helped by the correspondence of leading scholars with one another, even during the religious wars, and by the establishment of a *Royal Academy of Science* in France and England. *Sir Isaac Newton*, combining *Galileo*'s laws of terrestrial motion and *Johannes Kepler*'s laws of planetary motion, published a work on gravitational force called *Principia* (1687). The ideas in *Principia* impacted science and mathematics and helped lead to a new vision of the world. Many intellectuals thought that science showed that the world was ordered and rational and that natural laws applied to the rational and orderly progress of governments and society. This thinking is a key to the period of the Enlightenment.

The Enlightenment Leaving aside the old theological debates of *Scholasticism*, which concerned the relationship of faith to reason, the new debates turned on how best to apply reason to discover natural law and thus make infinite progress. Writers outside the scientific community, such as the *philosophes*, philosophers who popularized some Enlightenment ideals, worked to apply the principles to government and society. For example, the French writers Voltaire, Montesquieu, and Jean-Jacques Rousseau praised religious toleration and the English form of representative government; Denis Diderot edited a vast series of articles on science, the arts, and philosophy called the *Encyclopédie*. In America, such a philosophe was Benjamin Franklin, a writer and thinker who also dabbled in science. (To learn more about the Enlightenment period, see Chapter 21, "The Enlightenment, Nationalism, and Revolutions.")

Mercantilism, Early Capitalism, and Adam Smith

In the seventeenth century, Europeans generally measured the wealth of a country in how much gold and silver it had accumulated. Hence, countries set policies designed to sell as many goods as they could to other countries—in order to maximize the amount of gold and silver coming into the country—and to buy as few as possible from other countries—to minimize the flow of precious metals out of the country. This theory, known as *mercantilism,* called for heavy government involvement in the economy.

The accumulation of *capital*, material wealth available to produce more wealth, in Western Europe grew as entrepreneurs entered long-distance markets. Some merchant families became bankers, including the Medici of Florence, Sforzas of Milan, and Fuggers of Augsburg. Some entrepreneurs, partly to escape guild regulations, took cloth to rural households for local women to make into garments, beginning the practice of "putting-out," also known as *cottage industry*. Capital changed hands from entrepreneurs to laborers, putting laborers in a better position to become consumers. Despite restrictions by the Church, lending money at high rates of interest became commonplace. Actual wealth increased, too, as gold and silver were brought in from the Western Hemisphere.

Into this economic milieu of the eighteenth century stepped *Adam Smith*. Influenced by the new Enlightenment thinking and belonging to a group of economists called *physiocrats*, Adam Smith turned against mercantilism. In *The Wealth of Nations* (1776), Smith challenged the mercantilist belief that a nation's wealth should be measured by its accumulation of amount of gold and

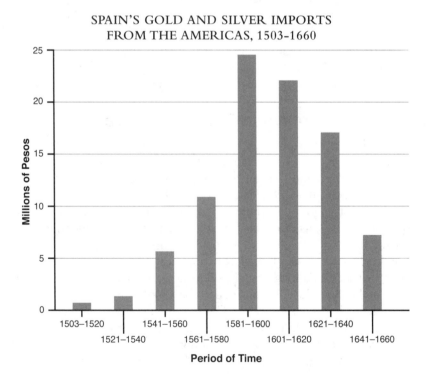

SPAIN'S GOLD AND SILVER IMPORTS
FROM THE AMERICAS, 1503-1660

Source: Earl J. Hamilton, "Imports of American Gold and Silver into Spain, 1503–1660." *The Quarterly Journal of Economics.* 1929.

silver. Hence, the extensive government regulations to promote exports and discourage imports were misguided. Smith argued that freer trade and greater trust in the laws of supply and demand would make everyone wealthier. He believed that allowing people to follow their self-interest, with some limits, would enable the market to regulate itself as if guided by an "invisible hand."

Commercial Revolution The *Commercial Revolution* that developed in the early modern period saw the transformation of commerce from local, small-scale trading mostly based on barter to large-scale international trade using gold and silver. The high rate of inflation, or general rise in prices, at this time is called the *Price Revolution*. The Commercial Revolution affected all regions of the world and resulted from four key factors: the development of European overseas colonies; the opening of new ocean trade routes; population growth; and inflation, caused partly by the pressure of the increasing population and partly by the increased amount of gold and silver that was mined and put in circulation.

Aiding the rise of this extended global economy was the formation of *joint-stock companies*, owned by investors who bought stock or shares in them. People invested capital in such companies and shared both the profits and the risks of exploration and trading ventures. Offering *limited liability,* the principle that an investor was not responsible for a company's debts or other liabilities beyond the amount of an investment, made investing safer. The developing European middle class had capital to invest from successful businesses in their home countries. They also had money with which to purchase imported luxuries. The Dutch, English, and French all developed joint-stock companies in the seventeenth century, including the British *East India Company* in 1600 and the Dutch East India Company in 1602. In Spain and Portugal, however, the government did most of the investing itself through grants to certain explorers.

Europeans in the Indian Ocean Trade Network

Demographic pressures pushed Europeans into exploration and trade. As the population grew, not all workers in Europe could find work or even food. Not all sons of the wealthy could own land because *primogeniture laws* gave all of each estate to the eldest son. In the early seventeenth century, religious minorities searched for a place to settle where people were tolerant of their dissent. All of these groups, as well as those just longing for adventure and glory, were eager to settle in new areas, resulting in a global shift in demographics.

Europe was never totally isolated from East and South Asia. The Indian Ocean trade routes had long brought silk, spices, and tea to the Mediterranean by way of the Red Sea. Islamic traders had long known land routes from China to the cities of Baghdad and Constantinople and from there to Rome. In the sixteenth century, however, more and more Europeans became active in the Indian Ocean, with hopes of finding gold and new converts as their twin motives. This often competed with Middle Eastern traders from Oman and other kingdoms in the *Omani-European rivalry*. Christopher Columbus's search for a new route to India was a way to avoid this competition. European traders would soon act as middlemen in the worldwide trade of sugar, tobacco, rum, and slaves across the Atlantic, while continuing to import silk, spices, and rhubarb from China and Southeast Asia. Spain, Portugal, Great Britain, France, and Holland established *maritime empires,* ones based on sea travel. Interestingly enough, the European traders in southeast Asia found themselves dealing with women. The markets, as well as money changing services, were traditionally handled by women.

New technology aided European seafarers in their explorations. Compasses developed by the Chinese replaced astrolabes. *Cartography,* or mapmaking, and knowledge of wind patterns also improved navigation. Ships moved more adroitly, aided by a new type of rudder, another idea imported from China. Newton's discovery of gravitation increased knowledge of the tides. The long-term result of combining navigational techniques invented in Europe with those from other areas of the world was a rapid expansion of exploration and global trade. About the only part of the Afro-Eurasia world not affected by the rapid increase in global trade was Polynesia, as it was far removed from trading routes.

The introduction of gunpowder, another Chinese invention, aided Europeans in their conquests abroad. Soon enough, however, sea pirates also used the new technology, particularly the Dutch pirates known as Sea Beggars.

Portuguese in Africa and India The small nation of Portugal, bounded as it was on the east by the Spanish kingdoms of Castile and Aragon, could expand only overseas. Its visionary ruler, *Prince Henry the Navigator* (1394–1460), became the first in a series of European royalty to sponsor seafaring expeditions, searching for an all-water route to the east as well as for African gold. Importation of slaves by sea began in this period, replacing the overland trans-Saharan slave route of earlier centuries. *Bartholomew Diaz* sailed around the southern tip of Africa, the Cape of Good Hope, in 1488. This was far enough into waters his crew did not know. Diaz feared a mutiny if he continued pushing eastward, so he returned home. *Vasco Da Gama* sailed farther east, landing in India in 1498, where he claimed territory as part of Portugal's empire. The Portuguese ports in India were a key step in expanding Portugal's trade in the Indian Ocean and with points farther east.

Early in the sixteenth century, the ruthless Portuguese admiral Afonso de Albuquerque won a short but bloody battle with Arab traders and set up a factory at Malaka in present-day Indonesia. He had previously served as governor of Portuguese India (1509–1515), sending strings of Indian ears home to Portugal as evidence of his conquests.

In the early sixteenth century, the Portuguese also travelled to Japan to trade, followed by Christian missionaries in 1549. They formed large Catholic settlements until the 1600s, when Japanese rulers outlawed Catholicism and expelled the missionaries.

Spanish in the Philippines Portuguese explorers such as Vasco da Gama were the first Western Europeans to reach the Indian Ocean by sea by going around the southern tip of Africa. Spanish ships, however, became the first to circumnavigate the globe when the government sponsored the voyage of *Ferdinand Magellan*. He died on the voyage in the Philippine Islands in 1522, but one of the ships in his fleet made it all around the world, proving definitively that the earth was round and could be circumnavigated. Spain annexed the Philippines in 1521 when Magellan's fleet arrived there. The Spanish returned in 1565 with strong forces and started a long campaign to conquer the Filipinos, who put up fierce resistance. *Manila* became a Spanish commercial center in the area, attracting Chinese merchants and others. Spain held on to the Philippines until the Spanish-American War in 1898. Because of the Portuguese and Spanish occupations, many Filipinos became Christians.

Dutch in Indonesia The Dutch arrived in India in 1595 and in Indonesia in 1619, using maps obtained from Portuguese sailors who had been there previously. The Dutch were soon competing with the British and French in the Indian Ocean region. Although the Dutch West India Company did not hold on to its North American colony after being forced out of New Amsterdam by the English in 1667, the Dutch East India Company was more successful in Asia. Both companies were dissolved in the 1790s.

France vs. England France and England continued to vie for dominance in North America. As English settlers moved into former Dutch territory in upper New York, the English began to form ties with the powerful Iroquois, who had been in conflict with the French over trade issues for decades. The English hoped that the Iroquois could frustrate French trade interests. Over time, the Iroquois began to realize that the English posed more of threat than the French. In a shift of alliances, The Iroquois and French signed a peace treaty known as the *Great Peace of Montreal* in 1701. This alliance would lead in time to the hostilities of 1756–1763 known in North America as the French and Indian War and in Europe as the Seven Years' War.

Trading Post Empires British trading posts in India were typical of the way European nations operated in the era of European exploration in foreign countries. Taking advantage of the differences between Muslims and Hindus in India and having limited forces that prevented penetration much beyond the coastal areas at first, the British East India Company's strategy was to build a fort, maintain soldiers, coin money, and enter into treaties with local Indian powers. All of this activity fell under the company's charters from the British government. At first, these trading posts were established on India's two coasts and solely focused on turning a profit. Then, with the help of European-trained Indian private forces called *sepoys*, the East India Company moved inland, spreading its influence. Later, officials of the company became embroiled in local Indian politics. Ultimately, Britain intervened in India politically and militarily to such an extent that it eventually controlled much of the subcontinent.

Indian products flowing through the trading posts were spices, cotton, tea, indigo dye, and saltpeter. As commercial treaties were concluded with the local authorities, the *factors,* or governors, for the British East India Company trained Indians as helpers. Travel back and forth to Britain could take up to two years, so the British traders were very isolated. Nevertheless, great fortunes could be made.

Thomas "Diamond" Pitt provides one example of how some were able to advance themselves in the new global economy. At age 21, Pitt travelled to India and operated on his own, illegally, since the British East India Company claimed a monopoly on trade in that area. By 1702, Pitt was so wealthy and successful at trade that the company hired him. While in India, he purchased a diamond that later became worth more than £135,000 after he had it cut in Amsterdam and sold to the regent of France. Pitt, the grandfather of William Pitt, the Earl of Chatham and the man for whom the city of Pittsburgh is named, used his wealth from a post in India to help his family rise to social prominence.

By establishing trading posts in Indian cities, the tiny nation of Britain paved the way for globalization. Each post became a node, an intersection of multiple points serving as a trade center for goods from many parts of the world.

Comparing Northwestern European Empires

The Netherlands, France, and England emerged as strong empires in the seventeenth century. They responded to similar challenges in distinct ways.

Commerce and Economics The Dutch were long the commercial middlemen of Europe, having set up and maintained trade routes to Latin America, North America, South Africa, and Indonesia. Dutch ships were faster and lighter than those of their rivals for most of the seventeenth century, giving them an early trade advantages. The Dutch East India Company was also highly successful as a joint-stock company. It made enormous profits in the Spice Islands and Southeast Asia.

Pioneers in finance, the Dutch had a stock exchange as early as 1602, and by 1609 the *Bank of Amsterdam* traded currency internationally. These developments placed the Dutch at the center of financial dealings in Europe. Their standard of living was the highest in Europe as such goods as diamonds, linen, pottery, and tulip bulbs passed through the hands of Dutch traders.

France and England were not so fortunate. Early in the eighteenth century, both countries fell victim to speculative financial schemes. Known as *financial bubbles*, the schemes were based on the sale of shares to investors who were promised a certain return on their investment. After a frenzy of buying that drove up the price of shares, the bubble burst and investors lost huge amounts of money, sending many into bankruptcy and inflicting damage to the economy at the same time.

In Britain, the crisis was called the *South Sea Bubble*, after the company that issued the shares. The British financial system was robust enough to absorb the shock of the crash and to avoid long-term economic impact. The same was not true with the *Mississippi Bubble,* the bubble in France. The French financial system could not absorb the losses and the country found itself unable to get credit from Europe's major banking families. The result was an ever-growing French national debt, which eventually contributed to the French Revolution.

Absolutist Control vs. Constitutionalism The Dutch and the British operated under constitutional liberties that they assumed to be right and natural and which became the basis of constitutional law. While the British government was centralized, it was not absolutist. The Glorious Revolution assured that the central government operated with the approval of Parliament, providing a check against the absolute power of the monarch. In a similar way, the Dutch provinces maintained autonomy, even after they banded together to form the central government known as the Dutch Republic in the 1648 Treaty of Westphalia. The French, on the other hand, were firmly under the absolutist control of Louis XIV and his successors, who continued to maintain the Sun King's policies, although less successfully.

Social Order In the Netherlands and Britain, the nobility held power and took an active part in the government. The Dutch landowners provided the stable support for local provincial government and in England large landowners controlled Parliament, although they had to contend with radical religious sects and the middle class, two growing segments of the social order.

In France, on the other hand, the nobles were often ignored by the absolutist monarchs. The Estates General in France did not meet during the period 1615–1789. France suffered socially from the inability of the growing *Third Estate*, comprised of the vast majority of France's population, to gain representation in the government. The members of this Third Estate remained legally subordinate to the clergy and nobles.

Growing Acceptance of Jews Jews began to have a larger role in these countries starting in the seventeenth century. In previous centuries, they had been expelled from England (1290), France (1394), Spain (1492), and Portugal (1497), as well as various independent kingdoms and cities in northern and central Europe. The explusion from Spain, by Ferdinand and Isabella, was particularly significant because so many Jews lived there. Jews from this area were known as Sephardic Jews.

Under the influence of the scientific revolution and the Enlightenment, old prejudices against Jews declined somewhat, and they began to move and settle more freely in Europe. They became particularly important in the banking and commercial sectors of the economoy. The Netherlands was especially tolerant of religious dissent and the Jewish minority faced less discrimination there than in most of Europe.

Comparing European States		
	Holland and Britain	**France**
Economic Trends	• Transoceanic trade flourished. • The government established overseas empires through East and West India companies. • Amsterdam emerged as Europe's financial center by 1609. • The government supressed guilds in order to encourage national and international markets.	• The government instituted costly and inefficient tax policies. • Government established overseas empires. • King Louis XIV set up tax-free areas, the Five Great Farms. • The government signed trading agreements with Ottoman Empire after 1535.
Power Dynamics	• The growing belief in natural rights limited the power of the monarchy. • The landed gentry was powerful. • The power of merchants increased. • The English Bill of Rights (1689) increased the power of Parliament and expanded the right of free speech.	• Absolutist French monarchs feared the power of their Hapsburg neighbors: the Holy Roman Empire and Spain. • *Parlements,* 13 traditional law courts overseen by nobility, could veto legislation. • The full Estates-General did not meet between 1615 and 1789. • Intendants carried out functions of government.
Class System, Role of Nobility	• Religious toleration increased. • Social mobility increased as feudal systems declined. • The Dutch commercial class, burghers, often had more wealth than nobles. • In the English Parliament, the House of Commons allowed some middle class representation, generally from country gentry or lesser nobility. The House of Lords was dominated by clergy and royal nobility.	• Ambitious bourgeoisie could rise socially by purchasing titles of nobility attached to land. People could also increase their status by being appointed to government positions. • The law established three estates: the clergy, the nobility, and everyone else. • The clergy were influential through annual financial grants to the monarchy.

Historians differ in assessing the progress made in women's rights during the early modern period of European history. Strong female rulers were an undeniable reality, including Elizabeth I (ruled England 1558–1603), Isabella of Castile (ruled in Spain 1479–1504), and Catherine de Medici (regent of France 1559–1589). Yet Shakespeare echoed most Renaissance writing when he had Hamlet declare, "Frailty, thy name is woman!"

Leading writers of the Protestant Reformation agreed with Martin Luther, who said in his 1532 work *Table Talk*, "No good ever came of female domination. God created Adam master and lord of all living creatures, but Eve spoiled it." Moreover, John Calvin, in his *Sermon #11*, admonished women "to be discreet, chaste, tarriers at home, good, subject to their husbands." Adding to the dismal prospects for women were the accusations of women's susceptibility to witchcraft. For example, the Dominican monk Heinrich Kramer, author of the widely used manual for witch hunters, *Malleus Maleficarum,* asked the rhetorical question, "Why is it that women are chiefly addicted to evil superstitions?"

Consequently, some historians today see the period as having "ambiguous implications for women" (Peter N. Stearns, et al. *World Civilizations*). In *A History of the Modern World*, R. R. Palmer points out a loss of opportunities for women with the decline of Roman Catholicism. The Church had provided positions of leadership in convents and inspired respect for women based on the position of the Virgin Mary in the Church. Some historians have further pointed out that although women spread the ideas of the Reformation, the Reformation did not markedly change their place in society.

Others have argued that opportunities for women in the early modern period began to increase because of the need for mothers to teach children to read the Bible. One popular textbook, *The Earth and Its Peoples* (Richard W. Bulliet, et al.), admits the lower status of women in the period but then adds that "recent research has brought to light the existence of a number of successful women who were painters, musicians, and writers. Indeed, the spread of learning, the stress on religious reading, and the growth of business likely meant that Europe led the world in female literacy."

KEY TERMS BY THEME

STATE-BUILDING: HISTORICAL FIGURES
Henry IV (Henry of Navarre)
Henry VIII
Anne Boleyn
Charles V, Holy Roman Empire
Philip II
Queen Isabella and King Ferdinand
James I
Charles I
Oliver Cromwell
Charles II
James II
William and Mary
Jean Bodin
Cardinal Richelieu
Louis XIV (the "Sun King")
Prince Henry the Navigator

STATE-BUILDING
Politiques
Spanish Armada
Schmalkaldic League
Peace of Augsburg
Edict of Nantes
Thirty Years' War
Peace of Westphalia
new monarchies
English Civil War
Puritan Revolution
Petition of Right
Glorious Revolution
English Bill of Rights
Toleration Act of 1689
divine right of the monarchy
intendants

Versailles
War of the Spanish Succession
Peace of Utrecht
Parlements
maritime empires
Great Peace of Montreal
sepoys

CULTURE: RELIGION
Huguenots
Cluniac Reforms
Lollards (John Wycliffe)
Hussites (Jan Hus)
Reformation
Huldrych Zwingli
Martin Luther
95 Theses
indulgences
simony
John Calvin
the elect
predestined
Reformed Church of Scotland
Puritans
Anglican Church
Counter-Reformation
Inquisition
Jesuits
Council of Trent
Index of Prohibited Books

CULTURE
Leonardo da Vinci
Michelangelo
Thomas Hobbes
John Locke
social contract

Francis Bacon
empiricism
Royal Academy of Science
Sir Isaac Newton
Johannes Kepler
Galileo
Scholasticism
philosophes

ECONOMICS
Five Great Farms
Bank of Amsterdam
joint-stock companies
mercantilism
capital
cottage industries
Adam Smith
physiocrats
The Wealth of Nations
laws of supply and demand
Commercial Revolution
Price Revolution
East India Company
Manila
factors
Thomas "Diamond" Pitt
financial bubbles
South Sea Bubble
Mississippi Bubble

SOCIAL STRUCTURES
Third Estate
primogeniture laws

ENVIRONMENT
Omani-European rivalry
cartography
Bartholomew Diaz
Vasco Da Gama
Ferdinand Magellan

1. Which of the following was a common result of the Protestant Reformation and the Counter-Reformation?

    (A) Rulers in Europe became less interested in overseas conquests because of religious problems at home.

    (B) Catholicism was limited to countries that were located close to Rome.

    (C) Religion in European colonies tended to follow the religion of the home country.

    (D) Christianity declined in Europe as Judaism, Islam, and Buddhism gained new converts.

Question 2 is based on the following excerpt.

IV. We [Louis XIV] enjoin all ministers of the said R.P.R. [Reformed Church], who do not choose to become converts and to embrace the Catholic, apostolic, and Roman religion, to leave our kingdom and the territories subject to us within a fortnight of the publication of our present edict, without leave to reside therein beyond that period, or, during the said fortnight, to engage in any preaching, exhortation, or any other function, on pain of being sent to the galleys. . . .

—From *Revocation of the Edict of Nantes*, October 22, 1685

2. Based on the excerpt, which choice faced people in France after the revocation of the Edict of Nantes?

    (A) Support King Louis XIV or join the Reformed Church

    (B) Leave France or convert to Catholicism

    (C) Join the Reformed Church or move to a territory

    (D) Become a preacher or be sent to the galleys

3. What were the two main opposing forms of government that played roles in state consolidation and expansion of empire in Western Europe 1450–1750?

    (A) Mercantilism and capitalism

    (B) Lollardism and Puritanism

    (C) Direct democracy and military dictatorships

    (D) Constitutionalism and absolutism

4. The Dutch were able to monopolize European overseas trade for most of the seventeenth century because they

   (A) had the largest maritime empire
   (B) had superior sailing technology
   (C) avoided using joint-stock companies
   (D) refused to lend money to foreign creditors

5. What was the main difference between the way Spain and Portugal financed foreign investment and the methods used by other European countries?

   (A) Spain and Portugal followed the principles of mercantilism
   (B) Spain and Portugal were slow to adopt joint-stock companies
   (C) Spain and Portugal had the earliest international banking system
   (D) Spain and Portugal had more middle-class investors.

Question 6 is based on the following map.

VOYAGES OF FERDINAND MAGELLAN AND FRANCIS DRAKE

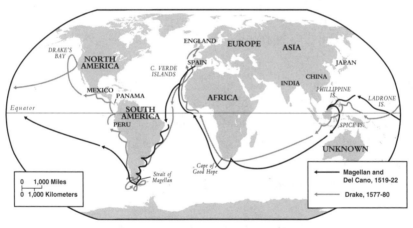

6. Magellan's and Drake's voyages differed from the Portuguese voyages of exploration in the late 1400s because they sailed

   (A) along the coast of Africa
   (B) westward from Europe to reach Asia
   (C) across the Indian Ocean
   (D) among the islands southeast of Asia

7. Which of the following was a result of the Thirty Years' War?
   (A) William and Mary took over as rulers of England.
   (B) Spain gained control of the Netherlands.
   (C) Protestants lost power throughout Europe.
   (D) The Holy Roman Empire became weaker.

8. Which of the following resulted from the English Bill of Rights of 1689?
   (A) The monarch won the right to choose the state religion.
   (B) The House of Commons had more rights than the House of Lords.
   (C) Rights of Parliament severely limited the monarch's power.
   (D) Women and men had equal rights in principle.

9. Which statement best describes European trading-post empires in this period?
   (A) They were a profitable way for Europeans to maintain a presence in Asia and Africa.
   (B) They required large numbers of European settlers to maintain control of foreign territories.
   (C) They were more expensive to maintain than trade using overland trade routes such as the Silk Road.
   (D) They had little lasting impact on the economies of Europe, Asia, or Africa.

10. Which of the following was supported by a policy of religious toleration in the Netherlands during this period?
   (A) The central government was strengthened.
   (B) Landowning nobility increased their wealth.
   (C) The commercial class grew stronger.
   (D) Peasants revolted against feudal landlords.

CONTINUITY AND CHANGE-OVER-TIME ESSAY QUESTIONS

Directions: You are to answer the following question. You should spend 5 minutes organizing or outlining your essay. Write an essay that:

- Has a relevant thesis and supports that thesis with appropriate historical evidence.
- Addresses all parts of the question.
- Uses world historical context to show continuities and changes over time.
- Analyzes the process of continuity and change over time.

1. Analyze continuities and change in government in England and France from 1000 to 1750.

Questions for Additional Practice

2. Analyze continuities and change in the role of any ONE of the following European nations in the Indian Ocean trade network from 1500 to 1750.
   - Portugal
   - Spain
   - Netherlands (the Dutch)
   - England

3. Analyze continuities and change in European economies from 1450 to 1750. Include details about overall policies and commercial institutions.

COMPARATIVE ESSAY QUESTIONS

Directions: You are to answer the following question. You should spend 5 minutes organizing or outlining your essay. Write an essay that:

- Has a relevant thesis and supports that thesis with appropriate historical evidence.
- Addresses all parts of the question.
- Makes direct, relevant comparisons.
- Analyzes relevant reasons for similarities and differences.

1. Analyze similarities and differences in the economic structures of TWO of the following sea-based empires between 1450 and 1750:
   - Portugal
   - Spain
   - France
   - England

Questions for Additional Practice

2. Analyze similarities and differences in the development and impact on politics of TWO of the following Protestant denominations:
   - Lutheranism
   - Calvinism
   - Anglicanism

3. Analyze similarities and differences in the role of religion between the Thirty Years' War and the conflict between the Ottoman Empire and the Safavid Empire.

THINK AS A HISTORIAN: PRACTICE INTERPRETATION

If an essays asks for an interpretation, you should explain how or why something happened. "Luther challenged Catholic practices" is not an interpretation. "Luther's deep personal faith led him to challenge Catholic practices" is because it explains his motivation. *Which TWO of the following sentences would best introduce an interpretive essay?*

1. "Paris is well worth a Mass," King Henry IV wrote in the sixteenth century, shedding light on how monarchs were newly willing to bargain and compromise, ruling with practicality rather than theology.

2. Martin Luther presented his "95 Theses" to Church leaders in Wittenberg, Germany, on October 31, 1517.

3. The final great religious war was the Thirty Years' War (1618–1648), which involved the Netherlands, Denmark, Sweden, France, and Spain.

4. Diamonds, linens, pottery, and tulip bulbs—all of these passed through the hands of Dutch traders, who were able to succeed because of their seaworthy ships, strong financial institutions, and geographical location.

WRITE AS A HISTORIAN: PROVIDE EXAMPLES

To make a generalization persuasive, support it with specific examples of individuals, locations, or events that demonstrate it. "Religious leaders were important" is a generalization. "Religious leaders such as Martin Luther and John Calvin were important in Europe in the sixteenth century" is more concrete and hence more powerful.

1. Select the TWO statements below that could best be used as examples in a paragraph about religious conflict in Europe during the sixteenth and seventeenth centuries.

   a. One of the kings of France tried to bring peace between religious groups, but he was not successful.

   b. The French Catholic monarchy battled the Huguenots for almost 50 years.

   c. The German Lutherans and Catholics fought over their beliefs in the 1500s.

   d. The European wars of the seventeenth century were terrible conflicts.

2. Select the TWO statements below that provide the best examples to use in a paragraph about the political developments in Western Europe in between the fifteenth and eighteenth centuries.

   a. Several important documents helped balance the power between England's Parliament and its monarchy.

   b. The French government further consolidated its authority and gave less power to their citizens.

   c. Writers such as John Locke and Thomas Hobbes commented on the ideas of government, which influenced the way powerful people ruled and what common people expected.

   d. The English Bill of Rights, signed in 1689, paved the way for guaranteed individual liberties for the English people.

16

The Americas in the Early Colonial Period

We are crushed to the ground; we lie in ruins.
There is nothing but grief and suffering in
Mexico and Tlatelolco, where once we
saw beauty and valor.

—from "Flowers and Songs of Sorrow," anonymous
Aztec poet, (c. 1521–1540)

The first transatlantic voyage by *Christopher Columbus* in 1492 was the initial event in what is known as the *Columbian Exchange*—the widespread sharing of animals, plants, cultures, ideas, technologies, and diseases between Afro-Eurasian cultures and the native peoples of the Americas.

European Interests in the Americas Columbus and other European explorers were seeking a new route to Asia and hoping to find gold, silver, and other valuable resources. The Spanish found so little of value in their first two decades of contact that they considered stopping further exploration. The English, after sponsoring voyages in the 1490s, made little attempt to explore or settle for almost a century.

However, European interest in the Americas was rekindled when the Spanish came into contact with the two major empires in the region, the Aztecs in Mesoamerica and the Incas in South America. These empires had the gold and silver that made exploration, conquest, and settlement profitable. In addition, Europeans soon realized that, by using enslaved Native Americans and later enslaved Africans, they could grow wealthy by raising sugar, tobacco, and other valuable crops.

Interaction of Cultures As the excerpt from the poem above suggests, initial contact and the subsequent conquest and colonization of the Americas did not bode well for the native peoples. Overpowered by superior weapons and decimated by disease, many native populations declined, dissipated, or were forced to submit to new rulers and a new religion.

Although European conquest seriously damaged entire native societies and their ways of life, eventually new ways of life developed out of the interaction of three broad traditions of culture: indigenous American, European, and African.

Why Did the Europeans Want to Explore?

There were several motives for the new age of European exploration that began in the late 1400s:

- Italian cities with ports on the Mediterranean had a monopoly on European trade with Asia. By controlling access to the trade routes, the Italians controlled prices of Asian imports to Europe, driving Spain and Portugal, and later France, England, and the Netherlands, into the search for new routes to Asia.

- Various inventions made it possible for Europeans to venture farther out into the ocean. The magnetic compass, originally invented in China, made it easier to steer a ship in the right direction. The astrolabe, improved by Muslim navigators in the twelfth century, allowed sailors to determine how far north or south they were from the equator. The *caravel*, a small, three-masted sailing ship developed by the Portuguese in the fifteenth century, allowed sailors to survive storms at sea better than earlier-designed ships.

- Many Europeans believed that it was their Christian duty to seek out people in other lands to convert them.

- Explorers hoped to find riches overseas, especially gold and silver.

Christopher Columbus was fortunate in 1492 to gain the support of the Spanish monarchs, Queen Isabella and King Ferdinand, for his voyages across the Atlantic. For his first voyage, he had the use of two caravels and one larger ship. Columbus was successful in reaching the Americas, although that had not been his intent: he had wanted to get to the East Indies or China.

Diseases and Demographic Catastrophe

Demography, which refers to population patterns and changes, was an important feature in the European conquest of the Americas. Up until this era, the peoples of the Western and Eastern Hemispheres had been almost completely isolated from each other. For that reason, the indigenous people of the Americas had no exposure to the germs and diseases brought by Europeans. Although European horses, gunpowder, and metal weapons were instrumental in subjugating indigenous Americans, disease was responsible for the majority of deaths, including those among the *Tainos,* a group of Arawaks native to the Caribbean. *Conquistadores*, Spanish conquerors such as Francisco Pizarro, Hernán Cortés, and Columbus, brought *smallpox* with them. Smallpox pathogens are spread through the respiratory system. When Europeans, who were largely immune had face-to-face contact with indigenous populations, they infected these populations with the deadly disease. In addition to smallpox, measles and influenza also killed many native peoples of the Americas. Historians estimate that the indigenous population fell by more than 50 percent through disease alone in less than a century. Some American lands lost up to 90 percent of their original populations. It was one of the greatest demographic disasters in history.

Columbian Exchange

Germ and disease transmissions were only one part of what is now called the Columbian Exchange. Another major component of the exchange was the sharing of new crops and livestock in both directions. Before the exchange began around 1500, Mesoamerican peoples consumed very little meat. Although contemporary Mexican food sold in the United States is reliant on pork, beef, and cheese, the indigenous people of Mexico knew nothing of pigs or cows until Europeans introduced them. These animals, along with Mediterranean foods such as wheat and grapes, were introduced to the Western Hemisphere and eventually became staples of the American diet. Another domesticated animal the European brought to the Americas, the horse, transformed the culture of the American Indians living in the plains region. Along with crops and livestock, the Europeans also brought with them vermin, such as mosquitoes and rats, adding to more environmental stresses to the American environment.

Conversely, European explorers took back Mesoamerican maize, potatoes, tomatoes, beans, peppers, and cacao to their home countries, where people started to grow them. Potatoes became so popular in Europe that they are often thought of as being native to certain regions, such as Ireland. The introduction of these vegetable crops caused tremendous population growth in Europe in the sixteenth and seventeenth centuries.

People themselves also became part of the exchange. The arrival of enslaved Africans to the Americas brought biological and demographic changes. For example, Africans brought okra and rice with them to the Americas. As part of the Atlantic Ocean slave trade, tobacco and cacao produced on American plantations were sold to consumers in Europe, Africa, and the Middle East. Despite the fact that slave traders kidnapped millions of Africans from their homelands, populations actually grew in Africa during the sixteenth and seventeenth centuries because of the nutritious foods that were introduced to the continent; yams and manioc, for example, were introduced to Africa from Brazil. (Test Prep: Write an outline of the effects of the Atlantic slave trade on Africa. See pages 323–327.)

Columbian Exchange				
Exchange	Plants	Animals	Disease	Technology/ Ideas
From Afro-Eurasia to the Americas	Wheat, grapes, okra, sugar, rice, barley, oranges, lettuce, coffee	Pigs, cows, horses, oxen, chicken, sheep, goats, rats	Bubonic plague, typhus, influenza, measles, smallpox	Written alphabet, farming technology, firearms, architecture, corporate structure
From the Americas to Afro-Eurasia	Potatoes, tomatoes, beans, peppers, yams, manioc, chocolate, tobacco, avocado, maize, squash, vanilla	Turkeys, llamas, alpacas, guinea pigs	Syphilis	Rubber, quinine

Economic Changes

The Western European search for profit began with Columbus. On his first voyage, he was convinced that gold was plentiful on *Hispaniola*, the name he gave the island now occupied by Haiti and the Dominican Republic. But gold was sparse in the Caribbean. Desiring to return home with something valuable, Columbus and his crew kidnapped Tainos and took them to Spain as slaves.

Coercive Labor In the early 1500s, the Spanish established a labor system called the *encomienda* to gain access to gold and other resources of the Americas. *Encomenderos*, or landowners, compelled indigenous people to work for them in exchange for food and shelter. This coercive labor system was notorious for its brutality and harsh living conditions.

Silver While gold did not yield riches for Spanish conquistadores, the discovery of silver in Mexico and Peru revived economic fortunes—for both individual explorers and Spain. The use of mercury to separate silver from its ore made silver mining more profitable. By the end of the sixteenth century, the cities of Zacatecas, in Mexico, and especially *Potosí*, in the Andes Mountains in modern-day Peru, became thriving centers of silver mining.

For this industry to flourish, Spanish prospectors needed labor. The indigenous populations would do all but the most dangerous work in the mines. In response, Spanish authorities in Peru transformed the traditional Incan *mit'a system* of labor obligation, in which young men were required to devote a certain amount of labor to public works projects, into a coerced labor system. Villages were compelled to send a percentage of their male population to do the dangerous work in the mines for a paltry wage.

The silver trade not only made individual Spanish prospectors wealthy, it also strengthened the Spanish economy. European powers at the time were adopting mercantilism, an economic system that increased government control of the economy through high tariffs and the establishment of *colonies*, claimed lands settled by immigrants from the home country. In the case of Spain, the main purpose of the colonies in the Americas was to supply as much gold and silver as possible. Another way to increase national wealth, according to the mercantilist system, was for a colonizing country to export more than it imported. A percentage of overseas silver production went directly to the Spanish crown. The empire used this wealth to build an impressive military and to establish trade with foreign lands.

Trade Across the Pacific China was a particularly enthusiastic consumer of this silver from the Western Hemisphere. Mexican silver, for example, made its way across the Pacific Ocean to East Asia in heavily-armed Spanish ships known as *galleons* that made stops in the Philippines. At the trading post in Manila, Europeans exchanged silver for luxury goods such as silk and spices, and even for gold bullion. The impressive Manila galleons allowed the silver trade to flourish. Indeed, the Chinese government soon began using silver as its main form of currency. By the early seventeenth century, silver had become a dominant force in the global economic system.

Sugar While Spain and Spanish America profited from silver, the Portuguese empire focused its endeavors on agriculture. Brazil, the center of the Portuguese-American empire, with its tropical climate and vast tracts of land, was perfect for *sugarcane* cultivation. As disease had decimated the indigenous population, however, there were not enough laborers available to do the cultivation. Moreover, many of the people who were forced to labor in the sugar fields escaped to the uncharted Brazilian jungle. In response, the Portuguese began to import enslaved people from Africa, especially from the Kongo Kingdom and cities on the Swahili coast.

Sugar's profitability in European markets dramatically increased the number of Africans captured and sold through the *transatlantic slave trade*. Sugar cultivation in Brazil demanded the constant importation of African labor. African laborers were so numerous in Brazil that their descendants became the majority population of the region. Slaves often died from backbreaking working conditions, poor nutrition, lack of adequate shelter, and tropical heat and the diseases that accompanied such heat. Sugar plantations processed so much sugar that they were referred to as *engenhos*, which literally means "engines" in Spanish. Because of the engenhos's horrible working conditions, plantation owners lost from 5 to 10 percent of their labor force per year. The Spanish noticed Portugal's success with plantation agriculture and returned to the Caribbean to pursue *cash crop* cultivation, such as sugar and tobacco. Cash crops are grown for sale rather than subsistence. Soon, sugar eclipsed silver as the main moneymaker for the European empires. (Test Prep: Write a paragraph comparing the economic practices of Spain's and Portugal's colonial empires with later European imperialism. See pages 465–477.)

Political Changes

In the late fifteenth century and early sixteenth century, the *Aztec* and *Inca Empires* collapsed relatively soon after the arrival of Europeans. (Test Prep: Write a brief outline of the Aztec and Inca Empires on the eve of the European conquests. See pages 258–264.)

The Fall of the Aztec Empire The Aztecs had accumulated numerous enemies throughout Mesoamerica as a result of the empire's militaristic actions toward its neighbors. In 1519, *Hernán Cortés* and his small band of conquistadors easily exploited the divisions among Mesoamerica's indigenous groups and marched on the Aztec capital of *Tenochtitlán*. The Aztecs offered Cortés gold to go away, but this gold made him even more determined. Helped by peoples that the Aztec ruled, Cortés's forces conquered the Aztec by 1521. Smallpox also aided his victory. The disease swept through Tenochtitlán, killing thousands and weakening the Aztecs' ability to defend their capital. Cortés quickly took control of the entire Aztec empire and founded the colony of *New Spain*. The Spaniards melted down the Aztecs' treasures and sent the gold back home. They destroyed Tenochtitlán and built their own capital, *Mexico City*, on its ruins.

The Demise of the Inca Empire In 1532, *Francisco Pizarro* and his crew attacked the Inca in Peru and captured their ruler, *Atahualpa*. Pizarro offered to release Atahualpa if the Inca would fill a large room with gold. The Inca complied, but in 1533 the Spanish killed Atahualpa anyway. By 1572, the Spaniards had completed their conquest of the Inca empire, which at its height had a population of 12 million. Some historians believe that European germs were more of a factor than guns and swords in drastically reducing the population of the Inca. The Spanish established a colonial capital in *Lima*, Peru, that administered lands from as far north as present-day Panama to as far south as Argentina.

SPANISH AND PORTUGUESE COLONIES, C. 1600

Other Regions of the Americas In the *Treaty of Tordesillas* of 1494, Spain and Portugal divided the Americas between them, with Spain reserving all lands to the west of a meridian that went through eastern South America while Portugal reserved all lands east of this north-south line. This arrangement put Brazil under Portugal's rule, while Spain claimed the rest of the Americas. In addition to establishing colonies in Mesoamerica and South America, Spain explored other parts of North America north of present-day Mexico. The explorer Pedro Menéndez de Avilés established a fort in St. Augustine on the east coast of Florida in 1565, which became the oldest continuous settlement in what later became the United States. Spain would not be able to control all of North America, however, because the French, British, and Dutch later made claims and settlements there.

Colonial Administration Indigenous political structures in Latin America were soon replaced by Spanish and Portuguese colonial administrations. Spanish royalty appointed *viceroys* to act as administrators and representatives of the Spanish crown. To keep these viceroys from operating independently of the crown, Spain established *audiencias*, or royal courts, to which Spanish settlers could appeal viceroys' decisions or policies. Slow transportation and communication networks between Europe and the Americas, however, made it difficult for the Spanish crown to exercise direct control over New Spain. As a result, the Spanish throne did not focus on the affairs of its colonies in the Western Hemisphere.

By 1750, those born in America of Spanish origin, or *creoles*, enjoyed political dominance in New Spain and soon began clamoring for independence from the Spanish throne. (Test Prep: In a brief paragraph or outline, trace the connections between creole elites and revolutions in Latin America. See pages 404–408.)

Cultural and Social Changes

Earlier land-based empires, such as those of the Romans, Muslims, and Mongols, all grappled with how to deal with conquered people's traditions and cultures. These empires either allowed traditions to exist or they tried to graft their ways onto those of their subjects. European empires in the Americas stand in stark contrast to these land-based empires. The Spanish and Portuguese empires managed to erase the basic social structures and many of the cultural traditions of the indigenous Americans within a century of when the first European explorers arrived. As discussed earlier in this chapter, the Europeans' actions almost depopulated the Americas. (Test Prep: Create a two-column table comparing the Spanish and Portuguese maritime empires with earlier land-based empires. See pages 77–70, 146–155, and 241–248.)

Cultural Changes The indigenous peoples of the Americas lost a great deal of their culture and history at the hands of conquerors. Conquistadors, such as Cortés in Mexico, ordered the burning of native books, which were thought to be unholy. Thus, very few original accounts written in *Nahuatl*, the language of the Aztec, exist today.

The relative scarcity of firsthand accounts from indigenous peoples has played a major role in how historians view this time and place in history. For example, because the Spanish burned nearly all Aztec documents, very few original sources exist from the Aztecs themselves. Most of the information that historians have about the Aztec comes from documents that were written by Spanish conquistadores and priests after the conquest. The Spanish point of view shows clearly in these accounts; the authors' biases and lack of familiarity with Nahuatl limits the value of these sources. However, there are some sources that are still considered reliable. For example, in 1545, a Spanish priest named Bernardino de Sahagún began compiling the *Florentine Codex*, one of the most widely cited sources about Aztec life before and after conquest. (A codex is a type of book.)

Spanish and Portuguese conquerors transplanted their own languages and religion into the Americas. The remnants of this cultural interaction are present today; although indigenous languages thrive in certain regions, in Guatemala and in the mountains of Mexico, for example, Spanish predominates through much of Latin America and Brazilians overwhelmingly speak Portuguese.

Religion in Latin America Several Catholic religious orders in Europe, such as the Dominicans, Jesuits, and Franciscans, sent missionaries to Latin America to convert people to Christianity. The missionaries were so successful that today, most Latin Americans are Roman Catholic Christians. In recent decades, Protestant denominations have begun to gain more members.

Numerous examples of religious syncretism originated in the Spanish colonies. Catholic saints' days that coincided with days honored by indigenous people were especially celebrated. In Mexico, a cult developed around the dark-complexioned *Virgin of Guadalupe*, who was revered for her ability to perform miracles. Meanwhile, certain syncretic religions developed that combined indigenous and Christian practices. *Vodun*, a descendant of West African animist traditions, is practiced mainly in Haiti and includes some elements of Catholicism. The religion is at times, often condescendingly, referred to as "voodoo." *Santeria* in Cuba shares many similarities with Vodun, combining Christianity and the traditions of the Aja people in Africa. *Candomblé* in Brazil combines Christianity with the traditions of the Yoruba from present-day Nigeria.

Social Changes Coupled with the arrival of Europeans was the importation of African slave labor. The combination of European settlers, imported Africans, and the conquered indigenous population led to the development of a new social hierarchy based on race and ancestry. At the top of the social pyramid stood the *peninsulares*, those who were born on the Iberian Peninsula. Next down the pyramid were the creoles, those of European ancestry who were born in the New World. Below these two groups were the *castas*, people of mixed-race ancestry. At the top of this group were *mestizos*, those of mixed European and indigenous ancestry, followed by *mulattoes*, those of mixed European and African ancestry, and *zambos*, those of mixed indigenous and African ancestry. Indigenous peoples and enslaved Africans made up the bottom ranks of the hierarchy. Skin color became a signifier of power and status in many parts of the Americas. Thus, racial and ethnic background defined social status in the Spanish and Portuguese empires in the Western Hemisphere for centuries following the Europeans' arrival.

The French Colonies

Spain's rivals in Europe also explored and claimed regions in the Americas. French, English, and Dutch explorers all looked for a *northwest passage*—a route through or around North America that would lead to East Asia. In the

1500s and 1600s, the French government sponsored expeditions for that purpose. In 1535, for example, French explorer *Jacques Cartier* sailed from the Atlantic Ocean into the St. Lawrence River at today's northern U.S. border. He did not find a new route to Asia, but he did claim part of what is now Canada for France. Eventually, explorers such as Cartier and *Samuel de Champlain* (explored 1609–1616) realized that there were valuable goods and rich resources available in the Americas, so there was no need to go beyond to Asia.

Like the Spanish, the French hoped to find gold. Instead, they found a land rich in furs and other natural resources. In 1608, they established a town and trading post that they named *Quebec*. French traders and priests spread across the continent. The traders searched for furs; the priests wanted to convert Native Americans to Christianity. The missionaries sometimes set up schools among the indigenous peoples. In the 1680s, a French trader known as La Salle explored the Great Lakes and followed the Mississippi River south to its mouth at the Gulf of Mexico. He claimed this vast region for France.

Unlike the Spanish—or the English who were colonizing the East Coast of what is now the United States—the French rarely settled permanently. Instead of demanding land, they traded for the furs trapped by Native Americans. For this reason, the French had better relations with natives than did the Spanish or English colonists and their settlements also grew more slowly. For example, by 1754 the European population of *New France,* the French colony in North America, was only 70,000. The English colonies included one million Europeans.

The English Colonies

In 1497, the English king sent an explorer named *John Cabot* to America to look for a northwest passage. Cabot claimed lands from Newfoundland south to the Chesapeake Bay. The English, however, did not have enough sea power to defend themselves from Spanish naval forces—although English pirates called "sea dogs" sometimes attacked Spanish ships. Then in 1588, the English surprisingly defeated and destroyed all but one-third of the Spanish Armada. With that victory, England declared itself a major naval power and began competing for lands and resources in the Americas.

At about the same time the French were founding Quebec, the English were establishing England's first successful colony in North America. In 1607, about one hundred English colonists arrived in a region called *Virginia*, previously named for Elizabeth I, England's virgin queen. At a location approximately 60 miles from the coast, they built a settlement on the banks of a river they called the James, after the current English monarch for whom they also named their settlement, *Jamestown*. This settlement was the first successful English colony in what would become the United States.

The *London Company*, a joint-stock company headquartered in England, owned Jamestown. In the hopes of making a profit, each English investor put up a portion of the money needed to fund the colony. Jamestown was not profitable at first, however; the colonists hoped to mine gold, but they found none. In addition, the town's swampy location caused many of its settlers to fall sick and die. Only food taken from the local Indians kept the colony alive. The

London Company replaced the deceased colonists by offering new settlers a free voyage to America.

Tobacco, a native plant grown by the Indians, proved profitable for the colony. By 1620, the colonists were growing a high-quality tobacco in great demand in Europe, spurring the establishment of more plantations in other parts of Virginia. As colonists took land for farming, however, local Native Americans attacked them. Not until the 1640s was the colony able to establish a peace with the local tribes.

The institution of *indentured servitude* became widespread in the English colonies of North America. An indentured servant was someone who contracted to work for an employer without pay for a set number of years in exchange for passage to America. In fact, the first Africans brought to Virginia in 1619 came as indentured servants. Virginia laws changed later in the 1600s, resulting in the enslavement of the African-American residents. Other Southern colonies enacted similar laws. Indentured servitude remained much more common in the northern English colonies, while slavery became the norm in the southern colonies.

FRENCH, ENGLISH, AND DUTCH COLONIES, C. 1650

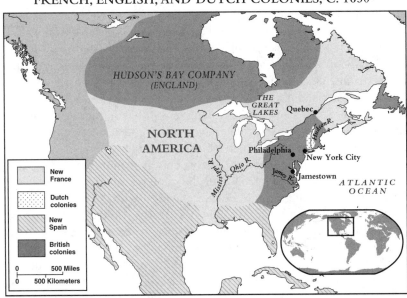

The Dutch Experience

In 1609, the Dutch sent *Henry Hudson* to explore the East Coast of North America. Among other feats, he sailed up what became known as the Hudson River to see if it led to Asia. He was disappointed in finding no northwest passage. But the Dutch used his voyage as the basis of claims to the Hudson River Valley and the island of Manhattan, where they set up a town called *New Amsterdam*. The Dutch used this port town as an important node in their transatlantic trade network. Dutch merchants bought furs from trappers and tobacco from Virginia planters; those goods and others went to the Netherlands in exchange for manufactured goods. In 1664, the English military forced the turnover of New Amsterdam to the English. Many Dutch settlers and merchants remained in Manhattan, however, and the Dutch language was spoken there for years to come.

Environmental Impact Contact between Afro-Eurasia and the Americas brought dramatic changes to both. Most changes resulted from the Columbian Exchange. In addition, though, Europeans used the land more intensely than did American Indians. Colonists cut down trees for farmland and created large fields that they cultivated year after year. As a result, deforestation and soil depletion became problems in the Americas.

HISTORICAL PERSPECTIVE: HOW HARSH WERE THE SPANISH?

After the first voyage of Christopher Columbus, Spanish conquistadors created a vast colonial empire in the Americas. In 1552, the Dominican friar Bartolomé de las Casas described the greed, ruthlessness, and cruelty toward the native populations practiced by Spanish officials. Ever since, historians have debated the accuracy of his observations.

Writing in 1914, Spanish historian Julián Juderías labeled this belief in the evils of Spanish rule as the Black Legend. He argued that during the sixteenth and seventeenth centuries, Europeans were jealous of Spanish wealth and power. As a result, they were inclined to believe the worst about Spain's rule. Juderías suggested that European historians focused so much on the Spanish as cruel, bigoted butchers that they ignored the positive achievements of Spanish colonialism.

Besides jealousy, another factor entering into how historians viewed Spain was religion. During the centuries of struggle between Protestants and Catholics, the Black Legend fit with the negative views many Protestants had toward Catholics. In the United States, where Protestants dominated the writing of history in the nineteenth century, acceptance of the Black Legend was common.

In the first half of the twentieth century, many Spanish historians shared the perspective of Juderías. Their works reflected the intense national pride that many Spaniards felt about their past. In defending Spanish colonization, they developed what their critics called a "white legend" to counter the Black Legend.

One American historian active in the debate over Spanish colonization was Lewis Hanke. He argued against the Black Legend by trying to show that Las Casas was just one of many Spanish reformers. Though the efforts of these reformers, Hanke, argued, the Spanish empire was "one of the greatest attempts the world has seen to make Christian precepts prevail in the relations between peoples."

Defenders of the Black Legend thought Hanke had exaggerated the strength of Las Casas and the reformers, thereby making the Spanish look better than they were. Others emphasized that, despite any attempts at reform, what actually happened was harsh.

In recent years, historians have compared colonial empires more systematically than in previous generations. While they often point out clear differences among the European colonies in the Americas, they have found ample examples of brutality in many colonies. Whether the Spanish were any worse than other Europeans remains hard to determine.

KEY TERMS BY THEME

STATE-BUILDING
Christopher Columbus
conquistadores
colonies
Aztec Empire
Inca Empire
Hernán Cortés
New Spain
Tenochtitlán
Mexico City
Francisco Pizarro
Atahualpa
Lima
Treaty of Tordesillas
viceroys
audiencias
Jacques Cartier
Samuel de Champlain
Quebec
New France
John Cabot
Virginia

Jamestown
Henry Hudson
New Amsterdam

ENVIRONMENT
caravel
smallpox
Hispaniola
Potosí
galleons
sugarcane
northwest passage
Columbian Exchange

CULTURE
Tainos
Nahuatl
Florentine Codex
Virgin of Guadalupe
Vodun
Santeria
Candomblé

ECONOMICS
encomienda
encomenderos
mit'a system
transatlantic slave
 trade
engenhos
cash crop
London Company
tobacco
indentured
 servitude

SOCIAL STRUCTURE
creoles
peninsulares
castas
mestizos
mulattoes
zambos

1. What is the most likely cause for the majority of the population losses among indigenous Americans after European contact?

   (A) Climate

   (B) Disease

   (C) Enslavement

   (D) Warfare

Question 2 is based on the following excerpt.

"The vivid scene of animals cavorting around the edge of lakes that once shimmered in Mexico City was painted by Aztec Indians in the early 1530s . . . .

"At the center of the 16-yard-long painting is a Christian cross in black and white, floating above a colorful, lively scene of fishermen, frogs, fish and other creatures.

"To the right of the cross and below it, the Indians painted an Ahuizotl, a mythical Aztec animal with paws resembling hands that was considered a servant or representative of the Aztec rain god, Tlaloc. To the left, there is a jaguar with a stylized plant on its back, upon which rests an eagle – a reference to pre-Hispanic place names and the kingdoms that ruled before the Spanish came.

"Indians also drew gracefully executed depictions of lakeside plants, some of which were used in traditional Aztec medicine."

—From "Aztec Mural Melds Cultures," by Mark Stevenson

2. Based on the excerpt, which statement best reflects the relationship between the Aztec and the Spanish in 1530?

   (A) The Aztec remained isolated from the influences of Spanish culture.

   (B) The Spanish had successfully converted most of the Aztec to Christianity.

   (C) Aztec religion and culture were very similar to Christianity and Spanish culture.

   (D) The Aztec maintained some of their culture in the face of Spanish influences.

3. What do the encomienda and mit'a systems used in Spanish colonies and the labor system used on Brazilian sugarcane plantations have in common?

   (A) Both were coerced labor systems designed to enrich European colonizers.

   (B) Both made use of enslaved Africans as agricultural workers.

   (C) Both were successful in teaching indigenous peoples European farming techniques.

   (D) Both were labor systems that provided economic opportunities for immigrants.

4. Which generalization best describes the cult of the Virgin of Guadalupe, Vodun, and Santeria?

(A) A mixture of Catholic and Protestant religious elements

(B) A mixture of indigenous and Christian religious elements

(C) A mixture of African and European religious elements

(D) A mixture of Christian, Jewish, and Muslim religious elements

Question 5 is based on the following table.

Transoceanic Voyages, c. 1300–c. 1800				
Sponsoring Empire	Explorer	Key Voyages	Purpose	Impact
China	Zheng He	To India, the Middle East, and Africa	To open up trade networks with India, Arabia, and Africa and to spread Chinese culture	China decided not to continue exploring
England	James Cook	To Australia, New Zealand, and Newfoundland	To collect botanical specimens, chart islands, and make astronomical observations	Europeans made contact with people in Australia and Hawaii, charted large areas of Pacific, and mapped Newfoundland
Portugal	Vasco De Gama	To India and western coast of Africa	To open a sea route from Europe to India and China	Portugal expanded trade and cultural exchange between India and Europe
Spain	Christopher Columbus	To the Americas	To find a sea route to India and China going west from Europe	Spain led the European exploration and colonization of the Americas
Spain	Ferdinand Magellan	Around South America to the Philippines	To demonstrate that Europeans could reach Asia by sailing west	Spain established links betwen the Americas and Asia across the Pacific Ocean

5. Which statement best compares the voyages of Zheng He with those of the Portuguese and Spanish explorers in the table?

(A) They resulted in closer contact between China and Europe.

(B) They focused on the Indian Ocean trading network.

(C) They shared some motives but had different results.

(D) They promoted more exploration in the Pacific Ocean.

6. Which economic system was largely responsible for the economic development of Brazil, Spanish America, and parts of western Africa in the sixteenth and seventeenth centuries?

(A) Columbian Exchange

(B) Feudalism

(C) Socialism

(D) Mercantilism

7. What factor played the greatest role in determining a person's social status in Spanish and Portuguese empires in the Americas by the seventeenth century?

(A) Commercial wealth

(B) Land ownership

(C) Racial ancestry

(D) Religious affiliation

8. Which statement best describes the way Spain ruled its American colonies in the sixteenth and seventeenth centuries?

(A) The monarch effectively maintained long-distance control of the colonies from Spain.

(B) Appointed officials represented the crown, overseen by royal courts in the colonies.

(C) Spanish colonial subjects elected their own rulers with the approval of the monarch.

(D) Spain adapted the political systems of the Aztec and Inca in ruling the colonies.

9. What conclusion about the results of the Columbian Exchange in the sixteenth century is most accurate?

(A) Africa benefitted more than Europe and the Americas.

(B) The Americas benefitted more than Europe and Africa.

(C) Europe benefitted more than Africa and the Americas.

(D) Africa, the Americas, and Europe all benefitted equally.

10. One characteristic of indentured servitude as a labor system was that

(A) servitude was passed from parent to child

(B) it involved a contract between master and servant

(C) servants had strong legal protections

(D) it was generally used only with skilled workers

CONTINUITY AND CHANGE-OVER-TIME ESSAY QUESTIONS

Directions: You are to answer the following question. You should spend 5 minutes organizing or outlining your essay. Write an essay that:

- Has a relevant thesis and supports that thesis with appropriate historical evidence.
- Addresses all parts of the question.
- Uses world historical context to show continuities and changes over time.
- Analyzes the process of continuity and change over time.

1. Analyze continuities and change in ONE of the following aspects of life in Latin Americas from 1492 to 1750:
   - demographics
   - political organization
   - social structure

Questions for Additional Practice

2. Analyze continuities and change in the global economy after Europeans began mining silver in the Americas in the 1500s.

3. Analyze continuities and change in religion in TWO of the following colonial empires in the Americas in the period 1492–1750:
   - Spanish
   - French
   - English

COMPARATIVE ESSAY QUESTIONS

Directions: You are to answer the following question. You should spend 5 minutes organizing or outlining your essay. Write an essay that:

- Has a relevant thesis and supports that thesis with appropriate historical evidence.
- Addresses all parts of the question.
- Makes direct, relevant comparisons.
- Analyzes relevant reasons for similarities and differences.

1. Analyze similarities and differences in the demographic effects of the Columbian Exchange on TWO of the following regions between 1492 and 1750:
   - Africa
   - The Americas
   - Europe

Questions for Additional Practice

2. Analyze similarities and differences in the goals and outcomes of exploration of the Americas by TWO of the following European powers from 1492 to 1750:
   - Great Britain
   - Netherlands (Dutch)
   - France

3. Analyze similarities and differences in the economic effects of mercantilism on TWO of the following European countries and its colonies between 1500 and 1750:
   - Great Britain
   - France
   - Spain

In chemistry, synthesis is the combination of one or more constituent elements into a single or unified entity. Similarly, in history to synthesize is to create a meaningful whole out of various pieces of information. *Which ONE of the questions and statements below would be least likely to prompt an answer that draws on synthesis?*

1. How were entire lifestyles and cultures destroyed due to the arrival of the European conquerors?

2. Explain the ways in which Italian trade monopoly, religious fervor, and economic motivations contributed to the rise of the Age of Exploration.

3. True or false: Germs caused more suffering to indigenous peoples than guns did.

4. Analyze the impact of the silver trade on the Spanish economy, European governments generally, the colonies in the Americas, and the global economic system.

Writing a generalization is one way to sum up information, but generalizing is sometimes justly criticized for leading to overly broad statement. To use it effectively, provide solid evidence to support your conclusions. *Which choice best supports the generalization below?*

During the exploration of the Americas by Western Europeans, demography (population patterns, shifts, and changes) played an important role in the European conquest of the Americas.

a. Up until the Europeans arrived, indigenous Americans had not been exposed to smallpox, influenza, and measles, which are estimated to have killed 50 percent of the indigenous population.

b. The indigenous people of Mexico knew nothing of pigs and cows until the Europeans introduced them.

c. Western Europeans traveled to the Americas mostly to make money, but some also had religious motivations.

Africa in the Early Colonial Period

We cannot reckon how great the damage is, since the mentioned merchants are taking every day our natives, sons of the land and the sons of our noblemen and vassals and our relatives, because the thieves and men of bad conscience grab them wishing to have the things and wares of this Kingdom.

—King Afonso, in a letter to the King of Portugal (1526)

In the quote above, King Afonso of the Kongo Kingdom was writing about the terrible devastation that the Trans-Atlantic slave trade wrought on his kingdom. The Atlantic slave trade was a pivotal development in the history of the African continent during the Early Modern Era. It contributed to the decline of many West African societies, but it also had ripple effects across the entire African continent; the changes it brought would make African societies of the year 1450 almost unrecognizable by 1750.

African Civilizations at the Beginning of the Era

As discussed in Chapter 9, the era from 600 to 1450 brought considerable change to Africa. South of the Sahara, the introduction of bananas from Southeast Asia spurred great population growth. In North Africa and in the trading cities along the east coast, Islam spread rapidly as a result of the phenomenal growth of the Abbasid Empire, centered in Baghdad, and the activities of Muslim merchants. Interactions among various cultures inside and outside of Africa brought extensive trade and new technology to the continent. (Test Prep: Create a timeline of the main changes in Africa during the years 600 to 1450. See pages 161–172.)

Songhay Empire The Songhay people were the main ethnic group in and around the city of Gao on the Niger River. Gao was conquered and the Songhay were absorbed into the Mali Empire. As the Mali Empire began to decline in the early 1400s, Songhay gained its independence. In 1464, *Sunni Ali* became ruler of Songhay and began to aggressively expand into territory on both sides of the Niger River. He took over Timbuktu with its famed center of Islamic scholarship. Although a Muslim himself, he instituted repressive

THE AFRICAN SLAVE TRADE

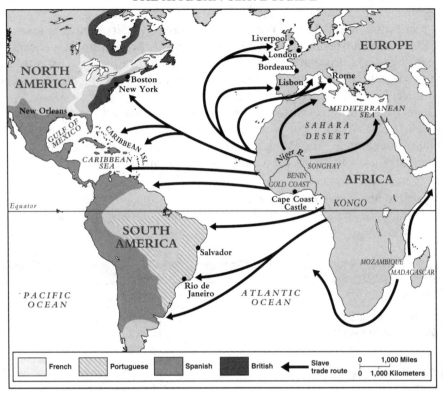

policies against some of the scholars there, particularly those associated with peoples he had overthrown in his empire-building campaign. By the 1480s, he had built an empire that surpassed that of the Mali Empire before him. The cause of Sunni Ali's death in 1492 is uncertain. According to some, he drowned while crossing the Niger River; others contend that he was killed by his sister's son in a bid for power. The Songhay Empire would last for 100 years, until its defeat by Moroccan forces wielding firearms, uncommon weapons for armies in Sub-Saharan Africa at that time.

Europeans Arrive Certain regions of East and West Africa were the targets of European conquest during the late fifteenth century. Portuguese ruler Prince Henry the Navigator was keenly interested in navigational technology. He financed expeditions along Africa's Atlantic Coast and around the Cape of Good Hope, exploring African coastal communities and kingdoms before other European powers.

With the cooperation of local rulers, first Portuguese and then other European traders set up trading posts along Africa's coasts. Some local rulers traded slaves to the Europeans in exchange for gunpowder and cannons, giving those coastal governments a military advantage when battling neighboring villages. Thus, many African city-states grew wealthy by agreeing to sell enslaved Africans to European slavers. *Dahomey*, in particular, grew stronger because it raided other villages for slaves and sold them to European merchants.

In central West Africa, Portuguese explorers, traders, and missionaries made inroads into the Kongo and Benin kingdoms. Artwork from these societies bears signs of European as well as African cultural influences. As early as the sixteenth century, Benin artisans incorporated images of the European "intruder" into their carvings and sculptures.

In 1498, Portuguese explorer *Vasco da Gama* invaded the Swahili city-states of East Africa, most of which were thriving commercial centers in the Indian Ocean trade. The Portuguese took over trade in Kilwa, Mombasa, and other city-states, throwing the region into a devastating decline.

Literature As in many other regions of the world, Africa produced influential literary works in the thirteenth, fourteenth, and fifteenth centuries. The oral history passed along by griots later became the basis for written poetry and novels.

Developments in Literature			
Works	**Country**	**Dates**	**Significance**
Collected works of William Shakespeare	England	1564–1616	Set the precedent for European styles in prose, poetry, and drama
***Don Quixote* by Cervantes**	Spain	1547–1616	Was the first great novel in European literature
Epic of Sundiata	Mali Empire in West Africa	1210–1260	Spead the story orally of the founder of the Mali Empire for generations before being written down
Journey to the West	China	1592	Used Buddhist, Taoist, and Confucian symbolism in the format of a novel
Kabuki Theatre	Japan	17th century	Dramatized love stories, conflicts, and other aspects of Japanese culture in a highly stylized and flashy form

Source: Wikimedia Commons, Adam Jones, Ph.D.

Source: Wikimedia Commons, Eupator

Source:

Before the use of gunpowder weapons, walls provided defense. Remnants of these defensive walls still stand throughout the world, including in West Africa (in Benin, above), Central Asia (in Kyrgyzstan, below left), and in East Asia (China, below right).

Africans and the Atlantic Slave Trade

Slavery had existed in Africa long before Europeans sought slave labor for their investments in the Americas. For example, in many societies, the entire community shared the land. In order to establish positions of wealth and power, individuals not only showcased the property they owned, but also showcased their slaves. Europeans were also not the first foreigners to seek out African labor. As discussed earlier, Arab merchants during the Post-Classical Era (600–1450) often bought slaves during their travels to the Swahili Coast of East Africa. However, it was the Atlantic slave trade that wreaked the most havoc on African societies. (Test Prep: Compose a graphic organizer that compares the forms of slavery during Sub-Saharan Africa's Early Colonial Period with slavery from 600 to 1450. See pages 161–172.)

Why Africans? Several factors converged to make Africa a target for slave raids by Europeans after 1450. As discussed in the previous chapter, slavery in Latin America and the Caribbean began toward the end of the sixteenth century, when European *conquistadores* sought fortunes in gold, silver, and sugar. Land was plentiful, but labor to make the land profitable was scarce.

Europeans initially forced indigenous people to do the hard labor of mining and farming, but European diseases wiped out large portions of these coerced laborers. The indigenous slaves who survived found it easy to escape bondage because they were more familiar with the territory, had social networks that could protect them, and could easily camouflage themselves within the native population. Repeated efforts to enslave Native Americans failed, although other efforts to coerce labor did have some success.

Labor for Plantations In North America, plantation owners recruited European indentured servants who would come to work for a specified period in exchange for passage, room, and board. However, most of these people were unaccustomed to the backbreaking agricultural working conditions and the climate of the Americas. In addition, indentured servants were required to work only for about seven years. If they survived their indenture, they became free laborers. Thus, landowners did not think of indigenous captives and European indentured servants as ideal workers.

During this era, Europeans sought sources of inexpensive labor in the Americas. Western European countries such as Portugal, Spain, and England were developing their naval technology, but Portugal was ahead of the others. In West Africa during the latter part of the 1400s, Portuguese trading fleets arrived in the Kingdom of the Kongo seeking slaves. Initially they took the enslaved Africans back to Europe to work as domestic servants.

Triangular Trade The Europeans' desire for slaves in the Americas coupled with Portugal's "discovery" of West Africa meant that Africa became the source for new labor. African slaves soon became part of a complex global trading system that was called the *Atlantic trading system* or the *triangular trade* based on a trade cycle with three "legs." One version of triangular trade involved the transport of European manufactured goods such as firearms to West Africa, and from there enslaved Africans were shipped to the Americas. The final leg involved the transport of American tobacco and other cash crops to Europe.

Once other European nations noticed the success that the Portuguese enjoyed with sugar plantations in Brazil, the English, Dutch, and French worked to replicate that success in the Caribbean; by the 1700s, sugar production and rum (made from sugar) were financing fortunes in Britain, and to a lesser extent in France and the Netherlands.

Capture and Shipment of Slaves to the Americas Capturing Africans for slavery was invariably a violent affair. When African leaders along the coast realized that their kingdoms could economically benefit from the slave trade, they invaded neighboring societies in a quest for slaves to take back to the coast. At times, African rulers were also willing to hand over individuals from the lower rungs of their own societies, such as prisoners of war, servants, or criminals. However, as King Afonso suggested to the King of Portugal in the quotation that opens this chapter, slave raids were not easily controllable. Though he had initially allowed slave trading in his kingdom, he had no intention of giving up his society's elite to slavery, nor did he want Kongo to be depopulated. King Afonso also saw that his authority was undermined because his subjects were able to trade slaves for European goods without his involvement. Before the Europeans came, he had been able to control all trade in his domain.

Captive Africans, swept away from their families, were taken to holding pens in West Africa known as *barracoons,* or "slave castles." The modern-day country of Ghana has preserved these "Points of No Return," where thousands upon thousands of Africans said goodbye to their homeland for the last time. Today, tourists can visit one such holding prison—the so-called House of Slaves on *Ile de Gorée* (Gorée Island), on the coast of Senegal.

From these holding pens, slave traders next crammed their captives into the dank cargo section of a ship, providing them little water, food, or even room for movement. The grueling journey across the Atlantic was known as the *Middle Passage*, because it was the middle part of the captives' journey. Many captured Africans staged rebellions en route, but most revolts were crushed. (The 1997 film *Amistad* provides an example of a successful Middle-Passage rebellion in 1839, in which Africans took control of the Spanish slave ship *Amistad*.) During the journey to the Americas, which usually took about six weeks, up to half of a ship's captives might die. Historians estimate that over the hundreds of years of the Atlantic slave trade from the early 1500s to the mid-nineteenth century, approximately 25 percent of all African captives perished before reaching the Americas.

African Presence in the Americas

African cultures were not completely lost once captives arrived in the Americas. In fact, during the *African Diaspora* (dispersion of Africans out of Africa), enslaved Africans managed to retain certain aspects of their cultures in their new environments.

Languages With a few exceptions, Africans were not able to transplant their languages to the Americas. The captives were spirited away from their communities, and they soon found themselves on ships among captives from all across West Africa (and, on some slave ships, from across East Africa as well). Since captives were taken from myriad African cultural groups, most did not share a common language. Understandably, they found it difficult, if not impossible, to communicate en route. Because of their linguistic isolation on the ships and in the Americas, most Africans lost their languages after a generation.

In spite of this forced isolation from their cultures, West Africans managed to combine European colonizers' languages (English, Spanish, French, or Portuguese, for example) with parts of their West African languages and grammatical patterns to create new languages known broadly as *creole.*

Because the Caribbean islands had a larger concentration of enslaved Africans than did North America, creole languages dominate there even today. In the United States, which had a smaller percentage of Africans in comparison to the total population, few examples of creole languages exist. One notable exception is the *Gullah* or *Geechee* language, of South Carolina and Georgia, in places where slaves once composed 75 percent of the population.

Religions African religions in the Americas provide powerful examples of religious syncretism, or the combining of different religious beliefs and practices. Africans melded aspects of Christianity that were introduced to them (or imposed upon them) with their West African religious traditions, such as drumming, dancing, and a belief in spirits that could "possess," or take over and act through a person, often in evil ways. The traditions of *Santeria* in Cuba, *Vodun* in Haiti, and *Candomblé* in Brazil were all combinations of Christian and traditional African religions. Enslaved Africans in the United States also laid the roots for the African-American church, a hybrid of Christianity and African spiritual traditions that remains one of the oldest and most stable institutions in African-American communities today.

Some of the enslaved Africans, maybe 10 percent, practiced Islam. While some of the men who sailed with Columbus may have been Muslims, these enslaved Africans became the first significant presence of Islam in the Americas.

Music Africans brought their music with them. Today's music, including gospel, blues, jazz, rock-n-roll, hip-hop, samba, reggae, and country music, are all influenced by African music. The syncopated rhythms and percussion in contemporary music can be traced back to West African musical traditions. Perhaps many African descendants maintained their musical traditions because enslaved Africans in America used music as a means of survival, singing tunes from home to help them endure long workdays as well as to communicate with other slaves, such as when planning an escape. They blended European Christian music with their own religious songs, known today as Negro spirituals— essential elements of American folk music history. Slaves also invented the banjo, which is very similar to stringed instruments found in West Africa.

Food Africans brought rice and okra (a green vegetable) to the Americas, as well as their knowledge of how to prepare these foods. The dish known as *gumbo,* popular in the southern United States, has roots in African cooking. With influences on language, music, food, and much more, African culture has had a profound and lasting impact on life in the Americas.

Effects of the Slave Trade on Africa

The Atlantic slave trade affected Africa in social, economic, and political ways. Those most affected were the peoples and civilizations of West Africa in present-day Ghana and Benin, from which most Africans were kidnapped or sold. Gender distributions in those regions became severely imbalanced, because more than two-thirds of those taken were males. The resulting predominance of women prompted a rise in *polygyny* (the taking of more than one wife) and forced women to assume duties that had traditionally been men's jobs.

Economically, African societies that conducted slave raids, such as the *Dahomey* and the *Oyo*, became richer from selling their captives to Europeans. This trade also had political effects, because when a society like Dahomey exchanged slaves for guns, its raiders easily took advantage of rival societies that had no firearms. Without firearms, it was hard for neighboring groups to resist slave raids, so raiding societies became even richer and more fortified with firearms. Intergroup warfare thus became more common and bloodier as a result of the slave trade.

The Trans-Atlantic slave trade permanently weakened several West African kingdoms (such as Kongo), largely because of the violence that it caused among their societies, but also because African slave-raiding kingdoms became economically dependent on goods from Europe. Such societies were slow to develop more complex economies in which they produced their own goods. Thus, the slave trade set the stage for European imperialism of the late nineteenth century. European colonizers would have an easier time further conquering the African continent in that era. (To learn about later European conquests in Africa, see pages 497–498.)

While the Atlantic trading system weakened Africa in many ways, it also ultimately spurred population growth through an improved diet. The Columbian Exchange introduced new crops to the continent, such as the American crops maize, peanuts, and manioc (also known as yucca or cassava), which became staples in the African diet.

The End of the Atlantic Slave Trade

Due to diverse factors, the slave trade ended in most places during the nineteenth century. In Europe, particularly Great Britain, political and social changes would drive the push for *abolition*. Enlightenment philosophers of the eighteenth century, such as Rousseau, wrote passionately about the right to freedom and the need for equality among all human beings. Enlightenment ideals formed the foundation for political revolutions in Europe and the Americas. Many intellectuals felt that slavery could not be reconciled with the Enlightenment values of democracy and equality, and thus the abolition movement was born. (See pages 394–413 for more information about the Enlightenment.)

People of European descent were not solely responsible for ending the slave trade in the Americas. Slave revolts were common, especially in those locations where enslaved Africans outnumbered free Europeans. In fact, slave revolts led by Toussaint L'Ouverture in the French colony of *Saint Domingue* in the late eighteenth century were so successful that they brought the end of slavery to the island in 1804, giving the newly independent nation of Haiti the distinction of being the first country in the Americas to end slavery. By 1888, slavery would be abolished throughout the Americas, usually through a gradual process of abolition. Haiti and the United States were the only two countries to end slavery through a full-scale war.

The Indian Ocean Slave Trade

Enslaved Africans were also sold from the eastern part of the continent. By land routes or by sea, slaves from Eastern Africa were sold to buyers in Northern Africa, the Middle East, and India. Many were transported to the islands off the southeast coast of Africa, such a as Madagascar.

HISTORICAL PERSPECTIVES: WHAT WAS THE SLAVE TRADE'S IMPACT?

Historians continue to study the impact of the Trans-Atlantic slave trade. In his book *Capitalism and Slavery* (Chapel Hill: University of North Carolina, 1944), historian Eric Williams, who was also the first prime minister of Trinidad and Tobago, posited that without slavery in the Americas, the European Industrial Revolution and capitalism as we know it would never have existed. Williams was thus one of the first to draw connections between the wealth of Western European countries and their involvement in the Atlantic slave trade. Thirty years later, Eugene Genovese's seminal work, *Roll, Jordan, Roll: The World the Slaves Made* (NY: Pantheon, 1974) described in great detail the social and cultural history of slavery, primarily in North America.

One public debate around African history in the Americas concerns the extent to which peoples of African descent actually retained remnants of African culture. The Black English controversy is a notable example of this debate. Linguists who study Creole and Black English have traced the grammatical patterns back to West Africa. For example, many West African languages do not conjugate the verb "to be," and linguists also observe this lack of conjugation among some people of African descent in the Americas. The validity of Black English as a dialect sparked a huge controversy in the media, touching on the question of whether Africa had a central place in the discussion about African-American history and culture.

Author Joseph Holloway addressed that issue in his book *Africanisms in American Culture* (Bloomington: Indiana University Press, 1999), showcasing research on the aspects of African culture that continue to exist in the Americas in music, religion, and other areas, with particular case studies of New Orleans and of Gullah culture in South Carolina. The book provides a unique perspective on the many connections among the cultures of the African Diaspora.

Most recently, in 2014, historian Edward E. Baptist published *Slavery: The Half That Has Never Been Told*. Baptist argued that the expansion of slavery and cotton production in the United States in the nineteenth century provided the foundation for the country's rise to its status as a global industrial power.

MULTIPLE-CHOICE QUESTIONS

1. The Middle Passage involved which of the following new connections in the era from 1450 to 1750?

   (A) It was the route of enslaved Africans from the interior of Africa to the African coast.

   (B) It was the voyage of enslaved Africans across the Atlantic Ocean to the Americas.

   (C) It was the triangular voyage of slave merchants between Europe, Africa, and the Americas.

   (D) It was the route of enslaved Africans leaving slave ships in the Americas and going to plantations.

2. Which statement is true about the slave trade in Africa?

   (A) The Atlantic slave trade was the beginning of slavery in Africa.

   (B) Portuguese traders were the first to capture slaves in Africa.

   (C) Slavery existed in Africa long before the arrival of Europeans.

   (D) Arab merchants of the Post-Classical Era were the first to trade for slaves in Africa.

3. What was one reason Africans became a prime target for slave traders?

   (A) Africans knew how to grow tobacco.

   (B) Africans were willing to travel to the Americas.

   (C) Africans had no prior experience with agricultural labor.

   (D) Africans did not succumb to illnesses common among Europeans.

Question 4 refers to the following image.

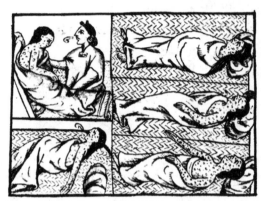

Source: Wikimedia Commons / CJLL Wright

4. The impact of the events portrayed in the image above led to

   (A) large-scale reduction in the population of indigenous peoples in the Americas

   (B) the violent capture of Africans to be sold as slaves in Africa

   (C) the harsh treatment of enslaved Africans on the voyage across the Atlantic

   (D) the enslavement of indigenous Americans by European *conquistadores*

5. What was a major effect in Africa of the Trans-Atlantic slave trade?

   (A) Most slave-raiding African groups became poorer because of the competition with other groups.

   (B) Warfare among African groups decreased in frequency and severity.

   (C) The influx of money caused economic growth.

   (D) The ratio of males to females became unbalanced.

6. What was the main cause of Haiti becoming the first land in the Americas to abolish slavery?

(A) political and social changes in Europe

(B) slave revolts there in the late eighteenth century

(C) slave revolts on ships during the Middle Passage

(D) the abolition movement in the United States

7. One similarity between the Swahili Coast and the West Coast of Africa is that local rulers on both coasts

(A) gained power by trading slaves for firearms

(B) used gunpowder and cannons to battle invading Europeans

(C) abandoned trade with other African kingdoms to trade with Europeans

(D) refused to participate in the slave trade that Europeans encouraged

Question 8 refers to the table below.

Destination of Enslaved Africans by Colonial Region	
Destination	**Percentage**
Portuguese Colonies	39%
British West Indian Colonies	18%
Spanish Colonies	18%
French Colonies	14%
British Mainland Colonies	6%
Dutch West Indian Colonies	2%
Other	3%

Source: Stephen D. Behrendt, et al. *Africana: The Encyclopedia of the African and African American Experience.*

8. Which statement is supported by the table above?

(A) Most enslaved Africans landed in regions that produced labor-intensive crops such as sugar.

(B) The labor needs of the Spanish Empire and British West Indian Colonies were the same.

(C) Slaves in the Dutch West Indies served primarily as domestic servants.

(D) About six percent of the population of British West Indian Colonies were enslaved Africans.

9. Which statement explains why Portugal became the first European nation to engage in widespread slave trading along the West Coast of Africa?

(A) The Portuguese were pioneers in gunpowder and cannon technology.

(B) The Portuguese were more skilled in setting up trading posts.

(C) Only the Portuguese were willing to trade cannons for slaves.

(D) The Portuguese were pioneers in naval technology.

10. Santeria in Cuba, Vodun in Haiti, and Candomblé in Brazil were all

(A) African religions that were the roots of today's African-American church

(B) African religions that included the belief in spirits that could "possess" a person

(C) Syncretic religions that combined aspects of Christianity with African religious beliefs and practices

(D) Syncretic religions that combined aspects of African religious tradition, such as drumming and dancing

CONTINUITY AND CHANGE-OVER-TIME ESSAY QUESTIONS

Directions: You are to answer the following question. You should spend 5 minutes organizing or outlining your essay. Write an essay that:

- Has a relevant thesis and supports that thesis with appropriate historical evidence.
- Addresses all parts of the question.
- Uses world historical context to show continuities and changes over time.
- Analyzes the process of continuity and change over time.

1. Analyze the continuities and changes on the African continent from 1450 to 1750 in one of the following areas:
   - Political and military power
   - Economic power

Questions for Additional Practice

2   Analyze the continuities and changes in networks of communication and exchange in Sub-Saharan Africa from the Post-Classical Era (600–1450, see Chapter 9) through the Early Colonial Era (1450–1750).

3. Analyze the continuities and changes in political power and the building of states in Sub-Saharan Africa from the Post-Classical Era (600–1450, See Chapter 9) through the Early Colonial Era (1450–1750).

COMPARATIVE ESSAY QUESTIONS

Directions: You are to answer the following question. You should spend 5 minutes organizing or outlining your essay. Write an essay that:

- Has a relevant thesis and supports that thesis with appropriate historical evidence.
- Addresses all parts of the question.
- Makes direct, relevant comparisons.
- Analyzes relevant reasons for similarities and differences.

1. Analyze the similarities and differences between slavery in Africa and in the Americas from 1450 to 1750.

Questions for Additional Practice

2. Analyze the similarities and differences in the culture of Africans living in Sub-Saharan Africa and enslaved Africans who had been sent to the Americas as part of the triangular trade.

3. Analyze the similarities and differences between slavery in Sub-Saharan Africa during the Post-Classical Era (600–1450) with slavery during the Early Colonial Era (1450–1750).

To correlate is to show a relationship between two or more things, events, people, or eras. For example, a historian might correlate evidence of climate change with the collapse of a civilization. *Select the statements below that express correlations.*

1. In the West Africa Empire of Songhay, Islam was related to economic interests; espousing Islam made it easier to do business with Muslim traders.

2. Prince Henry the Navigator financed expeditions along Africa's Atlantic Coast and around the Cape of Good Hope.

3. Coastal governments that traded in slaves had the wealth to buy firearms and gain military advantage over governments that did not engage in the slave trade.

4. Europeans were not the first foreigners to seek African labor; Arab merchants during the post-classical period bought slaves during their African travels.

Part of creating a strong argument is acknowledging and responding to evidence that does not support your thesis. *Identify the statements below that could be used as evidence AGAINST the thesis that new technology and products damaged Africa.*

1. Guns promoted the slave trade, which created problems for Africa's economic development.

2. Improvements in naval technology made shipping enslaved Africans to the Americas less expensive.

3. Imported manufactured goods from Europe slowed Africa's economic development

4. New food crops introduced into Africa from the Americas caused the population to grow.

18

Russia Unifies and Expands

I would not have guessed in 1700 that Reason, one day, would come to Moscow as the voice of a princess born in Germany. . .

—letter to Catherine the Great from the French writer Voltaire

Western Europeans were long unsure what to think of Russia: was Russia more European in its outlook and character, or was it more Asian? Not until modern times was there any agreement about where to place the geographical boundary between the European and Asian continents. Russia sprawled on both sides of the boundary finally agreed upon—the *Ural Mountains.*

Looking East

While Russia before 1750 was undoubtedly Christian, it was not the Roman Catholic or Protestant Christianity of the West. Instead, *Eastern Orthodoxy* had taken root in Russia. The rulers of Kievan Rus modelled the government and religious institutions on Constantinople, the seat of the Orthodox Byzantine Empire. This model was adopted by the princes of Moscovy. In time the tsars (Russian rulers) established the *Russian Orthodox Church* as a way to unite the people behind their leadership, claiming that they ruled by divine right through the Church. (Test Prep: Compose a brief outline of the connections between Russia and the Byzantine Empire. See pages 137–140.)

In the period when most of Europe was in the throes of the Reformation and the Renaissance, Russia experienced neither—the *Mongols* had tight control over the city-states and kingdoms that made up Russia and no such renaissance, or "rebirth," took place. However, Russian princes gained wealth and power as tax collectors for the Mongols, collecting what Russians had to pay in tribute (a sum paid in acknowledgement of submission). Eventually, their local dominance would give them the capacity to shake off the Mongols and become autonomous. (To learn about Mongol control of Russia, see pages 244–245.)

Russia was also in a pivotal position when it came to trade. It was able to exchange goods and services with other cultures farther east and west. To the east, Russian expansion into Siberia resulted in a robust *fur trade*, giving Russia an important export to Europe and China. Russia even gathered furs in North America and marketed them along the Pacific Coast as far south as

San Francisco. To the west, through its port of *Arkhangelsk (Archangel)* on the northwest coast, Russia could then import cloth from England, since trade agreements with the English had been drawn up in 1555. From the markets on the *Silk Roads* to the south, Russia could import silk from India and Persia. Exports from Russia in exchange included grain, leather, iron, hemp, wood, potash, pitch, and tar (for shipbuilding). In addition, Russian honey and caviar became famous worldwide. By the time of Peter the Great at the end of the seventeenth century, Russia would also bring in technicians from Western Europe to oversee the building of Russia's first shipyards.

Regardless of its expansion to the east, however, Russia remained tightly linked to Europe. Its capital—whether Kiev, St. Petersburg, or Moscow—was located in Europe. Although a product of Mongol influence from central Asia to the east, Russia was also a product of Europe as a result of Viking invasions and trading. Most important, rulers of the Russia Empire began to look west, first for technology and later for the ideals of the *Enlightenment*. (Test Prep: Create a graphic organizer showing Viking influences on Russia. See pages 221–222.)

Ivan III

Key figures often seem to make history, and historians see that pattern in Russia, which had a line of powerful, charismatic, and autocratic rulers. (This pattern continued into the twenty-first century with the Russian leader Vladimir Putin.) One such colorful leader was *Ivan III* (ruled 1462–1505), also known as "Ivan the Great." This prince of Muscovy (Moscow) threw off the "Mongol yoke" by refusing to pay tribute to the Mongols at a time when the Mongols were not powerful enough to enforce the collection. To legitimize his power, he unofficially called himself *tsar*. This term, derived from the Latin word *Caesar,* gave Ivan additional prestige through an assumed link to the Roman Empire. Ivan then married Zoe, the niece of the last Byzantine emperor, whose empire had fallen in 1453. This union gave Ivan's rule the religious legitimacy of the Orthodox Church.

Ivan III gained control over and united various Russian city-states, including longtime rival Novgorod, thereby gaining even more prestige and power. Through wars and diplomacy, he tripled the size of his state and became one of the longest-reigning rulers of Russia.

Moscow Physical changes in the city of *Moscow* showed the growing status and power of Russian rulers. Ivan rebuilt the walls of the *Kremlin*, the central citadel, adding towers designed by Italian architects. Located on a river in the midst of a forest, Moscow became a major trade center for furs and timber. *Kiev*, the location of a slave market, had formerly been the major link between trade routes that stretched from Scandinavia to the Islamic and Byzantine areas in the south and east. Kiev decreased in importance as Moscow's prominence rose. Later changes in Moscow would reflect the growing status of the tsars. (For more about Kiev, see pages 137–140.)

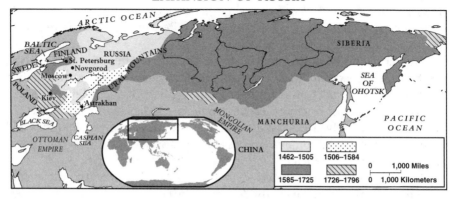

Social Classes Social hierarchy in Moscow was almost static—much as it had been in Kievan Russia earlier. The noble landowning class, the *boyars*, stood at the top of the social pyramid. Below them were the merchants. Last and most numerous were the peasants, who would gradually sink more and more deeply into debt and, as a result, into serfdom. *Serfs* were peasants who received a plot of land and protection from a noble. In return, the serf was bound to that land and had little personal freedom. Transfers of land ownership to another noble included ownership of the serfs on that land.

The boyar class would experience tensions with the rulers similar to the tensions between nobles and rulers in Western Europe. Boyars of Novgorod had opposed Ivan's expansionist policies, so Ivan punished them after his forces defeated Novgorod. Ivan confiscated the lands of his boyar opponents and forced them and their families to move to Moscow, where he could keep an eye on them.

Ivan IV

Another colorful leader was *Ivan IV* (ruled 1547–1584), called "Ivan the Terrible." Crowned tsar in 1547, he immediately set about to expand the Russian border eastward, first by taking control of the khanates of *Kazan*, *Astrakhan*, and *Siberia* held by the descendants of the "Golden Horde," the Mongolian conquerors. This expansion came to rely more and more upon the use of gunpowder. Ivan brought a Dane to Moscow in 1552 to help instruct his men in the use of land mines in the campaign. To commemorate the victories over Kazan and Astrakhan, Ivan commissioned the building of *St. Basil's Cathedral* (still standing in Red Square, Moscow), which served as a visual reminder to the nation that the tsar and the Church were united. The Russian government made great efforts to convert the population around Kazan to Orthodox Christianity, but most people remained Muslim.

Into Siberia Wanting to expand east to control fur trade, Ivan IV allowed the Stroganovs, major Russian landowners, to hire bands of fierce peasant warriors known as *Cossacks* to fight the local tribes and the Siberian khan. The

Stroganovs' forces were successful, gaining control of the *Volga River*, which flows into the *Caspian Sea*. Possessing this outlet to the sea, Moscow could trade directly with Persia and the Ottoman Empire without having to deal with the strong forces of the Crimean Tartars.

Russia would continue moving east into Siberia after the reign of Ivan IV. Fur traders and militias defeated one indigenous tribe after another. Missionaries followed, converting many to the Eastern Orthodox faith, although the local shamans, or religious leaders, continued to have influence. By 1639, the Russians had advanced east as far as the Pacific Ocean. Explorations and fur trading expeditions continued across the Pacific to *Alaska* (1741) and down the coast of North America to California (1814).

Russia's expansion eastward shared many features with the movement of Europeans westward in North America. In both case, the fur trade was important, and as people advanced they spread Christianity. And in both cases, indigenous people put up resistance, but succumbed to guns and diseases.

Violence and Expansion To control the boyars at home, Ivan established a paramilitary force loyal to him called the *Oprichnina*. Dressed in black and traveling quickly on horseback, the members showed fierce loyalty to Ivan. They were drawn from lower-level bureaucrats and merchants to assure their loyalty to Ivan rather than to the boyars. The Oprichnina's methods would be reflected later in the development of the Russian secret police.

After killing his son in a fit of rage, Ivan sank deeply into paranoia. He died in 1584, leaving Russia without a strong heir. Having killed not only his own son but also the inhabitants of entire cities, Ivan earned his name "the Terrible." But in spite of his reputation, he did add much territory to the Russian state and expanded its trade opportunities.

Time of Troubles and the Romanovs

In 1603, without a strong autocrat or family in control, Russia entered a phase historians call the *Time of Troubles*. Russia was nearly in a state of anarchy until 1613, when the national assembly, called the *Zemsky Sobor* (Assembly of the Land), chose Michael Romanov as leader, initiating the *Romanov Dynasty* that would lead Russia until 1917. The Romanovs held autocratic control, and (among other accomplishments) they pushed the borders of Russia east to Mongolia. In 1689, China's Qing Dynasty signed a border treaty with the Russians in the eastern town of Nerchinsk, Russia, to confirm this new border.

Peter the Great

Under the Romanovs, three main groups in Russia had conflicting desires and agendas: the Church, bent on conserving traditional values and beliefs; the boyars, desiring to gain and hold power; and members of the tsar's royal family. The rise to power of *Peter I*, also known as Peter the Great (ruled 1682–1725), illustrates these conflicting ambitions. First, to gain full control of the throne, Peter had to defeat his half-sister Sophia and her supporters, a boyar-led elite military corps called the *Streltsy*. He consolidated power by forcing Sophia into a convent. Later, after the Streltsy rebelled against Peter's reign, he temporarily disbanded them and gradually integrated them into Russia's regular army.

The Orthodox Church and Reforms Next, Peter moved against the Orthodox Church. The Church had long been the force unifying the Russian people and the tsars, who claimed to rule by divine right. Peter confirmed his power over the Church by abolishing the position of *patriarch*, the head of the Church, and incorporating the Church into the government. In place of the patriarch, he established the *Holy Synod*, composed of clergymen overseen by a secular official who answered to the tsar. Peter raised the minimum age for men to become eligible to be monks to 50, preferring that the young serve first as soldiers. Peter's reforms were not welcomed by many peasants and *Old Believers*, a sect that opposed earlier reforms.

Window on the West Peter visited Western Europe in 1697 to observe military and naval technology. He dressed simply and travelled under an assumed name. He was unable to keep a low profile, however, simply because of his great height—6 feet, 9 inches. His interest in European technology led him to hire technicians from Germany and elsewhere to help build Russia's military and naval power.

Russia's first use of this new military power was to seize lands on the Baltic Sea from Sweden. This conquest gave Russia its own warm-water port on the Baltic—*St. Petersburg*. Peter then moved the Russian capital from Moscow to St. Petersburg so he could keep watch on the boyars there, who were doing their required state service by working in his government.

The new city became a testament to Peter's determination to have his own capital. Architects laid out streets in a rectangular grid, unlike the irregular pattern of Moscow and other older cities. Peasants and Swedish prisoners of war were conscripted to work, draining marshes and building streets and government structures. In the mid-eighteenth century, workers would build the tsars' in-town home in St. Petersburg, the famous *Winter Palace*.

More of Peter's Reforms Peter wished the aristocracy of Russia to assume the manners and customs of the aristocrats he had seen in Western Europe. He insisted that beards be cut and sleeves be tailored to the style of Western dress. Often his manner of enforcement was extremely dictatorial, and he is said to have personally enforced his edicts by cutting some beards and sleeves himself. He also insisted that the boyars have their sons educated. In 1714, he introduced compulsory education in mathematics and geometry for sons of all nobility and government officials. He also established a school of medicine and a naval academy. These reforms did not reach the lower classes, however, where traditional customs remained strong.

Women benefitted somewhat from Peter's cultural outlook. He demanded that their traditional veils be removed and they be allowed to join men for some social events. He also insisted that they be allowed to marry of their own free will.

Peter established new industries owned by the state, especially shipyards in St. Petersburg and iron mines in the Ural Mountains. He also encouraged private industries. He brought in Western European naval engineers to build ships according to Western models.

When industrialization failed to bring in the revenue Peter needed for his military ventures, he raised taxes and began to compel workers to work in the shipyards—a sort of urban extension of serfdom. In 1718, the tax on land in Russia was replaced by a tax on heads (individuals), and peasants became more oppressed than ever. And yet, Peter simultaneously promoted men according to merit rather than social class. A new *Table of Ranks* listed military and governmental positions that could be filled by the best-qualified persons regardless of social status.

Peter reorganized the Russian government by creating *provinces* (first eight and later 50 administrative divisions). Provincial officials received a salary, replacing the old system of local officials "feeding off the land" (getting money through bribes, fees, and taxes). Another government reform was the creation of a senate, a council to advise government officials when Peter was away at war.

Nevertheless, Peter's reforms did not change the status and outlook of the majority of Russians to any great extent. In fact, many peasants sank deeper into serfdom as a result of increased taxation and forced labor on state projects such as shipyards. While the Russian upper class enjoyed reading French novels, speaking French to one another, and looking to the court of Louis XIV for fashion, not much improvement was seen for the lower classes.

Catherine the Great

Catherine II, also known as "Catherine the Great" (ruled 1762–1796), arrived in Russia as an educated, young, German-born Protestant. Her marriage to Peter III of Russia put Catherine in a position to take the throne after his death in 1762. Conspiracy theories abound about the death of Peter, but whatever its cause, Catherine became a powerful tsarina in her own right. In preparation to rule, Catherine had not only learned Russian but also had joined the Orthodox Church, illustrating once again how Russian rulers legitimized their power through union with the Church.

Catherine's education was apparent in all she did, from corresponding with the Western European thinkers known as the *philosophes* to attempting to codify Russian laws and end the state's use of torture. She met with resistance from the boyars on her reforms, however. Needing their support in case of peasant revolts, she gave in on some important revisions of the law. For example, in 1785 she finally exempted the boyars from paying taxes and performing the state service that had been required ever since Peter the Great's reign. After numerous failed attempts at rebellion by the peasants, Catherine allowed landowners to exert more control on the movement of their serfs. Ultimately, her enlightened principles gave way to her need for despotic control.

Eurasian Land Empires			
Empire	Important Leaders	Peak Period	Ethnic and Religious Conflicts
Ottoman Region: Southwest Asia, North Africa, Southeast Europe Key City: Constantinople	• Mehmed II • Suleiman I	1517–1699	The Ottomans, though tolerant of cultural diversity, ruled over diverse ethnic groups.
Mughal Region: India Key Cities: Agra, Lahore, Delhi	• Babar • Akbar • Shah Jahan • Aurangzeb	1556–1605	The Mughals were Muslims and they had conflicts with the Hindu-majority in the country.
Russian Region: North Europe and Asia Key Cities: St. Petersburg, Kiev, Moscow	• Ivan the Great • Ivan the Terrible • Peter the Great • Catherine the Great	1584–1682	The Russian rulers tried unsuccessfully to assimilate ethnic groups such as Ukrainians and Belarusians.
Manchu Region: East Asia Key City: Beijing	• Kangxi • Qianlong	1644–1690	The Manchus were an ethnic minority and were detested by most of the Chinese they ruled.

Expansion of the Empire Catherine II oversaw an significant expansion of the Russian Empire, adding Russia to the list of significant Eurasian land empires (see chart above). To the south, through the Russo-Turkish Wars (1768–1774 and 1787–1792), she gained the northern shore of the Black Sea and annexed the Crimean Peninsula from the Ottoman Empire. These lands secured for Russia a key trade route through the Black Sea and up the Danube River. To the east, Catherine expanded into the steppes beyond the Ural Mountains and along the Caspian Sea. By adding this land, Russia created a protective barrier for its agricultural settlements. To the west, she joined with Prussia and Austria in the *Partition of Poland*. The three powerful countries divided Poland among themselves. Poland would not reappear as an independent country until the twentieth century.

Expansion was costly. Not only was it expensive, but the new territory involved Russia more and more in the political and military struggle over the crumbling Ottoman Empire in the Balkans.

Some of Catherine's major successes at home were the establishment of schools for girls and the setting of a precedent for smallpox inoculations. Catherine continued the *Westernization* of Russia begun under Peter the Great. At the same time, a fear of losing their traditional culture grew among many Russians. These concerns had their most obvious expression in the conservative philosophical movement called *Slavophilism*. *Slavophiles* believed that Russia should base its development on its own history and character and not use Western European culture as a model.

The Pale of Settlement By 1795, the Partitions of Poland noted above gave Russia a far larger Jewish population. Although victims of discrimination, the free Jews in Poland had fulfilled important economic functions in Polish towns and villages. Jewish entrepreneurs and artisans in Russia, by contrast, were tied to landed estates and were not allowed the same independence as that enjoyed by Polish Jews. Catherine created a territory in which the Jews of Russia were required to live. This territory, or the *Pale of Settlement* (often referred to as "the Pale"), set the Jews apart and helped make them more vulnerable to anti-Semitism. By the nineteenth century, *pogroms*, or vicious anti-Jewish attacks, would occur frequently in Russia.

Russian Serfdom

While conditions had improved for serfs in Western Europe by the fourteenth century, the same was not true for the serfs in Russia. Wars during the fourteenth and fifteenth centuries weakened the central government and increased the power of the nobility. As demand for grain increased, nobles imposed harsh conditions on serfs. But Russian serfs had long suffered oppressive lives. First the Mongols and later the Russian princes collected heavy tribute and taxes (for services such as protection or to support the government's army) from the peasants. Consequently the peasants' debts increased, and over time more and more peasants lost their lands and were forced into serfdom. The practice of serfdom benefitted the government because it kept the peasants under control, regulated by the nobility. Serfdom also benefitted the landowners because it provided free labor. Although townspeople were likewise controlled and not permitted to move their businesses freely to other cities, the serfs were practically slaves, their labor bought and sold along with the lands of their owners.

As Russian territory expanded west to the Baltic and east to Siberia, the institution of serfdom expanded with it. An agricultural nation, Russia kept serfs tied to the land long after the practice had ended in Western Europe. For example, Elizabeth I freed the last remaining serfs in England in 1574. A law of 1649 chained Russian serfs to the lands where they were born and ensured their service to their landlords, who could buy and sell them and administer punishments. The *mirs* (village communes) also kept even the small landholders among the peasants in check. Serfdom would end in 1861 by decree of the tsar in the Emancipation Act.

Types Of Labor in the Early Modern Period			
Laborer	Location	Type of Work	Freedoms/Limits
Nomad	Europe, Asia, Africa	Animal breeding; pastoralism; sustenance gained from herding	Pasture land held temporarily; freedom to move; did not own land permanently
Slave	Americas, Africa	Domestic labor and agricultural labor	Slaves considered property; had few and sometimes no rights
Serf	Europe, India, China, Japan	Subsistence farming where majority of yield belonged to lord	Worker attached to land; property of the lord; not free to move; unpaid; little legal protection; could only be freed by lord or escape
Free Peasant	Europe, China	Varied lower class farming and craft jobs such as blacksmiths and weavers	Could work on own; could own businesses; paid taxes to lord and tithes to Church
Guild Member	Medieval Europe	One of an organized group of skilled crafts workers that set standards for quality and price	Included apprenticeship training; after which a member could start a business and sell in town

Cossacks and Peasant Rebellions

Southwest of Moscow, near the *Black Sea*, peasants who were skilled fighters lived on the grassy, treeless *steppes*. Many were runaway serfs who lived in small groups, influenced by the ways of the neighboring nomadic descendants of the Mongols. The fierce Cossack warriors were sometimes at odds with the central, autocratic government of the tsars. However, these fiercely independent warriors could also be hired as mercenaries to defend "Mother Russia" against Swedish, Tartar, and Ottoman forces. The Cossacks were thus important in Russia's expansion to the Ural Mountains and farther east into Siberia.

A Cossack known as *Yemelyan Pugachev* initiated a peasant rebellion against Catherine the Great in 1774. Falsely claiming to be Catherine's murdered husband, Peter III, Pugachev gathered a following of discontented peasants, different ethnic groups, and fellow Cossacks. At one point these groups controlled the territory between the Volga River and the Urals. Within a year, though, Pugachev was captured and executed. The *Pugachev Rebellion* only served to increase Catherine's oppression of the peasants in return for the support of the nobles to help her avoid future revolts.

France and Russia, 1750

One way to understand Russia during the period is to compare it with France. Such a comparison reveals important similarities. Each country was led by a well-known ruler: Louis XIV in France and Peter the Great in Russia. Unlike Britain, neither France nor Russia had an effective legislative body at this time; indeed, in France the Estates General did not meet once between 1614 and 1789. In Russia, no such body existed at all; Tsarina Elizabeth (ruled 1741–1762) ruled by decree and obtained advice from appointed advisors. Another similarity between France and Russia was the ruler's ambition for land expansion, which led each country to become involved in the Seven Years' War (1756–1763), with all its resulting financial burdens.

Differences between France and Russia are marked, however. Russian culture had not yet focused on the ideals of the Enlightenment, such as progress, reason, and natural law. There had been no Reformation in Russia, and Russian serfs would not be set free for another century. Consequently, the famous revolutions of each nation (1789, France; 1917, Russia), while sharing common causes, would be separated in time by more than a century. The chart below shows these comparisons in graphic form.

France and Russia in the Eighteenth Century		
	France	**Russia**
Politics	• Absolutist under Louis XV (ruled 1715–1774) • No effective legislative body • Royal ambitions to expand empire • Financial difficulties and class restrictions led to revolution in 1789	• Absolutist under Elizabeth (ruled 1741–1762) • No effective legislative body • Royal ambitions to expand empire • Financial difficulties and class restrictions led to revolution in 1917
Class	• Legal social classes divided into three estates • Women had few legal rights	• Legal differences between classes, especially between nobles and serfs • Women had few legal rights
Culture	• Center of baroque arts, fashion, and literature • Enlightenment ideas flourished	• Traditional in culture, although Peter the Great brought changes based on his travel to Western Europe • Enlightenment ideals not widespread until Catherine the Great became tsar in 1762

Students of history have long debated whether Peter's changes to Russia represented a true revolution or merely involved superficial "Westernizing." John G. Korb, an Austrian contemporary of Peter's, gave an outsider's view of Russia in Peter's day through the perspective of a Western European, *Diary of an Austrian Secretary of Legation at the Court of Czar Peter the Great.* According to Korb, Peter himself was fearless in his travels and praiseworthy for bringing the arts of Europe to his native people. On the other hand, Korb criticized the inhabitants of Russia as lacking manners and learning. He also mentioned the practices of slavery and serfdom and suggested that Russia as a nation disliked liberty. From Korb's description, the reader can infer that Peter had a difficult task in remaking Russian society into one more like that of France, Britain, or Korb's own Austria. It is interesting to contrast Korb's assessment with that of a historian writing about fifty years later. Edward Gibbons, in his classic work *The Decline and Fall of the Roman Empire,* noted that "Russia now assumes the form of a powerful and civilized empire."

Near the end of the twentieth century, Samuel Huntington, supporting his own famous "clash of civilizations" theory (*The Clash of Civilizations and the Remaking of the World Order*), echoed Korb in underscoring continuing differences between Russia's Slavic-Orthodox culture and Western civilization. Huntington's view was also greatly influenced by the belief that true "Westernization" was synonymous with modernization, and such change had not yet fully come to Russia. However, many reforms usually attributed to the West and begun by Peter the Great had in fact come to Russia—such as the ideals of gender equality.

Even with continued historical research, scholars today still disagree on the success of Peter's reforms. Jackson Spielvogel suggested that "too much has been made of Peter's desire to westernize his 'backward country' and his Europeanization was largely technical." On the other hand, R. R. Palmer, who one historian described as having "an optimistic and liberal view of French and European history," stated that Peter's programs of reform resembled a true social revolution, ending the isolation that had previously been characteristic of the country.

In *Russia and Asia: The Nomadic and Oriental Traditions in Russian History* (2007), Edgar Knobloch disputed the view that Russia had not tried to Westernize before Peter I. Moreover, he asserted that Russia after Peter I continued to be influenced by its Asian neighbors. Knobloch claimed that Peter's main Westernization efforts were in the military arena, the result of Peter's observation that the Ottoman Empire was overpowered by Austria and its allies, who had access to more modern military technology than the Ottomans. However, one reviewer of Knobloch's book explained the author's position as a one-sided view of Russia as a violent, despotic, non-European land, an opinion that is a holdover from the Cold War and earlier. Thus, even today, the questions about Russia and about the effectiveness and lasting impact of Peter's reforms remain open.

KEY TERMS BY THEME

ENVIRONMENT
Ural Mountains
Volga River
Caspian Sea
Alaska
Black Sea
steppes

CULTURE
Eastern Orthodoxy
Russian Orthodox
  Church
Enlightenment
St. Basil's Cathedral
patriarch
Holy Synod
Old Believers
St. Petersburg
Winter Palace
philosophes
Westernization
Slavophilism

STATE-BUILDING
tsar
Moscow
Kiev
Ivan III (Ivan the Great)
Kremlin
Ivan IV (Ivan the
  Terrible)
Kazan
Astrakhan
Siberia
Cossacks
Oprichnina
Time of Troubles
Zemsky Sobor
divine right
Romanov Dynasty
Peter I (Peter the Great)
St. Petersburg
Streltsy
Table of Ranks
provinces
Catherine II (Catherine
  the Great)
Partitions of Poland
Yemelyan Pugachev
Pugachev Rebellion

ECONOMICS
Arkhangelsk
  (Archangel)
Silk Roads
fur trade

SOCIAL STRUCTURE
Mongols
boyars
serfs (serfdom)
Pale of Settlement
pogroms
mirs

1. Which of the following statements best explains why Russian rulers established the Russian Orthodox Church?

   (A) To maintain closer relations with Western Europe

   (B) To adopt the religion of most Russian peasants and nobles

   (C) To unify Russians under the belief that the tsar ruled by divine right

   (D) To maintain closer relations with the Orthodox Church of the Byzantine Empire

2. Which of the following accurately describes the condition of serfs in Russia before the nineteenth century?

   (A) Most gained middle-class status by paying off their debts.

   (B) Most were freed and given lands neighboring those of their lords.

   (C) Most were tied to the land and could not move about freely.

   (D) They gained new constitutional rights through successful peasant revolts.

3. Russia's expansion eastward to Siberia and beyond created what new trade connection?

   (A) Export of fur to Europe, China, and North America

   (B) Export of cloth to England, India, and Persia

   (C) Import of caviar from markets on the Silk Road

   (D) Export of naval technicians to Western Europe

4. The movement of Russia's capital from Moscow to St. Petersburg reflected a new period in Russian history marked by a shift toward

   (A) a more agicultural economy

   (B) increased involvement with Western Europe

   (C) greater expansion into Siberia

   (D) more traditional Orthodox religious views

5. In which ways does Russian leader Vladimir Putin represent continuity with Russia from 1450 to 1750?

   (A) He is also the leader of the Russian Orthodox Church.

   (B) He is a descendant of the Romanov rulers.

   (C) He reflects the Enlightenment ideal of Peter the Great.

   (D) He is a powerful, charismatic, autocratic ruler.

6. The eighteenth-century French writer Voltaire wrote, "The sovereigns of Russia possessed the most extensive dominions in the world, and everything was yet to be done: at last, Peter was born and Russia was formed." By the phrase "everything was yet to be done," Voltaire probably meant that Russia

(A) Needed to collect much higher taxes in order to pay its bills

(B) Needed reforms of government and society like those of Western Europe

(C) Had a long way to go to achieve the goals of the Slavophiles

(D) Needed a stronger military force

Question 7 is based on the following photo.

Source: Library of Congress

7. The Kremlin in Moscow (strengthened with new walls and towers under the rule of Ivan III) best exemplifies which historical process?

(A) Displays of political power through monumental architecture

(B) Use of religious ideas to legitimate political power

(C) The growing power of local nobles over centralized rule

(D) The spread of Enlightenment ideas across Europe and Asia

8. For what reason did Tsar Ivan III engage in the following three activities?

- Refusing to pay tribute to the Mongols
- Taking the title of *tsar*, from the word *Caesar*
- Marrying the niece of the last Byzantine emperor

(A) To improve Russia's relations with the Byzantine Empire

(B) To share power with the Mongols and the Russian nobles

(C) To throw off Mongol rule and legitimize his own power

(D) To force the Mongols into a war with the Byzantine Empire

9. Which of the following was most responsible for making conditions worse for Russia's serfs in the fourteenth and fifteenth centuries?

(A) The growing power of the nobility

(B) The spread of Enlightenment ideas

(C) The growing power of Cossack warriors

(D) The rise in demand for fur

10. Which statement describes a change in social status caused by the 1795 Partitions of Poland?

(A) Catherine II gained more power to enforce her programs.

(B) Many more people were inoculated against the smallpox virus.

(C) Russian Jews had to live apart from the rest of the population.

(D) Many more schools for girls were established.

CONTINUITY AND CHANGE-OVER-TIME ESSAY QUESTIONS

Directions: You are to answer the following question. You should spend 5 minutes organizing or outlining your essay. Write an essay that:

- Has a relevant thesis and supports that thesis with appropriate historical evidence.
- Addresses all parts of the question.
- Uses world historical context to show continuities and changes over time.
- Analyzes the process of continuity and change over time.

1. Analyze the continuities and changes in Russian attitudes toward Western influences and how these influences affected Russia's political and social structures from 1450 to the end of the eighteenth century.

Questions for Additional Practice

2. Analyze the continuities and changes in Russia's economic system from Kievan Rus to Russia of the late eighteenth century in one of the following areas:
   - Labor systems
   - Trade networks

3. Analyze the continuities and changes in the power of the tsars and the nobles as well as the status of serfs in Russia from Kievan Rus to the end of the eighteenth century.

COMPARATIVE ESSAY QUESTIONS

Directions: You are to answer the following question. You should spend 5 minutes organizing or outlining your essay. Write an essay that:

- Has a relevant thesis and supports that thesis with appropriate historical evidence.
- Addresses all parts of the question.
- Makes direct, relevant comparisons.
- Analyzes relevant reasons for similarities and differences.

1. Compare serfdom in Russia to the coerced labor systems in ONE of these regions between 1450 and 1750:
   - Western Europe
   - British North America

Questions for Additional Practice

2. Analyze the similarities and differences between Russia and Western Europe from 1450 to 1750 in TWO of the following areas:
   - culture, including religion and technology
   - political structures
   - economic systems, including labor systems and trade networks

3. Analyze the similarities and differences between how Russia (from 1450 to the end of the eighteenth century) and the United States (after independence in 1776) each expanded its land empire.

THINK AS A HISTORIAN: APPLY THE USE OF HISTORICAL EVIDENCE

A key skill of historians is the ability to recognize good evidence and use it accurately. *Describe the kind of evidence—documents from the past such as maps, diary and journal entries, letters, treaties, statutes, archaeological findings, treaties, and more—that should be included in essays responding to each of the following questions.*

1. What were the ideals of the Enlightenment?

2. Why were the Crusades instrumental in Russia's expansion to the Ural Mountains and farther east into Siberia?

3. Was Peter the Great's revolution in Russia a true revolution, or did he merely make superficial changes?

4. What was it that set Russia apart from Europe? Why did it experience neither the throes of the Reformation or the Renaissance when most of Europe did?

5. How did physical changes in the city of Moscow show the growing status of Russian rulers?

WRITE AS A HISTORIAN: EXPLAIN CAUSATION

Often students are asked to explain why one event triggered changes in a society. For example, an essay question might ask students to explain the long-term impact on Russia of the Mongol invasion. *In each of the statements below, identify the ONE word which most clearly alerts you that the subject is causation.*

1. Because Russian princes became tax collectors, they grew enough in wealth and power to shake off Mongol rule.

2. Siberian expansion resulted in a robust fur trade, giving Russia an important export to Europe and China.

3. The use of gunpowder helped create the power of Ivan the Terrible, who used it to expand the Russian border eastward.

4. Peter the Great's interest in technology eventually permitted Russia to build up its military and naval power.

5. The Westernization of Russia can be attributed in part to Catherine the Great, who corresponded with Western European philosophers and added to Russian territory by partitioning Poland.

19

Islamic Gunpowder Empires

The conditions, customs and beliefs of peoples and nations
do not indefinitely follow the same pattern and adhere
to a constant course. There is, rather, change with days and
epochs, as well as passing from one state to another. . . .

—Ibn Khaldun, *Muquaddimah* (1377)

New patterns and change arise from many sources. One of these was technology: gunpowder. The term *Gunpowder Empires* refers to large multiethnic states in Southwest, Central, and South Asia that relied on firearms to conquer and control their territories. In addition to Russia, the Gunpowder Empires in the period from 1450 to 1750 included three in which Islam was strong: the Ottoman, the Safavid, and the Mughal Empires. Although their societies tended to be militaristic, all three left splendid artistic and architectural legacies.

The Ottoman, Safavid, and Mughal Empires would decline as Western Europe grew in strength economically and militarily—particularly in terms of sea power. Unlike these three Islamic empires, Russia modernized and reorganized its army, modeling it after the armies of England, France, and the Netherlands. The Islamic empires did not modernize, and, as a result, Russia remained powerful enough to survive as an independent nation-state, while the other Gunpowder Empires fell. The last to fall, the Ottoman Empire, came to an end following World War I with the formation of modern Turkey. The Safavid and Mughal Empires each had fallen long before. (For more on Russia's use of gunpowder and its military reforms, see page 337.)

Rise of the Islamic Gunpowder Empires

The warrior leaders of the Ottoman, Safavid, and Mughal Empires shared many traits. Besides being Muslims, they all

- were from nomadic Turkic backgrounds
- spoke forms of the Turkic family of languages
- took advantage of power vacuums left by the breakup of Mongol khanates
- relied on armies with artillery and cannons—and thus on gunpowder

The initial success of the Gunpowder Empires was a result of their own military might along with the weakness and corruption of the regimes that they replaced. Equally important to the history of these empires was the loose alliance of European nations that fought among themselves rather than uniting to topple the new powers growing in the east.

The Rule of Tamerlane The invasion of Central Asia and the Middle East by *Tamerlane* (Timur the Lame, a Mongol-Turkic ruler of the late fourteenth century) set the stage for the rise of the Turkic empires. Leading an army partly composed of nomadic invaders from the broad steppes of Eurasia, Tamerlane moved out from the trading city of *Samarkand* (in modern-day Uzbekistan) to make ruthless conquests in Persia (modern-day Iran) and India. The Eurasian steppes were also the birthplace of the *ghazi ideal*—a model for warrior life that blended the cooperative values of nomadic culture with the willingness to serve as a holy fighter for Islam. According to some historians, this ideal served for centuries as the model for warriors who participated in the rise of the Gunpowder Empires, and it was a model that fit Tamerlane well.

Some historians believe that Tamerlane's violent takeover of areas of Central Asia included the massacre of some 100,000 Hindus before the gates of Delhi in India. Violence continued to mark the pattern of conquest that resulted in new dynasties: the Ottomans, the Safavids, and the Mughals. Nonetheless, Tamerlane's rule in Samarkand also brought the encouragement of learning and the arts—a trend also typical of these later empires. For example, Tamerlane

TAMERLANE'S EMPIRE, C. 1400

championed literature, and he himself corresponded with European rulers and wrote his own memoirs. Buildings still standing in the city of Samarkand are testaments to his interest in architecture and decorative arts.

While the empire he created largely fell apart (except for the area that his descendant Babur would take over to create India's Mughal Dynasty), Tamerlane's invasions were a testament to the significance of gunpowder. He used it to build a government dependent upon his military and the use of heavy artillery. He also used it to protect land routes on the Silk Road. However, he failed to leave an effective political structure in many of the areas he conquered. Without effective government, the expenses of wars eventually ravaged the empire's economy.

Tamerlane's rule casts light on two major forces that had battled each other continually from the late tenth century to the fourteenth century—Mongols from the northeast versus Islamic forces from Arabia and the areas around the Mediterranean Sea. These forces would clash continuously with the rise and fall of the three Asian Gunpowder Empires that are the focus of this chapter.

The Ottoman Empire

Extending into modern-day Turkey as well as to the Balkan areas of Europe and parts of North Africa and Southeast Asia, the *Ottoman Empire* was the largest and most enduring of the great Islamic empires of this period. Founded by the Osman Dynasty in the 1300s, the empire lasted until its defeat in 1918 by the Allies in World War I. Thus, a single dynasty controlled the empire for over 600 years.

Mehmed II Called "the Conqueror," *Mehmed II* (ruled 1451–1481) firmly established the empire's capital after his forces besieged Constantinople (once the center of the Byzantine Empire) in 1453. Despite its triple fortifications, the city fell as its walls crumbled under the bombardment of Ottoman cannon. Under Mehmed II's rule, the city—its name changed to Istanbul—prospered due to its location, which was a nexus for trade; the city controlled the *Bosporus Strait*, the only waterway linking the Aegean Sea with the Black Sea. Under Mehmed II, Istanbul grew even more beautiful and expanded across both sides of the strait. One famous landmark is the royal residence of the sultans, *Topkapi Palace*, which began construction during the reign of Mehmed II.

The armies of Mehmed II next seized lands around the western edge of the Black Sea. Then they moved into the Balkans in Southeast Europe. To counter the power of Venice, Mehmed strengthened the Ottoman navy and attacked various areas of Italy. Although he did not conquer Venice, he forced the city to pay him a yearly tax. In the early sixteenth century, the Ottomans added to their empire lands in present-day Syria, Israel, Egypt, and Algeria. When the Mamluk Dynasty declined, Istanbul became a center of Islam. (For more on the Mamluk Empire, see page 150.)

To staff their military and their government, the Ottoman sultans used a selection system called *devshirme*, begun in the late fourteenth century and expanded in the fifteenth and sixteenth centuries. Through this system, Christian boys who were subjects of the empire were recruited by force to serve in the Ottoman government. Boys ages 8 to 20 were taken each year from conquered Christian lands in Europe. After converting to Islam, they were taught various skills in politics, the arts, and the military. The most famous group, called *Janissaries*, formed elite forces in the Ottoman army. Other boys were groomed to become administrators of the newly conquered territories; some were scribes, tax collectors, and even diplomats.

In some ways, becoming a Janissary provided a path of upward mobility in the Ottoman Empire, even though the Janissaries continued to be called "slaves of the state." Some parents even wanted their sons to be recruited into the service.

Suleiman I The Ottoman Empire reached its peak under *Suleiman I* (ruled 1520–1566). His armies overran Hungary in 1526 and, by 1529, were hammering at the gates of *Vienna*, the main city in Austria. Their attempt to take Vienna failed twice, but the ability of the Ottomans to send troops so far into the Christian Europe caused great fear there.

In 1522, Suleiman's navy captured the island of *Rhodes* (now part of Greece) in the eastern Mediterranean, which had long been a stronghold of Christian knights. In the 1550s, the Ottoman navy took control of Tripoli in North Africa.

THREE ISLAMIC EMPIRES IN THE SIXTEENTH CENTURY

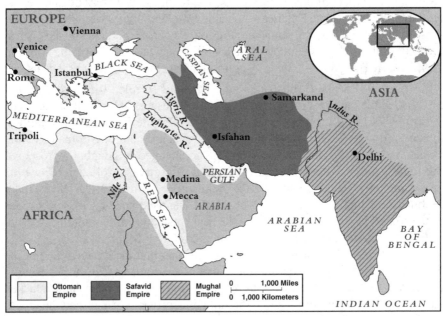

Suleiman ordered many mosques, forts, and other great buildings constructed in the cities under his control. For example, he ordered the construction in Istanbul of the magnificent *Suleimani Mosque*, which can be seen from the Golden Horn promontory that juts into the Black Sea at its convergence with the Bosporus. Suleiman also reformed the empire's legal system and thus came to be called "the Lawgiver."

Ottoman Economy Ottoman trade was energized in its early years by repeated expansion through conquest. Rulers forced people in occupied areas to send monetary tribute as well as goods to the central government in Istanbul. The Ottoman navy allowed traders to serve as *middlemen*, handling goods from both directions and receiving profit in exchange, in much the same way that the Dutch served as middlemen in Western Europe. In this way, some European styles and furnishings became popular in the empire.

Because of his control of the North African coast, the Ottoman sultan controlled the trade in gold and slaves. Eastern luxuries, particularly silk and spices, continued to be popular trade items, but the Ottomans also had a strong trade in creations of their own artisans: distinctive tiles, pottery, and rugs, for example.

To finance an economy backed by a powerful military, the Ottomans levied taxes on the peasants. Local officials and tax collectors, distant from the central government, grew wealthy and corrupt from skimming money from the taxes in their areas. Agricultural villages continued to be burdened with the upkeep of officers and troops. This burden of taxes and the military would eventually contribute to the economic decline of the empire.

An additional reason for the flourishing of trade in the early years of the empire was that the tolerant sultans allowed Christian and Jewish merchants to prosper as long as they paid taxes. Also, to increase commerce, the Ottomans signed *trade agreements* such as those with France that opened up commerce between the two powers. However, the terms of the agreements with France would ultimately diminish the Ottoman profits in the long term.

Many business agreements were signed in the empire's *coffeehouses*, settings not only of business transactions but also of cultural events such as poetry recitations and scholarly debates. They also hosted trade meetings with representatives of such areas as Yemen, the major exporter of coffee. Trade agreements made by the sultans allowed European importers to purchase coffee through the Ottoman Empire at rates cheaper than direct purchase from Yemen.

Interaction with the Americas led to the introduction of new crops on Ottoman lands that could be sold for cash. Near the city of Izmir, typical agricultural products such as dates, nuts, and olive oil were replaced by cotton and tobacco. Even though the use of the latter was officially prohibited throughout the Ottoman Empire, it quickly became popular among citizens.

By the seventeenth century, profits from imports dwindled. Problems in the neighboring Safavid Empire, for example, led to a reduction in silk production.

Social Classes The Ottoman social system was built around a warrior aristocracy that soon began to compete for positions in the bureaucracy with the *ulama* (scholars and experts in Islamic law). Within the military, more and more power and prestige was assumed by the Janissaries, who ultimately tried to mount coups against the sultans. The tension between the military elite and absolutist rulers became characteristic of all three Islamic Gunpowder Empires.

As sultans became less effective and less capable, strong advisors called *viziers* came to occupy influential positions in government, where they spoke for the sultan. Women also played social and political roles at court. Many wives and concubines of the sultan tried to promote their own children as likely heirs to the throne, giving rise to "harem politics," a reference to the *harem*, a residence where a man's wives and concubines lived.

Merchants and artisans formed a small middle class; below the middle class were the peasants, who were usually poor—particularly because they had to pay tribute to the government to help support the Ottoman armies. Below the peasants were slaves. They came from many areas as the Ottoman armies penetrated into Central and Eastern Europe, capturing prisoners of war in the Ukraine and elsewhere. Other European slaves were those captured by the *Barbary pirates* in the Mediterranean and then sold to the sultan or other high-ranking officials. Some people were *impressed,* or forced into service, in the navy as galley slaves—estimates of the number of people impressed go as high as a million or more between the sixteenth and nineteenth centuries.

One reason for the success of the empire was its relative tolerance toward Jews and Christians. The empire accepted Jews who had been driven out of Spain in 1492; Mehmed II issued an invitation to them to settle in Istanbul. Some members of the Jewish community, which expanded rapidly after 1492, became court physicians and diplomats; others contributed to the literary community and (according to some accounts) were responsible for bringing the printing press to the Ottoman Empire. Often, however, Jews were only permitted to live in specified areas of the cities. Under Suleiman, Christians and Jews were allowed to worship and live with few restrictions as long as they paid a tax required of all non-Muslims in the empire. The elite of the empire, however, were always Muslim.

Decline of the Ottoman Empire In 1571, after Suleiman's death, a European force made up mostly of Spaniards and Venetians defeated the Ottomans in a great naval conflict known as the *Battle of Lepanto*. After the reign of Suleiman, the Ottomans fell victim to weak sultans and strong European neighbors. In time, the empire became known as the "Sick Man of Europe." Successors to Suleiman were often held hostage to harem politics conducted by women and eunuchs. Although neither group would have the opportunity to rule, women and eunuchs nevertheless became powerful behind the scenes. The Ottoman Empire as a whole grew less tolerant of non-Muslims and more insular. Slavery there continued into the twentieth century.

Continuity and Change Under the Ottomans While tremendous changes in government and religion took place in the area controlled by the Ottoman Empire, the arts, culture, and the economy showed continuities. Until 1453, much of the area had been controlled by the Byzantine Empire and followed the Eastern Orthodox religion. After the fall of Constantinople, the area became Ottoman and the dominant religion became Islam. The emperor was replaced by a sultan, and the Byzantine Empire's Justinian Law was replaced by *shariah*. Shariah is a system of Islamic jurisprudence that deals with all aspects of life, such as criminal justice, marital laws, and issues of inheritance, to name but a few.

Despite the above differences, continuities existed. Constantinople, newly named Istanbul, remained the western end of the overland Silk Roads, and the *Grand Bazaar* there continued to be full of many foreign imports: amber and wood products from Russia, spices and silk from China, ivory and slaves from Africa, and carpets from Persia. Demand for goods that passed through Constantinople created an export market to other cities of the empire. Coffeehouses, although banned by Islamic law, continued to do a thriving business throughout the towns of the empire.

Istanbul remained a center of arts and learning. Poets and scholars from across Asia met in coffeehouses and gardens, creating a rich intellectual atmosphere as they discussed works by Aristotle and other Greek writers, as well as the works of many Arabic scholars, such as Ibn Khaldun, quoted at the beginning of this chapter. Cultural contributions of the Ottomans included the restoration of some of the glorious buildings of Constantinople, most notably the cathedral of Saint Sophia (which the Ottomans turned into a grand mosque) and the Topkapi Palace. From the time of Mehmed II, who established a workshop for their production, Ottoman *miniature paintings* and illuminated manuscripts became famous. As in Europe, artisans belonged to guilds that set high standards, particularly for artisans working in gold, silver, and silk.

The Safavids

Sandwiched between the other Islamic Gunpowder Empires, the *Safavids* had two problems: first, they were on the Arabian Sea but had no real navy; and second, they lacked natural defenses. Nevertheless, they rose to power in the 1500s due to their military might and strong leadership.

Ismail An early Safavid military hero named *Ismail*, whose ethnic background is much disputed, conquered most of Persia and pushed into Iraq. Although only 14 or 15 years old, he soon conquered all of Iran and was proclaimed *shah* (equivalent to king or emperor) in 1501. Using Shia Islam as a unifying force, Shah Ismail built a power base that supported his rule and denied legitimacy to any Sunni. This strict adherence Shia Islam caused frequent hostilities with the Ottoman Empire, stronghold of Sunni Islam. In 1541, Safavid forces were stopped by the Ottomans at Tabriz, a city in Persia that became part of the border between Sunni and Shia societies. The hostility between the two groups lives on in present-day Iraq and Iran.

Conflicts between Ottomans and Safavids were not entirely religious in nature, however. An additional conflicts arose over control of overland trade routes. The fighting between these two Gunpowder Empires kept both from becoming as much of a threat to Europe as they might otherwise have been.

Shah Abbas I Called "Abbas the Great," *Shah Abbas I* (ruled 1587–1629) presided over the Safavid Empire at its height. His troops, which were conscripted in ways similar to the recruitment of the Janissaries in the Ottoman Empire, included soldiers—often Christian boys pressed into service—from as far northwest as Georgia in Russia. Abbas imported weaponry from Europe and also relied on Europeans to advise his troops about this newly acquired military technology. Slowly, the shahs came to control the Iranian Shia religion as well as its politics. Using Shia practices to back up their legitimacy, Safavid rulers created a state religion and paved the way for the Iranian theocracy of today.

Abbas beautified the capital city of *Isfahan* (which is south of the modern Iranian capital of Tehran), adding broad avenues, parks, and numerous mosques and schools. He also encouraged craft production, although exports of crafts were not a large part of the Safavid economy as they were for their stronger neighbors to the east and west. The Safavids carried on some trade with the Portuguese fleet, which for a time held the *Strait of Hormuz*, a vital waterway between the Persian Gulf and the Gulf of Oman. Then, in 1622, Abbas took control of the strait with the help of English ships. This aid to the Safavid Empire began the long history of British interest in Iran.

The ineffectual leaders who followed Shah Abbas combined lavish lifestyles and military spending with falling revenues, resulting in a weakened economy. In 1722, Safavid forces were not able to quell a rebellion by the heavily oppressed Sunni Pashtuns in present-day Afghanistan. The Afghan forces went on to sack Isfahan and their leader, Mahmud, declared himself "Shah of Persia." While the Safavid Dynasty remained nominally in control, the resulting chaos was an impediment to centralization and tax collection. Taking advantage of the weakened Safavids, the Ottomans and the Russians were able to seize territories. The Safavid Dynasty declined rapidly until it was replaced by the Zand Dynasty in 1760.

Isfahan Despite the decline of Safavids, the city of Isfahan retained its beauty. The renowned gardens with fountains and pools made an inviting contrast to the harsh countryside outside of the towns and cities. The gardens were acclaimed by Englishman Thomas Herbert and Frenchman Jean Chardin in their travelogues of the period.

Women While Safavid women were still veiled and restricted in their movements, as was traditional in the region, they had access to rights provided by Islamic law for inheritance and, in extreme cases, divorce. Women, however, are barely mentioned in local Safavid histories, an indication of their lack of political influence.

Mughal India

Babur, a descendant of Tamerlane, founded a 300-year dynasty in the 1520s, during a time when India was in disarray. He completed conquests in northern India and, under the new Mughal name, formed a central government similar to those of Suleiman in Turkey and Ivan the Terrible in Russia. It would be Babur's grandson Akbar, however, who would achieve grand religious and political goals.

Akbar Ruling from 1556 to 1605, *Akbar* proved to be the most capable of the Mughal rulers. For the first 40 years of his rule, he defeated Hindu armies and extended his empire southward and westward. From his capital in *Delhi*, Akbar established an efficient government and a system of fairly administered laws. For example, all his people had the right to appeal to him for final judgment in any lawsuit. As Akbar's fame spread, capable men from many parts of Central Asia came to serve him. They helped Akbar create a strong, centralized government and an effective civil service. Paid government officials in charge of specific duties, such as taxation, construction, and water supply, were called *zamindars*. Later, they were given grants of land rather than salaries but were permitted to keep a portion of the taxes paid by local peasants, who contributed one-third of their produce to the government. The system worked well under Akbar. Under the rulers who came after him, though, the zamindars began to keep more of the taxes that they collected. With this money, they built personal armies of soldiers and civilians loyal to them.

Akbar was tolerant of all religions. He allocated grants of money or land to Hindus and Muslims. He gave money for a Catholic church in Goa, on the southwest coast of India. He provided land grants for the relatively new religion of *Sikhism*, which developed from Hinduism and, some believe, may have been influenced by the Islamic mysticism known as Sufism. He tried to mediate the conflict between Hindus and Muslims. He gave Hindus positions in his government—zamindars of both high and low positions could be Hindu—and he married Hindu wives. He exempted Hindus from the poll taxes paid by all non-Muslims in the empire. Because he enjoyed religious discussions, Akbar invited Roman Catholic priests to Delhi to explain Christianity to him.

Regarded as one of the world's outstanding rulers, Akbar encouraged learning and the growth of art, architecture, and literature. He is also noteworthy for trying (in vain) to prohibit child marriages and *sati*, the ritual in which widows killed themselves by jumping on the funeral pyres of their husbands. He died in 1605 without successfully converting his Hindu and Islamic subjects to the religion called *Din-i-llahi,* or "divine faith," which he had created for the purpose of reconciling Hinduism and Islam.

The Mughal Empire under Akbar was one of the richest and best-governed states in the world. Overseas trade flourished during the relatively peaceful period; commerce was carried out mostly by Arab traders, since Indian traders did not care for travel on the Indian Ocean. Traded goods included textiles, tropical foods, spices, and precious stones, all of which were often exchanged for gold and silver. Trade within the borders of the empire was carried on by merchant castes. *Castes* are social groupings in India, usually associated with specific occupations. Members of the merchant castes were allowed to participate in banking and the production of handicrafts.

Shan Jahan Mughal India flourished from Babur's time through the early eighteenth century. Magnificent architectural accomplishments included the *Taj Mahal*, built by *Shah Jahan* (ruled 1627–1658) as a tomb for his wife. Mughal rulers beautified Delhi and had forts built. The craftsmen and builders of Mughal India combined the arts of Islam (calligraphy, illumination of manuscripts, and ceramics) with local arts to create magnificent airy structures distinguished by their decorative geometric designs.

Aurangzeb Shah Jahan's son and successor, *Aurangzeb* (ruled 1658–1707), inherited an empire weakened by corruption and the failure to keep up with the military innovations of external enemies. Nevertheless, Aurangzeb hoped to increase the size of the empire and bring all of India under Muslim rule. Additionally, he wanted to rid the empire of its Hindu influences. In expanding the empire to the south, he drained the empire's treasury and was unable to put down peasant uprisings. Some of these uprisings were sparked by Aurangzeb's insistence on an austere and pious Islamic lifestyle. Under his rule, for example, music was banned. There were revolts as well among the Hindu and Islamic princes. The empire grew increasingly unstable after his death, which allowed the British and French to gain more and more economic power in India. The British would take political power away from the Mughals in the nineteenth century.

Source: Thinkstock

Source: Thinkstock

Source: Thinkstock

The Islamic Gunpowder Empires constructed monumental architecture with spiritual significance. The Ottomans built the Suleimani Mosque in Istanbul (upper). The Safavids built the Mosque of Ifshahan (lower left). The Mughals built the Taj Mahal, a mausoleum, in Agra (lower right).

Decline of the Gunpowder Empires

The decline of the Gunpowder Empires resulted from pressure from European trading companies, especially the British, and from competition among heirs motivated by harem politics. Aurangzeb, for example, seized the throne by killing his brothers. Other factors in the decline included weak or corrupt leadership and failure to keep in step with developments in military and naval technology. The expensive armies that each empire needed to keep under control placed harsh financial burdens on the peasants and villages forced to support them. Religious differences also created problems. In Mughal India, there was a deep religious division between Islam and Hinduism, and there were deep religious divisions between the Sunni Ottomans and Shia Safavids, setting the stage for conflict between the present-day countries of Iraq and Iran. (Test Prep: Write a paragraph comparing the decline of Mughal India with the decline of the Roman Empire. See pages 83–85.)

Ottoman, Safavid, and Mughal Empires, 1450–1750		
	Ottoman Empire	**Safavid Empire**	**Mughal Empire**
Religion	• Mostly Sunni with some measure of tolerance under Suleiman • Less tolerance under later rulers	• Mostly Shia • No tolerance; Ismail I made conversion mandatory for Sunni population	• Tolerance under Akbar, but his blend of Islam and Hinduism did not prove popular • Less tolerance under later rulers
Taxes	• Taxes on non-Muslims • Taxes on peasants	• Taxation policies used to encourage adherence to Shia Islam	• Taxes on unbelievers was abolished by Akbar but reinstated later • Taxes on peasants
Military	• Warriors (often trained Janissaries) were granted villages to provide their upkeep • Leaders made the military independent of central government • Strong navy	• Warriors were the Qizilbash, Turcoman militants who helped establish the empire • Leaders made the military independent of central government • No significant navy	• Warriors were granted villages to provide their upkeep • Officials known as zamindars made the military independent of central government • Small navy

HISTORICAL PERSPECTIVES: WHY DID THE ISLAMIC GUNPOWDER EMPIRES DECLINE?

The term "Gunpowder Empires" was coined by Marshall G.S. Hodgson in the 1970s to refer to the large land empires of Southwestern and South Asia that flourished during the period from 1450 to 1750 (*The Venture of Islam: The Gunpowder Empires and Modern Time*). Since Hodgson's massive work was published, the term has come into modern use in many books dealing with the rise and decline of the Ottomans, Safavids, and Mughals. As described by Kenneth Pomeranz and Steven Topik in their 2005 book *The World That Trade Created*, the empires became part of the growing global economy of the period. These authors, taking economic and social perspectives, use coffee as one example of the international character of consumer goods: "Coffee's role in sociability and prestige in Europe was enhanced by the arrival of emissaries of the Ottoman sultan in France and Austria in 1665–1666, who poured the exotic liquor for their aristocratic European guests during extravagant soirees."

However, the prosperity achieved by the Gunpowder Empires was not enough to sustain their independence indefinitely. Historians have given various reasons for their declines, but most fall into three categories: (1) ineffectiveness; (2) intolerance of minorities; and (3) failure to modernize. One reviewer summarized historian Vladimir Minorsky's reasons for the decline of the Safavid Empire:

(a) decline of theocratic ideology
(b) opposition between old and new elements in the military class
(c) disturbance in equilibrium among the service classes, which lost interest in the cause they were supporting
(d) the "shadow government" represented by the harem
(e) degeneration of the dynasty as a result of its insular nature

The reviewer's analysis illustrated the ways in which poor leadership affected the empires.

A recent work by Amy Chua, *Day of Empire: How Hyperpowers Rise to Global Dominance—and Why They Fall*, suggested a somewhat different reason for the eventual failure of the Gunpowder Empires. Her thesis was that intolerance ultimately became an obstacle to retaining great power. She suggested that the empires were successful in holding their power when they were at their most religiously and ethnically tolerant. This thesis can be used to explain why the Ottoman Empire, with its relative tolerance, outlived the more conservative Safavid and Mughal Empires. However, one reviewer criticized Chua's work for focusing on tolerance at the expense of other factors, such as military power.

Finally, William McNeill pointed out that rulers and military administrators did not try to keep up with "subsequent European innovations in military and naval matters, leaving them woefully exposed to attack." McNeill reminded his readers that the Ottomans' guns were able to defeat their Islamic rivals, the Safavids, because "until about 1600, the Ottoman army remained technically and in every way in the very forefront of military proficiency." Nevertheless, after the time of Suleiman, leaders did not themselves lead their men in battle, and military discipline declined at the same time that efficiency and technology began to lag behind Western Europe.

KEY TERMS BY THEME

ENVIRONMENT
Bosporus Strait
Strait of Hormuz

CULTURE
ghazi ideal
Suleimani Mosque
coffeehouses
ulama
Shariah Law
harem
miniature paintings
Sikhism
sati
Din-i-Ilahi
Taj Mahal

STATE-BUILDING
Gunpowder Empires
Tamerlane
Samarkand
Ottoman Empire
Mehmed II ("the
    Conqueror")
Topkapi Palace
Suleiman I
Vienna
Rhodes
viziers
Battle of Lepanto
Safavids
Ismail
shah
Shah Abbas I ("Abbas
    the Great")
Isfahan
Akbar
Babur
Delhi
Shah Jahan
Aurangzeb

ECONOMICS
middlemen
trade agreements
Barbary pirates
Grand Bazaar

SOCIAL STRUCTURE
devshirme
Janissaries
impressed
zamindars
castes

1. Which statement best summarizes the religious situation in Mughal India following the rule of Akbar?

   (A) Akbar's syncretic religion remained popular with the people as an alternative to either Hinduism or Islam.

   (B) Islamic influence slowly left the region.

   (C) Hinduism and Islam continued to coexist uneasily in the area.

   (D) Islam in the area was weakened by the fighting between Sunnis and Shias.

2. Which of the following descriptions comparing the Ottoman *devshirme* system with the Mughal *zamindar* system is accurate?

   (A) Both systems relied exclusively on officials who inherited their positions.

   (B) Both systems represented ways for central governments to recruit local and regional officials.

   (C) Both systems depended upon the spoils of war to support the officials.

   (D) Both systems included recruitment for the military as well as for local government officials.

3. Which of the following descriptions best characterizes European interactions with the Gunpowder Empires during the period 1450–1750?

   (A) The Gunpowder Empires were able to keep the European trading nations out of the Indian Ocean.

   (B) Arts, spices, and silk imported from the Gunpowder Empires were popular with Europeans.

   (C) The Gunpowder Empires were almost entirely unknown to the Europeans of the time period.

   (D) The isolated position of the Safavid and Mughal Empires restricted their ability to participate in regional and global trade patterns.

4. The careers of Suleiman and Akbar were alike because they both

   (A) Were intolerant toward non-Muslims

   (B) Kept the borders of their empires just as they had inherited them

   (C) Encouraged arts and learning in their capitals

   (D) Were overthrown by military coups

5. One reason that Russia evolved into a nation-state while the Islamic Empires declined is that between 1450 and 1740, only Russia
   (A) Modernized its army
   (B) Focused on becoming a sea power
   (C) Showed tolerance toward ethnic minorities
   (D) Had absolutist, charismatic leaders

Question 6 refers to the excerpt below.

Throughout the sixteenth century, the Safavi [Safavid] Empire remained a profoundly disturbing force in the [Muslim] world, dedicated to the defense and propagation of Shia doctrines at home and abroad. This policy implied a normal state of hostility with the Ottoman Empire, punctuated only briefly by periods of peace.

—William H. McNeill, *The Rise of the West:*
A History of the Human Community

6. Which of the following would be the most useful source of evidence to support McNeill's contention that "the Safavi [Safavid] Empire remained a profoundly disturbing force in the [Muslim] world"?
   (A) Writings by Safavids about Shia beliefs
   (B) Writings by modern-day Muslim historians
   (C) Writings by Ottoman religious leaders of that time about the Safavids
   (D) Writings by archaeologists about discoveries of Safavid and Ottoman religious relics

7. Which of the following was most directly a result of these three causes?
   - European nations fighting among themselves
   - the breakup of the Mongol khanates
   - Tamerlane's conquests in Central Asia and the Middle East
   (A) The rise of the Islamic Gunpowder Empires
   (B) The decline of the Islamic Gunpowder Empires
   (C) The rise of religious disputes between Jews, Christians, and Muslims
   (D) The rise of gunpowder as an important product for trade

8. Which reason best explains why Ottoman forces were able to break through the triple-enforced walls of Constantinople?
   (A) The ferocity of Ottoman warriors
   (B) The ability to find weak points in the walls
   (C) The willingness of the citizens to convert to Islam
   (D) The use of cannons

Question 9 refers to the image below.

Source: Thinkstock

9. The photo above of the Suleimani Mosque in Istanbul (built by Emperor Suleiman in the sixteenth century) best exemplifies which of the following historical processes?

(A) The development of syncretic belief systems

(B) European technological and architectural development

(C) Displays of magnificent architecture to legitimize state power

(D) New trade connections between the Ottomans and the Byzantines

10. The growth of Sikhism in Mughal India most closely represents which historical process?

(A) The expansion of older religions

(B) The development of new forms of religion

(C) The spread of Buddhism in Asia

(D) The spread of religion through conquest

CONTINUITY AND CHANGE-OVER-TIME ESSAY QUESTIONS

Directions: You are to answer the following question. You should spend 5 minutes organizing or outlining your essay. Write an essay that:

- Has a relevant thesis and supports that thesis with appropriate historical evidence.
- Addresses all parts of the question.
- Uses world historical context to show continuities and changes over time.
- Analyzes the process of continuity and change over time.

1. Analyze the continuities and changes in the political structure that affected the rise and decline of one of the following Islamic Gunpowder Empires:
   - the Ottomans
   - the Safavids
   - the Mughals

Questions for Additional Practice

2. Analyze the continuities and changes in the political power of one of the Islamic Gunpowder Empires in its interactions with other nations, focusing on how these continuities and changes strengthened or weakened that empire.

3. Analyze the continuities and changes in the treatment of minorities in ONE of the Islamic Gunpowder Empires, including how these continuities and changes influenced developments in that empire.

COMPARATIVE ESSAY QUESTIONS

Directions: You are to answer the following question. You should spend 5 minutes organizing or outlining your essay. Write an essay that:

- Has a relevant thesis and supports that thesis with appropriate historical evidence.
- Addresses all parts of the question.
- Makes direct, relevant comparisons.
- Analyzes relevant reasons for similarities and differences.

1. Analyze the similarities and differences in the effects of Islamic rule in the three Islamic Gunpowder Empires.

Questions for Additional Practice

2. Analyze the similarities and differences between Russia or Western Europe and one or more of the Islamic Gunpowder Empires from 1450 to 1750 in TWO of the following areas:
   - culture
   - technology
   - political structures
   - economic systems

3. Analyze the similarities and differences between Tamerlane's empire and one of the Islamic Gunpowder Empires in the strengths and weaknesses of the political structures they built.

THINK AS A HISTORIAN: USE CAUSATION

You may have heard of the domino effect, how the downfall of one country with a shaky regime might trigger the downfall of a neighboring country. That is an example of causation. *Which TWO of the prompts below would most likely result in a sound discussion about causation?*

1. Why did the Islamic Gunpowder Empires decline in strength as Western Europe grew in military and economic strength?

2. What did the Ottoman, Safavid and Mughal Empires have in common?

3. Do you agree with the values of the ghazi ideal, a model for warrior life?

4. What contributed to the falling apart of the violent Tamerlane's empire?

5. Did Mehmed ("the Conqueror") reflect the values of fifteenth-century East Asia?

WRITE AS A HISTORIAN: USE GENERALIZATIONS

When writing an essay, think of each statement as both an example and a generalization. Consider the phrase "Islamic Gunpowder Empires." It is an example of the broader idea of empires, as well as a generalization that covers three smaller topics: the Ottoman, Safavid, and Mughal empires. *For each of the following statements, select the letter of the generalization that includes it.*

1. Suleiman I was a great reformer.

    a. The Ottoman Empire had a series of strong leaders.

    b. Suleiman I revamaped the empire's legal system.

2. Leaders of the Safavid Empire were mostly Shia.

    a. The empires that controlled Turkey, Persia, and India in the sixteenth and seventeenth centuries were all Islamic.

    b. Shah Abbas used religion to unify the people of his empire.

3. Akbar shared similarities with the famous Persian ruler, Darius.

    a. Both practiced religious toleration.

    b. Many successful rulers followed the same policies.

East Asian Stability
Meets Foreign Traders

On this account men of all ranks and dignities whatsoever,
even nearest to him in blood, stand in his presence with the
deepest awe, and recognize him as sole ruler.

—Ferdinand Verbiest, a European missionary, on Emperor Kangxi

China's Yuan Dynasty, founded by Mongol invader Kublai Khan in 1271, was overthrown in 1368, after less than a century in power. The *Ming Dynasty* (1368–1644) assumed power. Ming rulers managed to stabilize the East Asian region for nearly 300 years. The Ming era would see the arrival of the Portuguese and other Europeans, who aimed to encroach on the Asian trade network. Then, in 1644, the powerful Manchu (from neighboring Manchuria) seized power and established the *Qing Dynasty*, which would rule until 1911. During both of these dynasties, Japan and Korea would experience parallel developments but with unique aspects.

Ming Dynasty

The economy of China, especially the silk industry, continued to grow under the stable and powerful Ming Dynasty. Both the northern capital, *Beijing*, and the southern capital, *Nanjing*, were beautified. In Beijing, members of the royal family lived in the *Forbidden City*, a walled compound of royal palaces.

The Ming Dynasty was conservative in the sense that it wanted to return to beliefs and customs from China's past, erasing the influence of the Mongol rulers under the Yuan Dynasty. For example, Mongol dress and names were discouraged, and rulers promoted the ancient ways of thinking and living of Confucianism. The Ming Dynasty also brought back the traditional civil service exam, improved education by establishing a national school system, and reestablished the bureaucracy, which had fallen into disuse under the Mongols. Europeans began to learn about and admire the civil service system, and in the eighteenth century it became a model for some European bureaucracies. (For more about Confucianism, see pages 100–101.)

The Ming Dynasty also expanded the size of China, conquering lands in Mongolia and Central Asia. It would not hold them for long, however; in the 1440s, Mongol armies defeated Ming forces and even took the Ming emperor prisoner. In reaction to renewed Mongol power, China's leaders looked to the Great Wall of China. The Wall had not been maintained under Mongol rule, but under the Ming Dynasty it was restored and expanded to help keep out invaders from the north. (Test Prep: Create a chart comparing the Ming and Yuan dynasties. See pages 246–247.)

The Voyages of Zheng He In 1405, the Ming emperor Yongle sent a Muslim admiral, *Zheng He* (1371–1433), on the first of seven great voyages. Zheng traveled to Indonesia, Ceylon, and other coastal areas on the Indian Ocean, to Arabia, and to the east coast of Africa as well as to the Cape of Good Hope. The main purpose of the voyages was to display the might of the Ming Dynasty to the rest of the world and to receive tribute from them. Zheng's fleet was certainly impressive: at its height, his fleet included more than 300 ships with crews totalling about 25,000 people. In contrast, about a century later, the European explorer Ferdinand Magellan would command only five ships.

The expeditions won prestige for the Chinese government and opened up new markets for Chinese goods. Zheng He and his crew returned to China with exotic treasures, such as the first giraffe the Chinese had ever seen. They also brought back a new understanding of the world beyond China's borders. The voyages inspired some Chinese people to immigrate to the ports that the expedition had visited in Southeast Asia and elsewhere.

Zheng He's voyages stirred controversy, though. Confucianism promoted a stable, agrarian lifestyle, and scholars worried that greater interaction and trade with foreign cultures threatened China's social order. Some critics simply looked down upon other cultures, deeming them barbaric and vastly inferior to Chinese culture. Emperor Yongle's successor, his son Zhu Gaozhi, thought the expeditions were too expensive.

THE VOYAGES OF ZHENG HE

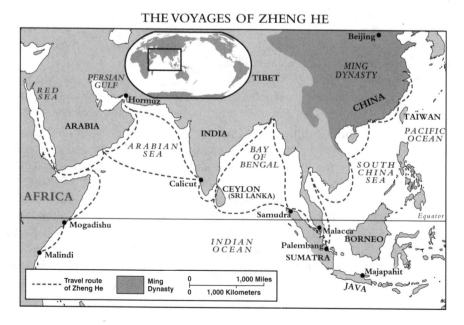

He not only ended Zheng He's travels but he also discouraged all Chinese from sailing away from China. To emphasize his point, he made building a ship with more than two masts a punishable offense.

The voyages had one positive short-term result: they put a stop to pirate activities off the coast of China and in Southeast Asia. However, after China stopped sending armed merchant ships into the ocean, the pirate activities resumed, especially on the China Sea.

A Portuguese Trading Empire in Asia

China's exploration of the outside world came to an end after Zheng He's final voyage in 1430. However, less than a century later, in 1514, the outside world arrived on China's doorstep in the form of Portuguese traders. At that time, Portugal's superior ships and weapons were unmatched among the Europeans. As a result of this advantage, the Portuguese had already won control of both the African and Indian coasts. They had won a decisive victory over a Turkish-Egyptian-Venetian fleet at Diu, India, in 1509. To ensure control of trade, the Portuguese had constructed a series of forts stretching from Hormuz on the Persian Gulf (built in 1507) to Goa in western India (built in 1510) to Malacca on the Malay Peninsula (built in 1511). The aim of the fort construction was to establish a *monopoly* (complete control over a market) over the spice trade in the area, and to license all vessels trading between Malacca and Hormuz. The forts gave Portugal a global trading post empire, one based on small outposts, not control of large territories.

Initial Portuguese visits had little impact on Chinese society. But the traders were followed by Roman Catholic missionaries, mainly Franciscans and Dominicans, who worked to gain converts among the Chinese people. The *Jesuits* soon followed and tried to win over the Chinese court elite. Scientific and technical knowledge were the keys to success at the court. Jesuit missionaries in *Macau*, such as Matteo Ricci (an Italian, arrived 1582) and Adam Schall von Bell (a German, arrived 1619), impressed the Chinese with their learning but were unable to win over many converts among the hostile scholar-gentry, who considered them barbaric. (For more about the expansion of Western European trade empires to China, see pages 288–291.)

Portuguese Vulnerability The Portuguese had success in global trade for several decades, but Portugal was a small nation, lacking manpower and the ships necessary for the enforcement and maintenance of a large trade empire. Many Portuguese merchants ignored their government and traded independently. In addition, there was rampant corruption among government officials, which further hampered the trading empire. By the seventeenth century, Dutch and English rivals were challenging the Portuguese in East Asia, including the islands that are today part of Malaysia and Indonesia. The Dutch captured Malacca and built a fort at Batavia in Java in 1620. From Batavia, the Dutch attempted to monopolize the spice trade. As a result, the English focused on India, pushing the Portuguese out of South Asia.

The Rise of the Qing Dynasty

During a famine in 1644, a peasant revolt led by a minor court official, *Li Zicheng*, conquered the Chinese capital, Beijing. The Manchu from Manchuria, the region northeast of China, saw the overthrow of the Ming Dynasty as an opportunity to seize power. They moved into China and pretended to help the Ming, but the Manchu easily ousted the inexperienced Li Zicheng and declared a new dynasty, the Qing Dynasty. People from Manchuria migrated into China to take advantage of the new lands and the high prestige of being part of the ruling ethnic elite. It took some 40 years before the Manchu pacified all of China, but then the Qing Dynasty was able to hold power for more than 250 years, until 1911.

The Qing Dynasty Like the Mongols some 400 years earlier, the Manchu were ethnically and culturally distinctive from the people they ruled. However, they were less tolerant than Mongol leaders, and they resolved to make their culture dominant in China. For example, men were obligated to dress in the Manchu style, wearing *queues* (braided pigtails), and those who refused were executed. Like the Mongols, the Manchurian-supported Qing put their own people in the top positions of government.

And like the Mongols, the Qing Dynasty did maintain continuity with some traditional Chinese practices. For example, they maintained the Chinese bureaucracy, including the civil service exams. In time, some, but not all, Chinese came to accept the Qing Dynasty as legitimate rulers of China.

Emperor Kangxi One of China's longest-reigning emperors, *Kangxi* (ruled 1661–1722) presided over a period of stability and expansion in China. Kangxi sent forces into Taiwan, Mongolia, and Central Asia, incorporating those areas into the empire. China also imposed a protectorate over *Tibet*, the mountainous land north of India, a policy reflected in China's control of the region today.

Kangxi had mixed policies toward Christian missionaries. At times, he showed great tolerance, and hundreds of thousands of Chinese people converted to Roman Catholicism. His successors were not as tolerant as he had been, and Chinese Catholics were forced to worship in secret. Nevertheless, Jesuits were respected by the Chinese because they learned how to speak and write in the Chinese language, they had high regard for Confucianism, and they were well educated and able to teach the Chinese the advances of European science.

Kangxi, a Confucian scholar and poet himself, urged the building of schools. He also authorized the compilation of the *Kangxi Dictionary*, with about 42,000 Chinese characters, which became the standard Chinese dictionary of the eighteenth and nineteenth centuries. Emperor Kangxi also sponsored a massive *Collection of Books*, comparable to Diderot's *Encyclopedia* during the eighteenth century in France.

Kangxi and Louis XIV		
Emperor Kangxi	**Both**	**King Louis XIV**
• Ruled Qing Dynasty China for 61 years • Encouraged introduction of Western education • Opened ports to foreign trade • Extended control over Tibet • Studied Western astronomy, physics, and medicine in spare time	• Became ruler during childhood • Excelled at horseback riding and archery • Spoke multiple languages • Supported the arts • Promoted study of sciences • Loved landscape gardens • Ruled during golden age of their empire	• Ruled France for 72 years • Known as the "Sun King" or Louis the Great • Built palace at Versailles • Extended France's eastern borders • Known as a symbol of absolute monarchy

Emperor Qianlong Another important Qing ruler was *Emperor Qianlong* (ruled 1736–1795), a poet, who was also knowledgeable in art and calligraphy. At the beginning of his reign, the country was well administered and government tax collections were at an all-time high. Qianlong initiated military campaigns in lands west of China, which led to the annexation of *Xinjiang* accompanied by the mass killings of the local population. Even today, parts of Xinjiang remain troubled, as the local Muslim population, called Uighurs, have never fully become incorporated into the rest of Chinese culture. Qianlong also sent armies into Tibet to install the Dalai Lama on the throne there. A campaign against the Nepalese was successful, forcing them to submit to Chinese rule. However, campaigns against Burma and Vietnam were unsuccessful and costly, resulting in the emptying of the empire's treasury.

Needing funds, the Qing Dynasty sold limited trading privileges to the European powers but confined them to *Guangzhou* (also known as *Canton*). The British were not satisfied with these limited privileges, so they asked for more trading rights in 1793. Emperor Qianlong responded by writing King George III a letter stating that the Chinese had no need for British manufactured goods.

During the later part of Qianlong's reign, the traditionally efficient Chinese bureaucracy became corrupt, levying high taxes on the people. In response to these high taxes and a desire to restore the Ming Dynasty, a group of peasants organized the *White Lotus Rebellion* (1796–1804). The Qing government supressed the uprising brutally, killing around 100,000.

Economic Changes China was a *proto-industrial* society in comparison to Western European nations, meaning that although some industry existed, the vast majority of people still worked on farms. As the population of China grew, the country experienced a land shortage, which the government attempted to rectify by setting laws that limited the amount of land people could own.

China's exports grew during the Qing Dynasty; China sold tea, silk, and porcelain products in Europe and India. The exports were largely purchased with silver, as China imported few goods. The demand for silk and the availability of silver for investing led to the creation of many silk workshops where former peasants could work for wages. The empire also instituted a tax on traded goods, which increased its wealth.

Chinese Society Social relations during this period reflected conservative adherence to Confucianism, which honored the family above the individual. Generations lived within the same household, and the elder generations were especially revered. Groups of extended families bonded into clans, and this solidarity helped to maintain social stability.

Women continued to have a lower status than men throughout the Ming and Qing dynasties. For example, formal education was restricted to men only, and divorce was not permitted. Pressure was put on widows not to remarry, and those new widows who committed suicide were honored after death. In addition, the traditional practice of binding women's feet continued to confer social status on women even as it greatly restricted their physical movement.

The Arts and Literature Some scholars argue that the modern novel can be traced back to *Journey to the West* (1590s), a fictional version of Xuanzang's pilgrimage to Buddhist sites in India. Twenty years later, China's first realistic novel was written by Lanling Xiaoxiao Sheng: *The Golden Lotus* (1610). Cao Xueqin penned *The Dream of the Red Chamber* (1791), a romance novel about life among the eighteenth-century aristocracy written in the Chinese vernacular based on Mandarin Chinese—a group of related languages spoken in northern and southwestern China.

Other types of art, such as fine Ming pottery and Manchu woodblock prints, also enjoyed a golden age in China during these dynasties.

Japan

Military leaders known as shoguns ruled Japan in the emperor's name from the twelfth to the fifteenth centuries. But then conflicts between landholding aristocrats called *daimyo* left Japan in disarray. Each daimyo had his own army of warriors known as samurai, ambition to conquer more territory, and power to rule his fiefdoms as he saw fit. Finally, just as gunpowder weapons enabled the rise of new empires in Turkey, Persia, and India, gunpowder weapons helped a series of three powerful daimyo to gradually unify Japan. (Test Prep: Write a paragraph connecting Shogun rule with the rule of the daimyo. See page 193.)

Powerful Daimyo The first of these powerful daimyo was *Oda Nobunaga*. Armed with muskets purchased from Portuguese traders, Nobunaga and his samurai took over *Kyoto* in 1568. He then began to extend his power, forcing daimyo in the lands around Kyoto to submit. Nobunaga had unified about one-third of what is today Japan when he was assassinated in 1582.

Nobunaga's successor, *Toyotomi Hideyoshi*, continued expanding the territory until most of what we now know as Japan was under his control. After his death in 1598, the center of power shifted to the city of *Edo* (Tokyo), controlled by the daimyo *Tokugawa Ieyasu* (ruled 1600–1616), who was declared shogun in 1603. His successors would continue to rule Japan into the mid-nineteenth century, in an era known as the *Period of Great Peace*.

Tokugawa Government The *Tokugawa Shogunate* set about reorganizing the governance of Japan in order to centralize control over what was essentially a feudal system. Japan was divided into 250 *hans*, or territories, each of which was controlled by a daimyo who had his own army and was fairly independent. However, the Tokugawa government required that daimyo maintain residences both in their home territory and also in the capital; if the daimyo himself was visiting his home territory, his family had to stay in Tokyo, essentially as hostages. This kept the daimyo under the control of the shogunate, reducing them to landlords who managed the hans, rather than independent leaders.

Social Changes As civil wars ended in Japan, the samurai warrior class declined in importance and many became unemployed. Some became *ronin*, samurai without masters. Some roamed the countryside, often becoming bandits. The government urged samurai to become bureaucrats, even though that profession did not pay as well as being a samurai had in the past.

Despite their unemployment, the traditional warrior class, including the daimyo, samurai, and ronin, remained near the top of the social pyramid in Japan, below only the emperor and the court. Below the warrior class, interestingly, were peasants and farmers, with artisans and merchants below them. Influenced by Confucian ideas, people viewed merchants as parasites because they made their profits from the work of others. Despite their low rank, some merchants became quite wealthy—wealthier than the daimyo, many of whom were becoming poorer as they lost power. Merchants and daimyo built lavish houses in the city of Edo. The very bottom rung of society was occupied by the *Eta*, a class comparable to the untouchables in India. The Eta were ostracized because they performed unclean jobs, such as executioner and butcher. Tightly regulated by the Japanese government, the Eta would not be emancipated until 1871. (Test Prep: Write a paragraph comparing Japan's class system with the caste system in India. See pages 92–93.)

Silk production flourished during the period of stability and the silver mine in Iwami Ginzan, one of the largest in the world, played an important role in trade. The use of banking and paper money also spurred commercial development. Agricultural production increased dramatically during the period, resulting in surplus crops of rice and cotton. Although the government restricted foreign trade, Chinese, Dutch, and Korean traders did well in Japan.

Arts and Literature During the prosperous Tokugawa Shogunate, Japanese arts and literature prospered. Wealthy merchants and daimyo spared no expense in constructing and decorating their residences. The Japanese refined the Chinese method of making woodblock prints. Arguably the most important contributor to literature of this period was the great poet *Matsuo Basho* (1644–1694), who developed and elevated the brief *haiku* form of poetry. Meanwhile, the stylized dance-drama called *kabuki theater* became extremely popular with audiences, who would often spend entire days watching performances. Fiction flourished as well. The stories of Ihara Saikaku, such as his *Five Women Who Loved Love* (1686), a collection of racy and down-to-earth stories about the exploits and adventures of five separate women, were very popular, particularly with the merchant klass.

Source: May S. Young / Flickr

The development of Kabuki theater in Japan (upper), and of Shakespearean plays in England (lower), emerged at opposite edges of Eurasia in the seventeenth century. Both types of drama appealed to an audience composed of people from the growing middle class.

Source: Dreamstime

Contact with Europeans European traders were initially welcomed when they arrived in Japan in the mid-sixteenth century. Christian missionaries were also tolerated at first. However, the thousands of new converts to Christianity were not especially tolerant of their old religions, and they were responsible for destroying some Buddhist shrines. In response, the then-regent Hideyoshi banned Christian worship in 1587, and missionaries were subsequently expelled. By the 1630s, nearly all foreigners were expelled from the country, and foreign books were prohibited. Japanese people could not travel abroad, and—as occurred in China—a ban on the construction of large ships was made official. The Japanese thought that they were through with the "uncouth" Europeans, but the Europeans would return in the nineteenth century. (For more about Japan's experiences with the West in the nineteenth century, see pages 454–458.)

Korea

Korea largely remained isolated from the rest of the world, earning it the title the *"Hermit Kingdom."* However, Korean culture continued to be strongly influenced by China. Korea, with assistance from the Ming, managed to turn away an attempted invasion by Japan in 1592. Years of fighting weakened Korea's military, enabling the Manchu to take over in the 1630s. Korea remained under the control of China under the Qing Dynasty. (For more on Korea's relationship to China, see pages 193 and 457.)

HISTORICAL PERSPECTIVES: WHY DID CHINA EXPLORE AND STOP?

Two historical debates swirl around the voyages of Zheng He. One focuses on the motive for the voyages. Historian Geoff Wade emphasizes international concerns. He argues that the voyages were motivated by a "proto-colonialistic" effort to control ports and trade routes throughout Asia. Other historians see the voyages as more benign, but still motivated by China's desire to establish a leading role in Asia.

In contrast, historians Jin Guo Ping (Sino-Portugal Cultural Research Center in Lisbon) and Wu Zhiliang (Macao) argue that international relations did not dictate the trips: domestic politics did. "It was that the Chinese people should recognize and acknowledge Emperor Yongle as the legitimate occupant of the throne." That is, the emperor sent Zheng He sailing in order to impress the people of China and win their support.

Historians also disagree on whether international or domestic concerns best explain why China did not follow up on Zheng He's travels. Some argue that stopping the voyages reflected China's low level of interest in the rest of the world: the kingdom considered itself the middle of the world and had no need for, or curiosity in, crops, animals, technologies, or ideas from foreign sources. Other historians focus more on internal politics. Zhang Jian, a historian at Sichuan University in China, suggests that the emperor stopped the voyages for very practical reasons: they were very expensive, and people complained about the cost, so the government decided to end them.

KEY TERMS BY THEME

ENVIRONMENT
Macau

CULTURE
Jesuits
Kangxi Dictionary
Collection of Books
Journey to the West
The Golden Lotus
The Dream of the Red
   Chamber
Matsuo Basho
haiku
kabuki theater

STATE-BUILDING
Ming Dynasty
Qing Dynasty
Beijing
Nanjing
Forbidden City
Zheng He
Li Zicheng
Kangxi
Tibet
Emperor Qianlong
Xinjiang
White Lotus Rebellion
Oda Nobunaga
Kyoto
Toyotomi Hideyoshi
Edo

Tokugawa Ieyasu
Period of Great Peace
Tokugawa Shogunate
hans
"Hermit Kingdom"

ECONOMICS
monopoly
Guangzhou (Canton)
proto-industrial

SOCIAL STRUCTURE
queues
daimyo
ronin
Eta

MULTIPLE-CHOICE QUESTIONS

1. Which of the following ways to determine historical periods would give historians the fullest picture of China from 1450 to 1750?
   (A) By foreign invaders who took control
   (B) By ruling dynasties
   (C) By European powers that arrived
   (D) By peasant revolts

2. Which of the following methods did China's Ming Dynasty use to improve the organization of its government?
   (A) Reestablished the traditional civil service exam and bureaucracy
   (B) Continued the governmental structures of the Mongol rulers
   (C) Copied the feudal system of Western Europe
   (D) Sent Zheng He to learn about government structures in other countries

3. A peasant revolt during the Ming Dynasty was one cause of
   (A) peasants reclaiming lands stolen by Manchu rulers
   (B) the Mongol Dynasty regaining power over all of China
   (C) the Manchu seizing power and establishing the Qing Dynasty
   (D) Europeans taking over key trade centers in China

4. Which of the following is most likely to have caused many Chinese people to emigrate to foreign lands in the first half of the fifteenth century?

   (A) the reestablishment of Confucianism

   (B) the fear of peasant rebellions

   (C) the influence of Zheng He's explorations

   (D) the influence of Portuguese traders

5. Which of the following statements best summarizes the status of women in China during the Qing period?

   (A) Women were considered equal to men according to Confucian principles.

   (B) Women were given more power than traditionally in China because the Manchu society was matriarchal.

   (C) Women were granted the right to divorce their husbands and inherit their property.

   (D) Women were regarded as inferior to men and could not obtain a formal education.

6. Which statement best describes the treatment of Christian missionaries by both China and Japan between 1450 and 1750?

   (A) Both were initially tolerant, allowing their subjects to convert to Christianity, but later banned Christian worship.

   (B) Both considered all Europeans to be "barbaric" and never allowed conversions to Christianity.

   (C) Both admired Western European learning and allowed their subjects to convert during the entire period.

   (D) Both initially banned Christian conversions, but then became more tolerant, allowing their subjects to convert to Christianity.

7. Which change in the structure of China's peasant labor system reflected a growing global demand for products?

   (A) the creation of workshops for silk workers

   (B) the reestablishment of China's civil service

   (C) the building of Portuguese outposts in China

   (D) the White Lotus Rebellion by angry peasants

8. Which statement best explains why the Portuguese were the first European traders to come to China?

(A) Portuguese ships and weapons were superior to those of other European powers.

(B) Portugal had a large enough population to maintain a long-term trading empire in Asia.

(C) Portugal succeeded in eliminating corruption among its government officials.

(D) Other European powers had no interest in building trade networks in Asia.

Question 9 is based on the quotation below.

The maritime forces sent abroad [by the Ming] in the first third of the fifteenth century were intended to achieve the recognition of Ming dominance. . . . To achieve this they used force, or the threat thereof. The number of Southeast Asian rulers travelling to China with the Zheng He missions suggests that coercion must have been an important element of the voyages. It was almost unheard of for Southeast Asian rulers to travel to other polities. . . . That such a large number of rulers did travel to the Ming court in this period suggests coercion of some form. "Gunboat diplomacy" is not a term which is usually applied to the voyages of Zheng He. However, given that these missions were nominally involved in diplomacy and it appears that the ships were indeed gunboats, with perhaps 26,000 out of 28,000 members of some missions being military men, this seems the appropriate term to apply to the duties of these armadas.

—From Geoff Wade, *The Zheng He Voyages: A Reassessment* (2004)

9. Which statement best summarizes the position of the historian of the above passage about the purpose of the Zheng He voyages?

(A) The purpose was primarily internal: to garner support for the emperor from the Chinese people.

(B) The purpose was to establish military dominance throughout the region.

(C) The purpose was to open new markets for Chinese goods.

(D) The purpose was to gather scientific knowledge from foreign lands.

Question 10 is based on the graphic below.

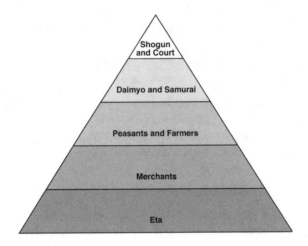

10. The social classes represented in this pyramid best represent which society or societies?

(A) China and Japan

(B) China

(C) Japan and Korea

(D) Japan

CONTINUITY AND CHANGE-OVER-TIME ESSAY QUESTIONS

Directions: You are to answer the following question. You should spend 5 minutes organizing or outlining your essay. Write an essay that:

• Has a relevant thesis and supports that thesis with appropriate historical evidence.

• Addresses all parts of the question.

• Uses world historical context to show continuities and changes over time.

• Analyzes the process of continuity and change over time.

1. Analyze the continuities and changes in the participation of China in the expanding global trade networks during the period from 1450 to 1750.

Questions for Additional Practice

2. Analyze the continuities and changes in the condition of the peasants in ONE of the following regions during the period from 1450 to 1750:
   - China
   - Japan
   - Russia
   - Western Europe

3. Analyze the continuities and changes in the role and power of political and economic elites in ONE of the following during the period from 1450 to 1750.
   - China
   - Japan

COMPARATIVE ESSAY QUESTIONS

Directions: You are to answer the following question. You should spend 5 minutes organizing or outlining your essay. Write an essay that:

- Has a relevant thesis and supports that thesis with appropriate historical evidence.
- Addresses all parts of the question.
- Makes direct, relevant comparisons.
- Analyzes relevant reasons for similarities and differences.

1. Analyze the similarities and differences in the maintenance of central governmental power and the recruitment and control of elites in China and Japan.

Questions for Additional Practice

2. Analyze the similarities and differences between the explorations of China's Admiral Zheng He and the Western European voyages of exploration of the fifteenth and sixteenth centuries.

3. Analyze the similarities and differences between the openness to technological and industrial advances of the East Asian nations with those of Western Europe in the period from 1450 to 1750.

THINK AS A HISTORIAN: RECOGNIZE PATTERNS OVER TIME

Learning to see patterns over time is an important skill for a historian. *Which ONE of the observations below describes a pattern of continuity and change over time?*

1. Emperor Kangxi, one of China's longest-reigning emperors, presided over a period of stability and expansion in China.

2. Wealth tends to bring about a flowering of culture, be it the golden age of pottery during the Ming Dynasty or the renaissance of literature during Japan's prosperous Tokugawa Shogunate.

3. The Ming Dynasty expanded the size of China, conquering lands in Mongolia and Central Asia.

4. Although strongly influenced by China, Korea remained isolated from the rest of the world during the period.

WRITE AS A HISTORIAN: USE QUOTATIONS

Quotations can bring history to life. The language of the past can be archaic, though, so it is important to understand what the words mean. *In the examples below, choose the best modern translations for the historic quotes.*

1. "You, Roman, remember to rule the peoples with power (these will be your arts.)"—Anchises

   a. Remember that wielding power well is a form of art.

   b. Artists should be part of the ruling class.

2. "On this account men of all ranks and dignities whatsoever, even nearest to him in blood, stand in his presence with the deepest awe, and recognize him as sole ruler."—Ferdinand Verbiest

   a. All men respect this ruler.

   b. His subjects could only stand in his presence, never sit.

3. "Your business is with action alone, not by any means with the fruit of the action."—*The Bhagavad Gita*

   a. To succeed in business, you have to be active.

   b. What matters is what you do, not what the results are.

PERIOD 4: Review

Thematic Review

Directions: Briefly answer each question in paragraph form.

1. **Interaction Between Humans and the Environment** Explain the effects of disease on the demographics of the Americas after European contact.

2. **Development and Interaction of Cultures** Compare the development of arts and literature during the Tokugawa Shogunate in Japan and the reign of Mughal emperors in India.

3. **Development and Interaction of Cultures** Explain how enslaved Africans preserved aspects of their culture in the Americas.

4. **State-Building, Expansion, and Conflict** Explain the reasons why England developed parliamentary rule while France became more absolutist during the period 1450 to 1750.

5. **Creation, Expansion, and Interaction of Economic Systems** Analyze the similarities and differences between the coerced labor systems in the Americas and serfdom in Russia between 1450 to 1750.

6. **Development and Transformation of Social Structures** Compare the social classes in Russia with those of the Ottoman Empire during the period 1450–1750.

TURNING POINT: WHY 1750?

Historians today often use 1750 to mark the end of the early modern period in world history. By then, two centuries of exploration and increasing trade had linked the world together. And around that date, people in Great Britain were beginning to use more and more machinery to produce goods, a shift that would spread throughout the world and become known as the Industrial Revolution. Historians focusing on the history of one country rather than the world might choose another date for the beginning of the modern industrial age. For example, Japan began to industrialize only after a domestic conflict known as the Meiji Restoration ended in 1868.

Some historians might start the modern period much earlier, in the sixteenth century. Indeed, the prestigious scholarly publication *Journal of Modern History* covers the period starting with the Renaissance. If the distinctive trait of the modern age is science, then the writings of Copernicus could be the starting point. Or if the modern age is the age of capitalism, then it could begin when mercantilism began to replace feudalism.

DOCUMENT-BASED QUESTION

Directions: The following question is based on the accompanying Documents 1–8. (The documents have been edited for the purpose of this exercise.)

This question is designed to test your ability to work with and understand historical documents. Write an essay that:

- Has a relevant thesis and supports that thesis with evidence from the document.
- Uses all of the documents.
- Analyzes the documents by grouping them in as many appropriate ways as possible. Does not simply summarize the documents individually.
- Takes into account the sources of the documents and analyzes the author's point of view.
- Identifies and explains the need for at least one additional type of document.

You may refer to relevant historical information not mentioned in the documents.

1. Using the following documents, describe the steps Peter the Great took in the late seventeenth and early eighteenth centuries to modernize Russia in order to transform the country into a major European power. What additional types of documents would be most helpful in furthering your analysis?

Document 1

Source: Bishop Burnet, of England, describing Peter the Great, 1698.

He was desirous to understand our doctrine, but he did not seem disposed to mend matters in Muscovy. He was, indeed, resolved to encourage learning and to polish his people by sending some of them to travel in other countries and to draw strangers to come and live among them. He seemed apprehensive still of his sister's intrigues. There was a mixture both of passion and severity in his temper. He is resolute, but understands little of war, and seemed not at all inquisitive that way.

Document 2

Source: Peter I, Decree Requiring Education of Russian Nobles.

Send to every gubernia [region] some persons from mathematical schools to teach the children of the nobility—except those of freeholders and government clerks—mathematics and geometry; as a penalty [for evasion] establish a rule that no one will be allowed to marry unless he learns these [subjects]. Inform all prelates to issue no marriage certificates to those who are ordered to go to schools.

Document 3

Source: Peter I, Decree on Foreigners, 1701.

Since our accession to the throne all our efforts and intentions have tended to govern this realm in such a way that all of our subjects should, through our care for the general good, become more and more prosperous. For this end we have always tried to maintain internal order, to defend the state against invasion, and in every possible way to improve and to extend trade. With this purpose we have been compelled to make some necessary and salutary changes in the administration, in order that our subjects might more easily gain a knowledge of matters of which they were before ignorant, and become more skillful in their commercial relations. We have therefore given orders, made dispositions, and founded institutions indispensable for increasing our trade with foreigners, and shall do the same in the future. . . . To attain these worthy aims, we have endeavored to improve our military forces, which are the protection of our State, so that our troops may consist of well-drilled men, maintained in perfect order and discipline. In order to obtain greater improvement in this respect, and to encourage foreigners, who are able to assist us in this way, as well as artisans profitable to the State, to come in numbers to our country, we have issued this manifesto.

Document 4

Source: Peter I, Decree on Wearing Western-Style Clothes, 1701.

Western dress shall be worn by all the boyars, members of our councils and of our court . . . gentry of Moscow, secretaries...provincial gentry, gosti [merchants], government officials, streltsy, members of the guilds purveying for our household, citizens of Moscow of all ranks, and residents of provincial cities . . . excepting the clergy and peasant tillers of the soil. The upper dress shall be of French or Saxon cut, and the lower dress . . . —waistcoat, trousers, boots, shoes, and hats— shall be of the German type. They shall also ride German saddles. Likewise the womenfolk of all ranks, including the priests', deacons', and church attendants' wives, the wives of the dragoons, the soldiers, and the streltsy, and their children, shall wear Western dresses, hats, jackets, and underwear—undervests and petticoats—and shoes. From now on no one of the abovementioned is to wear Russian dress or Circassian coats, sheepskin coats, or Russian peasant coats, trousers, boots, and shoes. It is also forbidden to ride Russian saddles, and the craftsmen shall not manufacture them or sell them at the marketplaces.

Document 5

Source: Statute for the College of Manufacturers, 1723.

His Imperial Majesty is diligently striving to establish and develop in the Russian Empire such manufacturing plants and factories as are found in other states, for the general welfare and prosperity of his subjects. He [therefore] most graciously charges the College of Manufacturers to exert itself in devising the means to introduce, with the least expense, and to spread in the Russian Empire these and other ingenious arts, and especially those for which materials can be found within the empire. . . . His Imperial Majesty gives permission to everyone, without distinction of rank or condition, to open factories wherever he may find suitable. . . .

Factory owners must be closely supervised, in order that they have at their plants good and experienced [foreign] master craftsmen, who are able to train Russians in such a way that these, in turn, may themselves become masters, so that their produce may bring glory to the Russian manufacturers.

Document 6

Source: Jean Rousset de Missy, *Life of Peter the Great*, c. 1730.

The tsar labored at the reform of fashions, or, more properly speaking, of dress. Until that time the Russians had always worn long beards, which they cherished and preserved with much care, allowing them to hang down on their bosoms, without even cutting the moustache. With these long beards they wore the hair very short, except the ecclesiastics, who, to distinguish themselves, wore it very long. The tsar, in order to reform that custom, ordered that gentlemen, merchants, and other subjects, except priests and peasants, should each pay a tax of one hundred rubles a year if they wished to keep their beards; the commoners had to pay one kopek each. Officials were stationed at the gates of the towns to collect that tax, which the Russians regarded as an enormous sin on the part of the tsar and as a thing which tended to the abolition of their religion.

These insinuations, which came from the priests, occasioned the publication of many pamphlets in Moscow, where for that reason alone the tsar was regarded as a tyrant and a pagan; and there were many old Russians who, after having their beards shaved off, saved them preciously, in order to have them placed in their coffins, fearing that they would not be allowed to enter heaven without their beards. As for the young men, they followed the new custom with the more readiness as it made them appear more agreeable to the fair sex.

Document 7

Source: Feofan Prokopovich's Funeral Sermon on Peter I, 1725.

O Russia, he . . . accomplished a deed unheard of in your annals, having introduced the building and sailing of ships. He gave you a new fleet that, to the wonderment of the world and surpassing all expectation, was in no way inferior to much older fleets, and he opened for you a path to all the ends of the earth, and spread your power and glory to the extreme corners of the ocean. . . .

It is known to the whole world how weak and impotent the Russian army was when it had no regular instruction, and how incomparably its strength was increased and became great and terrible when our august monarch, his Imperial Highness Peter the First, instructed it in a proper manner. The same is true of architecture, medicine, political government, and all other affairs.

But, most of all, that is true of the government of the Church: when there is not the light of instruction, the Church cannot have any good conduct, and impossibly can there be avoided disorder and superstitions that deserve a great deal of ridicule, as well as strife, and most foolish heresies.

Document 8

Source: Portrait of Peter the Great. Library of Congress.

PERIOD 5: Industrialization and Global Integration, c. 1750 to c. 1900

Chapter 21 *The Enlightenment, Nationalism, and Revolutions*

Chapter 22 *Industrial Revolution, 1750-1900*

Chapter 23 *Turkey, China, Japan, and the West*

Chapter 24 *Global Links and Imperialism, 1750-1900*

Period Overview

Beginning in the mid-eighteenth century, people began to build new and better machinery to replace human and animal power to perform work. These developments, known as the Industrial Revolution, caused manufacturing output to skyrocket and goods to become more plentiful than ever before. Among the several factors that helped cause the Industrial Revolution were increases in agricultural productivity, urbanization, the accumulation of money for investments, and the specialization of labor. The process began in Great Britain and spread throughout Europe and into the United States and Japan.

Products of industrialization such as railroads, steamships, and telegraphs expanded global trade and communications networks. These networks linked farmers, miners, manufacturers, and customers around the world. Industrial countries, to protect the access of their businesses to resources and markets, established overseas colonies. In response, colonies often rebelled. Some, such as the United States and Haiti, were successful right away. Others, such as India and China, laid the foundations for later success.

Even as countries such as Russia and China were expanding their empires, a new form of political organization was emerging: the nation-state. People increasingly felt that cultural and political borders should be the same. This feeling touched off waves of violent conflict. Some conflicts were rebellions to break up multi-ethnic empires such as the Ottoman Empire and Austria-Hungary into separate countries. Other conflicts, such as ones in Germany and Italy, united people who shared a culture but were divided into different states.

Disruptions caused by industrialization and political changes caused massive migrations of people. Some people moved voluntarily in search of work, including most Europeans who moved to the Americas, Southern Africa, India, or Australia. Others, such as the indentured servants from India who went to southern Africa, were semicoerced. Some people were captured by force, such as the Africans who were seized and taken to the Americas. The result of all this migration was greater ethnic diversity around the world.

Key Concepts

5.1. Industrialization and Global Capitalism

    I. Industrialization fundamentally changed how goods were produced.

    II. New patterns of global trade and production developed and further integrated the global economy as industrialists sought raw materials and new markets for the increasing amount and array of goods produced in their factories.

    III. To facilitate investments at all levels of industrial production, financiers developed and expanded various financial institutions.

    IV. There were major developments in transportation and communication.

    V. The development and spread of global capitalism led to a variety of responses.

    VI. The ways in which people organized themselves into societies also underwent significant transformations in industrialized states due to the fundamental restructuring of the global economy.

5.2. Imperialism and Nation-State Formation

    I. Industrializing powers established transoceanic empires.

    II. Imperialism influenced state formation and contraction around the world.

    III. New racial ideologies, especially Social Darwinism, facilitated and justified imperialism.

5.3. Nationalism, Revolution, and Reform

    I. The rise and diffusion of Enlightenment thought that questioned established traditions in all areas of life often preceded the revolutions and rebellions against existing governments.

    II. Beginning in the eighteenth century, peoples around the world developed a new sense of commonality based on language, religion, social customs, and territory. These newly imagined national communities linked this identity with the borders of the state, while governments used this idea to unite diverse populations.

    III. Increasing discontent with imperial rule propelled reformist and revolutionary movements.

    IV. The global spread of European political and social thought and the increasing number of rebellions stimulated new transnational ideologies and solidarities.

5.4. Global Migration

    I. Migration in many cases was influenced by changes in demography in both industrialized and unindustrialized societies that presented challenges to existing patterns of living.

    II. Migrants relocated for a variety of reasons.

    III. The large-scale nature of migration, especially in the nineteenth century, produced a variety of consequences and reactions to the increasingly diverse societies on the part of migrants and the existing populations.

Source: *AP® World History Course and Exam Description.*

21

The Enlightenment, Nationalism, and Revolutions

Every nation gets the government it deserves.

—Joseph de Maistre (1753–1821)

Like English statesman *Edmund Burke*, French thinker Joseph de Maistre was a conservative who went against the tide of Enlightenment thinking. In the view of conservative thinkers such as Burke and Maistre, revolutions were bloody, disruptive, and unlikely to yield positive results. However, try as conservatives might to quell revolutionary change, the desire of common people for constitutional government and democratic practices erupted in revolutions throughout the nineteenth century. And many nations did, indeed, get a new form of government that responded to the new wave of thinking with its key ideals: progress, reason, and natural law.

An Age of New Ideas

Growing out of the Scientific Revolution and the humanism of the Renaissance, the thinking of the Enlightenment was optimistic. Many writers believed that the application of reason to natural laws and rights would result in infinite progress. This idea, while not atheistic, nevertheless emphasized man's accomplishments in discovering the laws of the natural world. It led to the conclusion that natural laws governed the social and political spheres. While traditional religion did not disappear, it became less pervasive. The idea of *Deism*, the belief that a divinity simply set natural laws in motion and then did not interfere or cause miracles in the world, emerged. (Test Prep: Write a paragraph connecting the expression of Enlightenment ideals during this period with their expression from 1450 to 1750. See pages 286–288.)

New ideas emerged about how to improve society. Schools of thought including *socialism* and liberalism arose, giving rise to the period being called "the Age of Isms." Opposing socialism and liberalism were the currents of *conservatism*, particularly popular among European rulers, and *romanticism*.

The clash between new ideas and old political structures led to revolutions that often had two aims: independence from imperial powers and constitutional representation. The breakup of empires and the emergence of new forms of government often followed, developing out of the concept of *nationalism*, a feeling of intense loyalty to others who share one's language and culture. The idea that people who share a culture should also share a government threatened to destroy all of the multi-ethnic empires in Europe.

New Ideas and Their Roots

In the seventeenth century, Francis Bacon had laid the foundations for the empirical method of scientific inquiry, which is based on the observation of natural data. In the same century, philosophers Thomas Hobbes (author of *Leviathan*, 1651) and *John Locke* (author of *Two Treatises of Government*, 1690) viewed political life as the result of a *social contract*. Hobbes argued that people's natural state was to live in a bleak world in which life was "nasty, brutish, and short." However, by agreeing to a social contract, they gave up some of their rights to an absolutist monarch in return for law and order.

Locke, on the other hand, argued that the social contract implied the right, even the responsibility, of citizens to revolt against unjust government. Locke argued also that each man had a natural right—a right in the "state of nature"—to life, liberty, and the pursuit of property. Another of Locke's influential ideas is found in *An Essay Concerning Human Understanding* (1690), in which he proposed that children were born with minds like "blank slates" (*tabula rasa*) waiting to be filled with knowledge. In a world in which most people believed that an individual's intelligence, personality, and fate were heavily determined by their ancestry, Locke's emphasis on how environment shapes people was radical. It also implied that society should promote education.

The Philosophes In the eighteenth century, a new group of thinkers and writers who came to be called the *philosophes* explored social, political, and economic theories in new ways, popularizing concepts that they felt followed rationally upon those of the scientific thinkers of the seventeenth century. Taking their name from the French word *philosophe* ("philosopher"), these writers included Thomas Jefferson and Benjamin Franklin from America, Adam Smith from Scotland, and *Mary Wollstonecraft*, from England, who wrote *A Vindication of the Rights of Woman* (1792). Also prominent were French thinkers Diderot (editor of a vast encyclopedia) and three major Enlightenment philosophers: *Baron Montesquieu, Voltaire,* and *Jean-Jacques Rousseau.* These thinkers wrote extensively with one another, with some monarchs, and with the reading public throughout the Western world.

Of particular importance to writers of the new constitutions in France and America in the eighteenth and nineteenth centuries were the ideas of Baron Montesquieu. His famous work *The Spirit of Laws* (1748) praised the British government's use of checks on power by means of its Parliament. Montesquieu thus influenced the American system, which adopted his ideas by separating its executive branch (the president) from its legislative branch (Congress) and both from its third branch (the federal judiciary).

Francois-Marie Arouet, whose pen name was Voltaire, is perhaps best known for his social satire *Candide* (1762). He was famous during his lifetime for his wit and for his advocacy of civil liberties. Exiled for three years due to a conflict with a member of the French aristocracy, Voltaire lived in England long enough to develop an appreciation for its constitutional monarchy and regard for civil rights. He brought these ideas back to France, where he campaigned for religious liberty and judicial reform. His correspondence with heads of state (such as Catherine the Great of Russia and Frederick the Great of Prussia) and his voluminous writings, including articles in Diderot's *Encyclopedia*, are still quoted today. His idea of religious liberty influenced the U.S. Constitution.

A contemporary of Voltaire was the writer Jean-Jacques Rousseau, who expanded on the idea of the social contract as it had passed down through the work of Hobbes and Locke. Rousseau is often considered a pre-Romantic because his work seems to rebel against the social and political privileges of the French aristocracy as well as against scientific rationalism. One of Rousseau's early works was *Emile, or On Education* (1762) in which he laid out his ideas on child-rearing and education. A later work titled *The Social Contract* (1762) presented the concept of the General Will of a population and the obligation of a sovereign to carry out that General Will. An optimist who believed that society could improve, Rousseau gave the revolutionaries of the late eighteenth century hope of establishing better governments.

Salons and Coffeehouses Social gatherings of European intellectuals, or *salons*, took place in the homes of the rich and famous. As hostesses, some women made their marks on the eighteenth century by bringing together artists, politicians, philosophers, and popular writers who took the progressive ideas of the Enlightenment to the public. In addition to meeting in salons, writers and other intellectuals met in the coffeehouses of the major cities of Europe.

Such places became centers of the new economic thinking that changed radically in the eighteenth century. The *physiocrats*, as the new economic thinkers were called, often followed the ideas of *Adam Smith*. In his book *The Wealth of Nations* (1776), Smith argued for abandoning mercantilism in favor of free trade. His famous phrase *laissez-faire* (French for "leave alone") meant that governments should minimize their intervention in the economy. While Smith did support some regulations and taxes, he believed that everyone would be better off if the economic marketplace regulated itself more than it did under mercantilism. Smith also said that each person should act according to the dictates of his or her morals, with the result that good would filter through to all of society. (Test Prep: Create a chart or Venn diagram comparing and contrasting mercantilism and the free market. See pages 286–288.)

Deism The Enlightenment's emphasis on reason inspired new attempts among intellectuals to establish the relationship of humans to God or at least to God's natural world. *Deists* argued that God created the world and then sat back to observe its movements according to natural laws that could be discovered by scientific inquiry. *Thomas Paine*, never one to shrink from conflict, was militant in his defense of Deism in the book *The Age of Reason* (1794). Paine's previous work, *Common Sense* (1776), made him popular in America for advocating liberty from Britain, but his anti-church writings damaged much of his popularity. Deists compared the divinity to a watchmaker who makes a watch but does not interfere in its day-to-day workings: he creates a world and sits back to watch it move by its own natural laws. The Deists' relationship to God is consequently more impersonal and theoretical than those of Christians who focused on miracles and faith. Nevertheless, many of the Deists viewed regular church attendance as an important social obligation and moral guide.

European Intellectual Life, 1250–1789		
Period	Representative Thinkers	Characteristics
Medieval Scholasticism	• St. Thomas Aquinas (1225–1274)	• Used reason to defend faith • Argued through writing and debating • Relied heavily on Aristotle • Used little experimentation
Renaissance Humanism	• Erasmus (1466–1536) in Northern Europe • Mirandola (1463–1494) in Southern Europe	• Wrote practical books, such as Machiavelli's *The Prince* • Emphasized human accomplishments • Focused on secularism and the individual
Scientific Revolution and Enlightenment	• Francis Bacon (1561–1626) • Isaac Newton (1642–1727) • Thomas Hobbes (1588–1679) • John Locke (1632–1704) • French *philosophes*	• Emphasized collecting empirical data • Believed in natural rights, progress, and reason • Wanted new constitutions to improve governments • Supported religious toleration • Wrote for the reading public

Enlightened Despots

European monarchs of the Enlightenment period were often contradictory figures—they were enlightened in ideas of serving in the interest of their subjects and yet despotic in carrying out their ideas. They read about and believed in progress and reason, but also wanted the law to remain theirs to control. Enlightened despots would expand empires, build canals, invest in industry and education, and sometimes promote commoners on the basis of merit. They were unusually tolerant toward religions other than their own. On the other hand, they often suppressed dissent, using secret police forces to spy on their critics. They also insisted on ruling without the advice and consent of legislative bodies. While their goals were frequently progressive and reasonable, their methods could be tyrannical. Examples were Frederick the Great of Prussia (ruled 1740–1786), Maria Theresa of Austria (ruled 1740–1780), *Napoleon Bonaparte* of France (ruled 1799–1814), and Catherine the Great of Russia (ruled 1762–1796).

Only a few European monarchs could be called enlightened. Meanwhile, some Asian rulers in areas such as the "Gunpowder Empires" became less progressive and more despotic as their empires began to decline in territory and prestige. In the Ottoman Empire, for example, sultans who might have instituted Enlightenment reforms were violently opposed by conservative groups such as the Janissaries and the ulama (religious experts). The opposition forced Sultan Selim III (ruled 1789–1807) to suspend reforms to make his army more efficient, to centralize government, and to standardize taxes. He was executed before government forces could rescue him from a massive uprising of the Janissaries. (For more about the "Gunpowder Empires," see pages 353–363)

Revolutions and Reactions

Despite the few enlightened despots, conservative forces grounded in centuries of tradition and dynastic ambition resisted the new ideas of representative government. However, conservatives faced growing pressure to change. As urbanization increased and a new middle class rose out of the Industrial Revolution, people increasingly protested against governments that failed to recognize individual and natural rights. All over Europe and in its colonies, revolution—and reaction—were in the air in the late eighteenth century.

Periodization and Revolutions On the surface, modern revolutions appear to follow a similar pattern. In *The Anatomy of Revolution* (1938), Crane Brinton described the similarities of four political revolutions: the English Revolution of the 1640s, the American Revolution of 1776, the French Revolution of 1789, and the Russian Revolution of 1917. Brinton thought that all four revolutions went through four stages.

1. Citizens become dissatisfied with government.

2. Moderates gain more power.

3. Radicals take over in a "terror" phase.

4. The process culminates in a period of relative calm and acceptance, or what he calls the "Thermidorean Reaction."

Within this pattern, each revolution had unique revolutionary circumstances and outcomes. For example, Brinton acknowledged that the American Revolution, unlike the other three, lacked a "terror" phase. He concluded his study by noting that some top-down reforms imposed by government or elite leaders brought more lasting social change than the political revolutions he described. (For more about a top-down revolution, read about the regime of Mustafa Kemal in Turkey. See page 521.)

The American Revolution

The ideals that inspired the American Revolution had their roots in European Enlightenment philosophy. Despite being a conservative thinker, even the British writer Edmund Burke was willing to support the American Revolution. "No taxation without representation" was a distinctly English notion, demanded repeatedly and with increasing insistence from the time of the Magna Carta. Burke, though, would not be so generous toward the French Revolution, which followed the American one by about a decade.

The economic ideas of the physiocrats also played a part in the American Revolution, providing a defense of free market ideas in opposition to English mercantilism. Additionally, the American colonists had become more independent politically: colonial legislatures were making decisions usually made by Parliament. Moreover, great distances separated the colonists from Parliament and the king in London. With economic and political desires for independence grew a new social spirit. In America, chances for success were shaped less by the status of one's parents and more by one's own merit.

Declaration of Independence On July 4, 1776, the *Declaration of Independence* expressed the philosophy behind the Patriots' fight against British troops in America. In writing the document, Thomas Jefferson picked up the phrase "unalienable rights" from John Locke. For Jefferson, these rights were to life, liberty, and the pursuit of happiness. In the war that followed, the colonists received crucial help from Britain's long-time enemy, France, and eventually triumphed. With the British–U.S. Treaty of Paris of 1783, the 13 colonies won their independence from Britain.

New Constitution During the Revolutionary War, Americans created their own government under the Articles of Confederation. In it, they reacted against the excesses of the British government by setting up a weak central government. That government had no executive branch and no power to impose taxes, and it kept most authority with the individual states.

In a few years, many leaders began calling for a stronger central government. The result was the *United States Constitution*, which was ratified by the states in 1788. The U.S. Constitution, the oldest written constitution still in use in the world today, created a republic with a bicameral legislature (House of Representatives and Senate), an executive who was elected by the people through an Electoral College, and a judicial branch. These three branches of government illustrate the *separation of powers* so praised by the French writer Montesquieu: executive, judicial, and legislative. These branches provide important *checks and balances* on one another. Ten amendments to the Constitution, known as the Bill of Rights, were soon added to protect basic civil liberties such as freedom of speech and freedom of religion, as well as the rights of people accused of crimes.

The French Revolution

In France in the 1780s, revolutionary ideals took on their own spin, summarized in the slogan *liberté, égalité, et fraternité* (liberty, equality, and fraternity). These ideas were popularized through the writings of the *philosophes*.

Economic Woes However, there were additional causes that led to the French Revolution. France had long spent more money than it was taking in, partly to finance a series of wars against Great Britain and other countries.

Among this spending was the economic aid that France supplied the Americans in their revolution. In order to address its dire financial situation, the French government called a meeting of the Estates-General in the spring of 1789.

The chart below shows the social and legal breakdown of the French population in 1789. Note that the *First Estate* (the clergy) and the *Second Estate* (the nobility) paid almost no direct tax, and they resisted calls that they pay any more. The burden of taxation fell on the *Third Estate,* the common people, composed of peasants, urban workers, and the *bourgeoisie,* or middle class.

France's Estates in the Eighteenth Century			
Estate	Population	Land Ownership	Taxation
First: Clergy	Less than 1%	About 10%	Less than 1%
Second: Nobility	Less than 2%	About 25%	Less than 1%
Third: Commoners	More than 97%	About 65%	More than 98%

Since *King Louis XVI* (ruled 1774–1792) could not raise more money to finance the large and inefficient government, he called for the Estates-General to meet in 1789. Not having met since the days of Louis XIII in the early seventeenth century, the calling of the Estates-General caused excitement in France. Finance ministers had come and gone in the French government, fired when their plans for equalizing the tax burden had faltered. Now Louis XVI would be forced into some action.

The Revolution Begins When the Estates-General met, the First and Second Estate outvoted the Third Estate by a margin of two to one. Thus, the Third Estate withdrew to an indoor tennis court where they declared their intention to remain apart until a National Assembly could be formed that would grant one vote per member rather than one vote per estate. Representatives from the Third Estate supported this revolutionary idea with the *Tennis Court Oath*, which also called for a constitution limiting the king's power.

The early days of the French Revolution were exciting, as moderates like Marquis de Lafayette seemed to be on the point of establishing a constitutional monarchy. The National Assembly began meeting in Paris, but then the King threatened to arrest the leaders. Angry crowds rioted in Paris and elsewhere in France. On July 14, 1789, a crowd in Paris stormed the *Bastille*, a former prison that still symbolized the abuses of the monarchy and the corrupt aristocracy. In the French countryside, peasants rose up against nobles, even burning some manor houses. Some royal officials fled France. The king was forced to accept a new government with a National Assembly in charge.

The date July 14, 1789, became French Independence Day. The most permanent changes were enacted early in the Revolution—the abolition of feudalism and the adoption of the *Declaration of the Rights of Man*, a statement declaring basic human rights. However, one major problem for the new government was its creation of the *Civil Constitution of the Clergy*, which abolished special privileges of the Catholic Church in France and put it under state control. Condemned by the Pope and most of the French clergy, the document made the Church into a stronger opponent of the revolution. Louis XVI and the nobility refused to accept the limited monarchy, which led to dissatisfaction among radical groups such as the Jacobins and inspired the establishment of the First French Republic in 1792. It was from the Jacobins that sprang the Reign of Terror, a period during which the government executed thousands of opponents of the revolution.

Reign of Terror Among the first to die in the Reign of Terror was Louis XVI, who was executed by guillotine (beheading) in 1793. Louis' death raised grave fears among European leaders. Prussia and Austria were already at war with France. Britain, Spain, and Holland would join them. Besieged by enemies abroad and at home, the ironically named Committee of Public Safety, led by *Maximilien Robespierre*, sought to quell opposition by imposing the death penalty on opponents. They also started the *levée en masse*, or mass male conscription into military service. The idea grew from the revolutionary ideal of the democratic citizen, who, while assured of certain rights, was also given certain responsibilities, such as fighting for the security of the nation.

Also sent to the guillotine in 1793 was *Olympe de Gouges*, a French playwright. Her *Declaration of the Rights of Woman and the Female Citizen* (1791) alienated the male dominated leadership of the French Revolution. In pamphlets that she had written, she had asserted that French women should be given the same political rights as French men, and her work *Social Contract* called for marriages to be based on gender equality.

Conservative Reaction In 1794, moderates regained control of the French government and provided a return to a sense of security. They had Robespierre beheaded, thus ending the Reign of Terror. Yet another constituent assembly formulated a constitution. This period of relative calm became known as the *Thermidorean Reaction*, so named after *Thermidor*, the "month of heat" in the French revolutionary calendar when much of this reaction occurred.

As revolutionary vigor decreased in 1795, an oligarchic form of government called the Directory came to power. Under it, important reforms took place that preserved people's natural rights. The French had abolished slavery in the French colonies a year earlier, and now they reformed education and prohibited *primogeniture* (the right of an eldest son to inherit all his parents' property).

Nationalism increased in France and in other areas of Europe and in the Americas. More than in the past, people felt a common bond with others who spoke their language, shared their history, and followed their customs. Nationalism would contribute to the French people's willingness to support the 1799 coup led by the young general Napoleon, himself one of the directors of the new government. By 1804, France had returned to one-man rule governed by Emperor Napoleon Bonaparte (ruled 1804–1814). Meanwhile, nationalism was thriving in France and beyond its borders in areas conquered by Napoleon, particularly those in the Germanic areas of the declining Holy Roman Empire.

Napoleon's Reforms Coming to power later than the enlightened despots of the eighteenth century, Napoleon nevertheless shared many of their characteristics. He instituted a series of popular changes.

1. He made the tax burden more equal than it had been under the monarchy.

2. He had a new law code, the *Code Napoleon,* prepared. In it, all citizens were equal, and it provided for trial by jury and freedom of religion. It became the model for other law codes he imposed on lands he conquered.

3. Napoleon set up a public school system.

4. He sponsored archaeological expeditions in Egypt and elsewhere.

5. He established the French Legion of Honor (an honor society for those who served France well) and promoted government and military officials according to merit rather than family connections.

6. He even made peace with the Pope (Concordat of 1801), who had been distanced from France by the Civil Constitution of the Clergy.

Napoleon the Dictator Despite his achievements, Napoleon was despotic in his use of internal spies and control of government. More than any ruler, he showed the contradictions in the term "enlightened despot."

Napoleon's Foreign Policy In foreign affairs, Napoleon defeated the armies of Russia, Prussia, and Austria. His armies occupied northern Italy, knitting together a puppet kingdom out of several Italian states. Napoleon's conquests helped bring an end to the Austrian-dominated Holy Roman Empire and united several German states into a Confederation of the Rhine. He set up his relatives as "rulers" over France's satellite nations, such as Spain, Naples, and Westphalia. Part of his downfall came from instituting the Continental System, an international embargo of British trade. It failed because other nations refused to comply, and Britain retaliated with its own embargo.

Failure in the Peninsular Campaign Two poor military decisions led to Napoleon's downfall. France invaded Portugal in 1807, and soon Spain as well. Britain sent troops to help those countries fight France. This Peninsular Campaign tied up many French troops and other resources.

Disaster in Russia Five years into the Peninsular Campaign, Napoleon invaded Russia, using troops from all over Europe. At first, the campaign seemed successful. His forces were victorious at the Battle of Borodino, outside Moscow, and occupied the Russian capital. But *Tsar Alexander I* refused to sign a peace treaty. The Russian Army simply retreated farther east. Napoleon realized his army would never chase down the Russian army and destroy it. The French began to retreat. However, the harsh Russian winter set in. By the end of 1812, the French forces were suffering from hunger, cold, and disease. Napoleon had sent 600,000 soldiers to Russia. Only 100,000 returned. About half of the deaths were caused by typhus. The rest came from a combination of other diseases, battle wounds, the cold weather, hunger, and thirst.

Napoleon's military failure in the Peninsular Campaign and in Russia showed that he could be defeated. In 1814, France faced attack by the allied forces of Austria, Russia, Prussia, and Great Britain. After these forces took Paris, Napoleon abdicated. At the *Congress of Vienna* in 1815, the European powers, led by *Klemens von Metternich*, the conservative prime minister of Austria, exiled Napoleon to the island of Elba. Then, they set about restoring former boundaries and former dynasties. The Congress of Vienna marked the resurgence of conservative forces that opposed nationalist movements and revolutions. For much of the nineteenth century, these forces would try to keep peace by maintaining a *balance of power* among European nations and by opposing popular upheavals. Their biggest test came in 1848, when violent protests demanding wider participation in government broke out in Austria, France, Germany, Prussia, and Italy. All were defeated.

The Haitian Revolution

At the end of the eighteenth century, revolutionary forces were also at work in the rich French sugar and coffee colony of *Haiti* on the western end of the island of St. Domingue. Escaped slaves, called *Maroons*, revolted against their white masters, killing them and burning their houses. The examples of the recent American and French revolutions led former slave *Toussaint L'Ouverture* to join the revolts in 1791 and then to lead a general rebellion against slavery. Besides being well-read in Enlightenment thought, L'Ouverture proved to be a capable general. His army of enslaved Africans and Maroons established an independent government and played various forces of French, Spanish, and British against each other.

In 1801, after taking control of the territory that would become the independent country of Haiti, L'Ouverture produced a constitution that granted equality and citizenship to all residents. He also declared himself governor for life and declared complete independence of Haiti from France. Haiti next enacted land reform: plantations were divided up, with the lands being distributed among former slaves and free blacks.

L'Ouverture worked with the French but then he was betrayed by them. France promised to grant Haitian independence if L'Ouverture would abdicate, but then Napoleon had L'Ouverture captured and arrested. L'Ouverture was executed in France in 1803. Nevertheless, he had succeeded in establishing the abolition of slavery in Haiti and set Haiti on the road to complete independence from France.

In 1804, L'Ouverture's successor, Jean-Jacques Dessalines, took advantage of a distracted Napoleon and of an outbreak of yellow fever to declare Haitian independence permanently. Thus, Haiti became the first country in Latin America to win its independence and the first post-colonial, independent, black-led country in the world. It was also the only country to become permanently independent as a result of a slave uprising.

Comparing the Haitian and French Revolutions

Both the Haitian and French revolutions grew out of the Enlightenment's insistence that men had natural rights as citizens, and that legal restraints were limiting the freedom of people by forcing them into various estates (social classes). However, in the case of the Haitians, the restraints were more severe in that the rebellion was led by slaves who had no rights at all.

Long after its revolution, poverty would plague Haiti, while in France, protection of property and reform of taxation enacted during the French Revolution would help France's economic recovery. But the outcome in both cases was increased freedom. In France, the legal establishment of estates was abolished along with the last vestiges of feudalism. In Haiti, slavery was abolished and the rights of citizens were upheld. While class differences did not evaporate, legal discrimination was ended in Haiti even before its independence by the Constitution of 1801.

However, the Haitians had an additional wish—independence from France. While France wrestled with internal reform and the need for return to stability and order after the Reign of Terror, Haiti wrestled with the desire of foreign powers to exert control over them. Haiti succeeded in establishing the first independent republic in the Caribbean, although its economic success has been limited. France in the nineteenth century shifted between being a constitutional monarchy, a republic, and an empire, and back to being a republic. In both France and Haiti, aims of the Enlightenment were implemented. However, many necessary advances were yet to be made.

Creole Revolutions in Latin America

On the Latin American mainland, revolutionary ideals were taken up by *creoles*. Born of European parents in the Americas, the creoles were well educated and aware of the ideas behind the revolutions in North America and France. They considered themselves superior to the *mestizos*, who were born of European and Indian parents. Colonists who were born in Spain or Portugal, known as *Peninsulares*, felt superior to everyone. At the bottom of the social ladder were the African slaves, the indigenous population, and those of mixed African–indigenous heritage. (Some of these social distinctions remain today.)

There were many reasons for discontent in the colonies. Many creoles wanted independence from Spain because of Spain's mercantilist policies. These policies required that the colonists buy manufactured goods only from Spain and sell their products only to Spain. The creoles tended to be the wealthy landowners, mine owners, and businesspeople. As such, they were the ones most vocal against mercantilist policies.

Meanwhile, Spain tended to give important government jobs in the colonies to Peninsulares. Creoles resented this situation and wanted more political power. Mestizos also wanted political power, as well as a share of the wealth of the colonies. Many had jobs in the towns or worked in the mines or on the estates of the peninsulares and creoles.

Mexico Becomes Independent A Mexican village priest, Father *Miguel Hidalgo,* called on Indians and mestizos for support in his 1810 drive for Mexican independence from Spain. Hidalgo and his followers won several battles, but the previously sympathetic creoles turned on him when the revolutionaries began attacking and looting their property. As the owners of large ranches and mines, the creoles eventually supported the Spanish authorities, who came to represent law and order. The Spanish captured and then executed Hidalgo.

In 1821, a creole colonel named Agustín de Iturbide attracted the support of the Mexican army and the Roman Catholic Church to win freedom for Mexico City. Spain was so preoccupied with domestic problems that even Mexican conservatives were ready for independence from the home country. The leadership vacuum allowed Iturbide to declare Mexico an independent empire with himself as emperor. Opposition forces led by the conservative general Antonio López de Santa Anna soon overthrew Iturbide, and in 1824 Mexico became a republic. In the coming decades, Mexico would have many heads of government who had been successful military leaders.

The 1824 Mexican constitution guaranteed basic civil rights but did not address serious issues of inequitable land distribution, widespread poverty, the status of Mexican Indians, and inequitable educational access. The political environment featured *liberals* calling for reforms and *conservatives* opposing them. Liberals were influenced by the French and U.S. political models; they stressed the importance of individual rights and opposed the centralized state model of government. They wanted to limit the role of the Roman Catholic Church in politics and in education. Conservatives, by contrast, favored a centralized state in alliance with the Church.

Conflict with the United States In the 1830s and 1840s, the Mexican government was led by the *caudillo* (military dictator), General Santa Anna. Not everyone in Mexico accepted his rule. For example, Americans who had settled on Mexican lands disliked the Mexican law prohibiting slavery. Santa Anna, in between terms as president of Mexico, led Mexican forces in a brief war with Texas. After a defeat at the Battle of the Alamo in San Antonio, Texas, the Texans rallied under the leadership of American Sam Houston to defeat Santa Anna's forces. Mexico granted Texas independence in 1836, and it became the Republic of Texas and applied for admission to the United States.

A dispute over the border between Mexico and the United States resulted in the Mexican–American War (1846–1868). Mexico lost and was forced to cede vast territories from Texas to California to the United States in return for $15 million. Mexico also accepted an earlier U.S. annexation of Texas, with the Rio Grande as its southern border.

Benito Juárez A few years later, democratic reform would come to Mexico. *Benito Juárez,* an Indian lawyer from a background of poverty, became Mexico's president and eventually served five terms, breaking the patterns of military leadership and creole rule. He had led a liberal revolt called *La Reforma,* which resulted in a new constitution for Mexico in 1854. He also limited the power of both the Catholic Church and the Mexican army.

But European powers had not finished trying to control Mexico. In 1862, Napoleon III of France invaded, backing a conservative civil war against Juárez's institution of social reforms. His excuse was that Mexico had failed to pay debts owed to French citizens living in Mexico during the Mexican War with the United States. The French forced Juárez to flee Mexico City, they suspended the constitution, and they installed the Austrian *Archduke Maximilian* as emperor of Mexico. Juárez, however, organized resistance and drove the French army out in 1867, aided by some diplomatic pressure on France from the United States, which also wanted the French out of Mexico. Maximilian was captured and shot. Although constitutionally prohibited from serving more terms, Juárez continued to be reelected president until his death in 1872. Mexico had entered a period of political stability with a strong central government.

The Bolívar Revolutions Farther south, in South America, a desire for independence from Spain was also growing among the creole class. Fearing the masses, the creoles refused the support of mestizos, Indians, and mulattos (people of mixed African and European heritage). The creoles had seen the result in Haiti of a slave uprising as well as the excesses of the French Revolution during the Reign of Terror. Some creoles, such as *Simón Bolívar*, continued to push for Enlightenment ideals in Latin America. Never accepting a crown, he was instrumental in the independence of areas that became Venezuela, Colombia, Ecuador, and Peru.

Bolívar was born in Venezuela in 1783 to a family whose ancestors had been village aristocrats in Spain. The family had grown very wealthy in Venezuela, and Bolívar had access to this wealth for his revolutionary causes. After considerable military success in Latin America fighting the Spanish, his forces achieved the formation of a large area that he called Gran Colombia. He hoped it would become a federation similar to the United States, one based on Enlightenment ideals. He described himself as a liberal who believed in a free market and the abolition of slavery. Bolívar's goals and concerns for Latin America are outlined in his "Jamaica Letter" (1815): "Generous souls always interest themselves in the fate of a people who strive to recover the rights to which the Creator and Nature have entitled them, and one must be wedded to error and passion not to harbor this noble sentiment."

Bolívar served from 1819 to 1830 as president of Gran Columbia, a vast area of northern South America made up of present-day Colombia, Venezuela, Ecuador, northern Peru, western Guyana, and northwest Brazil. Due to its size and pressure from separatists, Gran Colombia split into the three successor countries Colombia, Venezuela, and Ecuador in 1830.

José de San Martín was another creole in South America who defeated royalists to establish an independent government. He led troops from his native Argentina over the Andes Mountains to set up independent republics in Chile and Bolivia. San Martín played the role of liberator in the southern part of South America much as Bolívar did in the northern part. He was hailed as the liberator of Argentina and the "Protector of Peru." Argentina achieved its independence in 1816 and Peru, in 1821, although consolidation of Peru's territories was not achieved until three years later. By 1825, most of Spanish America was independent; all the new republics had been born of the Enlightenment and nineteenth-century liberalism. Cuba and Puerto Rico, though, stayed under Spanish rule until 1898.

The new nations of Latin America suffered from the long wars of independence. Armies loyal to their generals led to the rise of the caudillos, who controlled only local areas. These men intervened in national politics to make or break governments. Sometimes the caudillos defended the interests of the regional elites and sometimes of the indigenous population and the peasants, but in general they disregarded representative forms of government and the rule of law.

Brazil As a Portuguese colony, Brazil's course was different from many other parts of Latin America. With creoles fearful of revolution, Brazilians were ruled by a prince who had fled Portugal in 1807 when Napoleon invaded. In 1821, the prince left Brazil and moved back to Portugal to become its constitutional monarch, King John VI. His son, Dom Pedro I, stayed in Brazil as regent. When the Portuguese government threatened Brazil's political autonomy, many Brazilians threatened revolution. In a surprising twist, Dom Pedro sided with the Brazilians and declared Brazil's independence from Portugal in 1822, one of the most nonviolent battles for independence in all of Latin America. He declared himself Emperor Pedro I and established a constitutional monarchy. Brazil remained a monarchy with the same social system in place until 1889 when it, too, became a republic after a conservative coup by the military and upper classes.

Results of the Creole Revolutions Although the constitutions of the newly independent countries in Latin America legally ended some social distinctions and abolished slavery, governments were often conservative. The first constitution of Peru, for example, forbade voting by those who could not read or write in Spanish, which effectively denied most Indians the vote until the constitution was changed in 1860. The creoles continued to form a powerful and conservative upper class, as they had before the wars of independence from the European nations.

Women gained little from the revolutions in Latin America. They were still unable to vote or enter into contracts. Most women received little education until late in the nineteenth century, and most remained submissive to men. One notable exception was Manuela Sáenz (1797–1856), who was the lover of Simón Bolívar. She actively participated in fighting alongside Bolívar, for example, in 1822 in a battle near Quito, Ecuador. An excellent rider as well as courageous fighter, she rose to the rank of colonel. On one occasion, she saved Bolívar's life, for which she received the nickname "Liberator of the Liberator."

INDEPENDENCE IN THE AMERICAS

UNITED STATES (1783)

REPUBLIC OF TEXAS (1836)

•San Antonio

Rio Grande R.

GULF OF MEXICO

MEXICO (1824)

Mexico City•

ATLANTIC OCEAN

HAITI (1804)

CUBA (Spanish Rule)

PUERTO RICO (Spanish Rule)

JAMAICA

CARIBBEAN SEA

San Salvador

Caracas

VENEZUELA

•Bogata

COLOMBIA

•Quito

Equator

ECUADOR

Amazon R.

LATIN AMERICA

PACIFIC OCEAN

SOUTH AMERICA

PERU (1821)

Lima•

•La Paz

BRAZIL (MONARCHY, 1822)

BOLIVIA

PARAGUAY

CHILE

Asunción•

Rio de Janeiro

Santiago•

ARGENTINA (1816)

•Buenos Aires

Newly Independent States

Independent Republics

Under Spanish Rule

Independent Monarchy

(_ _ _ _) Date when independence was achieved

| 0 | 1,000 Miles |
| 0 | 1,000 Kilometers |

The Age of Isms Continues

In Europe and America, Enlightenment thinkers reacted to the social ills caused by increasing urbanization and industrialization. Poverty in the cities increased; poor workers lived in slums without proper sanitation and without political representation. Various writers proposed solutions to the observable problems. Some wanted more government regulations and programs; many Christians called for greater private charity, and some conservatives blamed the poor themselves and called on them to change.

Utopian Socialism The economic and political theory of *socialism* refers to a system of public ownership or direct worker ownership of the means of production such as the mills to make cloth or the machinery and land needed to mine coal. Various branches of socialism developed in the nineteenth century, providing alternative visions of the social and economic future.

Those who felt that society could be channeled in positive directions by setting up ideal communities were often called *utopian socialists*. While they did not believe that governments could set up these ideal communities, they believed strongly in their own ability to do so. Each had a different vision. Although their experiments failed, each left a mark on history.

- *Claude Henri de Saint-Simon* advocated strongly for public works that would provide employment. He conceived the idea of building the Suez Canal in Egypt, a project that the French government eventually undertook and which opened in 1869.

- *Charles Fourier* identified some 810 passions that, when encouraged, would make work more enjoyable and workers less tired. One of his ideas, for example, was changing tasks frequently to prevent boredom. Fourier argued for an extension of women's liberties as well. Like other utopian socialists, Fourier believed that a fundamental principle of utopia was harmonious living in communities rather than the class struggle that was basic to the thinking of Karl Marx.

- *Robert Owen* established utopian communities at *New Lanark* in Scotland and *New Harmony* in the United States, where he insisted on providing some education for child workers.

- *Louis Blanc* worked to get France to set up national workshops.

In the later nineteenth century, socialist groups such as the *Fabian Society* formed in England. The Fabians were gradual socialists in that they favored reforming industrial society by parliamentary means. Writers H.G. Wells, Virginia Woolf, and George Bernard Shaw were just a few of the socially prominent Fabians. By the mid-twentieth century, many governments of the world, including Great Britain, France, and the Scandinavian countries, would be influenced by socialist principles. (Test Prep: Create a chart listing the ideas of Utopian societies and the thinking of Karl Marx. See page 432.)

Classical Liberalism Of more influence than Fabians in the period of revolution and reaction was *classical liberalism*. Being mostly professional people or intelligentsia, classical liberals believed firmly in natural rights, constitutional government, laissez-faire economics, and less spending on standing armies and established churches. Classical liberals in Britain pursued changes in Parliament to reflect changing population patterns so that new industrial cities would have equal parliamentary representation. The Reform Bills of 1832, 1867, and 1884, all of which broadened male suffrage, were backed by the classical liberals of the day. (Full female suffrage was not granted until 1928, although women over 30 who met minimal property qualifications were given the vote in 1918.)

On the European continent, classical liberals pursued constitutional governments in countries that had long had absolutist governments. In 1850, for example, liberals in Prussia achieved a constitution that allowed the election of deputies to a parliament. Prime Minister *Camillo Benso, Count of Cavour* (usually referred to as Cavour) of Piedmont-Sardinia, who helped to unify Italy as a constitutional monarchy, was also a classical liberal.

Romanticism The artistic movement known as *romanticism* spread widely in Europe and the Americas in the 1800s. It differed from rational classical liberal thinking in that romantics were fascinated with nature, the exotic, and emotion. They turned to instinct and sensitivity for inspiration rather than to reason. In music, composers such as Ludwig van Beethoven wrote passionate, expressive music. Writers often focused on the dark, the mysterious, or the exotic. For example, the words *gothic, bizarre, dark*, and *medieval* were often used in or to describe romantic poetry. In 1797, the British poet *Samuel Coleridge* wrote the poem "Kubla Khan," which he claimed was the product of an opium-induced dream. In Latin America, some poets and novelists began to see the native people as symbols of their national history. In 1876 *José Hernández* published *Martin Fierro* in 1876, an epic poem that romanticized the Argentine *gaucho* (a rough equivalent of the North American cowboy). Apolitical in nature, romantics focused on the history and distinctive traits of each culture. This fed opposition to Napoleon for his conquests, and fed sentimental nationalism throughout the continent.

Nationalism and Unification

Nationalism not only threatened large empires, but it also drove efforts to unite people who shared a culture into one political state. The unifying force of nationalism shaped new countries in Europe, the Middle East, Asia, and Africa.

Italian Unification Cavour, the prime minister of Piedmont-Sardinia, led the drive to unite the entire *Italian Peninsula* under the only native dynasty, the House of Savoy. At the time, the region was divided among a patchwork of kingdoms and city-states, and most people spoke regional languages rather than Italian. Cavour himself spoke French better than he spoke Italian. Like other classical liberals, he believed in natural rights, progress, and constitutional monarchy. But he also believed in the practical politics of reality, which came to be called *realpolitik*. Thus, he did not hesitate to advance the cause of Italian unity through manipulation. In 1858, he maneuvered Napoleon III of France into a war with Austria, hoping to weaken Austrian influence on the Italian Peninsula. Napoleon III backed out of the war after winning two important battles, partly because he feared the wrath of the Pope, who was not eager for his Papal States to come under the control of a central Italian government.

Nevertheless, it was too late to stop the revolutionary fervor, and soon several areas voted by plebiscite, or popular referendum, to join Piedmont (the Kingdom of Sardinia). To aid the unification effort, Cavour adopted the radical romantic revolutionary philosophy of *Giuseppe Mazzini*, who had been agitating for Italian resurgence (*Risorgimento*) since early in the nineteenth century. Cavour also allied with the Red Shirts military force led by *Giuseppe Garibaldi*, which was fighting farther south in the Kingdom of Naples.

Not all Italian troubles were solved by the unification that came in 1870, however. Poverty in Italy, more in the south than in the north, led to considerable emigration in the late nineteenth century—particularly to the United States and to Argentina, where the constitution of 1853 specifically encouraged *immigration,* the movement of people into the country from other countries.

WARS OF UNIFICATION IN EUROPE

German Unification In Germany, nationalist movements had already strengthened as a result of opposition to French occupation of German states under Napoleon Bonaparte. Following the Congress of Vienna, which settled the Napoleonic Wars in 1815, revolutions occurred in a number of European states, including Prussia and Austria. The revolutions of 1848 were the result of both nationalism (especially a desire for independence) and liberalism (a desire for representation under constitutions that recognized natural rights and civil liberties).

Prussian leader *Otto von Bismarck*, a practical politician like Cavour, used nationalist feelings to engineer three wars to bring about German unification. Bismarck manipulated Austria into participating in two of these wars, the first with Prussia against Denmark (1864) and the second against Prussia (Seven Weeks' War of 1866). After winning both wars, Bismarck manipulated France into declaring war against Prussia. His armies beat the French soundly in the Franco-Prussian War (1870). In each of these three wars, Prussia gained territory. In 1871, Bismarck founded the new German Empire, made up of many territories gained from the wars, including Alsace-Lorraine, a rich area long held by France on the border between France and the new Germany.

Kaiser Wilhelm I (ruled 1871–1888) of the Hohenzollern family was the nominal head of the new German Empire, but Bismarck, as chancellor, wielded great influence over government. He instituted old-age pensions and workers' compensation for injuries and illnesses; Germany's social insurance laws were the first by any country. Bismarck had set up workers' benefits to weaken German labor unions, which he violently opposed. Bismarck was forced to resign in 1890 shortly after Kaiser Wilhelm II (ruled 1888–1918) inherited the throne.

By 1871, two new powers, Italy and Germany, were on the international stage in an environment of competing alliances. Balance of power would be achieved briefly through these alliances, but extreme nationalism would lead to World War I.

Zionism Yet another "ism" in this age was the emergence of *Zionism*—the desire of the Jews of Europe and elsewhere to move to Israel and reestablish an independent homeland for the Jews after thousands of years of diaspora. Long the victims of oppression, anti-Semitism, and even pogroms, the Jewish population of Europe in the 1890s was shocked by a scandal known as the *Dreyfus Affair*, in which a Jewish military officer named Alfred Dreyfus was wrongly convicted of treason against the French government, based on forged documents. The Dreyfus Affair inspired a worldwide outcry, especially after French novelist *Emile Zola* took up Dreyfus's cause. Dreyfus was ultimately pardoned after having spent time in prison, but the case illustrated the anti-Semitic prejudice of the French government and its military. Discouraged Jews like *Theodor Herzl* (of the Austro–Hungarian Empire) believed that the case demonstrated that assimilation was not possible for the Jews, and that they instead needed a land of their own. Zionism was the outgrowth of his ideas. The establishment of the modern state of Israel in 1948 would partly result from this beginning.

Nationalism Spreads As nationalism spread beyond Europe, people often created an identity under one government where none had existed before. For example, in 1521, when Ferdinand Magellan claimed more than 7,000 islands off the southeast coast of Asia for Spain and named them the Philippines, no one called themselves "Filipino." The people on these islands spoke different languages, had different cultures, and were ruled by different governments. However, by the late nineteenth century, Filipinos had a strong enough national identity to begin to demand independence from Spain.

And no country called "Liberia" existed in West Africa before 1821. Beginning in that year, freed slaves from the United States and from slave ships captured by the British began settling in the region. However, native Africans already lived there. Over decades, people began to identify as Liberians, but the clash between the descendants of the native Africans and of the descendants of slaves has shaped Liberian politics ever since.

Philosphers Immanuel Kant and Moses Mendelssohn, and supporters of the Enlightenment in the late eighteenth century, were proud of its emphasis on reason. However, not everyone agreed with them. Edmund Burke, a British politician and political writer, challenged the wisdom of the Enlightenment's heavy reliance on reason. In light of the destructiveness of the French Revolution, Burke cast himself as the defender of tradition and opponent of rapid change. He doubted what he called the "conquering empire of light and reason" and defended instead the "latent wisdom" of ideas and practices that had developed slowly over generations. Burke feared that the emphasis on reason undermined long-practiced customs that held a community together. Throughout the nineteenth century, many Romantics and nationalists picked up on Burke's perspective and argued for the wisdom of tradition over reason.

A twentieth-century critic of the Enlightenment was the French scholar Michel Foucault. He argued that the legacy of reason was a legacy of repression. For example, governments used reason to justify colonizing other lands and putting dissidents in prison. Writing in an age when everyone from Nazis to Communists claimed to be acting according to reason, Foucault found many supporters.

However, the Enlightenment has always had strong defenders, particularly for its influence on government. Philosopher Kwame Anthony Appiah in his work *Cosmopolitanism: Ethics in a World of Strangers* (2007), credited the Enlightenment for producing ground-breaking ideas and documents such as the 1789 French Declaration of the Rights of Man and Emanuel Kant's proposal for a "league of nations." Historian Jonathan Israel, in *Democratic Enlightenment: Philosophy, Revolution, and Human Rights, 1750–1790* (2011), as well as in other works, argued that the Enlightenment had profound positive effects on the modern world. Among these were the establishment of successful republican and democratic governments.

Historian and political scientist Anthony Pagden in *The Enlightenment: And Why It Still Matters* (2013), praised the Enlightenment for preparing the world for a modern, global age. He credited the Enlightenment for clearing the intellectual arena of dogmatism and superstition and establishing, among other concepts, the basic understanding "that all human beings share the same basic rights and that women think and feel no differently than men or Africans from Asians."

KEY TERMS BY THEME

ENVIRONMENT
Italian Peninsula
immigration

CULTURE
conservatism
Deism
romanticism
nationalism
Mary Wollstonecraft
Voltaire
salons
Deists
liberals
Samuel Coleridge
José Hernández

SOCIAL STRUCTURE
First, Second, Third
   Estates
bourgeoisie
Tennis Court Oath
Bastille
Olympe de Gouges
primogeniture
Maroons
creoles
mestizos
Peninsulares
Zionism
Emile Zola

STATE-BUILDING: POLITICAL WRITERS & THOUGHT
Edmund Burke
John Locke
social contract
Baron Montesquieu
Jean-Jacques Rousseau
Thomas Paine
The Age of Reason
Declaration of
   Independence
United States
   Constitution
separation of powers
checks and balances
Declaration of the
   Rights of Man
Code Napoleon
balance of power
philosophes
Theodor Herzl

STATE-BUILDING: LEADERS
Napoleon Bonaparte
King Louis XVI
Maximilien Robespierre
Tsar Alexander I
Toussaint L'Ouverture
Miguel Hidalgo
Benito Juárez
Archduke Maximilan

José de San Martín
Simón Bolívar
Camillo Benso, Count
   of Cavour
Giuseppe Mazzini
Giuseppe Garibaldi
Otto von Bismarck

STATE-BUILDING
levée en masse
Congress of Vienna
Klemens von
   Metternich
Haiti
conservatives
La Reforma
realpolitik
Dreyfus Affair

ECONOMICS
socialism
physiocrats
Adam Smith
The Wealth of Nations
laissez-faire
utopian socialists
Claude Henri de
   Saint-Simon
Charles Fourier
Robert Owen
New Lanark
New Harmony
Louis Blanc
Fabian Society
classical liberalism

1. Which of the following pairs of terms best describes the Enlightenment ideas that were influential from 1750 to 1900?
   (A) empiricism and humanism
   (B) conservatism and aristocratic rule
   (C) worker ownership of industry and utopian communities
   (D) nationalism and instinct

2. Which of the following demonstrates that Toussaint L'Ouverture was greatly influenced by Enlightenment ideas?
   (A) He started the revolts in Haiti that ended slavery.
   (B) He negotiated with the Spanish against the French.
   (C) He won control of the territory that would become Haiti.
   (D) He produced a constitution that granted equality to all residents of Haiti.

3. Which would be the most useful source of evidence for understanding John Locke's influence on Thomas Jefferson?
   (A) a biography of Locke by written in 1748
   (B) a speech by Jefferson defending the Declaration of Independence
   (C) an essay by a current politician quoting Jefferson
   (D) collections of writings by Locke and by Jefferson

4. Which of the following would Adam Smith advocate most strongly?
   (A) implementing mercantilist policies
   (B) reducing government regulations on trade
   (C) increasing government controls over production
   (D) giving workers ownership of industries

5. Which of the following best describes an important demand that helped bring on the French Revolution?
   (A) The First Estate, or clergy, demanded that the Church have more power in government.
   (B) The Second Estate, or nobility, demanded that workers and peasants pay higher taxes.
   (C) The Third Estate, or workers, peasants, and bourgeoisie, demanded more equal taxation and a constitution.
   (D) King Louis XVI demanded more taxes from the First and Second Estates.

6. Which of the following is the best example of the concept of *realpolitik* in action?
   (A) Bonaparte's spread of French influence through the implementation of the Code Napoleon
   (B) Bismarck's support of old-age pensions to undercut the appeal of more radical ideas
   (C) Herzl's support for Zionism in hopes for finding a safe place for Jews to live
   (D) Robert Owen's establishment of the New Harmony community as an example for others to follow

Questions 7 and 8 are based on the following excerpt.

Do not adopt the best system of government, but the one which is most likely to succeed. . . . for it must be admitted that there is nothing more difficult in the political world than the maintenance of a limited monarchy. Moreover it must also be agreed that only a people as patriotic as the English are capable of controlling the authority of a king and of sustaining the spirit of liberty under the rule of scepter and crown.

—Simon Bolívar, letter to a Jamaican gentleman

7. Which statement most accurately summarizes Simon Bolívar's attitude toward establishment of new governments in the Americas?
   (A) It would be impractical for the new Latin American states to establish a limited monarchy like England's.
   (B) The Latin American states should establish absolute monarchies, not limited ones.
   (C) New Latin American governments should be based on conservative ideals.
   (D) It would be advisable for the new Latin American states to establish a limited monarchy like England's.

8. Which of the following concepts best summarizes the idea expressed in the first sentence of the quotation?
   (A) *laissez-faire*
   (B) *realpolitik*
   (C) nationalism
   (D) social contract

Question 9 is based on the following chart.

Italian Emigration to Argentina, 1857–1890	
Period	Number of People
1857–1860	6,743
1861–1870	49,638
1871–1880	37,235
1881–1890	201,218

9. Which of the following most likely caused the growth from 1881 to 1890?
   (A) economic conditions in Italy
   (B) the uniting of the Italian Peninsula under the House of Savoy
   (C) limited constitutional monarchy in Argentina
   (D) enlightened despotism in Italy after its unification

10. Which of the following events would advocates of the Enlightenment most likely use to vindicate the movement?
    (A) the advances in scientific knowledge
    (B) the use of *realpolitik* to accomplish real-world change
    (C) the establishment of nationalistic movements around the world
    (D) the development by European countries of colonial empires

CONTINUITY AND CHANGE-OVER-TIME ESSAY QUESTIONS

Directions: You are to answer the following question. You should spend 5 minutes organizing or outlining your essay. Write an essay that:

- Has a relevant thesis and supports that thesis with appropriate historical evidence.
- Addresses all parts of the question.
- Uses world historical context to show continuities and changes over time.
- Analyzes the process of continuity and change over time.

1. Analyze continuities and changes in the impact of Enlightenment thinking on ONE of the following regions between 1750 and 1815:
   - British colonies in North America
   - France
   - Haiti

Questions for Additional Practice

2. Analyze the continuities and changes in the condition of France's Third Estate (bourgeoisie, workers, and peasants) between 1750 and 1900.

3. Analyze continuities and changes of the impact of the shift from mercantilism to *laissez-faire* economics in ONE of the following regions between 1750 and 1900:
- British colonies/United States
- Great Britain

COMPARATIVE ESSAY QUESTIONS

Directions: You are to answer the following question. You should spend 5 minutes organizing or outlining your essay. Write an essay that:
- Has a relevant thesis and supports that thesis with appropriate historical evidence.
- Addresses all parts of the question.
- Makes direct, relevant comparisons.
- Analyzes relevant reasons for similarities and differences.

1. Analyze the similarities and differences in the political impact between the American Revolution and the Haitian Revolution.

Questions for Additional Practice

2. Analyze the similarities and differences in the meaning and impact of utopian socialism and classical liberalism.

3. Analyze similarities and differences between the ideas that shaped TWO of the following documents and between the influence of the two:
- Declaration of Independence
- Declaration of the Rights of Man
- Declaration of the Rights of Woman and the Female Citizen

THINK AS A HISTORIAN: USING PERIODIZATION

Periodization is a process by which historians divide the flow of history into meaningful periods. *Which TWO of the following statements contain periodization references?*

1. Growing out of the earlier intellectualism of the Scientific Revolution and the humanism of the Renaissance, the Age of Enlightenment was optimistic.

2. *Leviathan* was published by Thomas Hobbes in 1651. It was Hobbes who described life as "nasty, brutish, and short."

3. In the eighteenth century, a new group of thinkers and writers who came to be called the *philosophes* explored social, political, and economic theories in new ways.

4. Voltaire was famous for his wit and his advocacy of civil liberties. One of his most famous works was a social satire, *Candide*.

5. The Declaration of Independence became the philosophy behind the Patriots' fight against British troops in America.

6. Violence begets violence. It took the beheading of Robespierre to end the Reign of Terror.

WRITE AS A HISTORIAN: USING CONTRADICTORY INFORMATION

Part of writing a good history essay is to explain information that seems to be in conflict. If the contradiction simply reflects different points of view of two observers, explain each observer's perspective. If the contradiction reflects the behavior of an individual, explain the relationship between contradictory information. For example, perhaps the person changed positions over time.

Voltaire said, "Christians should tolerate each other." He also called Christianity "absurd." *Which THREE of the following sentences best explains the relationship between Voltaire's comments about Christianity?*

1. Voltaire held many different viewpoints. For example, he called for religious toleration and he was also critical of Christianity.

2. Voltaire had seen how Christians persecuted each other, which explains why he was both critical of Christianity and why he called for religious toleration.

3. Voltaire's comments on religion reflected his self-interest. He knew his views of Christianity were unpopular, so he urged others to be tolerant of diverse ideas.

4. Voltaire was consistently critical of Christianity, but sometimes he was gentle in his criticism and at times he was blunt.

5. It is hard to tell Voltaire's view of Christianity. Sometimes he was very critical of it. Other times, he was urging it to reform.

Industrial Revolution, 1750–1900

> *One man draws out the wire, another straightens it, a third cuts it,*
> *a fourth points it, a fifth grinds it at the top for receiving the*
> *head; . . . and the important business of making a pin is, in*
> *this manner, divided into about eighteen distinct operations.*
>
> —Adam Smith, *Wealth of Nations* (1776)

The quote above describes the rigid structure of early factory work, one of the most enduring images of the *Industrial Revolution.* The term *industrialization* refers not only to the increased mechanization of production, but also to the social changes that accompanied this shift. The Industrial Revolution began in Britain in the eighteenth century, and then it spread to other countries in northwest Europe and North America in the nineteenth century. Still later in the nineteenth century, it spread to Japan and Russia. In order to appreciate the impact of industrialization, it is important to understand its causes as well as what life was like prior to industrialization.

Preindustrial Societies

During the early eighteenth century, most families in Britain lived in rural areas, grew most of their own food, and made most of their own clothes. For centuries, wool and flax had been raised domestically, and people spun fabrics in their own homes.

However, one result of the East India Company's dealings with South Asia was that Indian cotton became available in Britain and before long it was in high demand. Wool and flax could not be produced as quickly or in as much quantity to compete with cotton imports. To compete with Indian cotton, investors in Britain began to build their nation's own cotton cloth industry. Using imported raw cotton produced by slave labor in the Americas, the British developed the *cottage industry* system, in which merchants provided raw cotton to women who spun it into finished cloth in their own homes.

Home spinning was hard work and did not pay well, but cottage industries gave women weavers a degree of independence. While working in their own homes, they were also within close proximity of their children. But this cottage industry, or *putting-out system* as it was called, was slow. Inventors demanded faster production, spurring the development of technologies that turned out cloth in more efficient ways.

Causes of Industrialization

The most obvious cause of industrialization was the development of technology. However, technological advances were not the only cause. Population growth and access to resources were other major contributors to Britain's industrialization. Yet analyzing historical causation is a complex process. Saying "A caused B" is often an oversimplification. Usually, historical causation is an expanding chain of causes and effects. For example, while the development of technology was one cause of industrialization, the growth of industrialization then spurred further advances in technology.

Growth of Technology By the mid-eighteenth century, the *spinning jenny* and the *water frame* reduced the time needed to spin yarn and weave cloth. The spinning jenny, invented by *James Hargreaves* in the 1760s, allowed a weaver to spin more than one thread at a time. The water frame, patented by *Richard Arkwright* in 1769, used waterpower to drive the spinning wheel. The water frame was more efficient than a single person's labor, and this mechanization doomed the household textile cottage industry, as textile production was moved to factories big enough to house these bulky machines. Arkwright was thus considered the father of the *factory system*.

Interchangeable Parts In 1798, *Eli Whitney*, best known for developing the cotton gin, created a system of *interchangeable parts* for manufacturing firearms for the U.S. military. In Whitney's system, if a particular component of a machine were to break, the broken component could easily be replaced with a new, identical part. Entrepreneurs adapted this method of making firearms to the manufacture of other products. The system of interchangeable parts was a pivotal contribution to industrial technology. Instead of relying on skilled workers to craft every component of a product, Whitney's standardized tools allowed unskilled workers to attach a particular piece to a product. This led directly to a *division of labor* among workers. In this system, each worker specializes in a specific task. For example, one worker might a cast a part. Once cast, the part is given to another worker, whose specific job it is to install the part on the finished product, and so on. In the early twentieth century, Henry Ford expanded the concept of the division of labor, developing the moving *assembly line* to manufacture his Model T automobiles.

Steam Engine The new machinery benefitted from a power source, one more mobile than rivers and streams. The *steam engine*, created by *James Watt* in 1765, harnessed coal power to create steam, which in turn generated energy for mechanical devices in textile factories. A steam-powered locomotive came almost 50 years later and produced power for railway trains.

Just as important was the development of the *steamship* in the late eighteenth century. Steam-powered ships were able to travel quickly upstream on rivers instead of having to sail up or be towed by people and animals along the shore. Steamships revolutionized transportation on lakes and the oceans as well, because ship captains were no longer dependent on winds for power. The need to travel long distances along ocean coasts led to the creation of coaling stations at critical points, such as in Cape Colony in South Africa and various islands in the Pacific.

Population Growth Slightly predating the Industrial Revolution during the early 1700s was an *agricultural revolution* resulting in increased productivity. *Crop rotation* (rotating different crops in and out of a field each year) and the *seed drill* (a device that efficiently places seeds in a designated spot in the ground) both increased food production. Additionally, the introduction of the potato from South America contributed more calories to people's diets. As nations industrialized, their populations grew because more food was available to more people. And because of improved medical care, infant mortality rates declined and people lived longer. With these demographic changes, more people were available to work in factories and to provide a market for manufactured goods.

THE GROWTH OF BRITISH CITIES, C. 1800

Urbanization However, the growing population would not remain in rural areas. Migration was sometimes the best of bad options. English towns had traditionally allowed farmers to cultivate land or tend sheep on government property known as "the commons." However, this custom ended with the *enclosure movement* as the government fenced off the commons in order to give exclusive use of it to people who paid for the privilege or who purchased the land. Many farmers became landless and destitute. The enclosure movement was thus instrumental in another wave of demographic change—forcing small farmers to move from rural areas to urban areas such as *Manchester* and *Liverpool,* and become the new industrial workforce.

Britain's Advantages Britain had many geographical advantages in the process of industrialization. Located on the Atlantic Ocean with its many *seaways,* the country was well placed to import *raw materials* and export finished goods. It also had the geographic luck of being located atop immense coal deposits. Coal was vital to industrialization because when burned it could power the steam engine. The burning of this *fossil fuel,* an energy source derived from plant and animal remains, was also essential in the process of separating iron from its ore. Iron production (and later steel production) allowed the building of larger bridges, taller buildings, and stronger ships. Coal mining became the major industry of northern and western Britain, including South Wales, Yorkshire, and Lancashire. When the United States industrialized, coal-mining areas developed in West Virginia, Pennsylvania, and Kentucky.

As a colonizing power, Britain also had access to resources available in its colonies, including timber for ships. Largely because of the wealth they accumulated during the trans-Atlantic slave trade, enough British capitalists had excess *capital* (money available to invest in businesses). Without this capital, private entrepreneurs could not have created new commercial ventures.

Britain, the northeastern United States, and other regions also had a natural network of rivers supplemented by publicly funded canals and harbors. These water routes made transport of raw materials and finished products inexpensive.

Britain also had the world's strongest fleet of ships, including commercial ships for trade and naval ships for defense. These ships brought agricultural products to Britain to be used to make finished products for consumers.

A final and vital factor that aided industrialization in Britain was the legal protection of private property. Entrepreneurs needed the assurance that the business they created and built up would not be taken away, either by other businesspeople or by the government. Not all nations offered these legal guarantees.

Spread of Industrialization

After Britain industrialized, Belgium, and then France and Germany followed. These countries possessed many of the characteristics that allowed Britain to industrialize, including capital, natural resources, and water transportation.

One factor that was not in France's favor was its sparsely populated urban centers, which limited the amount of labor available for factories. Another factor was the French Revolution (1789–1799) and subsequent wars involving

France and its neighbors, which consumed both the attention and the capital of France's elites. These factors delayed the Industrial Revolution for France.

Germany was politically fragmented into numerous small states, which delayed its industrialization. However, once Germany unified in 1871, it quickly became a leading producer of steel and coal.

The United States began its industrial revolution in the nineteenth century. By 1900, the United States was a leading industrial force in the world. The construction of railroads, including the *Transcontinental Railroad* that connected the Atlantic and Pacific oceans when it was completed in 1869, facilitated U.S. industrial growth. Like the canals, the railroads were heavily subsidized by public funds. The nation's vast natural resources, including timber, coal, and oil, contributed to its development as an industrial nation. *Human capital* (the workforce) was also a key factor in America's success. Political upheaval and widespread poverty brought a large number of immigrants to the United States from Europe and East Asia. These immigrants, as well as migrants from rural areas in the United States, provided the labor force to work in the factories. The development of the telegraph in the 1830s made long-distance communication easy for the first time in history.

The United States, Great Britain, and Germany were key players in what is known as the *second industrial revolution*, which occurred in the late nineteenth and early twentieth centuries. The innovations of the first industrial revolution were in textiles, steam power, and iron; the developments of the second industrial revolution were in steel, chemicals, precision machinery, and electronics. The development of chemical techniques to extract kerosene from petroleum in 1847 led to other developments such as the internal combustion engine, which in turn led to automobile and airplane technologies. Similarly, the harnessing of electrical power led to electrification—street lighting and electric street trains in the 1890s. Other technologies followed as well, such as the telephone (1876) and wireless communication and radio (1901).

Agricultural Products for Trade in the Nineteenth Century		
Product	Producers	Users (Finished Products)
Wheat	Russia, Britain	Britain (food)
Rubber	Brazilian Amazon	Britain (tires, footwear, fabrics)
Palm Oil	West Africa, Indonesia	Britain (cooking oil, soap)
Sugar	Caribbean Islands, Brazil	Britain (refined sugar)
Cattle and Hogs	United States, Ireland, Argentina	Britain, United States (meat)
Cotton	United States	Britain (textiles)

By the end of the nineteenth century, Japan also began the process of industrialization. Under the *Meiji* (1868–1912), Japan ended its self-imposed isolation from the rest of the world. It had been alarmed by the advanced navy and armaments produced by the industrial systems of the West—particularly those of Britain and the United States—and how they had humiliated China. Japan's leaders realized that their country needed to industrialize to protect itself. The leaders hired foreign experts to instruct their workers and business managers about modern industry. However, in replicating the "progress" made by Western countries, the Japanese also replicated some of industrial society's problems. For example, accounts of abuse and exploitation of female Japanese mill workers are similar to the experiences that British female mill workers had recorded decades earlier. (Test Prep: Write a brief paragraph comparing Japan's industrialization with developments in Europe and the United States. See pages 456–457.)

Russia also began to industrialize, focusing particularly on railroads and exports. By 1900, Russia had more than 36,000 miles of railroad, connecting its commercial and industrial areas. The *Trans-Siberian Railroad* stretched from Moscow to the Pacific Ocean, allowing Russia to trade more easily with countries in East Asia, such as China and Japan. The Russian coal, iron, and steel industries developed with the railroad, mostly in the 1890s. By 1900 Russia had become the fourth largest producer of steel in the world. However, the economy remained overwhelmingly agricultural until after the Communists came to power in a revolution in 1917.

Effects of the Industrial Revolution

The Industrial Revolution affected every aspect of society, transforming not only the way products were manufactured, but also the nature of work itself. Because of industrialization, people began to move from rural to urban areas, a trend that continued through the twentieth century. By the beginning of the 1900s, British society was more urban than rural. The new workplace and the growth of business created an entirely new class hierarchy. Women and children at every rung of society saw their roles in the family change dramatically.

Effects on Families Prior to industrialization, family members worked in close proximity to one another. Whether women spun fabric in their own homes or landless workers farmed the fields of a landlord, parents and children usually spent their working hours together. Industrialization disrupted this pattern. The machinery of industry needed to be operated in large factories, making it impossible to work from home. Thus, family members had to leave their homes and neighborhoods for a long workday in order to earn enough money to survive. Once at work, their schedules were nothing like those found on a farm or working at home in the cottage industry system. The shrill sounds of the factory whistle told workers when they could take a break, obviously a culture shock to ex-farmers who had previously completed tasks according to their own needs and schedules. Considering that workers commonly spent 14 hours a day, six days a week in a factory, exhaustion was common. Some of these exhausted workers operated dangerous heavy machinery, which regularly resulted in injury and death.

The low wages of factory workers forced them to send their children to work in the industries also. In the early decades of industrialization, children as young as five worked in textile mills. Because of their small size and nimble fingers, children could climb into equipment to make repairs or into tight spots in mines more easily than could adults. However, the dust from the textile machinery damaged their lungs just as much. Children who worked in coal mines faced even more dangerous conditions, working in oppressive heat and carting heavy loads of coal. Coal dust was even more unhealthy than factory dust, and mine collapses and floods loomed as constant threats to safety.

Source: Thinkstock

Source: Library of Congress

Industrialization created new jobs in factories (upper) and offices (lower) that pulled people from rural areas into urban areas, a process that continues around the world today.

Effects on Urban Areas Industrialization increased *urbanization* (the growth of cities). For the first half of the nineteenth century, urban areas grew rapidly and with little planning by governments. This left a damaging ecological footprint and created inhumane living conditions for the cities' poorest residents. Working families crowded into shoddily constructed *tenement* apartment buildings, often owned by factory owners themselves. Tenements were often located in urban *slums* (areas of cities where low-income families were forced to live), where industrial by-products such as polluted water supplies and open sewers were common. These unsanitary conditions were breeding grounds for diseases such as cholera, dysentery, and tuberculosis.

Effects on Class Structure As industrialization spread, new classes of society emerged in Britain. At the bottom rungs of the social hierarchy were those who labored in factories and coal mines. These slum dwellers were known as the *working class*. Though they helped construct goods more rapidly, the technology of interchangeable parts and the factory system's division of labor had deprived workers of the experience of crafting a complete product. In comparison to the craft workers and artisans of earlier generations, workers were low skilled and therefore easily replaceable, at least in the eyes of their managers, who were thus able to pay them lower wages.

Just as industrialization had created low-skilled jobs, it also required people with education and sophisticated skills to manage production of goods. A new middle class emerged, consisting of factory and office managers, small business owners, and professionals. *White-collar* jobs (those held by office workers) were also created during this time period. Unlike most factory workers, white-collar workers were literate and many could be considered middle class.

At the top of the new class hierarchy were the newly wealthy industrialists and owners of large corporations. These so-called *captains of industry* soon overshadowed the landed aristocracy as the power brokers and leaders of modern society.

Effect on Women's Lives The Industrial Revolution affected women in different ways, depending on their class position. Because their families needed the money, working-class women worked in coal mines (until the practice of hiring women for coal mining was declared illegal in Britain in the 1840s) and were the primary laborers in textile factories. Factory owners preferred to hire women because they could pay them half of what they paid men.

Middle-class women were spared factory work, yet in many ways they lived more limited lives than working-class women. Middle-class men had to leave the house and work at an office to provide for their families. If a wife stayed at home, it was an indication that her husband was capable of being the family's sole provider. Being a housewife thus became a status symbol. By the late 1800s, advertising and consumer culture contributed to a *cult of domesticity* that idealized the female homemaker. Advertising encouraged women to buy household products that would supposedly make the home a husband's place of respite from a harsh modern world. Pamphlets instructed middle-class women on how to care for the home, raise children, and behave in polite society and urged them to be pious, submissive, pure, and domestic. For working-class women the cult of domesticity was even more taxing, as they had to manage the household, care for their children, and work full time.

Industrialization also spurred feminism. When men left a community to take a job, their absence opened up new opportunities for the women who remained home. One political sign of this feminism came in 1848 at Seneca Falls, New York, when 300 people met to call for equality for women.

Effect on Mass Culture A culture of *consumerism* as well as of leisure developed among the working and middle classes of society in Great Britain. Consumption needed to keep up with production, so began to advertise heavily, particularly to the middle class whose members had some disposable income, or money that can be spent on nonessential goods.

Leisure activities such as biking and boating became popular during the late 1800s. Companies encouraged their workers to participate in athletics, because they believed that sports rewarded virtues such as self-discipline and playing by the rules. The sales of athletic equipment also generated business for those who made everything from soccer balls to sports stadiums.

Perhaps because workers spent most of their waking hours in a bleak industrial environment, material goods and leisure entertainment became important escapes. In Europe, soccer (known there as football), became popular, while baseball dominated sports in the United States.

Effects on the Environment The Industrial Revolution was powered by energy, specifically, the burning of fossil fuels such as coal, petroleum, and natural gas. Although burning coal, for example, produced more energy than burning wood, the effects on the environment were extremely harmful. Industrial towns during the late nineteenth century were choked by toxic air pollution produced by coal-burning factories. Water became polluted, also, as the new industries dumped their waste into streams, rivers, and lakes. (For more about the environmental consequences of industrialization, see pages 605 and 610–611.)

Effects on Business Organization New ways of organizing businesses arose during the Industrial Revolution. Some manufacturers formed giant *corporations* in order to minimize risk. A corporation is a business chartered by a government as a legal entity owned by *stockholders* (individuals who buy partial ownership directly from the company when it is formed or later through a *stock market*). Stockholders might receive sums of money, known as dividends, from a corporation when it makes a profit. If a corporation experiences a loss or goes bankrupt, the stockholders are not liable for the losses. The most that stockholders can lose is what they paid for the stock in the first place.

Some corporations became so powerful that they could form a *monopoly*, meaning that they controlled all aspects of a specific business and eliminated all competition. For example, Alfred Krupp of Essen, Germany, ran a gigantic company that used the *Bessemer process,* a more efficient way to produce steel, gaining a monopoly in the German steel industry. (In the twentieth century, Krupp's firm produced armaments that helped militarize Germany.)

Responses to the Industrial Revolution

The harsh conditions of urban industrial life provoked resistance. Some workers formed trade unions to advocate for higher pay and safer conditions. Social reformers campaigned for more humane living conditions in cities and working conditions in factories. Some activists went beyond demanding specific improvements; they instead rejected the norms of society produced by capitalism and called for an entirely new social and economic order.

Growth of Unions Dangerous and unsanitary working conditions, low wages, and long hours spurred workers to form *labor unions* (organizations of workers that advocate for the right to bargain over these matters with employers and put the resulting agreements in a contract). For most of the nineteenth century, unions in Great Britain had to organize in secret because the government treated them as enemies of trade. However, by the early twentieth century, unions became more acceptable and membership increased. Unions improved workers' lives by winning minimum wage laws, limits on the number of hours worked, overtime pay, and the establishment of a five-day work week.

Unions sparked a larger movement for empowerment among the working class. In 1832, 1867, and 1884, the British parliament passed reform bills to expand the number of men who could vote and give more representation to British cities. The acts reduced property ownership qualifications as a requirement for voting. These reforms laid the foundation for expansion of the franchise (right to vote) to all men in 1918. British women would not gain equal voting rights until 1928.

Social Reform Along with unions, social activists and reformers hoped to improve the living conditions of the least powerful in society. Reformers' achievements especially benefited children. A law in 1843 declared that children under the age of 10 were banned from working in the coal mines. In 1881, education became mandatory for British children between the ages of 5 and 10. This focus on education, as opposed to work for monetary gain, permanently redefined the role of children in urban society.

All industrializing nations grappled with the new challenges that factory life introduced. Among these nations, Germany implemented the most comprehensive set of social reforms to protect industrial workers. Under the leadership of Chancellor *Otto von Bismarck,* Germany started workers' accident compensation insurance, unemployment insurance, and old age pensions for employees. Bismarck was only somewhat interested in the health and security concerns. He was far more concerned that if his government did not address these problems, socialists and other more radical citizens would demand stronger government action, which would lead to social unrest.

Uniting the World One result of industrialization was to increase interdependence among people around the world. For example, British factories imported minerals from around the world to make into products. They purchased cotton from the United States, Egypt, and India to make textiles that they sold throughout Europe and other parts of the world. Similarly, the responses to industrialization built greater connections among people. Labor leaders advocated formation of international unions so that workers in various countries could unite to demand higher wages. Reforms that began in one country often spread. For example, Bismarck's social reforms spread throughout Europe, and eventually influenced much of the world.

Minerals for Trade		
Product	Important Producers	Important Users
Copper	Cuba, Mexico, Columbia, Peru, Chile, Australia, New Zealand	Europe, especially Britain
Gold	North America, South America, Africa, especially South Africa	Europe, especially Britain
Diamonds	Africa, especially South Africa	Europe, especially Britain
Guano	Mainly Peru, also Africa, and Caribbean and Pacific Islands	Europe, North America

The Intellectual Reaction

The rise of capitalism and industrialization caused people to think about society in new ways. Fresh ideas would shape all later economics and politics.

Adam Smith *The Wealth of Nations* by *Adam Smith*, first published in 1776, is considered a foundational text in support of *capitalism* and the establishment of private entrepreneurship. In this work, Smith describes his theory of the "invisible hand" of the market; if businesses were allowed to operate in their own interests, society in general would benefit. Though Smith recognized the need for some government regulations, his ideas were a precursor to the *laissez-faire* philosophy popular in the late nineteenth century, which opposed nearly all government regulations that limited business.

John Stuart Mill Others found that laissez-faire capitalism could be inhumane to workers, and they called for reform. The philosopher *John Stuart Mill* was a champion of social reforms of the industrial age, including labor unions, child labor laws, and laws ensuring safe working conditions in factories. Mill advocated a philosophy called *utilitarianism*, which sought "the greatest good for the greatest number of people." Utilitarians did not want to end capitalism; they wanted to address growing problems.

Utopian **Socialism** Unlike Mill, other reformers argued that capitalism was fundamentally flawed. Though it created tremendous wealth it also created tremendous suffering. They argued for *socialism,* a system in which major resources and industries would be owned by the workers or the government on behalf of all people. Some bought large tracks of land where they tried to establish new, ideal communities. (For more on utopian socialists, see page 409.)

Karl Marx The most influential advocate of socialism was *Karl Marx*, a German scholar and writer. In 1848, Karl Marx and *Friedrich Engels* published a pamphlet (now known as *The Communist Manifesto*) that summarized their critique of capitalism. According to Marx, capitalism divided society into two basic classes: the *proletariat* and the *bourgeoisie*. The proletariat was essentially the working class, working in factories and mines, often for little compensation. The bourgeoisie was the middle class and included the capitalists who owned the machinery and factories where the working class produced goods. Marx argued that in the capitalist system the bourgeoisie exploited the proletariat endlessly for the sake of profit. Because the bourgeoisie owned the *means of production*, such as machines, factories, mines, and land, they received most of the profits. The proletariat, who did the physical and dangerous work, received very little of the wealth they produced. Marx exhorted workers to take control of the means of production and share the wealth they created fairly. The end of capitalism, according to Marx, would usher in an era of equality and justice. Marxist socialism also became known as *communism*.

Anarchism Another response to capitalism was to see government itself as the problem. Anarchists argued for abolishing nearly all national government and allowing local communities to rule themselves. While several intellectuals supported this view, the movement became best known for assassinations of several European politicians in the late 1800s.

Industrial Revolution's Legacy

It is difficult to overstate the importance of the Industrial Revolution. Mass production made goods cheaper, more abundant, and more easily accessible to a greater number of people than ever before. Growth of factories was a primary factor driving people to move, both from rural areas to cities and from agrarian countries to industrial ones. Both low-skilled workers and high-skilled professionals moved to take advantage of new opportunities provided by industrialization. However, the natural by-products of industrial production polluted air and water supplies. Industry forever changed the nature of work and the lives of workers. Working populations became concentrated in urban centers, as opposed to being spread among rural areas. The workplace shifted from homes to factories, dramatically altering family life. The Industrial Revolution created a new—and many said unequal—working relationship between workers and owners.

Global inequalities also increased because of industrialization. Nations that industrialized early found that they needed more materials to power their production. They looked beyond their borders for raw materials, such as cotton and rubber. By exploiting overseas natural resources, they not only destroyed early industrialization in Egypt, China, and India, but they also ushered in a second wave of colonization. (For more on this second wave of colonization, see pages 493.)

HISTORICAL PERSPECTIVES: WHAT DEFINES INDUSTRIAL SOCIETY?

The social and economic upheavals caused by the Industrial Revolution prompted scholars starting in the mid-nineteenth century to suggest new perspectives for explaining the structure of modern society. British philosopher John Stuart Mill was one of a few thinkers who highlighted gender. He accepted the Enlightenment perspective of "man" as a rational being, but he included females as well as males in his definition of man. In his essay titled *The Subjection of Women* (1869), Mill argued that society would benefit from the inclusion of women in public life: "That the principle which regulates the existing social relations between the two sexes—the legal subordination of one sex to the other—is wrong itself, and now one of the chief hindrances to human improvement; and that it ought to be replaced by a principle of perfect equality, admitting no power or privilege on the one side, nor disability on the other."

As early as 1848, German philosopher and economist Karl Marx had also argued on behalf of equality for women. However, Marx focused more on class than gender. He saw the industrial world as divided into "two great hostile camps—bourgeoisie and proletariat." Since the bourgeoisie controlled the means of production and the proletariat did the work, Marx insisted that conflict was inevitable. His solution to the problems of modern industrialized society came from what he termed "scientific socialism" (as opposed to utopian socialism). Marx believed that communism was the only long-term answer for society.

Like Marx, German sociologist Max Weber analyzed the class system of the modern world, but considered more than economics. Rather, he included tradition, amount of power, and, most famously, religion. In *The Protestant Work Ethic and the Spirit of Capitalism* (1905), Weber suggested that in countries influenced by Reformation leader John Calvin, people worked hard because prosperity was a sign of God's favor, and this gave them assurance for salvation. In addition, people looked down upon showy displays of wealth so they saved their money. The combination of hard workers and ample capital for new investments provided ideal conditions for capitalism.

KEY TERMS BY THEME

ENVIRONMENT
spinning jenny
water frame
James Hargreaves
Richard Arkwright
Eli Whitney
interchangeable
 parts
steam engine
James Watt
steamship
crop rotation
seed drill
seaways
raw materials
fossil fuel
Transcontinental
 Railroad
second industrial
 revolution
Trans-Siberian Railroad
Bessemer process

CULTURE
urbanization
Protestant work ethic

STATE-BUILDING
Meiji
Otto von Bismarck

ECONOMICS
Industrial Revolution
industrialization
cottage industry
putting-out system
factory system
division of labor
assembly line
agricultural revolution
enclosure movement
Manchester
Liverpool
capital
human capital
consumerism
corporations
stockholders
stock market
monopoly

The Wealth of Nations
Adam Smith
capitalism
laissez-faire
John Stuart Mill
utilitarianism
socialism
utopia
Karl Marx
Friedrich Engels
*The Communist
 Manifesto*
means of production
communism

SOCIAL STRUCTURES
tenement
slums
working class
white-collar
captains of industry
cult of domesticity
labor unions
proletariat
bourgeoisie

Question 1 refers to the photograph below.

Source: Library of Congress

1. Which statement provides the best context for interpreting this photo showing a textile factory in the Industrial Revolution?
    (A) The machines used in factories were very similar to the ones used in homes.
    (B) Textiles were among the last products to be made in factories.
    (C) Middle-class females preferred working in factories to working at home.
    (D) Children provided a source of low-cost labor for factories.

2. One important reason rural residents in Britain migrated to cities during the eighteenth and nineteenth centuries was that they
    (A) lost the use of land through the enclosure movement
    (B) were part of the cottage industry system
    (C) wanted to live in urban tenements
    (D) preferred the factory work schedule over the farm one

3. Which of the following was an import that caused British entrepreneurs of the 1700s to search for faster and larger-scale methods of production?

   (A) machines from France and Germany

   (B) coal from the United States

   (C) cotton cloth from India

   (D) cotton cloth from Belgium

Question 4 refers to the quotation below.

The real grievance of the worker is the insecurity of his existence; he is not sure that he will always have work, he is not sure that he will always be healthy, and he foresees that he will one day be old and unfit to work. If he falls into poverty, even if only through a prolonged illness, he is then completely helpless, left to his own devices, and society does not currently recognize any real obligation towards him beyond the usual help for the poor, even if he has been working all the time ever so faithfully and diligently. The usual help for the poor, however, leaves a lot to be desired, especially in large cities, where it is very much worse than in the country.

—Otto von Bismarck, speech, 1884

4. The reforms that Bismarck passed based on the ideas expressed in his quote above are examples of

   (A) the "invisible hand" of the market and the *laissez-faire* economy

   (B) Marx's rejection of capitalism and free enterprise

   (C) reasons why Germany was slower than Britain to industrialize

   (D) social reforms to gain security for workers and prevent radical unrest

5. Which statement best reflects basic changes in life from 1750 to 1900 as a result of the Industrial Revolution?

(A) As the demand for food increased, the percentage of people who were peasants increased.

(B) As people switched from agricultural to factory work, families had less time to spend together.

(C) As industrialization increased production, people had to work fewer hours.

(D) As the demand for goods increased, the cottage industry system expanded.

6. The factor that most hindered French industrialization from about 1750 to 1815 was

(A) an autocratic system of government

(B) a series of wars, including the French Revolution

(C) a lack of natural resources

(D) an uneducated aristocracy

7. In England, harsh labor conditions and low wages during the Industrial Revolution were most responsible for which of the following developments?

(A) the enclosure movement

(B) worker unionization

(C) anti-labor laws

(D) specialization of labor

8. Which of the following developments during the Industrial Revolution best argues against Karl Marx's ideas that capitalism divided society into the proletariat and the bourgeoisie?

(A) the development of inventions to speed up work, such as the spinning jenny and water frame

(B) the decline of the cottage system and the movement of textile production to factories

(C) the rise of a new middle class of managers, office workers, and small business owners

(D) the legal protection of private property, minimizing risk for entrepreneurs and investors

9. Which of the following statements is true about the Industrial Revolution in both Britain and the United States?

(A) Both gained a large urban workforce as a result of the enclosure movement.

(B) In both nations, the federal government was in charge of industrial development.

(C) Both relied on coal to fuel factories and both had their own rich coal deposits.

(D) Both found early solutions to problems of air and water pollution from industries.

10. In what important way did the Atlantic slave trade help British capitalists invest in early industrialization?

(A) They used enslaved Africans as labor in some early factories.

(B) They accumulated the capital they needed for industrialization from the slave trade.

(C) By ending the slave trade, they were better able to focus on industry instead.

(D) Participating in the slave trade gave them connections on the global trade market.

CONTINUITY AND CHANGE-OVER-TIME ESSAY QUESTIONS

Directions: You are to answer the following question. You should spend 5 minutes organizing or outlining your essay. Write an essay that:

- Has a relevant thesis and supports that thesis with appropriate historical evidence.
- Addresses all parts of the question.
- Uses world historical context to show continuities and changes over time.
- Analyzes the process of continuity and change over time.

1. Analyze the continuities and changes in the social developments of the Industrial Revolution in Britain between 1750 and 1900, including ways in which workers, activists, and writers responded to these developments.

Questions for Additional Practice

2. Analyze the continuities and changes in industrial and technological development in Britain and the United States from the beginnings of the Industrial Revolution to 1900.

3. Analyze the continuities and changes in family dynamics and the role of women from 1750 to 1900 in countries that experienced the Industrial Revolution.

COMPARATIVE ESSAY QUESTIONS

Directions: You are to answer the following question. You should spend 5 minutes organizing or outlining your essay. Write an essay that:

- Has a relevant thesis and supports that thesis with appropriate historical evidence.
- Addresses all parts of the question.
- Makes direct, relevant comparisons.
- Analyzes relevant reasons for similarities and differences.

1. Analyze the similarities and differences in the political developments resulting from the Industrial Revolution in Great Britain and ONE of the following countries:
   - France
   - Germany
   - United States
   - Russia
   - Japan

Questions for Additional Practice

2. Analyze the similarities and differences between two of the following thinkers who responded to the Industrial Revolution and the development of capitalism:
   - Adam Smith
   - Karl Marx
   - John Stuart Mill
   - Max Weber

3. Analyze the similarities and differences between the urbanization of England during the Industrial Revolution with the formation of cities in Europe between 1000 and 1450.

THINK AS A HISTORIAN: APPLY THE USE OF COMPARISON

The examples below are first sentences of paragraphs, followed by possible second sentences. *Choose the second sentence that would best apply the use of comparison.*

1. Two inventions sped the process of weaving in the eighteenth century.

   a. The spinning jenny made it possible for one person to spin multiple spindles; the water frame increased the speed of the spinning jenny.

   b. James Hargreaves invented the spinning jenny and Richard Arkwright invented the water frame.

2. Steam power was an important development of the late eighteenth century.

   a. It triggered the creation of coaling stations at crucial points.

   b. On rivers, steam-powered ships could travel quickly upstream; on lakes and oceans, ships were no longer dependent on winds for power.

3. Japan and Russia had begun the process of industrialization by the end of the nineteenth century.

   a. Japan felt the need to catch up to the industrialized West and Russia built railroads that promoted trade.

   b. By 1900, Russia had become the largest producer of steel in the world.

WRITE AS A HISTORIAN: SUMMARIZE INFORMATION

In math, a sum is the total of two or more numbers. In writing, summarizing is adding up various pieces of information in order to present an accurate view overall. *Which THREE of the sentences below emphasize summary?*

1. During the early 1700s, most families in Britain lived in rural areas, grew their own food, and made their own clothes.

2. The burning of fossil fuel was essential in the process of separating iron from ore.

3. The Agricultural Revolution increased productivity as a result of crop rotation, the invention of the seed drill, and the introduction of the potato to people's diets.

4. Cottage industries gave women weavers a certain independence because they could work at home while minding their children.

5. Population growth, access to resources, and development of technology led to Britain's industrialization.

23

Turkey, China, Japan, and the West

"We should strive to maintain independence in the family of nations, and to spread our indigenous civilization as well as to enrich it by absorbing what is best in world civilization, with the hope that we may forge ahead with other nations towards the goal of ideal brotherhood."

—Sun Yat-sen, *Fundamentals of National Reconstruction,* 1923

Foreign challenges forced the Ottoman Empire, China, and Japan into modernization between 1750 and the early 1900s. Western domination and technology met with varying degrees of acceptance in each area. The Ottoman Empire was dismantled as a result of World War I. It was replaced by a smaller nation-state, the Republic of Turkey, and several independent countries. China, after undergoing a humiliating split into "spheres of influence" during the nineteenth century, shook off foreign domination and briefly became a republic. Japan, more swiftly than any other modern nation, developed into a technologically advanced and powerful civilization.

Although it was close to Europe geographically, the Ottoman Empire had refused to adapt to Western technology or to the ideas of the Enlightenment. Moreover, rampant corruption led to rapid decline and its nickname as "the sick man of Europe." Europeans feared what might happen in the power vacuum that would result from a collapse of the empire. They were equally aware of opportunities for increasing their own empires at the expense of the Ottomans. In its relative tolerance and diversity, the Ottoman Empire differed from both China and Japan. In politics and government, the empire became even more reactive rather than proactive. In Japan, by contrast, the central government grew stronger in its struggle to maintain independence and territorial integrity in the face of Western challenges. China, on the other hand, had to deal with the impact of the Opium War and Taiping Rebellion, which weakened the power of the central government and forestalled industrialization.

In the nineteenth century, Turkey, Japan, and China experienced competing pressures between preservation of traditional values and modernization, with the outcomes differing based on who was able to win that argument. Beginning in the nineteenth century, Japan became the first to widely accept technology from the West.

The Ottoman Empire

Suffering from problems of overexpansion and failure to modernize, the Ottoman Empire underwent palace coups, declining trade, and weakening leadership in the 1800s. The empire no longer covered the grand areas of Suleiman the Magnificent, who had taken his army to the gates of Vienna in 1529. (See the map on page 356.)

The Rise of Muhammad Ali One part of the Ottoman Empire where the sultan ruled in name but had little power was Egypt. In fact, the Mamluks, former Turkish slaves who formed a military class, had ruled there for some 600 years. In 1799, the French forces under a young general named Napoleon Bonaparte overthrew the Mamluks. Napoleon had to return to France to take control of his coup against the Directory. In his absence, the French generals had trouble ruling Egypt, and control fell back into the hands of the Mamluks. In 1801, the sultan sent an Ottoman army to retake Egypt. In the conflict with the Mamluks, an Albanian Ottoman officer, *Muhammad Ali*, rose to prominence, and local leaders selected him to be the new governor of Egypt. The sultan lacked the power to do anything but agree.

Ali Expands His Power Over the next ten years, Ali went on to consolidate his power by defeating Mamluk leaders. Meanwhile, in Arabia, an Islamic fundamentalist group called Wahhabis had taken control of Mecca and Medina from the Ottoman Empire. The sultan asked Ali to recapture Arabia, which his forces did in several campaigns over a number of years. Beginning in 1820, Ali then waged campaigns to the south to gain control of the Sudan for Egypt. This he accomplished without the sultan's permission.

Next, the sultan needed help in Greece, which was agitating for independence from the Ottoman Empire. In exchange for control of the island of Crete, Ali agreed to send an army and navy to Greece. Ali's and the sultan's forces were not strong enough to overthrow Greece's supporters— Russia, France, and Great Britain—in the naval *Battle of Navarino* (1827). As a result, the Egyptian navy was destroyed; Greece gained its independence in 1832.

Not content to sit back, Muhammad Ali sought control of Syria, with its valuable trading centers and natural resources. Ali's son Ibrahim led an Egyptian force to seize Syria in 1831–1832. He handily won there and went on to invade Anatolia itself, the heartland of the Ottoman Empire. Once again the European powers forced Egypt to withdraw in order to preserve the empire until *they* could decide what to do with its remains. The Europeans allowed descendants of Muhammad Ali to rule in Egypt until 1952—but with severely limited powers.

Ali as Reformer Although he did not break with the sultan totally, Muhammad Ali acted quite independently. One of his first reforms was to make over Egypt's army on a European model. He introduced the practice of *conscription*, compelling all men, even peasants, to become soldiers. By contrast, the sultan's army was composed of *Janissaries*—a highly organized elite military unit whose members were paid regularly and who wore distinctive uniforms—and citizens who were recruited as the need arose. These recruited Ottoman citizens were less disciplined soldiers than the regular standing army formed after 1826. For example, they sometimes had to depend on looting for their wages.

Muhammad Ali also established schools, sent officers to France for an education, and started an official newspaper, the first in the Islamic world. He also ordered many texts to be translated from French into Arabic.

As part of his reform of the Egyptian economy, Ali taxed the peasants at such a high rate that they were forced to give up their lands to the state. The government could then control the valuable cotton production and make money on the export of cotton and other agricultural products. Secularizing religious lands put more agricultural produce in the hands of the government, resulting in large profits during the period of the Napoleonic wars (1799–1815), when prices for wheat were high in Europe.

Muhammad Ali also pushed Egypt to industrialize. He had textile factories built to compete with those of the French and British. In *Cairo*, he had factories built to produce armaments. In Alexandria, he set up facilities to build ships so that Egypt could have its own navy. The city of Cairo had dozens of small shops turning out locks, bolts of cloth, and other parts for uniforms and weaponry. Ali is called the first great modern ruler of Egypt partly because of his vision of state-sponsored industrialization.

Selim III Reformist Sultan *Selim III* (ruled 1789–1807) attempted to reform the Ottoman army and bureaucracy after the pattern he saw in Europe, but two groups opposed these reforms. One group, Islamic scholars, fought the secularization of the government because it would reduce the power of religion. The other, the Janissaries, resisted reforms of their corps because they liked their privileges, including quarterly pay and a support corps providing medical care and other assistance when they were in camp or on marches during campaigns. They had a high standard of living and considerable social status, although they were not allowed to marry until retirement. Stymied by the opposition, Selim's military reforms were limited to new forces, which comprised only about 10,000 men in total. These new forces were organized into European-style formations and used European weapons and tactics. In 1807, Selim III was executed by conservatives supported by Janissaries.

Mahmud II Sultan *Mahmud II* (ruled 1808–1839) also enacted some reforms. In 1826, he abolished the corps of Janissaries, which had opposed him, and developed a new artillery unit trained by Europeans. When the Istanbul Janissaries revolted against Mahmud, he had them massacred. Although some Janissaries outlived Mahmud's attack, they were forced underground and became less threatening to the political balance. The abolishment of the feudal system in 1831 marked the final defeat of the Janissaries' power. Military officers were no longer able to collect taxes directly from the populace for their salaries. Instead, tax collections went directly to the central government, which paid military personnel, thus ensuring their loyalty.

Mahmud's reforms also included building more roads and setting up a postal service. To fight the power of the popular religious charities, he set up a government directory of charities. For the central administration of government, Mahmud II created European-style ministries.

Reorganization Reforms after Mahmud (during the years 1839–1876) are called *Tanzimat* (reorganization) and include the following changes:

- The sultans in this period worked to root out long-standing and widespread corruption in the central government.

- Education had long been under the control of the ulama, the educated class of Muslim scholars. Now the sultans created a secular system of schools. Thousands of primary schools were established, as well as some secondary ones, all under a ministry of education. Secular colleges were also gradually set up, one for each special purpose, e.g., military, engineering, translation, and civil service.

- As with earlier sultans, the Ottoman leaders of this period built more roads, but now they also constructed canals and railroads.

- The sultans codified Ottoman laws and created new ones, including a commercial code (1850) and a penal code (1858). These codes made it easier for foreigners to do business in the empire.

- In 1856, the sultan issued an edict known as the *Hatt-i Humayun* (Ottoman Reform Edict) that updated the legal system, declaring equality for all men in education, government appointments, and justice regardless of religion or ethnicity. The new legal system also regulated the millets, which were separate legal courts established by different religious communities, each using its own set of religious laws. Christians in the Balkans protested the new regulations because they felt that their autonomy was being threatened. Muslims, on the other hand, protested the reforms because they conflicted with traditional values and practice.

- One example of the Ottomans adapting to Islam is illustrated by a change in their military headgear in 1828 from caps to the fez. Wearing a cap with a bill did not allow for a soldier's forehead to touch the ground in prayer. The *fez*, not having a bill, allowed prayer in the manner of Islam.

Although not achieving religious equality, the Tanzimat reforms continued to have wide effect in areas such as the military and education even when succeeding sultans blocked the reforms. For example, in 1876, Sultan Abdulhamid II signed a constitution but then dissolved the parliament created by it.

Ottoman Loss of Territory In addition to the loss of Greece and the growing autonomy of Egypt, the empire lost power over other territories that became more independent during the nineteenth century. Estimates suggest that before 1850 a majority of all Ottoman subjects lived in the Balkans; the number dropped to about 20 percent in the early twentieth century. Bulgaria, Romania, and Serbia, as well as other Balkan territories, fell under the "protection" of either Russia or the Austro-Hungarian Empire. For example, Serbia, with the help of Russia, set up its own hereditary dynasty in the early 1800s and legally became a separate state in 1878 as a result of the *Congress of Berlin*, which met to reorganize the Balkans after the brief *Russo-Turkish War*.

The separation of these areas from the Ottoman Empire was, therefore, partly the result of a rise in nationalism in these areas and partly a result of decisions by the powerful nations of Europe. The Habsburg government of Austria-Hungary, for example, helped to administer the Balkan areas of Bosnia and Herzegovina and annexed them formally in 1908. The losses of the Ottoman Empire in the Balkans illustrate the increasing power of the European nations to make boundaries and impose control during the pre–World War I period.

On the coast of North Africa, France gained control of Algiers and made Tunis a protectorate by 1881. These Muslim areas were now firmly under French control, no longer belonging to the sultanate in Istanbul. In addition, Britain gained the island of Cyprus from the Ottomans, strengthening the British hold on shipping in the Mediterranean Sea.

These events limited the Ottoman Empire's holdings in Europe to a small strip of land protecting the Dardanelles and the city of Istanbul. The remainder of the land mass of the empire was now in Asia. (Test Prep: Write an outline in which you compare the decline of the Ottoman Empire with the decline of the Roman Empire. See pages 83–84.)

Ottoman Economy and Society After the Napoleonic wars ended in 1815, prices for food and other crops declined in the Ottoman Empire. However, a global economy was in place, built partially on the flow of wealth into the Mediterranean from European colonial expansion in the Americas. Ottoman workers were increasingly paid in cash rather than in goods. Financial enterprises such as banking increased.

These economic changes occurred along with the slow spread of industrialization. The growth of industry affected men and women differently. For example, most new industrial jobs went to men.

Legal reforms also benefited men more than women. Traditionally, under shariah, women had been allowed to hold money, to gain from inheritance, and to receive some education. The reforms of Mahmud II made the law more secular, and in doing so it ended the right of women to distribute their property or cash through trusts to family members. Although previously women had only indirect control of their property, the new nonreligious courts ended even these limited rights.

Many reforms had no effect on women. Since women were excluded from the army, the professions, higher education, and commerce, reforms in these areas did not affect women directly. The Tanzimat reforms of 1839 did not even mention women.

Nevertheless, by the end of the nineteenth century, girls attended many of the state primary schools. Some upper-class girls went to secondary schools, where they most often studied teaching or the fine arts. Overall, gender equality progressed slowly in the Ottoman Empire.

Economic Decline and European Investment Competing with other European nations, Germany presented an investment plan for a railway from Baghdad to Berlin. The Ottoman government accepted the plan and allowed foreigners to set up banking offices in Istanbul in order to provide additional loans for this and other investments. These foreigners lived in their own areas of the city and were granted *extraterritoriality*, the right of foreign residents in a country to live under the laws of their own country rather than those of their host country. Hence, foreigners could break an Ottoman law and not get punished for it. The Ottomans, like the Chinese and people in other places where foreigners successfully demanded extraterritoriality, found the practice demeaning.

Capitulations were concessions made by successive sultans to foreign nations. These capitulations allowed economic rights and privileges to subjects of foreign nations residing or trading in the areas dominated by the Ottomans. Drawn up to give the foreign nations favorable advantages in trade and import taxes, they frequently had the effect of draining resources from the Ottoman Empire. The capitulations agreements between Christian European nations and the Islamic Ottoman Empire had existed since 1500, when the earliest agreement was signed with France. They would not be formally abolished until the Treaty of Lausanne of 1923. Economic in nature, the agreements often contained a clause protecting the rights of Christians to worship when they were engaged in commerce in the Ottoman lands.

The Ottoman Empire had relatively few exports and a waning agricultural economy. The empire relied mostly upon its position as a trade center. Egypt, by contrast, continued to make profits from cotton.

As Ottoman prosperity declined, protest groups formed. Some scapegoated, or blamed, other groups for their economic problems, such as Armenians, a Christian minority, living and working in Anatolia. A new group, the *Young Turks*, became advocates for a constitution like those of the European nations as well as for *Turkification* of ethnic minorities. Turkification referred to a process of cultural change designed to make all citizens of the empire feel a part of a common Turkish heritage and society. For the Armenians hired to work on the German-owned railroads, such a cultural change was difficult as they were traditionally Christians.

Foreign investments, as well as resentment against other European nations that had imposed trade privileges unprofitable for the Ottomans, caused the Ottoman Empire to ally secretly with Germany and to become one of the Central Powers in World War I. (Test prep: Create a timeline showing the events that led the Ottoman Empire's role in World War I. See page 493–494 and 497–498.)

Qing Dynasty

The *Qing Dynasty* (1644–1911), the final dynasty for China, had many accomplishments, but Western intervention weakened it in the end.

Foreign Trade and Unequal Treaties In the late eighteenth century, Europeans interested in the China market could trade only in the city of Canton (Guangzhou). Europeans commonly bought tea, rhubarb, porcelain, and silk. In

Europe, Chinese fashions, table settings, and art objects were quite popular. The Chinese bought European silver at Canton but showed little interest in other European products. European trade missions, such as one led by *Lord Macartney*, a British statesman and foreign diplomat who became the first British envoy to China in 1792, were ineffective. Not only did the Chinese not desire the products Europeans wanted to sell, but they were suspicious of Europeans. People had heard that Macartney refused to *kowtow*, kneel and touch the forehead to the ground as a gesture of respect, to the Chinese emperor, causing distrust.

The British did have one product that appealed to many Chinese: *opium*. Grown in great quantities in British India and the Ottoman Empire, opium was easily imported into China. The Qing rulers had long forbade the importation of opium but did not enforce the law. However, as opium addiction became widespread, the Chinese government acted. In 1839, authorities enforced the law and seized shipments.

The Opium War (1839–1842) The seizure of opium infuriated the British. Ideologically, Britain said it violated the principle of trade. Economically, Britain considered the Chinese ban on opium to be a direct threat to its economy, which needed the Chinese market for the vast quantity of opium produced in the British colony of India. In 1839, the British went to war to protect their ability to sell opium in China, a conflict known as the *Opium War*. The Chinese, lacking a navy, quickly lost and were forced to negotiate the terms of the *Treaty of Nanking*. This 1842 treaty extended the old Canton trading-port rights of foreigners to four more Chinese ports. British citizens in China were granted extraterritoriality. In addition, Hong Kong became a long-term British colony, remaining in British hands until the late twentieth century. Other nations sought the same privileges that British traders received. Little by little, other European powers came to control trade in different parts of China. These areas were called *spheres of influence*. Until the late nineteenth century, gunboats from these nations frequented rivers far into the interior of China.

Meanwhile, the French, having established a number of Jesuit missions in Vietnam, encouraged Vietnam to ignore Chinese influence; the British encouraged Tibet to do the same.

Taiping Rebellion The Opium War left bitter feelings among the Chinese and anger at the Qing emperor for failing to protect China from "foreign devils." Other factors inflamed this anger. People resented the emperor because he was ethnically Manchu, not Chinese. They resented that he had granted extraterritoriality. They resented the presence of Christian missionaries who denounced Chinese traditions such as ancestor veneration and foot binding.

Not all Chinese resented the Christian missionaries. One who did not was Hong Xiuquan, a failed applicant for a civil service position. After converting to Christianity, he came to believe that he was the younger brother of Jesus, and that God wanted him to overthrow the Qing Dynasty and create a new Christian kingdom in Asia. A minor skirmish in 1851 quickly expanded into the *Taiping Rebellion*. Starving peasants, workers, and miners joined with others who opposed Qing rule, and Hong quickly built an army of perhaps a million fighters, with separate units for men and women. Beginning in southern China, they fought the imperial army for several years. Then in 1853, the Taipings seized the city of Nanjing and much of the Yangtze River Valley. They failed in a campaign against Beijing, the capital of the Manchu Empire, and another campaign against Shanghai. In 1864, the forces of the Qings, with help from some provincial warlords along with French and British intervention, were able to put down the Taiping Rebellion. Confucian principles of behavior also helped the cause of the Qings: Chinese subjects were supposed to respect their rulers, just as the rulers had a duty to rule virtuously.

In the midst of the war, the Yellow River (Huang He) changed course, flooding farmland in some areas and leaving others open to drought. With agricultural lands devastated, famine followed during which many Chinese starved to death. Adding to the troubles, the bubonic plague broke out at this time. By the end of the fighting, the rebellion was probably responsible for the deaths of more than 20 million people, more than half of whom were civilians.

Reform Efforts The Chinese government's major reform effort of the late nineteenth century (1861–1895) was known as the *Self-Strengthening Movement*. It developed as a way for the government to face the internal and external problems confronting China. Government officials hoped to strengthen China in its competition with foreign powers by advancing its military technology and readiness and by training Chinese artisans in the manufacture of items for shipyards and arsenals. French and British advisors helped Chinese reform efforts; one of these advisors served as inspector-general of the customs collection service. A stable government capable of collecting revenue allowed China to repay debts and participate in trade, which was an advantage for the Europeans. For the Chinese, their existence as an independent nation depended upon economic solvency. Reform in the name of modernization seemed inevitable.

As another step toward reform, the Chinese government set up its own diplomatic corps and a customs service to help collect taxes on imports and exports. The government's strategy in the reform efforts was to graft modern technology onto Chinese tradition rather than to create major change in cultural or political ideas.

Complicating the issue was the power of regional warlords whose help had been necessary to stop the Taiping Rebellion. These provincial leaders demanded certain *concessions* (rights to levy their own taxes, raise their own troops, and run their own bureaucracies) for remaining loyal to the central government. One such warlord, Zeng Guofan, maintained a personal army while also leading modernization efforts. To learn more about Western-style reforms, he hired American advisors to run his factories and shipyards and to encourage Chinese students to go abroad for their education.

Cixi's Conservatism Demand for reform increased after China's defeat in the Sino-Japanese War (1894–1895). People formed clubs to call for change. One club, led by a civil servant named Kang Youwei, gained momentum and was able to meet with Emperor Guangxu. Kang convinced the ruler to support a set of sweeping reforms known as the "Hundred Days of Reform." The reforms attempted to transform all aspects of Chinese society, including the abolition of the outdated civil servant exam, the elimination of corruption, and the establishment of Western-style industrial, commercial, and medical systems. However, the emperor's adopted mother, *Empress Cixi*, was a conservative who opposed the reforms and wanted to protect traditional social and governmental systems. In a coup d'état, Cixi imprisoned the emperor and immediately repealed his reform edicts. Cixi became known as the "Empress Dowager."

Cixi feared the influence of foreigners, so she resisted any new technology that would extend their reach into her country. For example, she stopped the extension of railroad lines and telegraph networks into the Chinese interior.

Reform of the Civil Service However, toward the end of Cixi's rule, she came to recognize the problems with the civil service system. It was designed according to Confucian ideals of respect for rank and hierarchy as well as values of civic participation and action. By the nineteenth century, though, the wealthy were using the civil servants to get favors. Revenue dropped off for the government as a result of bribes going into the pockets of corrupt civil servants. Moreover, non-qualified persons were purchasing civil service posts. In some cases, young men took the exams for others. In 1905, Cixi claimed that the exams did not meet the needs of a modernizing government since they were based on classical literature. China abandoned nearly 2,500 years of tradition, one that had yielded an educated bureaucracy of scholar-gentry. In spite of this concession, the empress's overall conservatism caused her to fail to cope with demands of modernity in China.

The Boxer Rebellion Cixi's fear of outside influence was shared by a group of Chinese named the *Righteous and Harmonious Order of Fists*, or, as Westerners called it, "the Boxers." It was a secret society in northern China that opposed the presence of all foreigners in the country. This society was a *millenarian movement*, in that it believed that after a sudden and violent change, a golden age would emerge. From 1899 to 1901, the central government in league with the society waged a violent anti-foreigner campaign known as the *Boxer Rebellion*. The campaign targeted Christian missionaries and converts.

However, provincial governors in southern China opposed the central government's actions and protected foreigners and Christians. In 1900, the British, the Americans, and the other foreign powers in China organized an international military force to put down the rebellion. The rebels and Chinese officials were forced to give way. The empress had to admit that she had erred, and the Chinese government was forced to pay an indemnity. Existing foreign powers in China retained their spheres of influence.

U.S. Open Door Policy At about the same time as the Boxer Rebellion, the United States became involved in diplomacy regarding China. Since the United States had no sphere of influence in China, Secretary of State John Hay asked the other foreign powers to agree to an *Open Door Policy*: all powers involved would have equal trading rights in China. Moreover, all the powers should respect China's territorial integrity. Answers to the United States demands were intentionally vague and evasive.

Russo-Japanese War In 1904–1905, Japan defeated Russia in a naval war. The Russians, feeling humiliated by their loss to an Asian country they considered inferior, were forced to withdraw from Manchuria. Removal of Russia left Manchuria open for the Japanese to move in, thus weakening China even more. (For more on the Russo-Japanese War, see page 454.)

Chinese Republic Although many Chinese had united behind the empress in 1899 to fight foreign influence, the Qing Dynasty's days were numbered. In 1911, the empire was overthrown by a revolutionary movement that established a Chinese republic with *Sun Yat-sen* as its first leader.

Although weak in the face of provincial warlords, the struggling republic tried to follow the three ideals of Sun Yat-sen, which he later elaborated upon in his book *The Three People's Principles*: democracy, nationalism, and livelihood.

- By democracy, he meant sovereignty, not for all the people but for those Chinese who were "able." In Confucian terms, this meant a country governed by the active and pragmatic experts in the name of the people. Not a Marxist, Sun Yat-sen nevertheless felt that expelling foreign capitalists from China would enable China to redistribute revenues from land taxes more fairly, since the revenues would not have to be used to pay debts to foreigners.

- By nationalism, he meant patriotism and loyalty, primarily to central authority.

- By livelihood, he meant an end to unequal distribution of wealth and economic exploitation.

Sun Yat-sen never ruled all of China, nor did he hold office long. Various warlords controlled the majority of the country. In fact, he was pushed out of office by a warlord in 1913. Nonetheless, his ideas formed the basis of the *Chinese Nationalist Party, Kuomintang*, which was to rule much of China for decades in the twentieth century.

Chinese Migrant Ethnic Enclaves Many Chinese emigrated in search of work during the end of the nineteenth century. European colonies in some areas of the world wanted a larger pool of laborers. For example, the British wanted more workers in the Caribbean to compete with the sugar plantations of Cuba and Brazil. Because the Taiping Rebellion had left millions of Chinese in poverty and ruin, many of them joined such a pool of workers. Other areas seeking more labor were newly industrializing countries such as Australia and Mexico, which became dependent upon Chinese labor for the building of their railroads and factories. Many of these laborers were *indentured servants*, bound for five to seven years of work to pay for their transportation.

While Chinese who migrated were common laborers, some were artisans or traders. Together, they spread Chinese culture across the world.

Source: Jakob Montrasio / Flickr

Jakarta

Source: rajkumar1220 / Flickr

Kolkata

Source: Thinkstock

London

The nineteenth-century migration of Chinese resulted in "Chinatowns" around the world, including in Jakarta, Indonesia (upper), Kolkata, India (middle), and London, England (lower).

Most emigrants were men who left wives and families in China. In some regions of China, the exodus of large numbers of men left openings for women to take up new roles in society.

The emigrants were interested in a new economic start but intent on taking with them their own traditions and culture. Chinese communities or ethnic enclaves (often called "Chinatowns") formed in almost every city of the world. In these areas inhabitants spoke Chinese, could easily find Chinese food, and could pursue a way of life similar to that which they had known in China.

Not all countries were happy to receive a large influx of Chinese immigrants. With many thousands of Chinese living in the United States by 1882, Congress banned further Chinese immigration by passage of the Chinese Exclusion Act. Initially limited to a 10-year period, the policy was extended periodically and made permanent in 1902. This act, which was finally repealed in 1943, gave testimony to ethnic and racial discrimination in the United States.

Common Limits to Reform In some ways, the reform movements of China and the Ottoman Empire reflected the revolutions and reaction movements going on in other parts of the world. In Latin America, for example, most nations had achieved self-government after rebelling against colonial governments sponsored by European imperialist nations. In Europe itself, new countries with constitutions had formed in Germany and Italy. Likewise, China and the Ottoman Empire were both responding to Enlightenment ideas, but they were both plagued by economic problems and by territorial encroachments by Europeans. Although each area modernized to some extent in the nineteenth century, the progress was slow and uneven due to conservative reaction.

CHINA AND JAPAN IN THE NINETEENTH CENTURY

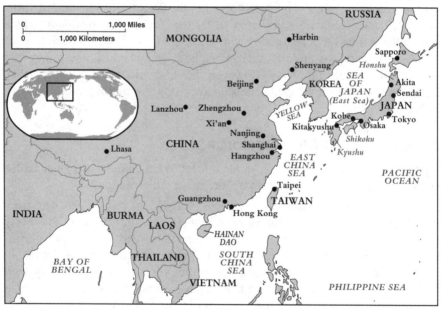

Ottoman efforts at internal reform were plodding, at best, although the Ottoman Empire did outlaw the Janissaries, attempt to modernize the army, and secularize the law under the Tanzimat. When the first Turkish parliament met, its' reforms were opposed by Sultan Abdulhamid, who used his new power to do away with the parliament. However, he did continue to emphasize primary education and secularization of the law. A few girls were allowed to attend girls' secondary schools by the beginning of the twentieth century.

Fearful of any "seditious" reform, the central government maintained tight control, driving the Young Turks into exile. The government also whipped up pogroms against minority groups, particularly Armenians and Assyrian

Christians. Between 1894 and 1896, between 100,000 and 250,000 Armenians were killed throughout several provinces in what has become known as the Hamidian massacres. The Ottoman authorities received little direction or help with their efforts at reform from Europeans, most of whom were intent on keeping the status quo and the balance of power in the Ottoman Empire.

In China, on the other hand, Europeans had much to gain from supporting a progressive central government. Even when reforms were met with the conservatism of Empress Cixi and the Boxer Rebellion, the Chinese government, including its provincial governors, continued to modernize, with some help from American and European advisors. Weakened by internal rebellion and fearing encroachment from Japan, China had to accept territorial "protection" from Western powers, who in return demanded trade concessions.

Following the ideas of Sun Yat-sen, the Chinese chose to become a republic. In addition, they resisted being swallowed up by their external enemies. China's attempts to preserve its territorial integrity benefited from the efforts of the United States to maintain stability in Asia by preventing Japan from encroaching farther on its territory after the Russo-Japanese War of 1905. United States efforts were exemplified by the *Treaty of Portsmouth*, which settled the war and was negotiated with the help of Theodore Roosevelt.

As will be discussed in later chapters, both Turkey and China progressed slowly into modern republics. However, due to conservative backlash, they lagged behind more developed nations in toleration of minorities and extending rights to women.

Japan and the Meiji Restoration

Japan's transition to a modern, industrialized country took less than half a century to accomplish. No country made such a rapid change.

A History of Isolation A conscious decision to remain isolated from outside influences dominated Japanese foreign policy from 1600 to 1854. Early brushes with Portuguese and Dutch traders (and the inroads made into Japanese tradition by Christian missionaries) made Japan withdraw into isolation. In 1614, the shogun, the country's supreme military leader, became uneasy with the increased number of Japanese Christian converts, and he issued a decree against them. Persecutions of the Christians intensified in 1617 and succeeded in removing the Christian presence from Japan, although some people continued to practice Christianity secretly. Dutch East India Company representatives were allowed to live on a small island in Nagasaki harbor but were kept in almost total seclusion. These traders introduced a few Western ideas about shipbuilding and medicine that made their way into the culture.

During this period, Japan continued some trade with the Chinese, mostly carried out by regional lords who were far from the capital city with easy access by sea to Korea, Taiwan, and Okinawa. Overall, though, Japan maintained its isolation under the authority of the various shogunates.

After two centuries of this self-imposed isolation, the islands of Japan yielded to American pressure in the form of a naval squad led by *Commodore Matthew Perry* in 1853. Four U.S. ships forced their way into Yedo and Tokyo Bay, asking for trade privileges. The next year, Perry returned with even more ships, demanding that the Japanese engage in trade with the United States. Faced with the power of the U.S. warships, the Japanese gave in to U.S. demands, and soon they yielded to similar ones by Britain, the Netherlands, and Russia. From the outside, it looked like Perry had "opened" Japan to the West. In reality, Japan opened itself to Western technology, while simultaneously avoiding the kinds of interference that the Chinese and the Ottomans were experiencing from Europeans. Although it rapidly modernized, Japan intentionally maintained many social customs, including a traditional family structure.

Impoverished Japanese nobles and samurai warriors, as well as merchants, pushed the signing of the commercial treaty with Perry to get themselves out of debt. The Japanese soon realized, though, that extraterritoriality and privileges for the foreigners were built into the early treaties. As a result, antiforeign feeling developed in Japan as it had in both the Ottoman Empire and China.

Collapse of the Shogunate In the Japanese hierarchy, the emperor was the supreme ruler. However, the emperor was in reality just a figurehead. Military dictators called shoguns had ruled Japan since the twelfth century. The nineteenth-century shoguns proved unable to govern in the face of conflict with Europeans and domestic critics. In one incident in 1862, the daimyo, or lord, of the far-western province of Satsuma resented the indemnity he had to pay because his samurai, the warriors under his command, had killed two Englishmen guilty of violating a point of Japanese etiquette. The Japanese government paid the indemnity instead. In a similar incident in 1864, after the lord of another far-western province, Choshu, had fired on passing foreign vessels, he was heavily fined by European nations and his forts and ships were destroyed. These incidents rankled both the foreign powers and many Japanese, further undermining the power of the shogunate.

The lords of the provinces of Choshu and Satsuma adopted Western military technology and forced the resignation of the shogun, who was unpopular for signing treaties with the West. The last shogun abdicated in 1867, and the emperor was "restored" to power. During the shogunate, it had been customary for the shoguns to run the government while the emperors stayed in remote palaces. There they practiced art and read classics but did not participate in the day-to-day running of government.

The new emperor who came into power, establishing what is now called the *Meiji Era* (1868–1912), was young and energetic. *Emperor Mutsuhito* was interested in abolishing feudalism and reorganizing Japan into *prefectures,* districts administered by the central government rather than provinces ruled by the daimyos, nobles who had supported the shogun. He was supported by young, energetic, far-sighted oligarchs, some of whom had been daimyos, but now were salaried members of the government. Daimyos who disagreed with the new administration retired. The new emperor also showed himself willing to meet with foreign envoys.

Reforms by the Meiji State The emperor instituted a number of reforms to bring his vision to reality. Under him, Japan

- formally abolished feudalism in 1868 by the *Charter Oath*, a statement of policy to be followed by the Japanese government in the Meiji Era
- borrowed Western ideas about justice, including the establishment of equality before the law and abolition of cruel and unusual punishments
- established a constitutional monarchy based on the Prussian model in which the emperor exercised political power and oversaw foreign policy, and the Diet focused on domestic policy
- remodeled the military, creating an army based on the Prussian army, building a new navy, and instituting conscription
- established a postal service
- created a new educational system modeled after Western systems, a reform that soon resulted in higher literacy rates
- promoted industrialization and financed it by both the Japanese government and by foreign investors
- started a railroad network in 1869, employing British engineers and rapidly expanding throughout the country

Some reforms worked better than others. The new schools quickly improved literacy rates, but the political changes did not result in a strong democracy. The lack of political parties meant that power fell mostly to army officers.

Samurai Resistance Just as China ended its long-standing civil service system, the Japanese also ended a traditional system of exercising authority. In 1871, Japan gave samurai a final lump-sum payment and legally dissolved their position. They were no longer fighting men and were not allowed to carry their swords. The *bushido*, their code of conduct, was now a personal matter, no longer officially condoned by the government

Some samurai adjusted to the change by serving the government as *genros* or elder statesmen. Others, particularly those from the provinces of Satsuma and Choshu, resisted the change. They defended their right to dress and wear their hair in traditional ways and to enjoy relative autonomy from the centralized government. The last battle between the samurai shogunate forces and those loyal to the emperor occurred in the 1870s. Dismayed by defeat, the samurai became the main victims of Japan's rapid modernization. (Test Prep: Write a brief paragraph comparing the samurai with the knights of medieval Europe. See pages 223–224.)

Industrialization and Economic Modernization The Meiji emperors wanted citizens who were educated and competent but also loyal and obedient. Industrialization, much of it paid for by careful government financing, created new jobs. The government provided massive subsidies for training new workers in the key industries of tea, silk, weaponry, shipbuilding, and a rice wine called sake. In addition, the government set up technical schools and instituted universal education. The central government modernized the transportation and communications systems, including new railroads and roads. A high agricultural tax financed much of the government investment that created new industries and jobs. The government's ability to collect increased taxes also provided revenue for the bureaucracy, now centered in Tokyo.

While the relationship between industry and centralized government was key to modernization in Japan, private investment from overseas was also important. Once new industries were flourishing, they were sometimes sold to *zaibatsu,* powerful family business organizations like the conglomerates in the United States. The prospect of attracting investors encouraged innovation in technology. For example, a carpenter founded a company in 1906 called Toyoda Loom Works that made an *automatic loom.* The company prospered, modified its name, and grew into today's Toyota Motor Company.

From Isolation to Imperialism Success in centralizing government, neutralizing the samurai, and building a conscript army led Japan away from isolationism to imperialism. Japan followed the pattern seen in other newly centralized nations such as Germany and Italy. It began to look outward for territorial gains.

Partially to relieve population pressures in rural areas and partially to gain knowledge of foreign places, the government began to encourage agricultural workers to take contract, or seasonal, work on Hawaii, Guam and other locations. Through a Colonization Society established in 1893, leaders began plans to establish colonies in Mexico and Latin America. By the early 1900s, Japan was looking to China, Korea, and Russia as areas where it could enlarge its holdings and influence.

A centralized government with an active emperor increased the feeling of nationalism throughout Japan. Population growth and economic needs also fueled the desire to expand. The new industries needed raw materials and expanded markets. Neighboring Korea in the late nineteenth century was having troubles of its own. When the Korean government invited China to help it put down a rebellion, the Chinese informed the Japanese, who objected. The brief *Sino-Japanese War* (also known as the Chinese-Japanese War) followed, which ended with a Japanese victory in 1895. The Chinese had to give up to Japan the island of Formosa (also known as Taiwan) and the Liaotung Peninsula on the continent. The Liaotung Peninsula was returned to China almost immediately through the intervention of Russia, France, and Germany. Russia was able to lease an area for a railroad in nearby Manchuria.

Russo-Japanese War In 1905, after the brief Russo-Japanese War (the first victory of an Asian nation over Europeans in the modern era), the Treaty of Portsmouth gave the Liaotung Peninsula back to Japan. The treaty also gave Japan a preferred position in Manchuria and a protectorate in Korea. As mentioned earlier in this chapter, the treaty was negotiated with the help of U.S. President Theodore Roosevelt in Portsmouth, New Hampshire.

The Russo-Japanese War exposed several Russian weaknesses and illustrated the growing strength of Japan. Japan believed that Russian railroad expansion through Manchuria to Port Arthur threatened its national security. Russia, on the other hand, wanted a more southerly port under its control than its port of Vladivostok. The attack, blockade, siege, and final fall of the Port Arthur harbor signaled the failures of the Russian navy. The defeat and resulting economic hardships at home plunged Russia into the Revolution of 1905, while the victorious Japanese enjoyed increased prestige throughout Asia.

HISTORICAL PERSPECTIVES: HOW STRONG WERE THE OTTOMANS?

Historians in the late-nineteenth and early-twentieth centuries, living in a period when Turkish power was low, generally viewed the Ottoman Empire as the "sick man of Europe." In his widely used college textbook, *A History of the Modern World* (first published in 1950), R.R. Palmer stated that the long slide of the nineteenth-century Ottoman Empire put the empire "behind modern industrial nations in its scientific, mechanical, material, humanitarian, and administrative achievements."

Recent historians, living in a period of increasing Turkish influence in the Middle East, have seen more vigor in all areas than previous scholars noted. They have credited the nineteenth-century reforms of the Ottomans with providing the stable foundation necessary to allow the success of the Republic of Turkey, established in 1923.

Donald Quataert pointed to the Public Debt Administration, which stabilized the economy and gave Europeans more confidence to invest in railroads, ports, and public utilities in the Ottoman Empire. These projects provided an increasingly modern infrastructure for the empire, although at the loss of some autonomy for the Ottoman government.

While acknowledging the difficulties that capitulations caused, Suraiya Faroqhi nevertheless emphasized that "more recent studies prove that Ottoman commerce and artisan production were more varied than they might appear at first glance" and that "production was now integrated into the world market."

Justin McCarthy called the changes in the Ottoman system "neither small nor cosmetic," pointing to "human rights, a constitution, Christians in high office, a parliament, the middle class in charge of the state, and the power of Islam eroded" as evidence of progress on multiple fronts. McCarthy further suggested that the empire fell not because of lack of successful reforms or the failure to modernize but because of the military power of the forces arrayed against it.

KEY TERMS BY THEME

STATE-BUILDING: LEADERS
Muhammad Ali
Selim III
Mahmud II
Qing Dynasty
Empress Cixi
Sun Yat-sen
Emperor Mutsuhito

STATE-BUILDING
Battle of Navarino
Janissaries
conscription
Cairo
Tanzimat
Hatt-i Humayun
Congress of Berlin
Russo-Turkish War
extraterritoriality
Opium War
Taiping Rebellion

Self-Strengthening Movement
concessions
The Three People's Principles
Chinese Nationalist Party (Kuomintang)
Treaty of Portsmouth
Meiji Era
prefectures
Charter Oath
Diet
Sino-Japanese War

CULTURE
Wahhabis
fez
Young Turks
Turkification
Lord Macartney
kowtow

Harmonious Order of Fists
Boxer Rebellion
millenarian movement
bushido
automatic loom

SOCIAL STRUCTURES
genros

ECONOMICS
capitulations
opium
Treaty of Nanking
spheres of influence
Open Door Policy
indentured servants
Commodore Matthew Perry
zaibatsu

MULTIPLE-CHOICE QUESTIONS

1. Which of the following statements provides the strongest evidence to support the interpretation of historians who argue that the Ottoman Empire instituted important reforms in the late nineteenth century?

   (A) The Ottomans created a network of state-run schools.

   (B) Janissaries were a powerful force.

   (C) Germany partially financed a railroad from Baghdad to Berlin.

   (D) The Ottomans lost control of the Balkans, Bulgaria, and Egypt.

2. Which of the following was most associated with Japanese industrialization during the Meiji Era?

   (A) daimyo

   (B) samurai

   (C) zaibatsu

   (D) bushido

Question 3 refers to the table below.

United States Population, 1840–1910			
Year	Total	Number of People of Chinese Heritage	Percentage of Population of Chinese Heritage
1840	17,069,453	NA	NA
1850	23,191,876	4,018	0.02%
1860	31,443,321	34,933	0.11%
1870	38,558,371	64,199	0.17%
1880	50,189,209	105,465	0.21%
1890	62,979,766	107,488	0.17%
1900	76,212,168	118,747	0.16%
1910	92,228,496	94,414	0.10%

Source: U.S. Census Bureau

3. The trend in the percentage of population of Chinese heritage (immigrants from China and their descendants) after 1880 is best explained by the
   (A) Boxer Rebellion
   (B) Open Door Policy
   (C) Chinese Exclusion Act
   (D) Self-Strengthening Movement

4. Which of the following characteristics were shared by the Boxer Rebellion and the Taiping Rebellion?
   (A) Each was religious in nature, one Buddhist and the other Confucian.
   (B) Each was an event in the twentieth century.
   (C) Each was an effort to start a new dynasty to rule an expanding Chinese empire.
   (D) Each was fueled by economic distress in China.

5. In contrast with Japan, the Ottoman Empire in the nineteenth century
   (A) was a model of tolerance to outsiders
   (B) had a weakening central government
   (C) was early to adopt Western ideas
   (D) grew through military conquests

6. The Turkification movement in the Ottoman Empire and the Boxer Rebellion in China both reflected

   (A) the need for modern militaries
   (B) an expansion of imperialism
   (C) a desire to lessen foreign influence
   (D) policies of the central governments

Question 7 refers to the excerpt below.

Her [Japan's] general progress, during the short space of half a century, has been so sudden and swift that it presents a rare spectacle in the history of the world. This leap forward is the result of the stimulus which the country received on coming into contact with the civilization of Europe and America, and may well, in its broad sense, be regarded as a boon conferred by foreign intercourse. Foreign intercourse it was that animated the national consciousness of our people, who under the feudal system lived localized and disunited, and foreign intercourse it is that has enabled Japan to stand up as a world power.

—Okuma Shigenobu, *Fifty Years of New Japan* (1910)

7. Which of the following events is most closely associated with what Okuma called Japan's "leap forward"?

   (A) The arrival of Commodore Matthew Perry
   (B) The refusal of Lord Macartney to kowtow
   (C) The end of the Russo-Japanese War
   (D) The death of Emperor Mutsuhito

8. Which of the following was a result of the Opium War between Great Britain and China?

   (A) China closed all its ports to foreign trade.
   (B) China was carved into spheres of influence.
   (C) The opium trade was outlawed in China.
   (D) Britain withdrew from the opium trade.

9. As a result of the Russo-Japanese War, Japan

   (A) formed an alliance with China against Russia
   (B) gained power at the expense of China
   (C) lost significant territory to Russia
   (D) gave up any imperial aspirations

10. Which of the following illustrates the contraction of the Ottoman Empire?

(A) Muhammad Ali's conquest of Anatolia

(B) The sultans' reforms of the Ottoman military

(C) The establishment of Balkan states

(D) Closer ties between Egypt and Greece

CONTINUITY AND CHANGE-OVER-TIME ESSAY QUESTIONS

Directions: You are to answer the following question. You should spend 5 minutes organizing or outlining your essay. Write an essay that:

- Has a relevant thesis and supports that thesis with appropriate historical evidence.
- Addresses all parts of the question.
- Uses world historical context to show continuities and changes over time.
- Analyzes the process of continuity and change over time.

1. Analyze continuities and change in the lives of members of ONE of the following groups between 1750 and 1900:

- Janissaries in the Ottoman Empire
- samurai in Japan

Questions for Additional Practice

2. Analyze continuities and change in the status of women in the Ottoman Empire between 1750 and 1900.

3. Analyze continuities and change in the central government of ONE of the following regions between 1750 and the early twentieth century:

- Ottoman Empire
- China
- Japan

COMPARATIVE ESSAY QUESTIONS

Directions: You are to answer the following question. You should spend 5 minutes organizing or outlining your essay. Write an essay that:

- Has a relevant thesis and supports that thesis with appropriate historical evidence.
- Addresses all parts of the question.
- Makes direct, relevant comparisons.
- Analyzes relevant reasons for similarities and differences.

1. Analyze similarities and differences in the role of Westerners in TWO of the following regions between 1750 and 1900:
   - The Ottoman Empire
   - Qing Dynasty, China
   - Japan

Questions for Additional Practice

2. Analyze similarities and differences in TWO of the following reform movements:
   - Tanzimat in the Ottoman Empire
   - Self-Strengthening Movement in China
   - reforms of Meiji Japan

3. Compare state-sponsored industrialization in Egypt under Muhammad Ali and in Japan during the Meiji Era.

Context helps us to understand a person, place, document, or period in history by grounding it with a time, a place, or surrounding circumstances. For example, a treaty's significance becomes clearer if we know how, when, and where it was created, what concessions the various parties made, and who signed it. Imagine you are a citizen of a distant past reading the day's newspaper. *Which THREE of the headlines below provide the most context?*

1. Sultan Sends Army to Egypt

2. Ali Debuts First Official Newspaper in Islamic World; Insists on Arabic, Not French

3. Workers Paid in Cash, Not Goods, as Post-War Wealth Grows

4. Much New Weaponry Is Produced Quickly

5. Religious Groups Protest New Laws That Ignore Shariah

A fundamental rule of writing is that if you want to be read, you must capture the reader's attention. *In the pairings below, choose the more compelling first sentence.*

1. Sultans and Reform

   a. Sultan Abdulhamid II signed a constitution but then dissolved the parliament created by that very constitution: Why?

   b. In the Ottoman Empire, it was not unusual for sultans to block reforms.

2. The Significance of Clothing

   a. Ottomans adapted to Islam in various ways, including in their clothing.

   b. Strangely, Ottoman adaptation to Islam can be illustrated by a change in military headgear from a cap to a fez (because a cap with a bill did not allow a soldier's head to touch the ground in prayer).

3. Decline of the Ottoman Empire

   a. After France took Algiers and Britain captured Cyprus, the once-mighty Ottoman Empire held only a small strip of land in Europe.

   b. The Ottoman Empire grew smaller and weaker just as the Roman Empire did, and in some of the same ways.

24

Global Links and Imperialism, 1750–1900

Take up the White Man's Burden—
Send forth the best ye breed—
Go bind your sons to exile
To serve your captives' need;
To wait in heavy harness,
On fluttered folk and wild—
Your new-caught, sullen peoples,
Half-devil and half-child.

—Rudyard Kipling, "The White Man's Burden"

The speaker in this poem by Rudyard Kipling, an English writer who spent his youth in British colonial India, views the whites of Western countries as superior and that they should take on the "burden" of colonizing and training the "half-devil" and "half-child" nonwhite peoples of the world. Whether Kipling actually supported imperialism is debatable, but the ideas in his poem were used to justify it. Countries built global empires upon such imperialistic and racist premises. During the nineteenth and early twentieth centuries, a number of Western European countries targeted lands in Africa and Asia to add to their empires. The United States became an imperial power in Latin America, the Caribbean, and the Pacific. Russia continued its expansion eastward and southward. The Russian-British rivalry for power in Central Asia was known as the *Great Game.* Japan concentrated its expansionist efforts in East Asia. Although ideological motives for imperialism were compelling, economics and politics primarily drove European countries to conquer more than 80 percent of the Earth's surface by the end of the nineteenth century.

Economic Motives for Imperialism

Though several motives drove imperialism, most historians agree that economics overrode all others. As you read in Chapter 22, Britain industrialized rapidly during the 1700s and 1800s. In order to feed industries' desires for raw materials, such as cotton, copper, and rubber, Europe looked to Asia and Africa. The people of these continents were also potential consumers of European manufactured goods. Finally, Europeans used colonial peoples as labor for large-scale projects, such as building railroads or telegraph lines. Colonial workers were paid meager wages for difficult and dangerous labor. In short, natural resources, new markets, and cheap labor drove economic imperialism.

Agricultural Resources from Colonies Instead of serving their own economic interests, colonies were turned into *export economies*, which meant that the goods they produced were not meant for domestic use but sent to colonial powers to sell for profit. The thirst for natural resources led to the development of *cash crops* within the colonies, such as tea, cotton, sugar, palm oil, rubber, and coffee. Imperial demand for cash crops had a deleterious effect on subject nations. For example, if a crop was particularly profitable, the colonized nation was forced to produce that crop in mass quantities. Farmers were allowed to raise only cash crops, such as sugar, cocoa, or groundnuts, at the expense of other agricultural products. This use of land led to *monocultures*, or a lack of agricultural diversity, particularly in African nations. The land's fertility quickly declined. Moreover, crop diseases and pests spread more easily when there was only one crop planted in an area. Today, many former African colonies have been unable to rediversify their land because the development of monocultures has badly damaged croplands. Many African nations must import basic agricultural goods in order to feed their people.

For centuries, India had been the world's number one supplier of finished cotton textiles. By the late eighteenth century, British traders from the British East India Company, who wanted a monopoly on the textile market, had pushed independent Indian textile artisans out of business. By the end of the nineteenth century, India was producing only raw cotton for Britain, not cotton textiles. After Britain's textile factories processed India's cotton, the colonial government sold some of its factory-made or "finished" textiles back to the Indian subcontinent at inflated prices.

Another example of economic imperialism involved opium, a harmful and hallucinogenic drug. It grew easily on South Asia's fertile lands, and selling it to the Chinese became quite profitable for Britain. The Chinese objected to the importation of opium, resulting in the Opium War. (For more information on the Opium War, see page 448.)

The Dutch East India Company first brought *tea* from China to Europe in 1610. Later, it became another profitable crop for the British, who introduced tea plantations to South Asia in the early nineteenth century. Tea became a cash crop in southern India and in Ceylon, modern-day Sri Lanka.

Railways in Colonies Europeans often pointed to their railroad projects as evidence that imperialism helped the peoples of Asia and Africa. However, providing new transportation technology to the colonies primarily served the interests of the colonizers. In India, the British built a complex railway network that stretched from the interior to the coasts in order to ship raw materials out of the country more easily. In Africa, a map of the railway system reveals that while many railroad tracks began in the interior of Africa, all lines reached the coasts.

British-born *Cecil Rhodes,* founder of De Beers Diamonds, was an especially enthusiastic investor in a railroad project that was to stretch from Cape Town, in modern-day South Africa, to Cairo, Egypt. Connecting all of the British-held colonies with a transportation network could make governance easier and aid in conducting a war, if necessary. The project was never completed because Britain never gained control over all the land on which such a railroad was to be built. The overwhelming majority of railway workers in Africa were natives who were paid far lower wages than their European counterparts. Thus, railroad technology was a means of extracting as many resources as possible from subject lands while paying colonial laborers as little as possible.

De Beers was one of many large transnational companies that emerged in the nineteenth century. Many, such as United Fruit Company, produced food or minerals. Others, such as Hong Kong and Shanghai Banking Corporation, focused on finance.

Japan Industrial countries outside of Europe also desired colonies. Japan, a small island nation with few natural resources and little arable land, sought lands and natural resources to fuel its own growth. It set up an empire in East Asia that included parts of China, Korea, Southeast Asia, and islands that lasted from the 1890s until World War II ended.

Labor Systems The desire for cheap labor was inextricably linked to the exploitation of natural resources in the system of economic imperialism. Although the African slave trade collapsed by the early nineteenth century, the demand for the agricultural goods that slaves had produced did not. Thus, European nations recruited new laborers to work on sugar and pineapple plantations. Indentured laborers came primarily from India and, to a lesser extent, from China and Japan. Indian laborers worked in British colonial possessions in the Caribbean as well as in Fiji and Dutch Guiana, present-day Suriname. Chinese and Japanese laborers migrated to Hawaii and later to Peru and Cuba. Their labor produced enormous wealth for the imperial nations.

Indentured laborers agreed to work for a period of years, during which time they sent money to their families and looked forward to returning home. However, most indentured laborers stayed in their new country. Some chose to stay and sent for their families to join them, while others simply could not afford the return journey. Regardless, indentured laborers brought their home cultures to their new lands and altered the demographics of these lands. For example, the cultures of Mauritius (in the Indian Ocean southeast Africa), Fiji (in the South Pacific), and Trinidad (in the Caribbean) show a strong Indian influence, and people of Asian descent form the majority of Hawaii's population.

Australia A different kind of labor system developed in Australia. In the late 1700s, Great Britain established a *penal colony*. The British government shipped *convicts* from England, Scotland, and Ireland as well as British colonies such as India to Australia, where they performed hard labor and suffered harsh treatment. Australia also attracted free settlers, especially after gold was discovered there in 1851. Some 50,000 Chinese came during this gold rush. Australia became one of Britain's most successful settler colonies.

Actual imprisonment of the convicts was rare. Most performed labor for free settlers, worked for the government in record keeping, or worked on government projects such as road and railway building. The majority of convicts earned their freedom after a prescribed number of years of service. Some were never allowed to return to Great Britain. In addition, because transportation back home was expensive, the majority decided to stay in Australia. By 1850, the British government ended the transport of convicts to Australia, largely because a stay in Australia was not considered much of a punishment.

The coming of the Europeans spread diseases among the indigenous *Aborigines* of Australia just as they had among Native Americans. In addition, the white settlers took over most of the lands of the Aborigines, dispersing them throughout the continent. A similar process took place in another British settler colony southeast of Australia, New Zealand. During the nineteenth century, the native *Maori* lost about 75 percent of its population to disease and warfare with the British. Although Australia was vastly underpopulated, the country was not open to immigrants from all parts of the world. The *White Australia Policy*, in effect from 1901 until 1973, restricted the immigration of nonwhites. (Test Prep: Write a paragraph comparing the effects of European settlement on Australian Aborigines to its effect on Native Americans. See pages 302–309.)

Political Motives for Imperialism

In Western Europe, revolutions, the rise of nationalism, and the creation of nation-states characterized much of the 1800s. Building an empire was one way for a country to compete for power and assert its national identity in the global arena. In the last quarter of the nineteenth century, Europe's "*Scramble for Africa*" epitomized such competition for colonies. European countries claimed African colonies, largely out of economic desires, but also in attempts to outdo each other. European nations most active in the scramble for territory included Great Britain, Germany, France, Belgium, Italy, Portugal, and the Netherlands. While Spain had led the quest for colonies in the first wave of imperialism during the sixteenth and seventeenth centuries, its power was greatly diminished by the nineteenth century. It did not play a dominant role in this second wave of imperialism.

Japan asserted its nationalist pride through incursions into Korea. This irritated China, a country that had exerted a strong presence in Korea for centuries. The conflict grew into the Sino-Japanese War (1894–1895). Japan's victory gave it control of Korea and Taiwan, which was known as Formosa from the time of Portuguese colonization in the sixteenth century until the end of World War II.

Ideological Motives for Imperialism

The Kipling quotation that opens this chapter epitomizes the racist attitudes shared by imperialism's proponents. Referring to colonized peoples as children makes colonizers seem like benevolent protectors rather than rapacious thieves. White racists' condescending attitudes toward the "darker corners of the earth" (Theodore Roosevelt, 1909) was not a reason for imperialism, but a justification for it.

The Misuse of Science Pseudoscientists strengthened racist justifications for conquest by claiming to have scientific proof of the intellectual and physical inferiority of nonwhite races. *Phrenologists*, people who studied skull sizes and shapes, claimed that a smaller skull size proved the mental feebleness of Africans, indigenous Americans, and Asians.

Legitimate science was also subverted for racist purposes. British scientist *Charles Darwin*'s nineteenth-century theory of evolution by natural selection stated that over the course of millions of years, biological competition had "weeded out" the weaker species in nature and that the "fittest" species were the ones that survived. Advocates of *Social Darwinism*, including British philosopher *Herbert Spencer*, used the "survival of the fittest" theory to justify European and U.S. dominance. Supporters of this theory claimed that whites had used their "biological superiority" to compete victoriously with the other races of the world. Writers and politicians used Social Darwinism to justify the actions of imperial powers around the world.

The Role of Missionaries Missionary work often combined humanitarian and religious motives. Some Christian missionaries, such as *David Livingstone* from Scotland, traveled to Sub-Saharan Africa where they worked to end the illegal slave trade. Others provided improved medicines and medical care in Africa. Most missionaries set up schools for instruction in religion and secular subjects. Missionaries spread their own religion and converted many non-Christian believers among Sub-Saharan Africans, who generally practiced ancestor veneration and animism.

Missionaries were sometimes criticized as supporters of imperialism. Because they tried to persuade people to give up their own sacred beliefs and adopt the faith common among Westerners, missionaries sometimes paved the way for others who were more focused on economic gain.

Imperialism in South Asia

In India, the British East India Company had established a commercial relationship with the Mughal Empire beginning in the seventeenth century. Britain did not have exclusive access to India, however. Portugal controlled a coastal trading post in the southwestern state of *Goa*, and France controlled *Pondicherry*, a city in the southeastern state of Tamil Nadu. During the mid-eighteenth century, France and England, along with their respective allies, competed for power on five continents in the Seven Years' War. Britain's victory in that war in 1763 drove the French out of India. The Portuguese remained in India until driven out in the mid-twentieth century.

Since the Mughal Empire was weak, the British East India Company easily encroached inland, using small forces of British soldiers to protect the firm's employees. As the British crept into India's interior, the British government began recruiting native Indians to join the British colonial army. By the mid-nineteenth century, *sepoys*, Indian soldiers under British employ, composed the majority of the British armed forces in colonial India. In 1857, the *Sepoy Mutiny* erupted among soldiers who believed that their rifle cartridges had been greased with the fat of cows and pigs. Hindus, who view the cow as sacred, and Muslims, who refuse to slaughter pigs, were both furious. They were convinced that the British were trying to convert them to Christianity. Their rebellion spread throughout cities in northern India, where the sepoys lashed out violently against British settlers and officials.

The British colonial government's response to the revolt was forceful and brutal. British counterinsurgency not only resulted in the deaths of thousands of Indian soldiers, but it also led the British government to take a more active role in governing India. Because of his involvement in the mutiny, the last Mughal emperor was imprisoned and exiled, marking the end of the empire. From 1858 until India finally won its independence in 1947, the British *Raj*, the colonial government, took its orders directly from the British government in London.

SOUTH ASIA

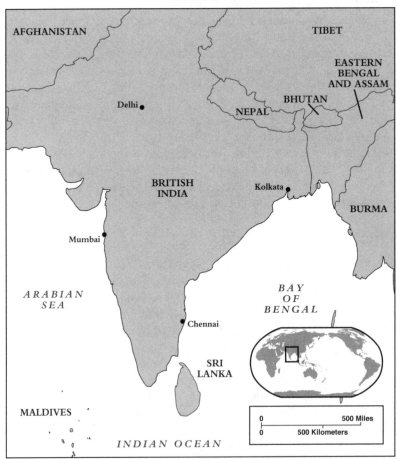

Imperialism in Africa

Europe had a long-standing relationship with Africa because of the slave trade. Although most European countries had declared the importation of slaves from Africa illegal by the early 1800s, Europeans continued to export guns, alcohol, and factory goods to Africa and import African natural resources, such as palm oil, gold, and ivory. England desired palm oil in particular because it kept the machinery in its textile factories from becoming rusty. In the last part of the nineteenth century, European tastes for African diamonds and ivory kept European empires thriving throughout the African continent. (Test Prep: Write a paragraph connecting late-nineteenth-century imperialism with the African slave trade. See pages 323–327.)

For most of the 1800s, European presence in Africa was minimal. The French seized Algeria in 1830, supposedly to prevent pirate attacks. Dutch immigrants had lived in South Africa since the 1600s; the British came to South Africa in 1806. In the second half of the nineteenth century, European nations expanded their presence in Africa with the help of better military technology; the discovery of *quinine*, a medicine that treats the tropical disease malaria; the steamship; and the early trips of individual explorers and business owners.

Congo By 1875, Western European nations were poised to penetrate Africa's interior. *King Leopold II* of Belgium (ruled 1865–1909) oversaw the invasion and pacification of the Congo, in central Africa. Unlike other European rulers, King Leopold owned the colony personally. That meant he kept the profits made by the *Congo Free State*, which totaled some $1 billion. Visitors to the colony reported on the terribly brutal conditions for the laborers who were forced to harvest ivory and rubber. For example, Leopold's agents severed the hands of Congolese workers in order to terrorize others into submission. Workers who could not meet their quotas were beaten or killed, while others were worked to death. Although the term "slavery" was not commonly used when describing imperial activities, laborers in the Congo often received no payment for their backbreaking work, and their spouses were held captive so that the workers would not run away. Overall, three million to eight million people perished under King Leopold's reign of terror in the Congo. In 1908, Belgium took over control of the Congo as a regular colony, and conditions improved. (Test Prep: Create an outline comparing conditions in the Congo with conditions in European colonies in South America. See pages 305–309.)

Suez Canal Europeans had long dreamed of dramatically shortening the route to Asia by building a canal connecting the Red Sea with the Mediterranean. This feat was finally accomplished when the *Suez Canal* was completed in 1869 by a French company using Egyptian *corvée laborers*. As many as 1.5 million of these unpaid workers were forced to work on the project, with thousands dying over the course of ten years. In 1882, Britain took over control of Egypt, still nominally part of the Ottoman Empire, because of unrest there that threatened British commercial interests. Britain also wanted to guarantee that the Suez Canal remained open.

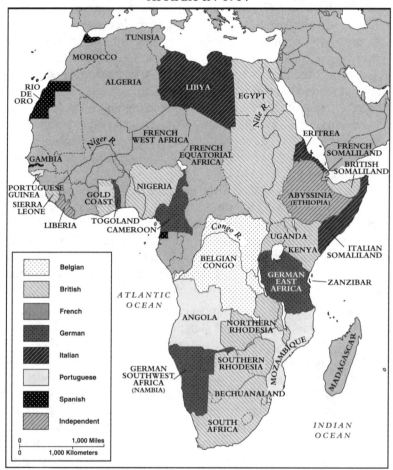

AFRICA IN 1914

Legend:
- Belgian
- British
- French
- German
- Italian
- Portuguese
- Spanish
- Independent

0 — 1,000 Miles
0 — 1,000 Kilometers

Scramble for Africa Fierce competition among European nations led to the *Berlin Conference* of 1884–1885 on the future of Africa. The purpose of this conference, held in Berlin, Germany, was not to divide Africa among the major Western powers but to set rules for establishing colonies there. However, it was clear that European powers were preparing to seize more land in Africa for colonies. No African representatives were invited to the conference.

By 1900, the only African countries unclaimed by Europeans were *Abyssinia*, modern-day Ethiopia, and *Liberia*, a country founded by formerly enslaved people from the United States. Because Liberia had a dependent relationship with the United States, it was not fully independent. Italy attempted to conquer Abyssinia in 1895, but the native forces were too strong for the Italians.

For the remainder of the continent, the new borders were merely artificial lines that meant little to the people who lived within them. Eventually, however, the borders became significant. Borders tore apart unified societies or placed rival groups under the same colonial government. For example, the Portuguese colony of Angola "united" ten major ethnic groups, including the Ambo, the

Herero, and the Kimbundu. The borders remained, even after African states won independence in the twentieth century. Although leaders have tried to develop a sense of nationalism, the borders have served to increase division instead of national unity. The lines drawn from afar set the stage for twentieth-century civil wars and created hundreds of thousands of refugees.

South Africa During the Napoleonic Wars (1799–1815), the British replaced the Dutch in the Cape Colony in the southernmost part of Africa. The British introduced the use of English but allowed people to use the Dutch language as well. Many of the Dutch-speaking *Afrikaners*, the descendants of seventeenth-century Dutch settlers, moved east of the Cape Colony, where they came into conflict with indigenous groups, including the Zulus, with whom they fought several wars.

From 1811 to 1858, the British fought the native Xhosa people, who did not want to be ruled by Europeans, whether Dutch or English. In 1856–1857, in the region east of the Cape Colony, some of the cattle of the local Xhosa were getting sick and dying, perhaps from catching an illness from the cattle of the British settlers. The Xhosa began to kill their cattle and destroy their crops in the belief that these actions would cause spirits to remove the British settlers from their lands. Some 400,000 head of Xhosa cattle may have been killed. The immediate result of the *Xhosa Cattle Killing Movement* was famine and the deaths of thousands of people; the British were not driven out of the area.

In 1849, the British sent a ship full of Irish convicts to the Cape Colony. This caused an uproar among the European settlers there, who did not want the land to become a convict colony like Australia. The British gave in and sent the ship on to Tasmania, an island south of Australia.

In the 1870s, the British fought the *Zulu Kingdom*, located on the South African coast of the Indian Ocean. At first, this *Anglo-Zulu War* went in favor of the Zulus, but eventually the British defeated them, and their lands became part of the British colony of South Africa.

Boer Wars Throughout the rest of the nineteenth century, the British and Afrikaners continued to fight over land. This conflict came to a boil in the *Boer Wars* (1880–1881, 1899–1902). These conflicts were bloody and brutal. In the end, the British army drove the Afrikaners and the Africans from their lands, forcing many into refugee camps. These settlements, which were segregated by race, came to be known as *concentration camps*. Medical care and sanitation were very poor, and food rations were so meager that many of the interned died of starvation. Once news arrived in Britain about the wretched conditions of the camps, activists tried to improve the lives of displaced refugees. However, white camps received the lion's share of attention, while conditions in black camps remained despicable. It is estimated that of the 100,000 blacks interned in concentration camps, nearly 15,000 perished.

By the end of the Boer Wars, the British had absorbed the settler colonies of British and Afrikaner peoples and the black Africans in the southern tip of Africa into its empire. Millions of Afrikaner and black African farmers had been displaced onto poor land, making it hard for them to earn a decent living.

Imperialism in China

China did not experience imperialism in the same way that South Asia or Africa did. Although the British were the first to establish a sphere of influence there with their victory in the Opium Wars (1839–1842), by 1898 other European countries had also set up spheres of influence in China. These "spheres" gave foreign powers exclusive trading rights and access to natural resources within their particular region. Internal problems within the Qing government, such as the Taiping Rebellion, made it easier for foreign countries to dominate the economic affairs of China. (Test Prep: Create a timeline tracing European imperialist actions in China between 1750 and 1900. See pages 447–454.)

Imperialism in Southeast Asia

The Dutch in Southeast Asia European imperialism in Southeast Asia began with a private company, just as it had begun in South Asia with the British East India Company. Dutch mariners arrived in the so-called "Spice Islands," modern-day Indonesia, and set up several trading posts on the archipelago. The Dutch East India Company, the VOC, extracted spices from the islands that became wildly popular in Europe. Although the trade was very profitable for the VOC, corruption caused the company to go bankrupt by 1800. Once the VOC folded, the Dutch government itself took control of the Dutch East Indies. By the middle of the nineteenth century, the islands were producing cash crops in order to support the Dutch economy.

Source: Xiengyod / Wikimedia Commons

The Southeast Asian country of Siam was one of the new states that people created in the nineteenth century in response to imperialism. Its flag featured a symbol of royal authority: an elephant.

Plantations produced tea, rubber, and sugar for export purposes, a situation that limited rice cultivation and eventually created enormous hardship for Indonesian farmers who relied on rice cultivation to survive. Although critiques of this agricultural policy forced the Dutch government to implement humanitarian reforms, the reforms were insufficient to meet the needs of the Indonesian people.

The French in Southeast Asia The French government also wanted an imperial presence in Asia. After it defeated China in the Sino-French War of 1883–1885, France gained control of northern Vietnam. France later pressured Siam to cede control of the territory of modern-day Laos to the French. By the 1890s, France controlled Cambodia, Laos, and all of modern-day Vietnam. French motives for imperialism were no different from those of the Dutch—a desire for cash crops. Soon rubber plantations began to dot the landscape of Cambodia and Vietnam. Dutch and French control of Southeast Asia continued until after World War II, when nationalist movements forced out the European powers.

One nation, Siam—modern-day Thailand—managed to escape the clutches of nineteenth-century European imperialism. Siam's monarchs deftly handled diplomatic relations with the British and French, whose colonies bordered Siam to the west and the east, respectively. The Siamese government also instituted a series of modernizing reforms, similar to Japan's Meiji reforms. The government began to industrialize by building railroads, and it set up Western-style schools in order to create an educated populace who would one day fill the ranks of an efficient government bureaucracy.

United States Imperialism in Latin America and the Pacific

The United States was not an established world power on the scale of Britain or France during most of the nineteenth century, but the Second Industrial Revolution brought newfound prosperity to the young republic. Economic considerations, as well as feelings of nationalism and cultural superiority, drove Americans' desire for territorial conquest. In 1823, President James Monroe issued the Monroe Doctrine, which stated that European nations should not intervene in the affairs of the countries in the Western Hemisphere. Although the doctrine on its face looks like an assertion of independence, it in fact masked the United States desire to be an imperial power in the Americas. This was borne out in the U.S. war with Mexico, 1845–1848, as a result of which the United States gained vast territories in the Southwest from Mexico.

Fifty years later, in 1898, the U.S. victory in the Spanish-American War brought Guam, Cuba, Puerto Rico, and the Philippines under U.S. control. President Theodore Roosevelt, a proponent of Social Darwinism and a believer in white cultural superiority, was especially eager to expand U.S. influence throughout the Western Hemisphere. The 1904 *Roosevelt Corollary* to the

Monroe Doctrine stated that if countries in Latin America demonstrated "instability," the United States would feel free to intervene. Indeed, in 1904 Roosevelt sent U.S. troops to occupy a Caribbean island nation, the Dominican Republic, until it repaid its foreign debts.

Comparing Three Types of Imperialism			
Type of Imperialism	Examples	Features	Outcomes
State-Run Colonies	• British West Africa • Belgian Congo	• Western education and political structures gradually replace the local culture • Often defended by claims of helping the indigenous population	• Exploitation of indigenous labor • Loss of indigenous culture • Creation of non-native elite and mixed native and non-native middle class • Imperialist countries rule by corporations or states modeled by Western policy
Settler Colonies	• British South Africa, Australia, and New Zealand • French Algeria	• Focus on control and use of land • Settlers remove or dominate the indigenous population • Often follows contact with sparsely populated lands	• Loss of indigenous culture; • Genocide • Spread of disease • Forced conversion to Western business, political, and religious ideas • Exploitation of indigenous labor • Forcing indigenous populations into extreme poverty and addiction
Economic Power	• British in China • French in China • United States in Latin America	• People, raw materials, and refined materials are main resources exploited • Cash crops and mineral resources are taken out on large scale	• Social destabilization based on economic exploitation • Opium Wars in China • Monoculture and lack of agricultural diversity caused by cash crops • Soil depletion • Long-range environmental damage

Responses to Imperialism

Nationalist movements emerged in response to imperialism in South Asia, China, and Africa. In each area, elite groups of Western-educated intellectuals led resistance to imperialism. Elite groups of Asians and Africans were educated in European schools and developed a deep understanding of Enlightenment ideals such as natural rights, sovereignty, and nationalism. Though they often worked in official posts in colonial government, elites eventually used the education that imperialism provided them to drive out their conquerors. In South Asia, such intellectuals established the *Indian National Congress* in 1885. Though it began as a forum for airing grievances to the colonial government, by the turn of the twentieth century the Congress began to fight for self-rule.

Organized African resistance to imperialism developed later than Indian resistance. Historians have different theories to explain this difference in timing. One theory is that European powers had been in India much longer than they had been in Africa. Another states that British colonial governments in India were partially run by Indians, while colonial governments in Africa were largely run by military officials from Europe. However, by the end of the First World War (1914–1918), Western-educated Africans had developed a sense of shared identity and nationalism known as *Pan-Africanism.*

HISTORICAL PERSPECTIVES: WHAT WAS IMPERIALISM'S IMPACT?

Historians still debate imperialism's overall impact. Many argue that imperialism did irreparable damage to colonial peoples, while some historians assert that imperialism overall was a positive development.

While many South Asians pushed the British to abandon their empire, some did not. One defender of British imperialism was Indian writer Nirad Chaudhari. His memoir, *Autobiography of an Unknown Indian* (1951), was hugely controversial when it was published—just four short years after India gained its independence. Chaudhari believed that the British Empire was not a source of India's problems, but had, in his opinion, brought the gift of British culture and civilization to his home country.

Rather than focus on one country and one colony, historian and political activist Walter Rodney, in *How Europe Underdeveloped Africa* (1972), looked broadly at imperialism by several countries in several regions. Rodney, from the South American country of Guyana, criticized the exploitation of African resources by imperialist powers and argued for Pan-African unity and socialism to solve post-colonial problems.

An even broader approach can be seen in *Orientalism* (1979) by Palestinian-American literary scholar Edward Said. He exposed the ideology of Western imperialism through close study of language that Western scholars use to describe the so-called "Orient." These scholars, Said says, assumed that Arabs and other Asians were backward and exotic, assumptions that justified European imperialism. Pro-imperial and pro-Western biases are evident even in contemporary Western scholarship about "Eastern" cultures, according to Said. His controversial work has influenced scholars to become more critical readers of historical texts.

Niall Ferguson, an economist and historian, defended British imperialism in his book *Empire: How Britain Made the Modern World* (2004). Ferguson said that Great Britain helped its colonies because it spread the rule of law, introduced the idea of parliamentary government, and built railroads. Most importantly, according to Ferguson, the British Empire was a force for globalization and free-market capitalism.

KEY TERMS BY THEME

GOVERNMENT
Great Game
imperialism
Scramble for Africa
sepoys
sepoy mutiny
Raj
King Leopold II
Congo Free State
Berlin Conference
Abyssinia
Liberia
Zulu Kingdom
Anglo-Zulu War
Boer Wars
Roosevelt Corollary
Indian National
    Congress
Pan-Africanism

ECONOMICS
export economies
cash crops
Tea
Cecil Rhodes
Goa
Pondicherry
corvée laborers
indentured laborers
penal colony
convicts

ENVIRONMENT
monocultures
quinine
Suez Canal
Charles Darwin

CULTURE
phrenologists
Social Darwinism
Herbert Spencer
David Livingstone
Afrikaners
Xhosa Cattle Killing
    Movement
concentration camps
Aborigines
Maori
White Australia Policy

Question 1 refers to the map below.

GLOBAL MIGRATIONS

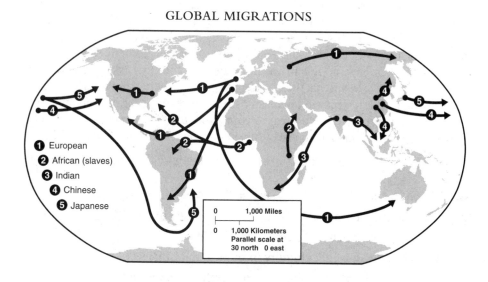

1. The migration from West Africa to the Americas was largely a forced migration. Which of these had elements of forced migration?

   (A) Migration 1: Britain to Australia

   (B) Migration 3: India to South Africa

   (C) Migration 4: China to Korea

   (D) Migration 5: Japan to North America

2. An economic motive for imperialism in the nineteenth century was a desire by industrialized countries

   (A) for natural resources, new markets, and cheap labor

   (B) for prestige among other nations

   (C) to improve health and living conditions of people around the world

   (D) to spread Christianity around the world

3. Which of the following was a long-lasting effect of the "Scramble for Africa" in the late nineteenth century?

   (A) Advances in self-government in African countries

   (B) Development of a more sustainable agricultural system

   (C) Growth of the United States as an imperial power

   (D) Creation of new borders that often led to conflict

Questions 4 and 5 refer to the excerpt below.

We find your country is sixty or seventy thousand li [three li equal about one mile, ordinarily] from China. Yet there are barbarian ships that strive to come here for trade for the purpose of making a great profit. The wealth of China is used to profit the barbarians. That is to say, the great profit made by barbarians is all taken from the rightful share of China. By what right do they then in return use the poisonous drug to injure the Chinese people? Even though the barbarians may not necessarily intend to do us harm, yet in coveting profit to an extreme, they have no regard for injuring others. Let us ask, where is your conscience? I have heard that the smoking of opium is very strictly forbidden by your country; that is because the harm caused by opium is clearly understood. Since it is not permitted to do harm to your own country, then even less should you let it be passed on to the harm of other countries—how much less to China!

—Lin Tse-Hsu, "Letter of Advice to Queen Victoria," 1839

4. Which statement would Lin Tse-Hsu agree with most strongly?
   (A) The British right to free trade should not be limited.
   (B) The British needed to sell opium in China.
   (C) The British were culturally inferior to the Chinese.
   (D) The British applied the same principles at home and in China.

5. What happened after the delivery of this message?
   (A) Britain stopped importing opium into China.
   (B) The United States and Germany began trading with China.
   (C) Relations between China and Britain worsened.
   (D) The Boxer Rebellion began in hopes of expelling foreign influence.

6. Which of the following was a major effect of the Sepoy Mutiny?
   (A) The abolition of the Indian caste system
   (B) The creation of the Indian National Congress
   (C) The withdrawal of British troops from India
   (D) The collapse of the Mughal Empire in India

7. In contrast to other nations in Southeast Asia, Siam
   (A) had no resources of interest to Western powers
   (B) used diplomacy to remain independent of Western control
   (C) defeated French and British forces with a strong military
   (D) refused to trade with Western countries

8. Which statement is true about British experience in its colonies?

(A) British faced European rivals for power only in West Africa.

(B) Britain encountered indigenous resistance to its power only in India.

(C) British citizens settled in large numbers only in South Africa.

(D) Britain defended the principle of free trade only in China.

9. Which motive best explains the reason for the actions of the British East India Company in India?

(A) Britain's desire to control strategic points in East Asia

(B) British industries' need for raw materials, such as cotton

(C) The Raj's plan to develop large military forces

(D) India's willingness to trade with British merchants

10. During the nineteenth and early twentieth centuries, the United States attempted to be an imperial power in which group of locations?

(A) Latin America, the Caribbean, and the Pacific

(B) The Caribbean, Africa, and the Pacific

(C) Africa, Asia, and the Caribbean

(D) India, Japan, and Latin America

CONTINUITY AND CHANGE-OVER-TIME ESSAY QUESTIONS

Directions: You are to answer the following question. You should spend 5 minutes organizing or outlining your essay. Write an essay that:

- Has a relevant thesis and supports that thesis with appropriate historical evidence.
- Addresses all parts of the question.
- Uses world historical context to show continuities and changes over time.
- Analyzes the process of continuity and change over time.

1. Analyze continuities and change in the response of native peoples to imperialism in ONE of these regions between 1750 and 1900:

- India
- Sub-Saharan Africa

Questions for Additional Practice

2. Analyze continuities and change in the role of technology in the development of Western colonial empires from the sixteenth century through the end of the nineteenth century.

3. Analyze continuities and change in British intervention in ONE of the following regions during the nineteenth century:
   - Sub-Saharan Africa
   - South Asia
   - China

COMPARATIVE ESSAY QUESTIONS

Directions: You are to answer the following question. You should spend 5 minutes organizing or outlining your essay. Write an essay that:
- Has a relevant thesis and supports that thesis with appropriate historical evidence.
- Addresses all parts of the question.
- Makes direct, relevant comparisons.
- Analyzes relevant reasons for similarities and differences.

1. Analyze similarities and differences between Western intervention in Africa and in ONE of the following regions between 1750 and 1900:
   - South Asia
   - Southeast Asia

Questions for Additional Practice

2. Analyze similarities and differences in the colonial labor systems in TWO of the following regions between 1750 and 1900:
   - the Caribbean
   - South Asia
   - Australia

3. Compare the first wave of colonialism in the sixteenth century to the second wave of colonialism in the nineteenth century in one of the following regions:
   - the Caribbean
   - North America
   - Africa

THINK AS A HISTORIAN: APPLY THE SKILL OF INTERPRETATION

To interpret history is not only to tell what happened in the past but also to explain how the past is viewed today. *In the sentences below, identify the verb that serves as a cue that you are reading interpretation.*

1. The words of Rudyard Kipling's poem "The White Man's Burden" are seen as racist today.

2. There were many motives for imperialism—among them acquisition of land and the quest for power—but most historians observe that economics overrode all of the others.

3. Europeans often claimed to undertake railway projects to benefit people in Asia and Africa; in retrospect, their motive can be perceived as pure self-interest.

4. The Berlin Conference of 1884–1885 on the future of Africa was ostensibly held for Western powers to set rules, but it appears to have been a buildup to a land grab.

5. Although the Monroe Doctrine looked like an assertion of independence, it masked the United States desire to be an imperial power.

WRITE AS A HISTORIAN: REVIEW THE MAIN POINTS

When you are writing about a multifaceted subject, it is a good idea to review the main points for the reader, who may be taking in the information for the first time. *Which THREE of the examples below best review the main points?*

1. Theodore Roosevelt is remembered as one of America's most colorful presidents, which is why many high schools are named for him.

2. Revolutions, nationalism, and the creation of nation-states were the chief characteristics of empire building in the 1800s.

3. During the imperialist era, legitimate science was subverted for racist purposes such as falsely claiming that whites were biologically superior.

4. The things that drove America's desire for territorial conquest were threefold: economic considerations, the rise of nationalism, and a feeling of cultural superiority.

5. In the second half of the nineteenth century, European nations were able to expand their presence because of better medical technology, the discovery of quinine to treat malaria, and the adventures of explorers and profiteers.

PERIOD 5: Review

Thematic Review

Directions: Briefly answer each question in paragraph form.

1. **Interaction Between Humans and the Environment** How did industrialization rely upon natural resources? What effect did industrialization have on the environment?

2. **Development and Interaction of Cultures** Explain how the ideas of Enlightenment thinkers compared to traditional religious beliefs.

3. **State-Building, Expansion, and Conflict** Describe similarities and differences in resistance to imperialism in India, China, and Africa in the nineteenth century.

4. **Creation, Expansion, and Interaction of Economic Systems** Explain how industrialization changed the nature of business in Britain.

5. **Development and Transformation of Social Structures** Analyze the causes and effects of the end of feudalism in Japan in the late nineteenth century.

6. **Development and Transformation of Social Structures** Explain the reasons for the social distinctions among various ethnic groups in Latin America in the nineteenth century.

TURNING POINT: WHY 1900?

The year 1900 marks the beginning of a new century. By that date, industrialization had spread globally, and Western imperialism was at its peak. The world was united into a tight economic network. Among the industrialized countries, faith in progress and reason was high. However, this faith would soon be shattered by World War I, which began in 1914. The British historian Eric Hobsbawm, using 1914 as a turning point, coined the phrase "the long nineteenth century" to describe the period from the start of the French Revolution in 1789 to the start of World War I. For historians who see the battle between capitalism and communism as the defining issue of the modern era, the success of the Communists in the 1917 Russian Revolution might be the turning point. Some historians even point to 1945 as the true turning point. Europe was the dominant world power in 1900, but by 1945, at the end of World War II, the continent had lost that status to the United States.

DOCUMENT-BASED QUESTION

Direction: The following question is based on the accompanying Documents 1–9. (The documents have been edited for the purpose of this exercise.)

This question is designed to test your ability to work with and understand historical documents. Write an essay that:

- Has a relevant thesis and supports that thesis with evidence from the document.

- Uses all of the documents.

- Analyzes the documents by grouping them in as many appropriate ways as possible; does not simply summarize the documents individually.

- Takes into account the sources of the documents and analyzes the author's point of view.

- Identifies and explains the need for at least one additional type of document.

You may refer to relevant historical information not mentioned in the documents.

1. Using the following documents, analyze the similarities in the role of women in Japan and Argentina in the period from the 1850s to the 1920s. Identify an additional type of document and explain how it would help your analysis of women's roles in these countries.

Document 1

Source: P. F. Siebold, *Manners and Customs of the Japanese in the Nineteenth Century,* 1852.

The position of women in Japan is apparently unlike that of the sex in all other parts of the East, and approaches more nearly their European condition. The Japanese women are subjected to no jealous seclusion, hold a fair station in society, and share in all the innocent recreations of their fathers and husbands. The minds of the women are cultivated with as much care as those of men; and amongst the most admired Japanese historians, moralists, and poets are found several female names. But, though permitted thus to enjoy and adorn society, they are, on the other hand, during their whole lives, kept in a state of tutelage; that is, of complete dependence on their husbands, sons, or other relatives. They have no legal rights, and their evidence is not admitted in a court of justice. [The husband] . . . also has the power of divorce, which may be considered unlimited . . . At home, the wife is the mistress of the family; but in other respects she is treated rather as a toy for her husband's amusement, than as the rational, confidential partner of his life.

Document 2

Source: Brian Platt, "Educational Reform in Japan (nineteenth century)," *Children and Youth in History.*

Enrollment in Japanese Primary Schools				
Date	Number of Schools	Percentage of Boys Enrolled	Percentage of Girls Enrolled	Percentage of All Children Enrolled
1873	12,597	40	15	28
1880	28,410	59	22	41
1890	26,017	65	31	49
1900	26,857	90	72	81

Document 3

Source: Oki Takato, Japanese Minister of Education, 1891.

If the aim of regular education is to make known the proper relations between man and man, to make the Japanese people understand their proper role, and to raise the quality and the welfare of Society and Nation, every person who lives in this country must receive a regular education. The country has the responsibility for achieving this end; but it is also the responsibility of each individual to dedicate himself completely, and every city, town, and village must—as they have been ordered—provide school facilities out of public funds, supervise all people involved, and see to it that children attend school . . .

Educational errors bring about harm—they may cause children to hate their family's occupation, despise their parents, acquire an appetite for luxury, seek to escape, and avoid work. Moreover, even poor people must attend school during their best years and if they fail to husband their resources and waste their time, they stir up unhappiness not only for themselves and their families but bring harm to the country as well. Therefore we must be careful that education not bring harmful effects, that girls, for example, do not lose their chastity and feminine ways (literally, beautiful manners), that children do not grow up incapable of doing proper work, or deficient in the ability to look after their households.

Document 4

Source: Baron Kikuchi, minster in the Japanese government, speech in 1907.

Our female education, then, is based on the assumption that women marry, and that its object is to fit girls to become good wives and wise mothers. . . . The house was, and still is, . . . the unit of society, not the individual . . . the object . . . of female education—in a word, to fit girls to become good wives and mothers, proper helpmates and worthy companions of the men of Meiji, and noble mothers to bring up future generations of Japanese.

Document 5

Source: Journalist describing the lives of female silk workers in Japan, 1898.

When I encountered silk workers I was even more shocked than I had been by the situation of weaving workers.... At busy times they go straight to work on rising in the morning, and not infrequently work through until 12.00 at night. The food is six parts barley to four parts rice. The sleeping quarters resemble pigsties, so squalid are they. What I found especially shocking is that in some districts, when business is slack, the workers are sent out into service for a fixed period, with the employer taking all their earnings... Many of the girls coming to the silk districts pass through the hands of recruiting agents. In some cases they may be there for two to three years and never even know the name of the neighboring town. The local residents think of those who have entered the ranks of the factory girls in the same manner as tea house girls, bordering on degradation. If one had to take pity on just one group among all these workers, it must be first and foremost the silk workers.

Document 6

Source: *International Statistics Annual,* 1920. All numbers are estimates.

Enrollment in Argentinian Schools			
Year	Total Number of Boys	Total Number of Girls	Total Number of Students
1896	150,000	130,000	280,000
1900	200,000	180,000	380,000
1905	290,000	170,000	560,000
1910	370,000	330,000	700,000
1915	480,000	450,000	930,000

Document 7

Source: Josefina Pelliza de Sagasta, "Women Dedicated to Miss Maria Eugenia Echenique," 1876.

Women should be educated; give them a solid education, based on wholesome principles, cemented with moral and sensible beliefs; they should have a general knowledge of everything that awakens ingenuity and determines ideas, but not for them are the calculation and egotism with which they instruct English women, not for them the ridiculous ideas of North American women who pretend in their pride to be equal to men, to be legislators and obtain a seat in Congress or be university professors, as if it were not enough to be a mother, a wife, a housewife, as if her rights as a woman were not enough to be happy and to make others happy, as if it were not enough to carry out her sacred mission on earth: educating her family, cultivating the tender hearts of her children making them useful citizens, laborers of intelligence and progress, with her words and acts, cultivating love in her children and the sentiments that most enhance women: virtue, modesty and humility. Girls, women someday, be tender and loving wives, able to work for the happiness of your life's partner instead of bringing about his disgrace with dreams and aspirations beyond your sphere.

Document 8

Source: Maria Eugenia Echenique, writing in response to Josefina Pelliza de Sagasta, 1876.

Every day we see men with unscrewed-on heads who have no love for order nor true affection for their families, who spend their lives on gambling and rambling around; cold-bloodedly, they leave their children on the street, because their wives, whose sphere of action is reduced only to love and suffering, do not know how to oppose forcefully the squandering nor how to stop in time the abuses from their husbands nor save in this way the interests of their children.

Emancipation protects women from this catastrophe. A woman, educated in the management of business, even if she does not make a profession of it, knows how to prevent or remedy the problem once it has occurred. She does not go through the pain of seeing her children begging for bread from door to door, because she has a thousand resources to satisfy their needs honorably. She goes to work, and thus she raises her children without the need for others' support that could lead her to corruption and to spend a miserable and humiliating life. Love can dry tears and sweeten the bitterness of life, but it cannot satisfy hunger nor cover nakedness. Love cannot be developed on a sublime and heroic level unless one is prepared to work, to put sentiment into practice.

Emancipation, conceding to women great rights, instills in them a great heart that takes them closer to the true perfection to which men can aspire here on earth. A woman who, to her physical beauty and spirituality, adds education and the ability to act for good in her vast sphere, is the ideal type imagined by Christianity, and she is going to carry out progress in this century.

Document 9

Source: The director of Argentinian census writing about women in the workplace, 1914.

Today women work for the city, the post office, customs, the telegraph company and in diverse public areas. The telephone service is almost exclusively their responsibility. This whole census was compiled by feminine hands. Beyond their mission as teachers, for which they are admirably prepared, women are each day making progress in industry, commerce, the professions. The job of typist is almost reserved for her. . . . There are women doctors, masseuses, translators, lawyers, professors, accountants, notaries, etc.

PERIOD 6: Accelerating Global Change and Realignments, c. 1900 to Present

Chapter 25 The World War I Era, 1900—1919

Chapter 26 The Interwar Years, 1919–1939

Chapter 27 World War II

Chapter 28 The Cold War Era

Chapter 29 Decolonization

Chapter 30 Post-Cold War World, 1990–Present

Period Overview

Scientific research after 1900 revolutionized how people thought, lived, and interacted with nature. Innovative theories reshaped human understanding of everything from how the universe began to the unconscious forces influencing individual behavior. Dramatic increases in agricultural productivity combined with medical breakthroughs such as the development of antibiotics to fight infections made people healthier and extended life, resulting in a population explosion. At the same time, new forms of birth control increased the control women had over their lives.

However, advances in technology and population growth intensified the human impact on the planet, resulting in air pollution, water pollution, deforestation, desertification, and global warming. In addition, improved military technology, including tanks, planes, and atomic weapons, increased wartime casualties.

The political order of the world in 1900 was dominated by a small number of countries in Europe, along with Russia, Japan, and the United States. Throughout the twentieth century, these states fought one another for power and struggled to maintain control of other lands. The result was a century with World War I and World War II, frequent large wars, endless small wars, and four decades of tense ideological conflict between the United States and the Soviet Union. By the end of the century, the old empires had collapsed, as most colonies had won their independence through negotiation or war.

The frequent wars and the rapid economic changes caused extensive global migrations as people fled violence and searched for economic opportunity. In the midst of all this upheaval, women were winning the right to vote and were challenging traditional divisions between the roles and opportunities for each gender.

In response to economic challenges, governments in Europe, the United States, India, and most countries increasingly influenced economic decisions. Communist governments such as the Soviet Union and China experimented with total control over the economy. The Soviets eventually abandoned the effort and China moved toward a more market-oriented approach.

The twentieth century featured the increasing role of transnationalism—the global reorganization of production in which the development of a product or service is split between multiple locations around the world. From regional organizations (the European Union) to collections of countries (United Nation) to humanitarian groups (Red Cross) to entertainment (Bollywood) to large corporations (Sony), people were working together across national borders in all aspects of life.

Key Concepts

6.1 Science and the Environment

    I. Researchers made rapid advances in science that spread throughout the world, assisted by the development of new technology.

    II. As the global population expanded at an unprecedented rate, humans fundamentally changed their relationship with the environment.

    III. Disease, scientific innovations, and conflict led to demographic shifts.

6.2 Global Conflicts and Their Consequences

    I. Europe dominated the global political order at the beginning of the twentieth century, but both land-based and transoceanic empires gave way to new forms of transregional political organization by the century's end.

    II. Emerging ideologies of anti-imperialism contributed to the dissolution of empires and the restructuring of states.

    III. Political changes were accompanied by major demographic and social consequences.

    IV. Military conflicts occurred on an unprecedented global scale.

    V. Although conflict dominated much of the twentieth century, many individuals and groups—including states—opposed this trend. Some individuals and groups, however, intensified the conflicts.

6.3 New Conceptualizations of Global Economy, Society, and Culture

    I. States responded in a variety of ways to the economic challenges of the twentieth century.

    II. States, communities, and individuals became increasingly interdependent, a process facilitated by the growth of institutions of global governance.

    III. People conceptualized society and culture in new ways; some challenged old assumptions about race, class, gender, and religion, often using new technologies to spread reconfigured traditions.

    IV. Popular and consumer culture became global.

Source: *AP® World History Course and Exam Description.*

The World War I Era, 1900–1919

If you could hear, at every jolt, the blood
Come gargling from the froth-corrupted lungs,
Obscene as cancer, bitter as the cud
Of vile, incurables sores on innocent tongues,—
My friend, you would not tell with such high zest
To children ardent for some desperate glory,
The old Lie: Dulce et decorum est
Pro patria mori.

—Wilfred Owen, from "Dulce et Decorum Est"

Britsh poet Wilfred Owen's "Dulce et Decorum Est" is one of the most famous war poems of the twentieth century. Most of the poem describes the horrors of modern warfare,and the final lines of the excerpt, translated as "It is sweet and noble to die for one's country," he labels "the old Lie." World War I, which lasted from 1914 to 1918, was known as *the Great War*, not because of its positive nature, but because of the immense scale of the fighting. No previous war had involved as many nations from different parts of the world and few had killed as many soldiers *and* civilians. However, World War I did more than create an enormous body count. It fundamentally weakened the Western European powers, thus encouraging the growth of nationalism and appeals for self-rule within European colonies in Asia and Africa. The treaties signed at the end of this war arguably set the stage for World War II. World War I was easily one of the most influential events of the twentieth century.

Immediate Causes of the Great War

The final straw in a series of events that led to World War I was *Gavrilo Princip*'s assassination of *Archduke Francis Ferdinand* and his wife, Sophie, on June 28, 1914. Princip, a Serbian nationalist, was a member of the *Black Hand*, a nationalist organization devoted to ending Austro-Hungarian presence in the Balkans. From the Austro-Hungarian perspective, the Black Hand was a terrorist group. Immediately following the assassinations, the Austro-Hungarian Empire sent an ultimatum to the Serbian government, demanding that it work to end all anti-Austrian agitation in Serbia. When the Serbian government rejected the ultimatum, the Austro-Hungarian Empire looked to its ally Germany, a stronger nation with more firepower, for military assistance to punish Serbia. Serbia, populated by ethnic Slavs looked to other Slavic countries, particularly Russia, for help. Russia and Germany's entrance into the conflict changed a minor issue into a large war in August 1914.

Long-Term Causes of the Great War

Princip's actions were not the sole cause of World War I. Rather, tensions in Europe had been simmering for decades. One way to remember the sources of such tensions is with the acronym MAIN: militarism, alliances, imperialism, and nationalism.

Militarism Defined as aggressive military preparedness, *militarism* celebrates war and the armed forces. European powers had been competing for dominance; one way to prove their strength was to invest in the military. Great Britain and Germany in particular spent a great deal of money on building up their armies and navies, heavily recruiting young men to join their armed forces, and buying more ships and other military hardware. A nation's militaristic attitude influenced its public to view war as a festive competition, more similar to a game than to a gravely serious matter.

Alliances In their quest for power, European nations also formed *secret alliances*, groups whose members secretly agree to protect and help one another when attacked. When one member of an alliance was attacked in any way, the other members of the alliance were expected to stand up for that particular member. This system explains why Russia and Germany were ready to jump into the conflict between Serbia and Austria-Hungary.

Further, countries that were allied with particular countries were also sworn enemies of members of other alliances. For example, Britain and France were allies with Russia in the *Triple Entente.*, but they also viewed Germany as a rival. France was bitter that Germany had taken French land during the Franco-Prussian War (1870–1871). Britain competed with Germany for colonies in Africa. After the war began, the Triple Entent added the United States, China, and Japan. This diverse group became known as the *Allies* during World War I.

The Allies' rival alliance before the war was known as the *Triple Alliance*, composed of Germany, Austria-Hungary, and Italy. However, when the war began, Italy remained neutral and then in 1915 switched its allegiance and joined the Allies. At the outbreak of the war, the Ottoman Empire joined the Triple Alliance, which was also called the *Central Powers*.

Imperialism The alliance system developed largely because Western European countries became bitter rivals for global domination. One of the most important ways these nations could assert their power and generate wealth was to own overseas colonies. During the latter half of the nineteenth century, for example, Western European countries scrambled for any available land in Africa to add to the colonies they already owned in South and Southeast Asia, in the Americas, and in the Pacific. Thus, imperialism was a driving force behind tensions in Europe leading up to the archduke's assassination.

Nationalism The assassination of the archduke in June 1914, the immediate cause of war, reflects the growth of nationalism, the final long-term cause of the Great War. On a basic level, nationalism originates from a feeling of pride in one's identity. Multinational empires such as the Ottoman Empire and the Austro-Hungarian Empire had to contend with nationalist movements among their subject peoples. Serbs, such as Princip, were eager to rid their land of Austro-Hungarian conquerors, and Arabs tired of the limitations imposed upon them by the Ottoman Empire. Both groups were seeking *self-determination*—the idea that peoples of the same ethnicity, language, culture, and political ideals should be united and should have the right to form an independent nation state. Militant nationalists among Serbs and Arabs fought on the side of the Allies, thus extending the boundaries of the Great War.

Understanding the role of militarism, alliances, imperialism, and nationalism during the years leading up to 1914 is essential to comprehension of this complicated conflict.

Changes in Warfare

Many modern-day films such as *Saving Private Ryan,* set during World War II, and *Platoon*, set during the Vietnam War, show that war is *not* a glorious experience, but most Europeans saw warfare differently during the first few months of World War I. Hundreds of thousands of teenage boys enthusiastically enlisted in the military, dreaming of heroism. Wartime assemblies sounded more like high school pep rallies, in which speakers naively predicted swift and easy victories in battles against supposedly inferior enemies. Leaders of some of the socialist parties were among the few Europeans who spoke out against the war. Even socialists were divided on the issue, however, as many supported the war effort of their nation.

At the time, few people actually understood how brutal twentieth-century warfare could be. Only over the years of fighting would the horrific effects of new advances in war technology and tactics, such as poison gas, machine guns, airplanes, submarines, tanks, and trench warfare become apparent.

- *Poison gas* was one of the most insidious weapons of the new style of warfare, with chlorine, phosgene, and mustard gas used during World War I. Soldiers were soon equipped with gas masks, which were effective when used in a timely fashion. Although fatalities were limited, the effects of a gas attack could be extremely painful and long-lasting. Many veterans suffered permanent damage to their lungs. After the war, international treaties outlawed the use of poison gas.

- Developed in the late 1800s, *machine guns* could fire more than 500 rounds of ammunition per minute, increasing the deadly impact of warfare. The weapon made it difficult for either side in a battle to gain new territory.

- Although *submarines* were used briefly in the American Civil War, they played a larger part in World War I, causing havoc on the shipping lanes of the Atlantic Ocean.

- *Airplanes* in 1914 were still light and small and unable to carry many weapons. Therefore, they did not present much of a threat to troops or vehicles on the ground or ships at sea. Planes were used mainly to carry on reconnaissance (observation) of enemy lines.

- *Tanks* allowed armies to move across vast areas of difficult terrain, even over trenches.

- The defining experience for most soldiers in this war was the time spent in the trenches, long ditches dug in the ground with the excavated earth banked in front in order to defend against enemy fire. *Trench warfare* was not a glorious way to fight a war. Combatant nations dug hundreds of miles of trenches facing one another, and soldiers slept, ate, and fought in the trenches for months at a time. Trenches were often cold, wet, muddy, and rat-infested. Many soldiers died from disease caused by the unhygienic conditions. Erich Maria Remarque's 1929 novel, *All Quiet on the Western Front,* and the 1930 film based on it, give a vivid sense of a soldier's life in the trenches during World War I. Remarque himself was a young German soldier during the war.

With both the Central Powers and the Allies using such brutal weapons and tactics, neither side could easily defeat the other, resulting in a bloody four-year *stalemate* in which neither side made significant progress. (Test Prep: Write a paragraph comparing and contrasting warfare during World War I with the warfare before and during World War II. See pages 516 and 542–543.)

United States Entrance into the War

Economic ties between the United States and the Allies comprised one of the underlying reasons for U.S. entry into the war in 1917. In addition, many Americans believed that the Allied nations were more democratic than the Central Powers were. A third reason was growing resentment against the Germans, especially for *U-boat* (submarine) attacks on ships carrying civilians, including Americans. On May 7, 1915, a German submarine attacked and sank the *Lusitania*, an ocean liner carrying more than 100 U.S. citizens among its passengers. The event that finally pushed the United States into the war was the interception of the *Zimmermann Telegram* in January 1917. In this document, the German government offered to help Mexico reclaim territory it had lost to the United States in 1848 if Mexico allied with Germany in the war.

The Russian Revolution

The Great War made an already unstable Russia even more chaotic. Russian troops suffered a number of defeats with devastating numbers of casualties. Government mismanagement led to fuel and food shortages during the winter of 1916–1917, causing popular uprisings in St. Petersburg. In March 1917, revolutionary groups overthrew Tsar Nicholas II. The Romanov dynasty, after 300 years of rule, collapsed.

The monarchy was replaced by a provisional government that included socialists, liberals, and conservatives. Vying for political power outside of the Duma, the Russian parliament, were several *soviets,* groups of workers or soldiers led by socialists, which promised the Russian people reforms such as land redistribution and better opportunities for education. A few months after the fall of the tsar, Vladimir Lenin returned to Russia from exile in Switzerland. He was the leader of the *Bolsheviks,* a party of radical socialists that seized power in November 1917, promising "peace, land, and bread" to hungry, war-weary Russians. (Test Prep: Create a chart that compares the Russian and the Chinese Revolutions. See pages 557–558.)

Throughout the 1917 upheavals, Russian troops continued to suffer an astounding number of casualties on the Eastern Front of the war against the Central Powers. Four months after he took control of the Russian government, Lenin appealed for peace with Germany. In March 1918, the leaders of the new *Soviet Russia* signed the *Treaty of Brest-Litovsk* with Germany, ending Russia's involvement in World War I. The treaty called for Russia to hand over to Germany an enormous amount of land, including most of Ukraine. But the treaty gave the new Bolshevik government time to concentrate on building a *Communist* state based on Marxist principles of common ownership of all property. The Bolshevik government also had to fight a civil war against anti-Communist forces that were supported by France, Britain, Japan, and the United States. In November 1920, the Russian government declared victory.

Total War

Combatant nations intensified the conflict in World War I by committing all of their resources to the war effort. This strategy, known as *total war*, meant that a nation's domestic population, in addition to its military, was committed to winning the war. Thus, millions of civilians, particularly women, worked in factories producing war materials. Entire economies were centered on winning the war. Governments set up planning boards that set production quotas, price and wage controls, and rationing of food and other supplies. They censored the media and imprisoned many who spoke out against the war effort.

Propaganda was another component of total war. *Propaganda* is communication meant to influence the attitudes and opinions of a community around a particular subject by spreading inaccurate or slanted information. Governments invested heavily in army and navy recruitment campaigns and other wartime propaganda. Posters and articles in newspapers and magazines often depicted the enemy crudely or misrepresented the facts of the war completely. For example, American and British propaganda demonized the German army, exaggerating reports of atrocities against civilians. Likewise, German propaganda demonized the Americans and the British. The use of highly emotional and often misleading information fomented hatred and bitterness across borders, among civilians as well as soldiers.

Source: Library of Congress

Source: Library of Congress

Posters recruiting sailors and soldiers for World War I in the United States and Great Britain reflected how governments used art and media to appeal to nationalist feelings in the early twentieth century.

A Global War

World War I was fought in Europe, Asia, and Africa and in the Pacific and Atlantic Oceans. Not since the Seven Years' War of the late eighteenth century had there been such a *global war*. Most of the major combatants in World War I ruled colonies in Asia, Africa, the Americas, and the Pacific. Competition for these colonies was one major reason for war. Imperialism extended the boundaries of the war, and major battles were fought in North Africa and the Middle East. Japan entered the war on the side of the Allies so that it could take control of German colonies in the Pacific: the Marshall Islands, the Mariana Islands, Palau, and the Carolines. Japan also occupied a German-held port in China: Qingdao.

The British were able to seize most of Germany's colonies in Africa, but the Germans held on to German East Africa, now Tanzania. The British also defended the Suez Canal from an attack by the Ottoman Empire.

Colonial troops reinforced their home countries' forces in several battles. Australian and New Zealand troops formed a special corps known as *ANZAC* and fought in a bloody year-long campaign at *Gallipoli*, a peninsula in northwestern Turkey, that resulted in heavy Allied losses with little to show for the effort. Canadian troops fought in several European battles. Britain drafted Africans and Indians for combat roles in Europe. Some 200,000 Gurkha soldiers from Nepal, India, served in the British Army in Europe and Southwest

Asia. France used Algerian, Chinese, and Vietnamese forces in support roles behind the lines. Some colonial troops fought in hopes that their efforts would gain them recognition from their colonizers, who often promised the colonies self-rule (ability to establish own government) after the war ended.

Arabs, long under the rule of the multinational Ottoman Empire, fought with the Allies because the British promised self-rule after the war if they were victorious. Arab troops attacked Ottoman forts in Arabia and present-day Israel and helped the British take over the cities of Baghdad, Damascus, and Jerusalem.

Source: Library of Congress

Source: Library of Congress

Source: Library of Congress

Source: Library of Congress

World War I armies included soldiers from Senegal in West Africa (upper left), France in Western Europe (upper right), India in South Asia (lower left), and Japan in Eastern Asia (lower right).

Casualties of the War

After three years of a bloody stalemate, the United States entered the war in 1917, despite considerable popular protests in the United States against American involvement. By the summer of 1918, when U.S. forces were finally in place in Europe, U.S. actions helped push the war in the Allies' favor. Allied advances against the Central Powers forced Germany to surrender on November 11, 1918, now known as *Armistice Day*.

Between 8 million and 9 million soldiers died in the Great War, with more than 21 million wounded. In France, Germany, Russia, and Austria-Hungary, less than half of all young men who fought for their countries returned physically unharmed. Soldiers who did return often bore emotional scars.

World War I Casualties				
Country	Alliance	Dead (in millions)	Wounded (in millions)	Imprisoned (in millions)
Germany	Central Powers	1.8	4.2	0.6
Russia	Allies	1.7	5.0	0.5
France	Allies	1.4	3.0	0.5
Austria-Hungary	Central Powers	1.2	3.6	0.2
Great Britain	Allies	0.9	2.1	0.2
Italy	Allies	0.5	1.0	0.5
Turkey	Central Powers	0.3	0.4	Not known
United States	Allies	0.1	0.2	Less than 0.05

Atrocities Civilian casualties were harder to record, but estimates range anywhere from 6 million to 13 million. This was one of the first modern wars where civilians were considered legitimate targets in battle. Although the Allies' propaganda often exaggerated accounts of atrocities, reports of German soldiers raping women and killing families during their march through Belgium were quite common.

The most shocking example of such atrocities was the death of between 600,000 and 1.5 million Armenians in Turkey. This action has been called the twentieth century's first *genocide,* the attempted killing of a group of people based on their race, religion, or ethnicity. The Ottoman government alleged that the Christian Armenians, a minority within the Ottoman Empire, were cooperating with the Russian army, the Ottoman's enemy during World War I. As punishment for this cooperation, the Ottoman government deported Armenians from their homes between 1915 and 1917 and forced them south to camps in Syria and Mesopotamia, present-day Iraq. Many Armenians died because of starvation, disease, or exposure to the elements, and some were executed by Turkish troops. Armenians have argued that the deaths constituted genocide, a Turkish attempt to eliminate the Armenian people. Turkish government have said the deaths were the result of actions of war, ethnic conflicts, and disease, but were not genocide. (Test Prep: Create a graphic organizer comparing the Armenian genocide with the Nazis' extermination of millions of Jews. See page 542.)

War-related deaths continued past Armistice Day. An *influenza epidemic* was another fatal blow that struck the globe at the end of the war. Under peacetime circumstances, a virulent disease might devastate a concentrated group of people in a particular region. However, in 1918, millions of soldiers were returning home as the war ended. As they did, they had contact with loved ones and friends, thereby facilitating the spread of the flu. In 1919, the epidemic became a *pandemic* (a disease prevalent over a large area or the entire world), killing 20 million people not only in Europe, but also in the United States and elsewhere around the world. India, for example, may have lost seven million people to the disease.

A more intangible casualty of the war was the loss of a sense of security and hopefulness. The term *Lost Generation,* used to describe a group of American expatriate writers living in Paris after the war, has been used more broadly to describe the shock that the war wrought on the generations that experienced the war.

Paris Peace Conference

The war itself inflicted significant damage on Europe. The treaty conference held in its wake, however, would have even more profound effects on the world as a whole. The leaders of victorious countries at the *Paris Peace Conference* became known as the *Big Four: Woodrow Wilson* (United States), *David Lloyd George* (Great Britain), *Georges Clemenceau* (France), and *Vittorio Orlando* (Italy). The Italians walked out of the peace conference in a rage because Italy would not get Fiume, a town they had been promised for joining the Allies. Soviet Russia, later called the *Soviet Union*, was not invited to the conference because it had undergone a Communist revolution. Western leaders shunned Russian leaders because they were terrified that Communist ideas would infiltrate their own countries. The leaders of the victorious countries had different visions of how to settle the peace.

President Wilson's pledge to establish "peace without victory," reflected his belief that no one country should be severely punished or greatly rewarded. France's Clemenceau could not have disagreed more: he believed that France, out of all the Allies represented at the conference, had suffered the most and thus deserved special considerations to be protected from Germany. He also argued that the victorious powers should seek some sort of revenge on the Central Powers for starting the war. Clemenceau complained that Wilson was an unrealistic idealist who was naive about European relations, even though Wilson had a Ph.D. in history. David Lloyd George tended to support Clemenceau's ideas, but he often acted as an intermediary between the two differing points of view.

Fourteen Points Despite Clemenceau's protests, Wilson pushed for his principles, which he outlined in a document called the *Fourteen Points*. He particularly wanted to create a *League of Nations*, an organization in which all nations of the world would convene to discuss conflicts openly, as a way to avoid the simmering tensions that had caused World War I. Although the other nations agreed to establish the League, the U.S. Senate voted against joining it and against ratifying the *Treaty of Versailles*, the 1919 peace treaty with Germany.

Wilson also believed that conquered peoples under the defeated Central Powers deserved the right to self-determination. Instead of the colonies and territories of the Central Powers being snatched up by the Allies, conquered peoples should have the right to decide their own political fate. Quite a few new nations were created or resurrected in Europe: Finland, Estonia, Latvia, Lithuania, Poland, Czechoslovakia, and Yugoslavia. The last three of these were home to Slavic peoples.

The Treaty of Versailles Because Wilson failed to convince France and Britain not to punish Germany, the Treaty of Versailles treated Germany harshly. Most notably, Germany had to pay billions of dollars in *reparations* (payment of money for wrongs committed) for damage caused by the war, give up all of its colonies, and restrict the size of its armed forces. Germans took the entire blame for the war. Signing the treaty was humiliating for German leaders. Moreover, the terms of the treaty caused tremendous damage to the nation during the decade following World War I. The German economy suffered from sky-high inflation, partly due to the reparations the country was forced to pay. The German people were bitter in the immediate aftermath of the Paris Peace Conference. Resentment toward the *Weimar Government*, which had agreed to the terms of the Treaty of Versailles, set the stage for an extreme and militaristic political party known as the Nazis to take power barely 15 years later.

Effects of the War

The effects of World War I were many and varied for different countries and areas of the world. For example, the United States experienced a tremendous surge in its economy because of all the war materials and agricultural products it sold to Britain and the other Allies. By contrast, the economies of those countries that experienced the greatest damage were devastated by the war.

Effects on Colonial Lands While nationalist movements had been brewing for decades in colonies in South Asia and West Africa, the war renewed the hopes of people in these regions for independence. African and Asian colonial troops contributed thousands of soldiers to the Allied war effort. In addition, this disastrous war showed colonial peoples that imperial powers such as Britain and France were not invincible or even formidable anymore. The colonized peoples thought that the principle of self-determination, as expressed in Wilson's Fourteen Points, would get them closer to self-rule. Nationalists in Africa and Asia hoped that the blood they had shed for their "home countries" would earn them some respect from Western Europe and thus begin a *decolonization* process.

The peace conference's *Big Three*—Lloyd George, Wilson, and Clemenceau—were not at all interested in freeing the colonies. Wilson even refused to meet with a young Vietnamese nationalist, Ho Chi Minh, who requested to speak with him about the independence of Vietnam from the French. This rejection only fueled stronger nationalist movements in colonies scattered across the southern rim of Asia and in parts of Africa. The seeds of African, Arab, and Asian, nationalism were sown largely in the aftermath of World War I. (and Test Prep: Write a brief paragraph connecting self-rule after World War I with later movements for independence. See pages 573–590.)

Mandate System Arab rebels of the former Ottoman Empire were especially insulted by the results of the peace conference. They had been promised self-rule if they fought with the Allies. Instead, the Allies forgot all of their promises and through the League of Nations established a *mandate system* to rule the colonies and territories of the Central Powers.

MANDATES IN THE MIDDLE EAST AFTER WORLD WAR I

Article 22 of the League of Nations charter specifically stated that colonized people in Africa and Asia required "tutelage" from more "advanced" nations in order to survive. For example, Cameroon, which had been a German colony, was divided and transferred to France and Britain as separate mandates.

Southwest Asia experienced enormous upheaval because of the fall of the Ottoman Empire. Palestine, Transjordan, Syria, and Iraq all became League of Nations mandates. These Arab states were not yet sovereign lands, but virtual colonies of Great Britain and France. This infuriated the Arabs who lived in these lands and set the stage for a nationalist movement known as *Pan-Arabism*—an ideology that called for the unification of all lands in North Africa and Southwest Asia.

Another source of conflict arouse in 1917 when the British government issued the *Balfour Declaration*, which stated that *Palestine* should become a permanent home for the Jews of Europe. Those who supported a Jewish homeland were known as *Zionists*. After the Allied victory in the Great War, European Jews moved in droves to Palestine, which was controlled by the British.

The mandate system existed in East Asia, as well. Japan, being a victorious ally, won spheres of influence in China that had formerly been controlled by Germany. The Chinese, who had also fought on the side of the Allies, were furious with the settlement, which ignored their demands that Japan stop occupying the Shandong Peninsula. Led by urban intellectuals and college students in Beijing, a series of nationalistic demonstrations, known as the *May Fourth Movement,* erupted in 1919 in response to the results of the Paris Peace Conference. The demonstrators also called for more democracy in China, much of which was controlled by war lords. Some of the leaders of the May Fourth Movement later became active in the new Chinese Communist Party.

HISTORICAL PERSPECTIVE: WAS THE PARIS PEACE CONFERENCE A SUCCESS?

The Paris Peace Conference, according to most scholars, was a major failure, but they have not agreed on what went wrong. British economist John Maynard Keynes was among the first critics with *The Economic Consequences of the Peace* (1919). As the title suggested, Keynes focused on the economic issues that emerged. In particular, he attacked the reparation policy, which he considered harsh and short-sighted. Partially due to the influence of Keynes' opposition to the reparations policy, the U.S. Senate rejected the Versailles treaty, and the United States never joined the League of Nations.

American journalist Ray Stannard Baker focused on the political consequences of the peace. During the conference, he had served as Wilson's press secretary, and afterwards he defended Wilson and criticized those who blocked his efforts to build a viable international organization. By 1941, Europe and East Asia were well into an even more bloody conflict, World War II, and Wilsonian internationalism looked even more attractive to some. Among these was American historian Paul Birdsall, whose book *Versailles Twenty Years After* was sympathetic to the efforts to unite the world against militaristic dictators.

By 2003, when Canadian historian Margaret MacMillan's book *Paris 1919: Six Months that Changed the World* was published, other problems from the conference were evident. At the conference, the borders in the Balkans and the Middle East had been redrawn. Wars and turmoil in both of these regions during the 1990s suggested that the settlement after World War I had failed to create viable states.

Not every scholar has focused on the shortcomings of the Paris Peace Conference. In 1996, Boston University historian William Keylor called for reevaluating the event. For example, he suggested that in light of the settlement of World War II, the treaties ending World War I do not look as harsh.

KEY TERMS BY THEME

STATE-BUILDING: HISTORICAL FIGURES
Gavrilo Princip
Archduke Francis Ferdinand
Woodrow Wilson
David Lloyd George
Georges Clemenceau
Vittorio Orlando
Ho Chi Minh

STATE-BUILDING: STATES, MOVEMENTS, & ALLIANCES
Black Hand
Triple Entente
Allies
Triple Alliance
Soviet Russia
Big Four
Big Three
Soviet Union
League of Nations
Weimar Government
Pan-Arabism
Zionists
May Fourth Movement

STATE-BUILDING
The Great War
militarism
secret alliances
Central Powers
self-determination
stalemate
Lusitania
Zimmermann Telegram
Treaty of Brest-Litovsk
total war
propaganda
global war
Gallipoli
ANZAC
Armistice Day
Paris Peace Conference
Fourteen Points
Treaty of Versailles
reparations
decolonization
mandate system
Balfour Declaration
Palestine

ENVIRONMENT
Poison gas
machine guns
Tanks
submarines
Airplanes
Trench warfare
U-boat
Influenza epidemic
pandemic

SOCIAL STRUCTURE
Soviets
Bolsheviks
Lost Generation

CULTURE
genocide
Armenians

MULTIPLE-CHOICE QUESTIONS

1. The long-term cause of World War I that was most responsible for expanding the scope of the war beyond Europe was
   - (A) alliances
   - (B) imperialism
   - (C) militarism
   - (D) nationalism

2. Women's participation in the labor force during the war
   - (A) decreased significantly
   - (B) increased only slightly
   - (C) increased greatly
   - (D) stayed basically at the same level

3. In the summer of 1914, the most popular view in Europe toward the prospect of war was widespread
   - (A) support for war
   - (B) opposition to war
   - (C) apathy toward war
   - (D) ignorance of a potential war

4. Why was World War I referred to as a total war?
   - (A) Nations committed all their resources to winning the war.
   - (B) All the European colonies were involved in the war.
   - (C) The European powers had large standing armies.
   - (D) Resulting social revolutions changed all aspects of European society.

5. Why is propaganda more common in a total war than in a traditional, more limited war?
   - (A) Very few people will volunteer if they think a war will be large.
   - (B) Propaganda primarily discourages enemy civilians from supporting a war.
   - (C) Only countries with totalitarian governments engage in total war.
   - (D) Winning a total war requires support from throughout society.

Question 6 refers to the cartoon below.

Source: Punch Limited

6. To which long-term cause of World War I does the cartoon refer to most directly?

   (A) new technology

   (B) militarism

   (C) nationalism

   (D) imperialism

7. What effect did the Russian Revolution have on Russia's actions in World War I?

   (A) Russia was instrumental in Germany's final defeat.

   (B) Russia made an early peace with Germany.

   (C) Russia turned against the United States and other Allies.

   (D) Russia enforced Communist principles at the Paris Peace Conference.

8. What alleged reason did the Ottoman Empire give for attacking the Armenian population in Turkey between 1915 and 1917?

   (A) Armenian collusion with the Russian Army

   (B) Cover-up of Ottoman military mistakes

   (C) Revenge for Armenian massacres of Muslims in the nineteenth century

   (D) Separatist movements within the Armenian population

9. Which of the conflicts below is a direct result of the mandate system?

   (A) World War II

   (B) Conflict in Vietnam

   (C) Nationalist conflicts in Africa

   (D) Palestinian and Israeli conflict

Question 10 refers to the excerpt below.

A free, open-minded, and absolutely impartial adjustment of all colonial claims, based upon a strict observance of the principle that in determining all such questions of sovereignty the interests of the populations concerned must have equal weight with the equitable claims of the government whose title is to be determined.

—From Woodrow Wilson, "Speech on the Fourteen Points," 65th Congressional Record

10. Based on the excerpt and information in the text, which statement best reflects Wilson's position?

    (A) Colonial powers should continue to determine a colony's future.

    (B) The Big Four should divide Germany's colonies among themselves.

    (C) Colonized peoples and colonizers should have equal say in a colony's future.

    (D) Colonized peoples should have an unlimited right to self-determination.

CONTINUITY AND CHANGE-OVER-TIME ESSAY QUESTIONS

Directions: You are to answer the following question. You should spend 5 minutes organizing or outlining your essay. Write an essay that:

- Has a relevant thesis and supports that thesis with appropriate historical evidence.

- Addresses all parts of the question.

- Uses world historical context to show continuities and changes over time.

- Analyzes the process of continuity and change over time.

1. Analyze the continuities and changes caused by nationalism from 1900 to 1920 in ONE of the following regions:

   - East Asia

   - Southwest Asia

   - Eastern Europe

Questions for Additional Practice

2. Analyze continuities and change in warfare from the Crimean War to the end of the Great War.

3. Analyze continuities and change in Russia's relationship with Western Europe in the late nineteenth century and the early twentieth century.

COMPARATIVE ESSAY QUESTIONS

Directions: You are to answer the following question. You should spend 5 minutes organizing or outlining your essay. Write an essay that:

- Has a relevant thesis and supports that thesis with appropriate historical evidence.
- Addresses all parts of the question.
- Makes direct, relevant comparisons.
- Analyzes relevant reasons for similarities and differences.

1. Analyze similarities and differences between the priorities of the United States and the priorities of Great Britain and France at the Paris Peace Conference.

Questions for Additional Practice

2. Analyze similarities and differences in the effects of World War I on TWO of the following countries and their empires:
   - France
   - Germany
   - Russia

3. Compare and contrast the effects of the Paris Peace Conference of 1919 with the effects of the Congress of Vienna in 1815.

THINK AS A HISTORIAN: APPLY SYNTHESIS

Synthesis is the process by which two or more things are joined together to create a new whole. For example, a synthesis of ideas to explain how World War I began might combine information about how the growth of militarism, the spread of nationalism, and the impact of alliances. Information about the number of deaths in the war probably would not fit into the synthesis. *Which THREE statements would be most useful in creating a synthesis to justify the name "The Great War" for the conflict now called World War I?*

1. The war included soldiers from all over the globe, including many from Africa and Asia fighting on behalf of a European country.

2. The alliance system that led to the conflict grew out of the Congress of Vienna, which has kept Europe relatively peaceful for a century.

3. The number of people killed and wounded in the conflict made it one of the costliest wars in human history to that time.

4. The conflict was total war, which meant that civilians were involved as providers of supplies for soldiers as never before.

5. Propaganda in the conflict often depicted the enemy crudely, and with little regard for accuracy.

WRITE AS A HISTORIAN: WRITE A STRONG LAST SENTENCE

The final sentence of an essay can have the most impact on a reader. Your last sentence should be compelling and solidify the points made in the body paragraphs. Summarize the contentions and restate the position from your introduction in order to firmly establish your stance. The closing sentence often resembles the thesis statement.

1. Choose the sentence that best concludes an essay about the causes of World War I.

   a. Several factors contributed to the Great War, including patriotism, expansionism, and military allies.

   b. The unwavering nationalism, strong alliances, and dominating imperialistic attitudes led to World War I.

2. Choose the sentence that best concludes an essay about the effects of the war on international relations.

   a. Germany's financial and political penalizations, the false hope of colonized peoples and the contradicting interests of nations generated the state of international relationships after World War I.

   b. In addition to nominal peace conferences, some countries felt excluded from such meetings which led to increased tension between nations.

26

The Interwar Years, 1919–1939

Has not this truth already come home to you now when this cruel war has driven its claws into the vitals of Europe? When her hoard of wealth is bursting into smoke and her humanity is shattered on her battlefields? You ask in amazement what she has done to deserve this? The answer is that the West has been systematically petrifying her moral nature in order to lay a solid foundation for her gigantic abstractions of efficiency.

—Rabindranath Tagore, *Nationalism*, written in 1917

History has underestimated the effects of World War I, or the Great War as it was called at the time. Perhaps because of World War II's unspeakable genocides, as well as its general carnage and destruction, much of the devastation of World War I has been forgotten.

The years following World War I brought economic depressions and hope to people around the world. From the perspective of Western Europe and the United States, the overall mood of the 20-year period was pessimistic. Colonized peoples, however, viewed a weakened Europe as an opportunity to fight for independence. As Tagore describes in the opening passage, Western Europe was beginning to implode. The troubles of the era moved many in the West to adopt radical philosophies, such as fascism and Nazism. Western countries grappled with new political landscapes and troubled economies. In the meantime, the colonized lands of the world were giving birth to nationalist movements and solidifying national identities. The interwar era, though short, was a time of daring new intellectual and artistic movements that emerged in response to the confusion and chaos of the time.

The Great Depression

World War I brought anxiety to the people that suffered through it. The Allied nations, though victorious, had lost millions of citizens, both soldiers and civilians, and had spent tremendous amounts of money on the international conflict. The defeated Central Powers, particularly Germany and the countries that emerged from the break-up of Austria-Hungary, suffered even greater losses. The Treaty of Versailles forced Germany to pay billions of dollars in reparations to the war's victors. War-ravished Germany could not make these payments, so its government printed more paper money in the 1920s.

This action caused *inflation*, a general rise in prices, which in turn caused the value of German money to decrease. To add to the sluggish post-war economy, France and Britain had difficulty repaying the money the United States had loaned them during the war, partly because Germany was having trouble paying reparations to them. In addition, the Soviet government refused to pay Russia's prerevolutionary debts.

Global Downturn Although the 1920s brought modest economic gains for most of Europe, the subsequent *Great Depression* ended the tentative stability. Agricultural overproduction and the United States' stock market crash in 1929 were two major causes of the global economic downturn. American investors who had been putting money into German banks removed it when the American stock market crashed. In addition to its skyrocketing inflation, Germany then had to grapple with bank failures. Germany thus suffered more than any other Western nation during the Great Depression. The economies of Africa, Asia, and Latin America suffered because they were dependent upon the imperial nations that were experiencing this enormous economic downturn. Japan also suffered during the Depression because its economy depended upon foreign trade. With the economic decline in the rest of the world, Japan's exports were cut in half between 1929 and 1931.

Keynesian Ideas The Great Depression inspired new insights into economics. British economist *John Maynard Keynes* rejected the laissez-faire ideal. He concluded that intentional government action could improve the economy. During a depression, he said, governments should use *deficit spending* (spending more than the government takes in) to stimulate economic activity. By cutting taxes and increasing spending, government would spur economic growth. People would return to work, and the depression would end.

The Global Economy, 1929 to 1938		
Year	Total Global Production	Total Global Trade
1929	100	100
1930	86	89
1931	77	81
1932	70	74
1933	79	76
1934	95	79
1935	98	82
1936	110	86
1937	120	98
1938	111	89

Source: Adapted from data in Barry Eichengreen and Douglas Irwin's, "The Protectionist Temptation: Lessons from the Great Depression for Today." voxeu.org. March 17 2009.

In this chart, the levels of production and trade for 1929 are represented by 100. The other numbers reflect changes from the 1929 level.

New Deal The administration of President Franklin Delano Roosevelt used Keynes's ideas to address the Great Depression in the United States. Roosevelt and his backers created a group of policies and programs known collectively as the *New Deal*. Its goal was to bring the country relief, recovery, and reform: *relief* for citizens who were suffering, including the poor, the unemployed, farmers, minorities, and women; *recovery* to bring the nation out of the Depression, in part through government spending; and *reform* to change government policies in the hopes of avoiding such disasters in the future.

By 1937, unemployment was declining and production was rising. Keynesian economics seemed to be working. However, Roosevelt feared that government deficits were growing too large, so he reversed course. Unemployment began to grow again. The Great Depression finally ended after the United States entered World War II in 1941, and ran up deficits that dwarfed those of the 1930s.

Depression Elsewhere The Great Depression that began in the United States spread to Western Europe and also powerfully affected nations in Latin America, Africa, and Asia, whose economies continued to be dominated by the Western powers. International trade experienced a downturn, as nations imposed strict tariffs, or taxes on imports, in an effort to protect domestic industries from foreign competition and to save jobs. By 1932, more than 30 million people worldwide were out of work.

In contrast, Japan dug itself out of the Depression much more rapidly than most other nations. Japan devalued its currency, which means that the government lowered the value of its money in relation to foreign currencies. Thus, Japanese-made products became less expensive than imports from places such as Britain. Japan's overseas expansionism also increased Japan's need for military goods, thus stimulating the economy.

Rise of Right-Wing Governments

Political upheavals characterized the interwar years. While the U.S. government became more liberal, governments in most countries moved to the political right out of a desire for stability and fear of uncertainty. In this environment, a new political system known as *fascism* flourished. Fascist regimes suppressed other political parties, protests, and independent trade unions. They used extreme violence to achieve their goals and were strongly anti-Communist.

Rise of Fascism in Italy Benito Mussolini coined the term fascism, which comes from the term "fasces," a bundle of sticks tied around an axe, an ancient Roman symbol for punishment. This violent symbol helped characterize Italy's fascist government, which glorified militarism and brute force.

The Italian fascist state was based on a concept known as *corporatism*, a theory based on the notion that the sectors of the economy, the employers, the trade unions, and state officials, are seen as separate organs of the same body. Each sector, or organ, was supposedly free to organize itself as it wished as long as it supported the whole. In practice, the fascist state imposed its will upon all sectors of society, creating a *totalitarian state*—a state in which all aspects of society are controlled by the government.

Mussolini Takes Control Even though Italy had been considered one of the major powers at the 1919 Paris Peace Conference—along with Britain, France, and the United States—Italy received very little territory from the Treaty of Versailles. This failure to gain from the war caused discontent in Italy. Amid the general bitterness of the 1920s, Mussolini and his allies managed to take control of the parliament. Mussolini became a dictator, repressing any possible opposition to his rule. Militaristic propaganda infiltrated every part of the fascist government. For example, school children were taught constantly about the glory of their nation and their fearless leader, "Il Duce."

Part of Mussolini's fascist philosophy was the need for his nation to conquer what he considered to be an inferior nation. During the imperialist "Scramble for Africa" in the nineteenth century, Italy seized *Libya* and colonized *Somaliland*, modern-day Somalia. However, the army was pushed back by Abyssinia, modern-day Ethiopia, in the 1890s. Under Mussolini in 1935, Italy crossed the border from Somaliland to Abyssinia, defying a mandate from the League of Nations. This time, the Italian army overpowered Abyssinia's while the global community did little to stop the conquest. In 1936, Mussolini and Germany's Adolf Hitler formed an alliance they hoped would dominate Europe. With the security of this alliance, Italy invaded and seized Albania in 1939.

Rise of Nazism Germany's defeat in 1918 brought an end to the kaiser's monarchical rule. The democratically elected *Weimar Republic* took its place. Under the terms of the Treaty of Versailles, the new German government not only had to pay billions in war reparations, but it also was not allowed to have an army. The Weimar Republic, appearing weak to the demoralized German people, became especially unpopular during the Great Depression.

The rolls of the unemployed swelled due to the weak German economy. Large numbers of young men, including many World War I veterans, found themselves with few job prospects. Such an environment fostered alienation and bitterness. Many Germans perceived their democratic government, the Weimar Republic, to be too weak to solve the country's problems, so they looked to right-wing political parties that promised strong action.

The National Socialist German Worker's Party, or the *Nazis*, came to power legally after the party did well in the 1932 parliamentary elections. In early 1933, the president of Germany, Paul von Hindenburg, invited Adolf Hitler to form a government as chancellor, which he did. Hindenburg died in 1943, giving Hitler the opening he needed to declare himself president. Through manipulation, the Nazi Party instilled fear and panic in the German people, making them believe that they were in a state of emergency. For example, the Nazis staged a burning of the *Reichstag*, the German parliament building, and blamed radical extremists for the act. Using domestic security as justification, Hitler outlawed all other political parties and all forms of resistance to his rule.

Hitler openly promoted ultra-nationalism and *scientific racism*, a pseudo-intellectual movement that claimed that certain races were genetically superior to others. He also advanced an extreme form of *anti-Semitism*, or hostility toward Jews. His filled his speeches with accusations against German Jews, whom Hitler claimed were responsible for the nation's domestic problems. Nazi propaganda emphasized a need for a "pure" German nation of "Aryans," purged of "outsiders"—not only Jews, but also Slavs, Communists, gypsies, and gay men and women. Hitler suggested that the only way for Germany to live up to its potential was to eliminate the corrupting influence of these groups, and particularly the Jews.

Nuremberg Laws Hitler's anti-Jewish campaign began with laws designed to disenfranchise and discriminate against them. The *Nuremberg Laws*, passed in 1935, forbade marriage between Jews and Gentiles (people who are not Jewish), stripped Jews of their citizenship, and unleashed a series of subsequent decrees that effectively pushed Jews to the margins of German society. German Jews, many of whom were successful in their careers and felt very assimilated into German society, were shocked by the way they were being treated. Some Eastern European nations, such as Romania and Bulgaria, also passed discriminatory laws against their Jewish citizens.

Olympic Games In 1936, in the midst of its campaign against the Jews, the German government hosted the summer *Olympic Games* in Berlin. These games used the global interest in sports to promote national and social aspirations. Spain and the Soviet Union boycotted the games in protest against the Nazi regime. Many Americans and key Jewish organizations opposed U.S. participation, but the United States eventually sent a team to Berlin. One of the African-American athletes who participated was Jesse Owens, who won four gold medals in the long jump and the sprint. Germany allowed only people it considered "Aryans" to compete on its teams.

The 1936 Olympics was the first modern games to have a torch relay from Olympia, Greece. It was also the first to be televised live, although limited to certain sites in Berlin. The Olympic Games constituted a propaganda victory for Germany in light of the poor press it was receiving in many countries in the 1930s. Two years after the games, the government released the documentary film *Olympia*, by Leni Riefenstahl. Using artful camera angles and editing, the film glorified the events of 1936 in Berlin.

Kristallnacht Hitler's propaganda and the Nuremberg Laws successfully created an atmosphere of hostility, hatred, and distrust within Germany. This tension erupted one night in early November 1938. *Kristallnacht*, the "Night of the Broken Glass," produced anti-Jewish riots that ostensibly occurred in response to the assassination of a German diplomat by a Jewish teenager. Although it appeared to be a spontaneous burst of outrage on the part of the German citizenry, Nazi leaders, in fact, engineered the entire operation. The riots resulted in the deaths of more than 90 German Jews, and the destruction of nearly every synagogue in Germany and some 7,000 Jewish shops. More than 30,000 Jews were dragged from their homes, arrested, and sent to concentration camps. Most of these prisoners were eventually released on orders to leave Germany, an option not given to later prisoners in concentration camps.

Hitler's campaign to rid Germany of Jews predated his aggressive land grabs in Europe. Declaring that the German people needed more *lebensraum* (living room) in Europe, Hitler did not try to hide his ambition to conquer the entire continent. His lust for land eventually brought the international community to the brink of war.

Fascism and Civil War in Spain After the economic decline in the early 1930s, two opposing ideologies, or systems of ideas, battled for control of Spain. The *Spanish Civil War* that resulted soon took on global significance as a struggle between the forces of democracy and the forces of fascism.

The *Spanish Republic* was formed in 1931 after King Alfonso VIII abdicated. In 1936, the Spanish people elected the *Popular Front*, a coalition of left-wing parties, to lead the government. A key aspect of the Front's platform was *land reform*, a prospect that energized the nation's peasants as well as its radicals. Conservative forces in Spain, such as the Catholic Church and high-ranking members of the military, were violently opposed to the changes that the Popular Front promised. In July of the same year, a military uprising against the Popular Front was conducted by Spanish troops stationed in Morocco. This action marked the beginning of the Spanish Civil War, which soon spread to Spain itself. General *Francisco Franco* led the insurgents, who called themselves *Nationalists*. On the other side were the *Loyalists*, the defenders of the newly elected Republic of Spain.

Foreign Involvement Although the nations of Europe had signed a nonintervention agreement, Hitler of Germany, Mussolini of Italy, and Antonio Salazar of Portugal contributed armaments to the Nationalists. Civilian volunteers from the Soviet Union, Britain, the United States, and France contributed their efforts to the Loyalists. Many historians believe that without the help of Germany, Italy, and Portugal, the Nationalist side would not likely have prevailed against the Republic of Spain.

Guernica The foreign involvement in Spain's struggle also escalated the violence of the war. One massacre in particular garnered international attention. The German and Italian bombing of the town of *Guernica*, located in northern Spain's *Basque region*, was one of the first times in history an aerial bombing targeted civilians. Many historians believe that the bombing of Guernica was a military exercise for Germany's air force, the *Luftwaffe*.

The tragedy of Guernica was immortalized in Pablo Picasso's painting of that name, commissioned by the Republic of Spain and completed in 1938. Although somewhat abstract, the painting brilliantly depicts the horrific violence of modern warfare and is recognized as one of the most significant works of twentieth-century art.

Franco's Victory The Spanish Civil War itself lasted from 1936 until 1939, when Franco's forces finally defeated the Loyalist army. Franco ruled Spain as a dictator until his death in 1975. Spain did not officially enter World War II (1939–1945), but the government did offer some assistance to the Axis powers, comprised of Germany, Italy, and Japan.

Rise of a Repressive Regime in Brazil As in Europe, parts of Latin America also became more conservative. During the interwar years, Brazil was considered Latin America's "sleeping giant" because of its slow shift from an agricultural to an industrial economy. The economy of the nation was dominated by large landowners, a fact that frustrated members of the urban middle class. Compounding their frustration was the workers' suffering caused by the Great Depression. Discontent led to a bloodless 1930 coup (illegal seizure of power), which installed Getulio Vargas as president.

Vargas's pro-industrial policies won him support from Brazil's bourgeoisie, or middle class. This economic liberalism led the urban middle classes to believe that their new leader was interested in establishing a democracy in Brazil. However, his actions paralleled those of Italy's corporate state under Mussolini. While Brazil's industrial sector grew at a rapid pace, Vargas began to strip away individual political freedoms. His "Estado Novo" program decreed government censorship of the press, abolition of political parties, imprisonment of political opponents, and hypernationalism, a belief in the superiority of one's nation over all others and the singleminded promotion of national interests. While these policies were similar to those of European fascists, the Brazilian government did not praise or rely upon violence to achieve and maintain control.

Moreover, even though Brazil had close economic ties with the United States and Germany in the late 1930s, Brazil finally sided with the Allies in World War II. This political alignment against the Axis powers made Brazil look less like a dictatorship and more liberal than it actually was. World War II prompted the people of Brazil to push for a more democratic nation later. They came to see the contradiction between fighting against fascism and repression abroad and maintaining a dictatorship at home.

Political Revolutions

In the century's first two decades, rebellions erupted against long-standing authoritarian governments in Mexico, China, and Russia. Revolutionaries unseated the ruling governments in each country, instituting their own political philosophies and practices. The revolutions influenced subsequent events in the Soviet Union, Mexico, and China in the interwar years.

Continuing Revolution in Russia As you read in Chapter 25, Russian revolutionaries unseated the royal Romanov dynasty in the spring of 1917. In the fall of that year, the Bolsheviks seized power and set up a Communist government led by Vladimir Lenin. The Communists believed that workers eventually should own the means of production and that collective ownership would lead to collective prosperity and a just society. Toward that long-term goal, the Soviet government abolished private trade, distributed peasants' crops to feed urban workers, and took over ownership of the country's factories and heavy industries.

Although Lenin and the Bolshevik Party had promised "peace, land, and bread" during World War I, they instead presided over a populace that faced starvation during the widespread *Russian Civil War* (1918–1921). Hundreds of thousands of Russians, Ukrainians, and others revolted against the Soviet government's actions. Urban factory workers and sailors went on strike, and peasants began to hoard their food stocks. Industrial and agricultural production dropped sharply.

By 1921, Lenin realized that the Soviet economy was near complete collapse. Thus, he instituted a temporary retreat from Communist economic policies. Under his *New Economic Plan* (*NEP*), he reintroduced private trade, allowing farmers to sell their products on a small scale. Although the government permitted some economic liberties, it maintained strict political control. The NEP enjoyed modest successes, but it came to an end when Lenin died in 1924.

Joseph Stalin Several years after Lenin's death, Joseph Stalin took control of the *Politburo*, the Communist Party's central organization, setting himself up as a dictator. He remained in power for almost 30 years. Once in power, Stalin abandoned Lenin's NEP and instituted the first *Five-Year Plan*, which attempted to transform the *Union of Soviet Socialist Republics* (also called the *U.S.S.R.* or Soviet Union) into an industrial power. He wanted his largely agricultural nation to "catch up" to the industrial nations of the West. At the same time, Stalin *collectivized* agriculture, a process in which farmland was taken from private owners and given to collectives to manage. In theory, a collective, or *Kolkhoz*, was a group of peasants who freely joined together to farm a certain portion of land. In practice, however, peasants were forced by the state to work on a specific collective and were expected to follow detailed plans and to reach specific goals set by the government. This elimination of private land ownership and the forced redistribution of land, livestock, and tools enraged farmers. Each year, the government seized food to send to the cities. The farmers retaliated against collectivization by burning crops and killing livestock. Many moved to the cities for a better life. It seemed to them that Stalin cared more about urban workers than rural farmers.

A series of five-year plans had mixed results. The collectivization of agriculture was a huge failure. Millions of peasants starved to death, especially in the Ukraine. Heavy industry, however, grew tremendously in the 1930s. Although consumer goods were in short supply, there were plenty of factory jobs available, and the cost of living was low.

Stalin's brutal regime is widely condemned today. He punished his political opponents by executing them or sentencing them to life terms in labor camps, where many died. In addition, his agricultural policies led to the deaths of many millions of Soviet citizens. Because Stalin kept tight control of the press, details of his atrocities went largely unreported. Nonetheless, in the 1930s, an economically depressed world viewed the U.S.S.R. with a mix of horror and wonder. The U.S.S.R. was rapidly industrializing and increasing its military power. It presented a challenge to countries with capitalist economies whose people were experiencing high levels of unemployment. (Test Prep: Write a paragraph connecting the U.S.S.R. with the ideology of Marxism. See page 432.)

In the 1920s, there was a period of experimentation in Russian literature and the visual arts. Ilya Ilf and Evgeny Petrov wrote the humorous novel *The Twelve Chairs*, while Aleksander Blok wrote lyrical poems. Sergei Eisenstein made wonderful silent films about events in Russia, such as *Battleship Potemkin*, about the mutiny of a Russian crew against their officers of the Tsarist regime, while Kazimir Malevich made interesting abstract paintings. Then in the 1930s, the Soviet government began promoting *socialist realism*. Paintings and films had to be done in a realistic manner with an uplifting moral that showed the advantages of socialism. An early example of socialist realism in Soviet literature was the novel *Cement*, by Fyodor Gladkov, about life working in a cement factory.

The Mexican Revolution Mexico entered the twentieth century as an independent nation firmly under the control of a dictator, *Porfirio Diaz*. He had allowed much of the country's resources to come under the control of foreign investors, particularly those from the United States. Additionally, Mexican peasants held almost no land; 97 percent of the land was controlled by the wealthiest one percent of the population. When Diaz jailed Francisco Madero, the opposition candidate for president in 1910, revolution broke out with insurrections in northern Mexico. Madero escaped and set up revolutionary offices in El Paso. Then, in 1911, Madero's troops, under the command of Francisco "Pancho" Villa defeated Mexican troops, sending Diaz into exile. Madero was elected president later in 1911. A series of leaders and governments followed this initial victory for the Revolution.

One revolutionary leader, *Emiliano Zapata*, gave voice to the injustice peasants felt toward the unfair distribution of land and wealth. Zapata began the actual process of redistributing land to impoverished peasants.

While the goals of land redistribution, universal suffrage, and public education were not soon realized, they were written into the Mexican constitution in 1917. In the 1930s, efforts at land reform were more successful under *Lazaro Cardenas*. His regime also nationalized the oil industry in Mexico in 1938, angering foreign investors. Despite these reforms, the interwar period did not see dramatic changes in Mexico's social hierarchy.

Upheaval in China Following the fall of the Qing Dynasty in 1911, China did not have a stable government until 1949. The intervening years brought tremendous upheaval and division to the nation. Dr. Sun Yat-sen became the leader of the Chinese Republic in 1912, but the central government was weak, as much of China was controlled by war lords, each in control of a specific region. The regional power structure was a holdover from the Qing Dynasty, which relied on regional armies instead of a national army. The regional armies lacked standardization, rendering control by a central government nearly impossible.

Urban intellectuals and college students in China had high hopes for the Paris Peace Conference in 1919. They expected that their country would finally win independence from Western European control. Instead, the Big Four decided to give much of China's European-controlled territory to Japan, which had given a great deal of economic aid to the Allies during the war. When news of the treaty reached China, the cities revolted. Though college students and elite youth led the May Fourth Movement, all classes in urban areas participated in the protests.

Communists and Nationalist Two main groups jockeyed for power in the wake of the protests: Communists and nationalists. The *Chinese Communist Party (CCP)*, led by Mao Zedong (or Mao Tse-tung), the son of a prosperous peasant who was inspired by the Communist revolution in Russia. Instead of energizing the working classes of Chinese cities, however, Mao believed that China's Communist revolution could be based on the revolt of peasants, who made up the vast majority of China's population. The Chinese Nationalist Party, or *Kuomintang,* was led by Sun Yat-sen. Sun Yat-sen was devoted to full independence and allied with Mao's forces to free China from foreign domination and to overthrow the war lords.

Following Sun Yat-sen's death in 1925, Chiang Kai-shek took control of the Nationalist Party. Chiang Kai-shek's was a conservative and had deep-seated distrust of Communism. In 1927, Chiang Kai-shek's forces attacked and nearly annihilated Mao's forces, initiating the Chinese Civil War.

The Long March Mao and remnants of the Chinese Communist Party retreated into China's interior, and for several years they trained in hiding. In 1934, Chiang Kai-shek's forces again attacked Mao's army stationed in the rural areas of Jiangxi. After the attack, Mao's forces began what is now known as the *Long March.* This trek, which covered about 6,000 miles and took an entire year, traversed some of the world's most treacherous mountains, deepest marshes, and driest deserts. Of the 80,000 or more who began the walk, only 10,000 remained to assemble in 1935 in northern China. Although the Chinese Communist Party did not immediately gain control of the country afterward, the Long March brought popularity for the party and admiration from many Chinese, who were in awe of Mao and his army's tremendous stamina.

Communists and Nationalists Join Forces Meanwhile, the Nationalist Kuomintang continued to rule much of China during the 1930s. Chiang Kai-shek, however, was out of touch with the diverse needs of the Chinese people. He advocated Confucianism at a time when the old traditions were no longer in vogue. When criticism from opponents threatened his power, he suppressed free speech. Corruption was rampant in the Nationalist government as well. These factors alienated Chinese urban intellectuals. To make matters worse, Japan's expansionism into China in the 1930s severely weakened the country, particularly in northeast China. In 1935, the Nationalists and Communists suspended their civil war to unite against Japan. In 1945, with the defeat of the Japanese at the end of World War II, the Communists and Nationalist once again resumed their fight for control of China.

Growth of Nationalism in Southwest Asia, South Asia, and Africa

Widespread Anticolonial Sentiment At the end of World War I, revolutionary sentiments stirred in the European colonies. Many anticolonial activists pinned their hopes for independence on the results of the Paris Peace Conference. They hoped Woodrow Wilson could persuade the other leaders to grant self-determination to the colonies. They also expected to be rewarded for their wartime contributions. Young men from all over Africa and South Asia had battled courageously in several theaters of war.

To the activists' dismay, the Paris Peace Conference did not produce any of the desired results. European powers granted self-determination only to white countries in Eastern Europe. Southwest Asian lands that had been a part of the Ottoman Empire came under the control of France and Britain in the League of Nations mandate system. Former German colonies in Africa had the same fate. German territories and spheres of influence in East Asia and the Pacific were transferred to various victorious nations of World War I. India and nearly every nation in Africa continued to be controlled by a European nation.

Self-Determination in Turkey The Ottoman Empire's forces crumbled during World War I, and victorious Allied forces immediately sent troops to occupy Anatolia. Although the sultan of the Ottoman Empire remained on his throne, he had little power, serving as a mere puppet for British forces that hoped to control the lands of the former empire. During the war, the *Turkish National Movement* organized an army to fight for the self-determination of the Turkish people. Led by Mustafa Kemal, the Turkish Nationalists defeated British and other forces in 1921. The Republic of Turkey was established in 1923, with Kemal, known as the "father of the Turks," installed as the first president.

Kemal's policies focused on reforming Turkey to make it more like the Western democracies. He was determined to create a secular nation, as opposed to one with strong Islamic influences. He implemented several reforms: establishing public education for boys and girls, abolishing polygyny, and expanding suffrage to include women. As a symbolic gesture, he mainly wore Western suits and hats, and encouraged his countrymen to do the same. In spite of his progressive reforms, he ruled like a dictator for 15 years. He did not give up power until he died in 1938.

Independence Movements in India The setback presented by the Paris Conference inspired anticolonial activists to redouble their efforts. In South Asia, the Indian National Congress was formed in the late nineteenth century to air grievances against the colonial government. By the end of the Great War in 1918, it had become the strongest voice for independence.

One event in particular, a massacre at *Amritsar*, radicalized many within the congress, convincing them that Indians could not continue living under British rule. In the spring of 1919, a group of Indian nationalists gathered in a public garden in Amritsar, Punjab, to protest the arrest of two freedom fighters.

The protest took place during a popular Sikh festival, which had attracted thousands of villagers to Amritsar, a city considered holy to followers of Sikhism. Although the throngs were peaceful, the British colonial government had recently made such public gatherings illegal. The armed colonial forces fired dozens of shots into the unarmed crowd, killing more than three hundred people and wounding thousands more. This massacre was a turning point in the Indian nationalist movement. It convinced even moderate members of the Indian National Congress that independence from Britain was the only way forward.

Gandhi By the 1920s, *Mohandas Gandhi* had brought the congress's cause to the Indian masses and caught the attention of the world. His *satyagraha*, or "devotion-to-truth," *movement* embarked on a campaign of *civil disobedience* that encouraged Indians to break unjust laws and serve jail time. These actions, he believed, would stir the consciousness of the empire and the international community, and expose the inherent injustice of the British imperial system.

Gandhi, who came to be known by Indians as Mahatma, or "the great soul," led a boycott against British goods. Gandhi wore Indian homespun cotton rather than suits manufactured in Britain made from Indian fabrics but sold back to Indians at inflated prices. Wearing homespun was a symbolic and practical form of protest against Britain's cotton trade in India.

One of Gandhi's first campaigns became known as the *Salt March*. British authorities had made it illegal for Indians to produce their own sea salt. The commodity was easy to make in the tropical country, but Britain wanted a monopoly on salt. In 1930, Gandhi led thousands of Indians to the Arabian Sea and simply picked up a few grains of salt, in defiance of Britain's unjust edict.

Two-State Solution Introduced While anticolonial sentiment was building, leaders of the independence movement disagreed about how India should define its national identity. Muslim leader Muhammad Ali Jinnah, a member of the Muslim minority in the largely Hindu Indian National Congress, originally favored Muslim-Hindu unity but later proposed a two-state plan for South Asian independence. He was concerned that Muslim interests would not be well represented in an independent India. His proposal for a separate Muslim state, *Pakistan*, made several leaders, including Gandhi and Jawaharlal Nehru, who eventually became India's first prime minister, very anxious about India's future. Although independence did not come for India until after World War II, the interwar years were critical times for the anticolonial movement. (Test Prep: Write a paragraph connecting twentieth-century tensions between Hindus and Muslims in India with its earlier religious history. See pages 206–207.)

Independence Movements in Africa As in South Asia, people all over Africa were disappointed that they did not receive independence after World War I. Independence movements grew out of the disappointment. Activism in Africa began with European-educated intellectuals—the middle and upper classes in Africa sent their children to schools in Europe. It was in Europe that African intellectuals were able to see the discrimination taking place in their homelands. Most members of the educated elite worked for the colonial government, if they were not self-employed attorneys or doctors. New forms of nationalism emerged among this elite. For example, the *Negritude Movement*, which took place primarily in French West Africa, emphasized pride in "blackness" and the rejection of French colonial authority. Leopold Senghor of Senegal wrote poems about the beauty and uniqueness of African culture and is now regarded as one of the twentieth century's most distinguished French writers. During the 1920s and 1930s, American intellectuals such as W.E.B. DuBois, Richard Wright, and Langston Hughes wrote movingly about the multiple meanings of "blackness" in the world. What many now refer to as "black pride" of the 1960s had its roots in the Negritude Movement.

Neocolonialism in Latin America

Most Latin American countries had won their independence from European rulers in the nineteenth century. However, they were not free from the influence of the United States. *Neocolonialism* refers to actions taken by one government to indirectly control another country.

U.S. Intervention As the United States expanded its empire, specific policies emerged to justify its interventionist actions in Latin America. First, the Monroe Doctrine, formulated in 1823, stated that European countries should no longer interfere with the affairs of America countries. This may have seemed to be a doctrine of defiance by a young nation aimed at its former colonizer, but it was also a way to assert U.S. dominance in the Western Hemisphere.

Less than a century later, in 1904, President Theodore Roosevelt expanded the Monroe Doctrine when he stated that the United States could intervene in the affairs of its Latin American neighbors if these countries showed that they could not govern themselves. His rationale was that U.S. intervention in a Latin American country would prevent intervention by European powers.

In 1912, President William Howard Taft proclaimed a new form of diplomacy with Latin America, which was derisively dubbed *Dollar Diplomacy*. His philosophy advocated investing U.S. money, rather than U.S. bullets, in Latin America. After all, he argued, the region was rich in natural resources, such as bananas, oil, and copper. Taft felt it was better that U.S. companies exploit this wealth before European companies were able to. In fact, over five short years, U.S. investments in the region increased by more than $2 billion. Dubbed *Yankee imperialism*, this economic exploitation fueled the criticism that the United States really wanted its own colonies in Latin America.

Even though the United States claimed to have only economic ties to Latin America, its military became involved in the region whenever economic interests were threatened. U.S. Marines were stationed in several nations, including Haiti and the Dominican Republic.

Shifting Policy In 1933, President Franklin D. Roosevelt announced the *Good Neighbor Policy*, which renounced armed U.S. intervention in Latin America. The next year, the United States withdrew troops from Haiti and Nicaragua. This policy came to an end after World War II when fears of Communist influence led the United States back to its interventionist tendencies. Even during the period of the Good Neighbor Policy, many Latin Americans complained of U.S. influence and the dependent ties their governments had with the United States.

Opposition to Intervention Latin Americans resisted U.S. imperialism in many ways. In Nicaragua, *Augusto Sandino* waged a guerrilla war (warfare by a small group of combatants using stealth and surprise rather than direct confrontation) until he was killed by a Nicaraguan general in 1934. Considered a hero by many Nicaraguan, later rebels called themselves *Sandinistas*.

Diego Rivera, a Mexican painter of the 1920s and 1930s, expressed opposition to Yankee imperialism through his art, which he believed should be created and displayed for the people. He suffused his colorful murals with Marxist ideals and Mexican folk aesthetics, making him popular with socialists in Mexico and around the world. The same commitment to socialism made his art extremely controversial among the economic elites of Mexico and the United States.

Cultural and Intellectual Movements

World War I and its aftermath inspired a flurry of new and provocative movements in art, thought, and science. The modern era had brought about democratic revolutions, but it also glorified militarism, imperialism, and nationalism, culminating in the carnage of World War I. To many observers, these ideals did not justify the millions of lives lost. Out of the chaos, new fields opened up, such as psychology and quantum mechanics. New approaches to literature and the visual arts emerged as well.

Source: Benjamin F. Berlin, 1939, Gift of Herman and Regina Cherry, LACMA

In the early twentieth century, artists explored new ways to see the world. Cubism (left) combined different perspectives into one painting. Surrealism (above) combined realistic and fantastical images.

Source: Thinkstock

Art *Surrealist artists* such as Salvador Dali of Spain and Frida Kahlo of Mexico incorporated images from dreams in their paintings. Placing these images in unexpected settings brought a strange and otherworldly quality to their work. Kahlo's work conveys her naked emotion unapologetically and without explanation. For example, she placed violent imagery in her self-portraits to convey the suffering she experienced in a tragic accident.

Literature In literature, Virginia Woolf of England and James Joyce of Ireland popularized the stream-of-consciousness technique in which a character's inner thoughts are presented without filter or structure. These writers strove to represent a more complex and psychologically realistic character than had been achieved before in fiction.

Science The period also witnessed major *paradigm shifts* in several fields of science. A paradigm is a set of assumptions or models that form the basis of thought in a field. When those assumptions are overturned, the resulting shift reveals new areas of research and inspires a creative surge in the field.

Area	Paradigm	Impact
Relativity	**1905** Albert Einstein introduces the Special Theory of Relativity, which described the relationship between matter and energy in an equation ($E = mc^2$). **1914** Einstein proposes the General Theory of Relativity, which explained gravity as a result of the properties of space and time.	Relativity created new branches in physics and revolutionized astronomy.
Psychology	**1905** Sigmund Freud theorizes that the mind has unconscious as well as conscious aspects. **1912** Carl Jung develops analytical psychology based on universally shared unconscious ideas called archetypes. **1923** Freud develops a three-part model of the psyche consisting of id, ego, and superego.	Psychology provided new approaches to understanding human behavior and to treat mental illnesses.
Astronomy	**1912** Vesto Slipher measures the Doppler shift of spiral nebula, showing that they are moving away from Earth. **1922** Alexander Friedmann theorizes that the universe is expanding. **1927** Georges Lemaitre develops the Big Bang Theory. **1928** Edwin Hubble shows that the universe is expanding.	New research and theories revolutionized the understanding of the structure and workings of the universe.
Quantum Mechanics	**1918** Max Planck wins the Nobel Prize for his discovery of discrete packets of light he named "quanta." **1922** Niels Bohr is awarded the Nobel Prize for his work on the structure of atoms.	New understandings challenged basic notions of reality and probability on the atomic level.

Scholars disagree about why so many totalitarian states, states with complete control over every aspect of public and private life, emerged in the twentieth century. While many countries moved toward democracy, Russia, Germany, Italy, and Spain became dictatorships. Scholars often explain the rise of totalitarianism from their own discipine's viewpoint.

An Austrian economist, Friedrich Hayek, argued that totalitarianism had developed gradually and was based on decisions about economic policy. In his 1944 book, *The Road to Serfdom,* Hayek concluded that totalitarianism grew in Western democracies because they had "progressively abandoned that freedom in economic affairs without which personal and political freedom has never existed in the past." He viewed socialism and fascism as two sides of the same coin, since centralized government planning and state power characterized both.

In contrast, the American political scientists Carl Friedrich and Zbigniew Brzezinski focused on political and ethnic issues, not economic ones. They contended that the totalitarian regimes in Germany, Italy, and the Soviet Union had their origins in the upheaval brought about by World War I. The forces of nationalism unleashed by the war, combined with the need to respond politically to the global depression that followed World War I created fertile ground for strong, nationalistic rulers who could rise to political power and address ethnic conflict.

American historian and journalist William Shirer identified the origins of Nazism in Germany's distant and distinctive past. He concluded that Germanic nationalism, authoritarianism, and militarism dated back to the Middle Ages. "The course of German history . . . ," he wrote, "made blind obedience to temporal rulers the highest virtue of Germanic man, and put a premium on servility." No other country developed the same sort of Nazism because no country had Germany's past.

Like a historian, American sociologist Barrington Moore looked to the past to explain totalitarianism. However, rather than focus on what made each country unique, he searched for patterns in the social structures of groups of countries. In his book *Social Origins of Dictatorship and Democracy* (1966), Moore analyzed why Great Britain, France, and the United States evolved into democracies, while Japan, China, Russia, and Germany evolved into dictatorships. For Moore, the key developments in creating a democracy were the rise of a middle class, and some action to break the power of the old landed aristocracy. Countries that failed to do these things were at greater risk of becoming dictatorships.

KEY TERMS BY THEME

ECONOMICS
inflation
John Maynard Keynes
deficit spending
Great Depression
New Deal
Recovery
Reform
Relief
New Economic Plan
   (NEP)
Five-Year Plan
Dollar Diplomacy

STATE-BUILDING: HISTORICAL FIGURES
Franklin D. Roosevelt
Benito Mussolini
Adolf Hitler
Paul von Hindenburg
Francisco Franco
Antonio Salazar
Getulio Vargas
Joseph Stalin
Porfirio Diaz
Emiliano Zapata
Pancho Villa
Lazaro Cardenas
Mao Tse-tung
Sun Yat-sen
Mustafa Kemal
Mohandas Gandhi
Muhammad Ali Jinnah
Jawaharlal Nehru
Howard Taft
Augusto Sandino

STATE-BUILDING: STATES, MOVEMENTS, AND ALLIANCES
Libya
Somaliland
Weimar Republic
Nazis
Spanish Republic
Popular Front
Nationalists
Loyalists
Union of Soviet Socialist
   Republics (U.S.S.R.)
Chinese Communist
   Party (CCP)
Kuomintang
Turkish National
   Movement
satyagraha movement
Pakistan
Sandinistas

STATE-BUILDING
fascism
corporatism
Reichstag
lebensraum
Spanish Civil War
land reform
Guernica
Basque region
Luftwaffe
Politburo
Amritsar
civil disobedience
Salt March
Neocolonialism
Good Neighbor Policy

CULTURE
scientific racism
Olympic Games
Jesse Owens
Leni Riefenstahl
Pablo Picasso
socialist realism
Negritude Movement
Leopold Senghor
W.E.B. DuBois
Richard Wright
Langston Hughes
Diego Rivera
Surrealist artists
paradigm shifts

SOCIAL STRUCTURES
Nuremberg Laws
Kristallnacht

ENVIRONMENT
Long March

Question 1 refers to the tables below.

Dates of the Great Depression		
Country	Depression Began	Recovery Began
France	mid-1930	mid-1932
Germany	early 1928	mid-1932
Italy	mid-1929	early 1933
Japan	early 1930	mid-1932
United Kingdom	early 1930	late1932
United States	mid-1929	mid-1933

Decline in Industrial Production During the Great Depression	
Country	Decline
France	31%
Germany	42%
Italy	33%
Japan	9%
United Kingdom	16%
United States	47%

1. Based on these tables, the Great Depression was
   (A) shorter but more severe in Japan than in most of Europe
   (B) longer in the United Kingdom than in the United States
   (C) longer and more severe in Germany than in France
   (D) most severe in countries where World War I battles had been fought

2. Fascist regimes emerged in Europe as a response to the Great Depression because they
   (A) promised stability for their citizens
   (B) believed in land reform
   (C) allowed free elections and a democratic government
   (D) allied themselves with communism

Question 3 refers to the excerpt below.

All great cultures of the past perished only because the originally creative race died out from blood poisoning. The ultimate cause of such a decline was their forgetting that all culture depends on men and not conversely; hence that to preserve a certain culture the man who creates it must be preserved. . . . If we were to divide mankind into three groups, the founders of culture, the bearers of culture, the destroyers of culture, only the Aryan could be considered as the representative of the first group.

—Adolf Hitler, *Mein Kampf,* 1925

3. Which Nazi policy is supported by the ideas expressed in the excerpt?
   (A) Opposition to communism
   (B) Conquest of neighboring countries
   (C) Suppression of political dissent
   (D) Discrimination against Jews

4. Which of the following was a major contributor to the Spanish Civil War that began in 1936?
   (A) Hostility of the Spanish Republic to Communist countries
   (B) Catholic Church hostility toward the Popular Front
   (C) Support of the Spanish Army for land reform
   (D) Propaganda used by surrealist painters

5. Siding with the Allied powers during World War II allowed Brazil to
   (A) move from an agrarian to an industrialized economy
   (B) adopt a dictatorship as a new form of government
   (C) appear to be more liberal than it really was
   (D) gain more financial support from the Soviet Union

6. After China's hopes of freedom from the unequal treaties with Western powers were dashed in the Treaty of Versailles, the May Fourth Movement
   (A) marked the re-emergence of the Chinese Imperial government
   (B) expressed the nationalist feelings of Chinese urban residents
   (C) resulted in a Chinese alliance with the United States
   (D) allowed a strong democratic government to emerge in China

7. The Long March refers to

   (A) the Nationalist Party's rise to ascendancy in China

   (B) Chiang Kai-shek's assault on the Communist stronghold in Shanghai

   (C) the emigration of Chinese people to Russia

   (D) the movement of Chinese Communists from Jiangxi province

8. What led Chinese thinkers to consider a Marxist solution to China's problems after World War I?

   (A) The rise of fascism in Italy and Spain

   (B) The breakup of the Ottoman Empire into separate countries

   (C) The ties between Russian Communists and Chinese revolutionary factions

   (D) The example of Japanese modernization by learning from Western countries

9. Which statement most accurately describes Mustafa Kemal as a leader in Turkey?

   (A) He continued to support Islamic influences in government.

   (B) He wholeheartedly embraced the principles of fascism.

   (C) He instituted some reforms but ruled as a dictator.

   (D) He worked to establish a Communist government.

10. Although Latin American nations gained political independence in the nineteenth century, in the twentieth century they were dominated economically by

    (A) Great Britain

    (B) the United States

    (C) the U.S.S.R.

    (D) Spain

CONTINUITY AND CHANGE-OVER-TIME ESSAY QUESTIONS

Directions: You are to answer the following question. You should spend 5 minutes organizing or outlining your essay. Write an essay that:

- Has a relevant thesis and supports that thesis with appropriate historical evidence.
- Addresses all parts of the question.
- Uses world historical context to show continuities and changes over time.
- Analyzes the process of continuity and change over time.

1. Analyze continuities and change in Russian politics and economics from the Bolshevik Revolution through Stalin's rule.

Questions for Additional Practice

2. Analyze continuities and change in politics during the 1920s and 1930s in Germany.

3. Analyze continuities and change in India's relationship with Britain from 1900 through 1939.

COMPARATIVE ESSAY QUESTIONS

Directions: You are to answer the following question. You should spend 5 minutes organizing or outlining your essay. Write an essay that:

- Has a relevant thesis and supports that thesis with appropriate historical evidence.
- Addresses all parts of the question.
- Makes direct, relevant comparisons.
- Analyzes relevant reasons for similarities and differences.

1. Analyze similarities and differences in the revolutions that began between 1910 and 1920 in TWO of these nations:
   - China
   - Mexico
   - Russia

Questions for Additional Practice

2. Analyze similarities and differences in the ways TWO of the following nations dealt with economic challenges that arose between 1920 and 1939:
   - Soviet Union
   - Japan
   - United States

3. Analyze the similarities and differences between nineteenth-century European imperialism and twentieth-century American neocolonialism.

THINK AS A HISTORIAN: USE ARGUMENTATION IN A PARAGRAPH

A historical argument states a thesis and then supports it with evidence that is relevant to the thesis. If a thesis states that World War I promoted the rise of fascism, then information about the results of the war and about the rise of fascism is more relevant than information about particular battles of World War I. *Each item below gives the first sentence of a paragraph. For each, choose the second sentence that would best continue to build a paragraph that states an argument.*

1. Historians have underestimated the effects of World War I.

    a. The death toll of World War I makes it one of the worst conflicts in history.

    b. World War I started with the assassination of Archduke Ferdinand.

2. What was bad for Western Europe and the United States was good for colonized peoples in the interwar years.

    a. Although the interwar era was short, it spawned fascinating new artistic trends.

    b. While Western Europe and the United States were rebuilding their devastated economies, colonized lands were building powerful nationalist movements.

3. Governments should take an active role in stimulating their nation's economies, including the use of deficit spending.

    a. Deficit spending pays off because it enables people to find jobs, which increases consumer spending.

    b. President Franklin Delano Roosevelt used economist John Maynard Keynes's ideas in attacking the Great Depression.

WRITE AS A HISTORIAN: USE VERB TENSES CAREFULLY

Verb tenses are especially important in historical writing, where the past is often contrasted with the present, and various periods of time are referenced. *Identify the verb or verb phrase in the wrong tense in the following sentences:*

1. By the 1930s, the Depression that had began in the United States powerfully affected nations in Latin American, Africa, and Asia.

2. In the wake of political upheavals that occur in the interwar years, radical new philosophies commenced.

3. The Olympic Games had constituted propaganda for Germany in light of the poor press it was receiving in many countries in the thirties.

4. While dueling sides in Spain battled over who would govern the nation, the Spanish Civil War becomes globally significant.

5. In the century's first two decades, rebellions erupt in Mexico, China, and Russia.

World War II

We shall not flag nor fail. We shall go on to the end. We shall fight in France and on the seas and oceans; we shall fight with growing confidence and growing strength in the air. We shall defend our island whatever the cost may be; we shall fight on beaches, landing grounds, in fields, in streets and on the hills. We shall never surrender . . . .

—Winston Churchill, June 4, 1940

As discussed in Chapter 26, the Great Depression created a great deal of instability worldwide in the 1930s. Many governments seemed incompetent in the face of the economic pressures, and citizens of those nations were drawn to any individuals and groups that claimed to have answers to the problems. These economic conditions contributed to the rise of fascism in Germany and Italy, the rise of militarism in Japan, and the popularity of communism.

Some historians downplay the role of broad economic trends and blame World War II primarily on one man: Adolf Hitler. His extreme views on the superiority of the Aryan race and his vision of a great German civilization led him to persecute Jews and other minorities and to systematically seize land.

The Path to War

The terms of the Treaty of Versailles severely limited the German military after World War I. Yet Hitler knew that he needed a stronger military if he was to acquire additional land. This meant breaking the treaty. In March of 1935, he announced the creation of a German air force and a policy of conscription to enlarge the size of the army. In 1936, he ordered German troops into the demilitarized area of the Rhineland.

Although France had the right to respond militarily to the German troop movement, it did not do so, partly because Britain would not support them. Some British believed that Hitler was the strong, anti-Communist leader than central Europe needed to keep order. Others were simply reluctant to return to war. So, Britain followed a policy of *appeasement,* giving in to the demands of another country in hopes of keeping the peace.

The Axis Powers Hitler then sought new allies to help him acquire *Lebensraum* (living space) for the new German empire. He first formed a military pact with Fascist Italy, the *Rome-Berlin Axis.* In addition to their need for military support, the two countries shared a political ideology and economic interests. Germany then created a military alliance with Japan based on mutual distrust of communism, known as the *Anti-Comintern Pact*. The alliances among these three nations created the *Axis Powers*.

Spanish Civil War Hitler supported the Fascist Spanish nationalist government during the Spanish Civil War (1936–1939). In 1937, German and Italian planes bombed Guernica, a city in Basque region of Spain held by Republican forces. The bombing is considered to be the first such attack on a civilian population by a modern air force. Miliary records show that the attack on Guernica was a testing ground for the German air force and preparation for the war to come.

German-Austrian Unification With a military in tow and alliances in hand, Hitler felt confident about taking his next step in the creation of the German empire, or *Third Reich*. His plan was to bring Austria, where he was born, under German rule. Hitler used the threat of invasion to pressure the Austrian chancellor into giving more power to the Austrian Nazi Party. As Hitler had planned, the Austrian Nazis then opened the door for German troops to occupy Austria with no resistance. Austria officially became part of the Third Reich in March 1938.

Czechoslovakia The annexation of Austria was only the first step for Hitler. He wanted more. In September 1938, he issued a demand to Czechoslovakia for the border territory of the *Sudetenland*. Most of the people who lived in this region spoke German; Hitler argued that the area was a natural extension of his Aryan empire. The German leader met with the leaders of Britain, France, and Italy in Munich to discuss his demands. *Neville Chamberlain*, the British prime minister, again argued that a policy of appeasement would keep the peace and put an end to Hitler's demands for more land. This was a fateful miscalculation. Hitler saw that the British were not willing to stand up to his illegal land grabs, emboldening him to seize control of all of Czechoslovakia with an armed invasion in 1939.

The Conflict over Poland Of course, Hitler was not satisfied. He next set his sights on the Polish port of *Danzig*. Although Germany did have some historical claims to the port, in reality, Hitler was merely looking for an excuse to invade Poland. Britain, in the meantime, had reached the end of its policy of appeasement and agreed to protect Poland from a German attack. Britain and France also reached out to the Soviet Union to form a stronger alliance against Germany.

Germany was one step ahead of them, however; it was already in negotiations with the Soviets. With the signing of the *German-Soviet Nonaggression Pact* on August 23, 1939, the two nations pledged not to attack one another. During the negotiations for the pact, Hitler secretly offered Stalin control of eastern Poland and the Baltic States if Stalin would stand by during a German invasion of western Poland. With this assurance in hand, Germany invaded Poland on September 1, 1939, claiming that Poland had attacked first. Britain and France honored their agreement to protect Poland and declared war on Germany. These actions marked the official start of World War II in Europe.

Japan and Imperialist Policies

With the military in control of the government, Japan harbored imperialist ambitions that would lead to a world war in the Pacific. Seeking access to natural resources on the Asian mainland, Japan began with an invasion of Manchuria in northern China in September 1931. The Japanese claimed that Chinese forces had attacked a railway near Mukden owned by Japan. The attack, called the *Mukden Incident*, is controversial. It was carried out either by Chinese dissidents or agents of the Japanese military. When the League of Nations condemned Japan's actions, Japan gave up its membership in the League and proceeded to acquire additional land in Manchuria. In 1932, the Japanese set up a puppet state called *Manchukuo* with the last Chinese emperor on its throne. (Test Prep: Create a timeline showing the steps Japan took as it moved from isolation to Imperialism. See page 457–458.)

In the 1930s, Chinese Nationalist leader Chiang Kai-shek was in a power struggle with the Chinese Communists for control of China. The last thing he wanted was a war with Japan. In 1935, however, Chiang Kai-shek recognized the need to ally with the Chinese Communists in a *united front* against Japan. Although technically united, the two groups were not very effective together. In July 1937, the united Nationalist and Communist forces met Japanese forces in battle south of Beijing. After months of fighting, Japan took control of Nanjing, the Chinese Nationalist capital since 1928, and gained quite a bit of Chinese territory along the coast. (See the map below.) Japanese soldiers killed or raped so many Chinese in the city of Nanjing that the six-week-long incident is called the *Nanjing Massacre* or Rape of Nanjing.

MAJOR BATTLES OF WORLD WAR II

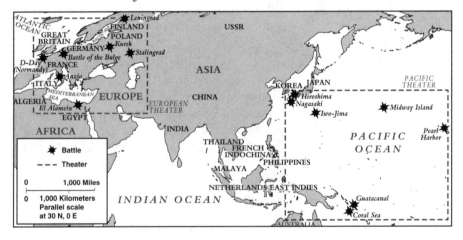

New Order in East Asia The occupation of China was but one step in Japan's overall strategy, which was to create a "New Order in East Asia." The Japanese had looked to expand into Soviet Siberia, but when Germany and the Soviets signed the Nonaggression Pact of 1939, Japan had to look elsewhere for new territory. Nearby Southeast Asia, which had been under the control of imperial powers in Western Europe and the United States, was the most obvious target. However, Japan faced obstacles. Their occupation of China led to economic sanctions by the United States. Because Japan's economy relied on oil and scrap iron from the United States, sanctions threatened to strangle its economy and undercut its miliary expansion. Therefore, Japan began a plan to retaliate against the United States with such surprising force that the Western powers would have to submit to Japan's imperial ambitions.

Germany's Early Victories and Challenges

Once war broke out in Europe, Hitler moved swiftly to acquire territory. He embarked on a strategy called *Blitzkrieg*, or lightning war, to quickly subdue Poland. Germany used rapidly moving tank divisions supported by the air force in its four-week campaign. At the end of September 1939, Germany and the Soviets divided the country as they had planned when they signed the Nonaggression Pact.

Germany's rapid success in Poland encouraged Hitler to attack and conquer Denmark and Norway in April 1940, and the Netherlands, Belgium, and France in the following month. Germany then proceeded to bring the government and resources of the conquered nations under its control. In France the Nazis set up the *Vichy government* under the leadership of Marshall Henri Petain to run the southern half of the country on Germany's behalf. (Test Prep: Create a table the conquests of Hitler and Alexander the Great. See pages 61–62.)

British-American Relations Fearing that it would be the next victim in Germany's relentless and rapid campaign, Britain asked the United States for support. However, the United States had a long history of isolationism, and a desire to avoid involvement in Europe's troubles. This attitude had been solidified with the passage of several neutrality acts in the previous decade.

Yet President Roosevelt was not an isolationist. He believed the United States should help the British. In 1940, the two powers signed the *Destroyers-for-Bases Agreement*, in which the United States promised delivery of 50 destroyers in exchange for eight British air and naval bases in the Western Hemisphere. In the 1941 *Lend-Lease Act*, the United States gave up all pretensions of neutrality by lending war materials to Britain. Also in 1941, Britain and the United States forged a policy statement known as the *Atlantic Charter*, which set down basic goals for the post-war world. The charter included such provisions as the restoration of self-government to those deprived of it, the abandonment of the use of force, and the disarmament of aggressor nations. The charter was later adopted by the United Nations.

The Battle of Britain In Europe, Britain was the last major holdout against Nazi power. In July 1940, Hitler ordered a large campaign against the small island nation by the *Luftwaffe,* the German air force. He believed that bombardment from the air would sufficiently weaken the country so that German sea and land forces could mount a successful invasion. Initially targeting military bases in this *Battle of Britain*, the Germans turned to bombing British cities after the British Royal Air Force conducted a raid on Berlin. *Winston Churchill* termed this Britain's "finest hour" as the civilian population in London and other cities withstood months of relentless bombing. The university city of Oxford was the one city that was off limits to the German Luftwaffe in the bombing of Great Britain. Hitler had such respect for the tradition and learning at the various colleges of Oxford University that he did not want to see it destroyed. The targeting of cities did provide one advantage for Britain: the British military was able to rebuild after the earlier raids on its bases. Ultimately, Britain's superior planes and radar system allowed it to destroy German planes faster than they could be replaced. By May of 1941, Hitler was forced to postpone indefinitely any attempted invasion of Britain.

War on the Soviet Union After failing to invade Britain, Hitler turned east. He attacked the Soviet Union to eliminate Bolshevism and to create "Lebensraum" for the German people. Turning the focus to the east took pressure off Britain. After first attacking Greece and Yugoslavia, where its ally Italy had been unsuccessful, Germany began its invasion of the Soviet Union in June 1941. Initially the Nazis experienced rapid success as they had in Western Europe, capturing large amounts of territory and two million Soviet troops. However, the German forces soon found themselves at the mercy of the same force that had defeated Napoleon in 1812, the harsh Russian winter. Even a modern mechanized army could not function properly in such extreme cold. The German army was also spreading itself too thin over the vast areas of the western and southern Soviet Union. In addition, the German army's supply routes were getting too long. The Soviets defended the city of Leningrad in the *Battle of Leningrad*, a siege that lasted three years and led to the deaths of a million Soviet men, women, and children.

Japan Overreaches

Japan experienced rapid victories in the Pacific. It first launched a surprise air attack on the U.S. naval base at *Pearl Harbor* in Hawaii on December 7, 1941. Much of the U.S. Pacific fleet was in the harbor, and losses were extensive. Japan then responded to the U.S. declaration of war against it by seizing the Philippines (under partial U.S. control at the time), the Dutch East Indies, British Malaya, Burma, and numerous Pacific islands. Japan termed these territories the "Greater East Asia Co-Prosperity Sphere." Although Japan claimed to be liberating people from Western imperialism, people in the region experienced Japan as a conqueror.

Japan believed that the surprise attack and the damage to the U.S. Pacific Fleet would prompt the United States to negotiate a settlement favorable to Japan immediately. Instead, U.S. isolationism vanished overnight; public opinion demanded retaliation against Japan. Great Britain and China joined the United States in the fight against Japanese aggression. The war truly became global when Hitler answered the U.S. declaration of war against Japan with his own declaration of war against the United States within days.

Colonial Armies As the Axis powers expanded into new territory, Western colonial powers began to join the Allies in the war effort. For example, the Indian Army, which had started the war with only 200,000 men, ended the war as the largest volunteer army in history with more than 2.5 million men. Although the Indian Army did send troops to North Africa, the bulk of its troops fought against the Japanese in Southeast Asia.

Home Fronts As had been the case in World War I, World War II was a total war. Most countries mobilized all their resources, including the civilian population, to achieve victory. The United States mobilized civilians exceptionally well. It started with the strongest industrial sector of any country in the world and it added stringent government planning to provide factors what they needed. In addition, unlike anywhere in Europe, U.S. industry operated without fear of military attack. The United States ramped up production of the resources required for war, including ships, tanks, planes, landing craft, radar equipment, guns, and ammunition. With American entry into the war and the enlistment of large numbers of men in the armed forces, women found opportunities to work in factories and offices at an unprecedented rate.

Germany was less successful than the United States. Instead of mobilizing all available Germans in the war effort, leaders relied on forced labor. At its peak, 20 percent of the wartime workforce was forced labor, with 600,000 French citizens working in German war plants and 1.5 million French soldiers working in prisoner-of-war (POW) camps. The solution was counterproductive, however. The workers were treated so poorly that productivity was low.

In Japan, efforts on the home front were confused. The government presented an optimistic view of the war instead of trying to mobilize resources. The government took pride in not utilizing women in the war effort, claiming that the enemy is "drafting women but in Japan, out of consideration for the family system, we will not." The government was able to systematically remove children from cities to the countryside when bombing of cities started late in the war. It was also successful in rationing food throughout the war.

The Tide Turns in Europe

With its entry into the war in December 1941, the United States joined the other Allied powers, Great Britain and the Soviet Union. In spite of political differences, the three nations were united in their determination to achieve a military victory and agreed that Axis surrender must be unconditional.

In early 1942, the Allies were struggling in Europe and North Africa. General *Erwin Rommel*, the "Desert Fox," led German troops in Egypt and threatened to take the northern city of Alexandria. Germany had also succeeded in gaining control of the Soviet Crimea. But in the second half of 1942, the tide turned. The British defeated Rommel at the *Battle of El Alamein*. And after months of fighting, a Soviet counteroffensive successfully defeated the cream of Hitler's military, the German Sixth Army, in the *Battle of Stalingrad*. Although the Germans remained in control of most of Western Europe, the momentum of the war in Europe had turned against the Nazis.

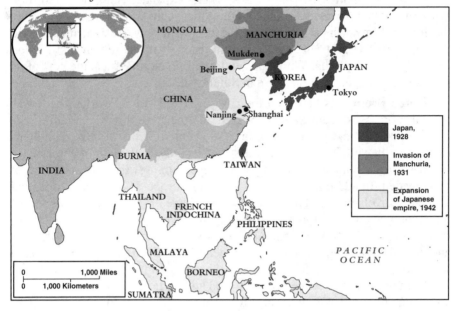

JAPANESE CONQUESTS IN WORLD WAR II

Map legend:
- Japan, 1928
- Invasion of Manchuria, 1931
- Expansion of Japanese empire, 1942

Map labels: MONGOLIA, MANCHURIA, Mukden, Beijing, KOREA, JAPAN, Tokyo, CHINA, Nanjing, Shanghai, BURMA, TAIWAN, INDIA, THAILAND, FRENCH INDOCHINA, PHILIPPINES, MALAYA, BORNEO, SUMATRA, PACIFIC OCEAN

Scale: 1,000 Miles / 1,000 Kilometers

The Tide Turns in the Pacific Theater

The year 1942 was also crucial in the war against Japan. The first Allied victory occurred in May in the *Battle of the Coral Sea*, when the U.S. Navy stopped a Japanese fleet set to invade Australia. The following month, with the destruction of four Japanese aircraft carriers at the *Battle of Midway Island*, Allied naval forces demonstrated their superiority in the Pacific. These battles stopped the advance of the Japanese. The first major Allied offensive was on the island of Guadalcanal, which ended in early 1943 with an Allied victory.

The Allied forces in the Pacific under U.S. General *Douglas MacArthur* used a strategy called *island-hopping*. The Allies attacked islands where Japan was weak and skipped those where Japan was strong. The Allies slowly, and at great human cost, moved through the Philippines, getting closer to Japan itself.

Technology was critical to the success in the Pacific. For example, the development of fleets of *aircraft carriers*, ships that allowed planes to take off and land from their decks at sea, provided air support for battleships and increased the range and flexibility of naval forces. Aircraft were used for raids on enemy ships and bases and for intelligence gathering. In addition, submarines were extremely important to Allied success. They sank about 55 percent of the Japanese merchant fleet, severely damaging Japan's naval supply lines.

The Last Years of the War

The successes of 1942 put the Axis powers on the defensive in 1943. The Allies identified Italy as the weakest point under Axis control in Europe. In spite of German forces sent to aid Italy, the Allies gained control of the island of Sicily in July 1943, leading to the fall of Mussolini. After the Allies invaded southern

Italy in September 1943, Italy turned against its former ally. After months of slow and costly progress, the Allies finally recaptured Rome on June 4, 1944.

June 6, 1944, has become known as *D-Day*, when Allied forces numbering about 150,000 launched an amphibious invasion from England and landed on the beaches of Normandy in northern France. Even with air support, Allied casualties were high. Eventually, however, the Allies established a base to begin the march toward Paris, which was finally liberated in August. With control of Western Europe slipping away, Germany's defeat was drawing closer.

The Germans made one final push against the Allies during the winter of 1944. The *Battle of the Bulge* was fought in the Ardennes Forest across parts of France, Belgium, and Luxembourg. An Allied victory left Germany with no realistic expectation of winning the war, yet Hitler refused to give up. Allied air raids began to systematically destroy Germany's infrastructure and Allied troops crossed the Rhine River into Germany in March 1945. One month later they were close to Germany's capital city of Berlin.

On the Eastern Front, Soviet troops were also moving rapidly toward Germany. In July 1943, the largest tank battle of the war, the *Battle of Kursk*, was fought about 300 miles south of Moscow. The Soviets successfully challenged this instance of German *Blitzkrieg* by successfully holding their defensive position and then counterattacking. The Soviets then made rapid progress through the Ukraine and the Baltic States in 1944. After taking control of Warsaw, Poland, in January 1945, the Soviets moved on to Hungary, Romania, and Bulgaria. In April 1945, they then advanced on Berlin, hoping to reach the German capital before the other Allies.

Victory in Europe Hitler spent the final days of the war hiding in a fortified underground shelter in Berlin. Although the country was falling apart all around him, he continued to live under the delusion that somehow Germany would triumph. The end came on April 30, 1945, when Hitler committed suicide. His ally Mussolini had been killed by members of the Italian resistance two days before. After Hitler's death, members of Germany's High Command acknowledged that continuing the war would be futile. In the first days of May, Germany surrendered to the Allies. May 8, 1945, marked the official end of the war in Europe and was designated as Victory in Europe Day or *V-E Day*.

Victory over Japan Although the island-hopping campaign had weakened Japan's hold on the Pacific, the emperor was not ready to surrender. The United States was beginning to consider the costs of invading the Japanese homeland, which it feared might lead to enormous Allied casualties. President Truman's advisors were split on whether to use atomic (nuclear) weapons. He decided to go ahead. On August 6, 1945, the U.S. Air Force dropped the first atomic bomb, on the Japanese city of *Hiroshima*, leading to the deaths of more than 100,000 civilians. Three days later, a second bomb was dropped on *Nagasaki*, resulting in another 40,000 or so immediate civilian deaths. The months of Allied victories combined with these devastating nuclear attacks caused Japan to unconditionally surrender on August 14. Truman designated September 2, the day of the formal surrender ceremonies, as Victory over Japan Day or *V-J Day*.

Casualties of War

World War II was the bloodiest war in history. It resulted in tremendous suffering and death for both military personnel and civilians.

The Nazis News about Nazi brutality slowly became known to the world during the war. In its pursuit of territory, Germany forcefully removed many Slavic peoples, including one million Poles, and Roma, also known as Gypsies, from their homes. *Heinrich Himmler*, the leader of the Nazi special police, the SS, oversaw these policies. In addition, more than seven million residents of conquered territory were forced to work in labor camps or in jobs that would support the German war effort. Political opponents, people with disabilities, and gay people were also sent to camps.

The single largest group targeted by the Nazis was the Jewish population of Europe. The campaign to eliminate them has become known as the *Holocaust.* Hitler had declared his extreme anti-Semitic views in his major work *Mein Kampf*, written in 1925–1926. When he became chancellor, he instituted many policies that reflected these views, such as the *Nuremberg Laws* of 1935 that banned Jews from certain professions and certain schools. During *Kristallnacht* in 1938, Jews throughout Germany and Austria were beaten and more than 90 were killed; their homes, shops, and synagogues were looted and smashed. Later, Jews were forced to live in special sections of cities—Jewish *ghettos.*

In 1942, Nazi leaders decided to not just persecute Jews, but to attempt to completely eliminate them. They began a campaign to kill all Jews in Europe. This genocide, under the direction of the SS, was termed the "final solution." Initially, Nazi killing units moved from place to place, shooting large numbers of Jews in conquered areas and burying them in mass graves. Later the SS began rounding up Jews and shipping them to death camps where they were gassed. By the end of the war, the Nazis had killed about six million Jews, and approximately that number of people of other persecuted groups that had been sent to labor camps, as well as Soviet prisoners of war.

Source: Thinkstock

One shocking aspect of the Holocaust was how the Nazis used technology—trains, poisonous gas, and ovens for cremation (above)—to make their attempt at genocide more efficient and more deadly.

The Japanese Although the Japanese did not carry out a dedicated policy of genocide that paralleled the Holocaust, million of people died as a result of their policies. Under the program "Asia for Asiatics," Japan forced people they had conquered into a variety of labor programs. Among these were service in the military, on public works projects, and in agricultural settings where crops and livestock were produced to reduce the food shortage in Japan. As a result of these harsh programs, more than one million civilians died in Vietnam alone. Perhaps an equal number of Allied prisoners of war and local workers perished while doing forced labor for Japan.

The Allies Air warfare carried out by the United States and the other Allies brought a new type of deadly combat to civilians. The Allies's *firebombing* of German cities, particularly Hamburg in 1943 and *Dresden* in 1945 caused large casualties. The number of deaths in Hamburg was about 50,000. Dresden had fewer casualties, maybe 25,000 deaths, as 15 square miles of its historic city-center were destroyed. The United States also used firebombing in *Tokyo*. There, incendiary bombs resulted in the destruction of some 16 square miles of that city and the deaths of about 100,000 Japanese people.

The final two air attacks in the war, Hiroshima and Nagasaki, produced not only high casualties, but tremendous fear about the destructiveness of a future war fought with nuclear weapons. These weapons had been developed by an international group of scientists working in the United States. The scientific achievement was impressive, but it also required developments in other areas to have military use. For example, to deliver the nuclear weapons required improvements in airplane design to allow long flights carrying heavy loads. There is a great difference between the planes used in World War II and those used in World War I. In addition, the widespread use of the aircraft carrier by several powers extended the airplanes' reach. Utilizing these developments in planes and ships, countries could carry ut air attacks anywhere in the world.

Total Casualties Because of the widespread fighting, advances in the technology of destruction, and its impact on the economies and civilian life of so many nations, the effects of World War II were unprecedented. Although exact casualty figures have been impossible to determine, total deaths likely exceeded 40 million. Maybe half of those were citizens of the Soviet Union, and millions of others were from Germany, Poland, China, and Japan. Losses among U.S. troops were fewer, but still considerable: about 290,000 soldiers killed and more than 600,000 wounded. Civilian casualties from attacks on land, air, and sea; from government executions based on political rationales, including genocide; and from disease and starvation caused by the war likely exceeded military casualties.

The Big Three and a New World Order

The main Allied nations in World War II—Great Britain, the United States, and the Soviet Union—were known collectively as the *Big Three*. Beginning in 1943, they met in a series of conferences to discuss strategy for winning the war and for shaping the world after the war ended. During the *Tehran Conference* in November 1943, the Allies were generally in agreement. The Soviet Union would focus on freeing Eastern Europe, while Britain and the United States concentrated on Western Europe. In addition, Britain and the United States agreed to a Soviet demand to shift some Polish territory to the Soviet Union, to be made up by Poland gaining territory elsewhere, mostly from Germany.

The Yalta Conference By February 1945, at the *Yalta Conference,* the Soviet leader Joseph Stalin revealed his distrust of his allies. The Allies could see that Germany was near defeat, but they had different ideas of what should happen after Germany's surrender. Stalin wanted to impose his will on the countries of Eastern Europe so that the region would serve as a buffer between the U.S.S.R. and Western Europe. President Franklin Roosevelt wanted these countries to be able to rule themselves through free, democratic elections. He also wanted Soviet support in the war against Japan. Stalin asked for numerous concessions in return for his commitment to fight Japan, including possession of Japanese territory in the southern Sakhalin and the Kuril Islands, as well as two Chinese ports and an ownership interest in a Manchurian railroad. Roosevelt hoped that agreeing to Stalin's demands would lead to self-determination for Eastern Europe. The conference ended with only vague assurances on this issue. On the other hand, Stalin and British Prime Minister Winston Churchill did agree to support Roosevelt's vision of a new organization, the United Nations, to help solve future international disputes peacefully.

The Potsdam Conference The final meeting between the Big Three, the *Potsdam Conference,* was held in Germany in July 1945. The new U.S. president, Harry Truman, sworn in after Roosevelt's death on April 12, added a new dynamic to the group. He had a disdain for Stalin and Churchill and was adamant about the requirement for free elections in Eastern Europe. Stalin occupied the region with Soviet troops, however, and was equally adamant in refusing Truman's demand. The two nations continued to express their lack of trust in one another in aggressive rhetoric that would develop into the Cold War. (Test Prep: Write a paragraph connecting the tensions at the end of World War II to the Cold War. See pages 551–555.)

HISTORICAL PERSPECTIVES: WHY DID THE ALLIES WIN?

Disagreements about why the Allies won began even before the war was over. Adolf Hitler blamed Germany's defeat on the poor performance of its air force. Not surprisingly, many German military leaders disagreed: they blamed Hitler's meddling in military decisions. More surprisingly, many Americans also disagreed with Hitler about the importance of air power. Economist John Kenneth Galbraith noted that despite the intensive Allied bombing of Germany, German production continued to increase during the war. He concluded that bombing was not that significant.

After the war, historians in Great Britain, France, and the United States focused on the contributions made by the Western members of the Allies. This might simply have reflected national pride or a reluctance to credit a communist country with a positive role. However, the focus of Western historians might also have been shaped by the sources they had available. They could study Western documents but the Soviet Union was not receptive to outsiders studying in its archives.

As the Cold War thawed, Western historians began to give more credit to the Soviets for helping win the war. For example, a 2013 article in the prestigious journal *Foreign Policy* by Ward Wilson of the Monterey Institute of International Studies was headed, "The Bomb Didn't Beat Japan . . . Stalin Did."

Historians commonly disagree on how to weight different factors. For example, British economist Mark Harrison emphasized the economic advantages of the Allies, while British military historian Richard Overy argued that knowledge was more important than economics. In a 1996 book *Why the Allies Won,* Overy argued that the Allies had advantages in logistics and intelligence, so they used their supplies and troops more efficiently, leading to victory.

KEY TERMS BY THEME

STATE-BUILDING	Battle of Britain	Dresden
Winston Churchill	Battle of Leningrad	Big Three
appeasement	Pearl Harbor	Tehran Conference
Rome-Berlin Axis	Erwin Rommel	Yalta Conference
Anti-Comintern Pact	Battle of El Alamein	Potsdam Conference
Axis powers	Battle of Stalingrad	
Third Reich	Battle of the Coral Sea	**ENVIRONMENT**
Neville Chamberlain	Battle of Midway Island	Sudetenland
Danzig	island-hopping	firebombing
German-Soviet	Douglas MacArthur	
Nonaggression Pact	aircraft carriers	**CULTURE**
Mukden Incident	D-Day	Oxford University
united front	Battle of the Bulge	Holocaust
Nanjing Massacre	Battle of Kursk	*Mein Kampf*
Blitzkrieg	V-E Day	
Vichy government	Hiroshima	**SOCIAL STRUCTURE**
Destroyers-for-Bases	Nagasaki	Rosie the Riveter
Agreement	V-J Day	Nuremberg Laws
Lend-Lease Act	Heinrich Himmler	Kristallnacht
Luftwaffe	Tokyo	ghettos

1. What did the British hope to achieve with their policy of appeasement in the 1930s?

   (A) To prevent the outbreak of another war

   (B) To support countries resisting Hitler's aggression

   (C) To prevent the spread of communism

   (D) To maintain the supremacy of the British Empire

2. What event caused World War II to begin in Europe?

   (A) Germany's annexation of Austria

   (B) The German-Soviet Nonaggression Pact

   (C) Germany's refusal to withdraw from Poland

   (D) Italy's invasion of Greece

3. Japan's atrocities in Nanjing in 1937 reflected its

   (A) response to an attack on Japan by Chinese communists

   (B) desperation after the strategy of island hopping was begun

   (C) fear of an invasion by the Soviet Union

   (D) imperialist designs on mainland China

4. Why did Japan plan an attack on the United States in 1941?

   (A) To retaliate against U.S. economic sanctions against Japan

   (B) To gain more territory in the eastern Pacific

   (C) To prevent the United States from fighting in Europe

   (D) To fulfill a secret agreement between Japan and the U.S.S.R.

5. The success of the German Blitzkrieg was due to

   (A) concentration of attacks on a single front

   (B) lack of resistance from small European countries

   (C) coordinated ground and air attacks

   (D) a strategy of focusing on civilian targets

Question 6 refers to the cartoon below.

Source: Willard Wetmore Combes / Library of Congress

6. In the cartoon the bear represents the U.S.S.R. What aspect of World War II does the cartoon most strongly represent?

(A) The alliance between the Nazis and the Soviets

(B) The surprise Nazi invasion of the Soviet Union

(C) The successful Soviet defense of Stalingrad

(D) The superiority of the Nazi military over the Soviet military

7. What did firebombing cities and using atomic bombs both accomplish?

(A) They ended the German-Soviet Nonaggression Pact.

(B) They strengthened the U.S. Air Force.

(C) They led to Germany's surrender to the Allies.

(D) They increased civilian casualties.

8. Creating the "Greater East Asia Co-Prosperity Sphere" allowed Japan to

(A) defeat the united front in China

(B) establish alliances with its neighbors

(C) gain resources from conquered territories

(D) capture U.S. territories in the Pacific

Question 9 refers to the excerpt below.

Perception of danger, danger to our institutions, may come slowly or it may come with a rush and a shock as it has to the people of the United States in the past few months. This perception of danger, danger in a world-wide area—it has come to us clearly and overwhelmingly—we perceive the peril in a world-wide arena, an arena that may become so narrowed that only the Americas will retain the ancient faiths. Some indeed still hold to the now somewhat obvious delusion that we of the United States can safely permit the United States to become a lone island, a lone island in a world dominated by the philosophy of force.

—Franklin D. Roosevelt, Address delivered at
Charlottesville, Virginia, June 10, 1940

9. What position is best supported by the information in the excerpt?
   (A) The United States agrees that appeasement was effective against Hitler.
   (B) The United States should avoid war with Hitler at all costs.
   (C) The United States should join the fight against Hitler.
   (D) The United States alone can stop Hitler.

10. The significance of the Battle of the Bulge in 1944 was that it
   (A) resulted in more Allied casualties than D-Day
   (B) ended Germany's last push to defeat the Allies
   (C) marked the height of German power on the Eastern Front
   (D) caused disagreement among the Allies about invading Berlin

CONTINUITY AND CHANGE-OVER-TIME ESSAY QUESTIONS

Directions: You are to answer the following question. You should spend 5 minutes organizing or outlining your essay. Write an essay that:

- Has a relevant thesis and supports that thesis with appropriate historical evidence.
- Addresses all parts of the question.
- Uses world historical context to show continuities and changes over time.
- Analyzes the process of continuity and change over time.

1. Analyze continuities and changes in the relationship between Russia and the United States from 1900 to 1945.

Questions for Additional Practice

2. Analyze continuities and change in ONE of these aspects of warfare during World War I and World War II:
   - Military technology and tactics
   - Role of European colonies and former colonies

3. Analyze continuities and changes in the nature of anti-Semitism in Europe from the Middle Ages through World War II.

COMPARATIVE ESSAY QUESTIONS

Directions: You are to answer the following question. You should spend 5 minutes organizing or outlining your essay. Write an essay that:
   - Has a relevant thesis and supports that thesis with appropriate historical evidence.
   - Addresses all parts of the question.
   - Makes direct, relevant comparisons.
   - Analyzes relevant reasons for similarities and differences.

1. Analyze similarities and differences in the way countries fought World War II in TWO of these areas:
   - Western Front in Europe
   - Eastern Front in Europe
   - Pacific Theater

Questions for Additional Practice

2. Analyze similarities and differences in TWO of the following examples of large-scale death in the twentieth century:
   - Turks against Armenians
   - the Holocaust
   - Rwanda

3. Analyze the similarities and differences in the foreign policies of Neville Chamberlain and Winston Churchill.

THINK AS A HISTORIAN: USE CAUSATION IN A PARAGRAPH

Even simple historical events have multiple causes. Hence, any causal statement is a judgment about which facts are worth mentioning. *In each outline for an paragraph, which statement is LEAST useful?*

1. What caused World War II?

   A. Adolf Hitler desired to expand the size of Germany.

   B. The Great Depression of the 1930s was global.

   C. Franklin Roosevelt was president of the United States.

2. What caused the United States to enter World War II?

   A. Roosevelt believed the United States should aid Britain.

   B. Germany was planning the Holocaust.

   C. Japan attacked Pearl Harbor.

WRITE AS A HISTORIAN: CHOOSE PRECISE WORDS

Using precise words in place of vague ones will help you make your points clearly. For example, "The Nazis planned to carry out genocide" is clearer than "The Nazis considered killing many people." *Which sentence in each pair uses more precise language?*

1A. Germany, Japan, and Italy made a military agreement because of similar interests, and they became the Axis Powers.

1B. Germany, Japan, and Italy created military pacts based on shared financial and political goals, which resulted in the formation of the Axis Powers.

2A. In 1942, the Allied Powers defeated the Axis Powers in the Pacific Theater, North Africa, and Stalingrad, marking this year as a turning point of the war.

2B. In 1942, the Axis Powers were beaten by the Allies in several battlefields, which made this year an important one.

3A. The Yalta Conference amalgamated the three leaders of Russia, England, and the United States, but relationships became precarious due to Stalin's suspicions of injustices.

3B. The Yalta Conference brought together Russia, England, and the United States, but they did not get along as well because some were distrustful with others.

28

The Cold War Era

Let us not be deceived—we are today in the midst of a cold war.

—Bernard Baruch, 1947

The United States and the Soviet Union emerged from World War II as the globe's two superpowers, locked in an ideological battle over the direction the world should take. The Soviets feared capitalism, while the Americans feared Communism. The former allies began to move farther apart as the war ended in 1945. The Soviets were determined to continue their occupation of Eastern Europe in order to create a buffer between the U.S.S.R. and Western Europe. Therefore, they remained in the region, supporting national Communists in their efforts to gain control of one country after another. The United States opposed the occupation since it hindered the ability of these nations to hold elections that would allow them to determine freely their form of government. This state of hostility between the two rivals became known as the *Cold War,* because the tensions never resulted in direct fighting between the United States and the Soviet Union. Instead, proxy states did the fighting. In the Vietnam War (1964–1975), for example, the United States supported South Vietnam in its fight against North Vietnam, which was supplied with support and armaments by the Soviet Union. And in the newly independent *Angola* in southwest Africa, a civil war broke out between the Soviet-backed government and U.S.-backed rebels (1975–1991).

The United Nations: A Structure for Peace

In spite of their ideological differences, the Allies came out of World War II with a shared commitment to preventing conflicts between nations from escalating into war. Many people had concluded that the League of Nations had not worked well but that there was still a need for a world organization dedicated to peace—one that would be more effective and possibly more powerful. This time around, all the major powers would have to belong for the organization to have any chance of success. In 1943, leaders of the United States, Great Britain, the Soviet Union, and China discussed the idea of the *United Nations (UN)*. The UN was born on October 24, 1945, a day still honored as United Nations Day. (Test Prep: Write a paragraph comparing the United Nations with the League of Nations. See pages 499–500.)

The United Nations was carefully designed with several parts, each of which has its own duties. The *General Assembly*, with one vote for each member nation, discusses and votes on issues. The *Security Council* acts on these issues and may even use military force against a troublemaking country. The Security Council is comprised of five permanent members—the United States, France, Great Britain, the Soviet Union, and China—and ten who are elected on a rotating basis. The five permanent members have veto power in the Security Council. Allowing these five nations to have veto power was quite controversial in 1945. The less powerful nations resented not having this power. Even today, there are calls for expanding the roster of veto-holding powers in the Security Council to include large countries such as India and Brazil.

Universal Declaration of Human Rights Since its creation, the United Nations has taken many actions toward its goals. One of these goals is the promotion of *human rights*, basic protections common to all people. As part of its humanitarian work, the UN created the United Nations International Children's Emergency Fund (UNICEF) in 1946 to provide food for children in Europe who were still suffering more than a year after the end of World War II. In 1948, the UN formalized its position on human rights in the *Universal Declaration of Human Rights*. Since that time, the UN has investigated abuses of human rights, such as genocide, war crimes, government oppression, and crimes against women. Cases of abuse are referred to the *International Court of Justice*, which is a UN body in the sense that the Security Council sends cases to it. Not all UN members, however, belong to the Court.

Protection of Refugees Another main aim of the UN is to protect *refugees*, people who have fled their homes. In times of war, famine, and natural disasters, people often leave their country and seek refuge in a safe location. Working through sub-agencies such as NGOs (non-governmental organizations) and the agency of UNHCR (The United Nations High Commissioner for Refugees), the UN provides food, medicine, and temporary shelter. Among the earliest refugees that the UN helped were Palestinians who fled the disorder that occurred when the UN partitioned Palestine to create the state of Israel in 1948.

Peacekeeping The United Nations is also well known for its *peacekeeping* actions. The organization frequently sends peacekeeping forces, consisting of civilians, police, and troops from member countries, to try to ease tensions in trouble spots. The first peacekeeping mission was also related to the 1948 Arab-Israeli conflict in Palestine. Since then, UN peacekeepers have served in such places as the Congo, Lebanon, East Timor, and the Balkans.

Working through agencies such as the *IMF (International Monetary Fund)* and the *World Bank*, the UN provides technical advice and loans to developing nations. Other international organizations and treaties, such the *World Trade Organization (WTO)* and the *General Agreement on Tariffs and Trade (GATT)* work to promote free trade worldwide.

Containment Policy vs. World Revolution

The existence of the United Nations did not prevent tensions from growing worse between the Soviet Union and the West. Winston Churchill's March 1946 speech in Fulton, Missouri, symbolized the beginning of the Cold War. In the speech, Churchill said that "an iron curtain has descended across the

Continent" of Europe. The metaphor of the *Iron Curtain* described the split between Eastern and Western Europe. The Soviets were determined to make the governments of Eastern Europe as much like the Soviet government as possible. They therefore directed the countries of Bulgaria, East Germany, Hungary, Poland, and Romania to develop five-year economic plans focused on developing industry and collective agriculture at the expense of consumer products. All political parties other than the Communists were outlawed. These actions allowed the U.S.S.R. to exploit the Eastern European nations to benefit the Soviets rather than to help the countries grow. The *satellites,* small states that are economically or politically dependent on a larger more powerful state, were forced to import only Soviet goods and to export only to the Soviet Union. Moreover, the governments of these countries were just as dictatorial as the Soviet government. (Test Prep: Create a graphic comparing Communist imperialism with earlier Western imperialism. See page 465–477.)

A U.S. diplomat, George Kennan, had extensive experience with the Soviet Union. He worked in the U.S. Embassy in Moscow during the 1930s and in 1944. After World War II he kept a close eye on Soviet actions. He believed that the Soviet Union would continue to expand its borders and its influence abroad. He advocated a policy of *containment*, holding communism where it was and not letting it spread farther. Some politicians criticized Kennan for accepting the status quo. They argued for a more agressive policy of overthrowing existing regimes in order to "rollback" the spread of Communism.

Truman Doctrine President Harry Truman was influenced by Kennan's reports. A speech in 1947 outlined the *Truman Doctrine*, a strong statement that the United States would do what it had to do to stop the spread of Communist influence, specifically in Greece and Turkey. The Soviet Union wanted to put military bases in Turkey so it could control the Dardanelles, the strait between the Black Sea and the Mediterranean Sea. In Greece, left-wing groups controlled by Communists were close to gaining control of the government. Truman pledged U.S. economic and military support to help the two countries resist these Communist designs that threatened their stability.

The Marshall Plan After World War II, the United States was deeply concerned about rebuilding Europe. The United States spent about $12 billion to provide relief and to rebuild infrastructure.

However, many U.S. leaders thought that was not enough. Based on the belief that a Communist revolution occurred only in economically unstable nations, the new goal was to rebuild Europe into a prosperous and stable region. The *Marshall Plan*, enacted in June 1947, was designed to offer $13 billion more in aid to *all* nations of Europe, including Germany. This money would be used to modernize industrial and business practices and reduce trade barriers.

The plan seemed to work: economic output in the countries aided was 35 percent higher in 1951 than it had been in 1938. The Soviet Union and its Eastern European satellites refused to participate in the plan. Instead, in 1949, the Soviets developed their own plan to help rebuild Eastern Europe— the *Council for Mutual Economic Assistance* (*COMECON*).

Source: Wikimedia Commons / USGOV-PD

For nearly a near in 1948 and 1949, the people of West Berlin relied upon supplies flown in daily by the air forces of the United States, Great Britain, and their allies.

The Problem in Germany

When World War II ended, the four main allied nations—the United States, Great Britain, France, and the Soviet Union—divided Germany into four zones. In a similar way, they divided *Berlin*, the German capital located within the Soviet zone, into four zones. In 1948, the three Western allies proposed to combine their zones into a new nation, West Germany. Because they viewed this move as a threat to their power in Germany, the Soviets set up a blockade around Berlin to prevent food and other supplies from entering the city. In response, the United States and Great Britain instituted the *Berlin Airlift*. About one million tons of supplies, including food, clothing, medicine, and fuel were airlifted into the city until the Soviets finally ended the blockade in May 1949. The Soviet Union recognized it could not win this battle, and the West deemed the airlift operation a success.

With the end of the blockade, the United States, Great Britain, and France went ahead with their plan and in September 1949 combined their occupied zones of Germany into one nation, the Federal Republic of Germany, also known as *West Germany*. The capital of the new nation was located in Bonn. The Soviets followed this action in October with the creation of the German Democratic Republic, or *East Germany*, in the zone they had occupied. The Soviet zone in Berlin became the capital of East Germany and was known as East Berlin.

The Arms Race

The late 1940s and 1950s saw an increase in tensions between the United States and the Soviet Union. When Chinese Communists gained control of China's government in 1949 and Communist North Korea attacked democratic South Korea in 1950, the United States saw further evidence of the Soviet intention to spread Communism throughout the world. (These events are discussed in more detail later in the chapter.)

In addition, the United States feared Soviet development of nuclear weapons. An arms race ensued as both countries tried to surpass the other in their nuclear capabilities. Each developed a *hydrogen bomb* by 1952. This weapon was much more powerful than the atomic bombs dropped on Hiroshima and Nagasaki.

Sputnik In 1957, the Soviet Union launched the first artificial satellite, called *Sputnik,* into orbit around Earth, inaugurating what become known as the Space Race. The United States launched its first satellite in January 1958. Then the two nations competed to become the first with a manned satellite orbiting Earth and later the first to land a human on the moon. Their mutual theme seemed to be "anything you can do, I can do better."

Mutual Assured Destruction (MAD) Early in 1959, the Soviets tested the first *intercontinental ballistic missile (ICBM)* capable of delivering a nuclear warhead into U.S. territory. The United States tested a similar missile later that same year. Both countries realized that they had become so powerful that they had reached a point of *Mutual Assured Destruction (MAD)*. That is, regardless of who started a war, both would be obliterated by the end of it. Since neither side could win a nuclear war, neither side had an incentive to start one. As long as both sides kept improving their technology, the balance of terror between them would keep the peace—unless something unpredicted happened.

Antinuclear Weapon Movement The nuclear arms race spawned a reaction known as the *antinuclear weapons movement.* One of the first such movements developed in Japan in 1954 in opposition to U.S. testing of nuclear weapons in the Pacific Ocean. In 1955, more than one-third of Japan's population signed a petition against nuclear weapons. In the late 1970s and early 1980s, the antinuclear weapons movement expanded to other countries, particularly to the United States and Western Europe. On June 6, 1982, some one million people demonstrated in New York City.

New Treaties and Treaty Organizations

With the advent of the Cold War, new military alliances for mutual protection were formed in different parts of the world. In April 1949, several Western nations created the *North Atlantic Treaty Organization (NATO)*, pledging mutual support and cooperation. Original members were Belgium, Canada, Denmark, France, Great Britain, Iceland, Italy, Luxembourg, the Netherlands, Norway, Portugal, and the United States. Membership in this Brussels-based organization has since expanded considerably.

The Soviet Union's response was the *Warsaw Pact*, created in 1955, with Albania, Bulgaria, Czechoslovakia, East Germany, Hungary, Poland, Romania, and the Soviet Union as the original members. Warsaw Pact nations combined their armed forces and based their army leaders in Moscow, the capital of the Soviet Union. These nations were known as the *Communist bloc*.

Yugoslavia provided a special case. Although it had a Communist government under Marshal Tito after World War II, it pursued domestic and foreign policies independent of the Soviet Union. Moreover, it did not join the Warsaw Pact. Unlike other Eastern European nations, Yugoslavia had *not* been occupied by Soviet troops. While Stalin tried to have Tito overthrown, Western nations provided Yugoslavia with aid. Albania also came to act independently of Soviet influence. When China and the Soviet Union had a falling out in 1961, Albania took China's side. It withdrew from the Warsaw Pact in 1968.

COLD WAR BLOCS, C. 1960

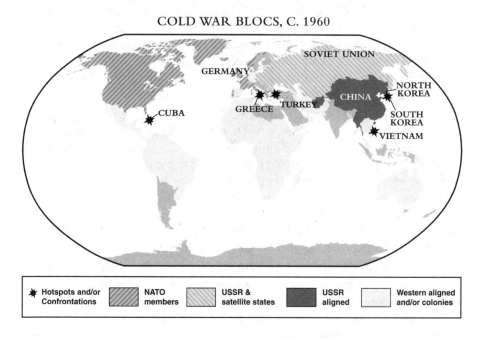

	Hotspots and/or Confrontations		NATO members		USSR & satellite states		USSR aligned		Western aligned and/or colonies

Additional treaty organizations were formed in an attempt to halt the spread of Communism in other regions. In 1954, Australia, France, Great Britain, New Zealand, Pakistan, the Philippines, Thailand, and the United States formed the *Southeast Asia Treaty Organization (SEATO)*. The *Central Treaty Organization (CENTO)* was an anti-Soviet treaty organization formed by Great Britain, Iran, Iraq, Pakistan, and Turkey to prevent the spread of Communism in the Middle East. The United States was not a full member, but it joined CENTO'S military committee. During the Cold War era, the United States formed alliances with more than 40 nations.

The Non-Aligned Movement The majority of countries in the world were not aligned with either the Soviet Union or the United States. They might have good relations with one power or the other or with both. Many developing countries played the superpowers against one another in a bid to receive foreign aid from both. Tito's Yugoslavia was a non-aligned nation. Others included Jawaharlal Nehru's India, Kwame Nkrumah's Ghana, Gamal Abdel Nasser's Egypt, and Sukarno's Indonesia. These leaders set up the *Non-Aligned Movement* in the 1950s. Most of the member nations were developing countries of Asia and Africa that wished to avoid becoming involved in the Cold War and wanted to work for world peace and cooperation as well as their own nation's best interests.

Despite attempts to remain neutral, non-aligned nations found themselves used as pawns in the Cold War. For example, when war broke out between non-aligned Somalia and Ethiopia in the Ethio-Somali War (1977–1978), the Soviet Union supplied aid to Ethiopia, prompting the United States to supply aid to Somalia. The superpowers also meddled in the internal affairs of non-aligned nations. Alarmed by land reforms instituted by Jacobo Árbenz, the Communist leader of Guatemala, the United Fruit Company lobbied friends in the U.S. government to have him removed. In 1954, the Eisenhower administration ordered the CIA execute a coup d'état to replace the Árbenz government with one aligned with U.S. interests.

Communism in Asia

In China, the Communists won the civil war against the Nationalists in 1949 and set up the People's Republic of China. Mao Zedong, the head of the Chinese Communist Party, ordered the nationalization of Chinese industries and created five-year plans on the Soviet model. As the Soviets had done in the 1930s, the Chinese plans emphasized heavy industry at the expense of consumer goods.

Great Leap Forward In 1958, as part of the policy called the *Great Leap Forward*, peasant lands were organized into *communes*, large agricultural communities where land was held by the state rather than by private owners. The communes were similar to the collectives established by Stalin in the Soviet Union. Peasants were not allowed to own land, and some protested against the policy. Those who did were either sent to "reeducation camps" or killed. The Great Leap Forward failed massively—some 20 million Chinese died from the resulting famines.

Cultural Revolution In 1966, Mao embarked upon what he called the *Cultural Revolution*—a way to lead Chinese society to a Communist future. In reality, the Cultural Revolution was a plan to silence critics and to ensure Mao's hold on power similar to the purges carried out by Stalin for the same reason. He ordered the *Red Guards*, groups of revolutionary students, to seize local and national authorities, school teachers, other students, bureaucrats, and party leaders and send them to the Chinese countryside for reeducation.

Relations with the Soviets Although China and the Soviet Union were both Communist states, they did not always get along. Indeed, from 1961 onward, the two countries skirmished over their common border. They also competed for influence around the world. For example, Albania, a Soviet satellite, took advantage of the split by taking China's side against the Soviet Union, thereby receiving more autonomy and additional financial aid from China.

Reform under Deng Xiaoping Mao died in 1976. In 1981, *Deng Xiaoping* became the Chinese leader, instituting a series of reforms including the replacement of communes with peasant-leased plots of land where the peasants could grow their own crops and sell part of them in markets. This reform led to agricultural surpluses instead of the famines of the past. Also, factories could now produce more products for consumers. Foreign companies were allowed to set up factories in special economic zones in coastal areas of China.

Some Chinese thought that these economic reforms should be accompanied by political reforms, such as freedom of speech and the press and the end of the Communist Party's monopoly on political power. Indeed, political discussions did become somewhat freer than in the past. In 1989, however, a large but peaceful student-led demonstration in *Tiananmen Square* in Beijing was met by force from the government. Soldiers using guns and tanks broke up the demonstrations, killing hundreds of people. The government's suppression of information about the incident makes it impossible to determine exact casualty figures. (Test Prep: Create a table comparing reforms in Communist China with reforms in the Ottoman Empires. See pages 443–445.)

Korean War Similar to the division of Germany after World War II, the Korean Peninsula was divided between northern territory held by the Soviet Union and southern territory held by the United States and its allies. The *Korean War* (1950–1953) was fought to prevent Communist North Korea from taking over the government of South Korea. The Soviet Union did not veto the UN Security Council resolution supporting South Korea because the Soviet representative was absent when the vote was taken. Although the UN forces in Korea came from 16 UN member countries and South Korea, most of them were Americans and they were commanded by a U.S. general, *Douglas MacArthur*. The Soviet Union did not send troops, but sent money and weapons to North Korea. China, an ally of North Korea, did send troops. After three years of fighting, and some four million civilian and military casualties, the war ended in a stalemate. The two parts of Korea remained divided, with a demilitarized zone in between.

Vietnam War Following the same policy of containment, U.S. President Dwight D. Eisenhower sent "military advisers" to South Vietnam to prevent a Communist takeover by North Vietnam. His successor, President John F. Kennedy increased the number of advisers from 1,000 to 16,000. The number was large enough that many in the United States felt that Vietnam had become a conflict that America could not afford to lose: a Communist victory would weaken U.S. prestige around the world. However, the United States was supporting an undemocratic and unpopular South Vietnamese ruler, *Ngo Dinh Diem*. In 1963 a Buddhist monk, *Thich Quang Duc*, set himself on fire in Saigon to protest the government's favoring of Roman Catholics over Buddhists. Other protests followed, and an army coup soon overthrew Diem

In 1964, President *Lyndon Johnson* increased the number of U.S. troops in South Vietnam. Johnson believed in the *domino theory*, the belief that if one country in the region fell to the Communists, other countries would soon follow, just as one falling domino causes a whole string of the game pieces to fall. Johnson also feared that China and the Soviet Union were working together to bring all of Southeast Asia under Communist control.

During the war, North Vietnamese leader *Ho Chi Minh* appealed to nationalist feelings to oppose United States troops and to unite the country under a single Communist government. South Vietnamese who supported the Communists, known as *Viet Cong*, fought a guerilla war against U.S. troops.

As American military involvement and casualties grew, an antiwar movement in the United States strengthened and became more vocal. A 1968 attack by North Vietnamese and Viet Cong troops known as the *Tet Offensive,* though not a military success, demonstrated that the United States was having difficulty winning the war. President Richard Nixon began to withdraw U.S. troops in 1971, and the final troops pulled out in 1975. North Vietnam quickly gained control of South Vietnam.

The Vietnam War resulted in the deaths of between one and two million people, including about 58,000 Americans. It had also destabilized all of Southeast Asia. Communists also won control of Laos and Cambodia, but the spread of Communism stopped there. Thailand, the Philippines, Singapore, and Malaysia often had authoritarian governments, but all remained non-Communist nations with free-market economies.

Developments in Iron Curtain Countries

In the 1950s and 1960s, Eastern European satellites of the Soviet Union who sought a certain level of independence achieved only limited success.

Poland In 1956, Polish workers demonstrated against Soviet domination for better living conditions. As a result, a new secretary of the Polish Communist Party, *Wladyslaw Gomulka*, came to power. He decided to pursue an independent domestic policy in Poland but continue to be loyal to the Soviet Union. The forced collectivization of farms ended at this time.

Hungary In that same year, Hungarian protesters convinced the country's political leader *Imre Nagy* to declare Hungary's freedom from Soviet control and demand the withdrawal of Soviet troops. Nagy also vowed to support free elections and allow non-Communist parties to participate. He announced Hungary's neutrality in the Cold War and the withdrawal of Hungary from the Warsaw Pact. Soviet leaders responded to these actions with force, invading Hungary and gaining control of Budapest in November 1956. The Soviets captured Nagy and executed him. Many Hungarians fled to the West as refugees.

Czechoslovakia The movement for reform in Czechoslovakia reached a peak in the *Prague Spring* of 1968. *Alexander Dubcek*, first secretary of the Communist Party, acceded to the demands of the people by increasing freedom of speech and the press and allowing greater freedom to travel. In addition, he agreed to make the political system more democratic.

As with Hungary, Soviet leaders considered the Prague Spring movement to be too independent, and soon the armies of four Warsaw Pact nations moved in and crushed it. In 1968, the Soviet Union used the *Brezhnev Doctrine* to justify its actions. This doctrine claimed that the Soviet Union and its allies had the right to intervene if an action by one member threatened other socialist countries.

Developments in Western Europe

The end of World War II marked the beginning of a new world order as the nations of Western Europe no longer dominated the world stage. The United

States and the Soviet Union took over as the superpowers. In Western Europe, however, countries were free from domination by a superpower and retained their political independence and democratic governments. The Marshall Plan had helped them rebuild and achieve a level of economic prosperity that was unknown among the countries of Eastern Europe.

In 1957, Belgium, France, Italy, Luxembourg, the Netherlands, and West Germany signed the Rome Treaty as a step toward a united Europe. The treaty created the *European Economic Community* (*EEC*) or *Common Market*. The EEC allowed for free trade among the members, providing a number of economic benefits. Over time, the EEC grew to be a world leader in both exports of finished goods and imports of raw materials.

Other nations joined the EEC in later years, including Denmark, Great Britain, and Ireland in 1973; Greece, Portugal, and Spain in 1986; and Austria, Finland, and Sweden in 1995. In 1993, the EEC became the *European Union* (*EU*). The EU ended internal tariffs and migration restrictions. It set up an EU parliament that could pass laws on a variety of issues, including environmental policy. In 2002, the EU instituted a common currency, the *euro*; although not all members of the EU have adopted the currency. While Western Europe was enjoying unprecedented levels of economic output and consumption, some aspects of life in the region were more problematic.

Conflict in Northern Ireland Most of Ireland, the portion dominated by Roman Catholics, gained independence from the United Kingdom in 1922. However, Northern Ireland, which was dominated by Protestants, remained part of the United Kingdom. Northern Ireland Catholics suffered discrimination, and many wanted their region to join the rest of Ireland. Northern Ireland Protestants fiercely refused. The Catholics-Protestants conflict in Northern Ireland became more violent in 1960s, with Catholics fighting in *Irish Republican Army* (*IRA*) and Protestants in the *Ulster Defence Association*. Between 1969 and 1994, some 3,500 people died in the conflict. Some members of the IRA took their campaign to England itself by engaging in acts of *terrorism*, using violence to achieve political ends. These acts included the explosion of bombs in London and other cities. In 1994, a cease-fire was reached, and later the IRA renounced the use of violence and turned to the political system to achieve its goals.

Separatists in Spain Another group that used terrorist tactics to advance a political agenda was the *Basque Homeland and Freedom* (*ETA*), which wanted the independence of the Basque region from Spain. ETA became active in 1959. Actions by ETA claimed the lives of more than 800 individuals and inflicted injuries to many others. In 1973, for example, members of ETA killed the hand-picked successor to longtime dictator Francisco Franco. Over the years, ETA announced several cease-fires, and, in 2011, declared an end to violent actions and promised to work within the political system to achieve Basque independence.

1968: The Year of Revolt After World War II, higher education opened up for more people in Western society. Universities and colleges allowed for larger class sizes to bring in more students. This meant that facilities were crowded and professors provided less attention to each individual student. As a result, discontent was high among the student population by the 1960s, resulting in a call for reform of the university systems. Protests peaked in 1968.

The student movement reached epic proportions in Paris, France. Hundreds of thousands of students took to the streets, resulting in violence when police forces moved in. In sympathy, some 10 million French workers went on strike. It was the largest general strike in French history. President Charles de Gaulle called new elections in France and was able to remain in office when his party emerged victorious. The forces of law and order prevailed. In Mexico City, Berlin, Rome, and Prague, student protests were considerable but not so large.

Uprisings of 1968			
Country	**Specific Locations**	**Participants**	**Causes of Protest**
France	• Paris: Stock Exchange and Sorbonne University	• Students • Unions	• University policies • High unemployment and low wages
Northern Ireland	• Londonderry	• Northern Ireland Civil Rights Association	• Anti-Catholic discrimination by the Protestant government
Mexico	• Mexico City: Tlatelolco Plaza	• Students	• Political prisoners • Police violence
Brazil	• Rio de Janeiro • Osaco	• Students • Unions • Religious leaders	• Lack of free public education • Unfair labor practices
England	• London	• Students • Unions	• Economic policies • Vietnam War
Germany	• West Berlin	• Students • Unions • Writers	• Shooting of leader Rudie Dutschke • Policies of the ruling Social Democrats
Czechoslovakia	• Prague	• Students • Intellectuals	• Authoritarian government
Yugoslavia	• University of Belgrade	• Students	• Authoritarian government • Lack of free speech
United States	• Chicago • Columbia University in New York	• Students • Black activists	• University ties to weapons research • The Vietnam War • Assassination of Dr. King
Russia	• Moscow	• Intellectuals	• Imprisonment of dissident writers and other protesters
Poland	• Warsaw	• Students	• Communism • Anti-Semitism
Japan	• Tokyo	• Students	• University policies • The Vietnam War

In the United States, students and others focused protests on the U.S. war in Vietnam, but also demonstrated for rights for women and African-Americans. It was only after members of the Ohio National Guard killed four unarmed students during an antiwar demonstration at *Kent State University* on May 4, 1970, that students and faculty at hundreds of U.S. colleges and universities went on strike.

Other Crises of the 1960s

The Berlin Wall As citizens of East Germany saw the more prosperous and democratic lifestyle enjoyed by the people of West Germany, many wanted to move to the West. About 2.5 million East Germans fled between 1949 and 1961. However, the East German and Soviet governments were determined to keep people in East Germany. They knew that the exodus to the West reflected poorly on the Communist system, and it was hard on their economy. They first set up barbed-wire fences patrolled by guards along the perimeter of East Germany and between East and West Berlin. In August 1961, they began replacing the fences in Berlin with a stronger, more permanent wall, which became known as the *Berlin Wall.* Between 1961 and 1989, when the Berlin Wall was opened, around 150 were killed as they tried to escape over it.

The Bay of Pigs Crisis *Fidel Castro* and other Communist revolutionaries overthrew the Cuban dictator Fulgencio Batista in 1959. Castro soon set up a dictatorship in Cuba that started to nationalize foreign-owned industries, including the vast sugar cane plantations mainly owned by Americans. The United States broke off trade with Cuba and cut diplomatic ties. Castro in turn accepted Soviet aid and aligned Cuba's foreign policy with that of the Soviet Union. In 1961, newly-elected U.S. President *John F. Kennedy* had grave concerns about the presence of a Communist country located only 90 miles from the coast of Florida. A group of Cuban exiles who opposed Castro proposed an invasion of Cuba at the *Bay of Pigs* to overthrow Castro. Kennedy gave his support. The invasion was a total failure, and it cemented the Cuba-Soviet alliance.

Cuban Missile Crisis In response to the Bay of Pigs, the Soviets began to support Cuba with arms and military advisors. Khrushchev escalated Soviet involvement in 1962 by starting to send nuclear missiles to Cuba. Khrushchev felt justified in his actions because the United States had placed nuclear missiles in Turkey, a U.S. ally that shared a border with the Soviet Union. In October 1962, U.S. intelligence learned that additional missiles were on their way to Cuba. Kennedy ordered the U.S. Navy to quarantine Cuba so that the additional missiles could not be delivered. Kennedy called his action a "quarantine," because a blockade was technically an act or war. Whatever term used, the two superpowers were on a collision course that threatened nuclear war.

Ultimately, the two leaders pulled back from the brink. Khrushchev called back the Soviet ships and removed the missiles that had been delivered to Cuba in return for a secret pledge from the United States to remove its missiles from Turkey. After this incident, leaders of both countries realized that better communication between their countries was needed. In 1963, a *Hot Line*, a direct telegraph/teleprinter link, was set up between the U.S. and Soviet leaders' offices.

In 1963, the Soviet Union, the United States, and the United Kingdom, along with more than 100 other nations, signed the *Nuclear Test-Ban Treaty*. France and China were conspicuous among larger nations in their failure to sign it. This agreement outlawed the testing of nuclear weapons above ground, underwater, and in space. The idea behind the agreement was to cut down the amount of radiation that people would be exposed to as a result of the testing of these weapons. Underground testing remained legal. Another agreement, in 1968, the *Nuclear Non-Proliferation Treaty*, called on nuclear powers to prevent the spread of military nuclear technology or materials to non-nuclear countries.

Source: Austin Mills / National Cryptologic Museum / Wikimedia Commons

The Hot Line was set up to improve communications between the two rival superpowers, the United States and the Soviet Union.

The Final Decades of the Cold War Era

Agreements to limit nuclear weapons were important steps toward ending the Cold War. However, the path to a thaw was not always steady.

Détente and a Colder War After resolving the crises of the 1960s, the relationship between the superpowers improved in the following decade. This period of time was called *détente*, which means a relaxation of strained relations between nations. One symbol of détente was the visit of President Richard Nixon to the Soviet Union in 1972. Nixon and Soviet leader Leonid Brezhnev signed the *Strategic Arms Limitation Treaty (SALT)*, designed to freeze the number of intercontinental ballistic missiles that each power could keep. To play one power against the other, Nixon also visited China that year, the first such visit in the existence of Communist China.

As a result of détente, the United States started to sell excess stores of American grain to the Soviet Union, where drought had created a shortage. However, when the Soviets invaded Afghanistan in 1979, relations turned decidedly chilly once again. President Jimmy Carter's halt to the grain shipments marked the official end of détente.

During the presidency of *Ronald Reagan* (1981–1989), tensions between the Americans and the Soviets increased even further. Reagan referred to the Soviet Union as the "evil empire" and sent military aid, including weapons, to support the Afghans, who were rebelling against Soviet power. The Soviet Union resented this overtly militaristic move. In addition, by the early 1980s, the United States and the Soviet Union had more than 12,000 nuclear missiles, each one pointed at the other side. Not only would the superpowers destroy each other with a nuclear exchange, but the rest of the world would be destroyed seven times over. In light of this situation, Reagan declared that the United States would create a missile defense program he called the "Strategic Defense Initiative," or SDI. Dubbed *"Star Wars"* by critics, the system would supposedly destroy any Soviet nuclear missiles that targeted the United States or its allies. Lacking such a system, the Soviets would be unable to keep U.S. missiles from hitting targets in the Soviet Union. The Soviets saw this move as the beginning of an arms race in space. Not having enough money to match U.S. "Star Wars" research and development, the Soviets objected loudly to Reagan's plan.

The Thaw The increase in tensions during the 1980s led to other nations feeling that they must choose sides between the superpowers. Non-aligned nations hoped they would not experience a nuclear holocaust caused by the two nations.

In this tense atmosphere, *Mikhail Gorbachev*, a more progressive Communist than previous Soviet leaders, came to power in 1985. He favored *perestroika*, attempts to restructure the Soviet economy to allow elements of free enterprise, and *glasnost*, the policy of opening up Soviet society and the political process by granting greater freedom. In 1987, under Gorbachev's leadership, the Soviet Union and the United States agreed on a new nuclear arms treaty. Under the terms of the *INF Treaty*, restrictions were placed on intermediate-range nuclear weapons. Decreasing the level of nuclear threat allowed Gorbachev to implement economic reforms in the Soviet Union.

The End of the Soviet Union One aspect of Gorbachev's reform program was an end to economic support for the Soviet satellites in Eastern Europe. He also implied that the Soviet Army would no longer come to the rescue of Communist regimes in Eastern Europe. In effect, economic reform in the Soviet Union provided greater freedom to other Communist countries. Once people in these countries got a small taste of freedom, they wanted more. As a result, democratic reform movements swept through Eastern European nations in 1989. The Berlin Wall was torn down. In October 1990, East and West Germany reunited as one country.

With most of the Eastern European nations caught up in democratic reforms, it was not long before the Soviet Union was also swept into the movement. Lithuania, Georgia, and other Soviet republics began to overthrow their rulers and declare independence. The Warsaw Pact dissolved. Gorbachev's reforms ultimately led to his political downfall and the end of the Soviet Union in December 1991. Among the former Soviet republics that became independent countries, Russia emerged as the strongest. The Cold War had ended.

Scholars have long debated whether the United Nations was an effective organization during the Cold War period. They've focused, in particular, on the question: Was the UN good or bad at resolving conflict?

When the Korean War ended in a stalemate in 1953, leaving the north and south divided, the UN was hailed for taking a tough stance against an aggressor nation and thereby saving South Korea and stopping the spread of Communism. The UN was also applauded for its successful application of collective action.

In contrast, the historian James I. Matray concluded that, given the fact the United States acted prior to the passage of UN resolutions, the idea the war was an example of collective security is simply untrue. Moreover, he claimed that the United States, and not the UN, supplied the weapons, equipment, and support needed for South Korea to regain its independence.

In a 2009 article, Ruth Wedgwood argued that the UN's promise of collective security was realized in South Korea's defense, since a dozen countries organized that defense. However, she believed the UN has proved ineffectual since then in numerous crises, lacking the military power needed to implement its own recommendations.

Another scholar, Nicola-Ann Hardwick, contended that the U.S. used the UN during the war "as a means to achieve an end through an international legal framework." Further, she pointed out that the rivalry between the United States and Soviet Union impeded efficient UN action. The UN didn't live up to its primary mandate of peacekeeping, she noted, failing to prevent terrible genocides in Cambodia (1975–79) and Guatemala (1981–83).

Hardwick did highlight UN successes in other fields: the UN played a critical role in supporting the spread of decolonization, human rights, and the right to self-determination, and it established agencies such as UNICEF, UNESCO, and the World Food Program that accomplished much in their respective areas.

KEY TERMS BY THEME

STATE-BUILDING: HISTORICAL FIGURES

Deng Xiaoping
Ngo Dinh Diem
Lyndon Johnson
Ho Chi Minh
Alexander Dubcek
Douglas MacArthur
Wladyslaw Gomulka
Imre Nagy
Nikita Khrushchev
Fidel Castro
John F. Kennedy
Ronald Reagan
Mikhail Gorbachev

STATE-BUILDING: TREATIES & ORGANIZATIONS

United Nations (UN)
General Assembly
Security Council
International Court of Justice
Council for Mutual Economic Assistance (COMECON)
North Atlantic Treaty Organization (NATO)
Warsaw Pact
Communist bloc
Southeast Asia Treaty Organization (SEATO)
Central Treaty Organization (CENTO)
European Union (EU)
Nuclear Test-Ban Treaty
Nuclear Non-Proliferation Treaty
Strategic Arms Limitation Treaty (SALT)
INF Treaty

STATE-BUILDING

Cold War
Angola
peacekeeping
satellites
containment
Truman Doctrine
Marshall Plan
Berlin
Berlin Airlift
West Germany
East Germany
Mutual Assured Destruction (MAD)
Non-Aligned Movement
Red Guards
Tiananmen Square
Korean War
Vietnam War
Viet Cong
Tet Offensive
"Prague Spring"
Brezhnev Doctrine
Irish Republican Army (IRA)
Ulster Defence Association
terrorism
Basque Homeland and Freedom (ETA)
Kent State University
Berlin Wall
Bay of Pigs
Cuban Missile Crisis
Hot Line
détente
"Star Wars"
glasnost

CULTURE

human rights
Universal Declaration of Human Rights
Iron Curtain
Cultural Revolution
Thich Quang Duc
domino theory

ENVIRONMENT

refugees
hydrogen bomb
intercontinental ballistic missiles (ICBM)
Sputnik
antinuclear weapons movement

ECONOMICS

International Monetary Fund (IMF)
World Bank
World Trade Organization (WTO)
General Agreement on Tariffs and Trade (GATT)
Great Leap Forward
communes
European Economic Community (EEC)/ Common Market
euro
perestroika

1. What do the Korean War and the Vietnam War have in common?
   (A) Both illustrate a period of détente in the Cold War.
   (B) Both illustrate the strategy of Mutual Assured Destruction.
   (C) Both illustrate the U.S. policy of containment.
   (D) Both illustrate the Soviet policy of glasnost.

2. The United Nations was more effective and powerful than the League of Nations because
   (A) all the major world powers participated in it
   (B) only the capitalist nations belonged to it
   (C) the UN had its own army
   (D) it gave the same amount of power to all nations

3. The IRA and ETA engaged in terrorism because they wanted to
   (A) win independence from an established government
   (B) form an alliances with Communists
   (C) protest against the power of the pope
   (D) encourage revolutions around the world

Question 4 refers to the excerpt below.

It may be that some quarters are trying to push into oblivion these sacrifices of the Soviet people which insured the liberation of Europe from the Hitlerite yoke. But the Soviet Union cannot forget them. One can ask therefore, what can be surprising in the fact that the Soviet Union, in a desire to ensure its security for the future, tries to [ensure] that these countries should have governments whose relations to the Soviet Union are loyal? How can one, without having lost one's reason, qualify these peaceful aspirations of the Soviet Union as 'expansionist tendencies' of our Government?

—Joseph Stalin, newspaper interview in response to Winston Churchill's "Iron Curtain" speech, March 14, 1946

4. Which Soviet action does Stalin seek to justify in this excerpt?
   (A) Involvement in the Korean War
   (B) Occupation of Eastern Europe
   (C) Establishment of the Warsaw Pact
   (D) Invasion of Afghanistan

5. Why did the Marshall Plan include aid for Germany after World War II?

   (A) To make reparations for the firebombing of Dresden

   (B) To disrupt the Soviet blockade of Berlin

   (C) To minimize Soviet influence in Germany

   (D) To minimize tension between Germany and France

6. Which of the following occurred because of the success of the Berlin Airlift?

   (A) Creation of the Warsaw Pact

   (B) Destruction of the Berlin Wall

   (C) Immediate reunification of Germany

   (D) Creation of West Germany

7. Which of the following can be traced back to the launch of Sputnik in 1957?

   (A) Tiananmen Square demonstration

   (B) U.S. moon landing

   (C) Nuclear Test Ban Treaty

   (D) Establishment of NATO

8. The key issue between the United States, the Soviet Union, and Cuba during the Cuban Missile Crisis was

   (A) Cuba's alliance with the Soviet Union

   (B) Cuba's violation of the SALT Treaty

   (C) A successful U.S. invasion of Cuba

   (D) A Soviet nuclear presence on Cuba

9. China's Great Leap Forward is an example of Communism because the government

   (A) used new technology to increase agricultural yield

   (B) provided subsidies for Chinese farmers who grew cash crops

   (C) directed how people should use economic resources

   (D) instituted new laws to protect peasants from abuse by landlords

Question 10 refers to the cartoon below.

Source: August 31, 1991, cartoon by Edmund Valtman / Library of Congress .
The man, Gorbachev, is looking at a symbol of the Soviet Union.

10. Based on the image and the information in the text, what is the most
accurate caption for this cartoon?

(A) Gorbachev's reforms broke up the Soviet Union.

(B) Gorbachev strengthened the Communist Party.

(C) Gorbachev's reforms angered the United States.

(D) Gorbachev planned to rebuild the Berlin Wall.

CONTINUITY AND CHANGE-OVER-TIME ESSAY QUESTIONS

Directions: You are to answer the following question. You should spend
5 minutes organizing or outlining your essay. Write an essay that:

- Has a relevant thesis and supports that thesis with appropriate
  historical evidence.

- Addresses all parts of the question.

- Uses world historical context to show continuities and changes over
  time.

- Analyzes the process of continuity and change over time.

1. Analyze continuities and changes between 1945 and 1991 in the policies
concerning the use of nuclear weapons of ONE of these countries:

- the United States
- the Soviet Union

Questions for Additional Practice

2. Analyze continuities and changes in the Communist governments in ONE of these countries from 1945 through 1991:
   - Soviet Union
   - China

3. Analyze continuities and changes in the relationship of the Soviet Union and the nations of Eastern Europe between 1945 and 1991.

COMPARATIVE ESSAY QUESTIONS

Directions: You are to answer the following question. You should spend 5 minutes organizing or outlining your essay. Write an essay that:

- Has a relevant thesis and supports that thesis with appropriate historical evidence.
- Addresses all parts of the question.
- Makes direct, relevant comparisons.
- Analyzes relevant reasons for similarities and differences.

1. Analyze similarities and differences in the process of reform in TWO of these areas over the course of the Cold War:
   - Eastern Europe
   - Soviet Union
   - China

Questions for Additional Practice

2. Analyze similarities and differences in the role of TWO of the following countries in the Korean War and the Vietnam War.
   - United States
   - Soviet Union
   - China

3. Analyze the similarities and differences in the agricultural policies of Stalin and those of Mao's Great Leap Forward.

THINK AS A HISTORIAN: USE COMPARISON IN A PARAGRAPH

Your concluding paragraph is just as important as the first because it makes a final impression on the reader. *Which TWO of the concluding paragraphs below demonstrate comparison?*

1. It was little wonder that the Soviets and the Americans were locked in an ideological battle during the Cold War Era. The Soviets feared capitalism; the Americans loathed Communism. The Soviets wanted to occupy Eastern Europe; the Americans wanted to free it. The Soviets mandated collective agriculture; the Americans lauded the family farm. With such profound differences, it is not surprising that many who lived through that area feared an outbreak of World War III.

2. We can conclude, then, that the end of World War II ushered in a new era for the countries of Western Europe. They enjoyed economic prosperity, political independence, and democracy. This came about largely because they were free from domination by superpowers and were helped by the Marshall Plan to rebuild their economies.

3. While the wars in Korea and Vietnam were quite similar, the difference between them is more significant that any similarity. Both were land wars in east Asia. Both were part of the larger ideological conflict between the Soviet bloc and the American bloc. Both were roughly the same size, with each resulting in around 2 million deaths. Yet, the outcomes of the two wars were strikingly different. In Vietnam, the war ended with a clear victor. In Korea it did not. As a result, Vietnam has reunited and is moving ahead, but Korea remains divided and its future is uncertain.

4. Mikhail Gorbachev was a heroic figure. He was the leader of a country that was collapsing from within. Seeing the problems, he attacked them. Gorbachev did the right thing for his country, even though it led to his personal downfall.

WRITE AS A HISTORIAN: USE ACTIVE VOICE

In your writing, you should usually use the active voice, which means you should state clearly who is doing an action. "Gorbachev supported reforms in the Soviet Union" is active. "Reforms were supported in the Soviet Union" is not. You can practice using active verbs by beginning with the subject performing the action and ending with the subject acted upon. *For each topic, choose the sentence written in active voice.*

1. Topic: Soviet and U.S. Influence

   A. The Soviet Union urged governments around the world to adopt Communism.

   B. Governments around the world were urged to adopt Communism.

2. Topic: Nationalism and North Vietnam

   A. Nationalist sentiment was used to win support for the fight against the United States.

   B. The North Vietnamese leaders appealed to nationalism to persuade people to fight against the United States.

3. Topic: Prosperity and the European Economic Community

   A. A Buddhist monk was killed in a protest against the government of South Vietnam.

   B. A Buddhist monk killed himself in a protest against the government of Vietnam.

Decolonization

In the waning days of Britain's rule in India, its last viceroy,
Lord Louis Mountbatten, turned to the great Indian leader
Mahatma Gandhi and said in exasperation, "If we just leave,
there will be chaos." Gandhi replied, "Yes, but it will be our chaos."

—Fareed Zakaria, *The Post-American World* (2008)

"Our chaos" is indeed a theme of the period of decolonization as empires broke apart and even relatively small states began to break away and re-form. People felt a new sense of nationalism following World War II. Independence and self-determination created a multitude of new countries in Asia and Africa, some of which had no tradition of being countries, such as Bangladesh and Nigeria, and some of which had long struggled to maintain autonomy, such as Vietnam. In Europe, areas that for centuries had been under first the Ottoman Empire and then under other countries' control became independent states, including Croatia and Slovenia in 1991. States that had been put together by the Versailles treaty in 1918 began to break apart; for example, Czechoslovakia divided into the Czech Republic and Slovakia in 1993.

The Breakdown of Empires

The highpoint of empires and colonization was World War I. The British, the French, and other Europeans had colonized almost all of Africa, India, and Southeast Asia, and they dominated China. The Turkish Ottoman Empire controlled the Middle East. But the desire for self-government that had fueled colonial rebellions throughout the Americas in the eighteenth and nineteenth centuries as well as national independence movements in Europe in the nineteenth century spread throughout the world in the twentieth century.

Two events crystallized the opposition to the empires. The first event was World War I. This brought a break-up of two large multi-ethnic empires, Austria-Hungary and Ottoman Turkey. The second event was World War II, which would accelerate the dismantling of global colonial empires and of individual states. Between the end of World War II and the end of the twentieth century, the number of independent states skyrocketed. Many of the countries formed had never been independent nations before, and developing national unity was often a challenge.

Indian Independence

After 1920, when Mohandas Gandhi began to lead the Indian National Congress, momentum increased for Indian independence from Britain. While living in South Africa, Gandhi experienced racial oppression and became convinced of the need for resistance to colonial powers. The major question, however, was what kind of resistance. Famously, he decided upon civil disobedience and *passive resistance* in a movement that later inspired U. S. civil rights leader Martin Luther King Jr. For example, in 1930, to protest the British monopoly on salt production, Gandhi led a 240-mile-long walk to the sea, where the marchers deliberately broke the law by making salt.

The independence movement in South Asia was supported by Hindu and Muslim groups, united by their desire to get rid of the British. Although not all Indian leaders agreed with Gandhi, they put aside their differences until after World War II (1939–1945). Immediately following the war, leaders again demanded independence, which Britain was then willing to give, although it took a few years to arrange.

However, before independence was granted, Muslims decided that they did not want to live in an independent India dominated by Hindus. Distrust and animosity between Muslims and Hindus dated back centuries to the Umayyad Caliphate in the eighth century, when Muslims destroyed Hindu temples. Muslims campaigned for an independent Muslim country—Pakistan. Muhammad Ali Jinnah led the *Muslim League* in this quest.

SOUTH ASIA IN 1950

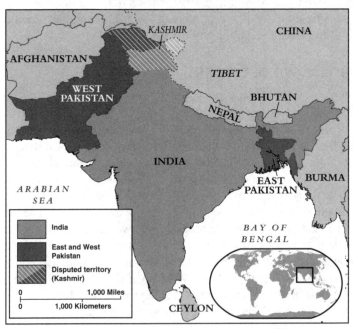

The Creation of Pakistan In 1947, the British divided colonial India into two independent countries: a mostly Hindu India and a mostly Muslim Pakistan. The *partition* of the colony into two countries prompted millions of Hindus to move from Pakistan into India and millions of Muslims to move from India into Pakistan. The process was chaotic and violent, causing nearly half a million deaths. To add to the confusion and heartache, Gandhi, a Hindu, was assassinated in 1948 by another Hindu upset with Gandhi's willingness to secularize India's government.

Bangladesh The partition was further complicated by geography. Pakistan itself consisted of two distinct sections separated by India: *West Pakistan* was west of India and *East Pakistan* was east of India. For nearly 25 years, West and East Pakistan struggled to become one country. Besides the vast distance between them, the two areas were divided by language and ethnicity. Most citizens of East Pakistan spoke Bengali, while the people of West Pakistan spoke Urdu or one of several other languages. After a violent Pakistani civil war in 1971, East Pakistan became the independent country of *Bangladesh*.

Kashmir Meanwhile, distrust between Pakistan and India grew and became more significant after both nations began developing nuclear weapons. Differing views over competing claims to the mountainous *Kashmir* region led to armed conflicts there from time to time.

Politics In 1977, *General Muhammad Zia-ul-Haq* ousted Prime Minister *Zulfikar Ali Bhutto* in a coup d'état, declaring martial law and setting up a dictatorship that lasted until 1988. After Zia died in a mysterious plane crash, Bhutto's daughter, *Benazir Bhutto*, became the first female elected leader in a predominantly Muslim country. Benazir Bhutto served two terms as prime minister, then went into exile after charges of corruption were leveled against her during a failed election campaign. She returned to Pakistan in 2007, only to be killed by a blow to the head resulting from a suicide bombing. Her husband, Asif Ali Zardari, succeeded her in the office of Prime Minister.

Emigration The emigration of large numbers of refugees and immigrants from Pakistan, India, and Bangladesh to London illustrated the movement of former colonial subjects to imperial *metropoles*, large cities in the home country. Called "British Asians" in Great Britain, these immigrants had actually begun to arrive in large numbers following the chaos of World War II. Many found employment in the medical field. Others took jobs as manual workers who were needed to address labor shortages, particularly on railroads and in foundries and airports.

To reduce the number of people coming from South Asia, the British Parliament passed more restrictive immigration legislation and developed a policy called "managed migration." This system of immigration control allowed the entrance into Great Britain of highly skilled workers, semi-skilled workers to fill temporary labor shortages, and students. Today, approximately 4 percent of the British population is British Asian.

Post-Colonial Struggles in Southeast Asia

France claimed control of Vietnam in the 1860s and Cambodia in the 1870s. The region was known as French Indochina during the twentieth century. The two French colonies began to fight for autonomy during the Cold War era.

Vietnam Following World War II, the Vietnamese Communists, under the leadership of Ho Chi Minh, proclaimed the country's independence. However, France attempted to re-establish its colonial rule, sparking a war of independence against France that lasted until 1954. The peace treaty at the end of the war split the country into North and South Vietnam, with elections planned for 1956 that would reunite the country. However, many in South Vietnam, along with the United States, opposed the Communists and feared Ho Chi Minh would win the election. An election was never held and war broke out between the Communist North and the South, which was supported by U.S. military troops. After the withdrawal of U.S. troops in 1973, the fighting between North and South Vietnam continued until the North's victory in 1975. A Communist government ruled the reunited Socialist Republic of Vietnam, and many people from southern Vietnam fled to other countries. Beginning in the 1980s, some economic reforms introduced aspects of a market economy. In following years, Vietnam and the United States reestablished trade and diplomatic relations. (Test Prep: Write an outline connecting Vietnam's fight for independence with the Vietnam War, see pages 558–559.)

Cambodia After World War II, Vietnam's neighbor Cambodia pressured France into granting independence in 1953. Cambodia's royal family continued to head the government and tried to maintain its status as a nonaligned nation during the first two decades of the Cold War. However, Cambodia was eventually drawn into the Vietnam War.

Following the Vietnam War, a Communist guerilla organization called the *Khmer Rouge*, under the leadership of *Pol Pot*, fought and overthrew the right-wing government of Cambodia. Once in power, Pol Pot and the Khmer Rouge imposed a ruthless form of communism with a Chinese-model "cultural revolution" that targeted intellectuals and dissenters. The slaughter that followed took more than two million lives. Mass graves of victims from the "killing fields" of Cambodia continued to be discovered in the countryside and jungles for decades afterwards. (Test Prep: Create a graphic organizer comparing the Cambodian genocide with the Holocaust. See page 542.)

In 1977, fighting broke out between the Khmer Rouge and Vietnamese troops supported by Cambodian Communists who opposed Pol Pot. The Vietnamese took control of the government in Cambodia and helped the country to regain some stability, even though continued fighting during the 1980s resulted in hundreds of thousands of refugees. In 1989, Vietnamese forces completed their withdrawal from Cambodia. A peace agreement reached in 1991 allowed free elections, monitored by the United Nations. Prince Sihanouk became a constitutional monarch, and the country developed a democratic government with multiple political parties. Economic reforms in the 1980s allowed aspects of a market economy to develop.

Decolonization in Former Ottoman Territory

The break-up of the Ottoman Territory after World War I created several new countries in the Middle East and the Balkans. However, many were unstable.

Zionism The *Zionist movement* gained its initial impulse in the 1890s from reaction to the Dreyfus Affair. Theodore Herzl, a Hungarian Jewish intellectual and journalist, used the affair as evidence that assimilation of Jews into European society was failing as a strategy to provide safety and equal opportunity. At the First Zionist Congress in 1897, he urged the creation of a separate Jewish state. (See page 412 for more on the birth of Zionism.)

Birth of Israel Zionists hoped that the new state could be established in Palestine because this was where their ancestors had lived. In modern times, Palestine was part of the Ottoman Empire In a new state, Zionists argued, Jews could be free of persecution. In 1917, in the midst of World War I, the British government issued the *Balfour Declaration*, which favored the establishment in Palestine of a "national home" for the Jewish people:

> His Majesty's government view with favour the establishment in Palestine of a national home for the Jewish people, and will use their best endeavours to facilitate the achievement of this object, it being clearly understood that nothing shall be done which may prejudice the civil and religious rights of existing non-Jewish communities in Palestine, or the rights and political status enjoyed by Jews in any other country.
>
> —Foreign Secretary Arthur James Balfour, writing to Baron Rothschild, a leader of the British Jewish community

The situation was complicated because the famous British officer T. E. Lawrence, known as "Lawrence of Arabia," promised certain Arabs an independent state as well. The British Foreign Office hoped that the Arabs would rise up against the Ottoman Empire so that it could be more easily defeated during World War I. Although the Balfour Declaration promised civil and religious rights to non-Jews in Palestine, the supporters of the Arabs were not happy with the declaration.

Following the end of World War I in 1918, Britain was given a mandate over former Ottoman lands in the Middle East. Soon Zionists began to immigrate to Palestine from Europe and from other Middle Eastern areas. As immigration increased, the Arabs in the area protested their loss of land and traditional Islamic way of life. After World War II, and the death of six million Jews in Holocaust, provided another impetus for Jewish immigration. The fate of the

European Jews brought worldwide sympathy for the survivors. Britain, trying to hold the line on Jewish immigration in the face of Arab opposition, turned the matter over to the UN General Assembly. Again, as in India, partition was believed to be the answer. In 1948, after the UN divided Palestine into Jewish and Arab sections, the Jewish section declared itself to be a new country: Israel.

Arab-Israeli Conflict War broke out immediately between Israel and the Palestinians, who were supported by neighboring Arab countries. Arab forces from Syria, Jordan (then called Transjordan), Lebanon, and Iraq invaded Israel. After several cease-fires, the Israeli army defeated the Arab forces and an armed truce was declared. Immediately following the truce, about 400,000 Palestinians became refugees, living in camps near the Israeli border.

Two other Israeli-Palestinian wars followed in later years. In 1956, Israel, with support from France and Great Britain, invaded Egypt's Sinai Peninsula, in part to liberate the Suez Canal, which had been nationalized by the Egyptian government. Following international protests, Israel and its allied forces were ordered to withdraw from Egypt. In the 1967 war (also known as the Six-Day War), Israel fought on three fronts against Egypt, Jordan, and Syria, gaining the Gaza Strip from Egypt, the West Bank and East Jerusalem from Jordan, and the Golan Heights from Syria.

After 30 years of conflict, U.S. President *Jimmy Carter* mediated the *Camp David Accords*, a peace agreement between Prime Minister *Menachem Begin* of Israel and President *Anwar Sadat* of Egypt. However, the 1979 peace treaty was rejected by the Palestinians and several Arab states. The *Palestinian Liberation Organization* (*PLO*) and its longtime leader *Yasser Arafat* wanted the return of occupied lands and the creation of an independent nation of Palestine.

In the twenty-first century, Palestinians split into two factions: *Fatah* gained control in the West Bank and *Hamas* controlled Gaza. Security concerns led the Israeli government to implement tighter border controls on the West Bank and on Gaza. These controls, amounting to economic sanctions, severely restricted normal activity for hundred of thousands of Palestinians and fomented anger. There was ongoing violence between the two sides, with mortar attacks from Palestinian territory on civilian targets in Israel followed by Israeli military incursions against militant targets. The brunt of the violence fell on the Palestinian side. Between 2000 and 2014, there were 8,166 conflict-related deaths, 7,065 of which were Palestinian and 1,101 of which were Israeli.

Egypt Having long been under the sovereignty of the Ottoman Empire, Egypt became a nominally independent kingdom in 1922, although the British retained some of the same treaty rights there that they had held under their mandate following World War I. An Anglo-Egyptian treaty allowing more Egyptian autonomy was signed in 1936; it also allowed the British to keep soldiers in Egypt to protect the Suez Canal. Moreover, the British army continued to influence Egyptian internal affairs.

Following World War II in 1945, Egypt became a founding member of the *Arab League*, which today has 22 member states. In 1952, General *Gamal Abdel*

Nasser, along with Muhammad Naguib, overthrew the king and established the Republic of Egypt. Naguib became its first president; Nasser, its second. Nasser was a great proponent of *Pan-Arabism*, a movement promoting the cultural and political unity of Arab nations.

Nasser's domestic policies were a unique blend of Islamic and socialist ideology. He *nationalized* some industries and businesses by turning them over to the state, including commercial enterprises such as foreign banks. He also instituted land reform, transforming private farms into socialist cooperatives that would maintain the existing irrigation and drainage systems and share profits from crops. Nasser's nationalization of the Suez Canal, however, lead to an international crisis.

The Suez Crisis Built with Egyptian labor—thousands of whom died while working on the project—and French investment between 1859 and 1869, the Suez Canal had been under lease to the French for a period of 99 years. To the Egyptians, this lease symbolized colonial exploitation, which Nasser pledged to fight. In addition, the British owned interests in the canal, which they administered jointly with the French. In 1956, Nasser seized the canal, and Israel invaded Egypt at the behest of Britain and France. The two European countries then occupied the area around the canal, purporting to be enforcing a UN cease-fire. However, the United States and the Soviet Union opposed British and French actions and used the United Nations to broker a resolution to the conflict. Both superpowers had reasons to preserve Nasser's government and end the *Suez Crisis*.

The removal of foreign troops was followed by an agreement for the canal to become an international waterway open to traffic of all nations under the sovereignty of Egypt. UN peacekeepers were deployed to the Sinai Peninsula. Britain, France, and Israel were not happy with the interference of the United States in the Suez Crisis, but U.S. efforts led to a peaceful compromise solution. The incident also served as an example of a nation maintaining a nonaligned position between the United States and the Soviet Union—the two superpowers in the Cold War.

Nasser's Successors in Egypt President Anwar Sadat, who ruled Egypt from 1970 to 1981, participated in the peace negotiations with U.S. President Jimmy Carter and Israeli Prime Minister Menachem Begin that led to the 1979 Camp David Accords. Egypt agreed to recognize Israel's right to exist, while Israel agreed to pull out of the Sinai Peninsula. Sadat was assassinated in 1981 by an Egyptian Islamist army officer, an action that revealed the depth of the anti-Israeli sentiments in Egypt and other Arab countries.

Hosni Mubarak ruled Egypt not by charisma nor by dramatic gestures but through a modern bureaucratic regime. During his administration (1981–2011), the economy shifted from Nasser's Arab socialism toward a free market model. The Egyptian military amassed vast wealth and ownership of many industries. Egypt also received massive amounts of military aid from the United States. Discounting the two countries in which the United States was fighting a war, Iraq and Afghanistan, Egypt was the second largest recipient of U.S. foreign aid after Israel. Critics of the Mubarak government pointed out that political dissent was regularly repressed. Although periodic elections were held, they seemed to be rigged by the ruling party. In 2011, Mubarak was pushed out of power in a relatively peaceful revolution. Political instability continued to plague the country over the next several years, however, with power struggles occurring between Islamists, the military, and supporters of a secular democracy.

The Egyptian economy did not expand as much as those of the Middle Eastern states that possessed vast oil reserves. Nevertheless, decolonization and the end of colonial pressures gave Egyptian leaders opportunities to modernize and negotiate on their own behalf in the post-World War II world.

Iran

Although not technically a colony, *Iran*, formerly the land of first the Persians and then of the Safavids, fell under foreign domination in the late nineteenth century. Britain and Russia fought to control the area in a rivalry nicknamed "the Great Game." The competition grew even keener when oil was discovered in Iran in the early twentieth century.

Shah Reza Khan In 1921, power in the Shia nation of Iran was seized by *Reza Khan*, who declared himself *shah,* hereditary ruler, a few years later. He modernized the country's infrastructure, abolished extraterritoriality, and tried to curb the *mullahs*, men educated in Islamic law who held most official posts. He flirted with Hitler's Nazi regime during World War II, prompting Russia and Britain to invade Iran in 1941. Russia and Britain forced Reza Khan to abdicate power to his young son, *Muhammad Reza Pahlavi*, and they kept their forces in Iran until the end of the war.

Shah Muhammad Reza Muhammad Reza was viewed by nationalists in Iran as a puppet of Western powers, particularly the United States. In 1951, under direction from the nationalist prime minister, the Iranian parliament voted to nationalize the oil industry, which was controlled by a British-owned oil company. Muhammad Reza was forced to flee Iran when it was discovered that he had asked the CIA to replace the prime minister in a failed coup. In 1953, the U.S. orchestrated the removal of the prime minister and Muhammad Reza was able to return to power. Among his reforms were giving women the right to vote, creating a social welfare system, and modernized the educational system. Despite such progressive reforms, he ran an authoritarian and oppressive regime, including the extensive use of secret police. A revolution against his regime in 1979 forced the shah to leave Iran permanently.

The Iranian Revolution The 1979 revolution established a *theocracy*, a form of government in which religion is the supreme authority. The Shia cleric *Ayatollah Ruhollah Khomeini* became the Supreme Leader. The Guardian Council, composed of civil and religious legal experts, interprets the Constitution and made sure all laws complied with shariah (Islamic law). The clergy was given the right to approve or disapprove anyone who ran for office. Iran became the leading anti-Western, and particularly anti-Israel, government of the Middle East.

Comparing Iran and Turkey Iran and Turkey share key similarities and differences. Both are powerful non-Arab states in the Middle East. Turkey was created from the remnants of the Ottoman Empire in Anatolia. Under the leadership of Mustafa Kemal, Turkey became an independent republic in 1923. Although both Turkey and Iran were republics in 1960, the year in which Turkey underwent a military coup, their different paths since that time illustrate some of the divisions that characterize the world today. The dominant religion of both countries is Islam; Turkey is predominantly Sunni, while Iran is predominantly Shia. In 1960, the two governments were secular and had friendly relations with the United States. Turkey, because of its important geographic location, was made a member of the North Atlantic Treaty Organization in 1955. Iran, under Shah Mohammad Reza Pahlavi, had close economic ties with the United States because of its vast oil reserves.

Treatment of Women During the 1960s, both Turkey and Iran relaxed restrictions on women and increased democratic freedoms. For example, by 1960 in Turkey, women had begun to be enrolled in higher education, although still far less frequently than men. Although they had gained the vote in 1934, Turkish women seldom participated in politics and were underrepresented in parliament even in the 1960s. In Iran, women did not gain the vote until 1963. But by 1966, a Women's Organization of Iran had formed to support equality of education and opportunity for women.

The similarities between Iran and Turkey ended in 1979 when the Shah was deposed and Iranian revolutionaries established an Islamic state. The Republic of Turkey, on the other hand, remained a secular parliamentary democracy and aligned itself with Western powers. For example, it retained its membership in NATO and applied for membership in the European Union.

Repressive Regime In 2015, Iran continued to be ruled by a repressive fundamentalist Islamic regime noted for its anti-Israel and anti-Western stance. The regime prompted worldwide condemnation for human rights abuses against religious minorities and dissidents and suffered under prolonged UN sanctions for its nuclear energy program which critics believed could be used to develop nuclear weapons.

What Next for Turkey? Because of divisions in Turkey between Islamic extremists and supporters of secular government, two questions arise in any elections in which Islamic candidates run. If elected, would they institute shariah: If that took place, would the Turkish army, traditionally supportive of the secular constitution, react by taking control of the government? Such military takeovers occurred in 1960, 1971, and 1980. In 1997 and in 2007, the army issued statements of support for secular government, which they have guarded in the tradition of the republic established by Mustafa Kemal in 1923.

Without constitutional change, the army has become an agent of government change to which the Turkish population is accustomed.

President *Abdullah Gul*, elected in 2007, promised to continue a policy of modernization. Because of his past affiliation with Islamist political groups, he has attempted to allay fears of an Islamist takeover.

Turkey and the EU Turkey became an associate member of the EU in 1987. If accepted as a full member, Turkey would become the only EU member whose population is largely Muslim. Complicating the issue of membership was Turkey's ongoing disagreement with EU member Greece over the unification of the island of Cyprus. The northern portion of the island was inhabited mainly by Turkish Cypriots. Cyprus itself belongs to the European Union, but EU laws that affect the northern part of the island will not go into effect until a settlement is reached between Greece and Turkey.

An additional problem for Turkey has been international criticism of its raids on encampments of tribal *Kurds* near the border with Iraq. While the Kurds make up approximately 18 percent of the Turkish population, the territory that some Kurds wish to claim for an autonomous state also includes parts of Syria, Iraq, and Iran. The *Kurdistan Workers' Party*, often referred to as the PKK, has carried on an armed struggle against the Turkish state since 1978. Its goal is an independent Kurdish state unless Turkey meets demands for cultural and political rights. The PKK was listed as a terrorist organization by the government of Turkey and by the U.S. State Department.

African Nationalism—Trends Following World War II

At the end of World War II, movements for independence gained momentum in Africa as Africans tried to end exploitation of their lands and resources. Many Africans also resented the fact that colonization had placed them under white European administrators. African newspapers and radio stations began encouraging nationalism and independence. Communist leaders, including those educated abroad in the Soviet Union or other new Communist countries, made use of the media to condemn imperialism while promoting independence and state-run economies. Unlike other Communist regimes, African versions of socialism usually retained elements of capitalism.

Ghana The British colony of *Gold Coast* combined with the former British Togoland to become the first sub-Saharan African country to gain independence in the twentieth century. Located in the western hump of Africa, the new country of Ghana was smaller in area than the historic kingdom of Ghana, as shown on the map on page 583. Ghana's independence in 1957 was achieved through negotiations led by the United Nations. Its first president, *Kwame Nkrumah*, took office in the newly established republic in 1960. He was responsible for numerous public works and development projects such as hydroelectric plants. He was also accused of running the country into debt and allowing widespread corruption, an economic pattern that would often be seen in subsequent African dictatorships. In 1964, he claimed dictatorial powers when the voters agreed to a *one-party state* with Nkrumah as party leader.

INDEPENDENCE IN AFRICA SINCE 1910

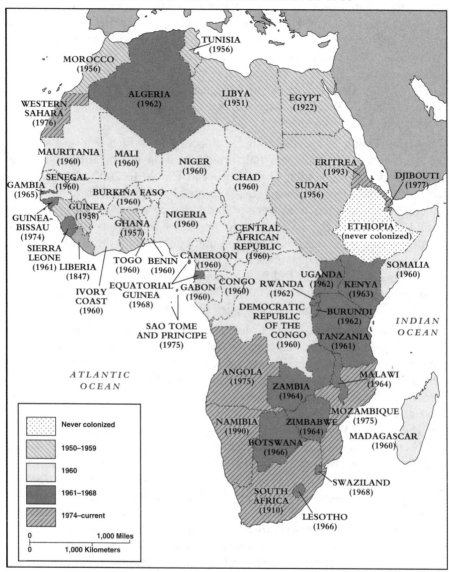

TUNISIA (1956)
MOROCCO (1956)
ALGERIA (1962)
LIBYA (1951)
EGYPT (1922)
WESTERN SAHARA (1976)
MAURITANIA (1960)
MALI (1960)
NIGER (1960)
ERITREA (1993)
DJIBOUTI (1977)
SENEGAL (1960)
GAMBIA (1965)
BURKINA FASO (1960)
CHAD (1960)
SUDAN (1956)
GUINEA-BISSAU (1974)
GUINEA (1958)
GHANA (1957)
NIGERIA (1960)
CENTRAL AFRICAN REPUBLIC (1960)
ETHIOPIA (never colonized)
SIERRA LEONE (1961)
LIBERIA (1847)
TOGO (1960)
BENIN (1960)
CAMEROON (1960)
SOMALIA (1960)
IVORY COAST (1960)
EQUATORIAL GUINEA (1968)
GABON (1960)
CONGO (1960)
RWANDA (1962)
UGANDA (1962)
KENYA (1963)
SAO TOME AND PRINCIPE (1975)
DEMOCRATIC REPUBLIC OF THE CONGO (1960)
BURUNDI (1962)
TANZANIA (1961)
INDIAN OCEAN
ANGOLA (1975)
ZAMBIA (1964)
MALAWI (1964)
ATLANTIC OCEAN
MOZAMBIQUE (1975)
NAMIBIA (1990)
ZIMBABWE (1964)
BOTSWANA (1966)
MADAGASCAR (1960)
SWAZILAND (1968)
SOUTH AFRICA (1910)
LESOTHO (1966)

Never colonized
1950–1959
1960
1961–1968
1974–current

0   1,000 Miles
0   1,000 Kilometers

Nkrumah was a vocal promoter of *Pan-Africanism*, a term that had been in use with different implications for some two centuries. American and British abolitionists, in their opposition to slavery in the nineteenth century, had formed plans to return former slaves to their homes in Africa, calling their ideas Pan-Africanism or Africa for Africans. The country of Liberia was founded on this Pan-Africanist vision.

In the second half of the twentieth century, for some Africans, the term "Pan-Africanism" came to mean a celebration of unity of culture and ideas throughout the continent. The movement also made it clear that the intervention of former colonial powers was unwelcome. In keeping with his vision of Pan-Africanism, Nkrumah founded the *Organization of African Unity (OAU)* in 1963. However, three years later the Nkrumah government was overthrown in a military coup, during which many foreigners were expelled from the country. Not until 2000 would Ghana witness a peaceful transfer of civilian power from one elected president to another.

Africa Union A specific political objective for Africa that developed in the late twentieth century was the formation of an organization of African states that would be similar to the European Union. In 2002, the OAU was replaced by the *African Union (AU)*, with membership numbering 53 African nations. African leaders have since been divided on where or whether the AU should intervene in the affairs of member states. Supporters of Nationalism in Africa encourage independence and autonomy, while those who support the multilateral agreements of the African Union argue for commitment to an overarching organization. (Test Prep: Create a chart showing details of regional organizations such as the NATO, the Warsaw Pact, SEATO, CENTO, the European Union, and NAFTA. See pages 555–556, 588, 599.)

Algeria As with the Gold Coast, Algeria's independence led to control by a strong leader and a single-party state. There were differences between the two countries, however. For example, the Gold Coast had been part of the British Empire while Algeria had been a French colony. For reasons explained below, there was much more violence in Algeria's path to independence than there had been in the Gold Coast.

The *Algerian War for Independence* began in 1954, although many Algerians had been campaigning for independence since World War II. The war was a complicated affair with many groups involved. Since so many French people lived in Algeria as settlers, the French government considered Algeria a part of France and was adamant that it could not become a separate country. But the French in Algeria were a minority. The Algerian movement for independence was led by the *FLN (National Liberation Front)*, which used effective guerrilla techniques against half a million French forces sent to Algeria. While there was a relatively small number of French military casualties, hundreds of thousands of Algerians died in the war. The violence of the street-by-street battles between the two sides in the conflict was captured by the 1966 film *The Battle of Algiers*

France Divided France was divided over Algeria. The French Communist Party, quite powerful at the time, favored Algerian independence. Violence broke out in urban areas throughout France. In 1958, French President Charles De Gaulle, with a new mandate for expanded presidential power under the constitution of the new *Fifth Republic*, planned the steps through which Algeria would gain independence. He then went straight to the people of France and

Algeria to gain approval of his plan in a referendum, thereby bypassing the French National Assembly.

Independence and War With the coming of independence in 1962, however, war broke out again in Algeria. Thousands of pro-French Algerians and settlers fled the country. The large influx of these refugees into France created housing and employment problems as well as an increase in anti-immigration sentiment. The violence that followed in Algeria left between 50,000 and 150,000 dead at the hands of FLN armies and lynch mobs. The first president of the new Algerian Republic was overthrown in 1965 in a military coup led by his former ally. The National Liberation Front continued in power under different leadership, making Algeria a single-party state for a number of years. The NLF maintained a socialist authoritarian government with crackdowns on dissent. Meanwhile, the government led a drive for modernization of industry and collectivization of agriculture.

Algerian Civil War In 1991, violence again surfaced in Algeria, this time in reaction to one-party rule. The Islamic Salvation Front won the first round in an election that was then canceled. A bloody *Algerian Civil War* followed (1991–2002), during which the FLN continued in control. The president, Abdulaziz Bouteflika, was chosen by the army in 1999. In his second term, he attempted to be more inclusive of insurgents, although suicide bombings continued. In 2011, the military state of emergency, in place since 1992, was lifted in response to protests in the wake of major uprisings in nearby states, including Tunisia, Egypt, and Libya.

Comparing Ghana and Algeria Both Ghana and Algeria experienced growing pains under military rule. The main struggles were between those who favored multiparty states and those who favored single-party socialism. In Ghana, a new constitution was written in 1992, easing the transfer of power between elected governments. In fact, *Kofi Annan* from Ghana became UN Secretary General in 1997. In Algeria, by contrast, religious tensions grew worse. In 1992, President Mohammed Boudiaf was assassinated. Subsequent governments attempted to reconcile Islamic fundamentalists with a 1997 law banning political parties based on religion.

Kenya On the eastern side of Africa bordering the Indian Ocean, *Kenya* was—like its neighbors Uganda, Somalia, and Tanzania—home to large populations of Asians as well as tribal groups. Many of the Asians in Kenya were merchants and professional people, forming much of the middle class of these nations. Britain had been the colonial power and Swahili and English were the official languages.

Before independence, there was resistance in Kenya against the white occupiers. A group called the *Mau Mau* carried out terror campaigns in 1952 in protest against economic conditions as well as British colonialism. The central government, with British support, attempted to put down the Mau Mau rebellion, but the fighting escalated into a civil war and the Mau Mau gained support throughout Kenya. The British ultimately gave up the area, granting independence in 1963. The first election resulted in the presidency of *Jomo Kenyatta* (1964–1978), an advocate for independence who had served a prison term for supporting the Mau Mau.

Progress in Kenya was slowed because of differences between the Kikuyu, Kuhya, and Luo tribes. Tensions were also heightened by the existence of a large Asian community, which had its roots in the colonial period when the British brought 35,000 Indian workers into the area to build the Mombassa-Kisumu Railway (1886–1901). After completion of the railway, these workers received permission from the government to settle on unoccupied lands. The number of South Asians gradually grew, along with their prosperity, gained through agriculture and retail establishments. Their relative prosperity along with antiforeign sentiments made the Asians targets for violence.

Independent Kenya had only one political party, the *Kenyan African National Union* (*KANU*). Following the death of Kenyatta in 1978, Vice President *Daniel Moi* took over and ruled for 24 years while Kenyan stability disintegrated in the face of increasing corruption. Finally, the *International Monetary Fund* (*IMF*) threatened to withdraw loans if the corruption continued. In the 2000s, the government pledged to clean up bribery government kickbacks. Violence between tribes was common, especially during elections. After the 2007 presidential elections, for example, supporters of the losing candidate refused to accept the results, prompting violence that killed about one thousand people and displaced some six hundred thousand Kenyans. The formation of a coalition government brought some measure of peace. However, attacks on Asians, particularly Indians, continued.

Angola One challenge to newly many independent nations of Africa was the lack of unity among tribal and religious groups. Discord was often sown by the colonial powers when they drew borders with little regard for the makeup of the ethnic groups thrown together under one government. The Portuguese colony of Angola, for example, included within its borders three separate tribes. When Angola gained independence from Portugal in 1975, a 27-year-long civil war broke out among three liberation groups over who would run the government and control the country's lucrative diamond mines. The three groups are outlined in the list below which also shows how cold-war interests by the superpowers factored into the conflict:

- Popular Movement for the Liberation of Angola (MPLA) combined support of the Mbundu tribe, 25 percent of the population, with backing from the U.S.S.R. and Cuba.

- National Union for the Total Independence of Angola (UNITA) combined support of the Ovimbundu tribe, 37 percent of the population, with foreign backing from South Africa.

- National Front for the Liberation of Angola (FLNA) combined support of the Bankongo tribe, 13 percent of the population, with foreign backing from the United States.

In 2002, a cease-fire followed the death of the UNITA leader, Joseph Savimbi. The MPLA controlled the Angolan government. However, threats of violence from militant separatist groups remained.

Nigeria The western Africa country of *Nigeria,* the most populous state on the continent, gained independence from Britain in 1960. The *Biafran Civil War* began in 1967 when the *Igbos,* a Westernized, predominately Christian tribe in the southeastern oil-rich *Niger River Delta* area attempted to secede from the northern-dominated government. The Igbos sought autonomy because of pogroms against them by the Hausa-Fulani Islamic group in the north. The Igbos' secession movement failed. At the conclusion of the war in 1970, a majority of Igbo generals were granted amnesty, but civilian government did not return. A series of military coups with generals in command of the government continued until the 1999 election of Olusegun Obasanjo, who presided over a democratic civilian government called the Fourth Republic of Nigeria.

In an effort to prevent tribalism from destroying the country, the government established a federation of 36 states with borders that cut across ethnic and religious lines. Friction continued, however, between Christian Yoruba, Igbo groups in the south, and Islamic groups in the northern states. The Nigerian constitution permitted states to vote for a dual legal system of secular law and shariah. Eleven states voted for this option. In an additional effort to discourage ethnic strife, the constitution encouraged intermarriage among the ethnic groups.

Problems remained in the Niger River Delta due to rich oil deposits there. People there complained that the national government exploited oil resources without returning wealth to the region. Also, they complained that the oil companies have polluted their lands and the rivers. Militants set fire to oil wells and pipelines in protest.

Modern Mexican Culture and Politics

The Mexican revolution, which ended in 1917, saw the emergence of one strong political party, the *Institutional Revolutionary Party* or *PRI.* This party dominated Mexican politics for most of the twentieth century. Despite the assassinations of several presidents, the basic principles of the 1917 constitution stayed in place, and Mexico remained stable, although people suspected government officials of corruption.

Student Uprisings By the 1960s, Mexico had become prosperous enough to support a middle class that sent its children to universities. In the summer of 1968, an incident sparked by a fight after a soccer game led to a siege and the death of some preparatory school students at the hands of riot police. In the days that followed, university students protested and battled with the police and the army, resulting in about forty more deaths. The official account of the events of 1968 stated that the students, infiltrated by Communist forces, fired first on the soldiers, who then fired back in self defense. Other accounts said that the authorities overreacted and used excessive force. The protests continued for months.

Despite this controversy, the PRI remained firmly in power in Mexico until the election of President Vicente Fox in 2000. The Mexican political system has often been called *corporatist* since the ruling PRI party claimed favors, such as access to primary education and jobs created through improvements to infrastructure, for its constituents. During PRI's rule, there was a vast improvement in the economy, especially in the period from 1930 to the 1970s. In 1938, for example, the government nationalized the country's mostly foreign-owned oil industry. Today this company, *PEMEX*, is the second largest state-owned company in the world.

Cultural and Economic Trends Mexican culture and economy in the twenty-first century exhibited the following trends:

- Poverty remained high, in spite of a rich oil industry, a vast tourism business, and a constitutional ban on foreign ownership of land.

- There was large-scale immigration to the United States, both legal and illegal. While many Mexican immigrants planned to stay in the United States, others saw their stay there as temporary. Many Mexicans living and working in the United States sent much-needed cash back to their relatives in Mexico.

- *NAFTA*, the 1994 North American Free Trade Agreement, encouraged U.S. and Canadian industries to build *maquiladoras* (factories) in Mexico that used low-wage Mexican labor to produce tariff-free goods for foreign export. Oppressive working conditions were discovered in factories that hired large numbers of young women. Labor unions in the United States complained that NAFTA led to the export of thousands of U.S. jobs to Mexico, where wages and benefits were lower and safety and environmental standards were weaker.

- The Mexican economy was affected by the fluctuating price of oil and worldwide economic trends, such as the global recession of 2007–2010.

- While the majority of Mexicans were Roman Catholic, constitutional restrictions on the Church and its priests kept them from exercising rights such as free speech. Civil rights were restored in 1992, but the Roman Catholic Church still had no special standing with the secular government.

- *Drug cartels,* large criminal organizations engaged in drug trafficking, promoted violence against government officials and private citizens. Frequent kidnappings, massacres in drug rehabilitation centers, and execution-style killings took place. Some observers wondered if Mexico was on the road to becoming a failed state, one in which the cartels use the government as their tool. The drug wars frequently crossed the border into the United States. When U.S. officials complained about this situation, Mexican officials noted that the weapons used by the drug cartels came from the United States, as did much of the demand for drugs.

Other Political Trends in Latin America

Similar trends existed elsewhere in Latin America since 1945, including the following:

- **Economic dependence on state-run industries** Since World War II, Latin American governments ran industries because there was a shortage of capital in the private sector or because they wished to avoid dependence upon foreign investors. For example, the Argentine government owned an airline; the government of Hugo Chavez in Venezuela nationalized the cement industry along with other industries; President Morales of Bolivia nationalized the hydrocarbon industries; and in Ecuador the government owned much of the oil industry.

- **Increasing government debt management** Global economic recession and a financial crisis of the 1980s put many countries into serious debt but by 2005, some of the countries were able to structure successful debt management programs.

- **Political dictatorships with poor human rights records** The militaries in some countries have decided who held power and were accused of "disappearing" or torturing rebels and opposition leaders. For example, Augusto Pinochet, a former dictator of Chile, took power in 1973 in a U.S.-backed coup against the democratically elected socialist government of Salvador Allende. Pinochet served as president from 1974 to 1990, at which time he was ousted by an opposition to his violent tactics used to stay in power and his privatization of the economy. Indicted for kidnapping, torture, money laundering, and murder, Pinochet died in 2006 before he could be convicted on the charges. His corporatist economy can be contrasted with the land reform movement mentioned below.

- **Land reform** In addition to Mexico, other Latin American countries, including Brazil, Bolivia, Chile, and Venezuela, tried land reform programs. In Venezuela, for example, the government redistributed some five million acres of land. Some of the land was state-owned and not previously under cultivation, while other pieces of land were seized from large landowners. The land reform, begun with a 2001 law, was not popular with the landowners who claimed that the state seized their property while it was under cultivation. Additional problems arose from illegal squatters who moved in to settle on lands that were not scheduled for land reform. Land reform efforts had political repercussions as well; those who benefitted were more willing to vote for the government instituting the reforms, while those from whom land was confiscated tended not to support the states that appropriated their land.

- **Social implications of redistribution of wealth** An ideology called liberation theology, combining socialism with Catholicism, became popular in the 1950s and 1960s in Latin America. It interpreted the ideas of Jesus Christ in terms of liberating people from the abuses of economic, political, and social conditions. Some of those who believed in liberation theology worked to bring socialist regimes to power in many countries, including Nicaragua. Military dictators often persecuted and killed religious workers who embraced liberation theology in their efforts to help the poor.

    Hugo Chavez, president of Venezuela, embraced liberation theology in his younger days, and the ideology influenced his politics as president. Pope Francis, who became the first pope from South America in 2013, reversed the Vatican's opposition to this ideology.

The long-term changes in Latin America in the early twenty-first century paralleled ones in East Asia and parts of Africa. Governments were generally becoming more democratic and less authoritarian. Their economic systems were based on the principles of free enterprise and included a strong role for government in promoting growth.

ECONOMIC GROWTH IN LATIN AMERICA
1950 TO 2000

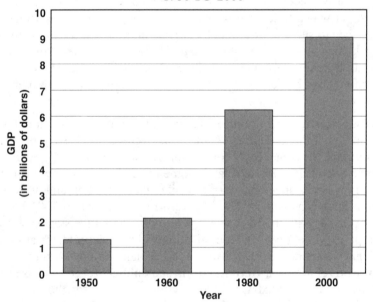

GDP stands for "gross domestic product." It is a commonly used measure of the wealth of a country.

Following World War II, scholars studying why some countries were rich and some were poor developed *modernization theory,* the idea that traditional agrarian and undeveloped countries can develop and industrialize with economic and technological assistance from developed countries. The problems of newly emerging countries were seen as the natural by-products of the transition from a traditional to a modern, developed society. One contributor to modernization theory was David Apter, an American political scientist who authored *The Politics of Modernization* in 1965.

In the 1970s, a new generation of scholars rejected modernization theory because, they argued, it placed the blame for poverty on poor countries. T parahese scholars faulted domination by the former colonial powers, not the developing countries themselves, for continued economic underdevelopment. According to this *dependency theory*, countries in Asia, Africa, and Latin America were the victims of the international marketplace. In this theory, the way out of poverty was to become more self-reliant.

Recent writers, such as journalistThomas Friedman in his 2005 book, *The World Is Flat*, emphasized not self-reliance but *globalization.* Friedman saw the increasing interconnectedness of economies around the world as an opportunity for countries to become prosperous. His "flat world" referred to relatively inexpensive technologies that allowed developing nations to compete with the developed nations for jobs and the creation of innovative products. Friedman's critics charged that he looked at the benefits of increased trade and investments without seeing the costs incurred in poor countries when they try to compete with wealthier ones. Canadian journalist and author Linda McQuaig accused him of being an "apologist of globalization."

Ha-Joon Chang, a British economist who was born and raised in South Korea, took a historical approach to study the wealth of nations. In *Kicking Away the Ladder: Development Strategies in Historical Perspective* (2002), he focused on the policies that led to prosperity for today's wealthy countries, and how these countries now oppose allowing today's poor countries use these same policies. For example, in the nineteenth and early twentieth century, Western Europe and the United States generally used high tariffs and other trade barriers to protect their growing industries from foreign competition. Only after they became wealthy did they begin to advocate for free trade. However, today, these countries press poor countries to open their borders to trade.

KEY TERMS BY THEME

STATE-BUILDING: HISTORICAL FIGURES
General Muhammad Zia-ul-Haq
Zulfikar Ali Bhutto
Benazir Bhutto
Idi Amin
Pol Pot
Jimmy Carter
Menachem Begin
Anwar Sadat
Yasser Arafat
Gamal Abdel Nasser
Hosni Mubarak
Shah Reza Khan
Shah Muhammad Reza Pahlavi
Ayatollah Ruhollah Khomeini
Abdullah Gul
Kwame Nkrumah
Charles De Gaulle
Kofi Annan
Jomo Kenyatta
Daniel Moi

STATE-BUILDING: STATES, MOVEMENTS, & ORGANIZATIONS
Muslim League
West Pakistan
East Pakistan

Bangladesh
Kashmir
Khmer Rouge
Palestinian Liberation Organization (PLO)
Hamas
Fatah
Arab League
Iran
Kurdistan Workers' Party (PKK)
Gold Coast
Organization of African Unity (OAU)
African Union
FLN (National Liberation Front)
Kenya
Mau Mau
Kenyan African National Union (KANU)
Nigeria

STATE-BUILDING
partition
Balfour Declaration
Suez Crisis
Camp David Accords
one-party state
Algerian War for Independence
Fifth Republic
Algerian Civil War
Biafran Civil War

CULTURE
passive resistance
Zionist movement
Theodore Herzl
Pan-Arabism
Pan-Africanism
Igbos
mullahs
theocracy
Kurds
modernization theory
Dependency theory

ENVIRONMENT
metropoles
Niger River Delta

ECONOMICS
nationalized
International Monetary Fund (IMF)
corporatist
PEMEX
NAFTA
maquiladoras
drug cartels
Institutional Revolutionary Party (PRI)
globalization

1. What do Pan-Arabism and Pan-Africanism have in common?
    (A) Both required communist governments to succeed.
    (B) Both promoted cultural unity across state borders.
    (C) Both were policies promoted by colonial powers.
    (D) Both led to government control of agriculture.

Question 2 refers to the excerpt below.

National integration shall be actively encouraged, whilst discrimination on the Grounds of place of origin, sex, religion, status, ethnic or linguistic association or ties shall be prohibited. . . .

[The constitution shall] encourage inter-marriage among persons from different places of origin, or of different religious, ethnic or linguistic association or ties.

—The Nigerian Constitution, 1999

2. Based on the excerpt and the information in the text, which of the following common problems is Nigeria seeking to address?
    (A) Rebellion against land reform
    (B) Protests against one-party states
    (C) Conflict between different tribes
    (D) Resistance to transnational organizations

3. Which term refers to the takeover of an industry by the government of a state?
    (A) Globalization
    (B) Militarization
    (C) Modernization
    (D) Nationalization

4. Mohandas Gandhi, Ho Chi Minh, and Kwame Nkrumah were all nationalist leaders who
    (A) challenged an imperial power
    (B) committed genocide against opponents
    (C) embraced the idea of passive resistance
    (D) supported communist governments

Question 5 refers to the table below.

Ten Countries with the Largest Number of Muslims			
	Muslim Population	Percentage of Population That Is Muslim	Percentage of World Muslim Population
Indonesia	221,147,000	87	13
Pakistan	189,111,000	96	11
India	165,624,000	13	11
Bangladesh	148,821,000	90	8
Nigeria	88,577,000	50	5
Egypt	86,895,000	100	5
Turkey	81,619,000	100	5
Iran	80,032,000	99	5
Algeria	38,424,000	99	2
Morocco	32,657,000	99	2

Sources: World Factbook, CIA, cia.gov.

5. Based on the information in this table, which statement best describes the distribution of Muslims in the world today?

 (A) The three countries that were at the centers of the Islamic Gunpowder Empires are majority-Muslim countries today.

 (B) The Muslim population of the world is spread evenly across the globe today.

 (C) Muslims dominate the region where Muhammad once lived.

 (D) Countries with the largest Muslim populations are mostly in the Middle East.

6. Which statement best describes the outcome of the Suez Crisis?

 (A) Relations between the United States and Egypt deteriorated.

 (B) Israel's power in the Middle East grew stronger.

 (C) Prestige of the United Nations declined.

 (D) Interests of Egypt and international trade were balanced.

7. What was a common result of the creation of the states of Pakistan and Israel?

   (A) Decrease in religious conflicts

   (B) Establishment of communist governments

   (C) Resettlement of large populations

   (D) Rise of military dictatorships

8. What effect of British colonialism created later tensions in Kenya?

   (A) Presence of a strong Christian minority

   (B) Presence of Islamist extremists

   (C) Presence of communist rebels

   (D) Presence of a large Asian population

9. What was the purpose of land reform in Latin American countries?

   (A) Improvement in agricultural practices

   (B) Redistribution of wealth to the poor

   (C) Promotion of economic competition

   (D) Solutions to environmental problems

10. In the 1980s, one major difference between the countries of Turkey and Iran was that

   (A) only Turkey had large oil reserves

   (B) only Turkey was an ally of the Soviet Union

   (C) only Iran had a government dominated by religious leaders

   (D) only Iran had a population that was mostly Muslim

CONTINUITY AND CHANGE-OVER-TIME ESSAY QUESTIONS

Directions: You are to answer the following question. You should spend 5 minutes organizing or outlining your essay. Write an essay that:

- Has a relevant thesis and supports that thesis with appropriate historical evidence.
- Addresses all parts of the question.
- Uses world historical context to show continuities and changes over time.
- Analyzes the process of continuity and change over time.

1. Analyze continuities and change in the relationship between Israel and Egypt between 1948 and the present.

Questions for Additional Practice

2. Analyze continuities and change in the national politics in ONE of these countries between 1900 and the present:
    - Turkey
    - Mexico

3. Analyze continuities and change in government control of the economy in a country in ONE of these regions between 1945 and the present:
    - Latin America
    - Africa
    - Middle East

COMPARATIVE ESSAY QUESTIONS

Directions: You are to answer the following question. You should spend 5 minutes organizing or outlining your essay. Write an essay that:

- Has a relevant thesis and supports that thesis with appropriate historical evidence.
- Addresses all parts of the question.
- Makes direct, relevant comparisons.
- Analyzes relevant reasons for similarities and differences.

1. Analyze similarities and differences in the process of achieving independence after World War II in TWO of these countries:
    - India
    - Algeria
    - Kenya

Questions for Additional Practice

2. Analyze similarities and differences in the challenges faced by TWO of the following leaders and how they responded to those challenges:
    - Gandhi
    - Ho Chi Minh
    - Kwame Nkrumah
    - Gamal Abdel Nasser

3. Analyze the similarities and differences in the partition of India in 1947 and the partition of Palestine in 1948.

For most of human history, continuity dominated and change occurred slowly. Today, change seems dominant, making continuity harder to see. *For each statement, decide if it represents change or continuity.*

1. "Our chaos" is indeed a theme of the period of decolonization as empires broke apart and . . . states began to break away and re-form.

2. During the 1960s, both Turkey and Iran relaxed restrictions on women and increased democratic freedoms.

3. Present-day Iran occupies much of the same territory that was held in its glorious past by the Persian Empire of 600 C.E.

4. Iran continued to be ruled by a repressive fundamentalist Islamic regime noted for its anti-Israel and anti-Western stance.

5. Zionists said that the land was where Israelites had lived thousands of years ago.

6. Turkey has been an associate member of the EU since 1987. If accepted as a full member, Turkey would become the only EU member whose population is largely Muslim.

WRITE AS A HISTORIAN: GROUPING INFORMATION

To help readers follow the story, a good writer will group related facts together by time period, by region, or topic. *Group these statements into two sets of three related comments.*

1. Hindus and Muslims were united in one goal: to get rid of the British.

2. In 1979, the Shia cleric Ayatollah Ruhollah Khomeini became the Supreme Leader.

3. Immigrants from Pakistan and India to London illustrated the movement of former colonial subjects to imperial *metropoles*.

4. Muslims decided that they did not want to live in an independent India dominated by Hindus.

5. Muhammad Reza was forced to flee Iran when it was discovered that he had tried to replace the prime minister in a failed coup.

6. In 1921, power in the Shia nation of Iran was seized by Reza Khan, who declared himself shah.

30

Post-Cold War World, 1990–Present

Mr. Gorbachev, tear down this wall!

—Ronald Reagan, speech in West Berlin, Germany, June 12, 1987

President Ronald Reagan's appeal to Soviet leader Mikhail Gorbachev came two years before the Berlin Wall fell in 1989. Two years after the fall, a coup ousted Gorbachev from power. The Soviet Union had officially collapsed. The Cold War was over, and communist governments remained in only a few countries, including China, North Korea, Cuba, and Vietnam. For some 45 years, the United States and the Soviet Union's rivalry had dominated the world stage. For much of that time the threat of nuclear war loomed large. However, after 1991, the world was not free of problems.

The end of a bipolar world presented myriad opportunities, as well as several formidable challenges. Political borderlines changed, and economic interactions among nations expanded. With this new openness, particularly with regard to trade, the world became more interconnected than ever before, which produced mixed results. The post-Cold War world had to grapple with new democracies, vast economic inequality, ethnic conflict and genocide, terrorism, environmental degradation, and global epidemics.

Economic Globalization

Globalization is the process of interaction among peoples, governments, and companies of different nations of the world. Although the Indian Ocean trade and European imperialism are both examples of globalization, the term usually refers to the fairly recent phenomenon of a global economy more integrated than ever before. Global trade exploded with the end of the Cold War. The Eastern Bloc nations that had been under Soviet control suddenly could trade freely with capitalist democracies. While several nonaligned nations during the Cold War era had strict government control over economic markets, many of these nations, including India, relaxed restrictions on trade in the 1990s. International trade agreements and organizations helped further integrate the world's economy. The new global economy emphasized the predominance of the market over any national government. While many rejoiced at this trend, globalization had its critics, who pointed to labor exploitation and environmental damage as results of free trade policies. (Test Prep: Write a paragraph comparing the Indian Ocean trade with contemporary globalization. See pages 164–166.)

Rise of East Asian Economic Powers Almost immediately following the end of World War II, the United States invested millions of dollars in Japan. The 1980s were an economic boom time for that small island nation. The end of the 1990s, however, brought a financial panic to Japanese markets. By 2015, its economy had still not fully recovered from the downturn and from the effects of a severe earthquake and tsunami in 2011 that destroyed part of the nuclear power industry and spread radioactivity over a part of the country.

Closely following Japan were the *Asian Tigers*—Hong Kong, Singapore, South Korea, and Taiwan. Like the eighteenth-century mercantilist countries in Europe, they had strong government economic policies that promoted exports. They enjoyed high economic growth starting in the early 1960s. These regions rapidly industrialized and became major exporters and international centers of banking, finance, and information technology.

China became a formidable economic competitor on the world stage after the government enacted reforms in the late 1980s and 1990s. The Communist government reopened the Shanghai stock market in 1989. It also allowed private ownership. These moves attracted investments by foreign firms who rushed to build factories in China to take advantage of low wage costs. In the years since, China's economy became the third largest in the world behind the United States and the European Union.

India, Brazil, and Russia In the early 1990s, India opened its markets and allowed foreign imports into the economy. With its highly educated English-speaking workforce, India was able to develop a software and information technology powerhouse, drawing investment from American and European companies who looked to outsource jobs and to take advantage of lower labor costs. Multinational corporations, such as *Microsoft* and *Google*, also invested in the Indian economy. The influx of corporate wealth and foreign goods created a thriving consumer culture among India's middle class, the ranks of which swelled tremendously after 2000. In 2014, the Indian middle class was estimated to be the largest in the world, with more than 350 million people.

In spite of India's prosperity, the majority of Indians continued to live in wretched poverty. India's growth had been limited to the private sector. The Indian government did little to address the problems of its poorest citizens, who did not have access to clean water, health care, education, or other social services. Although the government claimed to have built roads or other infrastructure projects in India's rural areas, many of the contracts existed only on paper. Corruption within the Indian government translated into people living without the tools that would allow them to rise into the middle class.

Another rapidly growing country in the 2000s was Brazil. Its agribusinesses and steel industries in particular brought considerable wealth to the nation. However, its urban poor continued to live in dire conditions in *favelas,* or slums, on the outskirts of major cities such as Rio de Janeiro.

Russia's oil wealth markedly expanded its economy after the end of the Cold War. In the early 1990s, Mercedes-Benz dealerships and high-fashion boutiques appeared in Moscow and Russia's wealthier citizens became accustomed to luxury goods and prosperity. Russia and other oil-producing countries prospered as long as the price of oil stayed high. When the price of oil dropped, however, the economies of these countries declined rapidly. The number of homeless and unemployed in Russia, for example, rose astronomically when oil prices dropped in the early 2000s.

International Trade Organizations Several organizations contributed to the growth of the global economy after the end of World War II. Signed in 1947, the *General Agreement on Tariffs and Trade (GATT)* lifted restrictive barriers to trade. *Protective tariffs,* taxes on foreign imports, had been at an average rate of 40 percent prior to the GATT. By lowering and eliminating tariffs, the agreement promoted more international trade and helped restore economic prosperity to war-ravaged nations. By the 1990s, average tariff rates had sunk below 5 percent, easing the movement of goods across national borders.

In 1995, the *World Trade Organization (WTO)* took over the GATT's operations. The WTO made rules that governed more than 90 percent of all international trade. For several reasons, the organization became controversial. Its meetings were closed to the public, and its board members represented mostly corporate interests. Also, the organization's rules tended to favor trade over other considerations such as moral issues. For example, through strict application of its rules, a member nation that refused to purchase clothing made from sweatshop labor could be sanctioned by the WTO.

Resistance to Globalization Critics of globalization asserted that free trade was not always fair trade. In an environment friendly to free trade, global corporations often ignored the rights of workers, disregarded environment impacts, and made it virtually impossible for small businesses to survive. Developing nations complained that their economies could not grow properly when their businesses had to compete with established corporations from the developed world.

In 1999, the WTO's meeting in Seattle was shut down by a variety of interest groups, including labor unions, environmental groups, and family farmers. Though the protests did not force the WTO to change its rules or to become a more inclusive organization, the WTO protests brought issues at the heart of the new global economy to the world's attention.

Globalization and the Role of Technology Globalization made the world feel smaller, as did advances in telecommunications technology. The *Internet,* first developed for the U.S. Defense Department during the Cold War, became a regular tool of communication for the public by the late 1990s. Not only had communication become easier, but information was also much more abundant and accessible than ever before.

Technology and Revolution Mobile technologies such as cellphones and other portable devices put the tools of information creation and dissemination into the hands of individuals around the world. Through social networking sites such as Twitter and Facebook, the "fourth estate" as the media was known in the United States, became accessible to anyone, anywhere. The impact of this revolution became apparent quickly. In the United States, videos taken on cellphone of police brutality sparked outrage, inquiries into racial profiling, and riots against injustices perceived in the justice system.

Arab Spring December 2010 marked the beginning of the Arab Spring, a series of popular uprisings in many Arab countries and Iran. The year of uprisings were sparked by an incident in Tunisia in which a man set himself on fire in protest after police confiscated his fruit stand. Videos of the protests that followed the incident were shared on Facebook, disseminating the story to millions who would not have learned of the incident had it gone through official news channels. In Egypt, protests against the regime of President Hosni Mubarak erupted in Cairo and other Egyptian cities in January 2011. The protests were organized through social media. One month later, Mubarak stepped down, handing power to his vice president. In February 2011 in Iran, thousands of people prompted by messages on social media, went to the streets in rare protests against the government. These and other similar uprisings revealed the power of new social media technologies.

Global Popular Culture Early in the twenty-first century, products and services began to be traded globally. Multibillion-dollar corporations were in the forefront of this development because they could afford to advertise and distribute their products and services globally. People around the world became familiar with *global brands* such as Apple, Nike, and Rolex and American celebrities became global superstars. Athletes such as Yao Ming and LeBron James were known around the world.

After 2000, The global cultural marketplace also became more diverse. Japanese *anime*, for example, became hugely popular among Western youth. And Indian musicals made in *Bollywood*, the popular name given to the film industry in Bombay (Mumbai), enjoyed popularity worldwide. The United States, however, remained the dominant transmitter of culture around the world.

Americanization of popular culture had several important impacts. People the world over learned more about Americans than Americans learned of the rest of the world. Corporations headquartered in the United States, which usually did business in English, brought their language with them to new markets. Those wanting to work for these corporations had to also speak English. Globalization thus brought the growing predominance of the English language, an imbalance that created resentment among those who felt that American popular culture diluted their unique cultural identity.

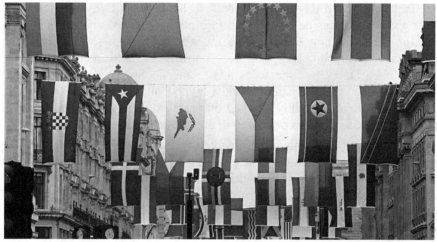

Source: Thinkstock

Since Olympic athletes represent their home nations, the games demonstrate the strength of nationalism. However, since the Olympics draw people together from nearly every country in the world, they are also an example of internationalism.

The globalization of popular culture was evident in sports as well. The establishment of the modern Olympic Games in 1896 reflected a growing sense of internationalism. In the 2000s, the opening ceremonies of the Olympics attracted nearly 200 million television viewers. The World Cup soccer competition also gained massive global audiences. In 2014, about 350 million watched it on television. Another sport that gained global popularity was basketball. Like soccer, it requires little equipment, so it can be played by almost anyone anywhere. In 2014, the premier professional league, National Basketball Association, included players from 30 countries or territories.

Additional evidence of globalization was the spread of new religious movements. In the early 1970s, the Hari Krishna movement, based on selected traditional Hindu scriptures, gained popularity in the United State and Europe after the former Beatles band member George Harrison released a song containing the words of a Hindu mantra, or sacred utterance. In what came to be called New Age religions, forms of Buddhism, shamanism, Sufism, and numerous other religions traditions were revived and repackaged for a largely Western audience. In China in the 1990s, Falun Gong, a syncretic movement composed of Buddhist and Taoist traditions gained popularity. Although the movement was initially supported by the Communist government, in 1999, the Chinese authorities began a nationwide crackdown on the practice. The suppression prompted international protests against the regime for human rights abuses.

Struggles for Democracy

The end of the cold war did not put an end to conflict. Indeed repressive regimes continued to exist, prompting democracy movements throughout the world.

South Africa Ends Apartheid South Africa's system of *apartheid*, which was put in place in 1948, institutionalized oppression in a nation that called itself a republic. Although white South Africans made up only 15 percent of South Africa's population, they were considered the only true citizens of the republic. So-called *pass laws* kept black South Africans from moving freely within their own nation. They were banned from living in certain areas of the country and had to carry passes when entering white areas, which they often had to do when traveling to their jobs. Mixed marriages were prohibited. For a while, schools for blacks were taught only in Afrikaans, the language of many of the white South Africans who ruled the nation. These dehumanizing decrees marginalized all South Africans of color who made up 85 percent of the population. (Test Prep: Write a paragraph connecting apartheid with South Africa's colonial past, see pages 471–474.)

In 1964, Nelson Mandela, a leader of the *African National Congress* (*ANC*), was imprisoned for life for agitating against apartheid. The ANC's primary goals were to end white domination and create a multiracial South Africa. Mandela's imprisonment throughout the 1960s, 1970s, and 1980s inspired a global movement to end apartheid. Black protests in South Africa, which were often peaceful, were crushed violently by the government's forces. South Africa's reputation grew worse in the eyes of the global community. Musicians staged concerts calling for Mandela's release from prison, college students urged their universities and corporations to divest from South Africa, and many countries voted for strict economic sanctions against the country.

As South Africa became a pariah state (undesirable state) in the 1980s, its leadership began to notice. Mandela himself began negotiations with the government in 1986 while still in prison. In 1989, F.W. de Klerk became the nation's acting president. Within six months, de Klerk announced Nelson Mandela's release from prison.

Although euphoria was high in the weeks following Mandela's release, apartheid remained the law of the land. Police violence against protesters persisted, which stalled negotiations between Mandela and de Klerk. However, a series of reforms in the 1990s ended apartheid. In 1994, South Africa held its first free elections. The African National Congress won the majority of the seats in the Parliament. The Government of National Unity was established with ANC members in the majority. On May 10, 1994, Nelson Mandela was sworn in as president, South Africa's first black leader.

One of the first acts of the Government of National Unity was to set up the *Truth and Reconciliation Commission* (TRC). Unlike the Nuremberg Trials that sought retribution for crimes against humanity committed by the members of Nazi regime during World War II, the TRC sought to restore and establish an atmosphere of trust in the new multiracial South Africa. The TRC set up a series of 19 public hearings designed to expose the truth of human rights violations that had occurred during apartheid, while at the same time granting amnesty to members of the apartheid regime who agreed to testify.

China's Citizens Protest for Freedom After economic reforms of the late 1980s and 1990s, China quickly became an economic powerhouse. The economic liberalization, however, was not matched by democratic reforms. The Chinese Communist Party (CCP) ruled the People's Republic with an iron fist. It censored the news industry and controlled what students were taught in primary and secondary schools. Such practices limited freedom of speech and thought. The CCP also required all non-state organizations and groups to register with the government. International nongovernmental organizations (NGOs) were not free to operate in China unless they were willing to undergo strict regulation. Opposition political parties did not stand a chance in China's governing system, although some debate was allowed in the legislative process. Overall, however, the governing system was designed to thwart all challenges to the CCP's authority. (Test Prep: Write a paragraph connecting China's government in the 2010s with the development of the Communist Party in China. See pages 557–558.)

Tiananmen Square Chinese intellectuals and college students had protested against their government before, including in the May Fourth Movement in 1919. In the spring of 1989, thousands of demonstrators, including students, professors, and urban workers staged a massive protest in Beijing's Tiananmen Square. The protests began when prodemocracy activists organized a public mourning of the death of a more sympathetic high official. The protesters demanded a chance to speak with Chinese leaders about freedom of the press and other democratic reforms. After the Chinese government refused to meet with activists, citizens in more than 400 Chinese cities staged sit-ins, refused to attend classes, and began hunger strikes. At the end of May 1989, the Chinese government declared martial law, and units of the army began to march into Beijing with orders to halt all protests. Beijing's citizens set up barricades to block the troops and even burned military vehicles. On June 4, the army arrived in Tiananmen Square, where most of the protesters had gathered and attacked unarmed protesters. The Chinese government claimed that nobody died in Tiananmen Square that day, but international organizations such as *Amnesty International* and the *International Red Cross* have made estimates of a few hundred to several thousand civilian deaths. Some *New York Times* reporters studied the numbers of admitted patients at nearby hospitals and estimated that anywhere from 200 to 400 civilians had perished.

Besides the loss of life, hundreds of prodemocracy activists were jailed. As late as 2015, the history of the Tiananmen Square crackdown remained censored. No mention of the event was included in school texts and all Web sites that discussed the Tiananmen Square incident and human rights abuses in China were blocked.

Minority Rights in China The Communist government in China struggled with the demands of its 55 ethnic minorities. Some prominent examples were calls by Tibetans for more autonomy or independence and the complaints of the Uighur people concerning religious and political discrimination in the northwest province of Xinjiang.

In 2011, some of the Mongolian people in China protested against the number of Han who have moved into Inner Mongolia, an autonomous region of northern China, and disrupted their pastoral way of life. The Mongolians staged protests against the environmental damage that came with settled agriculture, the strip-mining of coal, building of highways, damming of rivers, and overgrazing of land.

Environmental Degradation in China All provinces of China experienced environmental problems as a result of the rapid industrialization that started in the 1990s. Reduced rainfall coupled with development led to the expansion of the Gobi Desert, which covers large parts of China and Mongolia. At certain times of the year, Beijing's air filled with sand blowing in from the desert. All Chinese cities experienced *air pollution* resulting from the increased use of coal to run power plants and factories and the increased number of motor vehicles on the streets and roads. *Water pollution* was another serious problem. The Huang He, or Yellow River, was so polluted that it couldn't provide drinking water.

Water Problems in China Major construction projects in China had significant and widespread consequences. For example, the world's largest hydroelectric power station was built in the *Three Gorges Dam* on the Yangtze River. Its construction and the rising waters displaced some 1.3 million Chinese people. In the years after it was built, fears developed that the banks of the reservoir were collapsing and that earthquakes could cause landslides and massive flooding. The holding of so much water upstream deprived people who lived downstream of needed water for transportation and irrigation. Moreover, the building of the dam altered the ecosystem of the river.

Beijing and many other large cities used up the water in nearby aquifers and water had to be shipped in from elsewhere. These cities called for the construction of one or more large canals to divert water from the Yangtze or the Han rivers to more arid areas and cities in the north. This *South-North Water Diversion Project* would cost twice as much as the massive Three Gorges Dam and would require some 350,000 people to relocate.

Global Security

In the early 1990s, after the fall of the Soviet Union, President George H. W. Bush declared a *New World Order*, one in which the United States would take the lead in creating a unified and secure world. He believed the United States could bring Russia into the free market economy and world economic organizations led by the wealthiest nations. Bush also used the term in describing the coalition of nations that joined in the war against Iraq in 1991 after Saddam Hussein's forces invaded Kuwait. This *Persian Gulf War* resulted in Hussein's forces being driven out of Kuwait. However, the coalition, fearing that deposing Hussein was destabilize the Middle East, did not drive him from power.

Despite the lack of enmity between Russia and the West in the early 1990s, anger toward the United States existed in many regions of the world. Part of the anger was political. Other countries opposed how the United States exerted its influence as the world's sole superpower. Part of the anger was toward the Americanization of popular culture. Clerics in socially conservative societies, particularly those in the Middle East, objected to American media's permissive attitudes toward sex and gender roles. Ayatollah Khomeini of Iran was one of the first such clerics to reject American popular culture for such reasons.

Many Muslim nations were hostile to the United States, not simply because of Hollywood images or global brands. The United States donated millions of dollars to Israel every year, supplied its military with weapons, and did little to discourage Israel's occupation of Palestinian territory. Many people in Muslim nations felt that the United States had taken sides in the seemingly intractable Israeli-Palestinian conflict.

The Growth of Terrorism In the post-cold war period, open conflict between sovereign states were rare. Instead, individuals unaffiliated with any government formed *terrorist networks* that used violence and intimidation to make their point. Some of these networks, such as *Al-Qaeda,* advocated a fundamentalist interpretation of Islam. Financed by Saudi billionaire Osama bin Laden, Al-Qaeda carried out the devastating attacks of *September 11, 2001,* in which terrorists killed themselves and more than three thousand innocent people when they hijacked and crashed planes in New York City, near Washington, D.C., and in rural Pennsylvania.

In the years following the September 11 attacks, Al-Qaeda and similar groups carried out additional terrorist attacks that killed thousands of people. While high-profile attacks occurred in Madrid, London, and Paris, most victims were Muslims living in rural communities throughout the world. Several terrorists formed cells in Yemen—a poor country on the Arabian Peninsula—and used violence against the United States-backed government.

Other groups employed terrorist tactics as well. Basque separatists in Spain committed acts of violence to further their cause. Kashmiri separatists bombed a commuter train in *Mumbai*, India, in 2006. Two years later, a militant organization based in Pakistan staged bombing and shooting attacks in more than ten sites around Mumbai, killing more than 170 people.

Responses to Terrorism Within months of the September 11 attacks, U.S. President George W. Bush persuaded Congress to declare war on *Afghanistan,* the suspected hiding place of Osama bin Laden.

As war in Afghanistan heated up, the Bush administration began planning a war against Iraq. Members of the administration claimed that Iraqi dictator Saddam Hussein was stockpiling weapons of mass destruction and was connected to the September 11 terrorists. In spite of little evidence to support these claims, U.S. and a few allied forces invaded Iraq in May 2003. Resistance to the Iraq War emerged in the United States and around the world. The *Iraq War* (2003–2011) depleted much of the international community's post-September 11 sympathy for the United States.

In 2003, Saddam Hussein was captured, and in 2006 a special Iraqi tribunal prosecuted him for crimes against humanity and had him executed by hanging. Since 2003, no links of Saddam Hussein to Al Qaeda have been found, nor have any weapons of mass destruction been located in Iraq. In its first five years, the war killed more than 4,000 U.S. soldiers and untold numbers of Iraqi civilians. The war caused President Bush's popularity to plummet, and it tarnished the reputation of the United States throughout the world.

In 2011, U.S. forces located and killed Osama bin Laden. However, terrorism continued to threaten the United States and the world.

Countries with the Largest Defense Budgets, 2012	
Country	Total Defense (U.S. Dollars)
United States	$656 billion
China	$126 billion
Japan	$66 billion
United Kingdom	$61 billion
Russia	$59 billion
France	$51 billion
India	$45 billion
Germany	$41 billion
Saudi Arabia	$36 billion
Australia	$30 billion

Source: "U.S. Leads Global Arms Exports Surge," CNN Money. June 27, 2013. economy.money.cnn.com.

Genocide and Human Rights

The global community said "never again" to genocide after having experienced the horrors of the Holocaust. However, genocides continued to occur.

Bosnia Ethnic conflict drove the genocide in *Bosnia*. The end of World War I brought with it the creation of several new nations in Eastern Europe, including Yugoslavia, home to Serbians, who were Eastern Orthodox Christians; Croats and Slovenes, who were Catholic; and Muslims in the regions of Bosnia and Kosovo. Marshall Tito led Communist Yugoslavia from the end of World War II until his death in 1980. At times dictatorial, Tito managed to suppress separatist tendencies among the peoples of Yugoslavia.

After the collapse of the Soviet Union, Yugoslavia began to split apart as well. When Serbia, Slovenia, and Croatia declared independence, they each defined citizenship in terms of ethnic background and religion. Serbian nationalists led by the demagogue Slobodan Milosevic were particularly emphatic about ethnic purity. Serb forces, in attempts to dominate states such as Bosnia-Herzegovina and Kosovo, committed horrific acts of *ethnic cleansing* against Muslims from Bosnia and Kosovo, killing or driving people who were not part of the main ethnic group from their homes. Bosniaks, Kosovars, and Croats fought back, causing more casualties. Serb soldiers raped untold numbers of Muslim women. In total, more than 300,000 people in the region perished over the course of Yugoslavia's *balkanization*, or disintegration into separate states.

Rwanda One of the smallest countries in Africa, *Rwanda* was the site of one of the worst genocides in modern history. Ethnic hatred going back to the colonial era was behind the slaughter. Belgian colonizers had treated the minority *Tutsis* better than the majority *Hutus*. The latter group resented all the power that the Tutsis enjoyed. When Rwanda won independence from Belgium in 1962, the Hutu majority easily won control of the government and took revenge on the Tutsis by discriminating against them. In response, tens of thousands of Tutsis fled the country and formed a rebel army.

In 1993, Tutsi and Hutu forces in Rwanda began negotiations for a coalition government in which both ethic groups would share power. The negotiations were cut short in 1994 when Rwanda's president, a Hutu, was killed in a helicopter crash, supposedly shot down by rebel forces. This incident lit the flames of genocide. Over the next three months or so, between 500,000 and 1,000,000 civilians—mostly Tutsis—were killed. Perpetrators also targeted moderate Hutus. Some sources estimate that casualties were even higher.

International responses ranged from insufficient to callous. United Nations peacekeepers were instructed *not* to use force to restore order. There were also too few peacekeepers to protect all Rwandans. Individual countries, including the United States, evacuated their personnel from the country after Belgian peacekeepers were killed. UN peacekeepers and individual nations failed to evacuate any Rwandans. The Rwandan genocide focused attention on the lack of leadership in the international community. It became clear that the United Nations needed to think seriously about its role in violent conflicts if it wanted to effectively protect human lives and human rights.

Sudan Another genocide erupted in 2003 in *Darfur*, a region located in western Sudan. The people involved were all Muslims, but some were nomads of Arab descent while others are non-Arab farmers. The government of Sudan was controlled by Arab Muslims. Two Darfur rebel groups composed of non-Arabs took up arms against the Sudanese government in response to attacks from nomads. In response, the Sudanese government unleased Arab militants known as the *Janjaweed* on the region. Together with Sudanese forces, the Janjaweed attacked and destroyed hundreds of villages throughout Darfur, slaughtering more than 200,000 people, mostly non-Arab Muslim Africans. More than one million people were displaced, creating a refugee crisis that spilled into neighboring Chad. Despite negotiations, appeals, and actions taken by the International Criminal Court charging Sudan's President Omar Al-Bashir with war crimes, the genocide continued.

The genocides in Bosnia, Rwanda, and Sudan became stains on the conscience of the world. International organizations and the broad global community were supposed to defend human rights after the Jewish Holocaust. Considering the millions of lives lost and human dignity shattered, the failure of the international community appeared obvious. (Test Prep: Write a paragraph comparing recent genocides with the Holocaust. See page 542.)

Global Challenges

Alongside the challenges of global security and genocide, the global community had to grapple with hunger, environmental damage, and global epidemics.

Hunger There had long been relief organizations such as *CARE* and the UN's *World Food Program* that distributed food to starving people in times of emergency. Many people, however, looked for more long-term solutions to the problem through economic development and better farming practices.

The Green Revolution In the mid-20th century, the *Green Revolution* emerged as a long-range response. Scientists developed new varieties of wheat, rice, and other grains that had higher yields and greater resistance to pests, diseases, and drought. The new varieties were developed by *crossbreeding*—breeding two varieties of a plant to create a hybrid—and, more recently, by *genetic engineering*—using scientific techniques to manipulate a cell or organism to change its basic characteristics. Farmers also used more irrigation, fertilizers, and pesticides. In Brazil and elsewhere, forests were burned down and the land was plowed for agriculture. Acreage devoted to crops increased dramatically worldwide. Grain production increased sharply (see chart below).

The Green Revolution solutions were not free of problems. Many small farmers could not afford the new fertilizers or pesticides, reducing their ability to compete with large landowners. Many small farmers were forced to sell their land, increasing the holdings of large landowners even more. Also, since some of the techniques developed in the Green Revolution involved the use of mechanized equipment, fewer jobs were available for farm laborers. Finally, the heavy applications of chemicals damaged the soil and the environment.

Genetic engineering created its own set of concerns as well. Some argued that a genetic modification designed to give a plant resistance to insects might inadvertently cause a decline in the population of pollinating insects such as bees. Another problem was the loss of old seed varieties as new genetically engineered plants were adopted.

Environmental Challenges In the early twenty-first century societies were confronted by many environmental problems at once. Emissions of carbon dioxide caused by human activity, such as the burning of fossil fuels,

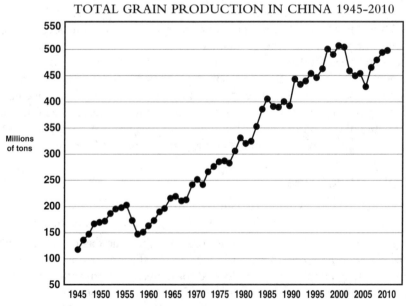

TOTAL GRAIN PRODUCTION IN CHINA 1945-2010

Source: National Bureau of Statistics of China, 2009.

began to increase the earth's temperatures. Scientists predicted that if nations did not curb their *carbon footprint*—the amount of carbon dioxide that each person produces—global warming would be catastrophic.

Many scientists believed that global warming was linked to more destructive natural disasters. Hurricane Katrina in 2005 was cited by some as evidence of this phenomenon. Severe flooding and droughts were also linked to climate change. It was understood that the blame for global warming could not be placed on one nation. But some nations clearly emitted more carbon dioxide than others. In 2007, China surpassed the United States as the world's biggest emitter of carbon dioxide. China's coal-powered energy plants and factories were mainly responsible. Also, automobile ownership had increased in China following the pattern in developed countries.

Efforts to Fight Global Warming It was difficult politically to get nations to agree on how to curb global warming. While developed nations in Western Europe and the United States focused some attention on the issue, rapidly developing nations such as China, Russia, India, and Brazil focused more on economic growth and viewed the environmental effects as an afterthought.

The international community organized around the goal of reducing carbon emissions. Most of the world's developed nations signed the *Kyoto Protocol* in 1997, but the United States refused to ratify it, making its provisions basically useless. Moreover, developing nations such as China and India were not required to agree to the strictest terms of the protocol. Following the failure of the Kyoto Protocol, scientists and diplomats worked to devise a new agreement acceptable to all carbon-emitting nations.

Earth Day Initiated in 1970, citizens in the United States designated April 22 each year as *Earth Day*, a day for people to focus on environmental themes such as recycling, developing alternative energy sources, eating locally grown and organic foods, and passing antipollution legislation.

Greenpeace With offices in some 40 countries, *Greenpeace* worked to counter deforestation, desertification, global warming, the killing of whales, and overfishing. The organization engaged in lobbying and direct action techniques, such as confronting whaling boats in the ocean.

Green Belt Movement Set up in 1977 by the National Council of Women of Kenya, the *Green Belt Movement* organized women in Kenya to plant trees to stop deforestation and soil erosion and to provide more fuel for home cooking. It also encouraged ecotourism. Green Belt organizations were set up in Tanzania, Uganda, Lesotho, Malawi, and Zimbabwe as well.

Alternative Energy As issues of global warming became more serious and immediate, companies and nations began to invest in alternative sources of energy, such as wind, solar, tidal, and geothermal power. Cost was a factor that slowed initial development of such sources. Over time, however, costs reduced enough that such sources became viable alternatives. While nuclear power was long considered a viable alternative to fossil fuels, serious accidents at three nuclear power plants—Three Mile Island in Pennsylvania (1986), Chernobyl in Ukraine (1989), and Fukushima in Japan (2011)—caused people to consider how to make this energy source safe.

Gender Issues In 1979, the United Nations adopted the Convention on the Elimination of Discrimination Against Women. The treaty outlined many rights and protections, including the right to vote and to hold office, the right to freely choose a spouse, the right to the same access to education as men, and the right to access to family planning resources and birth control. The convention also outlined laws against the trafficking of women and prostitution and against sexual assault.

Much progress was made since the signing of the convention. As of 2015, only two nations did not allow women to vote. The availability of microcredits allowed many women to start small businesses and to improve their economic condition and education and family planning improved the health of families.

Challenges remain, however. According to a report issued by the World Health Organization on March 8, 2012, "In many countries, women are not entitled to own property or inherit land. Social exclusion, 'honor' killings, female genital mutilation, trafficking, restricted mobility and early marriage among others, deny the right to health to women and girls and increase illness and death throughout the life-course."

Medical Challenges and Breakthroughs

Advancements in science and medicine eliminated many diseases. But some diseases persisted into, or emerged in, the early twenty-first century. Some of these related to poverty, including malaria, tuberculosis, and cholera. Others emerged as new global epidemics, such as HIV/AIDS and ebola. Yet others were known as lifestyle diseases such as diabetes and heart disease. Some conditions, such as Alzheimer's disease, mainly afflicted the elderly.

Antibiotics In 1928, Alexander Fleming was working in his lab in London when he accidently discovered that a particular fungus produced a substance that kills bacteria. He had discovered penicillin. Penicillin became the first *antibiotic*, a useful agent in curing infections.

Malaria A parasitic disease spread by mosquitoes in tropical areas, *malaria* killed more than 600,000 people per year, the majority of whom were young African children, in the early twenty-first century. The international NGO *Doctors Without Borders* treated about 1.7 million people annually with drugs. Preventative approaches were also developed, such as distributing mosquito nets treated with insecticide.

Tuberculosis A bacteria that affects the lungs causes *tuberculosis*. Before 1946, there was no effective drug treatment available, and many people died from the disease. A cure was developed involving antibiotics combined with extended periods of rest for the patient. In the early twenty-first century, a strain of tuberculosis resistant to the usual antibiotics appeared. The number of patients increased, especially in prisons, where people live in close quarters. For example, the Russian prison population suffered greatly. The *World Health*

Organization (*WHO*) began a worldwide campaign against tuberculosis in the 2010s.

Cholera A bacterial disease that spreads through contaminated water, *cholera* caused more than 100,000 deaths per year, mostly in developing countries. Methods to counter cholera include boiling or chlorinating drinking water or pouring water through cloth filters, a less effective form of prevention. Like tuberculosis and malaria, cholera is a disease that affects mainly poor people.

Smallpox The *smallpox* virus was a deadly killer through the centuries. The WHO's vaccination program eliminated the disease in the 1970s.

Polio Caused by water contaminated by a virus transmitted in fecal matter, *polio* once infected 100,000 new people per year. Dr. Jonas Salk first discovered an injectable vaccine against polio that was made available to the American public in 1955. An oral vaccine, developed by Dr. Albert Sabin, replaced the shots in 1961. The vaccines were adapted worldwide and polio infections were eliminated in all but three countries: Pakistan, Afghanistan, and Nigeria.

HIV/AIDS Between 1981 and 2014, the virus known as *HIV, Human Immunodeficiency Virus*, killed more than 25 million people. Although it began in Africa, the virus, which causes the disorder known as *AIDS, Acquired Immunodeficiency Syndrome*, claimed victims around the world. The virus attacks the body's T-cells, thus weakening the immune system. People who have AIDS more easily succumb to minor or major illnesses. AIDS patients are also susceptible to rare infections of the lungs and the surface of the brain.

Although HIV is preventable, misinformation regarding its spread persisted. HIV is contracted through the exchange of bodily fluids through unprotected sex or by sharing intravenous needles. A pregnant mother with HIV may infect her offspring during pregnancy, birth, or breast-feeding. Blood transfusions containing HIV antibodies also spread the virus. While nations in the developed world began screening blood donations for evidence of HIV, as late as 2014, many developing nations did not have the medical equipment necessary to screen blood. According to a WHO report, nearly 5 to 10 percent of all new HIV cases around the world were caused by blood transfusions.

Although a cure for AIDS has not yet been found, by the mid-1990s medical researchers had developed ways to treat the disease. *Antiretroviral drugs* stop HIV from weakening the immune system, thus allowing a patient to live with the virus for many years. Because these drugs are expensive, however, access to the latest drugs and proper treatment remained a challenge for most patients in the developing world. Since 2000, the United States government and private groups have increased funding for AIDS treatment in Africa, and the WHO has worked to increase funding for AIDS prevention programs and early treatment. However, the majority of infected people around the world still did not have access to the drug treatments that are available to patients in the developed world.

Ebola Discovered in the Congo in 1976, *ebola* is a deadly disease caused by a virus that infects the African fruit bat, humans, and other primates. Humans get the virus from exposure to fluids of infected people or animals. The disease causes extensive bleeding, organ failure, and, for the majority of infected people, death. In 2014, a massive outbreak in West Africa caused fear around the world. As of 2015, no effective treatment had been found.

Diabetes In 2015, almost 350 million people around the world had *diabetes*, a disease that affects how the body uses blood sugar. Considered a lifestyle disease, diabetes can damage a person's heart, kidney, eyes, and extremities. The treatments included an improved diet, regular exercise, weight control, and medications, including pills or insulin injections.

Heart Disease Like diabetes, *heart disease* is associated with lifestyle changes, genetics, and increased longevity. One of the major discoveries in fighting heart disease was the *heart transplant*, first performed by the South African Christiaan Barnard in 1967. Robert Jarvik led a team that designed an *artificial heart*, which was used as a temporary device while the patient waited for a compatible human heart. Less invasive procedures involved replacing valves, installing stents in arteries, and replacing the vessels leading to the heart. Many people with high cholesterol or triglyceride levels, both associated with heart disease, received medications to take on a daily basis. In the 2000s, many people with heart disease lived longer than similarly affected people did in the 1970s.

Alzheimer's Disease In the 2010s, a form of dementia known as *Alzheimer's disease* attacked a growing number of the elderly as well as some middle-aged people. Alzheimer's patients progressively lose their memory, eventually leading to a stage in which they do not recognize their loved ones. Some patients become aggressively angry. Since bodily functions are lost, the disease leads to death. As of 2015, Alzheimer's was incurable, although research aimed at a cure continued.

Annual Global Deaths by Infectious Diseases (in millions)		
Disease	**2004**	**2011**
Respiratory Infections	3.9	3.5
Diarrheal Diseases	1.8	2.5
HIV/AIDS	2.5	1.8
Tuberculosis	1.7	1.3

Sources: Center for Strategic Studies. smartglobalhealth.org; World Health Organization, who.int.

The end of the Cold War permanently altered the global paradigm. Inspired by the fall of the Soviet Union, the decline of communism, and the spread of democracy throughout the world, some intellectuals saw an optimistic future. In his provocatively titled 1992 book, *The End of History and the Last Man*, Francis Fukuyama posited that history as people knew it was over. He argued that democracy was the ideal form of government and capitalism was the best economic system, and they were spreading throughout the world. Eventually, all countries would adopt them and the political and economic conflicts that had driven wars in the past would vanish. Critics pointed out that 150 years earlier, Karl Marx had reasoned that scientific socialism would be the final phase of history, a prediction that had not come true.

One of Fukuyama's former teachers, Samuel Huntington rejected the entire end-of-history argument. In response, he wrote *The Clash of Civilizations and the Remaking of World Order* (1996). While Fukuyama was influenced by the end of rivalry between the United States and the Soviet Union, Huntington was struck by the increasing tensions around religion and culture. He claimed that people's beliefs and affiliations would draw the fault lines for conflicts in the post-Cold War world. Huntington cited several examples of cultural conflict, including Hindu and Muslim tensions in India and the rise of Islamic fundamentalism and its hostility toward Western culture.

Critics asserted that Huntington's generalizations were over-simplified and reflect a pro-Western prejudice. One of these critics, Nobel-prize winning economist Amartya Sen. In his 2006 work, *Identities and Violence: The Illusion of Destiny,* Sen rejected Huntington's suggestion that people of different beliefs and ethnicities could not get along, pointing to the existence of peaceful diverse societies around the world. Further, in an increasingly global world, people had many ways to identify themselves in the twenty-first century besides the old categories of religion and ethnicity.

The debate over the force shaping the post-Cold War world began before the Internet was part of everyday life for most people. By 2011, cell phones and other new technology were drawing people closer together around the globe. When physicist Mikio Kaku, published *Physics of the Future* (2011), he was optimistic that technology and trade could breakdown the cultural barriers that divide people. He did not predict the end of history, but he did hold out hope for material abundance and greater peace.

KEY TERMS BY THEME

ECONOMICS
Asian Tigers
Microsoft
Google
General Agreement
  on Tariffs and Trade
  (GATT)
Protective tariffs
global brands

ENVIRONMENT: ISSUES
favelas
air pollution
water pollution
Three Gorges Dam
South-North Water
  Diversion Project
Green Revolution
crossbreeding
genetic engineering
global warming
carbon footprint
fossil fuels
greenhouse effect
Kyoto Protocol
Earth Day
Greenpeace
Green Belt Movement
alternative energy
  sources

ENVIRONMENT: HEALTH ISSUES
antibiotic
malaria
tuberculosis
cholera
smallpox
polio
Jonas Salk
Albert Sabin
Human Immunodefi-
  ciency Virus (HIV)
Acquired Immunode-
  ficiency Syndrome
  (AIDS)
antiretroviral drugs
ebola
diabetes
insulin
heart disease
heart transplant
artificial heart
Alzheimer's disease

CULTURE
Internet
anime
Bollywood
Americanization
ethnic cleansing

SOCIAL STRUCTURES
apartheid
pass laws

STATE-BUILDING: HISTORICAL FIGURES
Nelson Mandela
F.W. de Klerk
Saddam Hussein
Osama bin Laden
Slobodan Milosevic
Omar Al-Bashir

STATE-BUILDING
World Trade
  Organization (WTO)
African National
  Congress (ANC)
Amnesty International
International Red Cross
New World Order
Iraq
Persian Gulf War
terrorist networks
Al-Qaeda
September 11, 2001
Mumbai
Afghanistan
Taliban
Iraq War
Bosnia
balkanization
Rwanda
Tutsis
Hutus
Darfur
Sudan
Janjaweed
South Sudan
World Health
  Organization (WHO)
Doctors Without
  Borders
UNICEF

1. Why do the majority of people in India continue to live in poverty despite their country's booming economy?

    (A) Because wealth from natural resources such as oil is not shared equally among all citizens

    (B) Because they have no representation in their country's elected government

    (C) Because the government has not provided needed services and infrastructure for all

    (D) Because ongoing ethnic conflict interferes with people's ability to find jobs

2. What is common to the free market economies now existing in former Communist countries?

    (A) Shift from an industrial to a service economy

    (B) Less government intervention in the economy

    (C) Nationalization of the most important industries

    (D) Elimination of all tariffs on imports

3. Which group is most likely to support the work of the World Trade Organization?

    (A) Corporate executives

    (B) Environmental activists

    (C) Labor unions

    (D) Leaders of small countries

4. Which of the following statements about globalization is most accurate?

    (A) Trade became global for the first time in human history during the twentieth century.

    (B) As global trade has increased, the world has become more culturally diverse overall.

    (C) Critics of globalization point out that many people work in very poor conditions.

    (D) Globalization has reduced the power of national governments.

Question 5 refers to the excerpt below.

The issue of a Truth and Reconciliation Commission has generated much public debate and some apprehension. The Minister of Justice is working to achieve broad agreement on this sensitive matter. In a nutshell, what this issue raises is how we deal with a past that contained gross violations of human rights—a past which threatens to live with us like a festering sore.

The question of amnesty for those who had done wrong is dealt with in the interim constitution. The challenge is to ensure that amnesty helps to heal the wounds of the past by also addressing the plight of the victims.

—Nelson Mandela, Speech to South African Parliament, August 18, 1994, after 100 days in office

5. Based on the excerpt and the information in the text, what can you conclude about how South Africa chose to move forward after the end of apartheid?

   (A) Black South Africans would get revenge against the white minority that had instituted apartheid.

   (B) Blacks and whites would seek ways to work together for the good of the whole country.

   (C) Punishment of those who committed violence during apartheid was the government's top priority.

   (D) The white minority government would not be held accountable for its actions during apartheid.

Question 6 refers to the map below.

GLOBAL WARMING

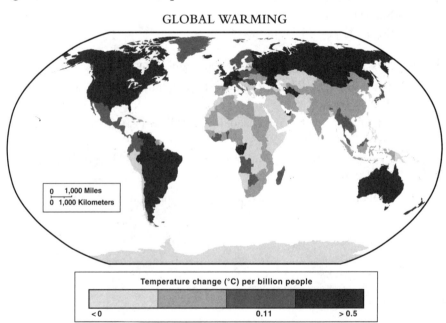

Temperature change (°C) per billion people

< 0   0.11   > 0.5

6. Which of the following statements is supported by the information shown on the map?

    (A) Countries with the largest populations are primarily responsible for global warming.

    (B) Highly industrialized countries have a large impact on global warming.

    (C) Developing countries have almost no impact on global warming.

    (D) Global warming is caused mostly by countries south of the equator.

7. Why have developing countries tended to place less emphasis on combating global warming than developed countries do?

    (A) Developing countries want the right to have a highly developed lifestyle.

    (B) Developing countries have few carbon emissions when they begin to industrialize.

    (C) Developing countries are rarely affected by global warming.

    (D) Developing countries are unaware of the problem of global warming.

8. Which of the following is true of terrorist groups and terrorist states?

    (A) They strike mainly against military targets.

    (B) They limit their fight to one region.

    (C) They strike military and civilian targets to influence the policy of one or more governments.

    (D) Membership in the group is limited to one ethnicity, religious affiliation, or ideology.

9. Which statement best represents the New World Order envisioned by President George H. W. Bush in 1990?

    (A) The United Nations would successfully resolve any conflicts between nations without the need of armed forces.

    (B) The new split in the world would be between the United States and Islamic countries.

    (C) The United States was ready to cede its global leadership to emerging economies such as China.

    (D) Other nations would follow the United States' lead to create a free and peaceful world.

10. What was a common cause of genocides in Bosnia, Rwanda, and Darfur?

    (A) Globalization

    (B) Independence movements

    (C) Ethnic and religious conflicts

    (D) Terrorism

CONTINUITY AND CHANGE-OVER-TIME ESSAY QUESTIONS

Directions: You are to answer the following question. You should spend 5 minutes organizing or outlining your essay. Write an essay that:

- Has a relevant thesis and supports that thesis with appropriate historical evidence.
- Addresses all parts of the question.
- Uses world historical context to show continuities and changes over time.
- Analyzes the process of continuity and change over time.

1. Analyze continuities and change in the attitudes toward the United States in ONE of the following regions from 1990 to the present:
   - the Middle East
   - East Asia
   - Latin America

Questions for Additional Practice

2. Analyze continuities and change in the economic development in ONE of these countries between 1980 and the present:
   - India
   - China

3. Analyze continuities and change between 1900 and the present, focusing on ONE of these topics:
   - agricultural innovations
   - diseases

COMPARATIVE ESSAY QUESTIONS

Directions: You are to answer the following question. You should spend 5 minutes organizing or outlining your essay. Write an essay that:

- Has a relevant thesis and supports that thesis with appropriate historical evidence.
- Addresses all parts of the question.
- Makes direct, relevant comparisons.
- Analyzes relevant reasons for similarities and differences.

1. Analyze similarities and differences between TWO of these examples of genocide in the late twentieth century:
   - Bosnia
   - Darfur
   - Rwanda

Questions for Additional Practice

2. Analyze similarities and differences between the goals and achievements of TWO of these international organizations:
   - United Nations
   - World Health Organization
   - World Trade Organization

3. Analyze the similarities and differences in the influenza pandemic of 1918–1919 and the HIV/AIDS epidemic that began in the 1980s.

THINK AS A HISTORIAN: USE SYNTHESIS IN A PARAGRAPH

When synthesizing information in an paragraph, the topic sentence should prepare the reader to see information from different sources or fields of study. Consider this sentence: "The conflict in Yugoslavia had religious, political, and historical roots." It suggests that the writer will follow-up with examples of three types of information that help explain the conflict in Yugoslavia. *Which of the TWO following statements would make the best topic sentence for a paragraph that emphasizes synthesis?*

1. With the new openness of the post-Cold War era—created by changed borderlines, expanded trade among nations, and more—the world is more interconnected than ever before.

2. Russia's oil wealth caused Mercedes-Benz dealerships and high-fashion boutiques to pop up in Moscow in the early 1990s.

3. Although the government claims to have built roads in India's rural areas, many contracts exist only on paper.

4. Japan had an economic boom in the 1980s, but by the end of the 1990s, a financial panic, a severe earthquake, and a tsunami combined to present severe challenges that are still delivering aftershocks today.

5. The Chinese government claimed that no one died in the Tiananmen Square protest, but Amnesty International and the International Red Cross have reported otherwise.

WRITE AS A HISTORIAN: USE COMMAS CORRECTLY

Commas provide guidance for natural pauses and breaks in the text. While writing essays, commas can help ensure that your sentences have rhythm and feel natural for readers. Using commas too often, however, can interrupt the fluidity of a passage. *Insert a comma (or commas) in the correct place in the following sentences. Not all sentences need a comma.*

1. Although India has experienced economic success in the past twenty years several social and political problems still plague the nation through poverty and corruption.

2. The Internet has enabled convenient communication accessible information and globalization.

3. Crimes against humanity still occur in the twenty-first century despite the advancements in equal rights for all people.

4. Serbian nationalists sought to eradicate the people of states like Kosovo and Bosnia-Herzegovina through ethnic cleansing.

5. If humans do not work to shrink our carbon footprint people will deplete the resources making the planet unsuitable for life.

PERIOD 6: Review

Thematic Review

Directions: Briefly answer each question in paragraph form.

1. **Interaction Between Humans and the Environment** Describe the environmental threats posed by global warming and explain the similarities and differences in the ways two or three countries have responded to these threats.

2. **Development and Interaction of Cultures** Describe two or three examples of the globalization of popular culture. Include an example of resistance to this trend.

3. **State-Building, Expansion, and Conflict** How did the two World Wars of the twentieth century affect the realignment, formation, and dissolution of states?

4. **Creation, Expansion, and Interaction of Economic Systems** How did global trade organizations that emerged after World War II change trade among nations?

5. **Development and Transformation of Social Structures** Explain the similarities and differences between the systematic anti-Semitism in Nazi Germany and the apartheid system in South Africa.

TURNING POINT: IS TODAY A TURNING POINT?

Looking for turning points in the present, historians try to see when change seems to outweigh continuity as they consider what might happen in the future. Some may argue that the end of the Cold War in 1989–1991 was the start of a new era, since conflicts no longer revolved around two superpowers. An event's significance may appear differently to people living through it than it does to historians. For example, the September 11, 2001, attacks seemed like a turning point at the time. Yet within 10 years, some historians view that attack as just one more event in an era of extremist violence. Historians who focus on how technology influences history might point to 2002, the year mobile phone usage surpassed landline phones and ushered in a new era of global communication. Maybe the great turning point of the era will be economic. It could be symbolized by when, as economists predict will soon happen, China becomes the world's largest economy.

DOCUMENT-BASED QUESTION

Direction: The following question is based on the accompanying Documents 1–10. (The documents have been edited for the purpose of this exercise.)

This question is designed to test your ability to work with and understand historical documents. Write an essay that:

- Has a relevant thesis and supports that thesis with evidence from the document.

- Uses all of the documents.

- Analyzes the documents by grouping them in as many appropriate ways as possible. Does not simply summarize the documents individually.

- Takes into account the sources of the documents and analyzes the author's point of view.

- Identifies and explains the need for at least one additional type of document.

You may refer to relevant historical information not mentioned in the documents.

1. Using the following documents, explain the factors that led Austria-Hungary to launch a war against Serbia. Why did Tsar Nicholas and Kaiser Wilhelm fail to prevent this regional war from becoming a general European war?

Document 1

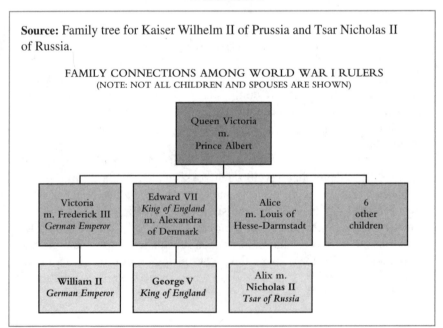

Source: Family tree for Kaiser Wilhelm II of Prussia and Tsar Nicholas II of Russia.

FAMILY CONNECTIONS AMONG WORLD WAR I RULERS
(NOTE: NOT ALL CHILDREN AND SPOUSES ARE SHOWN)

Document 2

Source: Baron Giesl von Gieslingen, ambassador of the Austro-Hungarian Empire, writing to the government of Serbia, in the summer of 1914

The July Ultimatum

In order to give these assurances a character of solemnity, the Royal Serbian Government will publish on the first page of its official organ of July 26/13, the following declaration: "The Royal Serbian Government condemns the propaganda directed against Austria-Hungary, that is to say, the whole body of the efforts whose ultimate object it is to separate from the Austro-Hungarian Monarchy territories that belong to it, and it most sincerely regrets the dreadful consequences of these criminal transactions.

"The Royal Serbian Government regrets that Serbian officers and officials should have taken part in the above-mentioned propaganda and thus have endangered the friendly and neighborly relations, to the cultivation of which the Royal Government had most solemnly pledged itself by its declarations of March 31, 1909.

"The Royal Government, which disapproves and repels every idea and every attempt to interfere in the destinies of the population of whatever portion of Austria-Hungary, regards it as its duty most expressly to call attention of the officers, officials, and the whole population of the kingdom to the fact that for the future it will proceed with the utmost rigor against any persons who shall become guilty of any such activities, activities to prevent and to suppress which, the Government will bend every effort."

Document 3

Source: *The Kaiser's Letters to the Tsar,* Isaac Don Levine, ed.

Tsar to Kaiser, July 29, 1914: Am glad you are back. In this serious moment, I appeal to you to help me. An ignoble war has been declared to a weak country. The indignation in Russia shared fully by me is enormous. I foresee that very soon I shall be overwhelmed by the pressure forced upon me and be forced to take extreme measures which will lead to war. To try and avoid such a calamity as a European war I beg you in the name of our old friendship to do what you can to stop your allies from going too far.

Document 4

Source: *The Kaiser's Letters to the Tsar,* Isaac Don Levine, ed.

Kaiser to Tsar, July 28, 1914 (this and the previous telegram crossed): It is with the gravest concern that I hear of the impression which the action of Austria against Serbia is creating in your country. The unscrupulous agitation that has been going on in Serbia for years has resulted in the outrageous crime, to which Archduke Francis Ferdinand fell a victim. The spirit that led Serbians to murder their own king and his wife still dominates the country. You will doubtless agree with me that we both, you and me, have a common interest as well as all Sovereigns to insist that all the persons morally responsible for the dastardly murder should receive their deserved punishment. In this case politics plays no part at all.

On the other hand, I fully understand how difficult it is for you and your Government to face the drift of your public opinion. Therefore, with regard to the hearty and tender friendship which binds us both from long ago with firm ties, I am exerting my utmost influence to induce the Austrians to deal straightly to arrive to a satisfactory understanding with you. I confidently hope that you will help me in my efforts to smooth over difficulties that may still arise.

Kaiser to Tsar, July 29, 1914: I received your telegram and share your wish that peace should be maintained. But as I told you in my first telegram, I cannot consider Austria's action against Serbia an "ignoble" war. Austria knows by experience that Serbian promises on paper are wholly unreliable. . . . I therefore suggest that it would be quite possible for Russia to remain a spectator of the Austro-Serbian conflict without involving Europe in the most horrible war she ever witnessed.

Document 5

Source: *The Kaiser's Letters to the Tsar,* Isaac Don Levine, ed.

Tsar to Kaiser, July 29, 1914: Thanks for your telegram conciliatory and friendly. Whereas official message presented today by your ambassador to my minister was conveyed in a very different tone. Beg you to explain this divergency! It would be right to give over the Austro-Serbian problem to the Hague conference. Trust in your wisdom and friendship.
Tsar to Kaiser, July 30, 1914: Thank you heartily for your quick answer. Am sending Tatischev this evening with instructions. The military measures which have now come into force were decided five days ago for reasons of defence on account of Austria's preparations. I hope from all my heart that these measures won't in any way interfere with your part as mediator which I greatly value. We need your strong pressure on Austria to come to an understanding with us.

Document 6

Source: *The Kaiser's Letters to the Tsar,* Isaac Don Levine, ed.

Kaiser to Tsar, July 30, 1914: Best thanks for telegram. It is quite out of the question that my ambassadors language could have been in contradiction with the tenor of my telegram. Count Pourtalès was instructed to draw the attention of your government to the danger & grave consequences involved by a mobilisation; I said the same in my telegram to you. Austria has only mobilized against Serbia & only a part of her army. If, as it is now the case, according to the communication by you & your Government, Russia mobilizes against Austria, my role as mediator you kindly intrusted me with, & which I accepted at you[r] express prayer, will be endangered if not ruined. The whole weight of the decision lies solely on you[r] shoulders now, who have to bear the responsibility for Peace or War.

Document 7

Source: *The Kaiser's Letters to the Tsar,* Isaac Don Levine, ed.

Kaiser to Tsar, July 31, 1914: On your appeal to my friendship and your call for assistance began to mediate between your and the Austro-Hungarian Government. While this action was proceeding your troops were mobilized against Austro-Hungary, my ally. thereby, as I have already pointed out to you, my mediation has been made almost illusory.

I have nevertheless continued my action. I now receive authentic news of serious preparations for war on my Eastern frontier. Responsibility for the safety of my empire forces preventive measures of defence upon me. In my endeavours to maintain the peace of the world I have gone to the utmost limit possible. The responsibility for the disaster which is now threatening the whole civilized world will not be laid at my door. In this moment it still lies in your power to avert it. Nobody is threatening the honour or power of Russia who can well afford to await the result of my mediation. My friendship for you and your empire, transmitted to me by my grandfather on his deathbed has always been sacred to me and I have honestly often backed up Russia when she was in serious trouble especially in her last war.

The peace of Europe may still be maintained by you, if Russia will agree to stop the milit. measures which must threaten Germany and Austro-Hungary.

Document 8

Source: *The Kaiser's Letters to the Tsar,* Isaac Don Levine, ed.

Tsar to Willy, July 31, 1914 (this and the previous telegram crossed): I thank you heartily for your mediation which begins to give one hope that all may yet end peacefully. It is *technically* impossible to stop our military preparations which were obligatory owing to Austria's mobilisation. We are far from wishing war. As long as the negotiations with Austria on Servia's account are taking place my troops shall not make any *provocative* action. I give you my solemn word for this. I put all my trust in Gods mercy and hope in your successful mediation in Vienna for the welfare of our countries and for the peace of Europe.

Document 9

Source: *The Kaiser's Letters to the Tsar,* Isaac Don Levine, ed.

Tsar to Kaiser, August 1, 1914: I received your telegram. Understand you are obliged to mobilise but wish to have the same guarantee from you as I gave you, that these measures **do not** mean war and that we shall continue negotiating for the benefit of our countries and universal peace.

Document 10

Source: *The Kaiser's Letters to the Tsar,* Isaac Don Levine, ed.

Kaiser to Tsar, August 1, 1914: Thanks for your telegram. I yesterday pointed out to your government the way by which alone war may be avoided. Although I requested an answer for noon today, no telegram from my ambassador conveying an answer from your Government has reached me as yet. I therefore have been obliged to mobilise my army.

AP® World History Practice Exam

Multiple-Choice Questions

Directions: Each of the questions or incomplete statements below is followed by four suggested answers or completions. Select the one that is best in each case.

1. Many archaeologists think that the first people migrated to the Americas by way of a land bridge across the Bering Strait. Which of the following types of evidence best supports this claim?

   (A) genetic similarity between modern Native Americans and Asians

   (B) spear points in America similar to those found in Europe

   (C) discovery of the site where maize was first cultivated in the Americas

   (D) the monumental architecture of the Chavin and Olmec cultures

2. After the Neolithic Revolution, which of the following characteristics was similar among both agriculturalists and pastoralists but different from earlier hunter-foragers?

   (A) People were living in settled communities.

   (B) People had mastered the use of fire.

   (C) People belonged to more clearly defined socio-economic classes.

   (D) People had begun to use stone and metal tools for farming.

Question 3 refers to the excerpt below.

By the immutable word of Enlil [a Mesopotamian god], king of the lands, father of the gods, Ningirsu and Shara set a boundary to their lands. Mesilim, King of Kish, at the command of his deity Kadi, set up a stele [a boundary marker] in the plantation of that field. Ush, ruler of Umma [a Sumerian city], formed a plan to seize it. That stele he broke in pieces, into the plain of Lagash [another Sumerian city, about 18 miles away] he advanced. Ningirsu, the hero of Enlil, by his just command, made war upon Umma. At the command of Enlil, his great net ensnared them. He erected their burial mound on the plain in that place.

—*Inscription by a Sumerian king*

3. Which of these effects of the development of civilizations can be inferred from this excerpt?

   (A) Civilizations developed new technologies of warfare.

   (B) Religion became separate from government power.

   (C) Violence became common as people became civilized.

   (D) Conflicts arose as communities established borders.

Question 4 refers to the map below.

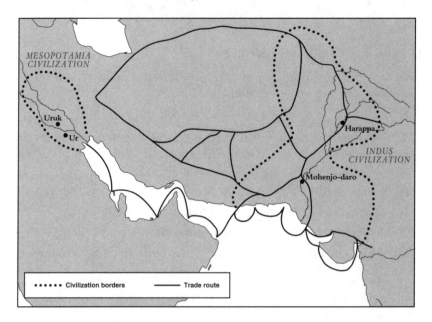

4. What characteristics of the development of civilizations is shown in the map?

   (A) The ability of some early states to conquer neighboring territories

   (B) The expansion of trade from local to regional

   (C) The diffusion of Vedic religion to Mesopotamia

   (D) The spread of new technology by pastoralists

5. Which of the following contributed most to the growth of the Jewish diaspora throughout the Mediterranean region before 600 C.E.?

   (A) Search for more fertile land

   (B) Missionaries' desire to spread the Jewish religion

   (C) Jewish involvement in the Silk Roads trade

   (D) Roman responses to Jewish revolts

6. Which of the following caused population decreases that contributed to the decline of the Roman Empire and the Han Dynasty?

   (A) Soil depletion from intensive agriculture

   (B) Religious warfare

   (C) Spread of diseases along trade routes

   (D) Climate change that affected crop yields

Question 7 is based on the following image.

Source: Wonderlane / Wikimedia Commons

7. This sculpture of the Buddha (1st–2nd centuries C.E.), from Gandhara in present-day Pakistan, reflects the influence of which of these empires on South Asia?

(A) Han

(B) Hellenistic

(C) Maya

(D) Persian

Question 8 is based on the following excerpts.

Hurt not others in ways that you yourself would find hurtful.

Udana-Varga [Buddhist]

Treat others the way you would have them treat you: this sums up the law and the prophets.

Gospel According to Matthew [Christian]

Do not do to others what you would not like yourself. Then there will be no resentment against you, either in the family or in the state.

Analects, 12:2 [Confucianism]

8. Which of these generalizations about new belief systems that arose between 600 B.C.E. and 500 C.E. is supported by the excerpts?

(A) They promoted universal truths.

(B) They came from a single source.

(C) They developed from ideas spread by trade.

(D) They were heavily influenced by local culture.

9. A common characteristic of the Mauryan, Han, and Hellenistic empires was

(A) heavy involvement in trade around the Mediterranean

(B) the imposition of political unity on previously competing states

(C) brutal treatment of conquered subjects

(D) promotion of a single state religion throughout the empire

10. Confucius's emphasis on honoring of ancestors and respecting and obeying parents supported a social structure in which gender and family relations were shaped by an earlier Chinese cultural pattern of

(A) egalitarianism

(B) legalism

(C) meritocracy

(D) patriarchy

11. Which of the following were used by the Mauryan and Roman empires to increase their military power and promote trade?

(A) Abolishing slavery within their borders

(B) Allowing local populations to join the army

(C) Building and maintaining roads

(D) Building walls and forts

12. The Greek and Mayan civilizations had which of the following in common?

(A) Both built pyramids as monuments to leaders.

(B) Both consisted of city-states.

(C) Both developed democratic governments.

(D) Both relied heavily on trade across seas.

13. Chang'an and Constantinople were similar in the seventh century CE. in that both were

(A) key cities on the Eurasian Silk Roads

(B) capitals, one of the the Mauryan Empire and one of the Byzantine Empire.

(C) wealthy port cities on Indian Ocean trade routes.

(D) religious centers, one for Confucianism and one for Islam

14. The Inca continued which pattern of labor from the earlier Andean civiliations including the Chavin and Moche?

(A) slave labor

(B) mit'a labor system

(C) encomienda

(D) tax and tribute

15. Which best describes the most significant cause of the split between the religious leaders in the Byzantine Empire and those in Rome?

(A) The Byzantine Empire evolved from a Christian theocracy to an Islamic theocracy.

(B) Leaders of Christian religious orders loyally supported the Byzantine emperor's decisions.

(C) The Byzantine emperor and religious leaders agreed to separate religion and politics.

(D) Byzantine Christians did not recognize the pope's supremacy.

Question 16 is based on the following map.

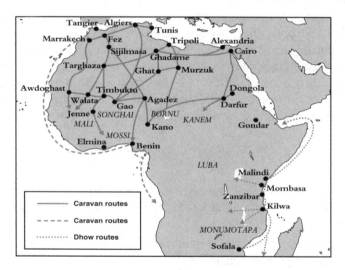

16. What significant economic developments are shown in the map above?

(A) Expansion of trade between Egypt and other African kingdoms before 600 B.C.E.

(B) Expansion of North African trade after the conquests of Alexander the Great.

(C) Expansion of trade after the arrival of Muslim merchants in the 700s C.E.

(D) Expansion of the African slave trade after 1500 C.E.

17. Similar to Jews, Christians, and Zoroastrians, followers of Islam

(A) believed that Jesus was divine

(B) honored spirits in nature

(C) revered a sacred stone

(D) worshipped one supreme deity

18. The return of Greek science and philosophy to Western Europe via Muslim al-Andalus in Iberia was the result of

(A) Muslim victory in the Battle of Tours

(B) increased cross-cultural interactions under tolerant rulers

(C) conquest of the region by Christian Crusaders

(D) the work of Muslim missionaries in the region

Question 19 is based on the following excerpt.

I saw a remarkable instance of the veneration in which the Damascenes hold this mosque during the great pestilence on my return journey through Damascus, in the latter part of July 1348. The viceroy Arghun Shah ordered a crier to proclaim through Damascus that all the people should fast for three days. . . . After the dawn prayer next morning they all went out together on foot, holding Korans in their hands, and the amirs barefooted. The procession was joined by the entire population of the town, men and women, small and large; the Jews came with their Book of the Law and the Christians with their Gospel, all of them with their women and children. The whole concourse, weeping and supplicating and seeking the favour of God through His Books and His Prophets.

Ibn Battuta, Travels in Asia and Africa 1325-1354

19. Based on the excerpt, which of these statements accurately reflects the extent of Ibn Battuta's intercultural knowledge and understanding about the Black Death?

(A) He observed that people of different faiths responded to the plague with similar religious practices.

(B) He doubted that fasting protected people from the plague.

(C) He understood that the plague affected people of all faiths.

(D) He noticed conflicts among people of various religious traditions about how to combat the plague.

20. The migration of the Bantu-speaking people throughout Sub-Saharan Africa was an example of

(A) the creation of a unified empire in an area of former competing states

(B) expansion of an existing long-distance trade network

(C) development of state-sponsored commercial infrastructure

(D) the spread of agriculture techniques to hunter-foragers

21. A common effect of the expansion of the Byzantine, Abbasid, and Mongol empires was

(A) development of decentralized governments

(B) facilitation of cross-regional trade and communication

(C) increase in agricultural productivity

(D) spread of Buddhism, Christianity, and Islam

22. A form of coerced labor that was common to Europe and Japan before 1450 was

(A) the encomienda

(B) indentured servitude

(C) serfdom

(D) slavery

Question 23 is based on the following excerpt.

Now that I have begun speaking of the Tartars [Mongols], I will tell you more about them. The Tartars never remain fixed, but as the winter approaches remove to the plains of a warmer region, to find sufficient pasture for their cattle; and in summer they frequent cold areas in the mountains, where there is water and verdure, and their cattle are free from the annoyance of horse- flies and other biting insects. During two or three months they go progressively higher and seek fresh pasture, the grass not being adequate in any one place to feed the multitudes of which their herds and flocks consist. Their huts or tents are formed of rods covered with felt, exactly round, and nicely put together, so they can gather them into one bundle, and make them up as packages, which they carry along with them in their migrations upon a sort of car with four wheels.

—Marco Polo, c. 1295

23. Which of these claims is supported by the evidence in the excerpt?

(A) Mongol women exercised more power and influence than women in Europe.

(B) Mongols used nomadic pastoralism as a form of labor organization.

(C) Significant cultural and technological transfers occurred across the Mongol empires.

(D) New forms of governance emerged in the Mongol Khanates.

24. What was the purpose of the construction of the Grand Canal under the Sui dynasty in China?

(A) to expand commercial growth within China

(B) to expand trade with the Abbasid Empire

(C) to provide irrigation for Chinese farmers

(D) to create a shortcut to the Indian Ocean sea lanes

25. The emergence of Zen Buddhism and Neo-Confucianism in China are examples of the
    (A) development of similar belief systems simultaneously in different regions
    (B) diffusion of cultural traditions through cross-cultural interactions
    (C) dominance of local cultural traditions over foreign influences
    (D) role of warfare in spreading cultural traditions

26. The growth of plantation economies in the Americas resulted in
    (A) diversification of agriculture
    (B) expansion of the number of landowners
    (C) increased demand for slaves
    (D) mechanization of farming

27. Which statement about cities is most useful in understanding the context in which urban populations changed during the period 600–1450?
    (A) Agricultural productivity changed in many civilizations.
    (B) Islam spread rapidly in the century following the death of Muhammad.
    (C) Latin evolved into several vernacular languages.
    (D) People learned how to use gunpowder in weapons.

28. What was a common characteristic of states in the Americas and in Afro-Eurasia in the period 600–1450?
    (A) Decentralized state government was the norm.
    (B) Older forms of state government persisted in all areas.
    (C) Social stratification declined in all states.
    (D) States expanded to control more territory

29. One result of the Columbian Exchange was that the population of indigenous people increased most significantly in
    (A) Europe
    (B) Africa
    (C) South America
    (D) North America

30. Which of these statements most accurately describes the role of sugar in the Columbian Exchange?
    (A) Sugar came from the Americas and became a staple crop in Europe.
    (B) Sugar came from Eurasia and became a cash crop in the Americas.
    (C) Sugar came from Africa and was grown by slaves in Africa.
    (D) Sugar came from the Americas and became a cash crop in Asia.

31. What effect did the increased interaction of hemispheres in the period 1450–1750 have on religion in the Americas?

(A) People blended elements of Christianity and indigenous faiths.

(B) Buddhism spread quickly throughout the region.

(C) Judaism became widely practiced in South America.

(D) Islam adapted to local cultural practices.

32. The Song Dynasty in China was the first state to mass produce steel primarily because China had long been advanced in science and technology and wanted steel for

A. stronger hulls for junks

B. replacing stone and iron bridges

C. weapons for its large army

D. stronger tools for peasants.

33. Portuguese travel to and trade with Africa starting in the late 1400s was an initial step in the

(A) voluntary migration of West African workers to Portugal

(B) large-scale migration of Portuguese settlers to Africa

(C) adoption by Africans of Portuguese agricultural practices

(D) establishment of Portugal's trading post empire in the Indian Ocean

Question 34 refers to the excerpt below.

Among the rights that the laws give the sovereign should be included [the right] to display all the signs of grandeur and majesty necessary to make manifest the authority and dignity of such wide-ranging and lofty power, and to impress veneration for it upon the minds of all subjects. For although they should see in it the power of God Who has established it and should revere it apart from any visible signs of grandeur, nevertheless since God accompanies His own power with visible splendor on earth and in the heavens as in a throne and a palace.

—*Jean Domat, The Civil Law in Its Natural Order, 1689*

34. This excerpt is from a book written during the reign of Louis XIV of France in the late 1600s. Which methods used by rulers to legitimize their power are supported by the excerpt?

(A) Use of military force

(B) Use of the arts and religious ideas

(C) Reliance on a social contract

(D) Appeal to legal precedent

35. Which statement correctly describes the difference between the Ottoman Empire and the Spanish Empire in the period 1450–1750?

(A) The Ottoman Empire was Protestant and the Spanish Empire was Catholic.

(B) The Ottoman Empire ruled Asia and the Spanish Empire ruled Europe.

(C) The Ottoman Empire was based on agriculture and the Spanish Empire was based on industry.

(D) The Ottoman Empire was land-based and the Spanish Empire was a maritime empire.

Questions 36 and 37 are based on the following chart.

Trans-Atlantic Slave Trade, 1514–1866			
	Total number of slaves	Total number of voyages	Average
Number leaving Africa	10,147,907	33,366	304 people
Number arriving in the Americas	8,752,593	33,047	265 people
Percentage of slaves embarked who died during voyage			12%
Length of Middle Passage			60 days
Percentage male			65%
Percentage children			21%
Size of vessel		17,606 tons	158 tons

Source: Adapted from the Trans-Atlantic Slave Trade Database, Emory University.

36. Which effect of the Atlantic slave trade on Africa is supported by the data in this chart?

(A) An increase in regional conflict

(B) A disturbance of the gender balance

(C) An improvement in African diet

(D) An increase in the death rate among children

37. Which statement about the sixteenth and seventeenth centuries provides the most useful context for understanding the significance of the information in this table?

(A) The Reformation in Europe created a split in Christianity.

(B) Global demand for sugar, tobacco, and coffee increased.

(C) The Manchus seized control of China.

(D) "Gunpowder" empires emerged in Turkey, Persia, and India.

38. Which development is most important for understanding the context of global economic change in the period 1450–1750?

(A) the Chinese began to use "flying cash"

(B) deposits of gold were found in West Africa

(C) the Spanish began exporting silver from American silver mines

(D) European banks began to issue letters of credit

39. Some world historians question the idea that Peter the Great's reforms in Russia in the early 18th century actually resulted in modernization. Which of these facts best supports their argument?

(A) Serfdom spread to Siberia and continued past the middle of the 19th century.

(B) St. Petersburg was laid out in an orderly fashion and infrastructure improved.

(C) The Russian aristocracy became better educated about European culture.

(D) Peter established state-sponsored industries in shipbuilding and mining.

40. One of the causes of conflict between the Ottoman Empire and the Safavid Empire was a religious clash between

(A) Catholics and Protestants

(B) Hindus and Muslims

(C) Jews and Christians

(D) Sunni and Shi'a Muslims

41. Which of these traditional trading regions was most affected by the Portuguese conquest of the Swahili city-states of East Africa in the late 1400s?

(A) Overland Eurasia

(B) Sahara

(C) Indian Ocean

(D) Mediterranean

42. The relationship between the shogun and the daimyo in Japan during the Tokugawa Shogunate and between Louis XIV and the French nobility are examples of

(A) the growth of representative government

(B) the fluctuating power of elites versus rulers

(C) the emerging power of merchants

(D) the oppression of ethnic minorities by conquerors

43. Which of the following changes best justifies the claim that a new period in world history began circa 1750?

(A) James Watt developed the first useful steam engine.

(B) The Ottoman Empire and the Manchu dynasty ended.

(C) Islam continued to spread through Africa and Asia.

(D) The British and French fought several wars involving their colonies.

44. Which statement most accurately explains a reason that a particular country industrialized successfully?

(A) France was heavily urbanized by the early nineteenth century.

(B) Germany was political united by 1848.

(C) The United States had a large quantity of human capital.

(D) Russia had large tracts of agricultural land.

45. Which factor was a key reason behind the emergence of Meiji Japan?

(A) Weakening of the power of the Japanese emperor

(B) Cooperation between Japan and Russia

(C) Contraction of the Ottoman Empire

(D) Increasing military and political pressure from Britain and the United States

Question 46 is based on the following graph.

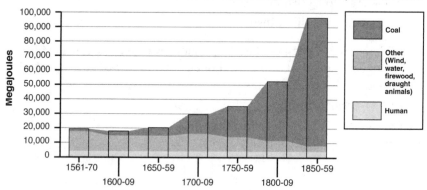

ANNUAL ENERGY CONSUMPTION PER PERSON IN ENGLAND AND WALES, 1561 TO 1859

Source: Wrigley, E. A., *Energy and the English Industrial Revolution.*

46. Which characteristic of the Industrial Revolution is shown in the graph above?

(A) Reliance on water power by early factories in Britain

(B) Growth in energy use from fossil fuels to power new machines

(C) Growth of empires based on the need for raw materials for industry

(D) Rapid increases in productivity under the factory system

47. Which of the following was both a factor that led to the rise of industrial production and a result of industrialization?

(A) Centralization of production

(B) Formation of joint-stock companies

(C) Growth of isolationism

(D) Increased urbanization

Question 48 is based on the following excerpts.

We hold these truths to be self-evident: That all men are created equal; that they are endowed by their Creator with certain unalienable rights; that among these are life, liberty, and the pursuit of happiness; that, to secure these rights, governments are instituted among men, deriving their just powers from the consent of the governed; that whenever any form of government becomes destructive of these ends, it is the right of the people to alter or to abolish it, and to institute new government, laying its foundation on such principles, and organizing its powers in such form, as to them shall seem most likely to effect their safety and happiness.

American Declaration of Independence, 1776

The representatives of the French people, organized as a National Assembly, believing that the ignorance, neglect, or contempt of the rights of man are the sole cause of public calamities and of the corruption of governments, have determined to set forth in a solemn declaration the natural, unalienable, and sacred rights of man, in order that this declaration, being constantly before all the members of the Social body, shall remind them continually of their rights and duties; in order that the acts of the legislative power, as well as those of the executive power, may be compared at any moment with the objects and purposes of all political institutions and may thus be more respected, and, lastly, in order that the grievances of the citizens, based hereafter upon simple and incontestable principles, shall tend to the maintenance of the constitution and redound to the happiness of all.

The French Declaration of the Rights of Man, 1789

48. Based on the previous excerpts, what is the common purpose of both of these declarations?

(A) To affirm that unalienable human rights must form the basis of government

(B) To justify a separation between a colony and an imperial power

(C) To outline the structure of a new form of representative government

(D) To promote an alliance between the United States and France

49. Which statement provides the clearest evidence of the role of South America in global trade in the period 1750–1900?

(A) Mexican mines produced copper for use in European industry.

(B) Brazil exported large quantities of sugar and coffee.

(C) Argentinian developed extensive internal trade networks.

(D) Bolivia took its name from a revolutionary leader.

50. Which provides the best evidence for the theory that developments in science and technology shape how people view society?

(A) arguing that the growth of the middle class led to new inventions

(B) proposing that workers should own the means of production

(C) explaining why material prosperity was a reflection of moral superiority

(D) using the ideas of Charles Darwin to justify imperialism

51. In what way were Qing China and the Ottoman Empire different from Japan in the late 19th century?

(A) Chinese and Ottomans expanded their empires while Japan remained isolated.

(B) Chinese and Ottomans often resisted industrialization while Japan embraced it.

(C) Chinese and Ottomans maintained strong central governments while Japan's became more decentralized.

(D) Chinese and Ottomans were tolerant of foreigners while Japan excluded them.

52. Which of the following is the best evidence that a new period in the structure of empires began in the mid-nineteenth century?

(A) the development of the palm oil industry

(B) the growth of urbanization

(C) the Indian Revolt of 1857

(D) the Taiping Rebellion

53. Which of the following was a result of the Latin American independence movements of the early nineteenth century?

(A) Strengthening of the mercantilist system throughout the region

(B) Increased power for creoles and local Roman Catholic leaders

(C) Increased political participation by Indians

(D) Greater equality for members of all racial and ethnic groups

54. Which statement provides the best evidence to support the idea that liberalism reflected discontent with monarchist and imperialist rule in nineteenth century Europe?

(A) the rise of constitutional governments

(B) the creation of government-sponsored utopian communities

(C) the emergence of public ownership of industries

(D) the evolution of workers' trade unions

55. How did global migrations in the ninetenth century affect the role of women?

(A) Women and men migrated equally throughout the word and competed for jobs in new industries.

(B) As men migrated away from Europe, women who did not migrate assume new roles outside of their homes.

(C) As men migrated away from Europe, women chose not to migrate because they were more focused on raising children.

(D) Women migrated more often than men did as a result of higher demand for women's skills in industry.

56. What did the United States and Russia have in common in the period 1750–1900?

(A) Both established settler colonies in Africa.

(B) Both experienced revolutions that established their independence from a colonial power.

(C) Both conquered neighboring territories to expand their borders.

(D) Both developed critiques of industrialization based on communist principles.

57. The new period in the history of the Middle East during the first two decades of the twentieth century was characterized by

(A) the spread of ideas such as cubism

(B) the end of the Ottoman Empire

(C) the establishment of Israel as a homeland for Jews

(D) the increased role of Russia in the region

58. One cause of the global conflicts in the first half of the twentieth century was great power rivalries between

(A) China and Japan

(B) France and Russia

(C) Germany and Great Britain

(D) the United States and the Soviet Union

Question 59 is based on the following image.

Source: National Archives and Record Administration / Wikimedia Commons
We French Workers Warn You... by Ben Shahn, 1942

59. Which characteristic of total war is reflected in this poster from World War II?

(A) Government use of propaganda to mobilize populations.

(B) Government use of colonial subjects as soldiers.

(C) Government use of military conscription to raise troops.

(D) Government use of war bonds to raise funds for the military.

60. One piece of evidence that World Wars I and II were global conflicts is that both

(A) started in Asia but were fought primarily in Europe

(B) included large battles in Latin America and Australia

(C) involved fighting by more soldiers from British and French colonies

(D) lasted far longer than previous wars

61. Which of the following was a consequence of India achieving independence from Britain in 1947?

(A) Violence between Hindus and Muslims after the region was divided

(B) Return of all Indians living in Britain back to India

(C) End of diplomatic relations between India and Britain

(D) Decrease in trade between India and Britain over the following century

62. Which statement best summarizes the process of decolonization in Ghana, Algeria, and Nigeria?

(A) Colonial independence usually required violence to succeed.

(B) Colonies achieved independence in a variety of ways.

(C) European countries generally supported orderly decolonization.

(D) Fighting for independence ended ethnic rivalries in African states.

Question 63 is based on the following excerpt.

"More than two years ago twenty nine governments of independent states convened together at the Bandung Conference to declare to the world at large that the tide of history has changed its course, and that Asia and Africa, which hitherto have been common play ground, where trespassers went by unheeded or a forest in which foreign beasts of prey roamed at leisure, have now become free world powers, majestic and serene, with a decisive role in shaping the future of the whole family of Nations. The Conference of Bandung was likewise convened to stress to the peoples of Africa and Asia the great importance of solidarity and the great weight they would have on the trend of world affairs when united."

Anwar el Sadat, speech at the First Afro-Asian People's Solidarity Conference, December 26, 1957

63. The ideas expressed in the excerpt are most supportive of the

(A) anti-globalization movement

(B) anti-nuclear movement

(C) Biafran separatist movement

(D) Pan-Africanism, Pan-Arabism, and Non-Alignment movement

64. Which of the following is the best generalization about the Green Revolution?

(A) It helped people return to traditional agricultural practices.

(B) It emphasized raising food for local consumption.

(C) It focused on reducing air and water pollution.

(D) It used modern technology to increase crop production.

65. Which event caused the governments of Europe and the United States to take a more active role in their nations' economies?

(A) Industrial Revolution

(B) Start of World War I

(C) The Great Depression

(D) End of the Cold War

66. Which of the following occurred as a result of the Cold War?

(A) Closer ties between the Soviet Union and China

(B) New regional trade agreements in North America

(C) Proxy wars in Asia, Africa, and Latin America

(D) Use of violence against civilians to achieve political aims

67. Which of these events is most often used by historians as the end of a period in history?

(A) President Nixon's visit to China marked the end of the rivalry between the United States and China.

(B) The collapse of the Soviet Union marked the end of the Cold War.

(C) The dropping of the first atomic bomb marked the end of Japan's rise as an industrial power.

(D) The end of the Vietnam War marked the end of the United States as a superpower.

Question 68 is based on the following graph.

GLOBAL GREENHOUSE GAS EMISSIONS BY SOURCE, 2004

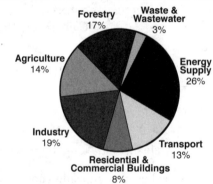

Source: Intergovernmental Panel on Climate Change, 2007

68. The data in this graph would most strongly support an argument about

(A) the effects of global warming on various industries

(B) how global warming affects different species

(C) which countries emit the most greenhouse gases

(D) how human activities contribute to global warming

69. Which generalization about world health at the end of the twentieth century is true?

   (A) Most contagious diseases were eliminated by improved public health.

   (B) Though most diseases persisted, medical innovations improved survival rates.

   (C) Similar diseases tended to dominate both rich and poor countries.

   (D) Global epidemics were less likely to occur than in the past.

70. Movements that protested increased global integration in the late twentieth century were generally concerned about

   (A) the inequality of environmental and economic effects of globalization

   (B) new international organizations that promoted global cooperation

   (C) the spread of communism that threatened democracy worldwide

   (D) the spread of disease pathogens along global trade routes

Free-Response Questions

PART A: DOCUMENT-BASED QUESTION

Directions: The following question is based on the accompanying Documents 1–10. (The documents have been edited for the purpose of this exercise.)

This question is designed to test your ability to work with and understand historical documents. Write an essay that:

- Has a relevant thesis and supports that thesis with evidence from the document.

- Uses all of the documents.

- Analyzes the documents by grouping them in as many appropriate ways as possible. Does not simply summarize the documents individually.

- Takes into account the sources of the documents and analyzes the author's point of view.

- Identifies and explains the need for at least one additional type of document.

You may refer to relevant historical information not mentioned in the documents.

1. Using the following documents, analyze continuities and changes in the relationship between China and Great Britain between 1792 and 1900. Identify an additional type of document and explain how it would help your analysis of these continuities and changes.

Historical Background: In the late eighteenth century, Europeans who wanted to trade with China were limited to the city of Canton (Guangzhou). In 1792, Lord Macartney, a British statesman and foreign diplomat, became the first British envoy to China and met briefly with Chinese Emperor Qianlong. At the time, opium was grown in great quantities in British India and the Ottoman Empire. The British East India Company, a joint-stock company chartered in 1600, represented the interests of the British government in Asia.

Document 1

Source: Chris Feige and Jeffrey A. Miron, "The Opium Wars, Opium Legalization, and Opium Consumption in China," Applied Economics Letters 15(12): 911–913.

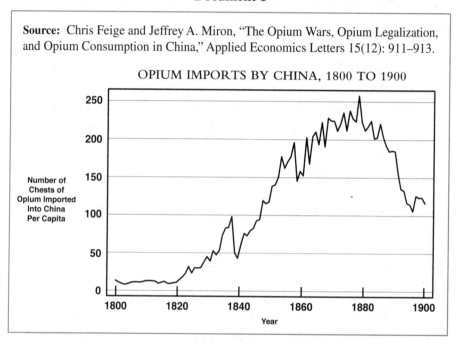

OPIUM IMPORTS BY CHINA, 1800 TO 1900

Number of Chests of Opium Imported Into China Per Capita

Document 2

Source: A Dutch version of a British cartoon showing the Chinese receiving Lord Macartney in 1792.

Source: Maastricht University Library / Wikimedia Commons

Document 3

Source: Chinese Emperor Qianlong's letter to Britain's King George III, 1793.

The Celestial Court has pacified and possessed the territory within the four seas. Its sole aim is to do the utmost to achieve good government and to manage political affairs, attaching no value to strange jewels and precious objects. The various articles presented by you, O King, this time are accepted by my special order to the office in charge of such functions in consideration of the offerings having come from a long distance with sincere good wishes. As a matter of fact, the virtue and respect of the Celestial Dynasty having spread far and wide, the kings of the myriad nations come by land and sea with all sorts of precious things. Consequently there is nothing we lack, as your principal envoy and others have themselves observed. We have never set much store on strange and ingenious objects, nor do we need any more of your country's manufactures.

Document 4

Source: Lord Macartney, describing his first visit to China. 1793.

Thus, then have I seen 'King Solomon in all his glory.' I use this expression, as the scene recalled perfectly to my memory a puppet show of that name which I recollect to have seen in my childhood, and which made so strong an impression on my mind that I then thought it a true representation of the highest pitch of human greatness and felicity.

Document 5

Source: Lin Zexu, Imperial Commissioner stationed in Canton. Letter to Queen Victoria, 1839.

We find that your country is sixty or seventy thousand li from China. Yet there are barbarian ships that strive to come here for trade for the purpose of making a great profit. The wealth of China is used to profit the barbarians . . . . By what right do they use this poisonous drug to injure the Chinese people?
I have heard that the smoking of opium is very strictly forbidden by your country; that is because the harm caused by opium is very clearly understood. Since it is not permitted to do harm in your country, then even less should you allow it to be passed on to do harm in other countries. Of all that China exports to other countries, there is not a single thing that is not beneficial to people: they are of benefit when eaten, or of benefit when used, or of benefit when resold: all are beneficial. This is for no other reason than to share the benefits with the people of the whole world . . . . We have heard heretofore that your honorable ruler is kind and benevolent. Naturally you would not wish to give unto others what you yourself do not want.

Document 6

> **Source:** Source: Lord Palmerston, British Foreign Secretary, letter to the Chinese government, 1840.
>
> It appeared that the Laws of the Chinese Empire forbid the importation of Opium into China, and declare that all Opium which may be brought into the Country is liable to confiscation. The Queen of England desires that Her Subjects who may go into Foreign Countries should obey the Laws of those Countries; and Her Majesty does not wish to protect them from the just consequences of any offenses which they may commit in foreign parts. But, on the other hand, Her Majesty cannot permit that Her Subjects residing abroad should be treated with violence, and be exposed to insult and injustice; and when wrong is done to them, Her Majesty will see that they obtain redress.

Document 7

> **Source:** Sir George Staunton, speech in the House of Commons on British trade with China, 1840.
>
> The course which I hope and believe Her Majesty's Government are about to take, is to make rational proposals to China — such proposals as China may accept without national dishonour or disgrace. But considering the character of its government, and all the events that have already taken place, no man can doubt the necessity of accompanying and supporting such propositions with a competent physical force (hear). The armament destined for this service has been condemned on account of its being supposed to be intended to support the trade in opium. On the contrary, I call on all those who would wish to see that detestable traffic really and effectually put down, to support a measure by which alone, I am convinced, such a wished-for consummation can ever be accomplished. Without a national treaty between the Governments of England and China, such as this armament may be hoped to lead to, and which it would be hopeless to expect otherwise, providing a plan of cordial co-operation between them for this end, it is but too certain that this detestable opium traffic must, in spite of every effort, not only flourish, but become every day more and more piratical and buccaneering in its character.

Document 8

Source: Articles of the Treaty of Nanking that ended the Opium War, 1842.

III.

His Majesty the Emperor of China cedes to Her Majesty the Queen of Great Britain, etc. the Island of Hong-Kong, to be possessed in perpetuity by her Britannic Majesty, Her Heirs, and Successors.

X.

[T]he Emperor further engages, that when British merchandise shall have once paid at any of the said ports the regulated customs and dues, . . . such merchandise may be conveyed by Chinese merchants to any province or any city in the interior of the Empire of China. . . .

XI.

It is agreed that her Britannic Majesty's Chief High Officer shall correspond with the Chinese High Officers, both at the capital and in the provinces, . . . on a footing of perfect equality.

Document 9

Source: John Ouchterloney, an engineer who served in the British Army in China during the Opium War, *The Chinese War,* 1844.

The balance of trade was, for some time, on the side of the Chinese, who received it in [silver] dollars from the East India Company; but by degrees the introduction of British manufactures, metals, cotton from India, and lastly opium, to a very considerable extent, turned the tide in our favour, and then the dollars and Sycee silver (the produce of their own country) began to ooze out in formidable quantities. The attention of the Imperial Cabinet being called to this national evil, orders were given to stop entirely the trade in opium, as that with which the empire could most safely and easily dispense. The importation of this article, about half a century ago, was inconsiderable, extending to not more than 1000 chests, but it had reached the immense quantity of 40,000 chests ; and as the people of all the southern portion of the empire were known to be all, more or less, addicted to the use of the drug, in smoking chiefly, it was an evil of gigantic magnitude. It was first introduced into China as a medical drug, under a fixed duty, and though hindrances were opposed from time to time by the Chinese authorities, the trade continued to thrive until 1820, when a proclamation was issued against it.

Document 10

Source: You Zan, Chinese economic scholar, 1894.

The Westerner's most effective weapon in butchering our financial well-being has been and still is opium, the poison of which permeates into every corner of the nation. We exchange precious silver for harmful drugs, and the total amount of silver that has flowed out of the country during the past fifty years is so large that we have ceased to count. The more we ban the opium traffic, the more the people violate the ban. Meanwhile the Westerners, sitting their (sic) comfortably and radiating a self-satisfied smile, collect their profit. They will not be satisfied until every Chinese looks like a skeleton and every Chinese penny goes into their pockets. They will not be happy until China, as a nation, has degenerated to such an extent that no recovery is remotely possible. Their strategy is clear: to prevent China from becoming strong, they have to keep her permanently poor.

PART B: CONTINUITY AND CHANGE-OVER-TIME ESSAY

Directions: You are to answer the following question. You should spend 5 minutes organizing or outlining your essay. Write an essay that:

- Has a relevant thesis and supports that thesis with appropriate historical evidence.
- Addresses all parts of the question.
- Uses world historical context to show continuities and changes over time.
- Analyzes the process of continuity and change over time.

1. Analyze continuities and changes in political, economic, or cultural life in ONE of the following interregional trade routes between circa 300 C.E. and circa 1500 C.E.

   - Eurasian Silk Roads
   - Trans-Saharan caravan routes
   - Indian Ocean routes
   - Mediterranean Sea routes

PART C: COMPARATIVE ESSAY

Directions: You are to answer the following question. You should spend 5 minutes organizing or outlining your essay. Write an essay that:

- Has a relevant thesis and supports that thesis with appropriate historical evidence.
- Addresses all parts of the question.
- Makes direct, relevant comparisons.
- Analyzes relevant reasons for similarities and differences.

1. Analyze similarities and differences between the way the Spanish dealt with the culture and traditions of conquered peoples in the Americas and the way leaders of ONE of the following empires dealt with conquered peoples' cultures and traditions.

- Roman
- Abbasid
- Mongol

Index

A

Abbas I (Abbas the Great), 359–360
Abbasids, 149–151, 186, 204, 232, 320
Abdulhamid II, 445
Abelard, Peter, 219, 231
Abolition, 327
Aboriginals, 39, 468
Abraham, 9, 22, 147
Absolute monarchies, 285, 292, 376
Abu Bakr, 148, 282
Abyssinia, 472, 514
Academy (of Plato), 56, 58
Achaemenid Empire, 58–61
Acquired immunodeficiency syndrome
    (AIDS), 613–614
Actium, Battle of, 77
Adulis, 29
The Aeneid (Virgil), 72
Aeschylus, 57
Afghanistan, 62, 148, 203, 360, 563, 580,
    606, 607, 613
Afonso (king), 320, 325
Africa. *See also* East Africa; *specific
    countries*; Sub-Saharan Africa
    agriculture in, 162, 466
    Bantu-speakers, 161–163
    borders in, 473
    Christianity in, 172
    city-states of, 321–322
    climate zones in, 23, 24
    colonial period in, 320–328
    colonies in, 469, 471–473
    Europeans in, 321–322
    expansion of trade in, 161–173
    geography of, 23
    history of, 173
    imperialism in, 471–473
    independence movements in, 522–523
    Islam in, 161
    migration out of, 3
    missionaries in, 469
    nationalism/nationalist movements in,
        477, 502, 582–587
    political structures in, 163–164,
        167–169
    Portuguese in, 289
    railroads in, 466–467
    religions of, 171, 326
    scramble for, 468, 472–473, 514
    slave trade and, 304, 306, 320, 323–327,
        471
African culture, 325–326, 328, 523
African Diaspora, 325, 328
African National Congress (ANC), 603
African Union (AU), 584
Afrikaners, 473
Afterlife, belief in, 5, 25, 27, 35, 80, 81, 94,
    102, 103, 147, 469
The Age of Reason (Paine), 396
Agricultural Revolution, 6, 423
Agriculture
    Africa, 162, 466
    Americas, 306
    ancient Egypt, 23–24, 26–27
    Aztec, 259
    Byzantine, 135
    cash crops, 306, 466
    China, 34, 35, 37, 38, 184–185
    collectivized, 518, 553
    development of, 6
    Early Middle Ages, 223
    Green Revolution, 610
    Indus Valley, 31
    Mayan, 115
    Mesoamerica, 38, 39, 114
    Mesopotamia, 17, 18
    Mississippian culture, 256–257
    as mistake, 11
    Moche, 112
    monoculture, 466
    Nile River Valley, 23–25, 27
    Ottoman Empire, 357
    Persian Empire, 60
    plantation, 306, 475
    slash-and-burn, 115
    Southeast Asia, 209, 211
    technological innovations in, 9, 20, 38,
        105, 185, 223–224, 423
    three-field system, 223
    trade crops, 425
Agrigentum, 58
Air pollution, 429, 490, 605
Aircraft carriers, 540, 543
Airplanes, 425, 494, 495, 543

Akbar, 341, 360–361, 363
Akhenaton, 26
Al-. *See word following the hyphen.*
Alamo, 405
Alaska, 3, 338
Albania, 514, 555–557
Albuquerque, Afonso de, 289
Alexander I, 402
Alexander the Great, 52, 62, 64, 75, 95, 97
Alexandria, 50, 62, 444, 539
Alexandrian Museum, 62
Alexius I, 137
Algeria, 355, 471, 498, 584–585
Algerian Civil War, 585
Algerian War for Independence, 584
Algiers, 446
Alhambra, 152
Ali (caliph), 148–149
Ali, Muhammad, 443–444
Ali, Sunni, 320–321
Alighieri, Dante, 233
All Quiet on the Western Front (Remarque), 495
Allah, 146–148, 206, 207
Allende, Salvador, 589
Alliances, 36, 242, 290, 412, 493, 494, 535, 555, 556
Allies, 54, 61, 168, 355, 469, 493–495, 497, 498–502, 514, 517, 520, 534, 539–541, 544–545, 551, 554, 558, 559, 564, 578
Alphabet
    Cyrillic, 134
    Phoenician, 54
Alphabetic script, 22
Alsace-Lorraine, 412
Alternative energy sources, 611
Alzheimer's disease, 612, 614
American Revolution, 398–399
Americanization, 601, 606
Americas. *See also* Latin America;
    Mesoamerica; North America; *specific*
    countries
    African culture in, 325
    colonial period in, 302–313
    early civilizations of, 112–118
    indigenous peoples of, 37–39
    Mississippian culture of, 256–258
    population of, in 1491, 265
    pre-European discovery, 256–265
    slavery in, 311, 323–328
Amistad, 325

Amnesty International, 604
Amritsar massacre, 521–522
Amu Darya, 246
An Lushan, 182
Analects (Selected Sayings), 100
Anarchism, 432
Anatolia, 443, 447, 521, 581
Ancestor veneration, 35, 163, 171, 172, 261–262, 448, 469
Ancient Egypt, 10, 23–29
    agriculture in, 23–24, 26–27
    cultural and scientific contributions of, 27–28
    government of, 25
    Middle Kingdom, 25–26
    New Kingdom, 26
    Old Kingdom, 25
    religion of, 27
    society of, 26–27
    transportation and trade in, 24–25
Al-Andalus, 152, 220
Andes Mountains, 10, 38, 112, 305, 406
Angkor Kingdom, 210
Angkor Thom, 210
Angkor Wat, 210, 211
Anglicanism, 280
Anglio-Zulu War, 473
Angola, 472–473, 551, 586–587
Animals
    Columbian Exchange and, 304
    domestication of, 6–8
    loss of diversity, 6
Anime, 601
Animism, 15, 00, 257, 263, 469
Annan, Kofi, 585
Antibiotics, 612
Anticolonial sentiment, 521, 522
Anti-Comintern Pact, 535
Antinuclear weapons movement, 555
Antiretroviral drugs, 613
Anti-Semitism, 342, 412, 515, 561, 577
Antony, Marc, 77
ANZAC, 497
Apartheid, 603
Apennine Mountains, 72
Appeasement, 534
Apter, David, 591
Aqueducts, 84–86
Aquinas, Thomas, 231
Arab League, 578–579
Arab merchants, 204

Arabian Peninsula, 146–148
Arabian Sea, 19
Arabic language, 148
Arabic numerals, 99, 209, 244
Arab-Israeli conflict, 552, 578
Arabs. *See also* Middle East
    World War I and, 498, 502
Arafat, Yasser, 578
Architecture. *See also* Pyramids
    ancient Greece, 57
    Gothic, 230
    Islamic, 152, 209
    Moche, 112
    Roman, 85
    Romanseque cathedrals, 230
    Zimbabwe, 169
Archons, 55
Argentina, 407
Aristocracy, 54, 55
    ancient Egypt, 25
    China, 184, 224
    Europe, 225, 291, 292, 293
    France, 400
    Japan, 192–193, 377–378
    Russia, 337, 339
Aristophanes, 57
Aristotle, 56–57
Arkhangelsk (Archangel), 336
Arkwright, Richard, 422
Armenians, 447, 453–454, 499
Armistice Day, 498
Armor, 242, 248
Armstrong, Karen, 106
Arrianus, Arrian Flavius, 65
Artifacts, 2, 4, 9
Artisans, 8, 26, 34, 35, 37, 113, 114, 358
Arts
    Africa, 172
    ancient Chinese, 35
    ancient Greece, 57
    Bantu-speakers, 163
    Byzantine Empire, 136
    China, 246, 377
    India, 98
    interwar years, 524–525
    Japan, 378–379
    Mayan, 118
    Mexico, 524
    Mississippian culture, 257
    Moche, 112–113
    Olmec, 38
    Ottoman Empire, 359

Paleolithic Period, 5
    post-classical China, 189
    Renaissance, 234
    Russia, 519
Aryans, 31–33, 52, 92
Ascetic, 94
Ashoka the Great, 97, 100
Asia. *See also* East Asia; South Asia;
    Southeast Asia; *specific countries*
    Central, 354–355
    communism in, 557–559
    Portuguese trading empire in, 374
    social classes in, 224
Asia Minor, 61
Asian Tigers, 599
Assembly lines, 422
Assyrians, 22, 29, 453–454
Astrakhan, 337
Astrology, 21
Astronomy, 21, 116, 118
Atahualpa, 306–307
Aten, 26
Athens, 54, 61, 73, 74
    democracy in, 55–56
    philosophy of, 56–57
    religion and culture, 57–58
Atlantic Charter, 537
Atlantic slave trade, 304, 306, 320, 323–328
Atomic bombs, 541, 543
Attila the Hun, 84
Audiencias, 308
Augustine, St., 82
Augustus (Octavian), 77–80
Aurangzeb, 362
Australia
    Aborigines of, 468
    penal colony of, 467–468
    White Australia Policy in, 468
Austria, 282, 356, 410, 411, 535, 559
Austro-Hungarian Empire, 446, 492–494
    break-up of, 573
Austronesians, 39
Automatic loom, 457
Averroes, 152
Avestas, 60
Avicenna, 150, 232
Axial age, 106
Axis powers, 516, 517, 534–535
Axum, 29, 172
Ayllus, 113
Al-Azhar University, 153
Aztecs, 256, 258–262, 306–308

B

Babur, 360
Babylon, 21
Babylonian Captivity, 225, 279
Babylonian Empire, 21
Bacon, Francis, 286, 395
Bactria, 97, 98
Baghdad, 149, 150–153, 204, 208, 232, 245, 264, 272, 320, 447
Baha'ism, 106
Bai, Mira, 207
Baibars, 246
Balfour Declaration, 502, 577
Balkanization, 608
Balkans, 445
Bananas, 162
Bangladesh, 575
Banjo, 326
Bank of Amsterdam, 291
Bank of England, 292
Bantu-speakers, 161–164
Barbary pirates, 358
Barley, 6, 23
Barracoons, 325
Barter, 31
Baruch, Bernard, 551
Baseball, 429
Al-Bashir, Omar, 609
Basho, Matsuo, 378–379
Basil II, 134
Basil the Copper Hand, 135
Basque Homeland and Freedom (ETA), 560
Basque region, 516
Bastille, 400
Batavia, 374
Battle of Actium, 77
Battle of Britain, 537–538
Battle of El Alamein, 539
Battle of Kulikovo, 244
Battle of Kursk, 541
Battle of Leningrad, 538
Battle of Lepanto, 358
Battle of Manzikert, 137
Battle of Midway Island, 540
Battle of Navarino, 443
Battle of Salamis, 61
Battle of Stalingrad, 539
Battle of the Alamo, 405
Battle of the Bulge, 541
Battle of the Coral Sea, 540
Battle of Thermopylae, 61

Battle of Tours, 152, 220
Batu, 244–245
Batwa, 162
Bay of Pigs, 562–563
Beans, 115, 304
Bedouin culture, 146, 153
Begin, Menachem, 578, 579
Beijing, 372, 449
Belgium, 424, 471, 537, 560
Benin, 172, 322, 323, 326
Benso, Camillo, 410
Bering Strait, 3
Berlin, 554
Berlin Airlift, 554
Berlin Conference, 472
Berlin Wall, 562
Bernard, Christiaan, 614
Bessemer process, 430
Bhagavad Gita, 92
Bhakti Movement, 207
Bhutto, Benazir, 575
Bhutto, Zulfikar Ali, 575
Biafran Civil War, 587
Bible, 81–82, 136, 231, 279
Big bang theory, 525
Big Four, 500, 520
Big Three, World War I leaders, 501
Big Three, World War II Allies, 543–544
Bill of Rights
    English, 285
    U.S., 399
Bin Laden, Osama, 606, 607
The Birds (Aristophanes), 57
Bishops, 225
Bismark, Otto von, 411–412, 430
Black Death, 228, 248, 279
Black English, 328
Black Hand, 492
Black Legend, 312–313
Black Sea, 341, 343, 355
Blanc, Louis, 409
Blitzkrieg, 537, 541
Blok, Aleksander, 519
Blyden, Edward Wilmot, 173
Boak, Arthur, 86
Bodin, Jean, 284, 285
Boer Wars, 473
Bohr, Niels, 525
Boleyn, Ann, 280
Bolívar, Simon, 406–407
Bolivia, 589

Bollywood, 601
Bolsheviks, 496, 517–519
Bonaparte, Napoleon, 397, 401–403, 411, 443
The Book of the City of Ladies (Pisan), 230
Book of the Dead, 27
Books, 189
Bosnia, 446, 607–608
Bosporus Strait, 131, 355
Boudiaf, Mohammed, 585
Bourgeoisie, 229, 432, 433
Bouteflika, Abdulaziz, 585
Bow and arrows, 26
Boxer Rebellion, 450, 454
Boyars, 138, 337–339, 340
Brahma, 32, 93
Brahmins, 32–33, 93
Braudel, Fernand, 40, 58
Brazil, 306, 307
    economic growth of, 599–600
    fascism in, 516
    independence for, 407
    uprising of 1968, 561
Breast-feeding, 5, 613
Brezhnev Doctrine, 559
Brinton, Crane, 398
Britain, 560. *See also* England
    Balfour Declaration by, 502, 577
    Boer Wars and, 473
    China and, 448, 474
    classical liberalism in, 409–410
    economy of, 291–293
    in Egypt, 471
    imperialism of, 465
    in India, 289, 466, 469–470, 521–522
    Industrial Revolution in, 421, 424
    in Kenya, 586
    migration to, 575
    militarism in, 493
    Romans in, 75
    in South Africa, 473
    urbanization in, 424, 428
    World War I and, 497
    World War II and, 537–538
British East India Company, 288, 290–291, 466, 469, 474
Bronze, 10, 34–36
Bronze Age, 10
Brzezinski, Zbigniew, 526
Bubonic plague, 105, 248, 449
Buddha, 94, 99

Buddhism, 92, 94, 96, 97, 99, 106, 182–183, 189–190, 193, 194, 206, 220, 282
Bukhara, 152
Bulgaria, 445, 553, 555
Bulgars, 132–133, 134
Bureaucracy
    China, 450
    Korean, 193
    Ottoman Empire, 357
    Qing Dynasty, 376
    Song Dynasty, 183–184
    Tang Dynasty, 182
    Vietnam, 194
    Western Europe, 226
Burghers, 229
Burial practices, in Paleolithic Period, 5
Burke, Edmund, 394, 398, 413
Bush, George H. W., 605
Bush, George W., 606–607
Bushido, 193
Business organizations, 429–430
Byzantine Empire, 131–139, 222, 229, 335, 355, 358
    arts and education, 136
    decline and fall of, 137
    economy and trade, 135
    government of, 132
    religion of, 134
    territory of, 131–133
Byzantium, city of, 131

C

Cabot, John, 310
Cacao, 260, 304
Caesar, Julius, 77, 85
Cahokia, 257, 258, 264, 272
Cairo, 152, 153, 444
Calendar
    ancient Chinese, 35
    Aztec, 260
    Egyptian, 28
    Inca, 262
    lunar, 21
    Mayan, 260
    Sumerian, 20
Calicut, 205
California, 338, 405
Caliphs, 148–149, 153
Calvin, John, 280, 294
Calvinism, 280, 282, 433

Cambodia, 209, 475, 558, 565, 576
Cambridge University, 231
Cambyses, 58
Camel saddles, 165
Camels, 165–166
Cameroon, 502
Camp David Accords, 578, 579
Canaan, 22
Canada, 310
Canals, 182, 424, 445
Candide (Voltaire), 395
Candomblé, 309, 326
Cannon, 248
Canon law, 445
Canon of Medicine (Avicenna), 232
The Canterbury Tales (Chaucer), 233
Canton, 376, 447, 448
Cape Colony, 473
Cape of Good Hope, 229, 289, 321
Cape Town, 467
Capet, Hugh, 226
Capital, 287, 424
Capital cities, 105
Capitalism, 286–288
    free-market, 477
    intellectual responses to, 431–432
Capitulations, 447, 458
Captains of industry, 428
Caracol, 116
Caravans, 60
Caravel, 303
Carbon dioxide, 611
Carbon footprint, 611
Cardenas, Lazaro, 519
CARE, 609
Caribbean, 305, 324–325, 467, 476
Carolingian Dynasty, 220, 222, 226
Carpa Nan, 264
Carter, Jimmy, 563, 579
Carthage, 22, 75–76
Cartier, Jacques, 310
Cartledge, Paul, 65
Cartography, 229, 289
Cash crops, 306, 357, 466
Caspian Sea, 338, 341
Castas, 309
Caste system, 92–93, 206, 207, 215, 224, 361
Castro, Américo, 155
Castro, Fidel, 562–563
Casualties
    of WWI, 498–500
    of WWII, 543

Catal Huyuk, 8
Catapults, 85
Cathedrals, 230
Catherine II (Catherine the Great), 340–342, 397
Catholic Church. *See* Roman Catholic Church
Catholic Reformation, 280–281
Catholicism, 309. *See also* Christianity
Cattle, 7, 425
Caudillo, 405
Cave paintings, 5, 6
Cavour, Count of, 410–411
CCP. *See* Chinese Communist Party (CCP)
Central Asia, 354–355
Central Powers, 493, 495, 496, 498, 511
Central Treaty Organization (CENTO), 556
Cervantes, 322
Ceylon, 97, 203
Chamberlain, Neville, 535
Champlain, Samuel de, 310
Chan Buddhism, 190
Chang'an, 105, 184, 185, 187, 192, 193, 264, 272
Chariots, 26, 31, 34
Charlemagne, 220, 221
Charles I, 284
Charles II, 284
Charles V, 280, 281
Charter Oath, 456
Chaucer, Geoffrey, 233
Chaudhari, Nirad, 477
Chavez, Hugo, 589, 590
Chavin civilization, 38
Chavín de Huántar, 38
Checks and balances, 74, 399
Chernobyl, 611
Chiang Jiang (Yangtze) River, 33–34, 604
Chiang Kai-shek, 520, 536
Chichén Itzá, 116, 258
Chickens, 7
Child development, 395
Child labor, 427, 430
Child marriages, 361
Child-rearing practices, in Sparta, 54–55
Chile, 261, 406, 431, 589
Ch'in Dynasty, 102–103
China
    agriculture in, 33–34, 35, 37, 184–185
    ancient civilizations in, 10, 33–38, 73
    arts and literature of, 246, 377
    Buddhism in, 99

Communist, 502, 520, 536, 556–557, 599, 603–604
Confucianism in, 100–101, 104, 187, 189, 193, 220, 372, 520
Cultural Revolution, 557
economy of, 184–187, 372, 376–377, 599–600
environmental degradation in, 605
fear of, 191
geography of, 33
Golden Age in, 36–38
Han Dynasty, 73, 103–105, 180, 184, 194
imperialism in, 474
intellectual and cultural developments, 189
Japan and, 191, 378, 450, 469, 520, 536
Korea and, 193, 380
mandate system and, 502
May Fourth Movement, 502, 520
Ming Dynasty, 247, 372–374
minority rights in, 604
modernization of, 442
Mongols in, 372–373
Neolithic Revolution in, 6
philosophies, 100–102
political structures, 180–181
Portuguese in, 374
post-classical period in, 180–190
protests in, 603–604
Qin Dynasty, 102–103
Qing Dynasty, 338, 375–377, 447–454, 474, 519
reforms, 449, 450, 453–454
religion in, 189–190, 220
society of, 101, 187–188, 377
Song Dynasty, 183–184, 186, 187, 188, 190, 224
Soviet Union and, 557
Sui Dynasty, 180–181, 185
Tang Dynasty, 181–183, 185, 190, 193, 194, 220, 224
trade, 83, 105, 106, 135, 185, 186, 205, 305, 448, 466
urbanization in, 185, 187
Vietnam and, 194
water problems in, 604–605
Yuan Dynasty, 246–247, 372
Zhou Dynasty, 36–38, 101
Chinampas, 259
Chinatowns, 452
Chinese Civil War, 520

Chinese Communist Party (CCP), 502, 520, 536, 556–557, 599, 604
Chinese Exclusion Act, 453
Chinese migrants, 451–453
Chinese Nationalist Party, 451, 520
Chinese Republic, 451, 454, 519–520
Chivalry, 193, 223
Chola Kingdom, 203
Christianity, 29, 30, 60, 79, 106, 147, 278, 282, 469. *See also* Roman Catholic Church
in Africa, 172
African Americans and, 325–326
Counter-Reformation, 280–281
Crusades and, 137, 151, 225, 227–229, 231
early, 81–82
Eastern Orthodox, 134, 136, 138–139, 224, 335, 338, 339, 340
Edict of Milan, 82
in Japan, 379, 454
in Latin America, 309
liberation theology, 590
Protestant Reformation, 278–280
in Roman Empire, 80–82, 86
schism, 134
Church of England, 280, 285
Churchill, Winston, 534, 538, 544, 552–553
Cicero, 75, 79, 80
Circumnavigation of globe, 290
Cities and towns. *See also specific cities*
ancient, 8
ancient Egyptian, 25
Aztec, 258–259
British, 423, 424
China, 37, 185, 187, 372
growth of, 8
India, 205
Mayan, 115, 117
medieval, 230
Mississippian culture, 257
Russia, 336, 339
slums in, 409, 428, 600
Sumerian, 17–18
City of God (St. Augustine), 82
City-states
Africa, 321–322
Greece, 53–58, 61, 64, 73
Mayan, 115–116
Sumerian, 18
Swahili, 166–167, 170
Civil Constitution of the Clergy, 400–401, 402

Civil disobedience, 522, 574
Civil liberties, 285
Civil service examination, 104, 182, 183, 193, 247, 372, 450
Civilization(s). *See also specific civilizations*
    Americas, 37–39, 112–118
    ancient Chinese, 33–38
    ancient Egyptian, 23–28
    ancient Greece, 52–58
    clash of, 615
    classical, 52–71, 72–86, 92–106
    core and foundational, 10
    cradle of, 17
    defined, 10
    development of, 40
    first, 10, 17–45
    Hebrew, 22–23
    Indus River Valley, 30–33
    Mediterranean, 52–53
    Pacific peoples, 39
Cixi (empress), 449–450, 454
Clans, 4, 170
    Aryan, 31
Clash of civilizations, 615
Class structure. *See* Social classes
Classic Period, of Mayan civilization, 114–115
Classical civilizations
    China, 100–106
    Greece, 52–58
    India, 92–100
    Macedonia, 61–62
    Persia, 58–64
    Roman, 72–86
Classical liberalism, 409–410
Clay pots, 9
Clemenceau, Georges, 500, 501
Clement V, 225
Cleopatra, 27
Clergy. *See also* Priests
    in France, 400, 401
Climate change
    desertification, 24, 25, 117, 490, 611
    global warming, 611–612
    human migration and, 2–3
    Little Ice Age, 229
    Moche civilization decline and, 113–114
Clovis (king), 219
Cluniac Reforms, 225, 279
Coal, 186, 422, 424–430
Coal mines, 427, 430

Code Napoléon, 402
Code of chivalry, 193, 223
Code of Hammurabi, 21
Codex, 309
Coffeehouses, 357, 359, 396
Cohen, Stephen P., 212
Coins, 37, 186
Colbert, Jean-Baptiste, 285
Cold War, 551–565, 598
Coleridge, Samuel, 410
Collection of Books, 375
Collectivized agriculture, 518, 553
Colleges, 231
Colonial period
    Africa, 320–328
    Americas, 302–313
Colonies
    administration of, 308
    African, 469, 471–473
    defined, 305
    Dutch, 311–312
    economic motivations for, 305, 465–469
    English, 290, 310–311
    French, 309–310
    India, 469–470
    labor from, 465–469
    mandate system and, 502–503
    North Africa, 446
    Portuguese, 307
    post-WWI, 501–503
    settler, 476
    Spanish, 305–308, 404–408
    state-run, 476
    in World War I, 497–498
    in World War II, 539
Columbian Exchange, 304, 312
Columbus, Christopher, 288, 302, 303, 305, 312
Comedies, 57
Commerce, 229
Commercial Revolution, 287, 288
Common Market, 560
Common Sense (Paine), 396
Communes, 557
Communism, 432, 433, 496, 500, 520, 534, 535, 553, 555–559, 582
The Communist Manifesto (Marx and Engels), 432, 433
Communists, 517–519, 520, 536, 551, 553, 554, 557, 576
Compass, 106, 186, 289, 303

Concentration camps
  in Boer Wars, 473
  Nazi, 515, 542
Concessions, 449
Confucianism, 100–101, 104, 187, 189, 193, 220, 372, 520
Confucius, 100–101
Congo, 471
Congo River Basin, 164
Congress of Berlin, 446
Congress of Vienna, 403, 411
Conquistadores, 303, 305–309, 324
Conscription, 443, 456
Conservatism, 394
Conservatives, 405
Constantine (emperor), 82, 131
Constantinople, 82, 83, 84, 131, 132, 133, 136, 137, 228, 278, 335, 355, 359
Constitutional Convention, 399
Consuls, 74
Consumerism, 429
Containment policy, 552–554
Continental System, 402
Cooking, fire and, 4
Copernicus, Nicolaus, 234
Copper, 10, 431
Copper coins, 186
Coral Sea, Battle of the, 540
Córdoba, Spain, 152
Core and foundational civilizations, 10
Corn, 6, 38, 39, 115, 304
Corporations, 429–430
Corporatism, 513–514, 588
Corpus Iuris Civilis (Body of Civil Law), 132
Corruption
  in Catholic Church, 225, 280
  in China, 448, 450, 520
  in India, 599
Cortés, Hernán, 261, 262, 303, 306, 308, 313
Cossacks, 337–338, 343
Cottage industry, 287, 421, 422, 426
Cotton, 39, 205, 357, 421, 425, 433, 466
Council for Mutual Economic Assistance (COMECON), 553
Council of ministers, 96
Council of Trent, 280
Counter-Reformation, 280–281
Cows, 304, 469
Cradle of civilization, 17
Creole languages, 325
Creole revolutions, 404–407

Creoles, 308, 404–407
Crete, 52–53, 443
Crimean Peninsula, annexed by Russia, 341
Crimean Tatars, 245, 338
Croatia, 573, 608
Cromwell, Oliver, 284
Cromwell, Richard, 284
Crop rotation, 423
Crops, 5, 6, 34, 38–40, 112, 115, 162, 256–257, 304, 306, 357, 425, 466
Crossbow, 38
Crossbreeding, 610
Crusades, 137, 151, 225, 227–229, 231
Ctesiphon, 64
Cuba, 407, 475, 562–563
Cuban Missile Crisis, 562–563
Cubist painting, 524
Cult of domesticity, 428–429
Cultural Revolution, 557
Culture
  African, 325–326, 328
  ancient Greece, 53, 57–58, 62, 63, 72, 79
  Aztec, 260
  Babylonian, 21
  Bedouin, 146, 153
  Chinese, 189
  colonial Americas, 308–309
  Egyptian, 27
  global, 601
  India, 208–209, 212
  interwar years, 524–525
  Islamic, 152–154
  mass, 429
  Mayan, 116, 118
  Mexican, 588–589
  Mississippian, 256–258
  Ottoman Empire, 359
  popular, 601
  South Asia, 208–209
  Sub-Saharan Africa, 172
  Sumerian, 19–20
  Vietnam, 194
Cuneiform writing, 19–20, 117
Currency
  China, 186
  Persian Empire, 60
Cuzco, 261, 262, 264, 272
Cyprus, 446, 582
Cyril, 134
Cyrillic alphabet, 134

Cyrus the Great, 58
Czech Republic, 573
Czechoslovakia, 501, 535, 559, 561, 573

D

Da Gama, Vasco, 289, 290, 322
Da Vinci, Leonardo, 278
Dadu, 246–247
Dahomey, 322, 327
Daimyo, 192–193, 455
Dali, Salvador, 525
Dali Lama, 376
Dalits, 93
Damascus, 149
Dao, 101
Dao De Jing, 101
Daoism, 101–102, 189, 190
Dar al-Islam, 148, 203, 204, 205
Darfur, 609
Darius I, 59–60, 64
Dark Ages, 219, 234. *See also* Middle Ages
Darwin, Charles, 469
David (Michelangelo), 278
Dawson, Christopher, 41
D-Day, 541
De Beers Diamonds, 467
De Gaulle, Charles, 561, 585
De Gouges, Olympe, 401
De Klerk, F. W., 603
De las Casas, Bartolome, 312–313
De las Casas, Pedro, 312
Death
    Egyptian beliefs about, 27
    Sumerian beliefs about, 19
Deccan Plateau, 96
Declaration of Independence, 399
Declaration of the Rights of Man, 400
Decline of the West (Spengler), 40
Decolonization, 501–503, 565, 573–592
    Africa, 582–587
    in former Ottoman territory, 577–880
    India, 574–575
    Iran, 580–583
    Southeast Asia, 576–577
Defense budgets, 607
Deficit spending, 512
Deforestation, 29, 31, 39, 50, 84, 262, 312, 490, 611
Deism, 394, 396–397
Deities

Greek, 57, 102
Mayan, 116
Roman, 80
Delhi, 203, 209, 360–361
Delhi Sultanate, 203–204, 209
Delian League, 61
Democracy, 54, 327, 451
    Athenian, 55–56
    direct, 55
    England, 227
    representative, 55, 84
    struggles for, 601–605
Demographic changes, 303
Deng Xiaoping, 557, 603
Denmark, 537, 560
Dependency theory, 592
Desert zone, 23
Desertification, 24, 25, 117, 490, 611
Dessalines, Jean-Jacques, 403
Destroyers-for-Bases Agreement, 537
Détente, 563
Development theories, 592
Devshirme, 355–356
Dharma, 32, 95, 190
Dhows, 152
Diabetes, 614
Dialects, 224
Dialogues (of Plato), 56
Diamonds, 431, 467, 471
Diamond, Jared, 302
Diaz, Bartholomew, 289
Diaz, Porfirio, 519
Dictatorships, 590
Diderot, Denis, 286, 375, 395, 396
Diet, 6, 456
Din-i-llahi, 361
Diocletian, 84
Direct democracy, 55
Directory, 401, 443
Disease. *See* Infectious disease
Districts, 97
The Divine Comedy (Alighieri), 233
Divine right of the monarchy, 36, 59, 284–285, 335, 339
Division of labor, 19, 30, 31, 422, 428
Divorce, 61, 79, 154, 248
Dnieper River, 138
Doctors Without Borders, 612
Dogs, 7
Dollar Diplomacy, 523
Dom Pedro I, 407

Dome architecture, 85
Domestic animals, 6, 7, 23, 29, 117, 304
Dominican Republic, 305, 476, 523
Domino theory, 558
Don Quixote (Cervantes), 322
Donation of Constantine, 225
Dowries, 154
Drama, 63
Dravidians, 30, 32, 33, 92
Dresden, 543
Dreyfus Affair, 412, 577
Drug cartels, 588
Du Fu, 189
Dubcek, Alexander, 559
DuBois, W. E. B., 523
"Dulce et Decorum Est" (Owen), 492
Dunn, Ross, 173
Dutch, 291–292, 374, 471
Dutch colonies, 311
Dutch East India Company, 288, 290, 292,
    454, 466, 474
Dutch explorers, 290
Dutch Republic, 292
Dynasty, 34

E

Early Middle Ages, 219–222
Earth Day, 611
East Africa. *See also specific countries*
    first humans in, 2
    kingdoms of, 169
    political structures, 169–170
East Asia. *See also specific countries*
    mandate system in, 502
    New Order in, 536
    post-classical period, 180–195
East Germany, 553–555, 562
East India Company, 288, 290–291, 421, 466,
    469–470, 474
East Pakistan, 575
Easter Island, 39
Eastern Europe, 543–544, 553, 558–559,
    564. *See also specific countries*
Eastern Orthodox Church, 134, 136,
    138–139, 224, 335, 338, 339, 340
Ebadi, Shirin, 581
Ebola, 612, 614
Economic globalization, 598–601
Economy
    Abbasid Empire, 151

Aztec, 259
    Byzantine Empire, 135
    capitalism, 287–288
    China, 184–187, 372, 376–377,
        599–600
    colonial period, 305–306
    England, 292
    France, 291, 292, 293
    global, 288, 598–601
    Incas, 261
    India, 599–600
    mercantilism, 286–287, 305, 399
    Mexican, 588
    Mississippian culture, 256–258
    Moche, 112–113
    Ottoman Empire, 357, 446–447
    South Asia, 204–206
    Sumerian, 19
    Zhou Dynasty, 37
Edict of Milan, 82
Edict of Nantes, 281
Edo (Tokyo), 377
Education
    Byzantine Empire, 136
    China, 189, 372, 377
    Enlightenment and, 395
    France, 402
    for girls, 446–447
    Islamic, 152
    Japan, 456
    in Middle Ages, 231
    Ottoman Empire, 445
    Russia, 339, 342
Egypt, 52, 75
    ancient, 10, 23–28, 73
    decolonization of, 578–580
    Hebrews in, 22
    industrialization in, 444
    Muhammad Ali and, 443–444
    Suez Canal and, 409, 471, 578, 579
    trade with, 19
    war with Israel, 578
Einstein, Albert, 525
Eisenhower, Dwight D., 558
Eisenstein, Sergei, 519
El Alamein, Battle of, 539
Elites, 8, 10, 476–477
Elizabeth I, 280, 294, 310
Emile, or on Education (Rousseau), 396
Empires, 21. *See also specific empires;*
    Trading post empires

Empiricism, 57, 286
Enclosure movements, 424
Encomenderos, 305
Encomienda system, 305
Encyclopedia (Diderot), 396
End of history, 615
Engels, Friedrich, 432
Engenhos, 306
England. *See also* Britain
    Asian migrants to, 575
    colonies of, 290, 310–311
    economy of, 292
    Glorious Revolution in, 284–285, 292
    Magna Carta, 226–227, 284, 399
    monarchy, 284
    Norman, 226–227
    Reformation in, 224, 280
    uprising of 1968, 561
English Bill of Rights, 285
English Civil War, 284–285
English language, 601
English Parliament, 227
Enlightened despots, 397–398
Enlightenment, 94, 286, 327, 336, 394–398,
    408–409, 413, 453
Environment
    adaption to, by early humans, 3
    current challenges with, 611
    Indus Valley, 31
Environmental degradation
    China, 604
    colonization and, 312
    Indus Valley, 31
    industrialization and, 429
    Mayan Empire, 117
    Roman Empire, 84, 117
Environmental movement, 611–612
The Epic of Gilgamesh, 20
Epic of Sundiata, 322
Epic poems, 94–95, 209
Epicureanism, 79
Epidemics, 499–500. *See also* Infectious
    disease; Black Death
    Han Dynasty, 105
    Roman Empire, 83–84
Equal-field system, 184, 192
Equestrian class, 78
Erasmus, Desiderius, 234
Essay Concerning Human Understanding
    (Locke), 395
Estates-General, 226, 292, 344, 399–400

Estonia, 501
ETA. *See* Basque Homeland and Freedom
    (ETA)
Eta, 378
Ethics, 56
Ethiopia, 29, 172, 472
Etruscans, 72–73, 75
Euphrates River, 10, 17
Eurasian land empires, 341
Euripides, 57
Euro, 560
Europe. *See also specific countries*; Western
    Europe
    balance of power in, 403
    imperialism of, 465–475
    Indian Ocean trade and, 288–291
    Jews in, 291
    Marshall Plan for, 553
    Renaissance, 232–234
    social classes in, 224
    unification, 410–412
    universities, 231–232
European Economic Community (EEC), 560
European explorers, 289–290, 302–303,
    308–310, 321–322
European Union (EU), 560
    Turkey associate member, 582
Evolutionary theory, 469
Export economies, 466
Extraterritoriality, 447, 455
Ezana (king), 29

F

Fabian Society, 409
Factories, 422, 432
Factors, 290
Factory system, 422
Factory workers, 426–427
Falong Gong, 106
Family
    Chinese, 101, 377
    Confucianism and, 101
    effects of industrialization on, 426–427
    nuclear, 4, 194
    Vietnam, 194
Farmers. *See also* Agriculture
    ancient Egypt, 26–27
    Neolithic, 7–8, 9
    Roman, 76

Farming. *See* Agriculture
Fascism, 513–516, 534
Fast-ripening rice, 185
Fatah, 578
Favelas, 599
Female infanticide, 154
Feminism, 429
Ferdinand (king), 284, 291, 303
Ferdinand, Archduke Francis, 492
Ferguson, Niall, 477
Fernández-Armesto, Felipe, 41
Fertile Crescent, 17, 18
Fertilizers, 610
Feudalism, 36, 184, 193, 220, 223–225,
    227, 456
Fez, 445
Fiefs, 223
Fifth Republic, 584
Fiji, 467
Filial piety, 101
Filipino, 290, 412
Film industry, 601
Financial bubbles, 291–292
Finland, 501, 559
Fire, control of, 4
Firebombing, 543
First Estate, 400
First Persian Empire, 58–61
Five Great Farms, 285
Five Pillars, 148
Five-Year Plan, 518
Flat world thesis, 592
FLN (National Liberation Front), 584–585
Floods, of Indus River, 31
Florentine Codex, 309
Florida, 307–308
Flutes, 5, 163
Flying buttresses, 230
Flying cash, 186
Food
    African, 326
    cooking and, 4
    surplus, 5, 8, 19
Foot binding, 188, 224, 377
Football, 429
Forbidden City, 323, 372
Forced labor, 539
Ford, Henry, 422
Formosa, 468
Fossil fuels, 424, 429, 611
Foucault, Michel, 413

Four Noble Truths, 94
Fourier, Charles, 409
Fourteen Points, 500–501
Fourth Crusade, 137, 228
France
    Algeria and, 584–585
    aristocracy in, 292, 293
    Capetian, 226
    Carolingian Dynasty, 220
    China and, 448
    colonies, 290, 309–310, 446, 469, 471
    economy of, 291, 292, 293
    as EEC member, 559
    Huguenots, 278, 280, 281
    industrialization in, 424–425
    monarchies in, 284, 285–286
    Napoleon Bonaparte and, 401–403
    in North Africa, 446, 471
    Reign of Terror in, 401, 404
    Russia and, 344
    in Southeast Asia, 475
    uprising of 1968, 560–561
    World War II and, 537
Francis (pope), 590
Franco, Francisco, 515
Franco-Prussian War, 411, 493
Franklin, Benjamin, 286, 395
Franks, 84, 219–220
Frederick the Great, 396, 397
Free trade, 287–288, 600
Free-market capitalism, 477
French and Indian War, 290
French Legion of Honor, 402
French Revolution, 292, 399–403, 404, 424
Freud, Sigmund, 525
Friedman, Thomas, 592
Friedmann, Alexander, 525
Friedrich, Carl, 526
Fugitivus, 79
Fujiwara clan, 192
Fukushima, 612
Fukuyama, Francis, 615
Fuller, Graham, 212
Funans, 209
Funeral rituals, of ancient Egyptians, 27
Fur trade, 310, 335–336, 338

G

Galbraith, John Kenneth, 544
Galen, 231

Galileo, 286
Galleons, 305
Gallipoli, 497
Gandhara Buddhas, 98
Gandhi, Mohandas, 522, 574–575
Ganges River, 31, 97
Gao, 168, 320
Gargoyles, 230
Garibaldi, Giuseppe, 411
Gate of All Nations, 60
Gauchos, 410
Gaul, 75, 84
Gautama, Siddhartha, 94
Gaza Strip, 578
Geechee language, 326
Gender roles, 10
    in Athens, 56
    in China, 101, 188
    in India, 95
    in Middle Ages, 230–231
    in Paleolithic Period, 4–5
    in Persian Empire, 60
    in Roman Empire, 76–77
    in South Asia, 207–208
    in Sparta, 54–55
    in Sub-Saharan Africa, 170–171
    in Sumeria, 19
General Agreement on Tariffs and Trade
    (GATT), 552, 600
General Assembly (UN), 551, 578
Genetic engineering, 610
Genghis Khan, 242–244, 249
Genocides, 499, 607–609
George III, 376
German Empire, 412
German language, 224
German-Austrian unification, 535
German-Soviet Nonaggression Pact,
    535–536, 537
Germany, 75, 447
    division of, 554
    industrialization in, 424, 425
    interwar years in, 512, 514
    militarism in, 493
    Nazi, 501, 514–516, 534–536, 542
    Treaty of Versailles and, 501, 511, 514,
    534
    unification, 411–412
    uprising of 1968, 561
    Weimar, 514
    World War I and, 495, 497, 501, 511
    World War II and, 534–541

Ghana, 168, 325, 326, 582, 585
Ghazi ideal, 354
Ghettos, 542
Gibbon, Edward, 86
Glaciation, 2–3
Gladkov, Fyodor, 519
Glasnost, 564
Global brands, 601
Global challenges, 609–612
Global economy, 288
    industrialization and, 431
    interwar years, 512
Global inequalities, 432–433
Global security, 605–607
Global war, 497–498
Global warming, 611–612
Globalization, 173, 291, 477, 598–601
Glorious Revolution, 284–285, 292
Glyphs, 40
Goa, 469
Goats, 7, 31, 80, 241, 248, 304
Gobi Desert, 33, 241, 604
Gods/goddesses. See Deities
Gold, 166, 169–170, 287, 305, 431, 467, 471
Gold Coast, 582, 584
Golden Age, 337
    China, 36–38
    Greece, 52, 55–56
    India, 98–100, 202
    Islamic, 150
    Kievan Rus, 139
Golden Horde, 139, 244–245, 247
Golden Mean, 56
Golden Rule, 101
Gomulka, Wladyslaw, 559
Good Neighbor Policy, 523–524
Google, 599
Gorbachev, Mikhail, 564, 598
Gospels, 82
Gothic cathedral, 230
Gothic literature, 410
Government(s)
    ancient Egypt, 25–26, 73
    ancient Greece, 54, 55–56, 73
    Aryan, 31
    Aztec, 259
    Byzantine, 132
    China, 182
    colonial, 308
    early forms of, comparison of, 73
    England, 226–227, 285
    feudal, 37

France, 285–286
Gupta Dynasty, 98
Han Dynasty, 73, 104–105
Incas, 261
Japan, 192, 456
Kievan Rus, 138
Korea, 193
Mauryan, 96–97
Mayan, 115–116
Mexico, 405
Mississippian culture, 258
in Neolithic era, 8–9
Persia, 150
Persian Empire, 59–60
representative, 84
right-wing, 513–517, 526
Roman influence on, 84
Rome, 73–75
Russia, 340
Sparta, 55
Sub-Saharan Africa, 164–165
Sumerian, 17–18
theocratic, 134
U.S., 399
Zhou Dynasty, 36–37
Grain production, 610
Grand Canal, 180–181, 185, 220
Great Britain. *See* Britain
Great Depression, 511–513
Great Game, 465, 580
Great Lakes, of East Africa, 162
Great Leap Forward, 557
Great Man Theory, 534
Great Peace of Montreal, 290
Great Pyramid, 259
Great Schism, 224, 225
Great Speaker, 259
Great Sun, 258
Great Wall of China, 373
Great War. *See* World War I
Great Zimbabwe, 170
Greece, 443, 553, 559, 582
ancient, 52–58, 73
city-states, 53, 54–58, 61, 64, 73
colonies, 58
compared with Persia, 64
geography of, 54
Golden Age, 52, 55–56
Minoans, 52
Mycenaens, 53
mythology of, 57, 80, 102
philosophy of ancient, 56–57

Roman rule of, 75
Greek culture, 53, 57–58, 62, 63, 72, 79
Green, Peter, 65
Green Belt Movement, 611
Green Revolution, 610
Greenhouse effect, 611
Greenland, 221
Greenpeace, 611
Griots, and griottes, 172
Grote, George, 65
Guam, 457, 475
Guangxu (emperor), 450
Guangzhou, 187, 376
Guano, 431
Guatemala, 565
Guerilla warfare, 194
Guernica, 515, 535
Guild, 187, 207, 230, 287, 293, 343, 359
Gul, Abdullah, 582
Gullah language, 326
Gumbo, 326
Gunpowder, 186, 195, 227, 244, 248, 289,
    303, 321, 323, 337, 353–364, 377, 398
Gunpowder Empires, 353–365, 398
    decline of, 363–365
    Mughal Empire, 360–363
    Ottoman Empire, 355–359, 363, 398
    rise of, 353–355
    Safavids, 359–360
Guns, 186, 195, 302, 494
Gupta Dynasty, 98–100, 202, 222
Gupta religion, 99
Gutenberg printing press, 278

H

Habsburgs, 446
Hagia Sophia, 132
Haiku, 378
Haiti, 305, 309, 327, 403–404, 523
Haitian Revolution, 403–404
Halakha, 445
Hamas, 578
Hamburg, 543
Hamid, Abdul, 453
Hamidian massacres, 454
Hammurabi, 21
Han Dynasty, 73, 103–105, 180, 184, 194
Han Fei Zu, 102
Han Wudi, 103–105
Hangzhou, 181, 185, 187
Hanseatic League, 229

Harappa, 30–31, 52
Hardwick, Nicola-Ann, 565
Harems, 154, 358
Harsgreaves, James, 422
Hatshepsut, 27
Hatt-i Humayun, 445
Hatto, A. T., 234
Hawaii, 39
Hayek, Friedrich, 526
Heart disease, 614
Heart transplants, 614
Heather, Peter, 140
Heaven, 60
Hebrews, 9, 22–23
Hegira, 147
Heian Period, 192
Hell, 60
Hellenistic Period, 62
Helots, 55
Henry IV, 278, 281, 284, 285
Henry of Navarre, 278
Henry the Navigator, 289, 321
Henry VIII, 280
Heraclius, 133
Hermit Kingdom, 380
Hernández, José, 410
Herodotus, 52, 54
Herzegovina, 446
Herzl, Theodor, 412, 577
Hidalgo, Miguel, 405
Hideyoshi, Toyotomi, 377
Hieroglyphics, 27, 29, 116, 117
High Middle Ages, 219, 227
Hijab, 154, 170
Himalayas, 33, 106
Hime, Henry, 195
Himmler, Heinrich, 542
Hindenburg, Paul von, 514
Hindi language, 31
Hinduism, 33, 92, 94–96, 99, 106, 206–207, 209
Hippocrates, 231
Hippodrome, 136
Hiroshima, 541, 543
Hispaniola, 305
The Histories (Herodotus), 54
History
    cyclical view of, 41
    end of, 615
Hitler, Adolf, 514–516, 534–539, 541, 542, 544
Hittites, 26

HIV/AIDS, 613–614
Ho Chi Minh, 501, 558, 576
Hobbes, Thomas, 285, 395
Hochschild, Adam, 471
Hogs, 425
Holland, 290–293
Holocaust, 542, 577–578, 609
Holy Land, 137, 231
    Crusades to, 137, 151, 225, 227–229, 231, 244
Holy Roman Empire, 220, 222, 226, 281, 282
Holy Synod, 339
Homo sapiens sapiens, 2
Hong Kong, 448, 599
Hong Xiuquan, 448
Horace, 79
Horse collar, 224
Horses, 7, 31, 223–224, 227, 303, 304
Hot Line, 563
House of Commons, 227
House of Lords, 227
House of Slaves, 325
House of Wisdom, 153
Housewives, 428
Hsuan Tsung (emperor), 182
Huaca, 263
Huaca de la Luna, 112
Huaca del Sol, 112
Huang He (Yellow) River, 33, 604
Huang He (Yellow) River valley, 10
Huayna Capac, 261, 264
Hubble, Edwin, 525
Hudson, Henry, 311
Hughes, Langston, 523
Huguenots, 278, 280, 281
Huitzilopochtli, 260
Hulegu, 245–246
Human capital, 425
Human immunodeficiency virus (HIV), 613–614
Human migration, in prehistoric period, 2–3
Human rights, 552, 607–609
Human rights abuses, 590
Human sacrifice, 113, 260, 262
Human settlements, earliest, 8
Humanism, 231, 232
Humans, first, 2
Hundred Years' War, 227, 278
Hungary, 553, 559
Hunger, 609–610
Huns, 84, 100, 222
Hunter-foragers/gatherers, 2, 4–5

Huntington, Samuel, 615
Hurricane Katrina, 611
Huss, John, 225, 279
Hussein, Saddam, 606–607
Hussites, 279
Hutus, 608–609
Hyksos, 26

I

Ibn Battuta, 161, 170
Ibn Khaldun, 353, 359
Ibn Rushd, 152
Ice Age, 5, 40
Ice ages, 38, 229
Iceland, 221
Iconoclasm, 134
Ides of March, 77
Idi Amin, 575
Ieyasu, Tokugawa, 378
Ifshahan, 362
Igbos, 587
Ile de Gorée, 325
Ilf, Ilya, 519
Iliad, 56
Il-khanate, 246
Illuminated manuscripts, 136
Imam, 149
Immigrants, 425, 451–453
Immigration laws, 452–453, 469
Imperialism
    in Africa, 471–473
    in China, 474
    economic motives for, 465–469
    European, 465–475
    ideological motives for, 468–469
    impact of, 477
    Japanese, 378–379, 536–537
    in Latin America, 475–476, 523
    political motives for, 468
    responses to, 476–477
    in South Asia, 469–470
    in Southeast Asia, 475
    U.S., 465, 475–476, 523–524
    World War I and, 493–494
Impressed labor, 358
In Praise of Folly (Erasmus), 234
Incas, 261–264, 306–307
Indentured labor, 311, 324, 451, 467
Independence movements, 521–522, 574. *See also* Revolutions
Index of Prohibited Books, 280

India
    ancient civilization in, 10
    Aryans, 31–33
    British in, 290–291, 465, 466, 469–470, 521–522
    caste system in, 32–33, 92–93, 207, 361
    culture of, 208–209, 212
    drama of, 63
    Dravidians, 30–31
    economic growth of, 599–600
    Golden Age in, 98–100, 202
    Gupta Dynasty, 98–100
    independence for, 574–575
    independence movement in, 476, 521–522
    Islam in, 203–204, 206–207, 212
    Mauryan Empire, 95–98
    Mughal Empire, 360–363, 469
    partition of, 574–575
    political structures in, 202–204
    Portuguese in, 289
    railroads in, 466
    religions of, 93–95
    social structures of, 207–208
    terrorism in, 606
    trade, 19, 98, 106, 135, 290–291
    in World War II, 539
Indian National Congress, 476, 521–522, 574
Indian Ocean trade, 98, 106, 165–166, 171–172, 203, 204–205, 288–291, 598
Indigenous peoples
    Americas, 38–40, 302, 303
    encomienda system and, 305
    Europeans and, 308–309, 310
    Pacific, 40–41
Indo-European languages, 31
Indonesia, 205, 209, 290, 474
Indulgences, 279
Indus River Valley, 10
    civilizations of, 30–33
Industrial Revolution, 398, 421–433
    effects of, 426–430
    legacy of, 432–433
    responses to, 430–431
    Second, 475
Industrial society, 376, 409, 426, 433
Industrialization, 408–409, 421, 444
    causes of, 422–424
    effects of, 426–430
    intellectual responses to, 431–432
    Japan, 456–457
    Ottoman Empire, 446

proto-industrialization, 185, 376–377
responses to, 430–431
spread of, 424–426
Industry
cottage, 287, 421
factory system, 422
nationalization of, 579
Russia, 340
state-run, 589–590
INF Treaty, 564
Infant mortality, 423–424
Infectious disease
Africa, 162
Black Death, 228, 248, 279
brought by Europeans, 261, 302, 303,
306, 307, 468
Han Dynasty, 105
influenza, 499–500
Roman Empire, 83–84
Inflation, 512
Influenza epidemic, 499–500
Inheritance laws, 79
Innovations. *See also* Technology
commerce and trade, 186–187
Inoculations, 98
Inquisition, 280, 292
Institutional Revolutionary Party (PRI),
587–588
Intellectuals, 476–477, 522–523, 524–525,
576, 603
Intendants, 285
Interchangeable parts, 422
Intercontinental ballistic missiles (ICBMs),
555
International Court of Justice, 552
International Monetary Fund (IMF), 552, 586
International Red Cross, 604
International trade organizations, 600
Internet, 600
Interregional trade, 186, 241, 248
Interwar years, 511–526
cultural and intellectual movements
during, 524–525
Great Depression, 511–513
nationalism in, 521–523
neocolonialism in, 523–524
political revolutions in, 516–520
rise of right-wing governments in,
513–516
Inti, 262
Inventions, 422–423
Invisible hand, 431

Iran, 64, 359–360, 580–583, 605
Iranian hostage crisis, 581
Iranian Revolution, 580
Iraq, 17, 64, 502
Iraq War, 606–607
Ireland, 559, 560
Irish Republican Army (IRA), 560
Iron, 29, 37, 162, 186
Iron Age, 37
Iron Curtain, 552–553
Iron Curtain countries, 558–559
Iroquois, 290
Irrigation, 24, 26, 38, 61, 115, 185, 210, 259
Irving, Washington, 155
Isabella (queen), 284, 291, 294, 303
Isfahan, 360
Isis, 27, 49, 80
Islam, 29, 146–155, 282, 359
Abbasid Empire and, 149–151
in Africa, 161, 165–167, 172
caliphs, 148–149
conversions to, 206–207
core principles of, 147
Five Pillars of, 148
Golden Age, 150
impact on trade, 164–165
in India, 203–204, 212
influence of, 134
in Mali, 169
Muhammad (prophet), 134, 146,
147–148, 153, 154
in practice, 148
prosperity under, 152
Shariah law, 148, 161, 358, 445
Shiite, 148–149
social and cultural life, 152–154
in South Asia, 206–207
in Southeast Asia, 211
in Spain, 152, 155
spread of, 133, 147, 148–149
Sufism, 155, 361
Sunni, 148–149, 359, 581
Umayyad Dynasty, 148–149
women in, 154, 360
Islamic gunpowder empires. *See* Gunpowder
Empires
Islamic Revolution, 580, 581
Islamic Salvation Front, 585
Island-hopping strategy, 540
Ismail, 359
Israel, 22, 355, 412, 498, 552, 577, 605
Arab-Israeli conflict, 552, 578, 579–580

creation of, 502, 577–578

Zionism and, 412, 577–578

Israelites, 22–23, 577

Istanbul, 131, 355, 359, 446

Italian Peninsula, 58, 410

Italy, 303, 472, 559

fascism in, 513–514

Renaissance, 233, 278

unification, 410–411

World War II and, 534–535, 540

Iturbide, Agustín de, 405

Ivan III (Ivan the Great), 336–337

Ivan IV (Ivan the Terrible), 337–338

Ivaylo, 135

Ivory, 166, 471

J

Jade, 34, 39

Jahan (shah), 361

Jain, Mahavir, 93

Jainism, 93–94

Jakarta, 452

James I, 284

James II, 284

Jamestown, Virginia, 310–311

Janissaries, 356, 398, 443–445, 453

Janjaweed, 609

Japan, 377–380, 561

arts and literature of, 378–379

atrocities committed by, 543

China and, 191, 378, 450, 469, 520, 536

daimyo, 377–378, 455

Europe and, 379–380

imperialism and, 378–379, 467, 469, 536–537

industrialization in, 426

interwar years, 513

isolation of, 454–455

Meiji Era, 425–426, 454–458

modernization of, 442, 455

Portuguese in, 289

post-classical, 190–193

post-WWII, 599

reforms in, 456

Russia and, 451

samurai in, 192, 377–378, 456

society of, 378

Tokugawa Shogunate, 378–379

United States and, 537

World War I and, 497

World War II and, 536–537, 538–541

Jarvik, Robert, 614

Jaspers, Karl, 106

Jatis, 93, 207

Jefferson, Thomas, 395, 399

Jericho, 8

Jerome, Saint, 231

Jerusalem, 23

Jesuits, 280, 374, 375

Jesus, 80–82, 147

Jewish Diaspora, 22–23, 80

Jews, 22–23

anti-Semitism and, 515, 542, 577

Nazis and, 515–516, 542

in Ottoman Empire, 358

pogroms and, 342, 412

in Roman Empire, 23, 80

Russian, 342

as scapegoats, 80

in Spain, 292

Zionism and, 412, 502, 577–578

Jihad, 148

Jinnah, Muhammad Ali, 522, 574

John VI, 407

Johnson, Lyndon, 558

Joint-stock companies, 288, 292

Journey to the West, 322, 377

Jousts, 227

Joyce, James, 525

Juárez, Benito, 405

Judaism, 9, 60, 106

Jung, Carl, 525

Junks, 186

Jupiter, 80

Jurchen, 241

Justice system, of Hammurabi, 21

Justinian code, 132

Justinian I (Justinian the Great), 132, 140

K

Ka'aba, 147

Kabir, Guru, 202, 207

Kabuki theatre, 322, 378

Kahlo, Frida, 525

Kaifeng, 184

Kailash, 202

Kalahari desert, 23

Kalinga, 97

Kang Youwei, 449

Kangxi (emperor), 375, 376

Kangxi Dictionary, 375
Kara Khitai Empire, 242
Karakorum, 243
Karma, 32, 94
Kashmir, 575
Kazan, 337
Keegan, John, 65
Kelly, Jack, 195
Kemal, Mustafa, 521, 581, 582
Kennan, George, 553
Kennedy, John F., 558, 562–563
Kenya, 585–586, 612
Kenyan African National Union (KANU), 586
Kenyatta, Jomo, 586
Kepler, Johannes, 286
Keynes, John Maynard, 502, 512
Khan, 242
Khan, Reza, 580
Khanate of the Golden Horde, 139
Khayyám, Omar, 152
Khmer Rouge, 576
Khmers, 209, 210
Khomeini, Ayatollah Ruhollah, 580, 606
Khrushchev, Nikita, 562, 563
Khwarazm Empire, 242
Kiev, 336
Kievan Rus, 137–140, 222, 335
Kilwa, 166, 167
Kin-based networks, 164–165
King, Martin Luther, Jr., 574
Kingdoms, 18
Kings, 223. *See also* Monarchy(ies); *specific kings*
    divine right of, 284, 285
    Egyptian, 25
    Mayan, 116
    philosopher, 56
    Southeast Asia, 209
    Sumerian, 18
Kinship groups, 4, 170
Kipling, Rudyard, 465, 469
Knights, 223, 224, 227, 248
Knights Templar, 231
Knossos, 52
Knossos Palace, 53
Knox, John, 280
Kolkata, 452
Kolkhoz, 518
Kongo Kingdom, 320, 322, 324, 327
Koran. *See* Quran
Korea, 182
    China and, 193, 380
    isolation of, 380
    Japan and, 378–379, 469
    post-classical period, 193
Korean War, 558, 565
Kosovo, 607–608
Kowtow, 182, 193, 448
Kramer, Heinrich, 294
Kremlin, 336
Kristallnacht, 515, 542
Krupp, Alfred, 429–430
Kshatriyas, 93
Kublai Khan, 229, 246–247, 372
Kulikovo, Battle of, 245
Kumbai Saleh, 168
Kumsong, 193
Kuomintang, 451, 520
Kurdistan Workers' Party, 582
Kurds, 582
Kuriltai, 242
Kursk, Battle of, 541
Kush, 29
Kushan Empire, 98
Kuwait, 605
Kyoto, 377
Kyoto Protocol, 611

L

La Reforma, 405
La Salle, 310
Labor
    child, 427, 430
    Chinese, 451–453
    colonial, 465–469
    convict, 467–468
    division of, 19, 422
    economic imperialism and, 467–469
    forced, 305, 306, 311, 324, 358, 539. *See also* Slaves/slavery
    guild, 187, 207, 230, 287, 293, 343, 359
    impressed, 358
    indentured, 311, 324, 452, 467
    nomad, 343
    peasant, 343
    serf, 343
    specialization of, 8
Labor movement, 430
Labor unions. *See* Unions
Laissez-faire, 396, 409, 431
Lake Texcoco, 259
Lake Victoria, 162

Land reform
    China, 184
    Latin America, 590–591
Landowners, in Byzantine Empire, 135
Landscape painting, 189, 190
Language(s)
    African, 325–326, 328
    Arabic, 150
    Aryan, 32
    Bantu, 161–164
    creole, 325–326
    dialects, 224
    English, 601
    Indo-European, 31
    Latin, 32, 85, 224
    Romance, 85
    Slavic, 134, 137
    Urdu, 209
    vernacular, 224, 232
Laos, 209, 475, 558
Laozi, 101
Lares, 80
Last Supper (Da Vinci), 278
Lateen sails, 206
Latifundia, 76
Latin, 32, 85, 224
Latin America, 453. See also specific
    countries
    creole revolutions in, 404–408
    land reform, 590–591
    neocolonialism in, 523–524
    political trends in, 589–591
    religion in, 309
    slavery in, 304
    U.S. imperialism in, 475–476, 523
    women in, 407–408
Latins, 72–73
Latvia, 501
Lawrence, T. E., 577–578
Law(s)
    Canon, 445
    child labor, 430
    Code Napoleon, 402
    Code of Hammurabi, 21
    Corpus Iuris Civilis (Body of Civil
    Law), 131
    English, 285
    immigration, 452–453
    inheritance, 79
    Justinian code, 132
    Nuremberg Laws, 515
    pass laws, 602

    primogeniture, 228, 288, 401
    private property, 424
    Rock and Pillar Edicts, 97
    Roman, 79
    Roman influence on, 84
    rule of, 74–75
    Russkaya Pravda, 139
    Shariah, 148, 161, 358, 445, 582
Laws of supply and demand, 288
Laws of the Twelve Tables, 74
Lay investiture controversy, 226
Lay people, 233
Lead, 86
League of Nations, 500, 501, 521, 551
Learning centers, 152, 153
Lebensraum, 534
Legal profession, 75
Legalism, 102
Legions, 76
Leisure activities, 429
Lemaitre, Georges, 525
Lend-Lease Act, 537
Lenin, Vladimir, 496, 517–518
Leningrad, Battle of, 538
Leo III, 133–134
Leo X, 279
Leopold II, 471
Lepanto, Battle of, 358
Levant, 137, 228
Leviathan (Hobbes), 285, 395
Li Bo, 180, 189
Li Si, 102
Li Yuan, 220
Li Zicheng, 375
Liaotung Peninsula, 378
Liberalism, 394, 409–410, 411
Liberals, 405
Liberation theology, 590
Liberia, 173, 412, 472, 583
Lima, Peru, 307
Limited liability corporation, 288
Literature
    African, 322
    ancient Greece, 56, 57
    Byzantine Empire, 136
    Chinese, 189, 246, 377
    developments in, 322
    interwar years, 525
    Islamic, 150, 152
    Japanese, 378–379
    Renaissance, 233
    Roman Empire, 79, 85

romanticism, 410
    Russian, 519
    Sub-Saharan Africa, 172
Lithuania, 501
Little Ice Age, 229
Liverpool, 424
Livestock, 5, 7, 304
Livingstone, David, 469
Livy, 79
Llamas, 39, 112
Lloyd George, David, 500, 501
Locke, John, 285, 395, 399
Logic, 57
Lollards, 279
London, 452
London Company, 310–311
Long March, 520
Longships, 221, 222
Lords, 223
Lost Generation, 500
Louis XIII, 285
Louis XIV, 285–286, 292, 344, 376
Louis XVI, 400, 401
L'Ouverture, Toussaint, 327, 403
Lower Egypt, 25
Loyalists, 516
Lu Yu, 185
Luftwaffe, 515, 537
Lunar calendar, 21
Lusitania, 495
Luther, Martin, 225, 279, 294
Lutheranism, 279, 281, 282
Luxembourg, 559
Lysistrata (Aristophanes), 57

M

MacArthur, Douglas, 540, 558
Macartney, Lord, 448
Macau, 374
Macedo, 75
Macedonia, 61–62
Machine guns, 494
MacMillan, Margaret, 502
Madagascar, 40, 162
Madero, Francisco, 519
Madison, James, 84
Magellan, Ferdinand, 290, 412
Magistrates, 74
Magna Carta, 226–227, 284, 399
Magnetic compass, 186, 303

Magnus, Lucius Pompey, 77
Magyars, 222
Mahabharata, 92, 94–95, 209
Mahmud II, 444–445, 446
Mahmud of Ghazni, 203, 206, 222
Maimonides, 152
Maistre, Joseph de, 394
Maitland, Samuel, 234
Maize (corn), 6, 37, 38, 115, 304
Majapahit Kingdom, 210
Malacca, 211
Malaka, 374
Malaria, 162, 471, 612
Malaysia, 205, 209
Malevich, Kazimir, 519
Mali, 161, 168–169, 320
Malindi, 166
Mamluks, 150, 443
Manchester, England, 424
Manchester, William, 234
Manchu Empire, 449
Manchukuo, 536
Manchuria, 375, 379, 451, 536
Mandate of Heaven, 36, 220
Mandate system, 502–503, 521
Mandela, Nelson, 603
Manhattan, 312
Manila, 290
Manorial system, 223–224
Manors, 223, 225, 229
Mansa Musa, 169
Manufacturing, 422
Manzikert, Battle of, 137
Mao Zedong, 520, 556–557
Maori, 468
Maquiladores, 588
Marathon, 61
Maria Theresa, 397–398
Maritime empires, 276, 278, 289, 308
Maritime trade, 166–167, 288–291
Marius, Gaius, 77
Maroons, 403
Marriage
    Athenian, 56
    Babylonian, 21
    child, 361
    polygamy. *See Polygyny.*
    polygyny, 146, 194, 326, 521
    Sumerian, 19
Marshall Plan, 553, 559
Martel, Charles, 220

Martin Fierro (Hernandez), 410
Martyrdom, 82
Marx, Karl, 409, 432, 433
Masonry, 264
Mass culture, 429
Mass production, 432
Mathematics, 98–99, 116, 152, 208–209, 264, 286
Matray, James I., 565
Matrilineal societies, 162–163, 258
Mau Mau, 585
Mauritius, 467
Maurya, Ashoka, 97, 100
Maurya, Chandragupta, 96
Mauryan Empire, 95–98
Maximilian (archduke), 406
May Fourth Movement, 503, 520
Mayans, 113, 114–118, 256, 258, 262
Mazzini, Giuseppe, 410
McCulloch, Diarmaid, 106
McQuaig, Linda, 592
Means of production, 432
Measles, 84, 105, 276, 303
Mecca, 146, 147, 149, 153, 169, 443
Medical science, 98, 152
    advances in, 612–614
    ancient Egyptian, 28
    Medical science, 231, 232
Medici, Catherine de, 294
Medieval period. *See* Middle Ages
Medina, 147, 153, 443
Mediterranean civilizations, 52–53. *See also specific civilizations*
Mediterranean climate zone, 23
Mediterranean Sea, 3, 6, 9, 19, 22–24, 52, 54, 83, 98, 219, 229, 280, 553
Mehmed II, 355–356, 358
Meiji Era, 425–426, 454–458
Mein Kampf (Hitler), 542
Melaka, 211
Memphis, Egypt, 25
Men. *See also* Gender roles
    in Paleolithic Period, 4
Menéndez de Avilés, Pedro, 307–308
Menes (king), 25
Menocal, Rosa Maria, 155
Mentuhotep II, 25
Mercantilism, 286–287, 305, 399, 404
Merchants, 54, 55, 153, 188, 204, 259, 287, 337, 358
Meritocracy, 183–184, 340

Merkits, 241
Meröe, 29
Mesoamerica. *See also* Americas
    ancient civilizations in, 10, 38–40, 112–118
    Aztecs, 258–261, 262, 306, 308–309
    Incas, 261–264, 306–307
    Mayans, 113, 114–118, 256, 258, 262
    Toltecs, 258
Mesopotamia, 10, 17–20, 21, 24–25
Mestizos, 309, 404–406
Metallurgy, 10, 39, 186
Metropoles, 575
Metternich, Klemens von, 403
Mexican Revolution, 519, 587
Mexican-American War, 405, 475
Mexico
    Aztecs in, 258–261, 262, 306, 308–309
    drug cartels in, 589
    independence for, 405–406
    modern culture and politics of, 587–589
    under Spanish rule, 305
    uprising of 1968, 561, 587
Mexico City, 306, 405
Michelangelo, 278
Microsoft, 599
Middle Ages, 219–232
    Crusades during, 137, 151, 225, 227–229, 231, 244
    Early, 219–222
    economic and social changes in, 229–232
    feudalism in, 223–224
    High, 219, 227
    political and social structures of, 219–220
    political trends in, 226–227
    population growth during, 229
    Roman Catholic Church in, 224–225
Middle class, 229, 284, 288, 358, 427, 428, 432
Middle East. *See also specific countries*
    Arab-Israeli conflict in, 552, 578
    decolonization of, 577–580
    mandate system and, 502–503
    Neolithic Revolution in, 5
Middle Kingdom, 25–26, 181–182, 190
Middle Passage, 325
Middlemen, 357
Midway Island, Battle of, 540
Migration

of Bantu-speakers, 161–164
by British Asians, 575
by Chinese, 451–453
in prehistoric period, 2–3, 38, 40
Militarism, 493, 534
Military
    conscription, 443, 456
    Islamic, 153
    Japan, 192, 456
    Ottoman Empire, 443–445
    Roman, 76, 77, 85
    technological innovations in, 83, 85,
        186, 195
Military society, of Sparta, 54–55
Mill, John Stuart, 431, 433
Miller, Mary, 118
Millet, 6, 29, 33, 162, 445
Milosevic, Slobodan, 608
Minamoto clan, 192
Minerals, 431
Minerva, 80
Ming Dynasty, 247, 372–374
Miniature paintings, 359
Minoan civilization, 52
Minority rights, 604
Minos (king), 52
Mirs, 342
Missionaries, 134, 225, 280, 289, 309, 310,
    374, 375, 379, 448, 469
Mississippi Bubble, 291–292
Mississippian culture, 256–258
Mit'a system, 305
Moche, 112–114
Model T, 422
Modernization theory, 592
Mogadishu, 166, 205
Mohenjo-Daro, 30–31
Moi, Daniel, 586
Moksha, 32, 33
Mombasa, 167, 205
Mombassa-Kisumu Railway, 586
Mommsen, Theodor, 234
Mona Lisa (Da Vinci), 278
Monarchy(ies), 54, 55, 232, 234. *See also*
    Kings
    absolute, 284, 285–286
    constitutional, 456
    divine right of, 284, 285
    new monarchies, 284
    of Rome, 72–73
    Western Europe, 226
Monasteries, 82, 94, 134, 190, 225, 231

Monasticism, 225
Mondal, Puja, 212
Money, paper, 186
Mongolians, 247, 604
Mongols, 139, 151, 184, 186, 204, 227, 229,
    241–249, 335, 336, 355, 372–373
Monocultures, 466
Monopoly, 34, 55, 291, 303, 374, 429–430
Monotheism, 9, 22, 60, 64, 106
Monroe, James, 475
Monroe Doctrine, 475–476, 523
Monsoon winds, 205
Montesquieu, Baron, 286, 395
Moravians, 134
Moscow, 244, 336
Moses, 22
Mosques, 169, 202, 356, 360
Mubarak, Hosni, 579–580
Mughal Empire, 202, 204, 341, 360–363, 469
Muhammad (the Prophet), 134, 146,
    147–148, 152, 153, 154
Muhammad, Ali bin, 171
Mukden Incident, 536
Mullahs, 580
Mulsim League, 574
Multinational corporations, 599, 601
Mumbai bombings, 606, 607
Mummification, 27, 28
Music, African, 172, 326
Musical instruments, 5, 36, 164, 326
Muslim Brotherhood, 445
Muslims
    in India, 522
    invasion of Western Europe by, 221
Mussolini, Benito, 513–514, 515, 540, 541
Mutshuhito (emperor), 455
Mutual assured destruction (MAD), 554–555
Mycenae, 53
Mystery cults, 80
Myths, 57, 80, 102

N

NAFTA. *See* North American Free Trade
    Agreement (NAFTA)
Nagasaki, 541, 543
Naguib, Muhammad, 579
Nagy, Imre, 559
Nahuatl language, 308–309
Naimans, 241
Nalanda University, 99, 182
Nanjing, 372

Nanjing Massacre, 536
Naples, 411
Napoleon III, 406, 410–411
Napoleonic wars, 444, 446
Nara, 192
Nasser, Gamal Abdel, 578–579
National Front for the Liberation of Angola (FLNA), 586
National Liberation Front (NLF), 585
National Union for the Total Independence of Angola (UNITA), 586
Nationalism, 227, 232, 394–395, 401, 410–412, 451, 469
    Africa, 582–587
    in interwar years, 521–523
    World War I and, 494
Nationalist movements, 476–477, 502
Nationalists, 515
Nation-states, 469
Native Americans, 290
    colonists and, 311
    Europeans and, 310
NATO. See North Atlantic Treaty Organization (NATO)
Natural disasters, 611
Natural gas, 429
Naval technology, 186, 205–206, 289, 303, 340
Navarino, Battle of, 443
Nazi atrocities, 542
Nazis/Nazism, 501, 514–516, 534–536
Needham, Joseph, 195
Negritude Movement, 523
Negro spirituals, 326
Nehru, Jawaharlal, 522
Neocolonialism, in Latin America, 523–524
Neo-Confucianism, 190
Neolithic Revolution, 5–10
Nepal, 376
Netherlands, 291–292, 312, 537, 559
New Amsterdam, 290, 311–312
New Deal, 513
New Delhi, 203
New Economic Plan (NEP), 518
New France, 310
New Guinea, 40
New Harmony, 409
New Kingdom, 26
New Lanark, 409
New monarchies, 284
New Order in East Asia, 536

New Spain, 306–308, 404–405
New Testament, 82
New World, 302. See also Americas
New World Order, 543–544, 605
New Zealand, 39, 468
Newfoundland, 310
Newton, Sir Isaac, 286, 289
Ngo Dinh Diem, 558
Nicaragua, 523, 590
Nicholas II, 495
Niger River Delta, 587
Nigeria, 573, 587
Nihilism, 41
Nile River, 10, 23, 24–25
1968, 560–562
95 Theses (Luther), 279
Nirvana, 94
Nixon, Richard, 558, 563
Al-Nizamiyya University, 153
Nkrumah, Kwame, 582
NLF. See National Liberation Front (NLF)
Nobility. See Aristocracy
Nobunaga, Oda, 377
Nomadic pastoralism, 7, 17, 21, 31, 162, 183, 241. see also Nomad, Pastoralism
Nomads, 3, 4, 6, 7, 8, 17, 21, 26, 31, 33, 35, 64, 76, 100, 103, 129, 139, 146, 153, 162, 165, 183, 184, 186, 220, 241, 248, 343, 353, 354, 609
Nonaggression Pact, 535–536, 537
Non-Aligned Movement, 556
Non-governmental organizations (NGOs), 552, 603
Normans, 137, 226–227
Norsemen, 221
North Africa, 446, 471
North America
    African culture in, 325–326
    colonies, 290, 310–311
    Mississippian culture, 256–258
North American Free Trade Agreement (NAFTA), 588
North Atlantic Treaty Organization (NATO), 555, 581
North Korea, 555, 557–558
North Vietnam, 576
Northern Ireland, 560, 561
Northwest passage, 309–310
Norway, 537
Novgorod, 136, 138, 140, 185, 336, 337
Nubia, 26, 29

Nuclear family, 4, 194
Nuclear Non-Proliferation Treaty, 563
Nuclear power, 612
Nuclear Test-Ban Treaty, 563
Nuclear weapons, 555, 575
Number system
 Arabic numerals, 98–99, 209, 232
 Egyptian, 28
 Olmec, 40
 Sumerian, 20
Nuremberg Laws, 515, 542

O

Obasanjo, Olusegun, 587
Obsidian, 114
Oceania, 39
Octavian (Augustus), 77–78
Odovacer, 84
Odyssey, 56
Offshoring, 592
Ogodei Khan, 243
Oil, 600
Old age pension, 430
Old Believers, 339
Old Kingdom, 25
Old Master, 101
Old Testament, 22
Oleg, 138
Oligarchy, 54, 55
Olmecs, 39–40, 112, 114, 256
Olympic Games, 58, 64, 515, 602
Omani-European rivalry, 288
One-party state, 584
Open Door Policy, 450
Opium, 448, 466
Opium War, 442, 448, 466, 474
Oprichnina, 338
Organization of African Unity (OAU), 584
Orient, 477
Orlando, Vittorio, 500
Orthodox Church. *See* Eastern Orthodox
 Church
Osiris, 27
Ostia, 83
Ostrogoths, 84
Otto I, 226
Otto of Freising, 140
Ottoman Empire, 278, 341, 353, 355–359,
 363–364, 398, 442, 494
 break-up of, 573

 decline of, 358, 379, 443–447, 502
 economy of, 357, 446–447
 European investment in, 447
 reforms, 444–445, 453–454
 society of, 357–358, 446–447
 World War I and, 521
Ottoman Turks, 137
Outsourcing, 592
Ovid, 79
Owen, Robert, 409
Owen, Wilfred, 492
Owens, Jesse, 515
Oxford University, 231
Oyo, 327

P

Pachacuti, 261
Pacific, U.S. imperialism in, 475–476
Pacific peoples, 40–41
Pack animals, 166, 259, 260
Pahlavi, Muhammad Reza, 580, 581
Paine, Thomas, 396
Painting
 Chinese, 189
 Cubist, 524
 prehistoric, 5
 Surreal, 524, 525
Pakistan, 203, 522, 574–575
Pale of Settlement, 342
Paleolithic Period, 3–5
Palestine, 8, 502, 552, 577–578
Palestinian Liberation Organization (PLO),
 578
Palestinian refugees, 578
Palm oil, 425, 471
Pan-Africanism, 477, 584
Pan-Arabism, 502, 579
Pandemic, 499–500
Papal States, 410
Paper, 105, 116, 149, 189
Paper money, 186
Papyrus, 27
Paradigm shifts, 525
Paris, 264, 272, 560
Paris, Matthew, 241
Paris Peace Conference, 500, 503, 520, 521
Parliament, 227, 284, 399
Parthenon, 55, 57
Parthians, 64
Partition of India, 574–575

Partitions of Poland, 341
Pass laws, 603
Passive resistance, 574
Pastoralism, 6–8, 23–24. *See also* Agriculture
Pataliputra (Patna), 97, 98
Patriarch, 134, 228, 339
Patriarchy, 10
Patriarchial societies, 4–5, 21, 188
Patriarchs, 134
Patricians, 74
Paul, St., 79, 81–82
Pax Mongolica, 243, 248
Pax Romana, 78
Pax Sinica, 105
Peace of Augsburg, 281
Peace of Utrecht, 286
Peace of Westphalia, 282
Peacekeeping actions, 552
Pearl Harbor, 538–539
Peasant rebellions, 343
Peasants. *See also* Serfs
    Byzantine Empire, 135
    China, 37
    Europe, 223
    Japan, 193, 378
    Ottoman Empire, 358
    revolts by, 135
Pechenegs, 139
Pedro I, 407
Peloponnesian League, 61
Peloponnesian War, 61
PEMEX, 588
Penal colony, 467–468
Penates, 80
Penicillin, 612
Peninsular Campaign, 402
Peninsulares, 309, 404
People of the Book, 147
Pepin (king), 220
Peppers, 304
Perestroika, 564
Pericles, 55–56
Period of Great Peace, 378
Perry, Matthew, 455
Persepolis, 59
Persia, 19, 150
Persian Empire, 58–61, 62–64, 95
Persian Gulf, 17, 19
Persian Gulf War, 605
Persian Wars, 54, 61
Peru, 305, 306–307, 407
Pesticides, 610

Petain, Marshall Henri, 537
Peter, St., 81
Peter I (Peter the Great), 336, 338–340, 344, 345, 388–391
Peter III, 340
Petition of Right, 284
Petrarch, 234
Petroleum, 429
Pharaohs, 25, 26
Philip II, 52, 61–62, 226, 281
Philip IV, 226
Philippines, 40, 289–290, 412, 475, 538, 540
Philosopher kings, 56
Philosophes, 286, 340, 395–396, 399
Philosophy
    ancient Greece, 56–57
    Chinese, 100–102
    Enlightenment, 286
    Roman Empire, 79
Phoenician alphabet, 54, 117
Phoenicians, 22, 54
Phrenologists, 469
Physiocrats, 396, 399
Picasso, Pablo, 515
Pictographs, 35–36
Pigs, 7, 304, 470
Pinochet, Augusto, 589
Pirates, 83, 230, 289, 310, 358, 374, 471
Pisan, Christine de, 230
Pitt, Thomas "Diamond," 291
Pitt, William, 291
Pizarro, Francisco, 264, 303, 306–307
PKK. *See* Kurdistan Workers' Party
Plagues, 83–84, 228
Planck, Max, 525
Plantations, 306, 47
Plants
    domestication of, 7
    loss of diversity, 6
Plato, 56, 58
Plautus, 85
Plebeians, 74
PLO. *See* Palestinian Liberation Organization (PLO)
Plows, 9, 38, 185, 223
Pochtec, 259
Poetics (Aristotle), 57
Poetry
    Chinese, 189
    epic, 94–95, 209
    Indian Ocean trade, 207
    Islamic, 150

Japanese, 378–379
Pogroms, 342, 412, 453–454
Poison gas, 494
Pol Pot, 576
Poland, 341, 501, 541, 553, 561
    communism in, 559
    conflict over, 535–536
    German invasion of, 537
Poleis, 54
Polio, 613
Polish Communist Party, 558–559
Politburo, 518
Political structures
    Africa, 168–170
    China, 180–181
    of Early Middle Ages, 219–220
    Greek city-states, 54
    South Asia, 202–204
Politics
    Athenian, 55
    harem, 358
    Late Middle Ages, 226–227
Politiques, 278
Pollution, 429, 604
Polo, Marco, 185, 229, 246
Polygamy. *See Polygyny.*
Polygyny, 146, 194, 326, 521
Polynesia, 39, 289
Polytheistic religions, 18–19, 27, 35, 80,
    202–204
Pondicherry, 469
Pontifex maximus, 80
Pope, 225, 233, 401, 410
Popular culture, 601
Popular Front, 515
Popular Movement for the Liberation of
    Angola (MPLA), 586
Popularis, 77
Population decline, in Roman Empire, 83–84
Population growth
    Africa, 327
    Europe, 304
    industrialization and, 423–424
    in Middle Ages, 229
Porcelain, 185, 205
Portugal, 559
    Asian trading empire of, 374
    colonies of, 306, 307, 407, 469
    slave trade and, 324
Portuguese explorers, 289, 321–322
Post-classical period

East Asia, 180–195
    South and Southeast Asia, 202–212
Post-Cold War era, 598–615
Post-colonial era
    India and Pakistan, 574–575
    Southeast Asia, 576–577
Potatoes, 37–39, 261, 264, 276, 304
Potosi, 305
Potsdam Conference, 544
Poverty, 408–409, 428
"Prague Spring," 559
Prakrit, 32
Prefectures, 455
Prehistoric period, 2–3, 8, 38, 40
Preindustrial societies, 421
Price Revolution, 288
Priests
    ancient Egypt, 26
    Mayan, 116
    in Neolithic era, 8–9
    Roman Catholic Church, 225
Primogeniture laws, 228, 288, 401
Princip, Gavrilo, 492, 494
Principality of Kiev, 138–140
Principia (Newton), 286
Printing press, 278, 358
Printing technology, 189
Private property, 8, 424
Procopius, 140
Proletariat, 432, 433
Prometheus Bound (Aeschylus), 57
Propaganda, 496
Property rights, 79, 231
Proselytizing, 134
Proselytizing religion, 206
Protective tariffs, 600
Protestant Reformation, 278–280
Protestant work ethic, 280, 433
Proto-industrialization, in China, 185,
    376–377
Provinces, 96, 340
Prussia, 282, 411, 412
Psychology, 525
Ptolemies, 62
Ptolemy dynasty, 62
Public debt, 590
Puerto Rico, 407, 475
Pugachev, Yemelyan, 343
Pugachev Rebellion, 343
Punjab, 203
Puritan Revolution, 284–285

Puritans, 280, 284
Putin, Vladimir, 336
Putting-out system, 421
Pygmies, 162
Pyramids
    Aztec, 259
    Egypt, 25, 27–28
    Mayan, 115
    Mississippian culture, 256
    Olmec, 38, 114

Q

Al-Qaeda, 605–606, 607
Qanat, 61
Qianlong (emperor), 376
Qin Dynasty, 102–103
Qin Shihuangdi, 102–103
Qing Dynasty, 375–378, 447–454, 474, 519
Quantum mechanics, 525
Quebec, 310
Quechua, 261
Quetzalcoatl, 114, 258, 260
Queues, 375
Quinine, 471
Quinoa, 39
Quipu, 264
Quran, 146, 147
Qutab Minar, 209

R

Ra, 27
Race, 309
Racism, 468–469, 514–515
Railroads, 378, 425, 426, 445, 447, 456,
    466–467, 586
Raj, 470
Ramadan, 148
Ramayana, 94, 95, 209
Ramses the Great, 26
Rape of Nanjing, 536
Raw materials, 424
Reagan, Ronald, 564, 598
Realpolitik, 410
Reconquista, 227
Red Guards, 557
Red Sea, 153
Reformation, 224, 280
Reformed Church of Scotland, 280
Refugees, 552
Reichstag, 514

Reign of Terror, 401, 404
Reincarnation, 94
Religion
    African, 172, 326
    ancient China, 35
    ancient Egyptian, 26, 27
    ancient Greece, 57–58
    animism, 257–258, 263
    Aryan, 32–33
    Aztec, 260
    Bantu-speakers, 163
    Buddhism, 92, 94, 96, 97, 99, 182–183,
        189–190, 193, 194, 206, 220, 282
    Byzantine, 134
    China, 189–190
    Christianity. See Christianity
    civilization and, 41
    Daoism, 189, 190
    Deism, 394, 396–397
    Eastern Orthodox, 134, 136, 138–139,
        224, 335, 338, 339, 340
    Gupta, 99
    Hinduism, 33, 92, 94–95, 96, 99,
        206–207, 209
    iconoclasm, 134
    Inca, 261–263
    India, 93–95
    Islam. See Islam
    Judaism, 9, 60, 80
    Latin America, 309
    Mayan, 116
    Moche, 113
    monotheism, 9, 60, 64
    Neolithic era, 9
    Paleolithic Period, 5
    Persian, 60
    polytheistic, 18–19, 27, 35, 80, 202–204
    proselytizing, 134, 206
    Roman, 80
    Russia, 339
    schisms, 282
    Sikhism, 106, 361
    South Asia, 206–207
    Sparta, 55
    Sufism, 155, 206–207, 211, 361
    Sumerian, 18–19
    syncretism, 57, 64, 80, 172, 190, 309
    Taoism, 101–102, 190
    Toltec, 258
    wars of, 281–283
    Zoroastrianism, 60, 64
Religious ceremonies/rituals, 9, 113, 116

Religious liberty, 396
Religious orders, 231
Religious tolerance, 278, 281, 291, 358, 361, 363–364
Remarque, Erich Maria, 495
Remus, 73
Renaissance, 227, 232–234, 278, 394
Reparations, 501, 511
Representative democracy, 55
Representative government, 84
The Republic (Plato), 56
Republic of Texas, 405
Republican government, 73, 74–75
Revolts
    of 1968, 560–562
    peasant, 135, 343
    slave, 171, 327, 403
Revolutionary War, 398–399
Revolutions. *See also* Industrial Revolution; Scientific Revolution
    Agricultural Revolution, 6, 423
    American Revolution, 398–399
    creole, 404–408
    French Revolution, 292, 399–403, 404, 424
    Haitian Revolution, 403–404
    interwar years, 516–520
    Iranian Revolution, 580
    Mexican Revolution, 519
    Neolithic Revolution, 6–11
    periodization and, 398
    Russian Revolution, 379, 495–496, 517–519
Rhodes, 356
Rhodes, Cecil, 467
Ricci, Matteo, 374
Rice, 6, 34, 185, 475
Richelieu, Cardinal, 285
Righteous and Harmonious Order of Fists, 450
Right-wing governments, 513–517, 526
Rig-Veda, 32–33
Risorgimento, 410
Rivera, Diego, 524
Roads
    China, 182
    Inca, 264
    India, 97
    Mongolian, 248
    Ottoman Empire, 445
    paved, 85

Roman Empire, 78
    Royal Road, 59
    Silk Roads, 82–83, 98, 99, 105, 135, 151, 186, 190, 220, 229, 241, 243, 336
    Zhou Dynasty, 38
Robespierre, Maximilien, 401
Rock and Pillar Edicts, 97
Rodney, Walter, 477
Roman Catholic Church, 81, 134, 219, 220
    Babylonian Captivity, 225, 279
    Counter-Reformation and, 280–281
    Crusades and, 228–229
    in France, 401
    indulgences and, 279
    in Latin America, 309
    in Mexico, 405, 588–589
    during Middle Ages, 224–225, 231
    Protestant Reformation and, 278–280
    religious orders, 231
Roman Empire, 62, 64, 77–86, 131
    Christianity in, 80–82, 86
    decline of, 83–84, 85–86
    Jainism and, 93–94
    Jews and, 23, 80
    legacies of, 84–85
    literature and philosophy of, 79, 85
    military, 76, 77, 85
    monarchy, 72–73
    religion of, 80
    roads, 78
    society of, 78–79
    trade networks, 29, 82–83
    women in, 79
Roman legions, 76
Romance languages, 85
The Romance of the West Chamber (Wang), 246
Romania, 85, 445, 553
Romanov, Michael, 338
Romanov Dynasty, 338, 495, 517
Romanesque cathedrals, 230
Romanticism, 394, 410
Rome, 134
Rome, republic of, 72–77
    civil wars, 77
    end of, 77
    expansion of, 75–76
    military, 76
    society of, 76–77
    women in, 76–77
Rome Treaty, 559

Rome-Berlin Axis, 534–535
Rommel, Erwin, 539
Romulus, 73
Ronin, 378
Roosevelt, Franklin Delano, 513, 523–524, 544
Roosevelt, Theodore, 379, 454, 475, 523
Roosevelt Corollary, 475–476
Rousseau, Jean-Jacques, 286, 327, 395, 396
Royal Academy of Science, 286
Royal ancestor cult, 261–262
Royal ancestor veneration, 261–262
Royal Road, 59
Rubber, 425, 433, 475
Rudder, 106, 186, 289
Rule of law, 74–75, 285
Rumi, 150
Russia, 446, 561, 605. *See also* Kievan Rus; Soviet Union
    arts and literature, 519
    Catherine the Great of, 340–342, 398
    Cossacks in, 343
    early modern period in, 335–346
    economic growth of, 600
    expansion of, 337–338, 341
    France and, 344
    imperialism of, 465
    industrialization in, 426
    Jews in, 342
    Mongols in, 244–245, 335, 336
    Napoleon invasion of, 402–403
    origins of, 137–140
    Peter the Great of, 336, 338–340, 344, 345, 388–391
    pogroms in, 342
    religion of, 335, 339
    Roman Empire and, 338
    serfs in, 342–343
    society of, 337
    Soviet, 496
    Time of Troubles in, 338
    trade, 335–336, 338, 341
    Westernization of, 339–340, 341
    in World War I, 495–496
Russian Civil War, 518
Russian Orthodox Church, 335
Russian Revolution, 379, 495–496, 517–519
Russkaya Pravda, 139
Russo-Japanese War, 378–379, 451, 454
Russo-Turkish Wars, 341, 446
Rwanda, 608–609

S

Sabin, Albert, 613
Sadat, Anwar, 578, 579
Saenz, Manuela, 407–408
Safavids, 359–360
Sahagún, Bernardino de, 256, 309
Sahara Desert, 23, 24, 165
Said, Edward, 477
Saikaku, Ihara, 379
Sailing technology, 205–206, 303
Saint Augustine, 82
Saint Domingue, 327
Saint-Simon, Claude Henri de, 409
Saladin, 228
Salamis, Battle of, 61
Salazar, Antonio, 515
Salerno Medical School, 231
Salk, Jonas, 613
Salons, 396
Salt March, 522
Samarkand, 83, 354–355
Samoa, 40
Samurai, 192, 377–378, 456
San Martí, José, 406
Sánchez-Albornoz, Claudio, 155
Sandinistas, 524
Sandino, Augusto, 524
Sanskrit, 31, 94
Santa Anna, Antonio Lopez de, 405
Santeria, 309, 326
Sarai, 244
Sarnath, 99
Sassanids, 64, 132, 133
Satellites, 553, 555
Sati, 361
Satrap system, 59, 64
Satyagraha, 522
Savanna, 23, 24
Savimbi, Joseph, 587
Scandinavia, 137, 221
Schall, Adam, 374
Schele, Linda, 118
Schism, 134
Schmalkaldic League, 281
Scholar gentry, 184, 187
Scholasticism, 231, 286
Scientific innovations. *See also* Technology
    Egyptians, 27–28
    Gupta Dynasty, 98–99
    Islam and, 150, 152
    Mayans, 116

Sumerians, 20
Scientific paradigms, 525
Scientific racism, 514–515
Scientific Revolution, 286, 394
Scientific socialism, 433
Scramble for Africa, 468, 472–473, 514
Scribes, 19, 231
Scutage, 227
Scylly Islands, 83
Sea dogs, 310
Sea levels, 39
Sea trade, 83, 98, 106, 166–167, 205–206, 288–291
SEATO. *See* Southeast Asia Treaty Organization (SEATO)
Seaways, 424
Second Estate, 400
Second Industrial Revolution, 475
Secret alliances, 493
Secret History (Procopius), 140
Secularism, 231
Security Council (UN), 551–552
Seed drill, 423
Seleucids, 62, 63
Self-determination, 494, 500, 501, 521, 565
Self-Strengthening Movement, 449
Selim III, 398, 444
Seljuk Turks, 137, 151, 227
Sen, Amartya, 615
Senate, Roman, 74, 78
Seneca, 79, 85, 429
Seneca Falls, 429
Senegal River, 166
Senghor, Leopold, 173
Separation of church and state, 82
Separation of powers, 399
Sephardic Jews, 291
Sepoy Mutiny, 470
Sepoys, 290–291
September 11, 2001, 606, 615
Serbia, 445, 492–493, 607
Serbs, 494
Serfs, 193, 223, 224, 225, 337, 340, 342–343
Settler colonies, 476
Seven Weeks' War, 411
Seven Years' War, 290, 344, 469, 497
Shahs, 359–360, 580
Shakespeare, William, 57, 294, 322
Shamanism, 5, 100, 602
Shang Dynasty, 34–36, 52, 103
Shariah, 148, 161, 358, 445, 581

Shaw, George Barnard, 409
Sheep, 7
Sheikhs, 146
Shia Islam, 148–149
Shihuangdi, 103
Shiites, 148–149
Shikibu, Murasaki, 192
Shipbuilding, 340
Shirer, William, 526
Shogun, 192, 455
Shotoku Taishi, 191
Shudras, 93
Siam Kingdom, 474, 475
Siberia, 337–338
Sicily, 58, 72, 75, 132, 137, 227, 540
Siege devices, 85
Siege weapons, 243, 248
Sikhism, 106, 361
Silk, 34, 98, 105, 135, 185, 205, 336, 372, 377, 378
Silk Roads, 82–83, 98, 99, 105, 135, 151, 186, 190, 220, 229, 241, 243, 336
Silla Kingdom, 182
Silt, 17, 23, 33, 117
Silver, 287, 305
Simony, 279
Sinai Peninsula, 26
Sind, 203
Singapore, 599
Singosari kingdom, 209
Sinification, 194
Sino-Japanese War, 378, 449, 468
Sistine Chapel, 278
Skin color, 309
Slash-and-burn agriculture, 115
Slaves/slavery
    abolition of, 327
    Americas, 306
    Aztec, 259
    capture of, 324–325
    cultural influences of, 325–326
    female, 154
    in Islamic society, 154
    Kievan Rus, 139
    Middle Passage, 325
    North America, 311
    Ottoman Empire, 358
    Persian Empire, 60
    religion and, 326
    revolts by, 171, 327, 403
    Roman Empire, 76, 79

Southwest Asia, 170–171
Sparta, 55
Sub-Saharan Africa, 171–172
Sumerian, 19
trade, 139, 171–172, 205, 304, 306, 320,
323–328, 471
Slavic languages, 134, 137
Slavic peoples, 137–140
Slavophilism, 342
Slipher, Vesto, 525
Slovakia, 573
Slovenia, 573, 607
Slums, 409, 428, 600
Smallpox, 83–84, 105, 303, 306, 613
Smelting, 186
Smith, Adam, 287–288, 395, 396, 431
Soccer, 429
Social classes
Asia, 224
caste system, 32–33, 92–93, 207, 361
China, 187–188
Europe, 224
industrialization and, 428
Islamic, 153
Japan, 193, 378
Ottoman Empire, 357–358
Roman Empire, 78–79
Russia, 337
Sumer, 19
Social contract, 285, 395, 396, 401
Social Darwinism, 469, 475
Social mobility, 224, 356
Social reforms, 430
Social stratification, 8, 10, 19
Socialism, 394, 409, 432, 433, 582
Socialist realism, 519
Society
ancient Egyptian, 26–27
Aztec, 259–260
Babylonian, 21
Bantu-speakers, 162–163
Chinese, 101, 187–188, 377
colonial Americas, 308–309
Early Middle Ages, 219–220
Greek city-states, 54
hunter-forager, 4–5
Incas, 261
industrial, 433
Islamic, 152–154
Japanese, 378
Middle Ages, 229

Mississippian culture, 258
Moche, 113
Olmec, 39–40
Ottoman Empire, 446–447
pastoral, 6–8
patriarchical, 4–5, 21
Persian, 60–61
roles in, 4–5, 8
Roman, 76–77, 78–79
South Asia, 207–208
Sparta, 54–55
Sub-Saharan Africa, 170–172
Sumerian, 19
Society of Jesus, 280
Socrates, 56
Socratic Method, 56
Sofala, 205
Soil erosion, 50, 84, 611
Solon, 55
Somaliland, 514
Song Dynasty, 183–184, 186, 187, 188, 190,
224, 246
Song Taizu (emperor), 183–184
Songhay Empire, 320–321
Sophocles, 57
South Africa, 467, 471, 473, 601–603
South Asia, 33, 222. *See also specific
countries*
culture of, 208–209
economic structures in, 204–206
imperialism in, 469–470
independence movements in, 521–522
nationalist movements in, 502
political structures in, 202–204
post-classical period in, 202–212
religion of, 206–207
social structures of, 207–208
South China Sea, 106, 186, 203
South Sea Bubble, 291
South Korea, 555, 557–558, 565, 599
South Vietnam, 576
Southeast Asia. *See also specific countries*
imperialism in, 474
nationalist movements in, 502
post-classical period in, 209–211
post-colonial struggles in, 576–577
Southeast Asia Treaty Organization
(SEATO), 556
Southern Song Dynasty, 184
South-North Water Diversion Project, 605
Southwest Asia. *See also specific countries*

ancient civilization in, 10, 17–20
nationalism in, 521–522
slavery in, 171–172
Sovereignty, 284
Soviet Russia, 496
Soviet Union, 500
in Afghanistan, 563
China and, 557
Cold War and, 551–565
dissolution of, 564, 598
German-Soviet Nonaggression Pact,
535–536, 537
interwar years in, 517–519
Korean War and, 557–558
satellite countries of, 553
World War II and, 538, 539–540, 541,
544, 545
Soviets, 496
Space race, 555
Spain, 559
colonies, 305–308, 404–408
fascism in, 515
imperialism of, 469
Islamic rule in, 152, 155
Philippines and, 290
reconquista, 227
Renaissance in, 233
separatists in, 560
Spanish Armada, 281, 310
Spanish Civil War, 515, 535
Spanish conquistadores, 303, 305–309,
312–313, 324
Spanish explorers, 290, 303
Spanish Inquisition, 292
Spanish Republic, 515
Spanish-American War, 475–476
Sparta, 54–55, 61
Spartacus Rebellion, 76
Specialization of labor, 8
Spencer, Herbert, 469
Spengler, Oswald, 40
Spheres of influence, 448, 474, 502
Spice Islands, 205, 474
Spices, 98
Spinden, Herbert, 118
Spinning jenny, 422
The Spirit of Laws (Montesquieu), 395
Sports, 58, 429
Sputnik, 555
Squash, 115
Squires, 224

Sri Lanka, 97, 203
Srivijaya Kingdom, 209
St. Augustine, Florida, 307–308
St. Augustine of Hippo, 82
St. Basil's Cathedral, 337
St. Petersburg, 339
Stalemates, 495
Stalin, Joseph, 518–519, 535, 544
Stalingrad, Battle of, 539
Star Wars, 564
State-run colonies, 476
State-run industries, 589–590
Steam engine, 422–423
Steamship, 422–423
Steel, 186
Steel industry, 429–430
Steppes, 343
Stern rudder, 206
Stirrups, 83, 224
Stock market crash of 1929, 512
Stock markets, 429
Stockholders, 429
Stoicism, 79
Stone Age, 3–5
Story-telling, 164, 172
Strait of Hormuz, 360
Strategic Arms Limitation Treaty (SALT),
563
Streltsy, 339
Student movements, 560–562, 603–604
The Subjection of Women (Mill), 433
Submarines, 494, 495, 540
Sub-Saharan Africa, 161. See also specific
countries
agriculture in, 162
Bantu-speakers in, 161–164
colonial period in, 320–328
cultural life in, 172
Islam in, 161, 165–167, 170, 172
political structures of, 164–165
slavery in, 170–171
social structures of, 170–172
trade in, 165–167
Sudan, 609
Sudetenland, 535
Suez Canal, 409, 471, 578, 579
Suez Crisis, 579
Sufism, 155, 206–207, 211, 361
Sugar plantations, 306
Sugarcane, 306, 425, 475
Sui Dynasty, 180, 185

Sui Yangdi (emperor), 180
Suleiman I, 356, 358
Suleimani Mosque, 356
Suleymaniye, 362
Sulla, 77
Sultans, 151, 357–358, 444–445
Sumerians, 17–20, 24
    cultural and scientific contributions of,
    19–20
    decline of, 20
    economy and trade of, 19
    government of, 17–18
    religion of, 18–19
    social structure of, 19
Sun Yat-sen, 442, 451, 454, 519, 520
Sundial, 20
Sundiata, 169
Sunni Islam, 148–149, 359, 581
Surreal painting, 524, 525
Swahili city-states, 166–167, 170
Swahili language, 172
Sweden, 559
Sweet potatoes, 39
Syncretism, 57, 64, 80, 172, 190, 309
Syracuse, 58
Syria, 75, 443, 502
Syrian dynasty, 133–134

T

Table of Ranks, 340
Tabula rasa, 395
Tacitus, 79
Taft, Howard, 523
Tagore, Rabindranath, 511
Taika Reforms, 191–192
Taiping Rebellion, 442, 448–449, 451
Taiwan, 40, 469, 599
Taj Mahal, 212, 361, 362
The Tale of Genji (Shikibu), 192
Taliban, 606
Tamerlane, 247, 354–355
Tamil Nadu, 469
Tang Dynasty, 181–183, 185, 190, 193, 194,
    220, 224
Tang Taizong (emperor), 182
Tangut Empire, 243
Tanks, 495
Tanzimat, 445, 446, 453
Taoism, 101–102, 190
Tariffs, 600

Tarquinius Superbus, 74
Tatars, 241
Taxes
    Babylonian system of, 21
    France, 400
    India, 204
    Mughal Empire, 361
    Ottoman Empire, 357
    Persian Empire, 59
    post-classical China, 185
    Russia, 340
Tea, 186, 288, 291, 377, 447, 466, 475
Technology
    agricultural, 9, 20, 38, 105, 185,
    223–224, 423
    Bantu-speakers, 162
    environmental adaptation and, 3
    globalization and, 601
    Han Dynasty, 105
    industrialization and, 422–423
    military, 83, 85, 186, 195
    naval, 186, 205–206, 289, 303, 340
    in Neolithic era, 9–10
    printing, 189
    sailing, 205–206, 303
    Zhou Dynasty, 37–38
Tehran Conference, 543
Telegram, 392, 450, 466, 495, 563
Temples
    Egyptian, 26, 27–28
    Mississippian culture, 257
    Moche, 112
    Olmec, 114
    Sumerian, 19
Ten Commandments, 22
Tenements, 428
Tennis Court Oath, 400
Tenochtitlán, 257–259, 264, 272, 306
Teotihuacan, 114
Terrorism, 560, 586, 605–607
Terrorist networks, 606–607
Tet Offensive, 559
Teutonic Knights, 231
Texas, 405
Textile mills, 427, 466
Textiles, 10, 98, 113, 205, 421, 466
Thailand, 209, 475
Thebes, 25
Theme system, 135
Theocracy, 134, 259, 360, 580
Theocrats, 25

Theory of relativity, 525
Thermidorean Reaction, 398, 401
Thermopylae, Battle of, 540
Thich Quang Duc, 558
Third Estate, 292, 400
Third Reich, 535
Thirty Years' War, 226, 282
Thompson, Eric, 118
Three Gorges Dam, 604
Three Mile Island, 611
Three Sisters, 115
Three-field system, 223
Tiananmen Square, 558, 604
Tiber River, 73
Tibet, 375, 376, 448, 604
Tigris River, 10, 17
Tikal, 118
Timbuktu, 169
Time of Troubles, 338
Timur the Lame, 247, 354–355
Tito, Marshall, 607
Tlaloc, 260
Tobacco, 304, 306, 311, 357
Tokugawa Shogunate, 378–379
Tokyo, 377, 543
Toleration, 60, 64, 147, 152, 278, 358,
    363–364
Toleration Act of 1689, 285
Toltecs, 256, 258
Tomatoes, 304
Tools, in Paleolithic Period, 3
Topkapi Palace, 355
Total war, 496
Totalitarianism, 514, 526
Tournaments, 227
Tours, Battle of, 152, 220, 221
Towns. *See* Cities and towns
Toyota Motor Company, 457
Trade, 9, 64. *See also* Trading post empires
    Abbasid Empire, 151
    Africa, 161–173
    agreements, 357
    ancient Egypt, 24–25
    ancient Greece, 54
    Aryans, 31–32
    Axum, 29
    Aztec, 260
    barter, 31–32
    Bedouins, 146
    Byzantine Empire, 135
    China, 83, 105, 106, 135, 185, 186, 205,
    305, 448, 466

European, 288–291, 303
    free, 287–288, 600
    fur, 310, 335–336, 338
    global, 229, 598–601
    India, 98, 106, 135, 290–291
    Indian Ocean, 98, 106, 166–167, 171–
    172, 203, 204–205, 288–291, 598–601
    Islamic world, 153, 165–167
    maritime, 83, 98, 106, 166–167,
    288–291
    Mediterranean, 221–222
    Mesoamerica, 114
    Moche, 112–113
    Ottoman Empire, 357
    overland routes, 146, 151, 229
    in Paleolithic Period, 4
    Persian Empire, 61
    Phoenician, 22
    Roman Empire, 82–83
    Russia, 335–336, 338
    sea routes, 83, 98, 106, 152, 205–206
    Silk Roads, 82–83, 98, 99, 105, 135,
    151, 186, 190, 220, 229, 241, 243, 336
    silver, 305
    slave, 139, 171–172, 205, 304, 306, 320,
    323–328, 471
    specialized products, 205
    Sumerian, 19
    transregional networks, 82–83
    trans-Saharan, 165–166
    triangular, 324
    Vietnam, 194
    Zhou Dynasty, 37
Trade union. *See* Unions
Trading post empires, 276, 290–291, 469,
    474
Tragedies, 57
Transatlantic slave trade, 304, 306, 320,
    323–328, 471
Transcontinental Railroad, 425
Transjordan, 502
Transnational corporations, 467
Transportation, 9. *See also* Roads
    ancient Egypt, 24–25
    canals, 424, 445
    railroads, 378, 425, 426, 445, 447, 456,
    466–467, 586
    steamships, 422–423
    Tang Dynasty, 182
Transregional trade networks, 82–83
Trans-Saharan trade, 165–166
Trans-Siberian Railroad, 378, 426

Treaty of Brest-Litovsk, 496
Treaty of Lausanne, 447
Treaty of Nanking, 448
Treaty of Portsmouth, 378–379, 454
Treaty of Tordesillas, 307
Treaty of Versailles, 500, 511, 514, 534
Treaty of Westphalia, 292
Treaty organizations, 555–556
Trench warfare, 495
Trevor-Roper, Hugh, 173
Triangular trade, 324
Tribes, 4
Tribunes, 74
Tributary system, 181–182, 193, 259
Tribute, 115, 139, 193, 245, 259, 357
Trinidad, 467
Triple Alliance, 493
Triple Entente, 493
The Trojan Women (Euripides), 57
The True Law of Free Monarchy, 284
Truman, Harry S., 541, 544, 553
Truman Doctrine, 553
Tsars, 336
Tuberculosis, 612
Tudor, Mary, 280
Tudors, 284
Tula, 258, 264, 272
Tumens, 242
Tunis, 446
Turkey, 8, 17, 442, 521, 581–582
Turkification, 447
Turkish National Movement, 521
Tutsis, 608–609
Two Treaties of Government (Locke), 285, 395, 399
Tyrants, 55, 74
Tyrrhenian Sea, 73

U

U-boats, 495
Uganda, 575
Uighurs, 182–183, 376
Ukraine, 518
Ulama, 357
Ulster Defence Association, 560
Umayyad Dynasty, 149–150, 203
Unemployment insurance, 430
Unification, 410–412
Union of Soviet Socialist Republics (U.S.S.R.), 518. *See also* Soviet Union
Unions, 430, 588

UNITA. *See* National Union for the Total Independence of Angola (UNITA)
United Fruit Company, 467, 557
United Kingdom. *See* Britain
United Nations, 544, 551–552, 565
United Nations International Children's Emergency Fund (UNICEF), 552
United Nations Refugee Agency (UNHCR), 552
United States
    Bay of Pigs and, 562–563
    Cold War and, 551–565
    Cuban Missile Crisis and, 563
    foreign policy of, 454, 475–476, 523–524
    Great Depression in, 512
    immigration policies, 452–453
    imperialism of, 465, 475–476, 523–524
    industrialization in, 425
    Iran and, 581
    Iraq War and, 606–607
    Japan and, 537
    Korean War and, 557–558
    Mexican immigrants to, 588
    New Deal in, 513
    post-WWI, 500–501
    as sole superpower, 605
    student movement in, 561, 562
    Vietnam War and, 558, 576
    World War I and, 495, 498
    World War II and, 537, 538–541
United States Constitution, 399
Universal Declaration of Human Rights, 552
Universities
    European, 225
    India, 99
    Islamic, 153
    Middle Ages, 231–232
University of Al Karaouine, 153
University of Constantinople, 136
University of Paris, 231
Untouchables, 93
Upanishads, 32, 33, 93
Upper Egypt, 25
Upper Nile Valley, 29
Ural Mountains, 335
Urban II, 228
Urban life, in Middle Ages, 230
Urbanization, 408–409, 424
    China, 37, 185, 187
    industrialization and, 428
    in Middle Ages, 229

Urdu, 209
Uruk, 17
Utilitarianism, 431
Utopian socialism, 409, 432

V

Vaishyas, 93
Valois, 284
Vandals, 76, 84
Vargas, Getulio, 516
Vassals, 223
V-E Day, 541
Vedas, 32–33, 99
Vedic Age, 32
Vedic religion, 9
Venezuela, 590
Venice, 137, 228, 355
Verbiest, Ferdinand, 372
Vernacular languages, 224, 232
Vernengo, Matias, 592
Versailles, 285
Viceroys, 308
Vichy government, 537
Vienna, 356
Viet Cong, 559
Vietnam, 194, 209, 475, 501, 573, 576
Vietnam War, 551, 558, 576
Vijayanagar, 203
Vikings, 137–138, 221–222, 226, 229, 336
Villa, Franisco "Pancho," 519
Villages. *See also* Cities and towns
    growth of, 8
A Vindication of the Rights of Woman
    (Wollstonecraft), 395
Vinland, 221
Virgil, 72, 79, 85
Virgin of Guadalupe, 309
Virginia, colony of, 310–311
Visigoths, 84
Visual arts. *See* Arts
Viziers, 150, 357–358
Vladimir I, 138, 139
VOC. *See* Dutch East India Company
Vodun, 309, 326
Volga River, 338
Voltaire, 286, 395–396
Voodoo, 309
Voting rights, 430
Vuh, Popol, 112
Vulgate Bible, 231

W

Wages, factory, 427, 428
Wahhabis, 443
Wang Mang, 105, 184
Wang Shifu, 246
War of the Spanish Succession, 286
Warsaw Pact, 555–556, 559, 564
War/warfare. *See also specific wars*
    atrocities committed during, 542–543
    changes in, 494–495
    global war, 497–498
    Mongolian, 242–243
    religious, 281–283
    slave trade and, 327
    total war, 496
    trench, 494, 495
    wars of unification, 410–413
Water frame, 422
Water pollution, 429, 605
Watt, James, 422
Wealth, accumulation of, 8, 10
The Wealth of Nations (Smith), 288, 396,
    421, 431
Weapons
    bronze, 35, 36
    guns/gunpowder, 186, 195, 227, 289,
        303, 494
    iron, 37
    nuclear, 555, 575
    siege, 243, 248
    technological innovations in, 38
    WWI, 494–495
Weaving, 8, 10
Weber, Max, 280, 433
Wedgwood, Ruth, 565
Weimar government, 501
Weimar Republic, 514
Wells, H. G., 409
West Africa, 166, 322, 324, 326, 327, 328
    kingdoms of, 167–169
    political structures, 167–169
West Bank, 578
West Germany, 554, 560, 562
West Pakistan, 575
Western Europe, 543–544. *See also specific*
    countries
    aristocracy in, 224, 284, 291, 292, 293
    during Cold War, 559–562
    comparisons of countries in, 291–293
    Counter-Reformation in, 280–281

early modern period in, 278–294
economies, 291–292
feudalism in, 223–224
Great Depression in, 512
invasions of, 221–222
in Middle Ages, 219–232
new monarchies, 284
Protestant Reformation in, 278–280
religious wars in, 281–283
Renaissance in, 232–234, 278
social classes in, 224
Wheat, 6, 23, 425
Wheel, invention of the, 9
Whirling dervish, 150
White Australia Policy, 468
White Huns, 100, 222
White Lotus Rebellion, 376
White Lotus Society, 247
White-collar jobs, 428
Whitney, Eli, 422
Wilhelm I, 412
Wilhelm II, 412
William and Mary, 284–285
William the Conqueror, 226
Wilson, Woodrow, 500–501, 521
Windmills, 223
Winter Palace, 339
Witchcraft, 294
Wollstonecraft, Mary, 395
Women
    in Africa, 326
    in ancient Egypt, 27
    Athenian, 56
    Aztec, 260
    in Babylonia, 21
    in China, 101, 188, 224, 377
    in Europe, 294
    impact of Industrial Revolution on,
    428–429
    in India, 95
    in Iran, 581
    Islam and, 154
    Islamic, 360
    in Latin America, 407–408
    in Middle Ages, 230–231
    Mongol, 248
    in Ottoman Empire, 358, 446–447
    in Paleolithic Period, 4–5
    Persian, 60
    in Roman Empire, 76–77, 79
    in Russia, 339

    in Safavid Dynasty, 360
    slaves, 154
    in South Asia, 207–208
    Spartan, 54–55
    in Sub-Saharan Africa, 170–171
    in Sumeria, 19
    in Turkey, 581
    in Vietnam, 194
    in World War II, 539
Wood-block printing, 188, 189, 191
Woolf, Virginia, 409, 525
Workers, factory, 426–427
Working class, 427, 428–429
World Bank, 552
World Cup, 602
World Food Program, 609
World Health Organization (WHO), 612–613
World Trade Organization (WTO), 552,
    600–601
World War I, 442, 446, 447, 477, 492–503,
    624–628
    casualties of, 498–500
    causes of, 492–494
    effects of, 501–503, 511
    as global war, 497–498
    New World Order, 543–544
    Paris Peace Conference, 500–501, 502
    reparations, 501, 511
    as total war, 496
    Treaty of Versailles, 501, 511, 514
    U.S. entrance into, 495, 498
    warfare during, 494–495
World War II, 515, 534–545
    Allied victories in, 539–541
    atrocities committed during, 542–543
    Axis powers, 534–535
    casualties of, 543
    causes of, 534–537
    colonial armies in, 539
    early German victories in, 537–538
    home fronts in, 539
    Japanese imperialism and, 536–537
    last years of, 540–541
    in the Pacific, 538–539, 540, 541
    Pearl Harbor, 538–539
    victory in, 544–545
Wright, Richard, 523
Writing
    alphabetic script, 22
    ancient Chinese, 35–36, 117
    Aryan, 32

cuneiform, 19–20, 117
Cyrillic alphabet, 134
development of, 8
early systems of, 117
Egyptian, 27, 117
hieroglyphics, 27, 29, 116, 117
Mayan, 116, 117, 118
Olmec, 40
Phoenician alphabet, 54, 117
pictographs, 35–36
Wu (empress), 220
Wu Li, 283
Wycliffe, John, 225, 279

X

Xerxes, 60, 61
Xhosa Cattle Killing Movement, 473
Xhosa people, 473
Xia Dynasty, 33–34
Xian, 184
Xin Qiji, 185
Xinjiang, 376, 604
Xiongnu peoples, 103–104
Xipe Totec, 260
Xuanzang, 182, 190

Y

Yalta Conference, 544
Yang, 101
Yang Guifei, 182
Yangtze River, 37, 180, 449, 605
Yankee imperialism, 523
Yaroslav I, 139
Yellow River, 33–34, 449, 605
Yellow Turban Rebellion, 105
Yemen, 29, 148, 357, 606
Yin, 101
Yin/Yang, 101
Yoke, 105, 224, 336
Young Turks, 447, 453
Yuan Dynasty, 184, 246–247, 372
Yugoslavia, 501, 561, 607–608
Yupanqui, 261

Z

Zacatecas, 305
Zaibatsu, 457
Zakaria, Fareed, 573
Zambos, 309
Zamindars, 361
Zand Dynasty, 360
Zanj Coast, 166
Zanj Rebellion, 171
Zanzibar, 166
Zapata, Emiliano, 519
Zarathustra, 60
Zardari, Asif Ali, 575
Zemsky Sobor, 338
Zen Buddhism, 190
Zeng Guofan, 449
Zheng He, 373–374, 380
Zhou Dynasty, 35–37, 100, 101
Zhu Yuanzhang, 247
Zia-ul-Haq, Muhammad, 575
Ziggurats, 19
Zimbabwe, 167, 169
Zimmermann Telegram, 495
Zionism, 412, 502, 577–578
Zionists, 502, 577
Zola, Emile, 412
Zoroastrianism, 9, 60, 64, 83
Zulu Kingdom, 473, 474
Zwingli, Huldrych, 279